A Good Cook... # TEN TALENTS

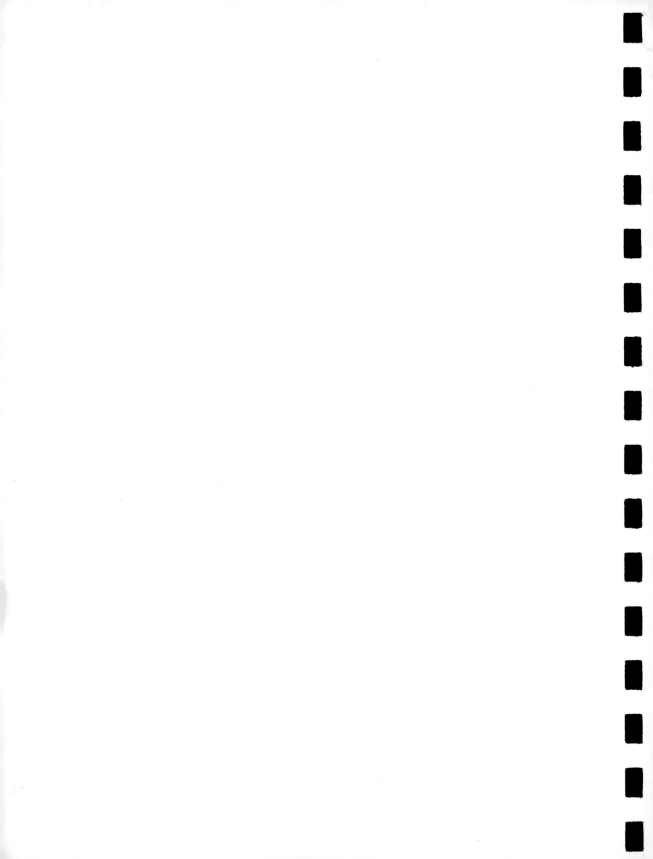

A Good Cook... TEN TALENTS

Rosalie Hurd, B.S.
and
Frank J. Hurd, D.C., M.D.

"The one who understands the art of properly preparing food, and who uses this knowledge, is worthy of higher commendation than those engaged in any other line of work. This talent should be regarded as equal in value to **TEN TALENTS***; for its right use has much to do with keeping the human body (organism) in health. Because so inseparably connected with life and health, it is the most valuable of all gifts."* E. G. White, Diet and Foods p. 251

New • Updated • Expanded
Pictorial Edition

Ten Talents...the classic natural foods vegetarian cookbook and health manual; emphasizing God's Original Diet for Man, from the Garden of Eden, as found in Genesis 1:29. Over 1,000 low fat, low sodium, high fiber, cholesterol - free, healthy recipes with the natural goodness of whole plant foods; including grains, raw fruits and vegetables, nuts, seeds, legumes and herbs, in proper combination, for peak endurance, optimum health and nutrition. Packed with information and compiled from the abundant storehouse of real foods, without the use of animal or dairy products, refined sugars, or harmful additives.

The 21 informative chapters include a *Glossary of Natural Foods*, *Simple Food Combining*, Baby Foods, Beverages, Meatless Main Dishes, Soups, Salads, Breads, Desserts, Sprouting, Sauces, Dips, Dairy Subsitutes, Sandwiches & Spreads, Meal Planning & Menus, Canning, Freezing, Drying Foods, Healthy Lifestyle Habits - Ten Principles for Abundant Health, and more.

This expanded edition is comprised of 675 pages, beautifully and artistically illustrated with more than 1,300 color photographs.

Publisher & Distributor

Dr. Frank J. and Rosalie Hurd
P.O.B. 5209 - Grants Pass, Oregon 97527
Telephone: (541) 472-1113
Phone or Fax Orders: 877-442-4425
www.TenTalents.net

TEN TALENTS COOKBOOK - Vegetarian Natural Foods • New • Updated • Expanded 2008 Edition	ISBN 978-0-615-25597-2
FOOD COMBINING MADE EASY CHART- (Laminated Edition) 4-color 18" x 24"	ISBN 978-0-9603532-3-1
FOOD COMBINING MADE EASY CHART- (Heavy Paper) 4-color 18" x 24"	ISBN 978-0-9603532-2-4
HERBS of YESTERDAY FOR TODAY - Herbal Charts #1, #2 - set (2 color 4" x 9" slide charts)	ISBN 978-0-9603532-8-6
DIEZ TALENTOS - Libro de Cocina (Spanish Edition) TEN TALENTS COOKBOOK	ISBN 978-0-615-26762-3
DIEZ TALENTOS - Tabla de Combinacion - FOOD COMBINING (4 color - Laminated Ed)	ISBN 978-0-9603532-6-2
DIEZ TALENTOS - Tabla de Combinacion - FOOD COMBINING (4 color - Heavy paper)	ISBN 978-0-9603532-7-9
VINYL LOOSELEAF BINDER - (with Index Dividers only) for 1968 - 1999 editions	ISBN 978-0-9603532-1-7
TEN TALENTS VHS/DVD - NATURAL FOODS - VEGETARIAN CUISINE / Lifestyle & Nutrition	ISBN 978-0-9603532-9-3
BETTER CHOICES - Raw Food & Favorites from Ten Talents - Fresh & Healthy Cuisine	ISBN 978-1-6136409-2-0

To order the above or other items: See Order Form at the back of this book
or Visit our web site: www.TenTalents.net

Printed in the U.S.A.

COLLEGE PRESS

Collegedale, TN 37315

Adventist Book Centers - Fulfillment and Distribution
Review & Herald Publishing Association

48th PRINTING - 2012
New • Updated • Expanded • Pictorial Edition

Library of Congress Control Number
(English) 2008909267
(Spanish) 2009901563

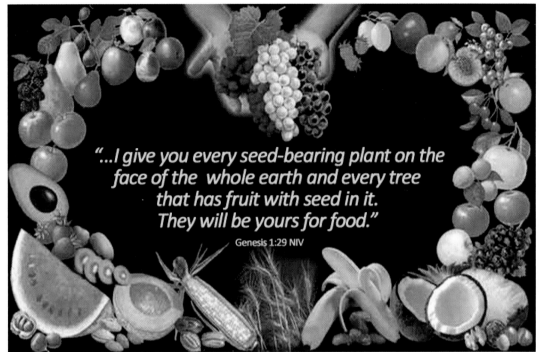

"...I give you every seed-bearing plant on the face of the whole earth and every tree that has fruit with seed in it. They will be yours for food."

Genesis 1:29 NIV

Dedication

This new edition is dedicated to every sincere wife, mother, parent, single or married person interested in promoting the health and spiritual well-being of themselves and others, and be prepared to meet the challenges of the age in which we live. Also to our 5 grown children and their families, who are forever encouraged to make wise choices, and enjoy the benefits and rewards of a healthy lifestyle.

To my devoted wife and faithful friend who has untiringly kept our family in excellent health for over 55 years, by using her culinary talents as a "good cook" to provide nourishing, attractive meals, and produce this beautiful cookbook/health manual. It is our desire the principles in this book will continue to inspire our readers to adopt new lifestyle habits and enjoy the most wholesome vegetarian cuisine.

Ten Talents, first published in 1968, has proved to be an indispensable kitchen companion and trusted resource of favorite recipes and information about foods that keep you healthy and feeling good.
*Along with this book we highly recommend the reading of **Counsels on Diet & Foods** and **Ministry of Healing** by E. G. White. These classics contain a wealth of inspiration to nourish body, mind, & spirit, and live an abundant life.*

Table of

Contents

Acknowledgments

First and foremost, are praises to our gracious **Heavenly Father** for the inspiration, the desire, steadfast purpose, and extended strength needed and given, in making this book possible. Without His guidance and help this project would not have been accomplished. The authors wish to acknowledge the **Lord's blessing** year after year, for the numerous phone calls, the letters of affirmation, the opportunities for service, and the favorable responses we have received in appreciation for better health and lifestyle changes, made by thousands who have acquired Ten Talents since it was first published in 1968.

Thank you **mother** (who lived nearly 105 years), for your example of healthy eating and for feeding our family simple wholesome food- fresh fruits and lots of vegetables (yes, even the bitter escarole). Thanks for teaching me all you did about good cooking, food shopping, kitchen economy, for singing while preparing meals, and for instilling in me a love for homemaking, sewing, and other domestic duties.

We are also very grateful to the **graphic artists, printers, family, relatives** and **friends**, whose ideas, suggestions, encouragement, and assistance, were so willingly shared.

Our heartfelt thanks to **Melissa** for her belief in this extended project, and for her excellent work in the interior design and layout of the book, even while she was learning new computer program skills herself.

Thanks for teaching me another meaning of the *menu bar* and *memory*, and how to play with a *mouse, scroll, open windows* and close *screens, copy and paste, maximize, minimize, browse, drag, delete,* transfer work to a *portable memory stick*, correct errors, find lost files, empty the *recycle bin*, pray when the computer *crashes*, and how to switch to *sleep mode* at the end of a long day! It was a lot of tedious work, but lots of fun too!

Our thanks to **Esther,** our youngest daughter, and her husband, for providing the sunniest room in their home, for me to stay as long as I needed to concentrate on the manuscript with no interruptions. Thanks for the quiet, peaceful surroundings, the comfortable computer chair, the excellent meals, daily walks in the sunshine (every day while waiting for baby to arrive), the talks, and for sharing your culinary skills, ideas and opinions. Thanks for allowing God to use you in making this book possible.

My appreciation goes out to **our family, our friends, patients, church family, and co-workers**. They intuitively understood the reasons for my refusal to take vacations, accept personal invitations, attend extra functions, decline requests to sing, forget to clean house or do laundry, neglect to answer the phone and mail in a timely manner, at times serving the family cold meals, or maybe no meal. During those times hubby would gladly make soup and sandwiches and volunteer to preserve the seasons' produce alone. This was life - while I sequestered myself to finishing the revision. Thanks to all of you for understanding!

Last but not least, our sincere gratitude to the **Review & Herald Publishing Association and Staff** for their continued e-mails and encouragement, for patiently waiting for the manuscript (and not giving up on me), and for finally facilitating the printing of this New Expanded Pictorial Edition. Thank You!

Cover Painting, Design - **Del Hearn**, Artist
Recipes, Food Preparation and Photography - **Rosalie Hurd**, author
Project Layout Design - **Melissa Ross**, graphic artist
Layout Logistics - **Brad Fisher,** Pre-press Coordinator

Ten Talents

A Word From the Doctor

The maxim "An ounce of prevention is worth a pound of cure" (Benjamin Franklin) is something to give more serious consideration to in this time of rising healthcare costs that are threatening our economy.

We are living in a fast-paced society that is making great demands upon us for peak performance and still keep healthy, through well-managed lifestyle habits. With all the devitalized, synthetic, and fast-foods tempting us today, it will require willpower to make wise choices in obtaining the necessary wholesome foods that will keep our bodies in optimal health.

Millions of hard-earned dollars are often wasted by way of our mouths. All of us are hungry for those necessary requirements that our "All-knowing Creator" designed our bodies should have, to maintain a healthy, vigorous, and responsive body. We must have a thorough understanding of our physiology and bodily needs, in order for us to acquire from nature's abundant storehouse that which will keep our body and mind in perfect health.

We have come face to face with three GIANTS in our modern society. These respectively are: our food producers, marketing agencies and supermarkets, and uninformed consumers and cooks who are responsible for the food that is set before us. The producers of our foods today find it difficult to be competitive and still grow foodstuffs without chemical fertilizers and harmful sprays. Because of this, we can hardly avoid buying contaminated foods. The marketing agencies do not want ripened fruits and mature vegetables for fear of losses due to spoilage and shipping. Therefore, many foods are forced-grown and harvested prematurely, which makes them inferior in nutritional values. The only safety is found in choosing the best quality of foods available or growing your own foods organically, if possible.

Fresh, ripened foods, in their natural state possess the highest nutritive value. In contrast foods that are improperly prepared, fermented, and or preserved with chemical additives only tends to destroy its value. Boiled vegetables that have been peeled and the water thrown away, taste of nothing, so something must be done to make them palatable. We "doctor them up" by mixing sugar, spices, butter, and different things together. We polish the rice, we remove the germ and the husk to make a refined flour for baking, we refine the sugars, or use harmful artificial sweeteners such as: Aspartame (NutraSweet), Sucralose (Splenda), Saccharin, and others.

We remove the skins, seeds and cores of apples and pears; we peel the potatoes and scrape the carrots. We make beverages from coffee, cocoa beans and tea, all containing stimulating poisons. We use wonderful fresh grapes to make fermented and intoxicating drinks which in time paralyze the brain and nervous system. Meat, fish, cheese, and eggs supply us with an enormous amount of animal protein. We even preserve good food with chemicals such as sulfurous acid, salicylic acid, nitrates, and benzoic acid.

Because these devitalized and tampered-with foods cannot readily supply our body with what it needs, but takes nourishment from it, depleting our store of physical and nervous energy - we take a sedative, tranquilizer, or aspirin which eventually makes our condition worse.

If we would learn to eat more fresh raw foods in their whole natural state, the common ailments we now have, would be few. Sickness would be replaced with health. The fresh complexion, sound teeth, lustrous hair, vigorous build, perfect posture, and natural graces of the body would present the strongest argument in favor of natural living.

Much praise can be given to the mother, daughter, nurse, doctor, or any other person who realizes our bodies must not be defiled, and who provides for these "temples" a healthful dietary that will radiate a natural beauty.

My good wife deserves much praise on my behalf. Her efforts have been continuous in providing our family with the proper nutrition for optimal health. You will find in this volume the personal touch of her hands and heart, to assist you in finding a better way to enjoy better health.

Yours for Abundant Health,
Frank J. Hurd, D.C., M.D.

TEN TALENTS Acronym for Abundant Health

T **Trust in Divine Power**

E **Exercise**

N **Nutrition**

T **Temperance**

A **Air, Pure**

L **Light, Sunshine**

E **Energizing Water**

N **Nightly Rest**

T **Thankfulness**

S **Service**

The
10 Principles for Abundant Health have been arranged
to form an acronym that coincides with the title of this book TEN TALENTS.
(See **Healthy Lifestyle** chapter 21 of Ten Talents for a brief description of these principles)

 Nedley Clinic

1045 15th Ave. NW Ardm[...]

The first edition of the **Ten Talents Cookbook**, published more than 44 years ago, was a pioneering work in providing recipes for simple, practical, yet healthful cooking. It was my pleasure to recommend the **Ten Talents Cookbook** to readers of my book **Proof Positive**, and I am happy to recommend, with confidence, this updated pictorial edition today.

Dr. Frank and Rosalie Hurd are to be commended for their balanced approach to "getting back" to the original (and biblical) diet prescribed for man. Whole plant foods and low fat recipes have been scientifically shown to enhance physical well-being and promote peak mental performance. Those are the types of recipes provided in this book. The appealing photos, new look, and updated recipes will certainly ensure the continued place of **Ten Talents** as a favorite cookbook in kitchens around the world.

While some individuals hold work in the kitchen to heavy drudgery or even a sort of slavery, it is, in the words of one of my favorite authors, "a science above all other sciences." Those who understand this science, and can share it, should be highly commended, for a knowledge of healthful cooking is worth more than "ten talents". Because of its inseparable connection with life and health, the talent of being a chef is truly one of the highest of gifts.

Over the years, many healthful living initiatives have emphasized acronyms for health-promoting lifestyle habits. The creators of the **Ten Talents Cookbook** have adopted ten principles of their own— principles which, if followed, will surely lead to abundant health. These principles include many of the tenets we have utilized with great success in the *Nedley Depression Recovery Program.*

T Trust in Divine Power
E Exercise
N Nutrition

T Temperance
A Air, Pure
L Light, Sunshine
E Energizing Water
N Nightly Rest
T Thankfulness
S Service

I recommend that you try these principles, together with the healthful recipes provided for you in the **Ten Talents Cookbook**. If faithfully followed, these principles and recipes will have a lasting and positive impact on your health, and, if you are cooking for others, they will no doubt contribute to the happiness, digestive tranquility, and health of those around you as well.

Neil Nedley

Neil Nedley, M.D.

Internal Medicine Physician
Author of **Proof Positive: How to Reliably Combat Disease and Achieve Optimal Health through Nutrition and Lifestyle**
Author of **Depression: the Way Out**
Author of **Nedley Depression Recovery Programs**
Author of **Achieving Peak Mental Performance Programs**
President, **Weimar Center of Health and Education**
www.drnedley.com

Introduction...by Hans Diehl, DrHSc, MPH, FACN

A Better Way to Better Health
LIFESTYLE MEDICINE INSTITUTE

Hans A. Diehl, DrHSc, MPH
Founder and Director

Le
Un

Board Member
American College of Lifestyle Medicine

Although much information about good nutrition is readily available, the American public is bombarded with advertising that encourages the eating of a rich diet, which has created a paradox—people are overweight and undernourished.

This has contributed to an avalanche of chronic diseases. They include heart disease, cancer, diabetes, hypertension, arthritis, and depression. Circulatory diseases in particular, accounting now for almost every second death in North America, are closely related to a Western lifestyle that is largely characterized by poor nutrition, smoking, and a lack of consistent exercise. This, in turn, also contributes to lower productivity at work and to hyperactive children at school.

It will be the power of choice that will determine whether our diet is nutritionally adequate or not. Just eating less fat and more nutrient-dense, fiber-rich foods, and exercising more consistently will make a huge difference in being able to lose extra pounds and feeling better. Using more whole grains, fresh fruits and vegetables, and legumes—instead of meat, pies and pastries, whoppers and cheese—will drastically benefit our health and well-being.

For most of us, it is not enough to make some cosmetic changes, such as exchanging white meat for red meat, or skim milk for whole milk, or cutting back on our fast food fare. If we want to reverse disease and improve our health, we must become more serious about bringing our eating habits more closely into alignment with natural law. Failing to make these changes and instead relying on prescribed drugs for our common Western diseases may lead to disappointment. It's not enough to treat the symptoms of these diseases. We must attack and remove their causes.

Food needs to taste good and look good to do us good. The recipes in *Ten Talents* meet these needs as we learn and enjoy our new way of eating. Over the years, *Ten Talents* has been used in conducting classes in healthful cooking and seminars in nutrition, lifestyle medicine, depression and stress management. It has also been very helpful in conducting programs dealing with diabetes and weight control and with our CHIP (Coronary Health Improvement Project) program.

Ten Talents is more than a cookbook. If you missed the 60's, here's a book that brings back that cozy, hopeful, idealistic time. When first published in 1968, *Ten Talents* provided everything that new vegetarians and simple-living-seekers needed—all in one place. It showed them how to make soy milk, yogurt, tofu, wheat gluten, nut butters, soups and salads, and how to sprout seeds. It offered instruction for bread making, feeding baby and nursing mothers. It had numerous glossaries and charts describing natural foods, how to choose fresh produce, tables on vitamin needs, simple food combining, beneficial use of herbs, general kitchen helps, and a section with milk and eggs for people in transition from the usual diet.

Ten Talents has stood the test of time. And, even now after 44 years, it is still considered one of the best vegetarian cookbooks around. This edition of *Ten Talents* still contains all the foundational building stones and the favorite recipes, but it has been expanded to include more recipes, and has a fresh new look with lots of attractive pictures of fruits and vegetables, whole grains, legumes, and nuts, all provided by our Creator as the original and optimal diet.

The authors created *Ten Talents* to be a lifestyle cookbook with practical information including an expanded variety of plant-based recipes that are very low in fat, low in salt and sugar, and high in fiber. It's a book for people concerned about health, ecology and lowering the costs for food and medicines. It's a book for intelligent people who are looking for a rational choice amidst a world of sensational claims and promises. It's a book that will deliver on its promises.

You are invited to practice the principles and enjoy the heart-healthy recipes and see your health make a quantum leap forward.

Bon Appétit!

Hans A. Diehl

Hans A. Diehl, DrHSc, MPH, FACN

Founder and Director of the CHIP Program
Lifestyle Medicine Institute, Director
Clinical Professor of Preventive Medicine, School of Medicine,
   Loma Linda University
www.CHIPhealth.com

Food - Man's Medicine

"The doctor of the future will give no medicine, but will interest his patients in the care of the human frame and in the cause of and prevention of disease."
Thomas A. Edison 1847-1931

My personal observation is that what we eat and drink is directly responsible for how we think and feel, as well as our personal relationship to our Creator. Many times I have talked about our human digestion and how our well-being is affected by the complicated mixtures and poor combinations of perfectly good food we ingest. The poorly digested foods and the apparent symptoms of indigestion, such as burping, belching, abdominal gas, acid reflux, etc. contribute to the diseases that bring on aging and premature death . These symptoms are in reality an indication that the systems of our body are not standing up to the abuses of our daily habits. The most irregular and daily abused habit is that of eating. Thus I would say, look to this avenue for the trouble and take action to remedy the condition.

The all-American diet of hamburgers, hot dogs, potato chips, ice cream, and soda pop, can hardly be labeled "vital food" and creates acid residues which are responsible for all kinds of health problems.

We should eat to enhance our immune system, by including in our diet at least 65 - 75 % raw food (fresh fruits, vegetables, nuts, etc.) – simply combined with other wholesome and properly prepared foods that can be easily digested.

Even if not one year was added to our life, the rewards of living, and the increased quality of life when eating for health reasons, instead of merely for the gratification of appetite, could be enjoyed an hundred-fold more in physical, mental, and spiritual attainment.

"If you will diligently hearken to the voice of the Lord your God, and do that which is right in His eyes, and give heed to His commandments, and keep all His statues, I will put none of the diseases upon you which I put upon the Egyptians; for I am the Lord, your healer." Exodus 15:26

Frank J. Hurd, D.C., M.D.

Ten Talents

Printers Prologue...by Noble Vining, B.A.

Fifty Years Before "Ten Talents"

Noble was born September 2, 1918 in Atlanta, Georgia. He attended the Seventh-day Adventist Church School, graduating from the 10th Grade in spring of 1933. That summer he worked in a bakery from 9 to 10 hours each day for $1.00 per day, saving enough for his entrance deposit to Southern Junior College, Collegedale, Tennessee.

That fall he left home to attend school, the youngest boy in the dormitory. On a previous visit he had toured The College Press and from that visit he wanted to work there. His dream came true in January, 1934. A few months later the National Recovery Act came into being under President Franklin D. Roosevelt, and Noble received a pay increase from .14 per hour to .34 per hour, under the first Minimum Wage Law.

Noble worked his way in printing through 5 years at SJC and 3 years at Emmanuel Missionary College (now Andrews University) to graduate, with a major in business administration, the summer of 1941, just in time to be drafted into the Army, October 16, 1941. After serving with the 84th (WZ) Fighter Squadron, as the Flight Surgeon's Assistant, three of these years being with the Eighth Air Force in England, he was discharged October 14, 1945.

From then until 1968 he was Manager of The College Press, Collegedale, Tennessee; Production Manager of the Stanborough Press, England; Manager and Treasurer of Philippine Publishing House, Manilla, Philippines; Manager of The College Press, South Lancaster, Massachusetts; Production Manager of Southern Publishing Association, Nashville, Tennessee; then to become in 1966, Manager of The College Press, again at Collegedale. In these various facilities he had a part in designing and producing many books. Perhaps this background was training for the challenge of producing the first edition of "Ten Talents" in 1968. Having seen the Atlanta Airport grow from two old WWI airplanes to, at times, first in the nation, and looking forward to seeing the first Model A Fords, and from hand setting printer's display type to what everybody can now do on their computers, you can appreciate my enthusiasm and perspective regarding the production of this new pictorial revised **"Ten Talents"**.

Looking at proofs of the attractive cover and some of the pages of this revision of **"Ten Talents"**, I am thrilled and reminded of a text in Daniel that ". . . many shall run to and fro, and knowledge shall be increased." You may wonder why I, a technical person, would think of this scripture. As manager of The College Press and thirty-five years after I started in printing, Rosalie and Frank Hurd showed me a box of recipes, each on a separate piece of paper, some even handwritten, and in 1968, from that box of recipes came the initial printing of **"Ten Talents"**. I had to convince the Linotype operator to put each individual recipe on his copy board instead of the double spaced typewritten copy that all writers were mandated to submit for publication.

In the last 40 years, knowledge has not only increased, it has literally mushroomed. God has provided almost unbelievable Technical Knowledge in the area of worldwide communication, and in printing and the Graphic Arts. This knowledge has made possible this beautiful book with color photos and original art throughout. None of this was possible when the first **"Ten Talents"** was published. How nice to see photos of the actual recipes as they look when prepared.

More important, the content of the book, I'm sure has kept pace with increase in knowledge. It contains along with the recipes, helpful instructions such as how to cut and serve a mango. Health principles with a thread of Divine guidance are also included in **"Ten Talents"** by Rosalie and Frank.

The photos of Rosalie are ageless. I even asked her when they were taken? She said, "About a year ago." I'm convinced there must be something to her way of life that maintains her youthful vitality.

My last big project before retirement in 1985 was a revision of **"Ten Talents"**. It was originally typeset in hot metal on a Linotype so revisions were still set on the Linotype, however we were beginning to use computers in the industry which enabled us to easily produce the cross- referenced Index in that 376 page revision, which was set by a Photo Typesetter, now obsolete.

This "knowledge shall be increased", state-of-the-art cookbook/manual, should find a place in every home. May God bless in its message and circulation.

Noble Vining

Noble Vining, BA
Manager, retired - The College Press
Compiler, designer of: The Bible Textionary

Author of: "A 6-day Creation Week"
Box 555 - Collegedale, TN 37315
www.Bibletextionary.org

From Our Hearts to Your Home....

Dear Reader,

..."Of making many books there is no end (so do not believe everything you read), and much study is a weariness of the flesh." also ..."that which has been done is that which will be done again; and there is nothing new under the sun." These words were written by the wisest King Solomon. (Ecc. 1:9, 12:12 The Amplified Bible)*

This could include cookbooks too! So you ask – then.. "Why another book?" That's a valid question. Actually it's the same title, and basically the same message, but with updated recipes, many favorite familiar ones, many new healthy-for-you, with lots of pictures, just 40 years later.

Ten Talents *contains the basic information you need to choose the right foods, and prepare them simply and healthfully, in an attractive manner that will invite the appetite, and nourish the body.*

This new expanded edition will take you right back to our Creator's health principles... back to the Garden of Eden*, the Tree of Life*, and the foods God has so bountifully provided for us, in the original diet given at creation*.

And... hopefully it will inspire you to treat your body as a temple, to care for it, by following the Ten Principles for Abundant Health, so you may enjoy a better quality of life here, and delight in the pleasures of eternity in the earth made new.

Friend, there is a definite connection between what you eat, how you think and feel, and the quality of your life. One of my favorite authors puts it this way:

"Few... understand how much their habits of diet have to do with their health, their characters, their usefulness in this world, and their eternal destiny." *Ellen White, Counsels on Diet and Foods, pg. 51*

There is more to life than just living here. I am interested in your total well-being, physically, spiritually, and emotionally. ***"I hope all is well with you, and that you are as healthy in body as you are strong in spirit".*** *3 John 1:2, New Living Translation*

Yours for More Abundant Health,

Rosalie Hurd

Rosalie Hurd

*Texts for your perusal: Genesis 1: 29; 2:7-9; Rev. 22: 1, 2, 14

Clergy Comments...by Marvin Clark, Senior Pastor

Pastor Marvin Clark

Why would a person be concerned about what kind of food he eats? Why would someone choose to walk 3 or 4 miles every day? Why would a person be sure to drink 8 glasses of water each day? Most of us would probably answer the above question with a response similar to this:

"I am careful about what I eat and how much I exercise so I can have a healthy body. I don't want my body to wear out early, and I don't want to get cancer or have a heart attack. So I treat my body with respect, feeding it the most healthful food, and giving it adequate rest and exercise."

This is a good answer, but there is something more that needs our consideration------

The Spiritual Dimension

One of my favorite passages in the Bible is found in the Old Testament book of Isaiah, chapter 7, verse 14 and 15.

> ***"Therefore the Lord Himself will give you a sign: Behold, the virgin shall conceive and bear a Son, and shall call His name Immanuel. Curds and honey He shall eat, that He may know to refuse the evil and choose the good."***

These verses are clearly a prophecy that directs our attention to the birth of Jesus Christ, about 700 years after Isaiah stated it. But these amazing verses also give us a valuable insight into the diet of Jesus, and why He selected that particular diet.

Notice, in verse 15, how He chose a very simple, basic diet of curds and honey. The curds were probably a yogurt or cottage cheese. The honey was the same honey we eat today. Now, most importantly, we are given the reason why Jesus Christ chose to eat a very basic, simple, low-fat diet---

> ***"That He may know to refuse the evil, and choose the good."***

Here we are given a most amazing principle regarding the intimate connection existing between our mind and our body. Between the body and mind there is a mysterious and wonderful relation. They react upon each other. A healthy body contributes to a clear and healthy mind. A healthy mind enables us to make choices that build a Christ-like character. Because the body is the only medium through which the mind and soul are developed for the building of a Christian character, it is eternally important that we use discretion in choosing what we eat, and how we treat our body.

King David wrote in Psalms 34:8, "O taste and see that the Lord is good: blessed is the man who trusts in him." This reminds me of how much God cares for His creation, for He has abundantly provided good foods for us to eat.

The cookbook you are holding is filled with the simple good foods God has provided to keep our body and mind in a healthy condition. **Ten Talents** was first published in 1968. I purchased my first copy in 1969, while working as a manager of a vegetarian restaurant in San Diego, California. During this time, I used several **Ten Talents** recipes as part of my restaurant menu. Since that time, I have purchased and given away many copies of **Ten Talents**. Now with this new revised edition, I am even more enthused and excited to distribute copies to my family and to my friends.

Ten Talents contains a gold mine of physical, mental, and spiritual information to get you healthy, and to keep you healthy.

I trust that you will enjoy this book as I have for the last forty years.

Marvin Clark

Marvin Clark, Senior Pastor
Grants Pass, Oregon
www.gpsdachurch.com

What Others Have Said...

*"The health message is the right arm of the Gospel and I appreciate Dr. Frank and Rosalie Hurd for their work in this area. I became acquainted with Frank and Rosalie in 1993 when 3ABN produced a series of ten cooking programs the Hurds entitled Lifestyle & Nutrition Seminars. These half hour programs aired on 3ABN for several years and were very much appreciated by the 3ABN family viewing audience. The Hurds ministry to provide both good food and instruction for a more healthy lifestyle through their cookbook **Ten Talents** is vitally needed in these closing moments of Earth's history."*

  – Danny Shelton, Founder and Corporate Consultant,
    Three Angels Broadcasting Network (3ABN)

*"It is a privilege to endorse this new edition of **Ten Talents**. It has been among my valued cookbooks for many years, actually virtually since its inception in 1968. Being the very first vegan vegetarian cookbook ever published to our knowledge, and despite the plethora of excellent new vegan cookbooks on the market since then, **Ten Talents** still ranks very high in the minds of many, as the vanguard of books of its kind four decades ago, and even now.*

With the obesity, diabetes and cardiovascular epidemics going at such a momentum, this 'classic' is more needed than ever. May its circulation continue to bless and edify those who read it and put its principles into practice."

  – Roby Angelina Sherman, MD, Associate Medical Director,
    Wildwood Lifestyle Center & Hospital, Wildwood, GA

*"**Ten Talents**.... In several editions, because I keep splattering 'cashew white sauce' on them....is a kitchen companion I can't think of doing without. Love it, love it, love it! I raised my daughter on these recipes and she asked for a copy of **Ten Talents** as a wedding gift."*

  – Victoria Moran, author of Fit From Within and The Love-Powered Diet

*"The **Ten Talents** cookbook of natural foods has been a part of my kitchen for over 15 years. I have found **Ten Talents** to be more than a cookbook. It is a guide to healthful living aimed to improve health and extend life. I am excited about this revised edition knowing that it offers more of the best.*

A special thanks to Rosalie and Frank Hurd for dedicating their lives to the mission of extending life and health."

  – Sharon Erickson, President, Mid-America Union Chapter of ASI

*"When you have the best; Forget the rest! Get back to health with **Ten Talents**. It's the best cookbook- but not 'just a cookbook'. Congratulations for over 40 years of feeding so many of us so well! "*

  – Dana Huff, California

"The Library of Congress requests permission for TEN TALENTS to be transcribed into embossed form for the blind....Your cooperation is sincerely appreciated."

  – The Library of Congress

"In the early 1960's I was diagnosed as having hypoglycemia. As a result, I went on a quest to learn about foods, and more in depth to know what, when, and how much to eat, that would control my blood sugar.

"*Ten Talents* is more than recipes! It is an informative text book including proper food combining, meal planning, and the wonderful spiritual quotes throughout the book. Surely the Lord has blest with the preparation."
– Jo Ann Fjarli, Southern Oregon Builders

"*Ten Talents*...No other cookbook looks like it....or sells like it.... A proven best-seller. Every vegetarian needs this all-time 'classic' book."
– Royal Publications

"......No-nonsense cookbook. We've handled it for years and still highly recommend it. *Ten Talents* in our opinion is excellent for the beginner or the more advanced."
– North American Vegetarian Society

"A basic manual on vegetarian cooking, gracefully sprinkled with SDA philosophy and quotations....These elite authors have left lasting impressions and changed vegetarianism for the better."
– Vegetarian Times

"A novice to vegetarianism, I purchased *Ten Talents* years ago, hoping to gain some insight and expertise in the area of a vegetarian diet, as I wish to adopt such a lifestyle. The cookbook exceeded my expectations, and continues to do so with each reading. I love it! it's thorough without sacrificing charm. I'm so grateful to the person who recommended your book."
– C. Bender, New York

"*Ten Talents* not only taught me vegetarianism, it taught me to cook. I was twenty years old when I discovered *Ten Talents* and although I've grown tired of other cookbooks, this is my perennial favorite. Although I'm on my third copy, the various spots and splatters of cream of tomato soup, and that wonderful cheeseless macaroni and cheese attest not only that I'm a rather messy cook, but that this is still my most used cookbook. The recipes are healthy, wholesome, and they're for real food, comfortable food. Not only that--and this is almost a miracle--they always turn out the way they're supposed to. But there's more to *Ten Talents* than good food: the knowledge and commitment of Rosalie and Dr. Frank Hurd are on every page, along with their mission to help make this world a saner, healthier place for us all."
– V. M. , Author, Free-lance writer

"A good friend gave me your book *Ten Talents*...I have a radically replaced hip and the orthopedic surgeon said "better lose some weight." I lost 20 lbs. after applying the "Healthy Lifestyle Principles" found in your book. The two-meal-a-day plan, with a light or no supper works great; and my "sugar fix" was satisfied with your simple healthy recipe 'Vanishing Fruit-Nut-Balls.'"
– Gary R Crabtree – www.TheLegalTree.com

A Virtuous Wife

Who can find a wife of noble character? She is worth more than the costliest jewels. Her husband has confidence in her abilities. He will never be poor. All her life she will do him good and will never do anything to harm him. She supplies her house with wool and linen, and does her work eagerly. She supplies her home with food brought by ships from all over the world. She rises while it is still dark to lay out the day's food for the family and plan the day's work for her servant girls.

She looks at some land and buys it; with her earnings she plants a vineyard. She works with energy and puts all her strength into her tasks. She knows the value of what she sells and often works late into the night.

She spins her own thread and weaves cloth with her own hands. She gives generously to the poor and helps those who are in need. She doesn't worry about her family in winter. They have double garments for warmth. She makes her own curtains and bedspreads; her clothes are tasteful and beautiful. Her husband is respected because of her and is chosen to sit with the city officials. She markets beautiful clothes and belts, and sells them to the merchants.

She's respected in her own right and is not afraid of the future. She speaks words of gentle wisdom and teaches kindness to others. She is never lazy and watches over the affairs of her family. Her children respect her and say so, and her husband praises her saying, "Many women do wonderful things, but you surpass them all."

Charm is deceptive and beauty disappears, but a woman who honors the Lord will be praised. Reward her for what she has done. Let her works be praised by everyone In the city.

Proverbs 31: 10-31 The Clear Word

Natural Foods
and Daily Needs

Index - Chapter 1

Chapter Cover Photo: *Rosalie Hurd at Home in her Kitchen*

Fresh Fruit & Vegetable - Amounts

Fruits, Fresh	Your Recipe States	Approx. Amount
Apples	1 cup sliced or chopped	1 medium (6 ounces)
	1 pound	3 medium
Bananas	1 cup sliced	1 medium or 2 small
	1 cup mashed	2 medium
Cranberries	4 cups	1 pound
Lemons or Limes	2 to 3 Tbs. juice	1 medium
	2 to 3 tsp. grated peel	1 medium
Melons,	1 medium	3 pounds
Cantaloupe or honeydew	2 cups 1-inch chunks	1 pound
Oranges	1 to 2 Tbs. grated peel	1 medium
	1/3 to 1/2 cup juice	1 medium
Peaches or Pears	2 cups diced	3 medium (1 pound)
Pineapples, fresh	4 cups cubed	1 medium
Pomegranates	1 1/3 cups seeds	1 medium
Strawberries	4 cups sliced	1 quart

Vegetables, fresh	Your Recipe States	Approx. Amount
Asparagus	16 to 20 stalks	1 pound
Beans, green or yellow wax	3 cups 1-inch pieces	1 pound
Broccoli, fresh	2 cups flowerets or 1-inch pieces	6 ounces
Cabbage, Chinese (napa)	1 medium head	1 1/4 pounds
Cabbage, green or red	1 medium head	1 1/2 pounds
	4 cups shredded	1 pound
Carrots	1 cup shredded	1 1/2 medium
	1 cup sliced, 1/4-inch	2 medium
Cauliflower	3 cups flowerets	1 pound
Celery	1 cup thinly sliced or chopped	2 medium stalks
Corn, sweet	1 cup kernels	2 small ears
Cucumbers	1 cup chopped	3/4 medium
Eggplant	1 medium	1 1/4 pounds
Garlic	1 tsp. finely chopped	2 medium cloves
Leeks	2 cups thinly sliced	1 medium
Lettuce, romaine	1 medium head	1 1/2 pounds
	6 cups bite-size pieces	1 pound
Mushrooms, fresh	6 cups sliced	1 pound
Onions, green with tops	1/4 cup sliced	4 medium
Onions, yellow or white	1/2 cup chopped	1 medium
Parsnips	3 cups 1/2-inch slices	1 1/4 pounds
Peas, green	1 cup shelled	1 pound in pods
Peppers, bell	1 cup chopped	1 medium
Potatoes, new	10-12 small	1 1/2 pounds
Potatoes, red, white, sweet	1 medium	5 to 6 ounces
	1 cup 1/2-inch pieces	1 medium
Pumpkin	1 cup mashed, cooked	1 pound, uncooked or 1 cup canned
Rutabagas	2 cups 1/2-inch pieces	12 ounces
Spinach	4 cups leaves	6 ounces
Squash, Summer (yellow, zucchini)	2 cups sliced, chopped, shredded	1 medium
Squash, Winter (acorn, buttercup butternut or spaghetti	1 medium	1 1/2 to 2 1/2 pounds
Tomatoes, fresh	1 cup chopped	1 large
Turnips	1 cup 1/2-inch pieces	1 medium

Foods, Other	Your Recipe States	Approx. Amount
Bread, whole wheat	1 cup soft crumbs	2 slices
	1 cup dry crumbs	4-5 slices, oven-dried
Buttery Spread or Soy Margarine	1/2 cup	1/4 pound (1 stick)
Cheese, Soy or Tofu	2 cups	16 ounces (1 pound)
Coconut, fresh	1 1/2 cups shredded or flaked	4 ounces
Nuts, (shelled) chopped	1 cup	4 ounces
Pasta, macaroni, spaghetti	4 cups cooked	6 to 8 ounces dried, uncooked
Rice, long grain	3-4 cups cooked	1 cup uncooked
Yogurt, soy	1 cup	8 ounces

Glossary of Natural Foods

AGAR-AGAR

Vegetable gelatin from sea weed (algae). It is a tasteless, non-irritating, non-habit forming colloid which absorbs moisture rapidly and retains it. This rapid absorption of moisture throughout the intestinal tract supplies bulk and lubrication and increases peristaltic action. A gentle relief for constipation. Agar is used as a jelling agent in salads, soups, non-dairy cheese recipes, and desserts in place of animal gelatin or pectin. It jells readily at room temperature and a little goes a long way. May be used in low carbohydrate, low protein and other special diets.

Basic Proportions: 3 ½ cups liquid and 2 Tbs. agar flakes or 3 ½ cups liquid and 1 Tbs. granulated agar. For softer jell: 2 cups liquid and 1 Tbs. agar flakes. Bring to a boil. Cool to jell. Proportions may vary with the addition of fruit. (see recipes)

AGAVE

A natural sweetener made from various cactus plants of the agave family cultivated for their fiber or sweet sap. The natural nectar is approximately 1½ times sweeter than sugar (see Substitutions for Sugar in **Misc.** chapter). Agave syrup has a low glycemic index, which in small amounts may be suitable for diabetics.

ALMONDS

Almonds are rightly called the "King of the Nuts." Fruit of the almond tree, highly nutritious, containing 84 grams of good quality protein per pound. Almonds, when compared to other nuts contain more Vitamin E, which is associated with a decreased risk of heart disease. A good source of Riboflavin, Magnesium, and Iron. [1]

Almonds contain all the essential amino acids, as well as Calcium, Phosphorus, Potassium, Niacin, and other vitamins and minerals. High in mono-unsaturated fat. Used moderately, and in combination with grains and fruit or vegetables will supply an adequate protein with no cholesterol or toxic effects.

Almonds, like other nuts, are best eaten in their raw natural state. Try soaking them in water, overnight, until plump. See chapter on **Nuts,** and recipes for making almond milk, almond butter, etc.

ARROWROOT FLOUR

A pure nutritious starch also known as arrowroot starch or powder. Arrowroot powder is made from the beaten pulp of tuberous rootstocks of a tropical American plant. It is not a refined product but simply a smooth textured dried and powdered root, yielding an easily digested starch with a calcium ash, and some trace minerals. Suitable in infant and convalescent diets and can be used in place of cornstarch to thicken fruits, soups and gravy.

Basic proportions: 1 cup water and 1 ½ Tbs. arrowroot. Bring to a boil to thicken.

BARLEY MALT

Germinated barley grain, softened by steeping in water. Its carbohydrate content (dextrin, maltose), a diastase (converting starch into sugar) and its protein content, is responsible for its use as a wholesome nutrient. Promotes bowel regularity.

Malt can be used in milk drinks or sprinkled on fruit. An excellent addition to bread recipes, promoting yeast activity. Malt, a complex sweetener, gives better body and texture, while enhancing flavor of other ingredients.

BRAGG LIQUID AMINOS ®

Formulated from soybeans and purified water, with no fermentation. An excellent substitute for soy sauce which often contains colorings, chemicals, alcohol, and other additives. A pleasant tasting seasoning which can be used on salad in place of salt, in soups, gravies, casseroles, rice, tofu, stir-fry, etc. Similar to Dr. Bronner's Balanced Mineral Bouillon, but with a lighter flavor.

CAROB

Commonly called "St. John's Bread," Honey Locust. Finely ground pods from budded treed are made into carob flour. Carob powder is a rich source of the following important nutrients: Thiamine-B1, Riboflavin-B2, Niacin, Vitamin A, and Calcium. Carob also contains Potassium, Phosphorus, Magnesium, Silicon, and Iron. Rich in natural sugars, low in starch, low in fat (only 2% fat as commonly compared with 52% fat in chocolate).

Carob powder contains Pectin, good for regulating digestion. Delicious in brownies, pudding, hot drinks, cakes, and "confections without objections." 3 Tbs. Carob and 2 Tbs. water equal 1 square of chocolate. Good for babies too-supplying extra calcium and phosphorus for teeth and bones. Resembles cocoa in appearance and flavor. For those who wish to restrict their intake of sugar, caffeine, and saturated fats, carob is the healthy alternative to chocolate.

CASHEWS

A kidney shaped fruit of a tropical American tree of the sumac family. Actually the seed (appendage) of the fleshy pear-shaped cashew apple. A versatile nut for the vegetarian cook. Cashews can be used in making delicious cream soups, milk, nut butters, ice cream, as a binder in vegetarian entrée, or just eaten as they are.

Because the cashew nut is soft, it can be blended to a smooth white liquid with no residue. Moderately high in protein, unsaturated and saturated fatty acids. Source of magnesium, phosphorus, B1,B2, Niacin, Iron and potassium. Having a mild flavor, this nut can be incorporated into many dishes. Cashew Nut Milk may be used in most recipes, to replace whole dairy milk. Lightly toasted cashews can be made into a delicious butter, a nice alternative to peanut butter. (see chapter **Nuts, Seeds & Olives**)

COCONUT

The edible fruit of the coconut palm. A most important product of the tropics. The "milk" is a sweet and nutritious beverage and can be used as liquid in recipes. The fresh or dried "meat" is delicious and when pressed yields an edible oil which is used in making buttery spreads, soaps, shampoo, lip balm, etc. *Cold-pressed* coconut oil is rich in saturated fat, and has a lower melting point than vegetable shortening and margarine that has undergone "hydrogenation". It will partially solidify at room temperature, but will melt in the palm of your hand. Coconut oil should be used in moderation, as with any other oil. Coconuts are a source of insoluble fiber, and beneficial fatty acids: lauric, myristic, caprylic, oleic, and linoleic. Coconuts are best eaten in their whole natural state. (see chapter **Nuts**)

COFFEE SUBSTITUTES

Beverages made from a healthful blend of natural ingredients such as barley, carob, chicory, figs, beet roots, roasted cereals or beans. A variety of brands are available: *Bueno, Cafix, Pero, Postum, Roma,* and *Teeccino.* These are non-addictive and 100% caffeine free!

DATE SUGAR

Dates (many varieties) grow in thick clusters on giant date palm trees. It takes 100 years for the tree to produce dates. It requires 6 pounds of dates to produce 1 pound of date sugar. The dried dates are ground into a fine texture resembling brown sugar. A concentrated form of a very sweet natural whole food, date sugar contains vitamins and minerals including A, B, C, Potassium, and fiber. Dates and date sugar can be used in muffins, bread, granola, etc. in place of refined sugar.

EMES-JEL®: replace with Agar, Gefen, or KOJEL®

Emes-Jel®, no longer available, can be replaced with Kojel® or Gefen made from vegetable gums, or Agar-Agar, a vegetable gelatin from seaweed (see **Agar-Agar**).

Basic Proportions using plain unflavored jel: 1 Tbs. to 2 cups liquid, or follow package directions. Cool to set.

KoJel® info: call 1-800-835-6535; for Gefen, call 1-718-369-4600, 1-800-765-6955

ENER-G® (Substitutes)

Egg Replacer, Baking Powder, and Baking Soda replacements are produced by Ener-G Foods (www.ener-g.com) using ingredients such as: Potato starch, Tapioca Flour, Citric Acid, Calcium Carbonate, and Calcium Lactate (plant source). The simplicity of the formulas require the use of double the amount of baking powder and soda generally listed in many recipes, and following the package instructions carefully, for mixing and baking, in order to achieve optimum results.

FEARN® Products

Soya Powder - purely soybeans which are pre-cooked to enhance nutrition, digestibility, and flavor; used in baking, and making soya milk. *Soya Granules* are small nuggets of toasted soybeans with a nut-like flavor, added to meatless dishes, soups, baked goods and cereal. Other products: *liquid lecithin* and *lecithin granules.*

FLAXSEED

Golden or Brown flax is high in unsaturated fatty acids. Flax Seed is the richest source of essential Omega-3 (linolenic acid). Other plant foods include English and black walnuts, soybeans, spinach, green leafy vegetables and almonds. The Omega-3 fatty acids have been shown to reduce the risk of heart disease, benefit rheumatoid arthritis, depression, and improve memory and brain function. 1 Tbs. of flaxseed oil, is at the top of the list with approximately 7500 mg. of Omega-3 as compared to 1 Tbs. of wheat germ oil which has approximately 925 mg.[2]

Flaxseed also contains Phosphorous, Iron, Niacin, Protein and Fiber. (see recipes in chapter **Nuts, Seeds & Olives**).

GRAINS

Cereal grains-an important staple food. Each grain kernel is actually a single-seeded fruit of various cereal grasses, including Wheat, Barley, Buckwheat, Millet, Corn, Oats, Rice, Rye, etc.

A single kernel can be separated into 3 parts, mainly the germ or heart of grain, which sprouts when the seed is planted, the bran layers or covering of the grain; and the endosperm, or largest part of the grain.

Grains contain approx. 25-300 vitamins and minerals and are primary sources of B1, B2, B6, and Protein, also containing other nutrients such as Calcium, Iron, Phosphorus, Magnesium, etc.

Freshly ground flour made from wheat and other whole grains may be used in making wholesome breads, thus preserving many naturally occurring nutrients which are lost in the milling process. Grains and bread, often referred to as "the Staff of Life" are a principle part of a wholesome diet. (see chapter on **Grains**)

HONEY

The natural pre-digested food produced by honey bees from the nectar and pollen of flowers, differing widely in flavor, color, and trace elements. Honey, a unique food with a long and fascinating history, is the oldest sweet known to mankind. Mentioned in the Bible over 50 times, it is the only natural sweet available that is not manufactured by man. Used in moderation, it is well tolerated by both adults and children. Other beneficial products of the beehive include pollen and royal jelly.

Natural raw honey has been used throughout the centuries for its therapeutic and medicinal values, since bacteria will not grow in raw honey, and has been found to possess antiseptic, wound-healing properties.

Honey is a carbohydrate made up of two invert or simple sugars - levulose (fructose or fruit sugar) and dextrose (glucose or grape sugar) readily absorbed and easily digested. Natural raw, unfiltered (unclarified*) honey contains small amounts of minerals, traces of protein and B vitamins as well as vitamin K, which is known to inhibit tooth decay by halting the formation of acid bacteria in the mouth. Cane sugar loses its Vitamin K in the process of refining. [3]

Refined Sugar, which is 99.95% sucrose, is known as being an "empty calorie" type of non-food. It is white because the vitamins and minerals needed by the body to metabolize the sugar have been processed out. Brown sugar is white sugar to which a small amount of molasses has been added for coloring. Studies and experiments by Dr. John Yudkin, renowned physician-author of Sweet and Dangerous, and
other researchers reveal potential risk to the health of the heart, as well as other health hazards from refined sugar consumption such as: obesity, arthritis, diabetes, tooth decay, etc. [4]

Honey Headlines: It requires 556 bees to gather a full pound of honey. The bees have to fly 35,584 miles to gather this pound, or more than once around the world. Honey in the honeycomb, as "mother nature" provided, nothing added, nothing taken away, is the best way to eat it. Read Proverbs 24:13; 16:24; 25:16; 25:27.

*Clarifying is a process which removes the slight cloudiness, that may be present, resulting in crystal-clear, brilliant honey, but less nourishing. Processed honey that is heated to keep it from crystallizing, causes the honey to lose some of its medicinal properties.

INSTANT CLEAR JEL ®
(Also known as Modified Food Starch) A versatile instant product used commercially in a wide range of applications. Made from pre-gelatinized, stabilized waxy maize starch. Hydrates quickly. Provides high viscosity *without cooking*. Sprinkle in slowly while blending. Used as a thickener and binder for instant puddings, pie fillings, soup, sauces, gravy, or salad dressings. Good freeze-thaw stability. Does not add to the nutrient content of food.

LECITHIN
A food extracted from the soybean containing phosphorus, choline, and inositol. Lecithin is an important constituent of all organs of the human body, and especially the brain, heart, liver, kidneys, and nervous tissue. Lecithin helps to emulsify fat and cholesterol in the body, and may prevent accumulation of fat in the liver, as well as aid in the absorption and utilization of fats. It plays an important part in maintaining a healthy nervous system. Lecithin is available in liquid or granular form. When used in bread and other baked goods - results in a more tender crust, better texture, grain, and keeping quality.

LEGUMES
Pulse / Beans - The seed of a pod bearing plant such as peas, beans and lentils. A rich source of protein, B vitamins, iron, calcium, and phosphorus. When legumes are combined with grains and seeds, the limiting amino acids will balance or complement each other, resulting in a complete protein equal or exceeding that of meat, eggs, cheese or milk. Sprouting legumes increases the Vitamin content, and often assists those who may have difficulty in digesting beans. (see chapter on **Sprouting**)

MALT SYRUP
A sweetener made from grains, mostly barley. The process of malting barley produces enzymes during germination. The aqueous extract is concentrated into syrup or powder, rich in diastase (a type of amylase), used in the digestion of starch. (see Barley Malt)

MAPLE SYRUP
A concentrated golden brown sweetener, made by boiling down the watery sap of sugar maple trees. Maple syrup has a slight caramel flavor, and is often used as a topping.

MOLASSES
A thick syrup which is separated from raw sugar in the process of refining; ranging from light to dark brown with a sweet distinctive flavor. Blackstrap molasses, a bit stronger in flavor, and richer in nutrients, is the residue left from further refining sugar from the cane or beet. Molasses contains iron, calcium, potassium, magnesium, phosphorus, and other trace minerals and vitamins, in lesser amounts. **Sorghum Molasses,** which is less refined, is made from sweet sorghum grain.

NUTS
See chapter on **Nuts, Seeds, and Olives.**

OILS

In vegetable form, **unsaturated fats and fatty acids** are abundant in raw nuts and seeds, legumes, various grains and in fruits such as olives and avocado. Cold-pressed oils as Flax, Olive, Sesame, Canola, and Soybean, are also good sources.

Unsaturated fats are an essential part of the diet, providing energy, as carriers for the fat-soluble vitamins A, D, E, and K, aiding in the absorption of vitamin D and Calcium, etc. Diets deficient in unsaturated fats and fatty acids could lead to excess loss of weight and eczematous conditions of the skin.

Saturated fats are usually solid at room temperature and primarily from animal sources such as butter, lard, and cream. Vegetable shortening and most margarine have undergone *"hydrogenation"* a process of heating the oil under pressure, which converts the liquid oil into a more *"saturated"* or solid form. This process adversely alters the fat molecules into *trans fats* which significantly raise LDL and cholesterol levels.

Oils and margarine from a culinary point of view, add texture and flavor to plain food. The choices and methods of extracting and processing are many; the nutritional value of pure cold-pressed oils is only a portion of the value found in the whole seed, nut or fruit.

The **unsaturated fats and fatty acids**, as provided by nature in the nuts, fruits, seeds, legumes, and grains, are the best suited for digestion and optimal health. For more information on **Oils,** see chapter 5: **Breads**, Staff of Life; chapter 11: **Nuts, Seeds and Olives** (Olives); and chapter 13: **Salad Dressings** (Salad Oils).

SEA SALT

Sea Salt harvested from seawater, carefully sifted to remove natural debris, then dried by sun and wind, or other low temperature drying methods which do not alter the molecular structure of the salt. Methods for producing natural sea salts vary widely. Celtic Sea Salt contains trace amounts of more than 80 vital minerals, not found in common table salt. These beneficial trace elements partially compensate for the harmful effects of excess sodium. When used in moderation, it is a universally prized seasoning.

Rock salt mined from inland salt mines may contain some trace elements. These salts may be slightly off-color as compared with refined common table salt. Salt plays an important role in many body functions; however only a small amount is needed. The daily need for salt is mainly provided in foods naturally; adding salt should be sparingly.

SEAWEED

Sea vegetation or marine plant species, varying in color from red to purplish-black. Seaweed is harvested off the coastlines of U.S., Japan, Korea, Canada, and Norway, where some of the finest seaweed farming is established. Edible varieties include Dulse, Nori, Kelp, Kombu, Wakame, Hijiki, Spirulina, and Agar. Sea vegetables, or marine algae, provide a rich source of trace elements and minerals including iodine, iron, calcium, potassium, also vitamin A, B, C and protein. Nori, Kelp, and Dulse have been found to contain Omega 3, and traces of Vit. B12. [5]

Seaweed is low in fat; a good source of dietary fiber and chlorophyll. Valued by weight watchers, pregnant women, nursing mothers, and those who want to grow healthy hair.

The dried sheets are used for wrapping sushi and rice balls, in grain or bean dishes. The powdered form is often used as a salt substitute, in salads, soups, and vegetables. An important source of nutrients especially for the total vegetarian, plant based diet.

SESAME SEED

Originally a staple food of the Middle East. A nutritious, small flat seed, yielding an oil which is used as food, in natural cosmetics, and in making soap. Sesame seeds are an excellent source of Calcium, Phosphorus, and Protein. High in Iron, mono-unsaturated fat, and containing a good percentage of the 8 essential amino acids, especially methionine-important to maintaining healthy liver function. Food values tend to be higher in whole brown sesame seeds, and in the mechanically hulled sesame seed versus the chemically hulled. See chapter on **Nuts and Seeds & Olives**, and recipes.

SOYBEANS

Widely grown in China, Japan, and the U.S. A legume which yields oil, flour, and meal. The soybean (both plant and bean) is cultivated for its many uses and known as the "wonder" crop. Soybeans are the "meat" of the Orient, and serve as the major source of protein in the plant based vegetarian diet. There are more than 2,000 kinds of soybeans, with numerous varieties being cultivated in the U.S. Fully mature, dry soybeans, are light tan to yellow in color.

The soybean is rich in food values. Soybeans (weight for weight) contain approximately twice as much protein as navy or lima beans, twice as much protein as meat or fish, four times as much protein as eggs, and twelve times as much protein as milk. Soybeans contain an average of 18% fat, chiefly consisting of the essential unsaturated fatty acids. This "wonder" bean is also the richest source of lecithin, surpassing that which is found in eggs (yolk). Some authorities list by analysis the presence of Vitamin B12 in soybeans. [6]

Soybeans are both economical and very useful. Can be made into milk, bean curd (tofu), meatless dishes, added to soups, made into flour to enhance the food value of bread (1 part to 7 parts wheat), baked, boiled, or sprouted (increased vitamin C, and cooking time shortened when sprouted). Soybean milk can be used to replace dairy milk in recipes, with good results.

SPROUTS

See chapter on **Sprouting**.

STEVIA

This herbal sweetener (Stevia Rebaudiana) is approx. 80 times sweeter than sugar. Stevia is from South America, and has been used there for centuries. Though fairly new in the U.S. it is often used for low sugar, low carbohydrate, and weight-loss diets. A pinch of the powdered herb will sweeten a cup of herbal tea; 4-5 drops of the liquid extract equals 1 tsp. sugar.

SUCANAT ®

Unrefined evaporated 100% cane juice, with only the water removed. The nutritional analysis of Sucanat shows it to contain up to 3% mineral salts and trace elements, as compared to common table sugar (sucrose) which contains none. Sucanat has a rich, full flavor, containing all the molasses, and is used cup-for-cup, to replace sugar in recipes.

SUGAR SUBSTITUTES

Avoid artificial chemical sweeteners such as: Aspartame, Equal, NutraSweet, Splenda, Saccharin, Sucralose, etc. See natural sweeteners: Agave Syrup, Barley Malt, Date Sugar, Natural Raw Honey, Maple Syrup, Molasses, Rice Syrup, Sorghum, and Sucanat.

SUNFLOWER SEEDS

One of the richest foods in nutritional value. Sunflower seeds are a good source of protein, vitamins, and minerals. The protein content of sunflower seeds is approximately 30-35%, being equal to that of meat, with no putrefying bacteria, and containing 45-50% oil which is highly unsaturated.

Sunflower seeds excel in Phosphorus and contain good amounts of Calcium, Potassium, Magnesium, Niacin, Iron, Vitamin A, B1, and B6. Lesser amounts of Copper, Zinc, Silicon, and Fluorine are also included, making sunflower seeds a good survival food.

The excellent teeth of the Russian peasants may be due to the fact that they eat so many sunflower seeds, which provide magnesium and fluorine, so necessary for healthy teeth.

Delicious added to cereal or fruit, in granola, cookies, breads, meatless entrée, or just eaten out of hand. The kernels can be crushed, ground fine , or made into seed butter. Try sprouting them! See chapters on **Nuts and Seeds** & **Sprouting**.

TAHINI

Also known as sesame tahini or sesame seed butter. Tahini is made from the hulled sesame seeds which have been ground to a fine paste. Rich in unsaturated fatty acids, protein, vitamins, minerals, and trace elements. Approximately 45% protein and 55% oil. Rich in calcium and phosphorus and containing similar nutrients as whole sesame seed. An easy-to-digest versatile food, used in a variety of recipes. An important ingredient in Hummus, a dip of pureed garbanzo beans. Tahini can be mixed with peanut butter or honey for a delicious spread. A nutritious addition to nut milk and soymilk, dairyless cheese, cream soup, salad dressing, spreads, baby foods, desserts, etc. (see recipes)

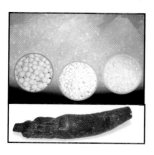

TAPIOCA

A granular preparation of the cassava root (also called yucca of the agave family). A good choice for thickening foods especially fruits, puddings, pies, and foods that will be frozen. Unlike flour or cornstarch frozen tapioca mixtures retain their thickness when thawing and reheating. Tapioca is a nutritious and easily digested starch, available in large or small pearl and the convenient granulated or powdered form.

TOFU

Soybean curd, bean curd (dòufu) or soy cheese. A staple food in the Orient, much like potatoes in America. Tofu, is rich in protein, cholesterol free and low in sodium. A popular plant-based choice for vegetarians, low fat diets, and weight-loss pro-grams. Tofu is made by curdling soy milk. Although almost tasteless by itself, tofu acts like a sponge, easily absorbing other flavors. A versatile and delicious food that can be made at home for less than .25¢ per pound, and available at most markets, as water-packed, fresh, or seasoned and ready-to-eat. A rich source of tryptophan, an important amino acid, needed to optimize melatonin levels. [7] A good source of calcium, phosphorus, iron, plant estrogens, and the essential amino acids. Especially nutritious when combined with the complementary protein in grains.

Tofu can be prepared in a variety of ways: scrambled (resembling eggs), baked, in soups, salads, meatless entrees, on pizza, in cheesecake, salad dressing, dips, and spreads (see recipes). Store tofu in the refrigerator (unless in an aseptic package). Once opened, refrigerate, covered with water up to 1 week, changing water daily. Tofu can be frozen, which results in a change of texture, which is more spongy.

VANILLA BEAN

The seed-pod of a tropical climbing orchid, used in making vanilla flavoring. The vanilla bean is 8-10 inches long, and has a pleasant sweet odor. Most of the flavor is in the tiny seeds of this thin pod. When the pod is split and the seeds scraped out, they bring an intense vanilla flavor, and dark brown confetti-like flecks to dishes. *Pure vanilla* extracts (brown, clear, powdered) although more expensive, impart a richer flavor. Pure *white vanilla powder* or *clear vanilla,* are substituted in dessert recipes, where color is a factor. For making homemade vanilla flavoring, see recipe in Miscellaneous chapter.

WHEAT GERM

Untreated raw embryo of select wheat. The heart (life) of the kernel. Wheat germ, is a rich source of Protein and Vitamin E. Also a good source of the B-vitamins, especially Thiamine (B1), Phosphorus, Iron, and Magnesium. Vitamin E, found in raw wheat germ oil, is necessary for a healthy heart. The widespread practice of milling wheat into refined white flour has resulted in a loss of Vitamin E. Vitamin E is associated with a decreased risk in heart disease and a deficiency of this antioxidant is linked to the staggering rise in cardiovascular disease. [8]

Wheat germ can be used in bread, on cereal, and fruit. When lightly toasted it has a nutty flavor. Keep refrigerated.

YEAST

Dried (inactive) nutritional food yeast has been recognized as an excellent source of many nutrients such as protein, vitamins, and minerals. *Primary grown yeasts* are pure strains of microscopic one-celled plants grown in purified cane and beet molasses under controlled conditions, yielding top quality food yeast. Primary yeasts are not obtained as a by-product of the brewery or any other manufacture.

Nutritional food yeast may vary in color, flavor, and texture, containing 50% high quality protein (all the essential amino acids), a rich source of B-complex vitamins including Niacin, also Iron, Phosphorus, and trace minerals. Some types contain Vitamin B-12, [9] an important factor in the total vegetarian diet. The flaked or powdered form is easily dispersed in liquids, and can be stirred into tomato juice for a quick pick-up. Used in cooking (see recipes), or sprinkled on toast, popcorn, or spaghetti in place of cheese. Tasty and nutritious!

Note: This glossary of Natural Foods provides a description and/or composition of the foods and does not imply that any single food will provide the minimum daily requirement of the nutrients listed.

1 **Taber's Cyclopedic Medical Dictionary**, 14th ed., (Philadelphia: F.A. Davis Co., 1981)

2 Nedley, Neil M.D., **Proof Positive**, Ardmore, OK., 1999 pgs. 122-123, 273

3 Miller, William, "Honey in Nutrition," Lee Foundation for Nutritional Research, Milwaukee, Wis.
Norris, P.E.; **About Honey: Everything You Want to Know**, (New York: Pyramid Communications, Inc., 1975) pgs. 9-54
"I'll take Honey, Thank You," Prevention Magazine, (Emmaus, Pa.: Rodale Press, August 1976) pgs. 132-74

4 "What's So Bad About Sugar?" Executive Fitness, Editors, (Emmaus, Pa.: Rodale Press, 1978)

5 Binding, G. J., and Moyle, A., **About Kelp: Seaweed for Health and Vitality,** (London: Thorsons Publ., 1976) pgs. 28-31
Shurtleff, W.R., and Aoyagi, A., **The Book of Tofu**, (Tokyo: Autumn Press, 1975) pgs. 326-28
Kirschmann, John D., **Nutrition Almanac**, (Nutrition Search, Inc., New York: McGraw-Hill Paperbacks, 1984) pg. 235
"Dulse: A Natural Marine Plant," Atlantic Mariculture Ltd., New Brunswick, Canada
Balch, James F., M.D. and Balch, Phyllis A.,C.N.C., **Prescription for Nutritional Healing,** (Avery Publishing, 1990) pgs. 43, 55
Pamplona-Roger, George D., M.D. Enclopedia of Foods and Their Healing Power, Toledo Spain, 2004 (distributed in USA by Review & Herald Publishing Assoc., Hagerstown, Maryland) pgs. 134-135

6 Chen, Philip S., Ph.D., and Chung, Helen D., M.S., **Soybeans: For Health and a Longer Life**, (New Canaan: Keats Publ., 1973) pgs. 3-24
Heinz Nutritional Data, 6th ed. (Pittsburgh: Heinz International Research Center 1972) pgs. 60-61
Oliver, Martha H., **Add a Few Sprouts**, (Conn.: Keats Publ., 1975) pg. 49 quoted from: Rohatgi, K., Banerjee, M., "Effect of Germination on VitaminB12 values of pulses (leguminous seeds)," Jour, Nut. 56:403-408

7 Nedley, Neil M.D., **Proof Positive**, Ardmore, OK., 1999 pg. 204

8 Shute, Wilfrid E., and Taub, Harold J., **Vitamin E for Ailing and Healthy Hearts**, (New York: Jove Publ., 1983)

9 **Heinz Nutritional Data**, 6th ed. (Pittsburgh: Heinz International Research Center, 1972) Vit. B12 in foods - pg. 61 Red Star, **Primary Grown Nutritional Yeasts Report**, 1977

"If we plan wisely, that which is most conducive to health can be secured in almost every land. The various preparations of rice, wheat, corn and oats are sent abroad everywhere, also beans, peas and lentils. These, with native or imported fruits, and the variety of vegetables that grow in each locality, give an opportunity to select a dietary that is complete without the use of flesh meats."
E. G. White, Ministry of Healing, pg. 209

Fruits, Vegetables, Legumes and Grains contain thousands of phytochemicals (complex substances found only in plant-based foods) that stimulate the body's natural immunity and act as antioxidants in the prevention of disease.

Our Daily Food Needs

	A (Provitamin, Carotene)	**B₁** (Thiamin)
VITAMIN	Found in nature, as the orange-yellow pigment carotene, which is changed into vitamin A in the body. Exists as pre-formed vitamin A in fish-liver oil, milk fat, and eggs. **Fat soluble.**	One fraction of B complex. Widely distributed in nature, especially in the germ of cereals and in the outer layers of whole grains. Destroyed by long exposure to heat and oxidation. **Water soluble.**
FUNCTION IN BODY	Essential for normal growth and development, normal tooth formation, proper functioning on the body, healthy skin and mucous membranes. Prevents development of nrutitional night blindness. Maintains normal infection resistance, and normal pregnancy and lacation.	Essential for normal growth, proper utilization of sugars and starches, normal functioning of the nervous system, maintenance of appetite, noral tone and functioning of the digestive tract. Healthy nerves, promotes appetite, normal pregrancy and lactation.

VALUABLE SOURCES

A		**B₁**	
Apricots	Papaya	Apples	Legumes
Avacados	Parsley	Alfalfa sprouts	Nuts
Broccoli	Peaches	Avacados	Milk
Cantaloupe	Peas	Bananas	Soybean milk
Carrots	Pumpkin, cooked	Brewer's yeast	Sunflower seeds
Collards	Red bell peppers	Carob	Peas
Dark green salads	Spinach	Citrus fruits	Wheat germ
Green beans	Sweet potatoes	Grapes	Whole grain cereals
Green & yellow vegetables	Tomatoes	Green leafy vegetables	Vegetables
Kale	Turnip greens		
Mango	Watercress		
Mustard greens	Winter squash		

Avoid adding soda to vegetables (increases destruction of thiamin).

RECOMMENDED DAILY ALLOWANCES

	A		**B₁**
Adults	5,000 units	Adults	1.2-2.0 mg.
Pregnancy	6,000 units	Pregnancy	1.3 mg.
Lactation	8,000 units	Lactation	1.7 mg.
Children	2,000-5,000 units	Children	0.7-1.8 mg.
Infants	1,500 units	Infants	0.4-0.5 mg.

Muscular activity, pregancy, and lactation increase need for thiamin.

Approximate values:

	A		**B₁**
Apricots, dried (4 halves)	1,500 units	Beans, navy, dry (1/2 cup cooked)	0.27 mg.
Butter (1 Tbs)	400 units	Bread, 100% whole wheat (6 slices)	0.45 mg.
Carrots (1 medium)	11,000 units	Soybeans, dry (1 1/2 c. cooked)	0.40 mg.
Egg yolk	800 units	Whole wheat cereal, (1 oz dry)	0.15 mg.
Milk, 1 qt.	1,500-2,000 units		
Potato, sweet (1 medium)	4,500 units		

RESULTS OF LACK OR DEFICIENCY

A	**B₁**
• Retarded Growth • Respiratory Infections • Night blindness • Rough, dry skin	• Mild: Loss of appetite • Impaired digestion of sugars and starches • Constipation or diarrhea • Emaciation • Severe: Beriberi Nervous disorders of various types

B_2
(Riboflavin)

Found in wide variety of plant and animal foods. Heat stable. Unstable to light. **Water soluble.**

Essential for normal growth and development, and along with other fractions of the B complex, for utilization of food energy. Involved specifically in process of oxidation within the cells of the body. Healthy skin and eyes.

Apricots	Nuts
Bananas	Peas
Beans	Seeds
Brewers' yeast	Soy milk & cheese
Carob	Sprouts: alfalfa, soy
Citrus fruits	Tomatoes
Eggs	Wheat germ
Legumes	Whole grains
Milk & cheese	

Adults	1.6-2.5 mg.
Pregnancy	2.0 mg.
Lactation	2.5 mg.
Children	1-2 mg.
Infants	0.4-0.9 mg.

Approximate values:

Bread, 100% whole wheat (6 slices)	0.16 mg.
Broccoli (3 stalks with buds)	0.40 mg.
Milk, whole (1 qt.)	1.80 mg.
Soybeans, dry (1 cup dried)	0.65 mg.
Turnip greens (1/2 cup cooked)	0.40 mg.
Yeast (1 Tbs.)	0.44 mg.

- Impaired growth
- Lassitude
- Weakness - fatigue
- Pale lips
- Rough red tongue
- Headaches, Digestive disturbances

Niacin - B_3
(Niacinamide - Nicotinic acid)

Found in natural foods in small amounts. Not destroyed by heat, light, or air. **Water soluble.**

Essential for normal growth and development. Associated with other B vitamins in utilization of food energy. Healthy clear skin.

Alfalfa sprouts	Mushrooms
Brewers' yeast	Natural rice
Broccoli	Peanuts (very high)
Carrots	Tomatoes
Green leafy	Wheat germ
vegetables	Whole grains
Legumes	

Adults	12-20 mg.
Pregnancy	15 mg.
Lactation	15 mg.
Children	8-21 mg.
Infants	6-7 mg.

Approximate values:

Bread, 100% whole wheat, 6 slices	5.1 mg.
Bread, white enriched, 6 slices	3.8 mg.
Milk, 1 quart	1.6 mg.
Potato, 1 sweet	1.9 mg.
Peanuts, 1 cup	23.3 mg.
Yeast, 1 Tbs.	2.9 mg.

- Mental disturbances
- Gastro-Intestinal disturbances
- Pellagra
- Dermatitis
- Black tongue (in dogs)

C
(Ascorbic acid)

Widely distributed in natural staple foods, especially among fruits, particularly citrus fruits. **Water soluble.**

Essential for normal growth and development, maintainance of practically all body tissues, especially those having to do with joint structures, the ligaments, bones, teeth, and gums. Promotes healing. Increased resistance to infections.

Asparagus	Mangoes
Avacado	Mustard greens
Berries	Oranges
Cantaloupes	Papaya
Currants	Pineapples
Green leafy	Potatoes
vegetables	Strawberries
Grapefruit	Sweet peppers
Lemons	Tomatoes

Most fruit & vegetables

Adults	75-100 mg.
Pregnancy	100 mg.
Lactation	150 mg.
Children	35-100 mg.
Infants	30 mg.

Approximate values:

Grapefruit, 1/2	50 mg.
Green cabbage, 1 cup shredded	40 mg.
Green pepper, 1 raw	76 mg.
Guava, 1	200 mg.
Orange juice, 1/2 cup	60 mg.
Potato, baked, 1 large	12 mg.
Tomatoes, fresh (1 medium)	30 mg.
Tomato juice, 1/2 cup fresh or canned	30 mg.

- Bleeding gums
- Lowered resistance to disease
- Tender joints
- Susceptibility to dental caries
- Scurvy

Our Daily Food Needs (continued)

	D	**B$_{12}$** *(Cyanocobalamin)*
VITAMIN	Natural food sources of Vitamin D are meager. Stable under refrigeration. Stored in liver. **Fat soluble.**	Soluble in water or alcohol.
FUNCTION IN BODY	•Essential for normal growth and development. •Promotes use of calcium and phosphorus in formation of bones and teeth. •Especially needed for infants, children, and women during pregnancy and lactation. Deficiency leads to rickets.	•Essential in the formation of red blood cells. •Produces remision in pernicious anemia. •Proper digestion and absorption promotes normal growth and development.
VALUABLE SOURCES **Lesser or Trace Amounts**	Sunlight Dairy products (fortified with Vit. D) Fish-liver oil Ultraviolet rays from special lamps acting on the skin Soy milk (enriched) [9]Yeast [7](fortified) [10]Sea Vegetables (Dulse, Nori, etc)	Dairy products Human milk Soy milk (fortified) [12]Barley [11]Soybeans [10]Sea Vegetables (Dulse, Nori, etc) [12]Spinach [13]Sprouts Sunlight [11]Wheat, corn [9]Yeast
RECOMMENDED DAILY ALLOWANCES	Adults - none except in pregnancy Pregnancy 400 I.U. Lactation 400 I.U. Children & Infants 400 I.U. *Approximate values:* Milk, whole, fortified with Vitamin D, 1 quart 400 I.U.	3.5 micrograms (1 millionth of a gram)
RESULTS OF LACK OR DEFICIENCY	•Mild: Interferes with utilization of calcium and phosphorus in bone and teeth formation. •Irritability •Weakness Severe: Rickets	•Anemia •Nerve problems

[9] Taber's Cyclopedic Medical Dictionary 14th ed., (Phil; F. A. Davis Co., 1981) app. 139
[10] Binding, G. J., and Moyle, A., *About Kelp: Seaweed for Health and Vitality*, (Londan: Thorsons Publ., 1976) pgs 28-31
  "Dulse: A Marine Plant," Atlantic Mariculture Ltd., New Brunswick, Canada
  Shurtleff, W. R., *The Book of Tofu*, (Tokyo: Autumn Press, 1975) pgs. 326-28
[11] Red Star, Primary Grown Nutritional Yeasts Report, 1977
  Heinz Nutritional Data, 6th ed. (Pittsburgh: Heinz International Research Center, 1972) pgs 60-61
[12] Rodale and Staff, Hylton, W. H. (ed), *Rodale Herb Book*, (Emmaus, Pa.: Rodale Books, 1974) Comfrey pgs. 410-14
[12] Campbell TC. B$_{12}$ Breakthrough: Missing Ingredients Found in Plants. New Century Nutrition 1996 Nov 2 (11):1-2
  Gates J. Vitamin B$_{12}$: When Myth Meets Discovery, New Century Nutrition 1996 Nov 2 (11):3.
[13] Rohatgi, K.: and Banerjee, M., Effect of Germination on Vit. B$_{12}$ values of pulses (leguminous seeds)" 1955. Jour. Nutrition 56:403-408

# E *(Alpha tocopherol)*	# K *(Blood coagulation vitamin)*	# Folic Acid *(Folate, folacin)*
Fat soluble Stable to heat	Fat soluble	Coenzyme with B_{12} and Vitamin C Heat and water soluble.
• Antioxidant • Protects red blood cells • Anti-clotting factor • Improved heart & brain function • May retard aging • Protects against environmental products	• Normal clotting of blood. • Anti-hemorrhagic • Essential for good circulation	• Red blood cell formation • Body growth and reproduction of cells • Utilization of proteins • Promotes brain function
Cold-pressed oils (wheat germ, corn, safflower, soy, etc.) Dark green leafy vegetables Grapes Legumes Lettuce varieties Nuts (almonds), seeds, etc Wheat germ Whole grains	Alfalfa Cabbage Green leafy vegetables Kale Oats Rye Wheat	Asparagus Avacados Black-eyed peas Broccolli Cauliflower Dark green leafy vegetables Fenugreek (sprouts) Legumes (garbanzos, limas, lentils, pintos, etc) Nuts (almonds, filberts, etc.) Whole grains Yeast, nutritional food
10-30 mg.	up to 100 mcg. (depending on age, sex)	400 micrograms (adult) 600 mcg. (lactation) 800-1000 mcg. (pregnancy)
• Fragility & rupture of red blood cells • Muscle & tissue degeneration • Faulty absorption of fat, iron, and soluble vitamins (A, D, F, K) • Heart related diseases • Anemia of newborn, premature births, miscarriages, infertility	• Prolongs blood clotting. • Causes hemorrhages.	• Poor growth • Macrocytic anemias • Intestinal disorders • Dizziness, fatigue

There are other vitamins and minerals not listed that have a role in human nutrition such as B_6, (Pyridoxine), Biotin, Choline, Pantothenic Acid, etc.

When a large variety of whole plant based foods are properly combined and included in the diet, the nutrients needed for proper nutrition and optimum health are usually supplied. However, to avoid deficiency, vitamin and other food supplements are readily available to those who wish to insure an adequate supply of those limited nutrients (such as B_{12}) present in a plant based total vegetarian diet.

Four Main Minerals

There are seventeen or more mineral elements in the body, thirteen of which are known to be absolutely essential. If we obtain adequate amounts of calcium, phosphorus, iron, and iodine each day in our foods, it is likely that we shall not be lacking in the other mineral elements.

	## Calcium	## Phosphorus
AMOUNT IN BODY	1.5% of body weight. 99% of this in bones. (About 2 ¼ pounds in average man.)	Calcium and phosphorus comprise 95% of minerals found in bones. There is twice as much calcium and phosphorus in body as all other minerals put together.
NEEDED FOR	• Contributes to formation of strong bones and teeth. • Helps to clot blood, regulate heart-beat, maintain mineral balance in all body tisues. • Calcium, phosphorus, and Vitamin D help prevent softening of bones as occurs in rickets. • Vitamin D must be present for proper calcium utilization.	• Combines with calcium, helps form and maintain bones and teeth. • Found in nucleus of each cell. • Assists body cells to absorb food and get rid of wastes. • Abundant in nervous tissue (brain & nerve cells). • Found in blood stream and muscle tissue. • Essential to normal glandular system. • Vitamin D is important in absorption of phosphorus.

GOOD SOURCES	Grams of Calcium per 100 grams fresh substance (100 grams = approx 3 ½ oz)		Grams of Phosphorus per 100 grams fresh substance (100 grams = approx 3 ½ oz)	
	Almonds	0.25	Almonds	0.45
	Beans, dried	0.15	Barley	
	Carob flour		Bran	
	Figs, dried	0.16	Dried fruit	
	Green Leafy Vegetables :		Legumes	
	Broccoli	0.30	Lentils	0.38
	Collards	0.20	Milk, dairy products	
	Kale	0.28	Nuts and seeds	
	Mustard greens	0.25	Oatmeal	0.38
	Turnip greens	0.35	Peas, dried	0.41
	Milk, dairy products		Peanuts	0.39
	Molasses	0.25	Soybeans	0.66
	Oranges		Vegetables (many)	
	Pineapple		Whole grains	
	Sesame, sunflower seeds			
	Soybeans, dried	0.23		
	Tofu, soy cheese			
	Whole grains			

DAILY ALLOWANCE	Calcium in foods is measured in grams One ounce equals about 30 grams.		Phosphorus in foods is measured in grams. One ounce equals about 30 gr.	
	Adults	0.8 grams	Adults	0.88 - 1.5 grams
	Pregnancy	1.5 - 2 grams	Pregnancy & lactation	1.5 - 2 grams
	Lactation	1.5 - 2 grams	Children	1.0 - 1.6 grams
	Children	1.0 - 1.4 grams		

DEFICIENCY	• Brittle bones and nails • Dental Caries • Rickets • Poor bone development • Excessive bleeding • Muscle cramps	• Perverted appetite • Retarded growth • Loss of weight • Weakness • Imperfect development of bones, and teeth

Iron

Total amount of iron found in the body is less than the weight of a penny. About 3 grams in actual weight, or .004% of body composition.

- Small amount of iron in all blood cells.
- Most of iron in red blood cells.
- Helps to form hemoglobin: red coloring matter of red blood cells.
- Vital to transporting oxygen to every body cell.
- Insufficient iron in diet causes anemia.

Milligrams of Iron per 100 grams fresh substance (100 grams = approx 3 ½ oz)	
Beans (dried)	10.5
Egg yolk	8.6
Fruits (dried):	
Apricots	7.6
Peaches	6.1
Prunes	2.8
Green leafy vegetables:	
Chard, Collard, Kale,	
Turnip greens	2.5-3.5
Molasses	7.3
Peas (dried, split)	5.7
Soybeans	8.8
Whole-grain cereals:	
Oatmeal	5.2
Quinoa	5.4

Iron is measured in milligrams. The head of a common pin weighs about one milligram.

Adults	12 mg.
Pregnancy & Lactation	15-18 mg.
Children	8-12 mg.

- Anemia
- Pale complexion
- Lowered vitality
- Retarded development
- Decreased red blood cells and hemoglobin
- Brittle hair

Iodine

Only 1/100th os much iodine as iron in the body - less than a grain of wheat. About 50 milligrams of iodine in whole body.

- Essential to thyroid gland in making a hormone which regulates the rate food is burned in the body.. This hormone is important for proper growth and development.
- Deficiency of iodine causes simple goiter, an enlargement of thyroid gland, prevalent around the Great Lakes and Pacific Northwest regions.

- Kelp
- Dulse
- Iodized salt
- Green leafy vegetables grown near seashore, or in soil not depleted of iodine content

Note: Knowledge is lacking of exact amounts of iodine in many foods, owing to difficulty of measuring such minute quantities.

Needed in only trace amounts. Iodine is measured in milligrams; 1,000 mg = 1 gram.

Estimated .05 - 0.1 milligrams per day. Growing children and pregnant women need several times as much as adults.

- Simple goiter
- Retarded physical, sexual and mental development in the young (cretinism).

Other Minerals

MINERALS	BODY FUNCTION	GOOD SOURCES	
CHLORINE - (digestive system)	• Body Cleanser • Expels wastes	Beets Coconut	Radishes Sea Salt
FLUORINE - (bones, teeth)	• Disease resister • Knits bones • Body beautifier	Brussel Sprouts Cabbage Cauliflower Spinach	Sprouts Tomatoes Watercress
MAGNESIUM - (nerve and muscle support, digestive, laxative)	• Promotes new cells • Relaxes nerves • Prevents & relieves constipation • Activates enzymes • Assists in calcium & phosphorus uptake	Apples Avacados Bananas Barley Coconut Eggplant Figs Grapefruit	Garlic Green leafy vegetables Kelp Oranges Sesame Seeds Tofu Whole Grains
MANGANESE - (hemoglobin - enzyme activator)	• Aids in forming hemoglobin • Activates enzymes • Improves memory • Helps protein & fat metabolism • Helps blood sugar regulation	Avacados Bananas Beans Beets Blueberries Bran Chard	Leafy greens Nuts Pineapple Seaweed Seeds Spinach Whole grains
POTASSIUM - (cell and tissue secretion mineral)	• Healthy nervous system • Helps regulate heart rhythm and acid-base balance • Maintains weight • Muscle toner • Good for nerves, good disposition, grace, beauty	Almonds Apricots Avacados Bananas Beans Blueberries Cabbage Coconut Dandelion Dried fruits Fresh vegetables	Grapes Legumes Molasses Nuts Olives Parsley Potato skins Watercress Whole grains
SILICON - (skeleton structure, bones, teeth, hair, skin, nails)	• Hard teeth • Glossy hair • Sparkling eyes • Keen hearing • Tones up body, gives resistance	Alfalfa Asparagus Barley Cabbage Cucumbers Flax	Oats Seeds Spinach Strawberries Tomatoes
SODIUM - (body fluids maintainer)	• Normal heart action • Body equilibrium • Preserves balance between calcium and potassium • Regulates body fluids • Aids digestion	Asparagus Beets Carrots Celery Coconut Cucumbers Most foods contain some sodium	Figs Oatmeal Okra String beans Turnips
SULPHUR - (brain and tissue)	• Synthesis of body proteins • Ion balance of tissues • Resists bacteria • Healthy hair, nails, & skin	Almonds Asparagus Bell peppers Broccoli Brussels sprouts Cabbage Cauliflower Chestnuts Eggplant Garlic	Kale Legumes Lentils Mustard greens Nuts Onions Soybeans Turnips Whole grains

Other Dietary Essentials

FUEL (Carbohydrates and fats)	PROTEINS (Building blocks)	FIBER & BULK (Soluble and Insoluble)	WATER (Principal chemical constituent of body: 75%)
Function:	**Function:**	**Function:**	**Function:**
• Supplying heat and energy to the body	• Essential for growth • Building new tissue • Repairing broken-down tissue • Heat and energy in body	• Intestinal cleansing action • Prevents constipation • Powers blood circulation • Lowers blood cholesterol • Stabilizes blood sugar levels	• Digestion & absorbtion of food • Transport waste products • Most universal solvent • Important in regulation and maintenance of body temperature • Principal constituent of all body fluids • Circulation, excretion
Sources:	**Sources:**	**Sources:**	**Sources:**
Avacado & Olives Breads Cereals Fats & Oils Fruits Legumes Nuts & Seeds Starchy vegetables Whole Grains	Legumes, Peanuts Nuts, Seeds MIlk & Eggs Soybeans Soy milk & cheese Whole grains	Beans Carob flour Coconut Fruits & vegetables Nuts & seeds Oat bran, Rice bran Whole grains	Pure clear soft water Fruits Melons
Daily Amount:	**Daily Amount:**	**Daily Amount:**	**Daily Amount:**
(Varies with age, sex, lifestyle, body size, etc) Carbohydrates 60-75% of diet; Fats (mainly unsaturated) 15-25% of diet	Approx. 10 - 20% of diet (Best = plant sources) Children - 2-3 grams p er kilogram of body weight Divide normal weight by 2.2 to find amount needed in diet.	Adequate / abundant in a plant based diet.	4 - 8 glasses daily in addition to juice, milk, soup, fruits
Deficiency:	**Deficiency:**	**Deficiency:**	**Deficiency:**
• Loss in weight • Lessened energy	• Stunted growth • Early aging • Lessened vigor • Craving for sugar *Excess protein may result in calcium loss	• Various diseases • Obesity • Constipation • Colon cancer • Heart disease • Other disorders	• Many ailments • Constipation • Dehydration • Toxic condition • Imbalance in body fluids

Natural Food Equivalents

	Unit	Approx. Measure
AGAR flakes	1 lb.	10 cups
AGAR flakes	1 oz.	⅝ cup
AGAR granulated	1 lb.	4 cups
AGAR granulated	1 oz.	¼ cup
ALFALFA SEED	1 lb.	2 ¼ cups
ARROWROOT POWDER	1 lb.	3 cups
BERRIES, fresh	1 lb.	3-4 cups
CAROB POWDER	1 lb.	5 ⅓ cups
CEREAL/GRAINS, dry		
Barley, whole	1 lb.	2 ½ cups
Buckwheat Groats	1 lb.	2 ¾ cups
Corn Meal, yellow	1 lb.	3 cups
Corn, whole popcorn	1 lb.	2 ⅓ cups
Millet, whole	1 lb.	2 ½ cups
Oat Groats, whole	1 lb.	2 ¾ cups
Oat Meal, quick	1 lb.	6 cups
Rye Flakes	1 lb.	5 cups
Rice, Brown, whole	1 lb.	2 ⅔ cups
Wheat Flakes	1 lb.	4 ½ cups
Wheat, whole	1 lb.	2 ½ cups
CHEESE, soy or cottage	1 lb.	2 cups
COCONUT, Shredded	1 lb.	4 ¾ cups
EGGS, whole	3 med.	½ cup
FLOUR		
Corn	1 lb.	4 ½ cups
Graham	1 lb.	4 cups
Oat	1 lb.	4 ¼ cups
Rye	1 lb.	6 cups
Soy	1 lb.	4 cups
Unbleached white	1 lb.	4 cups
Whole Wheat	1 lb.	3 ½ cups
FRUITS, Dry		
Apricots, unsulphured	1 lb.	3 ½ cups
Dates, pitted	1 lb.	2 - 2 ½ cups
Figs, black	1 lb.	2 ½ cups
Peaches, unsulphured	1 lb.	3 cups
Prunes, whole	1 lb.	2 ½ cups
Raisins	1 lb.	3 cups

LEGUMES, Dry

Fava Beans	1 lb.	3 cups
Garbanzos (chick peas)	1 lb.	3 cups
Lentils	1 lb.	2 ½ cups
Mung Beans	1 lb.	2 ¾ cups
Navy Beans	1 lb.	2 ¼ cups
Peas, green split	1 lb.	2 ¼ cups
Soy, green dry	1 lb.	2 ½ cups
Soy, yellow dry	1 lb.	2 ½ cups
Soy, yellow soaked	1 lb.	6 ½ cups (2 ¼ lb.)

MILK, Whole, Soy, Nut	1 lb.	2 cups
MILK, Soy powder (dry)	1 lb.	4 cups

NUTS, raw shelled

Almonds	1 lb.	3 ½ cups
Brazil	1 lb.	3 cups
Cashews	1 lb.	3 ½ cups
Chestnuts, dry tree	1 lb.	3 cups
Filberts	1 lb.	3 ½ cups
Peanuts	1 lb.	3 cups
Pecans	1 lb.	4 cups
Pine Nuts	1 lb.	4 cups
Walnuts	1 lb.	4 cups
Nuts in Shell	1 lb.	½ lb. shelled

OIL, Olive, Canola, Soy	1 lb.	2 ¼ cups
ONION FLAKES, Dry	1 lb.	5 ½ cups
PEANUT BUTTER	1 lb.	2 cups
SALT	1 lb.	1 ½ cups

SEEDS, raw

Flax Seed, whole	1 lb.	3 cups
Pumpkin Seeds	1 lb.	3 cups
Sesame Seed, whole	1 lb.	3 cups
Sunflower Seed	1 lb.	4 cups

SWEETS, natural

Honey, raw	1 lb.	1 ½ cups
Maple Syrup	1 lb.	2 cups
Molasses	1 lb.	1 ½ cups
Sugar, date	1 lb.	2 ¼ cups
Sugar, raw	1 lb.	2 ¼ cups

TOFU, Firm	1 lb.	2 cups
WHEAT GERM, flakes	1 lb.	4 cups
YEAST FLAKES, nutritional	1 lb.	8 cups

Abbreviations Commonly Used

tsp (or t) – teaspoon	qt – quart	doz – dozen
Tbsp (or T) – tablespoon	pkg – package	mod – moderate
C – cup	bu – bushel	° (or dg) – degree
gal – gallon	min – minute	sub – substitute
oz – ounce	hr – hour	pd – powder
lb (or #) – pound	sec – second	fl – flake
pt – pint	"(or in.) – inch (2.5 cm.)	gr – granulated

Oven Temperatures

Slow: 250-300° F
Mod. Slow: 325° F
Moderate: 350° F
Mod. Quick: 375° F
Mod. Hot: 400°F
Hot: 425 - 450° F
Very Hot: 475 - 500° F

Common Weights

1000 milligrams = 1 gram (.035 ounce)
1 oz. (dry wt.)   = 28 grams (approx.)
1 lb. (#, pound) 16 oz. = 450 grams
1 quart = 2 pints (dry) = 1.101 liter
2.20 lbs. (#, pounds) = 1,000 grams (1 kg)
1 gallon (dry wt.)   = 4.404 liters

Measurements

1 inch	2.5 centimeters
3 inches	7.5 centimeters
6 inches	15.0 centimeters
12 inches	30.5 centimeters

Contents of Different Sized Cans

8-ounce	1 cup
Picnic	1 ¼ cups
No. 300	1 ¾ cups
No. 1 tall	2 cups
No. 2	2 ½ cups
No. 2 ½	3 ½ cups
No. 3	4 cups
No. 10	13 cups (approx. 3 qts.)

Storage Temperatures

Fruits and Vegetables	34-45°F
Soy or Dairy Products	38-40° F
Frozen Foods	0-20° F

Temperature Equivalents

32° F	0° C
212° F	100° C
250° F	120° C
275° F	140° C
300° F	150° C
325° F	160° C
350° F	180° C
375° F	190° C
400° F	200° C
425° F	220° C
450° F	230° C
475° F	240° C
500° F	260° C
Broil	Broil

Metric Conversion Guide

pinch	= ⅓ ml (milliliter)
⅛ tsp. (t, teaspoon)	= 0.5 ml
¼ tsp.	= 1 ml
½ tsp.	= 2 ml
1 tsp.	= 5 ml
1 Tbs. (T, tablespoon)	= 15 ml
2 cups = 1 pint	= 500 ml, approx.
1 qt (quart) liquid	= 1 liter, approx.
1 gallon (gal) liquid	= 3.785 liters

Equivalent Measures

Dash or pinch	=	less than ⅛ tsp.
60 drops	=	1 teaspoon
3 tsp.	=	1 Tablespoon (15 ml.)
2 Tbs.	=	⅛ cup or 1 fl. oz.
4 Tbs.	=	¼ cup or 2 fl. oz.
8 Tbs.	=	½ cup or 4 fl. oz.
16 Tbs.	=	1 cup or 8 fl.oz.
1 cup	=	½ pint or 8 oz.
2 cups	=	1 pint (16 oz. or ½ quart)
4 cups (2 pints)	=	1 quart (32 ounces)
8 cups (4 pints)	=	½ gallon (64 ounces)
4 qts.	=	1 gallon (128 ounces)
8 qts.	=	1 peck (solid)
4 pecks	=	1 bushel
8 oz.	=	½ pound
16 oz.	=	1 pound
4 Tbs.	=	¼ cup
5 ⅓ Tbs.	=	⅓ cup
8 Tbs.	=	½ cup
12 Tbs.	=	¾ cup
14 Tbs.	=	⅞ cup

Standard Conversion Guide

Cup	Fl. oz.	Tbs.	Tsp.	MIliliter
1 cup	8 oz.	16 Tbs.	48 tsp.	237 ml
¾ cup	6 oz.	12 Tbs.	36 tsp.	177 ml
⅔ cup	5 ⅓ oz.	10.6 Tbs.	32 tsp.	158 ml
½ cup	4 oz.	8 Tbs.	4 tsp.	118 ml
⅓ cup	2 ⅔ oz.	5.3 Tbs.	16 tsp.	79 ml
¼ cup	2 oz.	4 Tbs.	12 tsp.	59 ml
⅛ cup	1 oz.	2 Tbs.	6 tsp.	30 ml
–	½ oz.	1 Tbs.	3 tsp.	15 ml

Cooking Terms and Techniques

Al dente – *An Italian term used to describe pasta that is cooked, but still firm "to the teeth".*

Baste – *To moisten at intervals with a liquid (pan drippings, etc.) especially during cooking.*

Beat – *To make a mixture smooth by rapidly mixing with a spoon, fork, wire wisk, or electric mixer.*

Blanch – *To immerse food in boiling water (scald), or place over steam for a brief time, to partially cook, then plunge into cold water to stop the cooking process, preserve color and nutrition or to loosen and remove the skins from peaches, tomatoes, almonds, etc.*

Blend – *To combine two or more ingredients with a mixer or blender or food processor, until smooth and uniform in texture, color and flavor.*

Boil – *To heat liquids until bubbles form that cannot be stirred down. When boiling 10.5*

Bread – *To coat food evenly by dipping into a liquid, then into fine cracker crumbs, cornmeal, or seasoned breading meal, before baking or browning in pan.*

Broil – *To cook by radiant dry heat, (approx. 4 to 6 inches) under a red-hot heating unit.*

Brown – *To cook foods quickly in a skillet or oven, to develop flavor and a rich desirable color on the outside, while retaining moistness on the inside.*

Candied – *A food, usually a fruit, citrus peel or nut, that is boiled or baked with a syrup.*

Chill – *To place food in the refrigerator or over ice, until thoroughly cold.*

Chop – *To cut food into course, fine, or irregular shaped pieces, using a knife, food processor, food chopper, or blender.*

Combine – *To place several ingredients in a single bowl or container and thoroughly mix.*

Core – *To carefully remove the center of fruit such as apples, pineapples, pears which contain the seeds or are woody. To remove the core from iceberg lettuce, strike the core end against a flat surface, then twist and lift it out.*

Crisp-tender – *A term used to describe vegetables that are cooked until just tender but somewhat crunchy, retaining more nutrients than vegetables that are overcooked.*

Cube or Dice – *To cube, using a knife cut fruits or vegetables into ½ in. to 1 in. pieces that are square. To dice, cut foods into smaller chunks ⅛ in. to ¼ in. in size.*

Crimp or Flute – *To pinch or press pastry or dough into a V or other shape, with your fingers or fork to create a decorative impression around edge of pie.*

Dash / Pinch-Dash – *a measure less than ⅛ teaspoon that is used for herbs, spices, or salt.*

Pinch – *a very small amount-taken between the finger and thumb (non-accurate measures).*

Emulsify – *To combine through a whisking action two liquids that traditionally separate, such as oil and lemon juice, into a mixture that will not separate upon standing.*

Fold – *To gently overturn or mix light or delicate ingredients without stirring or decreasing their volume.*

Garnish – *To decorate food and add visual appearance to a finished dish by using food accents of contrasting colors or textures such as parsley, radishes, olives, nuts or berries.*

Glaze – *To spread, drizzle, or brush the surface with an ingredient (milk, honey, jam, melted carob) on hot or cold food to moisten, give a glossy appearance, or hard finish.*

Grate – *To cut into tiny particles by rubbing food across a rough surface as the small holes of a grater, as in grating lemon zest.*

Grill – *To toast or fry on a griddle. Also, a cooking utensil of parallel bars, on which food is exposed to heat as from gas or electricity; or from charcoal (not recommended).*

Hull or Husk – *To hull with a knife or berry huller to remove leafy part and stem from soft fruits such as strawberries. To husk by removing the outer shell (coconut) or outer leaves (corn on the cob).*

Julienne – *To cut foods into long thin slices. Stack slices and cut into match-like sticks about 2 ½" long and ¼" thick.*

Moisten – *To add enough liquid to dry ingredients while stirring gently to make a slightly wet not runny mixture, as often used in the preparation of muffins.*

Knead – *To work or press dough into a mass that is smooth and elastic, with your hands or mixer. Kneading develops the gluten and improves the texture of the finished product.*

Marinate or Macerate – *To allow food to soak in a marinade- to add flavor or tenderize. Vegetables / tofu can be marinated in a savory sauce for 1 hour or more, till seasonings are absorbed. To macerate (usually fruit), is to soften and infuse flavors by steeping in a liquid.*

Mince – *To cut food into very fine, tiny bits, smaller than chopped pieces.*

Mix or Stir – *To combine ingredients together until they are evenly blended, using any method, or to stir in a circular or figure eight motion with a spoon to mix or to prevent foods from sticking during cooking.*

Parboil – *To boil briefly in water or vegetable stock, until partially cooked.*

Pare or Peel – *To remove, trim, or cut off the outer covering of a fruit or vegetable, using a vegetable peeler, small knife, or with your fingers, as when peeling a banana.*

Poach – *To cook foods (partly submerged) in simmering liquid just below the boiling point, until tender.*

Process – *To prepare food in a mini-chopper or food processor to blend, chop, grind, knead or liquify. To process is also to preserve food at home by the canning method.*

Puree – *To process, mash or blend food until very smooth and creamy, using a blender, food processor or sieve. Puree also refers to the resulting mixture.*

Reconstitute vs. Reduce – *To restore or reconstitute food, such as dried fruit, dehydrated vegetables or frozen juice concentrate to its original state by adding water. To reduce the volume of liquids, as in boiling the soup or sauce, to thicken and intensify the flavor.*

Roasting – *To cook by exposure to dry heat in an oven, as roasting vegetables in a shallow pan uncovered, without adding liquid; or before a fire, surrounded with hot embers or stones, as in roasting corn on the cob, or potatoes.*

Saute' – *To stir and cook diced, chopped, or shredded vegetables, in an open pan, over medium-high heat, in a nonstick skillet or a little oil, till vegetables are shiny and tender.*

Shred – *To cut or tear into long, thin strips using a shredder, knife or food processor as in shredding carrots or cabbage.*

Sift or Strain – *To put dry ingredients especially flour through a sifter or sieve to remove lumps and incorporate air. Strain liquid by pouring through a fine sieve or strainer to remove larger particles.*

Simmer – *To stew gently in a liquid just below the boiling point. Simmering is done after reducing heat from a boil; bubbles rise slowly and break just below the surface.*

Steam – *To cook food in the vapor given off by boiling water, by placing it on a rack or steamer basket over a small amount of boiling water in a covered pan.*

Steep – *To soak food in water or liquid, at a temperature just below the boiling point, in order to extract the essence, flavor, and color, as steeping herbs in making herbal tea.*

Stir-fry – *Oriental method of quick cooking sliced / cut vegetables over high heat in a preheated nonstick skillet or lightly oiled wok, lifting and stirring constantly with a turner or wooden spoon. Vegetables prepared in this way are crisp-tender and retain their color.*

Toast – *The process of browning, crisping, or drying a food (as in making zwieback) by exposing it to heat. Occasionally nuts, seeds and coconut are toasted to bring out flavor.*

Toss – *To mix with a quick, light, lifting motion, using a spoon and fork. Often used in tossing salad greens with dressing or pasta with sauce.*

Whip – *To beat ingredients rapidly using an electric mixer or wire whisk, to add air and increase volume until light and fluffy.*

Zest – *To remove the outer colored layer of citrus fruit, using a grater, peeler, knife or citrus zester. The peel of oranges, lemons or limes that contains aromatic oils and flavor. The zest is used as flavoring in a variety of dishes, including desserts, salads and sauces.*

Prescription for Health

"My son, be attentive to my words; incline your ears to my sayings. Let them not escape from your sight; keep them within your heart. For they are life to him who finds them, and healing to all his flesh." Proverbs 4: 20-22 RSV

America has the best hospitals, fully equipped, the most doctors per capita, the highest rate of obesity, and the most sick people per capita with shorter life spans than 41 other countries in the world. On the contrary, Hunza land has no hospitals or doctors and is one of the healthiest nation in the world, with people living up to 150 years old.

When your physician makes a prescription out for you, it usually involves a specific formula for a certain condition or reaction that has taken place in the body. Many doctors fail to consult the manual that our Creator has given us, by which we could have perfect health. Man cannot improve his condition of health by following any other method inferior to those our Creator has outlined in His manual.

"The living organism is God's property....A failure to care for the living machinery is an insult to the Creator." Counsels on Diet and Foods, pg.16

The very first provision for man, after God created the human body, was his food. The second provision provided for man was a beautiful home. The third provision was in giving man the power of choice, in that there was one tree in the garden which man should not eat of, lest the process of death would begin to take place. It is this third provision, the power of choice, that we need to understand, and put to work. There are many examples in the Bible, where a choice of dietary restrictions produced blessings in both physical and spiritual well-being.

The problem is so simple that most of us overlook it at every meal. The restrictions call for moderation and simplicity of diet, which our food fads, and refined food diets, with their abundance of variety, completely overlook. Overeating with its resulting indigestion has a depressing way of benumbing our sensibilities. The ability that is manifested in the power of choice comes from the alert thinking forebrain. Anything that would suppress this power of choice, whether it be medicine, chemicals, overeating, or just poor food combinations, certainly ought to be eliminated.

For those who find themselves living in the cities, the ability to have clear thoughts may be compromised by the lack of fresh air, pure water, and other negative environmental factors. I would very definitely encourage anyone living in the city, who desires a better state of health, to make plans to enjoy the benefits of country living. Country living provides the natural foods, clean environment, and quietness so necessary to the health of body, mind, and spirit. The times in which we are living demand a move to the country.

Remember, the Life you save may be your own!

Original Diet

Index - *Chapter 2*

Chapter cover photo: *Fresh Fruit - A Vital Part of the Original Bible Diet*

Original Bible Diet - Best for Man Today

Fruits and Vegetables, whole grains, legumes, nuts and seeds, and various herbs, all of plant origin, are rich in fiber, vitamins and minerals, protein, antioxidants, and phytochemicals needed to maintain good health and well being.

The **optimal or ideal diet** is low in fat, high in fiber, and rich in complex carbohydrates. This is the **"original diet"** given to man, consisting of fruits, Grains, Nuts and Vegetables.

"And God said, Behold I have given YOU every herb bearing seed, which is upon the face of all the earth, and every tree, in the which is the fruit of a tree yielding seed; to you it shall be for meat." Genesis 1:29, KJV

A more modern New King James Version reads:

"And God said, *See, I have given YOU every herb that yields seed which is on the face of all the earth, and every tree whose fruit yields seed; to you it shall be for food."* Genesis 1:29, NKJV

Note: The following explanation of **Genesis 1:29**, lists the foods that would be included *as we know them today.*

"BEHOLD I HAVE GIVEN YOU EVERY HERB BEARING SEED...."
(Herb bearing seed or seed bearing plant – plants which do not develop persistent woody tissue)

> **GRAINS** – wheat, corn, rye, barley, rice, millet, oats, kamut, spelt, quinoa, buckwheat, teff, amaranth, etc.
>
> **SEEDS** – sunflower, sesame, flax, pumpkin seeds, etc.
>
> **LEGUMES** – soybeans, black beans, lima beans, lentils, navy beans, pinto, garbanzos, kidney beans, fava and mung beans, peas, cranberry beans, azuki beans, anasazi beans, peanuts, and other legumes, etc.
>
> **HERB (SUCCULENT PLANTS) BEARING SEED AND SEED POD** – green beans, eggplant, tomatoes, cucumber, okra, summer and winter squash, pimentos, bell peppers, pumpkins, edible pod peas, sweet corn, melons, etc.

"...and EVERY TREE, in which is THE FRUIT OF A TREE YIELDING SEED..."
(A woody perennial plant, shrub, or bush having a single elongate main stem)

> **FRUITS** – oranges, lemons, limes, grapefruit, apples, peaches, pears, apricots, nectarines, cherries, mangos, papaya, persimmons, plums, figs, grapes, berries, pineapple, bananas, dates, carob, avocado, olives, etc.
>
> **NUTS** – almonds, walnuts, pecans, cashews, brazil nuts, filberts, pistachio, pine nuts, macadamia, chestnuts, coconut, etc.

"...to YOU it shall be for MEAT." Genesis 1:29 KJV

The following pictures simply illustrate the abundance of natural foods available. See **Food Combining Made Easy Chart,** for assistance in planning balanced meals.

1. FRUITS, Citrus + Acid – (citrus – Oranges, Grapefruits, Lemons, Limes, Tangerines, Tangelo, Kumquat, Ugli fruit, Pummelo); (acid – Cranberries, Currants, Gooseberry)

2. FRUITS, Sub-Acid – Apples, Apricots, Pears, Peaches, Nectarines, Kiwi, Persimmons, Cherries, Plums, Mango, Papaya, Pomegranate, Star fruit, etc. (vine & bush fruits: Grapes, Strawberries, Blueberries, Raspberries, Boysenberries, Blackberries, etc.)

Fruits, sweet-dried

Barhi Dates

Calmyrna Figs

White Figs

Dried Bananas

Apricots

Black Mission Figs

3. FRUITS, Sweet – Dates, Black Figs, White Figs, Raisins, Prunes, Carob, (sun dried Apricots, Pears, Peaches)

4. FRUITS, palm – Bananas, Dates, Pineapple, Coconut, etc.

Fruits, palm

Note: The fruits shown may be included in more than one group. (Example: grapes in group 2, are also listed in group 3 as raisins; coconut in Fruits, palm is also listed with nuts; etc.) The four fruit groups shown combine well, as illustrated in the **Simple Food Combining** chart. The composition of groups pictured in this chapter simply illustrate the abundant variety of natural foods included in the original Bible diet.

Fruits, neutral

5. FRUITS, Neutral – Avocados, Olives, and Oils

Nuts

6. NUTS – Almonds, Cashews, Brazil Nuts, English Walnuts, Filberts, Pecans, Pine Nuts, Macadamia, Hickory Nuts, Pistachio, Chestnuts, Black Walnuts, Coconut, etc.

Seeds

7. SEEDS – Sunflower, Sesame, Flaxseed, Pumpkin, Squash Seeds, etc (grains and nuts are also seeds, but not commonly called such).

8. GRAINS – Wheat, Oats, Barley, Millet, Rye, Rice, Buckwheat, Corn, Spelt, Quinoa, Kamut, Tritacale, Teff, Amaranth, etc.

Grains

9. LEGUMES –
Soybeans,
Lima Beans,
Garbanzo beans,
Black-eyed Peas,
Lentils, Great
Northern beans,
Fava Beans,
Pinto Beans,
Kidney Beans,
Navy Beans,
Black Beans,
Mung Beans,
Azuki beans,
Anasazi beans,
Cranberry beans,
Peanuts, Alfalfa,
etc.

10. MELONS – Watermelon, Honeydew, Cantaloupe, Casaba, Crenshaw, Pepino, Persian, etc. (any of various typically sweet gourds, usually eaten raw as fruits)

Vegetables, succulent —

herb bearing seed
and seed pod

11. VEGETABLES, Succulent – (Herb Bearing Seed and Seed Pod) - Tomatoes, Eggplant, Bell Peppers, Pimento, Pumpkins, Cucumbers, Okra, Green Beans, Yellow Wax Beans, Peas, Edible Pod Peas, Sweet Corn, Zucchini, Summer and Winter Squash, etc. (these Succulent foods –the herb bearing seed and seed pod - the "fruit"or end-product of the plant or vine, including tomatoes - are commonly known and eaten as vegetables).

Note: Definition of **"Fruit"** from Taber's Cyclopedic Medical Dictionary: "A ripened ovary consisting of a seed or seeds and the surrounding tissue. Example: pod of a bean, nut, grain, pome, or berry. Also, the edible *end-product* of a *plant* consisting of ripened seeds and the enveloping tissue." Webster's Dictionary definition of **"Fruit"**- a product of plant growth (as grain, vegetable, or cotton); a succulent plant part, etc. Pome: A fleshy fruit (as an apple or pear...)

The foods in groups 1-11 are *tree fruits or end-products* of herbaceous plants. Keep in mind the word "fruit" has several meanings, including the phrases *"the fruit of our labor," "to bear fruit," "the fruits of the Spirit," "the fruit of the earth"* etc. Therefore, care should be taken when combining foods. **Keep it simple,** for optimum digestion. *Example:* Peaches and bananas combine and digest better with other fruits, grains, seeds or nuts, rather than serving them at a meal with peppers, tomatoes, eggplant, or beans. These *"fruits of the earth"* such as beans, squash, peppers, tomatoes, and eggplant, which are known as common garden **vegetables** combine best with grains, nuts, seeds, legumes and other vegetables, rather than with tree fruits (apples, peaches, pears, bananas, etc.)

Another example: Let's look at the word **"Berry"** which also has several meanings (as strawberry, blueberry or cranberry), (as wheat or rye berry), (as grape–a smooth skinned juicy berry), (as tomato- a pulpy berry*). Note: **wheat "berry"** is commonly known and used as a **grain**, not a berry.

Tree fruits* are assimilated and digested quickly, however when eaten with legumes (group 9), or with vegetables (as those in group 11-14), which require more complex digestion = it results in a poor combination, which tends to ferment, and create putrefaction and flatulence (gas), or faulty, incomplete digestion. Therefore, it is best to know the different kinds of food, and avoid complicated mixtures. Learn how to **simply** and **properly combine foods** for optimum health and nutrition. (*most)

Notice the importance placed on proper food combining, by a noted and respected author:

"Knowledge in regard to *proper food combinations* is of great worth, and is to be received as *wisdom from God.*" E.G. White, *Diet & Foods,* pg.109

*See **"Tomatoes - Fruit or Vegetable?"** in **Salad** chapter; also **Food Combining Made Easy** chart--back of book.

The Green Herb - Originally Animal's Food

..."*And to every BEAST of the earth and to every FOWL of the air, and to every THING that creepeth upon the earth...I have given every GREEN HERB for MEAT: and it was so.*" Genesis 1:30 KJV

After man sinned, he was driven out of the Garden of Eden, and no longer had access to the wonderful tree of life. Man had to gain his livelihood by tilling the earth, and the "Green Herb" (originally food for the animals) was added to his diet.

"*And unto Adam He said, Because thou hast harkened unto the voice of thy wife...cursed is the ground for thy sake...and thou shalt eat the HERB of the Field.*" Gen. 3: 17, 18 KJV

(**Herb** - A plant that does not develop persistent woody tissue, but dies down at the end of a growing season)

Leafy and Stem: Asparagus, bok choy, Brussels sprouts and cabbage, celery, chard, collard greens, escarole, endive, fennel, kale, kohlrabi, lettuce (all varieties), mustard and turnip greens, parsley, rapini, spinach, radicchio, watercress, rhubarb stalks,etc.

Flower: Broccoli, cauliflower, globe artichoke, etc.

Root: Carrots, beets, parsnips, potatoes, radishes, turnips, Jerusalem artichoke, rutabaga, jicama, yams, etc. (bulb) onion, garlic, leek, etc. (fungi-spore) mushrooms.

Although vegetables (green herbs, plants, roots) were not part of the original diet given to man, they were added to man's diet after he sinned, and are an important part of our diet today.

"*Grains, fruits, nuts, and vegetables constitute the diet chosen for us by our Creator.*"

-E. G. White, *Diet and Foods*, pg. 81

Vegetables, leafy

12. VEGETABLES, Leafy – Kale, Swiss Chard, Spinach, Collard and Mustard Greens, Escarole, Rapini (broccoli raab), Lettuce, (many varieties), Parsley, Cilantro, Florentine Fennel, Endive, Beet / Turnip Greens, Salad Savoy, Radicchio, Red and Green Cabbage and Brussels Sprouts (form heads), Asparagus, Bok Choy, Celery, Kohlrabi, Rhubarb stalks, Watercress, etc.

Vegetables, flower

13. VEGETABLES, Flower - Globe Artichokes, Broccoli, Cauliflower, etc.

Vegetables, root

14. VEGETABLES, Root – Carrots, Beets, Rutabagas, Turnips, Parsnips, Radishes, Jicama, Jerusalem Artichoke, Celery Root, Potatoes, Sweet Potato, Yams; Garlic, Leeks, Shallots, Onions (bulb); Mushrooms (spore)

Principles of Food Combining and Eating

UNDIGESTED FOODS HAVE NO NUTRITIONAL VALUE. Consequently, *proper food combining* is of the utmost importance in the *digestion* and *assimilation* of starches, sugars, protein, and fats. In turn, proper digestion enhances nutrition and provides protection against fermentation and putrefaction, the result of incomplete or poor digestion. ***"Knowledge in regard to proper food combinations is of great worth, and is to be received as wisdom from God."*** CDF 109. Listed are a few guidelines:

1. Fruit and vegetables are best if not combined at the same meal. It is better to have fruit at one meal, and vegetables at another. ***"Fruit and vegetables taken at one meal produce acidity of the stomach; then impurity of the blood results, and the mind is not clear because the digestion is imperfect."*** [14]

2. In order to avoid a sour stomach (which may lead to a sour disposition), **keep the combinations simple**; avoid combining **many different kinds of food** [15] at the same meal. A well-balanced nutritious meal can be planned with just two or three different kinds (food groups), and still have a nice variety.
Example: A salad may have 4 or 5 different varieties of leafy greens (romaine, endive, escarole, spinach, bib lettuce, etc.) *but* they are all in the same *kind* or group of leafy greens. You may also plan at that meal, a protein dish made of legumes; and you may want to include some squash and/or green beans. This dinner meal (example), has several different varieties of foods, but only 3 *kinds*: Leafy vegetables, Legumes, and Succulent foods. These 3 groups are compatible with each other. Bread and olives or avocado may also complement the meal.

3. ***"Do not have too great a variety at a meal. Three or four dishes are plenty."*** [15] These dishes should be made of the kinds of foods that combine well and are compatible with each other. Avoid heavy and complicated mixtures which is a frequent cause of indigestion. The more simple the meals, the better.

4. When planning a meal, choose complex carbohydrates, such as whole grain cereals and breads, vegetables, and naturally sweet fruits. These contain nutrients and fiber that are often lacking in refined carbohydrates, such as white flour products and refined sugars. Choose proteins of vegetable sources such as legumes. These are adequate when combined with grains and nuts.
Note: Those who have difficulty digesting legumes and beans such as: soybeans, mung beans, lentils, garbanzo beans, etc., may find them easier to digest when **sprouted,** lightly steamed, and eaten in proper combination with other foods, such as a green salad. (see chapter - **Sprouting**)

5. Avoid the use of "grease" in foods (primarily animal fats- butter and lard), which makes the food difficult to digest. Reducing the total intake of fat in food preparation, including vegetable fats, especially those which have been hydrogenated is a heart-healthy step in the right direction. The use of liquid oils such as cold-pressed canola, corn or olive oil (which dates back to ancient Bible history), should be used *sparingly,* to enhance the flavor of food, and make it more appetizing. With a little culinary skill and practice, often the oils, that are naturally found in seeds, nuts, avocado and olives, is all that is needed, to make a tasty dish.

6. When planning meals, concentrate on the fresh raw salads, and main dish, keeping the sugary sweet desserts to a minimum.

"Sugar is not good for the stomach. It causes fermentation, and this clouds the brain and brings peevishness into the disposition." [16]
"Milk and sugar clog the system, irritate the digestive organs, and affect the brain...Sugar when largely used is more injurious than meat." [17]

Eating the natural unrefined sugars that are packed with adequate nutrients and fiber, such as is found in fresh and dried fruit, is the most beneficial to the digestive system. On the contrary, diets high in refined sugars and starches such as white sugar and white flour products, are detrimental and often crowd out the desire for more wholesome foods, resulting in nutritional deficiencies.

Pure refined sugar, being the most depleted of "foodless foods" makes demands on the pancreas, and body's store of vitamins and minerals (especially B-vitamins) for its assimilation. Research and evidence agree that although sugar may pamper and satisfy your sweet tooth, it acts as a sneaky and insidious thief of your health. Unfortunately, it has only gained popularity as being the "sweet killer". [18]

7. Eat **slowly**, chewing the food **thoroughly**, so it will be well mixed with saliva. Digestion begins in the mouth. It is best to avoid drinking with the meals. Washing the food down with water, dilutes the gastric juices needed for digestion. The more liquid taken into the stomach at mealtime, the more difficult it is for the food to be assimilated. Savor the flavor while chewing; once food is swallowed the zest is gone!

8. Foods that are **too hot** or **too cold** should not be eaten. Very hot soups and drinks tend to debilitate the stomach, and are best when partly cooled. Very cold foods require the vitality of the system to warm them, until they are the same temperature as the stomach, before the work of digestion can be carried on.

9. Eat fresh food in its natural state. Include in the diet more **raw fruits and vegetables**. A large raw salad eaten **before** the main course, is a good practice to follow. This will often stimulate and assist digestion, satisfy the appetite, and help avoid overeating of other cooked foods, an excellent routine for weight control. "....even fruit should not be eaten **after** a full meal of other foods." [19]

10. Eating a variety of fruits, grains, vegetables, nuts and plant-based proteins, in proper combination, will adequately provide, all the vitamins, minerals, and building blocks, needed for life, health, and vitality. Eat with thanksgiving, and forget to worry about what you have eaten. Remember, *"A merry heart does good, like medicine, but a broken spirit dries the bones."* Proverbs 17:22

Note: Dairy products are not essential for a well-balanced diet, and have not been included with the natural food groups, however, they are generally compatible with the natural foods.

14 White, Ellen G., *Counsels on Diet and Foods*, (Wash., D.C.: Review and Herald Pub., 1976) pg. 113
15 *Ibid.*, pg. 109-110
16 White, Ellen G., *Counsels on Diet and Foods*, pg. 327
17 *Ibid.*, pg. 328
18 "The Sweet Killer in Your Cupboard," Wade, Carlson, Spec. Report on Sugar (Natural Food and Farming, October, 1978)
19 White, Ellen G., *Counsels on Diet and Foods*, pg. 309

To simplify and assist in Food Combining and Meal Planning, the *FOOD COMBINING MADE EASY* chart, **18" x 24",** illustrated in full color, is available. (See order form at the back of book)

Simple Food Combining

FOOD GROUPS	Fruits #1-4	Fruits (neutral), Nuts, Seeds #5, 6, 7	Grains #8	Legumes #9	Melons #10	Vegetables #11-14
KEY: **XX**-Combines well	**X**-Fair compatibility		**NR**-Not recommended		**No**-Not compatible	
1. **Fruits,** citrus - acid	XX	XX	X	X - NR	X	No X Lemon
2. **Fruits,** sub - acid	XX	XX	XX	X - NR	X	No
3. **Fruits,** sweet - dried	XX	XX	XX	No	X	No
4. **Fruits,** palm	XX	XX	XX	NR	X	No
5. **Fruits,** neutral	XX	XX	XX	XX	X	XX
6. **Nuts**	XX	XX	XX	XX	X	XX
7. **Seeds**	XX	XX	XX	XX	X	XX
8. **Grains**	X - XX	XX	XX	XX	X	XX
9. **Legumes,** & bean sprouts	NR X Lemon	XX	XX	XX	NR	XX
10. **Melons**	X	X	X	NR	XX	NR - No
11. **Vegetables,** (Succulent: herb-bearing seed & seed pod)	NR X Lemon	XX	XX	XX	NR	XX
12. **Vegetables,** leafy	No X Lemon	XX	XX	XX	No	XX
13. **Vegetables,** flower	No X Lemon	XX	XX	XX	No	XX
14. **Vegetables,** root	No X Lemon	XX	XX	XX	No	XX

Original Diet

Ten Talents

64

"If we would preserve the best health, we should avoid eating vegetables and fruit at the same meal...Have fruit at one meal and vegetables at the next..." E.G.White, *Diet & Foods*, p. 395

Simple Food Combining

Basic 4 - Food Groups

Fruits

Neutral - Olives, Avocado

AVOID

Grains

OATMEAL HELPS REMOVE CHOLESTEROL

QUICK-1 MINUTE

QUAKER OATS

100% WHOLE WHEAT

All Purpose

FLOUR

Nuts

Seeds

Vegetables

Legumes

*"**Grains, Fruits, Nuts, and Vegetables, in proper combination,** contain all the elements of nutrition; and when properly prepared, they constitute the diet that best promotes both physical and mental strength.* E. G. White, **Education**, pg. 204-5

Healthy Lifestyle Habits

OUR HEALTH IS OUR GREATEST TREASURE. Better than wealth, honor, and education, **good health is our most precious temporal possession.** It should be guarded as carefully as our character. All the laws of nature were designed by our Creator for our highest development. If followed we could slow down the aging process, add years to our life, and enjoy better health, peace, and happiness as a result.

Listed are a few simple suggestions to help you get started on a healthier regime.

1. Drink **plenty of water** on arising and between meals. Water is the best liquid possible to cleanse the tissues and purify the blood. Two glasses of water on arising with a little freshly squeezed lemon juice- is a great way to start the day! Drink a short while *before* breakfast.

2. Eat a **substantial breakfast**. In the morning, after a good night's rest, the stomach is better able to digest a hearty meal than at any other time of the day. The practice of eating little or no breakfast and a heavy supper, may be conducive to putting on "unwanted" pounds.

3. Eat at regular intervals, allowing 5-6 hours before the next meal, with nothing between. **Avoid snacking** between meals. This is a bad habit to overcome once started. If there is a feeling of hunger between the meals, look at the clock; and if it is not time to eat, take a big drink of life-giving cool water. (Hunger pangs after a full meal are generally a sign of indigestion)

4. Eat "for strength and not for drunkenness." The benefit you derive from your food, does not depend so much on the quantity eaten, as on its thorough digestion. Neither does gratification of taste depend so much on the amount of food swallowed, as on the length of time it remains in the mouth. Overeating weakens the digestive organs and lessens brain power.

5. Avoid eating just before going to bed. The stomach must not be constantly at work, but must have periods of rest. When you retire, the stomach should have its work all done, so it may rest with you. If you feel that you must eat, take a drink of cold water, or juice. In the morning you will feel much better for not having eaten, and have a good appetite for breakfast.

6. Take time to eat and *enjoy mealtime*. Avoid eating when overtired, hurried, in pain, emotionally upset, or compulsive eating (when not hungry). Instead, sip on your favorite herbal tea, relax in a tub of warm water, or take a leisurely walk.

7. Generally, two meals a day are better than three – but if a third meal is eaten at all, it should be light, and several hours before going to bed. Suggested times for two meals are: at 8 a.m. and 2 p.m. Three meals: at 6 a.m., 12 p.m. and 6 p.m.

8. Have regular hours for sleep in a well-ventilated room. ***Two hours of sound sleep before midnight, is worth far more than four hours after midnight.*** Sleep, nature's sweet restorer, invigorates the tired body.

9. Basic Guidelines for **Good Eating Habits**:

> a. Include in the dietary a ***wide variety*** of fresh fruits and vegetables, dark leafy greens, whole grain cereals and breads, vegetable proteins from sources such as dry beans and peas, sprouted lentils and other legumes, tofu, nuts and seeds, soybean milk, etc.

> b. Reduce the intake of salt, sugars, visible fats and oils, in the diet.

> c. Avoid high cholesterol foods such as: eggs, cheese, butter, and meat.

> d. Refrain from alcoholic and caffeinated beverages (coffee, tea, cola).

"In Grains, Fruit, Vegetables, and Nuts are to be found all the food elements that we need." [20]

10. Take time for a brisk walk after meals. **Exercise** is probably just as important as what you eat.

> ***"Exercise will aid the work of digestion. To walk out after a meal, hold the head erect, put back the shoulders, and exercise moderately, will be a great benefit. The mind will be diverted from self to the beauties of nature. The less the attention is called to the stomach after a meal, the better. If you are in constant fear that your food will hurt you, it most assuredly will. Forget self, and think of something cheerful."*** [21]

Note: In addition to above comments, see the ***10 Principals for Abundant Health*** found in chapter 21 of this book.

Some of the expression and enthusiasm noted in *Healthy Lifestyle Habits* and *Principals of Food Combining and Eating*, have been gleaned from the perceptive writings and manuscripts of Ellen G. White.

20 White, E. G., *Counsels on Diet and Foods*, pg. 363
21 White, E. G., *Counsels on Health*, pg. 53

***"Blessed Art Thou, O Land,
when thy princes
Eat...for strength
and not for drunkenness."***

Ecclesiastes 10:17 KJV

Flesh Meat – Man's Food??

" The diet appointed man in the beginning did not include animal food. Not till after the Flood, when every green thing on the earth had been destroyed, did man receive permission to eat flesh. " - E. G White, **Ministry of Healing**, pg 311

It was not until nearly 1,700 years after creation that the Lord allowed man to eat flesh. This was to shorten man's sinful life of indulgence. Because of man's unnatural craving for flesh, his life was rapidly shortened, so that by 3,000 years after creation, the life span was only three score and ten – (not much more than it is today).

Our Creator designed that human beings should live forever. Even after sin, man lived to be as much as 969 years old. We cannot hope to live that long today, in this degenerate age, but we can follow a plan which will help us to gain eternal life, and at the same time be able to enjoy healthy bodies, and clear minds, for the mere three score and ten years allotted to this life.

Flesh eating today does not always appear to lessen the three score and ten, but with all the diseases that can be traced to the eating of flesh today – and the abundance of food provided by our Creator, we should certainly avoid eating the carcasses of dead animals.

We have an ample supply of grains, fruits and nuts, which will, along with vegetables, in the proper combinations, more than satisfy our physical needs.

"Meat is not essential for health or strength,… All the elements of nutrition are contained in the fruits, vegetables, and grains." E. G. White, **Healthful Living**, pg. 96

The history of Vegetarianism, dating back through the centuries, has been based on deep religious and humanitarian views. The benefits of a plant-based dietary have achieved wide recognition, resulting in an increased vegetarian population. Just a few of the advantages, of switching to a plant-based, vegetarian diet are:

1. Less expensive	5. Appetizing	9. Satisfying/delicious
2. Disease free	6. Wholesome	10. Ecological reasons
3. Easier to digest	7. Varied choices	11. Adequately nutritious
4. Increased lifespan	8. Healthier lifestyle	12. Greater endurance

For those who are still using flesh foods:

1. A classification of "clean" and "unclean" creatures is recorded in Lev. 11:1-30.

2. Remove fat from meat. (Leviticus 7:23-24)

3. Eat no blood of animals. (Leviticus 7:26-27)

4. Avoid eating meat conjointly with milk. (Exodus 23:19)

"When flesh food is discarded, its place should be supplied with a variety of grains, nuts, vegetables, and fruits, that will be both nourishing and appetizing." E. G. White, **Diet and Foods**, p. 315

"THE GRAINS, WITH FRUITS, NUTS, AND VEGETABLES, CONTAIN ALL THE NUTRITIVE PROPERTIES NECESSARY TO MAKE GOOD BLOOD." – **Diet and Foods**, p. 313

Baby Foods

Index - *Chapter 3*

Parents - Advantage of Early Years — Children - Right Habits

"The lessons learned, the habits formed, during the years of infancy and child-hood, have more to do with the formation of the character and the direction of the life than have all the instruction and training of after years." E. G. White, Child Guidance, pg. 184

"Too much importance cannot be placed on the early training of children. The lessons that the child learns during the first seven years of life have more to do with forming his character than all that it learns in future years." E.G. White, Child Guidance, pg. 193

Note: Child Guidance, along with other volumes by Ellen G. White, are saturated with insightful truths, and helpful advice in nurturing and raising our children. Her publications are highly recommended.

Chapter cover photo: *Simple Natural Foods to Guard Your Baby's Health*

Your Baby: A Precious Bundle of Love

"Train up a child in the way he should go; and when he is old, he will not depart from it." Proverbs 22.6

What a wonderful and sacred responsibility rests with parents! The following quotation is from the chapter *"The Mother"*, in the book **Ministry of Healing**. It is one of my favorites, and has been an inspiration to many mothers. It would be well for parents to review the entire chapter often.

"The mother's work often seems to her an unimportant service. It is a work that is rarely appreciated. Others know little of her many cares and burdens. Her days are occupied with a round of little duties, all calling for patient effort, for self-control, for tact, wisdom, and self-sacrificing love; yet she cannot boast of what she has done as any great achievement. She has only kept things in the home running smoothly; often weary and perplexed, she has tried to speak kindly to the children, to keep them busy and happy, and to guide the little feet in the right path. She feels that she has accomplished nothing. But this is not so. Heavenly angels watch the care-worn mother, noting the burdens she carries day by day. Her name may not have been heard in the world, but it is written in the Lamb's book of life...No other work can equal hers in importance!" E. G. White, *Ibid* pg. 371-8

Let's Have Healthy Children

Mother's milk is superior to any other milk or formula for infants. It supplies the necessary protein, vitamins, and minerals, most adapted to the infant's needs in a fresh, clean, warm, bacteria-free, and inexpensive form. Although infant formulas may approximate the composition of human milk, no formula can transfer the immune antibodies present in mother's milk, nor satisfy mother's maternal instinct in nursing her child.

The diet and habits of the mother during pregnancy and lactation will largely affect the production of milk. Care should be taken that the diet include an abundant variety of wholesome natural foods, carefully chosen and combined.

Beginning with the infant at its mother's breast, habits of regularity and discipline should begin. Many children suffer today from irregular and poor eating habits.

Good eating habits are developed (not inherited), and need to be instilled in the child while very young. Nutrition is of utmost importance during the early years of rapid growth and development. Attention should be given in educating the child's tastes and appetites for nourishing and healthful foods. Their food should be simple and in as near-natural a state as possible, given at regular mealtime with nothing in between. Teach good habits by example. Children learn more from actions than from words. Practice what you preach, and you will be healthier too!

Points for Parents to Ponder

1. The best food for the infant is the food that nature provides – Mother's Milk. It is the ideal perfect food for baby, providing all the necessary nutrients in proper balance, as well as antibodies that protect the child against infectious disease.

2. The child should be given food only at regular intervals – the training should begin with the infant in its mother's arms.

3. It should not be given sweets, or the food of older persons, which is more difficult to digest. Avoid the use of non-pasteurized honey for infants younger than 1 year of age.

4. Care and regularity in feeding will promote health and lay the foundation of habits for future years. This will help to establish the principle that "We should eat to live - rather than live to eat."

5. Nothing should be eaten between meals. Irregularity in eating destroys the healthful tone of the digestive organs.

6. The more quiet and simple the life of the child, the more favorable it will be to physical and mental development.

John

7. Everything about the child should be clean and sweet. During sleeping or waking hours they should breathe a pure, invigorating atmosphere.

8. Let mealtime be a cheerful, happy time. Let all the sunshine of love possible enter your hearts and pervade in the home.

9. The first education children should receive from the mother in infancy should be in regard to their physical health.

10. The proper diet and lifestyle of the mother (as well as father) should begin before conception and the birth of her children. It has a greater influence than once thought on the health of the future child. If parents set the right example, the children will soon follow.

"That our sons may be as plants (well nurtured), grown up in their youth; that our daughters may be as corner stones (pillars), polished after the similitude of a palace." Psalms 144:12 KJV (NIV)

"Sons are a heritage from the Lord, children a reward from him" Psalm 127:3 NIV

> "The best food for the infant is the food that nature provides."
> E. G. White, Diet & Foods p. 226

BREASTFEEDING IS BEST - NURSE THE CHILD IF AT ALL POSSIBLE – MORE IS IMPARTED TO THE CHILD THAN JUST THE MILK.

Oatmeal Gruel for Nursing Mothers
(Good for baby too!)

Simmer gently 20 minutes:

**1 qt. pure water
    or herb tea***
½ cup oats, quick
pinch of sea salt

Stir or blend and strain.
Blend again with:

**2 tsp. agave, molasses
    or honey**
**1 Tbs. soy milk
    or soya powder**

Drink while warm to help increase flow of milk.

*Part herb tea may be used (fennel, fenugreek)

Note: For extra nutrition blend with a little tahini or flaxseed meal.

Ways to Increase Mother's Milk

1. Drink 8-10 cups fluid daily- pure water, vegetable broth, herbal tea - aniseed, fennel, fenugreek (tend to promote healthy lactation), coriander, chamomile, clover, spearmint.

2. Drink 2-3 glasses of Soybean Milk or Oatmeal Gruel, see recipes.

3. Use whole grains (corn, buckwheat, millet, oats, rice, barley, quinoa, spelt) - excellent for breakfast, in place of refined and sugar-coated cereals so popular on store shelves today.

4. Diet should include an ample supply of fresh fruits, dark leafy green salads, vegetables, wholesome bread, raw nuts, sesame, sunflower seeds, seaweed, and fortified food yeast.

5. Include in the dietary fresh sprouts (alfalfa, clover, fenugreek, lentil, mung bean, soy).

6. Get plenty of rest at night, and a nap during the day if possible.

7. Maintain a calm, restful attitude while nursing your baby.

Natural Food Formulas

Beverages for babies who are weaned from the breast (not intended to replace mother's milk).

Nurse as long as possible, weaning should be gradual; usually by 12 - 18 months, baby should have a good start in life.

In a blender, start with ingredients using half the amount of water, gradually add remaining water while blending until smooth. Put through a fine strainer into glass, cup, or bottle. Pulp may be added to cereals, bread, or cookies.

No. 1

1 cup almond, blanched
1 qt. pure water, divided
1 Tbs. agave or honey
¼ tsp. lecithin, opt. creamier milk
few grains sea salt

No. 2

½ cup almonds, blanched
½ cup cashews or sesame seeds
1 qt. pure water, divided
1 Tbs. agave or honey

No. 3

1 cup soya milk powder
2 Tbs. sesame tahini
1 qt. pure water, divided
1 Tbs. agave or honey
few grains sea salt

No. 4

½ cup almonds, blanched
½ cup coconut, fresh shredded
2 Tbs. sesame tahini
5 dates, pitted
5 cups pure water
  or liquid from coconut

No. 5

1 qt. Soybean Milk, see recipe
1 Tbs. sunflower or sesame seeds
2 tsp. flaxseed meal
agave or honey, to taste

Note: For blanching almonds and nutritive value of nuts- see chapter Nuts, Seed, Olives

Beverages for Baby

Ideally mothers milk is sufficient; plain water and other beverages may be offered as baby grows.

1. Pure soft water (may sweeten with a bit of molasses, agave or barley malt).

2. Fresh apple, orange, or tangerine juice after 3-4 months (may dilute).

3. Herbal tea (chamomile, catnip, clover) between meals if baby is colicky*.

4. Brown Rice or Barley water, vegetable broth

5. Grape juice, liquid from coconut, fresh fruit "smoothies" and vegetable drinks. (see chapter **Beverages).**

6. **Oatmeal Gruel** and **Graham gruel**, see recipes.

7. **Natural Food Formulas** (complementary beverage offered from a cup after feeding) – not intended to replace mother's milk.

8. **Never** give your child alcohol, soft drinks, coffee, or tea.

*Infants that are breast-fed and not given solid foods too early (which may cause them to become "gassy" should not be disturbed with colic. However, if your baby occasionally suffers from colic, the simple old-fashioned herbal remedy mentioned above, given in small doses, will often bring relief.

Note: Beverages may be given ½ -1 hour before feeding time (Natural Food Formulas, Oatmeal Gruel and fruit "smoothies" are best given after feeding).

B is for Baby - Bananas are for Baby

When babies are 4-6 months old, they can start to enjoy many fruit blends.

Introduce one new item at a time over several days; first to see how baby responds to each new food, and second, to allow the baby's digestive system to adapt to the change. Pears are a very good start.

Bananas also are a favorite solid food for babies. Good source of vitamins and minerals- including vitamin B1, B2, B6, A, C, E, K, potassium, magnesium iron, niacin, phosphorus, folate and other nutrients. Bananas are satisfying and easy for baby to digest, but they should be fully ripe (speckled). Bananas contain natural sugars, a good source of energy for baby, and bulk (fiber) needed to help maintain normal digestive functions. Fresh flaxseed meal and prune purée also provide bulk.

Laura

Bananas are packaged by nature in individual containers; sprays, dust, and bacteria do not reach fruit. Ripen at room temperature for ideal flavor and consistency. Bananas, fully ripened, can be mashed, sieved in a baby food mill, or blended. For baby start with small portions of 1-2 teaspoons.

Bananas may be sliced lengthwise and dried. These can be stored in a jar or freezer and are excellent for older children to chew.

Fruits for Baby

Try these combinations:

Bananas + avacado
Bananas + pears
Bananas + apricots
Bananas + peaches
Bananas + blueberries
Bananas + applesauce
Bananas + mango
Bananas + papaya

Note: Try freezing individual portions in ice cube tray. Convenient to use when traveling, just thaw prior to feeding time.

Avocados are also a good starter food and can be mashed with ripe banana or other fruits. Ripe fruits are naturally sweet, and need no additional sweetening. It is unnecessary to spend money for processed baby foods cooked with sugar and starch; just whiz fresh fruits in your blender or put through a baby food mill. Your baby may not be fat – but will be healthier. Use fruits that are fully ripe. Listed are a variety of healthy fruit blends:

Avocado + applesauce   **Applesauce + pear**
Avocado + pear   **Kiwi + Strawberries**
Blueberries + Peaches   **Prunes, stewed, puréed**
Peaches + pears   **Apricots + prunes**
Apricots + pineapple   **Pears + persimmon**
Strawberries + Banana   **Mango + peaches**

Seeds, such as **flaxseed meal** & **sunflower seed meal**, may be added to fruit. When your baby is old enough to have cereal, simply combine fruit and seeds with cereal.
(see **Baby and Cereal**)

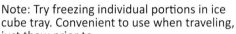

Baby Teething Biscuits

Your baby won't mind cutting teeth while sucking and mealing away on these healthy crackers. Brother and sister will want some too - they're hard and chewy - and taste really good!

½ cup barley flour
2 Tbs. oat flour + 2 Tbs. soya powder
1 cup whole wheat pastry flour
2 Tbs. arrowroot or flaxseed meal
¼ tsp. sea salt
¼ tsp. anise seed, ground
½ tsp. pure vanilla
⅓ cup maple syrup, agave,
    or part molasses
¼ cup milk, soy or nut
¼ cup orange juice concentrate

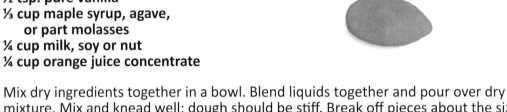

78

Mix dry ingredients together in a bowl. Blend liquids together and pour over dry mixture. Mix and knead well; dough should be stiff. Break off pieces about the size of a walnut; with hands roll pieces 2" long, tapering slightly at one end. Press flat with spatula to ¼" thick. Bake in a 275° -300° oven 25-30 min. Yield: 12 biscuits; these freeze well.

Graham Gruel

...most palatable and healthful...Diet and Foods pg. 315

Good for baby when starting on cereals. Use **coarse graham flour**. Simmer in same proportions as mentioned for **Oatmeal Gruel**. Strain, add **milk**; drink warm.

Rice Water

Drain liquid off cooked brown rice or whole barley. Add to baby's formula, or blend with fruits or vegetables.

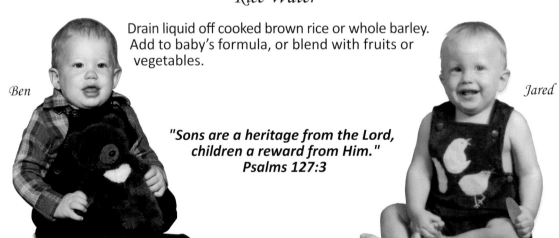

Ben

Jared

**"Sons are a heritage from the Lord,
children a reward from Him."
Psalms 127:3**

Salads for Baby

Your baby can have **fresh tender salad greens** by blending to a purée with **pure water**. Add **mashed avocado** for the dressing and combine until smooth. Delicious!

Vegetables for Baby

Your baby can learn to like vegetables starting at 6 months. Steam vegetables until tender and purée in blender or baby food mill. Fresh organic vegetables such as carrots, squash, and peas are superior to frozen, canned, or processed baby foods.

The need for salt is usually covered by the naturally occuring salt in the foods; if some is needed, a pinch of sea salt will suffice (babies cannot tolerate much salt). When your baby is old enough, cooked grains may be combined with the vegetables. Try blending these vegetables to a smooth purée:

Green Beans
Sweet Potatoes
Parsnips
Squash, varieties
Beets + Potatoes

Peas + or Carrots
Mixed Vegetables
Spinach + Tofu
Tofu + Broccoli
Carrots + Lima Beans

Soups for Baby

Your baby will enjoy these soups with added pieces of dry bread (zwieback) soaked in soup. Soups are a good way to include protein in the diet. Meat and eggs are often recommended for babies when just a few weeks old; however, that is not the ideal diet. Babies will thrive on natural plant based foods – just as surely as growing children or adults. The smooth texture and digestibility of tofu and tahini provide excellent nutrition to supplement baby's diet. Tofu and sesame tahini may be blended with vegetables or soups for extra protein. Blend smooth or chunky, as to age. Start with small portions.

Best Barley Soup

More Soups to try:

Garden Vegetable Soup
Cream of Celery Soup- add tofu
Vegetable Soup with Rice
Almond Cream - add tofu
Cream of Broccoli Soup
Escarole Garbanzo Noodle Soup
Split Pea Soup
Pumpkin or squash soup

Note: see chapter - **Soups and Stews** for recipes. (modify seasonings for baby feeding)

Potato Soup

Baby and Cereal

When a baby is approx. 10-12 months old, and has a set of baby teeth, saliva secretion (and ptyalin) increases, which assists in digesting carbohydrates (the starches) in grains. Up to that time, it is not recommended that babies have much cereal. Baby's main food should be **milk** (ideally mother's milk) and some fruits, vegetables and hard-dry bread or zwieback. **Zwieback** (twice-baked bread) is more easily digested than fresh bread or cereal, and like teething biscuits, provides good chewing and massage for baby's teeth and gums.

Grains should be well cooked for baby (see *Methods of Cooking Grains* - chapter **Grains**). Sprouted grains require less cooking, but should be blended smooth for baby. Blend grains with **nut, seed or soy milk**, or any of the **Natural Food Formulas** listed.

Dates, date sugar, seeds or **fruits** may be blended with cereal for a sweeter taste. Here are some possible combinations that your baby will love. Whiz in blender until very smooth.

Incidentally, if there are leftovers after your baby is fed, you may want to enjoy it too!

Natural Brown Rice
Dates, pitted
Nut or soymilk

Kasha (buckwheat)
Flaxseed meal
Date sugar
Soy or nut milk

Corn meal
Raisins, soaked
Sunflower or flax meal
Almond milk

Spelt, steamed
Dates, chopped
Flaxseed meal
Almond milk

Barley, whole steamed
Raisins, soaked
Almond or Cashew milk

Rye flakes or kernels
Black Figs
Almond Milk

Whole kernel wheat
Dates, pitted
Sesame tahini
Soymilk or nut milk

Rosalie's Raw Granola
Date Butter
Almond Milk

Millet, whole steamed
Prunes, stewed
Almond milk

Quinoa, steamed
Dates or date sugar
Cashew or coconut milk

Mixed grain cereal
Prunes, puréed
Coconut or cashew milk

Mixed grain cereal
Apricots, unsulfured
Pumpkin seeds, meal
Cashew milk

Sprouted grains, steamed
Apricots or apples
Coconut or Almond milk

Oatmeal, quick, cooked
Applesauce
Sunflower or flax meal
Soymilk or Cashew milk

Oatmeal, cooked
Dates, pitted
Coconut, grated
Soy or almond milk

Wheat or barley flakes
Raisins, soaked
Pine Nuts
Almond milk

Steamed Spelt with dates, almond milk

David

A baby's body grows and develops more in the first three years of their life than in all the remaining years. Therefore what a child is fed during these highly development years is of primary importance.

"Let every father and mother realize that when their child is three years of age, they have done more than half they will ever do for its character."
-Horace Bushnell

"He (Jesus) grew in wisdom and stature, in favor with God and men..."
Luke 2:52 NIV

**Sow a thought
and reap an Act
Sow an act
and reap a Habit
Sow a habit
and reap a Character
Sow a Character
and reap a Destiny!**
-author unknown

A Healthy Baby is a Happy Baby

River

**Stewed Prunes
Flaxseed meal**

Hannah

Kelsey

Riley

Beverages

Index - Chapter 4

Beverages

84

Ten Talents

Chapter cover photo: *Peach Blush, page 90*

Water the best beverage...

"In health and in sickness, PURE WATER is one of heaven's choicest blessings. Its proper use promotes health. It is the beverage which God provided to quench the thirst of animals and man. Drunk freely, it helps to supply the necessities of the system, and assist nature to resist disease."
E. G. White, Counsels on Diet & Foods 419

*D*o all in your power to secure the best possible PURE WATER for your family, free from additives and impurities. City water today is no longer pure, but treated with Chlorine, Fluorine, Iodine, Softeners, and other inorganic chemicals for protection against disease. A wealth of information has been published on the benefits of drinking water. Water plays a vital role in all of our bodily functions and is rated second to oxygen as essential for life. Thirst signals the body's need for water, however many do not realize a dehydrated body craves fluid before thirst occurs, and we need about eight 8-oz. glasses each day. On the average, each day we lose one and a half cups through breathing, one and a half cups through the skin, and four or five cups through the kidneys. Drink freely of pure soft water on arising and between the meals. One or two glasses (preferably hot) in the morning, with fresh squeezed lemon, is an excellent way to start. At mealtime, our food should not be washed down by diluting with water. Water taken with the meal hinders the flow of the salivary glands, and makes the food more difficult to digest; for the liquid must first be absorbed. Pure water, juices, and other healthful beverages may be taken a short while before the meal or in the evening for a light supper. Nourishing and healthful drinks may be made with simple combinations of natural foods. In this chapter you will find a variety of refreshing beverages, delicious fruit drinks, smoothies, vegetable juices, tasty herb teas; nut, seed, and soymilk, and nutritious chocolate and coffee substitutes. After you have tried them, you may want to go on and experiment with your own combinations.

Fruit Beverages

Three-Fruit Frosty

Naturally sweet and simply delicious!

2 cups blueberries, frozen or fresh
2 cups peaches, sliced fresh / frozen
¼ cup raspberry frozen juice concentrate
1 cup soy milk, vanilla
1 cup soy yogurt
¼ tsp. pure coconut extract, opt.

Combine blueberries, peaches and soy milk in a blender. Cover and process until smooth. Add the raspberry frozen juice concentrate, yogurt and coconut extract. Blend again. Pour into 4 glasses. Garnish with blueberries if desired. Serve immediately.

Tangerine Orange Grape Quencher

2 cups fresh
   or frozen orange juice
1 cup white grape juice
1 cup frozen
   or fresh tangerine juice
1 cup water +
½ tsp. lemon zest

Blend together until smooth. Serve at room temperature, or on a hot summer day with crushed ice, and a wedge of lemon.

Strawberry - Pineapple Blend

2-3 cups pineapple juice
2 cups fresh strawberries
1-2 bananas (fresh or frozen)
honey to taste, optional

Pour part of the pineapple juice into blender. Add the fresh or frozen strawberries; blend briefly. Add the rest of juice and bananas; continue blending until creamy smooth. Pour into 3 or 4 serving glasses and decorate with strawberries and bananas.

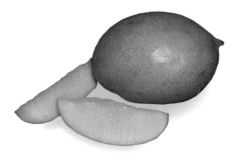

Mango-Orange Cooler

2 cups fresh orange juice
1 cup fresh cut mango

Blend together until smooth; sweeten with honey, if desired. Delicious!

Morning Eye-Opener

1 cup pineapple juice
1 cup grapefruit juice
½ cup orange juice
2 Tbs. lime juice

Stir or shake the juices together until blended. Use freshly squeezed fruits whenever available. A refreshing healthy beverage to start the day. Servings: 2

Golden Apricot Nectar

1 cup pineapple juice
1 cup orange juice
¼ tsp. orange zest
4-5 apricots, fresh or canned

Pour the pineapple and orange juice in blender. Add the zest and apricots. Process until smooth. Garnish with fresh apricot slices if desired. Serve chilled.

Tropical Island Delite

(Simply Delicious)

2 cups pineapple juice
    or Dole® Pineapple Mango juice
1 cup fresh or frozen strawberries
1 cup mango* fruit, diced
½ cup lite coconut milk
    or 2 Tbs. soy milk powder

Blend until smooth. If desired, add
1 tsp. light raw honey.

* Peaches may substitute in this satisfying breakfast beverage.

Raspberry Lemonade

3 cups water
¾ cup fresh lemon juice
½ cup raspberries*
2-3 Tbs. light honey, to taste

Blend all ingredients together.

*raspberries can be fresh or frozen. Strain beverage. Garnish with **lemon slices** and **mint**.

Limeade

Substitute **¾ cup fresh squeezed lime juice** (about 7 limes) for the lemon juice, and omit raspberries. Stir in **honey** to taste. Garnish with **lime slices** and **strawberries** if desired.

Cran-Raspberry Sunrise

½ cups 100% cranberry juice
½ cup orange juice
1 cup fresh raspberries
1 Tbs. lemon juice

Put all ingredients in blender or food processor and blend until smooth. Decorate with **slices or spirals of fresh orange or lemon**. Serve immediately.

Cashew-Orange Breakfast Drink

¼ cup raw cashew nuts
2 cups orange juice
2 Tbs. soy milk powder
1 tsp. honey to taste, optional

Blend cashew nuts with 1 cup orange juice until creamy and smooth. Add remaining juice, soy milk powder and honey if desired. Decorate with **orange slice**. Serves 2.

Pineapple Grapefruit Tango

Juice **fresh grapefruits**. Mix with equal part of **pineapple juice**. Float chunks of fresh grapefruit or pineapple in glass. A refreshing morning beverage.

Lemon Sorbet

Make your own fruit flavored ice with fresh squeezed lemons - a refreshing summer treat.

2½ cups pure cold water
4 Tbs. light honey, or to taste
6 lemon juice cubes, fresh-frozen
lemon zest, optional

Blend water and honey on low speed to combine. Add frozen lemon juice cubes and zest. Blend until smooth. Pour into a shallow square dish and freeze, stirring several times to keep mixture smooth. Sorbet should be firm in 3-4 hours. Garnish with lemon zest. Servings: 4

Boysenberry-Cherry Soda

1 part Boysenberry 100% Juice or Frozen Juice Cubes
1 part Cherry 100% Juice or Frozen Cherry Juice Cubes
1 part unsweetened Mineral Water or Sparkling Water

Mix equal parts of each juice, with one part of mineral or sparkling water. Add a little lemon and sweeten with raw honey, to taste, if desired. Fill glasses and serve. OR: Put 4 Frozen Juice Cubes in each glass. Fill will Mineral or Sparkling Water. For an extra treat – add a scoop of sherbet on top.

Peach Blush

¾ cup milk (your favorite)
3 cups peach slices, fresh, frozen or canned
1-2 Tbs. golden flaxseed meal
2 fresh apricots, cut in half
1 cup fresh strawberries
1-2 bananas, sliced/frozen
4-5 ice cubes, optional

Pour the milk into a blender or food processor. Add the peach slices and ground flaxseed and process until combined. Add the apricots, strawberries, bananas and ice cubes and process until creamy smooth. Pour into glasses; decorate with fresh peaches. Delicious!

Lemon and Lime Sparkle

Juice of one lemon + two limes
3 cups unsweetened mineral water
2 Tbs. raw honey, to taste
¼ tsp. lemon or lime zest

Combine or blend until smooth. Serve with a slice of lemon or lime and sprig of mint, if desired.

Pineapple Cream Float

1 qt. pineapple juice, cold
2 cups orange juice, cold
+ 1 tsp. orange zest
4 Tbs. cashew butter

Blend until creamy. Pour into 4 tall glasses. Float a scoop of **homemade ice cream** or **fruit sherbet** in each glass. Serve with a spoon. Delicious!

Beauty Beverage

2 cups watermelon chunks
1 cup fresh strawberries
1 cup peaches, sliced, ripe
1 tsp. lime juice

Blend together. Sweeten with a little agave syrup or raw honey, if desired.

Grape Apple Drink

2 cups pure grape juice
2 cups pure apple juice
2 cups pure water
juice of 2 limes or 1 lemon
honey to taste, if desired

Combine all ingredients together in a large pitcher, chill and serve; or pour over ice cubes in a punch bowl or individual glasses. Decorate with slices of lemon or lime, if desired.

Wedding Punch

Serves 50

100% White Grape, frozen juice concentrate
100% Cranberry-Raspberry, frozen juice concentrate
2 cups Lemon or Lime Juice, freshly squeezed
6 quarts Pure Water
Ice cubes

Mix 2-12 oz. each, unsweetened frozen fruit juice concentrate with 6 qts. water. Add 2 cups juice from freshly squeezed lemons or limes (approx.8 - 12). Place 4 cups ice cubes in large punch bowl and pour over blended juice. Decorate with thinly sliced **lemon rings** or **fresh floating raspberries**. Makes 8 quarts approx. 50 5-oz.servings)

Note: Other combinations of frozen 100% fruit juice concentrates can be substituted:

Apple/Grape/Raspberry,
White Grape/Peach,
White Grape/Raspberry,
Concord Grape,
Orange/Peach/Mango,
Pineapple,
Pineapple/Apple/Banana,
Orange /Banana/Strawberry,
Pineapple/Apple/Strawberry

Melon Refresher

1 cup plain soy yogurt
½ cup honeydew, chunks
½ cup crenshaw or other melon
½ cup cantaloupe, chunks
½ cup watermelon, chunks
6 ice cubes

Pour the yogurt and cantaloupe into blender and process until smooth. Add the rest of melon chunks along with the ice cubes and process until smooth. Pour the drink into glasses and decorate with a wedge of melon. Serve at once.

Summer Fruit Slush

¼ cup orange juice
1 Tbs. lime juice
¼ cup sparkling water
2 cups frozen melon
6 ice cubes, berry juice
fresh raspberries, optional

Pour the orange juice, lime juice and sparkling water into a food processoror blender. Add the frozen melon chunks (or berries), and frozen berry juice cubes. Process until a slushy consistency has been reached. Pour into glasses. Decorate with fresh raspberries, if desired and serve.

Frosty Cranberry Cocktail

A very pretty, surprisingly sweet, and really good-for-you beverage

1 qt. pineapple juice, cold
1½ cups cranberries, fresh or frozen
1-2 drops mint extract, opt.

Whiz in blender until very smooth and foamy. Pour into glasses; garnish with fresh mint if desired. Serve immediately to avoid settling. This healthy beverage is naturally sweet-tart without sweetening!

Homemade Grape Juice

Fresh Grapes and other softskin fruits (apples, berries, cherries, pears, plums, etc.) are easily made into *pure, undiluted*, fruit juice with a steam process, stainless steel juice extractor *(such as the *Mehu-Maija® – available, from the authors)*. Simply place washed grapes or other fruit in the top holding pan. The pure juice quickly collects (by steam process) in the juice kettle and is easily drawn off by the drain tube. Simply fill glass bottles and seal with a lid, for winter use. No further processing is needed. A sure method of extracting pure undiluted fruit juice from a variety of fruits!

* See photo in **Miscellaneous** chapter.
Note: **Fresh Juices that Freeze Well** (see chapter- Misc. Canning, Freezing Drying)

Fruit "Smoothies"

Incredibly quick and easy to make, homemade "Smoothies" are a delicious way to enjoy fruit all year round. What better way to enjoy the variety of colorful fruits available to us, even when they are out of season, than by whipping them up into a tasty and nourishing drink? Smoothies can be served at breakfast, alone as a light meal, or for a simple satisfying supper. Fruit smoothies can be made with a base of pineapple or orange juice, soy, nut, or coconut milk, and a variety of fresh, frozen, dried, or canned fruits. The addition of nuts or seeds will enhance the food value. Blend until creamy smooth and serve in tall glasses.

Strawberry-Banana Smoothie

2 cups soy milk, vanilla
1-2 ripe bananas, frozen
1 cup ripe strawberries, fresh or frozen
4 Tbs. orange juice concentrate
2 Tbs. golden flax seed, fresh ground
1 Tbs. honey, opt.
1 cup soy yogurt, opt.
¼ tsp. vanilla, clear, opt.

Blend all ingredients 1-2 minutes until smooth and creamy. Serves 2-3. Simple and delicious!

Pina Colada Fresca

¼ cup frozen 100% pineapple juice, concentrate
1 cup soymilk, vanilla
½ cup coconut milk
¼ cup water
¾ tsp. pure coconut extract, flavor
2 bananas, frozen
½ cup pineapple chunks, frozen

Pour the pineapple juice (undiluted), soymilk, water, coconut milk and extract into the blender. Blend together. Add the frozen bananas (cut in pieces), and frozen pineapple chunks. Blend until creamy and smooth. Fill glasses, add straws and serve.

2

1 cup pineapple or orange juice
½ cup soy yogurt
2 cups ripe persimmons, fresh
  or frozen
1 ripe banana, fresh or frozen, cut

Melissa's Tropical Fruit Smoothie

2 cups white grape juice
2 cups pineapple chunks, fresh or
  canned
2 cups canned or fresh cut pears
¾ cup (½ - 12 oz. can) coconut milk
1 ripe banana, fresh or frozen, cut
1 golden delicious apple

Blend grape juice and pineapple until
smooth; add rest of ingredients and
continue blending until very creamy
and smooth. Delicious!

3

3 cups pineapple juice
2 cups pears,
  fresh or canned
1-2 bananas
1 Tbs. sesame
  tahini

Simple Smoothie Ideas

Frozen fruits may substitute for fresh, in
the suggestions listed below:

1

2 cups creamy coconut
  or almond milk
2 cups ripe peaches,
  fresh or frozen
1 ripe banana, frozen
1 cup pineapple juice
1-2 Tbs. almond butter

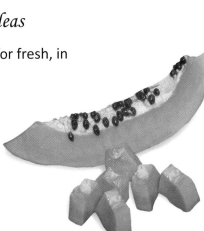

4

2 cups ripe papaya
  pureé or juice
1 cup ripe pears
  or raspberries
2 cups pineapple juice
1 Tbs. cashew butter
2-3 Tbs. Soymilk
  powder

Very-Berry Smoothie

2 cups Silk® Soy Milk, vanilla
1-2 medium bananas, ripe, frozen
1 cup strawberries, fresh or frozen
1 cup mixed berries, fresh or frozen
 (raspberries, blueberries, blackberries)
1 Tbs. honey, to taste
½ cup soy yogurt, optional

In a blender container combine soy milk and fruit. Cover and blend until puréed and smooth. Serve in 2 tall glasses. If desired, top with a few fresh berries.

5

2 cups blueberries or peaches,
 fresh or frozen
1 cup pineapple juice
1 cup orange juice
1 cup soy yogurt, vanilla
1 Tbs. flaxseed meal

6

1 cup orange juice
½ cup soy milk, vanilla
1 cup strawberries, ripe
1 banana, frozen or fresh
1-2 Tbs. golden flaxseed, fresh ground

7

2 cups apricots, fresh, frozen or canned
3 cups orange juice
1-2 bananas
2 Tbs. sunflower or flaxseed meal
1 cup soy yogurt, optional

Raw Vegetable Juices & Drinks

"Home Therapy"

Fresh fruit and vegetable juices can serve as a nutritious supplement to the diet. These nutrient rich juices contain vitamins, minerals, and enzymes, in an easily digested form.

For those who cannot eat sufficient raw foods to supply their daily needs without upsetting their digestion, fresh juices are suggested. Fruit juices generally are cleansing (Grape, Berry, Apple, Citrus, Pineapple, Papaya, Prune). Vegetable juices are builders and regenerators (Carrot, Beet, Celery, Cabbage, Tomato, Parsley, Spinach, Watercress, Barley and Wheat grass). Raw fruit and vegetable juices are very perishable. Drink after juicing or keep refrigerated in a tightly closed jar, for up to one day.

Further reference:
Live Food Juices, by Dr. H. Kirschner,
Fresh Vegetable & Fruit Juices,
by Dr. N. W. Walker,
 How to Keep Slim, Healthy and Young with Juice Fasting, by Paavo O. Airola, N.D., Ph.D.
*Contact the authors for information on **Juicers**, and *BarleyLife* or *Garden Trio* juice powders

Spicy Vegetable Juice

2 cups carrot juice
1 cup celery or cabbage juice
2-3 cloves garlic, fresh
3 ripe tomatoes, cut
1 romaine lettuce, small head
2 Tbs. lemon juice, fresh
¼ tsp. sea salt, to taste
cayenne or paprika, to taste
½ cup pure cold water

Put the carrot and celery juice, garlic, and tomatoes in blender. Blend lightly. Add the washed romaine leaves, lemon juice, seasoning, and pure water (or ice cubes).Process in blender until combined and smooth.
Pour into 4 glasses.
Garnish with a
parsley sprig.

Vital Green Drink

2 cup fresh celery or tomato juice
½ cup fresh alfalfa sprouts
¼ cup fresh parsley or watercress
2 Tbs. sunflower seeds
5 almonds, blanched

Liquify the seeds and nuts with ¼ - ½ cup pure water until smooth. Add rest of ingredients and blend until smooth, diluting with pure water (or for a cold drink with frozen vegetable juice cubes), if desired. Serve immediately.

Dinner Appetizer

2 cups fresh celery juice
1 cup cabbage or kraut juice
1 cup alfalfa sprouts, 1" long
pinch of cayenne, opt.

Blend the above ingredients 10 seconds. Serve immediately. Need not be strained.

Blood Builder Beverage

½ cup fresh beet juice
1 cup fresh carrot juice
1 Tbs. Barleylife® powder
or wheatgrass juice

Wash, peel and juice beets; clean and juice carrots. Add **Barley-life** powder to juice. Stir with a spoon to combine or shake in a jar with tight fitting lid. Drink before a vegetable meal.

Garden Green Drink

2 stalks celery
¼ head cabbage,
watercress or parsley
fresh spinach
or 1-2 comfrey leaves
pure water

Combine cut celery, cabbage, handful of watercress and spinach leaves, with a little pure water. Blend until smooth; strain. Add a squeeze of **lemon juice**. Serve at once.

Fresh Carrot Juice

Juice **fresh clean garden carrots**. Drink immediately after juicing. Carrot juice is a good source of carotene, which may improve eye function. The remaining moist pulp, a source of fiber, may be added to bread, cookies, muffins, or patties.

Carrot-Coconut Drink

2 cups fresh carrot juice
½ cup lite coconut milk

Stir to combine. Serve as a dinner appetizer, with a **sprig of fresh mint**, if desired.

Tangy Tomato Juice

2 cups tomato juice, fresh or frozen
1 cup sauerkraut juice or part celery juice
Serve in small glasses, as an appetizer before dinner.

Alfalfa Energizer

3 cups fresh cabbage juice
2 cups alfalfa sprouts, rinsed
4 Tbs. raw almond or cashew butter
Squeeze of lemon juice, optional

Blend in blender until smooth and creamy. Serve before a vegetable meal.

Three C Veggie Builder

Cabbage juice
Watercress
Carrot juice
Spinach leaves
Celery juice
Parsley sprig

Combine equal parts of cabbage, carrot and celery juices. Blend together with a handful of the leafy greens until smooth. An excellent potassium-rich tonic.

Appetite Booster

½ cup fresh tomato juice
½ cup fresh cabbage juice
¼ cup cucumber juice
¼ cup red or green pepper juice

Blend together. Strain if desired. Drink before a vegetable meal. Serves 2.

Fresh Tomato Juice

Fresh ripe tomatoes
Lemon squeeze
pinch of salt, to taste

Blend until smooth. Strain if desired, to remove the seeds.

Note: As a supplement for B vitamins, add **1 Tbs.** of nutritional yeast.

Grape-Nog Pick-Up

Blend:

1 healthy egg into
1 glass pure grape juice

"When you see that you are becoming weak physically, it is essential for you to make changes, and at once...Get eggs of healthy fowls...Drop them uncooked into the best unfermented wine (grape juice) you can find. This will supply that which is necessary to your system."

E.G. White,
Counsels on
Diet & Foods
page 367

Rhubarb Spring Tonic

**pure water
rhubarb stalks,
fresh crisp
strawberries, fresh
or frozen
honey, to taste**

Process fresh crisp rhubarb stalks through a juicer. Blend whole strawberries. Mix equal parts of rhubarb juice and strawberry purée together. Add ½ part pure water to dilute. Blend or stir thoroughly. Sweeten to taste with honey, if desired.

Skin Toner

**3 garden cucumbers, small
½ cup alfalfa sprouts**

Blend until smooth adding pure water as needed. Strain and chill before serving.

Stimulating Drinks Information

Our society is plagued with an endless variety of advertisements encouraging the use of Tea, Coffee, Cocoa, Alcoholic drinks, Soft Drinks artificially sweetened, and Tobacco. These are all stimulating and contain poisons to a greater or lesser degree. They are not only unnecessary, but harmful and should be discarded, if we want to enjoy the best of health.

Caffeine is an alkaloid, considered a psychoactive drug, and classified as a central nervous system stimulant. It is present naturally in coffee beans and tea leaves, and added to many soft drinks consumed by millions today.

Cocoa beans also contain some caffeine, but much higher levels of another bitter alkaloid called theobromine, closely related to caffeine.

When caffeine is removed from the source plant, it is reduced in form to a white powder, which is very bitter. For this reason, many beverages containing caffeine, also contain copious amounts of sugar or other artificial sweeteners.

Caffeine has many side affects, including:

1. Sleep patterns, altered
2. Nervousness
3. Dizziness
4. Headaches
5. Habit Forming
6. Impaired Brain Function
7. Gastrointestinal problems
8. Heart palpitation- rhythm changes
9. Link to other Diseases
10. Drug withdrawal reactions

Caffeine content of some common drinks (based on 8- ounce beverage)

Source: National Soft Drink Assoc., US Food and Drug Admin.

8-ounce Beverage	milligrams
Coffee, Drip, Brewed	15-175
Coffee, Espresso (2 ounces)	100
Coffee, Instant	65-100
Tea, brewed, iced	47-60
Dr.Pepper, Diet Coke, Jolt	41-71
Pepsi Diet, Cola, Mountain Dew	36-55
Tea, green, instant	15-30
Decaf Tea, White tea, Hot Cocoa	10-15
Sprite, 7-Up, Fresca, artifically sweetened	0
Herbal Tea, Fruit Juices,	0

Note: There are a variety of tasty beverages available at whole food markets made from a healthful blend of natural ingredients such as barley, carob, chicory, figs, beet root, roasted cereal grains, garbanzos and soybeans. These good-for-you substitutes have the aroma and flavor of coffee, are non-addictive and 100% caffeine free!

Listed are a few favorite brands: **Bueno, Cafix, Roma, Pero, Postum, Teeccino**.

Herb Teas & Coffee Substitutes

The glow of health is soon lost by those who drink stimulating beverages. In place of these nerve irritants, choose beverages beneficial to health. In the book **Counsels on Diet and Foods,** by Ellen G. White, there is an enlightening chapter on "Beverages." We recommend this excellent reading.

How To make Herb Teas:

For each cup of boiling water add:

1 Tbs. dry herb tea leaves or
2 Tbs. fresh herb tea leaves

Bring water to a boil
Add tea leaves. Remove from heat.
Let stand. (do not boil leaves)
Steep 10-30 min.
Strain, serve hot or cold; may sweeten with honey.

A bit of **orange peel** dropped into some teas gives a delightful flavor. Among the many herbs, **Spearmint, Peppermint, Alfalfa, Clover, Rose Hips, Fennel, Chamomile,** and others may be used alone or in combination, to make delicious or medicinal teas. Herb teas may be served hot or cold, plain or sweetened with honey.

See chapter on **Herbs** for growing, gathering, drying, storing, and use of herbs.

Also see: **Herbs of Yesterday for Today** charts, a handy guide for the use of Medicinal Herbs in the back of **Ten Talents**.

Note: The common tea leaves cultivated in China, Japan, and India, which are used in making tea and which millions of people are drinking, is injurious to the system. Tea and coffee are artificial stimulants.

Vanilla Creme Latte

Enjoy a *caffeine-free beverage with no harmful stimulating effects. Delicious hot or cold.

2½ cups soy vanilla or cashew milk
1 Tbs. honey or agave
1 Tbs. carob powder
½ tsp. pure vanilla
2 tsp. instant *Pero, Roma, or Cafix
¼ tsp. lecithin granules, opt.

In a saucepan, heat soymilk to desired temperature. Pour into blender. Add rest of ingredients and blend until smooth and frothy. Serve in cups.

Good Night Cap

¼ oz. chamomile flowers
¼ oz. mint or catnip leaves
¼ oz passion flower herb
¼ oz. valerian herb

Bring 1 quart of water to a boil. Remove from heat. Add the herbs. Cover and let steep for 10-15 to infuse. Strain. Sip a cup slowly while reading inspirational verses; then retire.

Milk Drinks
(non-dairy)

Soybean Milk # 1
(Mild flavor- approx. 16¢ per qt.)

1 lb. dry Soybeans = 2 ½ cups
** (makes 6 ¼ qts. milk)**
2 cups dry Soy Beans makes 5 qts. milk
1 cup dry beans = 2 ½ cups when soaked

Recipe for 2 qts. soymilk:

2 cups soaked soybeans
2 qts. pure water (less for richer milk)

   Step 1. Soak 1 cup of dry Soybeans (preferably in refrigerator) for at least 12- 24 hours. Drain and rinse several times, covering with clear fresh water.

   Step 2. Purée 2 cups soaked soybeans with 2 qts. pure water, blending until creamy, one cup beans with one cup water (go to step 3). Repeat the process using all the water and beans, re-blending the pulp to extract all the milk possible.

   Step 3. Strain through clean towel, or flour sack cloth, squeezing to extract all liquid.

   Step 4. Bring to a boil, stirring to prevent boil over; then reduce heat and simmer for 30 minutes stirring frequently; or transfer milk to a double boiler (no need to stir).

Step 5. Cool milk a few minutes, then pour through fine mesh strainer into blender.

Homemade Soy Coffee

Several instant caffeine-free beverages are available in stores - see Coffee Substitutes in the Glossary of Natural Foods. However for those who want to experiment at home, here is a starter recipe:

Prepare beans: Spread **dry yellow soy beans** on a shallow pan. Roast in oven, very low temperature (200˚) till roasted through and dark brown coffee color, (several hours). Process roasted beans through a medium fine coffee grinder. Store in a glass jar with tight fitting lid to retain flavor.

½ cup ground roasted soybeans
1 quart pure water

Bring to a boil and simmer for 20 min. Let stand. The longer it steeps the richer the flavor. Good the next day. Strain. Re-heat and serve black or with honey and nut cream.

Quick Cafix

1 cup pure hot water
1 heaping teaspoon Cafix
1 tsp. molasses or honey, opt.
soy milk, to taste

Stir Cafix into hot water; add molasses and milk to taste. Enjoy!

For each quart of milk, add and blend:

1 Tbs. honey, to taste
½ tsp. soy oil, opt.
¼ tsp. sea salt
½ tsp. pure vanilla, opt.

Pour milk into quart jars and store in refrigerator-will keep sweet for several days. This delicious milk can be used in many ways (see recipes). The soybean pulp remaining (okara) after straining the milk, can be added to bread, patties, etc. (Okara is a good source of fiber).

Hint: For an intense flavor, split a **vanilla bean**, scrape out the seeds, add to simmering soymilk.

Soybean Milk # 2

(made with Soya Starter)

1 cup Soya starter*, plain
½ tsp. oil or lecithin granules, opt.
1 qt. pure water
1 Tbs. honey, to taste
¼ tsp. salt; ¼ tsp. pure vanilla, opt.

Blend all ingredients together in blender until very smooth (1-2 min.)

Variation: Sweeten with **maple or agave syrup** instead of honey.

*Soya Starter- see misc. chapter

For **Carob Soymilk:** Add **2-3 Tbs. Carob powder**, **½ tsp. pure vanilla**, and **1 Tbs. honey** or **4 soft dates** to above recipes. Blend till smooth. Serve hot or cold.

Note: If lecithin is used instead of oil, the milk will remain in suspension with no settling.

Hot Carob Cocoa

Carob is the ideal replacement for cocoa. A good source of nutrients, natural sugars, low in fat. (see description of Carob in Glossary of Natural Foods)

1 qt almond or soy milk, vanilla
3 Tbs. carob powder
6 soft dates or 2 Tbs. honey
½ tsp. pure vanilla
½ tsp. lecithin granules, opt.
pinch of sea salt

Blend above ingredients until creamy smooth, starting with only 1 cup of the milk. The addition of lecithin granules make for an extra creamy drink. Add remaining milk. Blend again. Warm on stovetop, but do not boil. Enjoy hot or cold!

Malted Carob Milk

Cocoa and chocolate are products of the cacao bean. It has properties similar to those of caffeine a harmful stimulant. Carob, on the other hand, is a product of the honey locust tree, naturally sweet, with high nutritive value. See Carob in Glossary of Natural Foods..

1 qt. milk: cashew-rice, or soy
3 Tbs. carob powder
2 tsp. malt powder or syrup
½ tsp. pure vanilla

Blend above ingredients until smooth. Add **1-2 Tbs. honey** to taste. Blend. For creamier malted milk, add **¼ tsp. lecithin granules.** Chill. Serve.

Rice Dream Milk

Cooked grains can be used alone or combined with raw nuts in making tasty, and nourishing beverages at a fraction of the cost of prepared commercial drinks. Here is one that is easy to prepare.

½ cup cooked brown rice
3 Tbs. cashew nuts
    or 2 Tbs. tahini
1½ cups pure water
2-3 tsp. honey
    or maple syrup
¼ - ½ tsp. pure vanilla
¼ tsp. sea salt

Blend cooked, warm rice and cashews together with 1 cup of the water until smooth and creamy (2-3 min). Add rest of ingredients and ½ cup more water or sufficient to make desired consistency. Blend again. Strain if desired.

Note: **Millet** or **Barley** can be used to replace the brown rice with good results; also almonds or coconut in place of cashews. Try other combinations.

Almond – Coconut Milk

Follow directions for making **Almond Milk.** Use part **almond** and **part fresh shredded coconut.** Sweeten with **4-5 dates** instead of honey. Strain if desired.

Almond Milk

1 cup soaked almonds, blanched
1 quart pure water
1-2 tsp. honey or maple syrup
¼ tsp. pure vanilla, opt.
½ tsp. malt, optional
⅛ tsp. sea salt, to taste

Blanch soaked* almonds. (Pour boiling water over nuts. Wait one minute, drain, remove skins by rubbing between fingers).*soaking/blanching: see chapter-**Nuts**. Blend ingredients in blender (using half of the water) 2-3 minutes, until smooth and creamy. Add remaining water and blend again. Delicious on hot/cold cereal!

Note: Almond milk prepared with soaked/blanched almonds will be smooth, creamy and white. Straining the milk is unnecessary. If straining is preferred, use the remaining pulp in granola, etc.

Almond – Cashew Milk

Use equal amounts of **Almonds** and **Cashews** (clean, raw) and follow directions given for almond milk. This tasty combination is good on granola, for making desserts, smoothies, creams, sauces, and for gravy (omit sweetening and vanilla when used for gravy; blanching almonds is optional).

Vanilla Tofu Milk

Very easy to make, just blend and serve.

8 oz. firm silken tofu, rinsed
2 cups pure water
1 Tbs. honey
½ tsp. pure vanilla
¼ tsp. sea salt
¼ tsp. lecithin
  granules, opt.

Drain and rinse tofu with clear water; drain again. Place tofu, water, honey, vanilla and salt in blender. Whiz until smooth. The addition of lecithin keeps milk in suspension and adds a bit of creaminess.

Note: To enhance the nutritive value of the milk, add **1 Tbs. sesame tahini** while blending.

Fresh Coconut Milk

1 cup fresh shredded
  coconut
3 cups pure water
  or coconut liquid
honey, to taste
pinch of sea salt

Whiz in blender until creamy smooth, using half the water. Add remaining water, honey and salt and blend again. Use on cereal as is, or strain and use pulp in crumb crust. Note: Other combinations of milk using coconut are delicious. Try these suggestions:

1. Coconut – Almond
2. Coconut – Sesame
3. Coconut --Cashew
4. Coconut – Carob Soy

Note: **Unsweetened dried coconut** may be used for milk. Soak in water before blending.

Almond – Sesame Milk

Use **¾ cup blanched Almonds** and **2 Tbs. Sesame Tahini**. Follow directions for **Almond Milk. 3 Tbs. whole or hulled sesame seeds** may substitute for tahini. Strain milk.

Cashew Nut Milk

The smooth creamy white texture of this mild flavored milk, makes it adaptable for many recipes. Simple to make.

1 cup raw cashews
½ Tbs. honey or maple syrup
¼ tsp. salt
1 qt. pure water
½ tsp. lecithin granules or oil, opt.
½ tsp. pure vanilla, opt.

Blend nuts, sweetening and salt, with half of the water, for 2-3 minutes until very smooth. Add the rest of water, lecithin and vanilla, if desired; blend again. Refrigerate. Can be used the same way as whole milk or combined with other non-dairy milk, such as coconut.

Note: For a richer Cashew milk or creamer (for fruit topping), use 1/2 the amount of water.

Milkless Milk Shakes

Strawberry Milk Shake

Follow recipe for **Vanilla Ice Cream #1** (omit freezing). Add **½ cup water** or **4 frozen pineapple juice cubes**, omit vanilla. Blend in **2 cups strawberries** (fresh or frozen). Pour into tall glasses. Servings: 4

Carob Banana Milk Shake

2 cups cashew/rice or soymilk
1 ripe banana, fresh or frozen
2 tsp. honey or molasses
1-2 Tbs. carob powder
1 Tbs. soy milk powder, opt.
¼ tsp. pure vanilla

Blend all ingredients 1-2 min. until smooth and creamy. Serve in tall glass. Delicious!

Vanilla Milk Shake

Use **Vanilla Ice Cream recipe # 2**. Reduce oil to 3 Tbs. Blend until smooth (omit freezing) Chill 1 hour, blend again. Yield: 4 servings.

"Chocolate" Milk Shake

Follow method for **Vanilla Milk Shake**. Add **2 Tbs. carob powder**, and **½ cup more water**; sweeten to taste. Whip. Chill. Servings: approx. 4

Date Milk Shake

2 cups almond milk or other
1-2 bananas, fresh or frozen
8-10 dates, soft, pitted
1 tsp. molasses

Blend half of the milk with the dates, till smooth. Add remaining milk, molasses and fresh or frozen banana. Whiz again in blender until very smooth. Serve.

Variation: **Carob Date Milkshake**: add **1 Tbs. carob powder**.

Cashew - Fig Milk Shake

2 cups cashew or coconut milk
2-4 Tbs. fig syrup
1 Tbs. soy milk powder
¼ tsp. pure vanilla, opt.

Blend well until smooth. Drink hot or cold.

Molasses Milk Shake

1 cup rice, soy or nut milk
1 Tbs. molasses

Add molasses to milk. Shake or blend thoroughly. Serve cold or hot.

Note: 1 Tbs. blackstrap molasses contains: Iron: 3.2 mg., Calcium: 176 mg.

Yogurt Notes

Yogurt is a natural food for the acidophilus or friendly bacteria within the colon. One of the finest health drinks, extolled by nutritionists and beauty advisors for its youthful elements.

Yogurt is consumed today by approximately 500 million people. However, in this country, very little yogurt is produced on a commercial basis. Yogurt can be made at home much cheaper, fresher, and tastier, using the milk of your choice.

1. Any kind of milk is used: powdered, sealed in carton, or fresh soybean milk.

2. Heat milk to just below boiling. Maintain this temperature for1-2 min. Let the milk cool down to 109° - 112°. Stir occasionally.

3. Add fresh culture to the warm milk,110° is ideal (too hot will destroy culture). Check temperature of milk with a food thermometer to be sure. Follow the incubating directions that come with the specific yogurt maker used.

4. Fresh *freeze-dried cultures* are available from health food stores, or use plain fresh yogurt for your culture. Fresh soy yogurt is also available in most stores.

5. Yogurt is a prime source of pre-digested protein. When selecting commercial varieties, look for natural plain yogurt with no artificial flavors, color or sugar.

6. Reserve some fresh yogurt to use as a starter for making the next batch. Twice as much yogurt culture may be used for quicker results. Rice starch, modified food starch or vegetable gelatin is sometimes added for a firmer consistency. After making several batches of yogurt, start over with a fresh culture.

7. Add fresh, frozen, canned fruits or flavors after yogurt is made.

Flavored Yogurt Suggestions

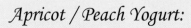

Strawberry / Raspberry / Blueberry / Cherry Yogurt

Add **¼ cup fresh or frozen berries or fruit** to each serving of yogurt. Sweeten with **honey** or **agave**, if desired.

Apricot / Peach Yogurt:

Add **¼ cup chopped dried and soaked, or canned fruit**.

Prune Yogurt:

Blend **soaked pitted prunes** to a puree. Add **3 Tbs.** to each serving

Molasses Yogurt:

Stir in **2-3 tsp. rich molasses** just before serving.

Date Yogurt:

Add **soft chopped dates** to **date puree**. Mix together; add to yogurt.

Honey Yogurt:

Stir in flavors of **natural honey** and/or **1-2 drops pure vanilla**.

Pineapple Yogurt:

Add **¼ cup crushed pineapple** to yogurt just before serving.

Lemon / Lime Yogurt:

Add **½ tsp. lemon or lime zest** or **2 tsp. lemon or lime juice** to each serving; add **honey** if desired. Mix together.

Bread, Yeast

Index - CHAPTER 5

Breads, Yeast

110

Ten Talents

Chapter cover photo: ***A Variety of Whole Grain Breads, the "Staff of Life"***

"Bread is the real staff of life, and therefore every cook should excel in making it...It is a religious duty for every Christian girl and woman to learn at once to make good, sweet, light bread from unbolted wheat flour. Mothers should take their daughters into the kitchen with them when very young, and teach them the art of cooking'." E.G. White, Diet and Foods, 315, 316

Bread - The Staff of Life

Everyone loves the pleasing aroma of fresh home-baked bread. It is amazing to me that such simple ingredients as flour, water, yeast, salt, and perhaps a little honey and oil when skillfully combined and baked in the oven, do come out tasting so good, and so good for you!

The basic ingredients have different functions, and if combined with fruits, nuts, seeds or vegetables, in the right proportions, result in a variety of breads of many tastes, textures, colors and shapes, that can be made at home, in your own kitchen.

The **flour*** or sprouted grain is the base for bread. Wheat is the primary grain, and the flour from hard wheat contains the right amount of gluten needed to facilitate the rising of bread. Spelt is another favorite grain for making bread. Barley is light and since the gluten content is low, barley flour is good for making flat bread, buns, crackers, or piecrust. Other flours such as rye, millet, oats, rice and soybean can be used in small amounts with good results.

The **water** should be warm, pure and soft. Other liquids such as potato water, vegetable broth, milk, or juice, can be substituted depending on the kind of bread made.

The **yeast** is a living organism that grows and converts its food to carbon dioxide bubbles that make the dough rise. Yeast is very sensitive; high heat will kill it, cold will stunt it's growth. Proof yeast or check for freshness (be sure it has not passed the expiration date).

**The amount of flour used can vary in a recipe, due to moisture content, type and age of grain (in bread making you will "feel" the dough – flour measurements are generally approximate).*

Salt is the flavoring needed to control the growth of the yeast, and prevent the dough from rising too much. Too much salt can kill the yeast; too little lets the dough rise so fast, it may cause the bread to collapse. If salt is decreased or omitted, decrease the rising time as well.

The **sweetening**, whether honey, molasses, sugar, maple or malt syrup, provides "food" for the yeast to help it grow, and enhances the flavor of the bread.

Oil adds tenderness, better texture and flavor to bread. The oil from the olives dates back to Bible times and was used in bread, even during times of famine (read 1 Kings 17: 11-14); also expended as a precious commodity to be sold to pay one's debt (read 2 Kings 4: 1-7). Lecithin can also be added to bread (see description - in Glossary of Foods).

And now that we have identified the basic ingredients, come with me into the kitchen and let's start making a batch of bread.

"Mothers should take their daughters into the kitchen when very young and teach them the art of cooking"
Esther Hurd (age 11) is putting to practice what she has learned, by eagerly making another batch of delicious wholesome bread (see simple steps and her finished bread).

Note: Flour, freshly ground from whole grains will yield a loaf of bread that is superior in flavor, texture and nutrition. For best results mill grains just before making bread, and use the flour while still warm (valuable nutrients begin to oxidize shortly after milling).
*Compact flour mills (hand or electric mills) are available- for more information, contact the authors.

Types of Wheat Flour

100% Whole Wheat Flour – Made from the whole kernel of wheat - nothing removed. *Hard red winter wheat* and *hard red spring wheat* are low in moisture content and contain higher gluten-forming protein (about 14%) which gives more structure to baked goods and is best for making bread. ***Hard white wheat*** (whole kernel) is comparable in protein to red wheat. It yields a loaf that is lighter in texture and color, and can be used in making bread, crackers, quick breads, or cookies. MIll flour fresh or store in the freezer or refrigerator to keep the fat in the wheat germ or grain from becoming rancid.

Whole Wheat Pastry Flour – Made from the 100% soft white wheat kernel which has less gluten than hard bread wheat, is lower in protein and higher in carbohydrates. A good choice for tender biscuits, pie crust, pancakes, quick breads or cookies.

Gold'n White w/Germ – Milled from *hard* red spring wheat – contains all the vital germ; some bran is left in flour. An all-purpose creamy colored flour for lighter baking. (available from Natural Way Mills - see *Index - Sources of Natural Foods*)

Graham Flour – Coarsely ground, unsifted flour, made from the whole wheat kernel, yielding a nutty flavor and dense texture to baked goods (named after Sylvester Graham, a nineteenth century dietary reformer).

Gluten Flour – The protein from wheat in concentrated form made from the refined flour of hard red wheat. A small amount added with other flours gives the dough a spongy, elastic texture which results in a chewy light bread. **Spelt**, an ancient grain is made into flour for bread, to adequately replace wheat, for those who have an intolerance to gluten.

All-purpose White Flour – Made from selected wheats blended for all kinds of baking, however the vital germ and bran (fiber) layers containing many nutrients have been removed. The unbleached variety is best combined in baking with 100% whole wheat and other whole grain flours.

Unbleached White Flour – Milled from the kernel of *hard* red spring wheat, however the vital germ and bran (fiber) layers have been removed.

Unbleached White Pastry Flour – Milled from the *soft* white winter wheat; the bran and germ are removed.

Note: Gluten restricted diets, replace wheat with brown rice, millet, oats, spelt, barley, quinoa, corn, teff.

100% *Whole Wheat Bread*

Into a bowl put:

5 cups pure warm water
3 Tbs. dry active yeast
1 Tbs. honey or sweetening
4 cups 100% whole wheat flour

Mix and let rise twice, stirring down sponge each time. Add in the order given:

3 cups 100% whole wheat flour
2 Tbs. lecithin or ¼ cup olive or soy oil
1 Tbs. sea salt
4 Tbs. honey or molasses

Mix bread adding more flour (approx. 6-7 cups) or enough to make a soft dough. Avoid adding too much flour. Knead dough 10 minutes until soft and springy. Shape into 4 loaves. Let rise in pans until almost double. Bake at 350° for 45-50 min.

Rye Bread

Into a bowl put:
1 qt. pure warm water
2 Tbs. dry active yeast
5 Tbs. pure sorghum or molasses
2 Tbs. liquid lecithin

Let set 10 minutes. Add and combine with mixer:

1 cup grated raw potato
   or ½ cup mashed potato
2 tsp. sea salt
2 Tbs. crushed caraway seed
4 Tbs. soy sauce or liquid aminos
2 cups rye flour
4 cups 100% whole wheat flour
¼ cup soy flour
4 ¾ cups gold'n white or barley flour

Knead bread 10 minutes, using the last ¾ cup golden white flour as needed. Add just enough flour to make a soft but not sticky dough. Let rise in a warm place until almost double. Shape into 5 loaves. Let rise in pans until almost double. Bake at 350° for 50 - 60 min. or until done – depending on size of loaves. Dough may be formed into buns, breadsticks, or rolls of different shapes.

"Zwieback, or twice-baked bread, is one of the most easily digested and most palatable of foods...." E.G. White, **Diet & Foods**, *p. 317*

"Bread dried in the oven is one of the most wholesome articles of diet." Ibid

7 Tips for Better Yeast Bread

• For the best bread start with fresh-milled whole grain flour. Have flour and all ingredients ready for mixing at room temperature.

• Proof the yeast in warm water **120° - 130°** (not too cold or hot), with a little added sweetener, before adding to bread mixture, *or* check the expiration date to be sure the yeast is fresh, so bread will rise properly.

• Start with the minimum amount of flour in recipe and slowly knead in the remaining flour, just enough to make a springy, soft, pliable dough.

• Knead bread thoroughly, either by hand or with a mixer, for about 10 minutes. Kneading develops gluten from the protein in flour and produces a smooth, even texture. If dough isn't kneaded enough, the bread may be coarse, crumbly, heavy and dry.

• Proof (raise) the dough in a warm, draft free place. *Oven proofing* works well. Place a bowl of very hot water on bottom of unheated oven; place bowl of dough on rack above it; close oven door. Let dough rise until *almost*, but not quite double.

• Form loaf, place in pan and bake *before* it rises to double in size (this will produce the nicest shape and texture of loaf). Bread will continue to rise in the oven while baking.

• To check the doneness of yeast bread, tap the bottom or top of loaf with fingers. The bread should sound hollow when it is baked. Remove from pans; cool thoroughly.

Simple 1-Loaf Recipe for Children
(Laura, age 12, adds sprouted wheat to this simple bread children enjoy making)

"Before children take lessons on the organ or piano, they should be given lessons in cooking." E. G. White, Diet and Foods pg. 263

1 cup pure warm water
1 pkg. dry active yeast (2 ¼ tsp.)
2 Tbs. maple syrup, honey or molasses
1 tsp. sea salt
1 cup whole wheat flour

In a mixing bowl, mix above ingredients together and let stand 10 minutes. Stir down, let stand 15 minutes, then add:

2 tsp. lecithin
1 ½ - 2 cups gold'n white, whole wheat, or barley flour

Knead for 5-7 minutes until smooth and elastic. Shape into 1 large or 2 small loaves. Let rise in prepared non-stick pans, until almost double. Bake at 350° for 45 minutes. Tap bottom of loaf; a hollow sound means loaf is done. Remove from pans, cool thoroughly on wire rack. Good warmed the next day. Serve with a little nut butter and honey.

Note: Chopped dates, nuts, flax seed or ground wheat sprouts may be added before last flour, if desired.

Simple Steps to Shaping a Loaf

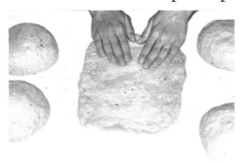

1. With fingers press and flatten dough into an oblong to remove air bubbles.

2. Fold ⅓ of narrow end diagonally into center. Press flat.

3. Repeat with other side, overlapping slightly. Press flat.

4. Starting at narrow end, roll dough up tightly, tucking in ends as you roll.

5. Finished loaf should be slightly longer than pan. Place seam down in *prepared pan.

6. Let rise in warm place until almost double. Bake until tests done according to recipe.

*Pan Coat: To **prepare pan** for easy removal of baked goods:
Stir and combine ¼ cup canola oil + ½ tsp. liquid lecithin. Lightly brush on baking sheet, bread pan or muffin cups. Store this ready-to-use mixture in a covered jar; use as you would a non-stick spray.

Raisin and Nut Bread

2 cups pure warm water
1 Tbs. dry active yeast
¾ cup sucanat, date sugar or honey
2 tsp. lecithin or 3 Tbs. soy oil
2 tsp. sea salt
3 cups whole wheat flour

In a mixing bowl combine the water, yeast, sweetening, lecithin or oil and salt. Let set 5 minutes then gradually add the 3 cups whole wheat flour. Beat with spoon or electric mixer 5-8 minutes. Cover and let stand until mixture forms bubbles. Stir down and add:

1 Tbs. ground cinnamon substitute
1 cup chopped walnuts or pecans
1 ½ cup raisins, brown or golden
3 cups gold'n white or w.w. pastry flour

Mix until dough pulls from bowl to form a soft ball. Knead dough, adding flour as needed until smooth, soft and elastic. Cover and let rise in a warm place until almost double. Shape into loaves or rolls and let rise in prepared pans. Bake in pre-heated 350° oven 45 minutes or until golden brown. Remove from pans; lightly oil tops to keep crust soft. Cool thoroughly, wrap and store.

Note: When using date sugar, less flour is needed.

Pumpernickel Rye Bread #1
Pumpernickel – A dark coarse bread made with unbolted (unsifted) rye flour.

2 cups hot water, + 1 Tbs. cafix or pero
¼ cup dark honey (i.e. buckwheat)
2 Tbs. dark molasses
2 tsp. sea salt
2 Tbs. pure olive or soy oil
¼ cup gluten flour + ¼ cup soy flour
1 cup coarse rye flour
1 cup graham flour
1 tsp. crushed caraway seeds
2 tsp. onion powder

Add the above ingredients to the hot water. Mix or beat thoroughly. Let sponge stand 10-15 minutes. Sprinkle and stir in yeast, then add remaining flour to make a soft, not sticky dough:

1½ Tbs. (2 pkg.) of dry active yeast
2 cups graham or whole wheat flour
1-2 cups gold'n white, or w. w. flour

Knead well 8-10 minutes. Let rise (proof) in oven or warm place until almost double in bulk. Punch down and shape into loaves; let rise in pans until almost double. Bake at 350° 45-50 min. Baked bread will sound hollow when tapped. Remove bread from pans, thoroughly cool on wire rack before wrapping. Yield: 3 1-lb. loaves.

Pumpernickel Rye Bread #2
(no fat, fine grain, dark rye)

Combine:

1 cup pure warm water
2 pkg. (1½Tbs.) dry active yeast
¼ cup dark molasses

Mix. Let stand 5 minutes while you blend:

1 cup water with 1 cup grated raw potato
2 Tbs. carob powder + 1 Tbs. cafix or pero

Combine the two mixtures, then add:

2 tsp. sea salt
1 Tbs. liquid lecithin, optional
3 cups whole wheat flour
2 cups rye flour
¼ cup gluten flour
¼ cup barley flour or corn meal
2 tsp. crushed caraway seeds

Mix well – and knead in approximately:

2 ½ cups whole wheat or gold'n white flour

On lightly floured board, knead bread 8-10 minutes until smooth and elastic. Dough should be moderately firm. Place in oiled bowl. Cover, let rise until almost double. Punch down. Divide dough for loaves or rolls. Shape and put into prepared pans. When almost double in bulk, bake at 350° 45-55 min. Yield: 3- 1 lb. loaves.

100% Whole Wheat – Rye Bread

Into a mixing bowl combine:

3 cups pure warm water
2 pkg. dry active yeast
3 Tbs. molasses or raw sugar

Let stand 10 minutes until bubbly, then add:

1 raw potato blended with 1 cup hot water
1 Tbs. sea salt, scant
1 Tbs. lecithin + 2 Tbs. oil
1 Tbs. ground caraway seed
¼ cup pure sorghum
5 cups 100% whole wheat flour

Beat 5 minutes with electric mixer. Let sponge set in a warm place 35-40 minutes. Mix again while adding:

2 cups rye flour
3 cups whole wheat or gold'n white flour

Knead well for 8-10 minutes until dough is smooth and elastic but not sticky. Divide into 4 pieces; shape each loaf. Let rise in prepared pans until almost double. Cut ⅛" slashes if desired. Bake in pre-heated 350° oven, 50-55 minutes until tests done.

Sprouted Wheat Bread or Buns

3 cups lukewarm water, divided
2 Tbs. dry active yeast
¼ cup honey or part molasses
1 Tbs. sea salt
3 Tbs. soy or olive oil
4 cups whole wheat flour
2 cups wheat sprouts
gold'n white flour, as needed

Dissolve yeast in 1 cup of the water. Add honey, salt, oil, and whole wheat flour. Beat well. Let this sponge rise in a warm place. To raised sponge add: 2 cups ground sprouts (blend with remaining 2 cups of water in recipe or put through a food grinder). Add more flour, enough to make a smooth soft dough that is not too sticky (no measurement for flour is given because some flours absorb more moisture). Knead well until smooth and elastic – adding suffi-cient flour or oiling hands to keep from sticking. Place in lightly oiled bowl. Cover. Let rise in warm place until almost double.

A Slice of Advice

Bread should be thoroughly baked, inside and out. Slow down and take time to chew it well. Digestion begins in the mouth!

Shape into loaves or buns. Place in non-stick or pre-pared bread pans. Let rise until almost double. Bake in 350° oven for 1 hour. Remove from pans. Cool thor-oughly and wrap. Yield: 4-5 loaves.

Note: Part of the sprouts may be used without grinding. If desired, add 1 more cup of sprouts; shape into bread, rolls or buns; let rise, bake until golden brown.

*Devitalized white bread made from highly refined flour cannot be compared in nutrition to wholesome bread, the **"staff of life"** made with whole grains and freshly milled flour.*

Beginners Bread in a Bag

This fun and easy way is a start for children or anyone learning to make bread. Start with a simple loaf using lighter flours, until you get "the feel of the dough".

2 cups flour, (mixed whole wheat, all-purpose or barley flour)
1 pkg. (2¼ tsp.) yeast, quick-rising
2 tsp. sucanat, honey or other sweetening
½ tsp. sea salt
1 Tbs. soy or olive oil
1 cup pure warm water (120° - 130°)

1. Combine all dry ingredients in a 1 qt. zip-lock plastic bag; close bag and shake.

2. Mix liquid ingredients together in a measuring cup; add to dry ingredients in the bag.

3. Close the bag and work dough with fingers thoroughly, adding a little more flour if needed, to make a soft dough that pulls away from sides of bag.

4. Turn dough out onto a lightly floured surface and knead for 5-7 min. until it forms a smooth and elastic ball. Cover the dough with the plastic bag and let it rest for 10 min.

5. Divide in half; flatten each piece of dough into a rectangle. Starting at small end, roll tightly to form a loaf. Place seam-side down in non-stick, lightly sprayed loaf pan. Let rise until almost double (about 30 min.)

6. Bake in pre-heated 375° oven for 30 minutes or more until tests done (loaf should sound hollow when tapping bottom of bread). Remove bread from pans and thoroughly cool on wire rack. Yield: 2 small loaves.

Soy Bread or Rolls

In a mixing bowl stir:

3 cups pure warm water
2 Tbs. dry active yeast
1 Tbs. honey

Let stand until dissolved then add:

¼ cup light molasses
¼ cup soy or olive oil
1 Tbs. sea salt

Add slowly while mixing:

3 cups whole wheat flour
¼ cup soy flour
4½-5½ cups gold'n white flour

Mix with wooden spoon or mixer, then knead for 10 minutes until smooth and elastic. Let rise in a warm place until almost double. Shape into loaves or rolls. Cover, set in warm place or proof in unheated oven with pan of hot water until very light. Bake at 350° to golden brown.

For soft crust: lightly brush tops with oil. This bread has a wonderful texture.

"...Form classes, where you may teach the people how to make good bread, and how to put together ingredients to make healthful food combinations..."
E.G. White, Medical Ministry p. 267

Shape into 1 large or 2 small loaves or rolls by flattening out with palms of hands to remove air bubbles. Roll up tightly sealing ends. Place in non-stick or prepared bread pan. Let rise until almost double. Bake at 375° for 10 min. – then at 350° for 35 min. or until golden brown and tests hollow when tapped on the bottom. Remove from pan. For soft crust, *lightly* brush top with oil. Cool thoroughly; best eaten next day. Enjoy!

Italian Loaves

Follow the recipe given for **Soy Bread** or **Variety Dinner Rolls**. Shape into narrow 8" or 9" long loaves, with the ends of loaf slightly tapered. Roll back and forth on counter to smooth top of loaf. Let rise on floured baking sheet 4" apart until almost double. Carefully cut ¼" deep diagonal slashes on top of loaves with sharp serrated knife. Brush with milk and sprinkle with sesame or poppy seeds if desired. Bake at 400° for 30-35 minutes or until loaves are golden and sound hollow when tapped. **For crusty loaves:** Omit or reduce oil in recipe to one-half. Lightly *mist loaves with cool water after shaping them, while rising, and after placing them in oven to bake.

   *Use a spray bottle with a fine spray to mist loaves. This adds moisture, and as water evaporates in the oven, it dries the surface of the bread and forms a crust.

Note: Lean dough products - flatbread, rolls, pizza – have a chewy texture. Use a little gluten flour or hard wheat flour – high in protein.

One-Loaf Whole Wheat Bread

"Mothers should take their daughters into the kitchen with them when very young, and teach them the art of cooking." - E. G. White, Child Guidance, p. 374

Mix together, let set 5 min. until bubbly:

1 cup pure warm water
1 pkg. active dry yeast (2 ¼ tsp.)
2 Tbs. molasses or honey

Stir in:

1 Tbs. soy oil
1 tsp. sea salt
1 cup 100% whole wheat flour
¼ cup quick oats, uncooked

Mix thoroughly then add:

1 Tbs. soy or gluten flour
1 Tbs. wheat germ
1 cup whole wheat or gold'n white flour

Knead dough on lightly floured surface for 6-8 minutes, adding enough flour to make a soft dough that is smooth and elastic. Place dough in oiled bowl; cover and set in a warm place to rise (an oven with pilot light or pan of hot water in oven works well). Let rise until almost double in size. Punch down and let rest 15 minutes.

Oatmeal Pecan Bread

Mix in bowl:

**2 cups pure warm water
1 Tbs. dry active yeast
1 Tbs. dry malt, opt.
2 Tbs. honey + 2 Tbs. sucanat
1 cups quick oats or cooked oatmeal
1 cup barley or gold'n white flour
2 tsp. lemon or orange zest
2 tsp. lecithin or 1 Tbs. soy oil**

Let stand few minutes to soften oats, then add:

**¼ cup cooked mashed potatoes, opt.
2-3 cups graham or gold'n white flour
2 tsp. sea salt
2 cups whole wheat or gold'n white flour
   (or replace 2 Tbs. with soy flour)
1 cup chopped pecans**

Knead 8-10 minutes, adding just enough flour to make a soft, springy dough. Cover and let rise to almost double in bulk. Knead down and divide into 3 parts. Let rest for 15 minutes. Shape into loaves; put into prepared pans. Let rise to almost double. Bake in 350° oven for 50- 55 minutes. Remove from pans – lightly oil tops for a soft crust. Yield: 3-1 lb. loaves

Ezekiel Bread

" Take wheat and barley, beans and lentils, millet and spelt, and put them into a single vessel, and make bread of them." Ezekiel 4:9 RSV

**4 cups pure hot water, (divided, 3+1)
¼ cup sucanat or honey
2 tsp. liquid lecithin or granules
1 Tbs. sea salt
1 cup barley flour
1 cup sprouted lentils, chopped fine
½ cup cooked millet or ⅓ cup millet flour
½ cup whole cooked spelt, coarse chop, opt.
¼ cup cooked oatmeal
½ cup gluten flour or other flour
1 Tbs. soy flour
2 Tbs. active dry yeast
6-8 cups whole wheat or spelt flour**

In a large mixing bowl, put 3 cups hot water, and all ingredients, except last 2 above. Mix well. Add the yeast (proof with remaining cup warm water + ¼ tsp. honey) and 2 cups of the flour. Mix sponge on low speed for 3-4 minutes, then let sponge set 30 minutes. Slowly add, while mixing, 5-6 cups more flour to make a soft, not sticky dough that pulls away from sides of bowl; let rest in bowl 15 minutes. Turn out on floured board and knead until smooth and elastic. Divide; form into loaves or rolls. Let rise in prepared pans until almost double. Bake at 350° 45-60 minutes, until loaves sound hollow when tapped on bottom.

Mix with electric mixer or spoon adding flour to make a moderately firm dough, not too sticky. Knead 10 minutes until smooth and elastic. Put in lightly oiled bowl. Cover, let rise in warm place to almost double. Punch down; let rise again. Divide in 6 pieces; shape into loaves or rolls. Put into prepared non-stick bread pans. Let rise until almost double. Bake at 350° for 50-60 minutes; baked loaves sound hollow when tapped. Remove from pans. Lightly oil tops if soft crust is desired. When cool, wrap. Best eaten next day. Yield: 6 loaves.

Multi-Grain Bread or Rolls

Stir together in mixing bowl:

1½ qts. pure warm water
4 Tbs. dry active yeast
¼ cup honey

Let dissolve then add:

¼ cup molasses
3 Tbs. lecithin or ⅓ cup soy oil
½ cup flax or corn meal
2 cups quick oats or barley flour
2 cups rye flour
¼ cup soy flour + ¼ cup gluten flour
5 cups whole wheat flour
1 ½ Tbs. sea salt
6-7 cups gold'n white or w.w. pastry flour

Walnut Date Loaf

Follow recipe for **Oatmeal Pecan Bread** with the following changes:
For the sweetening: Use **maple syrup** and **date sugar.** Omit mashed potatoes- substitute **2 Tbs. gluten flour**.
Add **1 cup chopped dates and walnuts,** instead of pecans.
Walnut Date Round Loaf: Brush or spray 46-oz. juice can with non-stick coating. Place dough in prepared juice can up to ½ full. Let rise to nearly double. Bake round loaf at 350° for 45 minutes or until loaf sounds hollow when tested. Remove from can, cool thoroughly before slicing.

until almost double in bulk. Dough is ready if indentation remains when touched. Punch down and shape into loaves or buns. Let rise almost double. Bake in 350° oven 50 minutes or until loaves sound hollow when tapped on bottom of loaf. Remove from pans to wire rack. Cool thoroughly.

No-Crumble Whole Wheat Bread

2 cups pure warm water
1 Tbs. dry active yeast
⅓ cup light molasses
1 Tbs. liquid lecithin or granules
1 Tbs. olive or soy oil, opt.
5-6 cups whole wheat flour, divided
2 tsp. sea salt

Dissolve yeast in warm water in large bowl. Stir in molasses, olive oil and lecithin. Stir in 3 cups of the whole wheat flour and salt. Beat with electric mixer 1-2 minutes. Add enough remaining flour to make a soft dough, easy to handle. Place dough on lightly floured surface. Cover loosely with plastic wrap and let rest 15 minutes. Knead 8-10 minutes or until smooth and elastic. Place dough in large, lightly oiled bowl. Cover loosely and let rise in a warm place about 1 hour

Spelt Bread

This ancient grain, rich in protein and fiber, is used in making bread. An excellent alternative for those who are sensitive to wheat or gluten.

2¼ cups spelt flour or part whole wheat
1 pkg. dry yeast (2 ¼ tsp), quick-rising
2 Tbs. sucanat or honey
1 cup pure warm water
½ tsp. sea salt
1 Tbs. olive oil or 1 tsp. lecithin

Combine the flour, yeast, salt and sweetening in a bowl. Stir in water and oil or lecithin. Mix to form dough. Turn dough out onto floured board and knead 5 minutes until smooth and elastic, adding more flour as needed to make a soft dough. Place dough in oiled bowl, cover and let rise in warm place until nearly double. Form into a round or regular loaf. Place in prepared pan, Cover and let rise until almost double. Bake at 350° to golden brown 45 minutes or until loaf sounds hollow when tested.

Marbled Loaf

A bread with lots of eye appeal that tastes as good as it looks. Simple to make,
yet adds a special touch to the meal- perfect for any occasion.

Use the **Oatmeal Pecan Bread, Sweet Rolls, Perfect Pecan**, or **Dinner Rolls** recipe.
Divide 1-lb. of dough in half. To one portion add enough gold'n white flour to make a
moderately stiff dough; knead 5-6 minutes until smooth and elastic (finely chopped
pecans or walnuts may be added to dough, if desired). To the other portion add
1½ Tbs. molasses and **2-4 Tbs. carob powder**. Knead into dough 5-6 minutes until
smooth and thoroughly combined. Cover dough portions; let rest 5-10 minutes
before making loaf. *(If dough has not risen, set in bowls to rise then punch down and*
let rest before making loaf).

To Form Loaf: Roll each dough portion into a 12"x 8" rectangle. Place dark dough
on top of light dough. Starting at a short end, roll up dough. Place seam side down
in non-stick bread pan. Cover, let rise to nearly double. Bake at 350° 45 minutes or
until bread sounds hollow when lightly tapped on bottom of loaf. Remove from pan.
Cool on rack.

Bagels

Make recipe for **Special Health Bread** or **Sweet Dough** or your favorite bread recipe. After first rising, remove dough from bowl, divide into equal portions. Roll each piece into a smooth ball about 2½" in size. With thumb and index finger press through the center to form a large hole, and stretch to form shape of bagel. Place on non-stick or floured surface. Cover and let rise (proof) in oven or warm place for 20-25 minutes. In a wide kettle, boil 4 quarts of water and 2 Tbs. honey or molasses. Carefully transfer three or four bagels at a time to boiling water. Gently simmer bagels 3-5 minutes, turning bagels over during simmer. Remove from water, drain on paper towels. Repeat process for all bagels. Place bagels on lightly coated non-stick baking sheet; bake at 375° for 30-35 minutes or until golden brown and well baked. Yield: 1 dozen approx.)

Note: If desired, brush tops with flax jel and sprinkle with sesame seeds before baking.

Pita (Pocket) Bread

You'll want to experience making your own pocket bread at least once. See how thinly rolled pita rounds magically puff up and form a pocket almost instantly while baking in a very hot oven. It's fun to watch!

1 cup pure warm water
1 pkg. quick-rising dry yeast (2½ tsp.)
2 tsp. honey, molasses, or other sweetener
½ tsp. sea salt
1 Tbs. gluten flour
2 ¾ -3 cups whole wheat
   or pastry flour, mixed

1. In a mixing bowl, combine water, yeast, and honey. When bubbly add half of the flour and salt. Mix or beat until smooth. Continue adding flour ¼ cup at a time until a medium soft dough is formed.

2. Turn out onto floured board; knead 5-7 minutes until smooth and elastic, adding flour to keep from sticking. Place dough in an oiled bowl, cover and let rise (proof) in oven or warm place until *almost* double in size.

3. Punch down and shape dough into a long 2" roll. Cut slices 1¼" wide. Roll each piece into a smooth ball. Let rest 5-10 minutes.

4. On a lightly floured surface, roll each ball of dough out evenly from center to form a 6" circle ¼ " thick. Place circles on a clean cloth that is lightly floured; lightly dust tops with flour, cover with saran wrap; let rise in warm place 15-20 minutes.

5. Pre-heat oven (including one middle rack) to 500°, also pre-heat a large baking sheet (turned upside down) or a cast-iron flat griddle.

6. Carefully remove circles from cloth and place on pre-heated baking sheet in hot oven three or four at a time. Bake 5-7 minutes or until puffed and lightly browned.

7. Remove from oven and place in a covered kettle. When cool, cut in half, store in plastic bag to keep soft and pliable. Pitas also freeze well. **To serve:** Stuff pockets with desired filling. Yield: approx. 12 pitas.

Note: Occasionally a pocket will not puff evenly, don't worry; just use as Greek pita flat- bread with spread; or wrap around salad greens, stir-fry or sandwich fixings; also perfect for miniature pizza crust, pita wedges or baked chips.

Sprouted Sunflower or Wheat Bread

3 cups warm water, divided
1 ½ Tbs. active dry yeast
1 Tbs. honey
2 Tbs. molasses
1 Tbs. lecithin or 2 Tbs. olive oil
4 cups 100% whole wheat flour
1 Tbs. sea salt
1 raw medium potato, with skin
2 cups sprouted wheat
  or sunflower seeds
3 cups gold'n white flour
  (or mix spelt, barley, oat)

Method for sprouting sunflower seeds: Soak seeds in jar of water for a few hours. In the morning drain water. Leave seeds in a dark place for 1-2 days, until sprouts are ⅛-¼" long. (If sprouts get too big, they will have a strong flavor). Rinse the sprouts once or twice a day to prevent drying out; drain well.

1. In a mixing bowl, put 2 cups warm water, yeast, honey, molasses, lecithin and whole wheat flour. Mix well to form a sponge. Set aside while preparing the rest.

2. Next, in blender put the remaining 1 cup water; add the salt, potato (scrub and cut). Blend until smooth. Add 2 cups sprouted sunflower seeds or wheat. Blend briefly.

3. Combine the sponge and sprout mixtures, stirring and mixing well to combine. Gradually add the rest of flour, sufficient to make a soft dough that is easy to handle – but not too stiff. Turn out on board; knead well 5-7 minutes, oiling hands to prevent sticking.

4. Place dough in oiled bowl; let rise in warm place until almost double. Divide dough into 4 pieces and shape into loaves. Let rise in pans until almost double. Bake at 350° for approximately 50 minutes or until done when tested. Remove from pans; cover with clean towel. Cool thoroughly. Wrap and store or freeze. Yield: 4 small loaves

Variations: When shaping loaves add one of the following:

Onion Bread: spread dough with sautéed onions.

Parsley/Herb Bread: sprinkle with dry parsley, garlic powder, rosemary, or other herbs.

Tomato Rosemary Bread

*The rich flavor of dried tomatoes and
fresh rosemary permeate Aunt Joan's savory loaf.*

20 dried red tomato halves*
1¼ cups boiling water
1 packet dry active yeast (about 2 ½ tsp.)
3½ - 4 cups whole grain flour
  (wheat, spelt, barley)
¾ tsp. sea salt
1½ Tbs. virgin olive oil
2 -3 Tbs. rosemary, fresh or dried

**The water used to re-hydrate the tomatoes is
used in the bread.*

Combine boiling water and dried tomatoes in a bowl. Cover and let stand 30
minutes until tomatoes are soft. Drain
tomatoes, reserving the liquid. Finely
chop or blend tomatoes. In large mixing
bowl, dissolve yeast in warm reserved
tomato liquid. Add 3 cups flour, tomatoes, sea salt, olive oil and crushed
rosemary. Mix and knead 8-10 minutes
until a soft dough forms. Turn dough
out onto a floured surface. Knead until
smooth and elastic; add remaining
flour as needed, to prevent dough from
sticking to hands. Place dough in oiled
bowl; cover and let rise in warm place
until almost double. Punch down, let
rest 5 minutes. Form into 1-2 loaves.
Cover and let rise until almost double.
Place in pre-heated 375° oven, reduce
heat to 350° and bake 45-50 minutes or
until loaves sound hollow when tapped.
Remove from pans; cool bread thoroughly before slicing or wrapping.

Pizza Dough

*Save time with this light, wholesome crust that
is pre-baked- simple and ready-to-use.*

2½ - 3 cups flour (whole wheat, barley)
2 tsp. honey or other sweetening
1 pkg. (2¼ tsp.) active dry yeast
1 tsp. sea salt
1 cup very warm water
1 Tbs. olive oil

Mix 2 cups of the flour, yeast and salt in a
large mixing bowl. Add the warm water,
sweetening, and olive oil. Combine and
stir until smooth, or beat with electric
mixer on medium speed for 3 minutes.
Stir in enough remaining flour to form a
medium stiff dough that pulls away from
sides of bowl. Turn dough out on lightly
floured surface; knead until smooth and
elastic about 8 minutes. Place in oiled
bowl; cover and let rise in warm place
25-30 min. or until nearly double. Prepare two 12" round pizza pans or baking
stones; lightly oil or use non-stick spray
and sprinkle with cornmeal, if desired.
Divide dough in half, let rest 10 min. Pat
each half into 12-inch circle, transfer to
pizza pans or baking stones* ; let rise a
little. Partially bake in 375° oven for 15-
20 min. or until crust begins to brown.
**Remove from oven, cool crusts, stack
and freeze**** (or remove from oven,
spread with sauce, veggies and cheese).
Bake 20-25 minutes more, until well
baked and bubbly.

****Baking stones** duplicate effects of brick-lined
ovens for crispier crust. Use seasoned stoneware, sprinkle surface with cornmeal or apply a
non-stick spray. Pre-heating stoneware is optional.*
****When ready to use, remove from freezer,
add sauce and toppings.** Bake in 400° oven
15-20 min., until well baked and bubbly.

Beet* Bread

1 cup cooked beets
1¼ cups warm water or beet liquid
3 Tbs. honey
1¼ tsp. sea salt
1 Tbs. dried parsley
3 Tbs. olive oil or 1 Tbs. lecithin
¼ cup soy flour
¼ cup flaxseed, whole
2 ½ cups whole wheat flour
1¼ Tbs. dry active yeast in
  ¼ cup warm water + 1 tsp. honey
2½ cups gold'n white flour

Blend first 3 ingredients; pour into mixing bowl, add next 6 ingredients. Then add the yeast (dissolve in the ¼ cup water + honey; let set 5 min. before adding). Next stir in the golden white flour, enough to make a soft dough. Knead 5 min. until smooth and elastic. Place in oiled bowl. Cover and let rise in a warm place until almost double. Shape into 3-4 loaves. Place in oiled bread pans and let rise until almost double. Bake at 375° for 45-50 min. or until done (baking time depends on size of loaves - bread should sound hollow when tapping the bottom). Remove from pans. When thoroughly cooled, wrap and store. Delicious flavor!

Note: If part beet juice (liquid) is used for water, the bread will be a deeper red color.
*Squash, Pumpkin or Sweet Potato may subsititute.

Kalamata Olive & Tomato Bread
The tart flavor of sun-dried tomatoes combined with the piquant flavor of Greek Kalamata olives gives this bread a unique taste.

1¼ cups very warm water, divided
⅓ cup chopped dried tomatoes
3½ - 4 cups whole grain flour
  (wheat, barley)
1 packet dry active yeast (about 2 ½ tsp.)
1 Tbs. sucanat or other sweetening
½ cup pitted Kalamata olives, drained
1 Tbs. dry crushed basil leaves
1 Tbs. virgin olive oil
¾ tsp. sea salt

1. In a small bowl mix the dried chopped tomatoes with ¼ cup of the very warm water. Set aside until softened and re-hydrated.

2. In the meantime, in a large bowl, combine the remaining 1 cup of warm water with 2 cups flour, the yeast, and sweetening. Beat with electric mixer or wire whisk to form a sponge; cover and let stand until bubbly, about 45 min.

3. Place re-hydrated tomatoes in a food processor, add the pitted olives and process until finely chopped. Pour mixture over flour sponge in bowl. Stir in basil, oil and salt. Add more flour, ¼ cup at a time, until a soft dough forms.

4. Turn onto floured board, knead 8 -10 min. until dough is smooth and springy; add a little flour as needed to keep from sticking. Place dough in oiled bowl; cover and let rise (proof) in oven or warm place until almost double.

5. Punch down; shape into round or 12" long loaves. Place on prepared non-stick baking pans sprinkled with flour and cornmeal. Cover with plastic wrap and let rise until *almost* double.*

6. Bake in pre-heated 400° oven for 10 minutes; reduce temperature to 375°, bake 40-45 minutes to deep golden brown or until loaves sound hollow when tapped. Remove from pans; cool bread thoroughly before slicing or wrapping.

Note: *For a crisp crust and decorative top, *carefully* cut 1/4" deep diagonal slashes across top of loaf with a sharp serrated knife. Spray loaves with cool water before baking.

Special Health Bread

1 qt. pure warm water
3 Tbs. dry active yeast
3 Tbs. honey, molasses or raw sugar
1 cup quick oats, raw*
1 Tbs. lecithin
2 Tbs. olive oil
1 Tbs. sea salt
½ cup rye flour
¼ cup soy flour
¼ cup wheat germ*
¼ cup flax seed, sesame
   or chopped sunflower seeds
5 ½ cups 100% whole wheat flour
4 cups gold'n white, barley,
   or whole wheat, mixed flour

* Flour may replace oats or wheat germ

Dissolve the yeast in ½ cup of the warm water. Add the rest of the water and the sweetening. Add oats, lecithin, oil, and salt. Combine the rest of ingredients in a large bowl. Gradually add dry ingredients to yeast mixture beating after each addition. Continue adding flour as needed to make a moderately firm dough that is not too sticky. Knead dough 8-10 min. until smooth and elastic. Place in oiled bowl, turn it over. Cover and let rise in a warm place (80-85° or set in oven with a pan of boiling water to proof). When almost double in bulk, punch down. Let rise the second time. Punch down and divide into loaves. Let rise in prepared bread pans until almost double. Bake in

350° oven about 50 min. depending on size of loaves. Remove from pans. For a soft crust- lightly brush tops with oil. When thoroughly cool, wrap and store. Best when day old. Yield: 4 loaves.

Note: Experiment with your bread machine by replacing the whole wheat flour with small amounts of other flours (rye, spelt, oat, barley,) sprouted grains, wheat germ, herbs, or dried fruit.

Les' Home Bakery Bread
(for automatic Bread Machine)

1½ cups pure warm water
3½ cups flour (whole wheat,
   barley, spelt)
1 Tbs. gluten flour
1 tsp. sea salt
2-3 Tbs. honey or other sweetening
1 Tbs. lecithin liquid or granules
2 Tbs. flax seed, opt.
1 Tbs. olive oil, opt.
1½ tsp. active dry baking yeast

Pour warm water into bread pan. Add all ingredients in order given. Press start button, or follow baking method on bread machine. Your oven fresh bread will be ready in approximately 4 hours. Remove and allow to cool thoroughly before slicing.

Easy 100% Whole Wheat Bread
(for automatic Bread Machine)

Pour into mixing pan in order given:
1½ cups warm water
3 Tbs. honey or sucanat
¾ tsp. sea salt
**3½ cups 100% whole
   wheat bread flour**
1½ tsp. active dry yeast
2 tsp. lecithin liquid or granules, opt.

Press the start button and follow directions as given with bread machine. Remove bread from pan after baking. Allow to cool thoroughly before slicing. Best eaten next day.

Note: Bread can be mixed and baked in Bread Machine or remove dough from machine after mixing. Let rise, form into rolls or loaf and bake in conventional oven.

Light and Easy Biscuits

½ cup pure warm water
1 Tbs. dry active yeast
1 Tbs. honey
2½ cups flour, any combination*
1 tsp. sea salt
3 Tbs. olive oil or soy spread
½ cup water or soymilk

Dissolve yeast in water, add honey. Let rise to proof. In a bowl, sift flours and salt together. Using a pastry blender, cut in the oil or soy butter until mixture resembles coarse crumbs; add rest of liquid. Add yeast mixture. Mix and knead lightly. Roll out ¾" thick on floured surface. Cut with biscuit cutter. Let rise 20 minutes. Bake at 375° 25-30 minutes. Yield: approx. 1 dozen.

Note: *whole wheat pastry, barley or oat flour, + 1 Tbs. soy for extra nutrition is a good combination.

Sweet Dough

This light dough works well for Swedish tea ring, rolls, fruit buns, doughnuts, etc.

1 ½ cups pure warm water
⅓ cup honey or raw sugar
2 cups whole wheat or gold'n white flour
3 Tbs. soy oil + ½ tsp. lecithin, opt.
1 tsp. sea salt
¼ cup soy flour or barley flour
1 Tbs. dry active yeast
2-3 tsp. grated orange or lemon zest
¼ tsp. ground anise seed, opt.
2-3 cups gold'n white, or w. w. pastry flour

In a large mixing bowl make a sponge with the first six ingredients. Mix with electric mixer or wooden spoon 3-5 minutes. Let rest 15 minutes. Sprinkle on dry active yeast, beat well 5-7minutes. Add rest of ingredients, and just enough flour to make a soft dough that is smooth and elastic. Place in oiled bowl to rise until almost double. May shape as desired after one rising. Let rise again and bake.

Pecan Nut Bread: spread with honey, chopped pecans, sprinkle on coriander; form loaf.

Raisin Cinnamon Loaf: spread with honey; sprinkle on raisins, cinnamon substitute.

Braid: Roll 3 pieces of dough into 1" rope like strips. Braid; pinch ends or turn under.

Honey Balls: Shape piece of dough into 1" ball; while holding lightly dip in liquid soy spread and honey, then place in bread pan. Repeat until pan is 2/3 full. Let rise and bake. Enjoy eating loaf by pulling balls apart.

Super Cinnamon Rolls or Bread

2 cups pure warm water
1 Tbs. dry active yeast
⅔ cup light honey
2 tsp. lecithin + 2 Tbs. oil
1½ tsp. sea salt
3 cups whole wheat + gold'n white flour
1 Tbs. cinnamon substitute
1 cup chopped pecans and walnuts
1 ½ cup raisins
1 Tbs. lemon or orange zest

Add gradually:

3 cups whole wheat pastry
   or gold'n white flour
   (or replace ¼ cup with:
2 Tbs. soy + 2 Tbs. wheat germ)

In a mixing bowl dissolve the yeast and honey in the 2 cups warm water. Add the lecithin, oil, salt and first 3 cups flour. Beat with a spoon 5- 8 minutes. Cover and let stand in warm place until sponge mixture forms bubbles. Stir down then add next 4 ingredients. Mix dough with a spoon or mixer until it pulls away from sides of bowl. Knead well for 10 minutes, oiling hands or adding a little flour if needed to make a soft, but not sticky dough. Cover and let rise until almost double. Shape into loaves or divide and roll out to form a rectangle. Brush with soy spread, thread on honey or sprinkle with date sugar and cinnamon substitute (see recipes). Roll up tight like a jelly roll. Cut into 1" slices. Place cut side down in pan with non-stick coating. Let rise and bake 40-45 minutes in 350° oven. Dough may be shaped in cloverleaf rolls or any desired shape. Delicious!

Swedish Tea Ring

A delicately sweet, elegant fruit and nut bread perfect for holidays and simple to make in 3 easy steps. One of our favorite demonstrations at cooking schools.

Follow recipe given for **Sweet Dough**. After one rising:

1. Roll dough into oblong 10" x 20". Spread lightly with oil or **homemade butter** and **honey** or **date sugar**. Sprinkle with **cinnamon substitute**, 1 **cup raisins and ½ cup chopped walnuts, filberts, pecans, or other nuts**.

2. Roll up tightly, beginning at wide side. Seal well by pinching edges together. Place sealed-edge-down in shape of a ring, on prepared or non-stick baking sheet. Join ends of ring, pinch to seal.

3. With scissors, make cuts ⅔ of the way through the ring at 1½" intervals. Turn each section on its side. Let rise until almost double in bulk (about 35 min.) Bake in 375° oven 35-45 minutes or until golden brown and baked through. Let cool on rack; add frosting and decorate with nuts and fruit (see photo below).

Clockwise from bottom left: Oatmeal Crackers, Sesame Soup Thins, Wheat Germ Wafers, Raisin Nut Bread, Italian Loaf, Oatmeal Pecan Bread, Rye Bread, Soya Bread or Rolls, Bread Sticks, Perfect Pecan Rolls, Swedish Tea Ring (center), Sweet Dough.

Perfect Pecan Rolls

In mixing bowl combine:
2 cups warm vanilla soy milk
1½ Tbs. dry active yeast
½ cup honey
¼ cup soy oil + 1 tsp. lecithin
Stir to dissolve then add next 4 ingredients:

1 Tbs. orange zest (no color added)
2½ - 3 cups whole wheat or pastry flour
1 tsp. sea salt
2½ cups gold'n white + ¼ cup soy, mixed
1 cup pecans, chopped
½ cup soft raisins

Turn dough onto lightly floured surface. Knead until smooth and elastic. Place in oiled bowl, cover. Let rise in warm place to almost double. Punch down; divide in 2 pieces. Roll each half into a 12" x 8" rectangle. Spread with soy spread, sprinkle on sucanat, date sugar or honey and cinnamon substitute. Sprinkle on half of the chopped pecans and raisins. Starting at wide end, roll up dough like a jelly roll; cut into 12-1" pieces using *floss, thread or serrated knife. Put **Pecan Topping** (below) in prepared pan or muffin cups. Lay slices on topping. Let rise until double. Bake at 350° 35-40 min. or until light brown (cover with foil last 5 min. to prevent over browning). Remove from oven; turn pans upside down so topping drips over rolls. Cool, wrap to store. Reheat before serving if desired. Yield: 24 rolls.

*Note: To cut even slices, slide a piece of floss or thread under the roll, bringing ends of thread up, then criss cross, pulling ends of thread.

Topping for Pecan Rolls

4 Tbs. melted soy butter, see recipe
4 Tbs. honey, sucanat or date sugar
2 Tbs. pure water or orange juice
4 Tbs. chopped pecans or walnuts

Butter bottom of pan. Spread with above topping. Place rolls cut side down in pan. Let rise in warm place to almost double; bake according to directions.

No-Fry Health Doughnuts
(Easy-baked)

Surprise the family with a batch of really good doughnuts! Follow recipe given for **Sweet Dough**. Let rise one time. Roll out to 5/8" thick. Cut with doughnut cutter or use a wide mouth jar ring and a large thimble for the hole. Lay on non-stick cookie sheet 1" apart. Let rise to almost double until light. Bake at 400° for 10 min. then reduce heat to 350° and bake for 25 min. or until golden color. Remove from oven and dip one side in glaze. Put on tray lined with waxed paper in refrigerator to set glaze.

Glaze for Doughnuts

2 Tbs. Creamy Whipped Butter (see recipe)
1-2 Tbs. carob powder
2 Tbs. thick honey
¼ tsp. pure vanilla or maple flavor

Carob Glaze: Melt butter over low heat. Stir in carob, honey and flavoring. Dip top of doughnut into glaze; set in refrigerator to harden. For light color glaze: omit carob, add **soy milk powder** and **ground coconut** or make **Lemon Glaze**. (see recipe)

Whole Grain Rice Rolls

2 cups pure warm water
⅓ cup cooked basmati rice
or 1 Tbs. potato flour

Mix above ingredients; add whole wheat flour, enough to make a batter. Beat thoroughly, let stand 15 minutes; then add:

1 Tbs. active dry yeast
2 Tbs. honey or molasses
1½ tsp. sea salt
2 tsp. liquid lecithin
more flour for a soft dough (5-6 cups)

Knead 10 minutes until dough is smooth and elastic. Let rise until almost double. Divide into balls. Let rest 10 min. Shape into rolls. Let rise until almost double. Bake at 350° 35-45 min. or until done and sounds hollow when tapped. Cool on wire racks.

Dinner Rolls

2 cups warm soy milk or water
1½ Tbs. active dry yeast
⅓ cup honey
2 tsp. sea salt
2 Tbs. olive oil + 1 Tbs. lecithin granules
3-4 cups whole wheat flour
2 cups gold'n white flour
   (replace 2 Tbs. with soy)

In mixing bowl stir together warm milk, yeast, honey, oil, lecithin and salt. Gradually add the flour, mixing well to form a soft dough. Turn out on lightly floured bowl and knead well until smooth and elastic. Place dough in oiled bowl and let rise until almost double in warm place. Punch down, divide dough into 4 parts, let rest hile preparing pans. Form rolls; place 2"apart on non-stick baking sheet or in pans. Cover let rise until nearly double in bulk. Bake at 350° 25-35 minutes until done and golden brown.

Cloverleaf Rolls:
Shape pieces of dough into a ball, pulling edges under to make a smooth top. Place 3 balls in each prepared muffin cup, smooth sides up.

Butterhorns:
Roll dough into 12" circle, lightly brush with olive oil. Cut circle into 12 wedges. Starting at wide end, loosely roll toward the point. Place point-side down on pan.

Parker House Rolls:
Roll dough ⅓" thick, cut into 2 ½" rounds. Brush with olive oil. With a dull knife make an off-center crease. Fold on cease so the top ⅔ of roll projects beyond the lower ⅓. Press folded edge firmly.

Knots / Rosettes:
Roll a piece of dough into 8" long rope. Tie in a loose knot. For rosette cut 12" long, tie knot leaving 2" long ends. Tuck top end under knot and bottom end into top center of knot.

Barley Buns

Use **Dinner Rolls** recipe – except replace **1 cup Whole Wheat flour with 1 cup Barley flour or use soaked ground or steamed barley.** Follow directions for mixing and rising. Shape into buns and bake as directed.

Maple Walnut Rolls

1 cup warm water or soy milk
1 pkg. active dry yeast (2½ tsp.)
3 Tbs. honey or fructose
2 Tbs. soy or walnut oil
½ tsp. sea salt
1 tsp. lemon or orange zest
1 tsp. coriander, optional
2½ - 3¼ cups w.w. flour,
   golden white or other

Topping / Filling:

¾ cup pure maple syrup
2 Tbs. apple juice concentrate
¼ tsp. butter flavoring, opt.
¾ cup chopped walnuts
¼ cup raisins, optional
honey; cinnamon substitute

1. In a mixing bowl, dissolve yeast in the warm water or soy milk. Add the sweetening, oil, salt, lemon zest, ground coriander, and half of the flour. Beat 1-2 minutes on medium speed or mix well to form a soft sponge. Let rest 5 minutes. Stir in just enough remaining flour to make dough easy to handle.

2. Knead 4-5 minutes on floured surface until dough is smooth and spongy. Place in lightly sprayed or oiled bowl. Cover and let rise 30-35 minutes. Dough is ready if indentation remains when touched.

3. Make Topping. Mix the maple syrup, juice concentrate, and flavoring. Pour into prepared rectangular pan, 13x9x2 inch. Sprinkle with half of the walnuts.

4. Gently push dough to deflate. Flatten into 15 x 10 inch rectangle. Spread with honey, cinnamon substitute, raisins, and remaining walnuts. Roll up tightly beginning at 15 inch side. Stretch and shape until even. Cut roll into fifteen 1-inch slices with dental floss or serrated knife. Place slightly apart in pan over topping. Cover with plastic wrap and let rise in warm place until almost double.

5. Bake in 350° oven 35-40 minutes or ntil golden brown. Remove from oven and let stand 2-3 minutes. Immediately turn upside down onto tray or serving plate. Let stand 1 minute so topping can drizzle over rolls; remove pan. Cool thoroughly before serving.

Banana Bran Muffins

½ cup warm water or soy milk
1 Tbs. dry active yeast
½ cup honey, raw or date sugar
¼ cup soy or grape seed oil
2-3 chunky smashed bananas
1 tsp. pure vanilla
1 cup 100% Bran or crude bran
2 cups flour: whole wheat pastry
   or gold'n white
½ tsp. sea salt

In a small bowl stir the warm water or soy milk and yeast. In a mixing bowl, blend the sweetening and oil together. Add the bananas, vanilla and yeast mixture; fold in the bran. Let set about 10 - 15 minutes until the bran is soft, then add the flour and salt. Fill non-stick or prepared muffin cups ¾ full. Let rise only 10 min. Bake at 350° 30-35 min.

Optional (but good): *A little grated orange rind (zest) adds a wonderful flavor.*

Banana Nut Bread

Follow recipe given for **Banana Bran Muffins**. Add **½ cup chopped walnuts** and **1 tsp. grated orange rind**. Fill 2 small non-stick loaf pans ¾ full. Let rise 10-15 min. Bake at 350° for 45-55 min. Loaves may settle a little but will have a delicious flavor.

Breakfast Cup Cakes

*These sure and simple muffins are easy to make;
light, dry and delicious!*

In a mixing bowl dissolve:

2 Tbs. active dry yeast
1 tsp. honey
½ cup pure warm water

Whiz in blender:

1 cup pure warm water
⅓ cup soy or sunflower oil
1 cup date sugar or raw sugar
½ cup whole wheat pastry
or gold'n white flour
1 Tbs. pure vanilla
1 tsp. sea salt

Add the above to yeast mixture; stir as little as possible. Fold in:

1 more cup flour

Set in a warm place to rise 15-20 min., not more. Fold in:

1¾ cups more flour

Prepare non-stick muffin cups (lightly coat with cooking spray or oil and flour) Fill muffin cups ½ full. Let set for 5-6 minutes, not more. Bake at 350° for 30 minutes. Yield: 24 small muffins.

Variations: **Pecans, raisins, or walnuts** may be added, when folding in last flour. These muffins are not soggy, the amateur cook can make them dry and delicious.

Walnut Date Muffins

Follow recipe given for **Breakfast Cup Cakes**. Add **¾ cup finely chopped dates** and **½ cup chopped walnuts**, when folding in the last flour. Bake as directed above.

Blueberry Breakfast Muffins

*Enjoy the flavor and nutrition of fresh blueberries
in these easy to make muffins*

In a mixing bowl dissolve:

2 Tbs. active dry yeast
1 Tbs. honey
½ cup pure warm water

Let set for 5 minutes while blending:

1 cup pure warm water
1 Tbs. pure vanilla
1 cup dried date pieces or date sugar
1 tsp. sea salt
¼ cup soy oil

Stir this into the yeast mixture – then fold in:

1 ½ cups whole wheat pastry flour

Let rise 15-20 minutes in a warm place; then fold in:

1 ¾ cups flour (gold'n white, soy, barley)
2 cups fresh, frozen, or dried blueberries

Fill non-stick or treated muffin cups (brush with non-stick coating or oil and flour muffin cups). Let set for 10 minutes *not more*. Bake at 350° for 35-40 minutes. Cool thoroughly and wrap. Warm in oven if desired, serve plain or with your favorite nut butter or spread. Yield: 15 large muffins.

Note: For extra nutrition ½ cup chopped walnuts or filberts may be added when folding last flour.

Corn Bread

This yeast-raised cornbread is good with baked beans, chili, soup, or salad.

2 cups. pure warm water
1 pkg. dry active yeast
2 Tbs. honey or sorghum
2½ cups yellow corn meal
1½ cup soft wheat flour
1¼ tsp. sea salt
2 Tbs. corn or soy oil

Dissolve yeast and honey in water, let rest until bubbly. Mix dry ingredients together. Add oil and salt. Add yeast mixture all at once to corn mixture. Stir just enough to evenly mix. Spoon into lightly coated non-stick baking dish 1½" thick, or treated iron skillet. Let rise 15 min. Bake at 375° 40 minutes to golden brown or until done. Cool thoroughly.

Variation: Add ½ cup whole kernel corn to mixture for cornbread that is moist and tender.

Golden Grain Muffins

In a mixing bowl, stir together:

**1 pkg. yeast in 1 cup warm water or milk
3 Tbs. molasses
2 Tbs. soy or olive oil
½ cup bran or oat flour**

Let set 10 minutes. Sift together then add:

**1 cup flour, gold'n white + 2 Tbs. soy
½ cup spelt, barley or rye flour
¼ tsp. sea salt**

Mix together lightly. Fill non-stick or prepared muffin cups ¾ full. Let set 10 minutes (not more). Bake at 350° 35-40 min. Remove from muffin cups; cool on wire rack.

Zwieback / Rusk

A form of bread, biscuit or rusk, that is baked, sliced and slowly toasted until dry and crisp.

Zwieback (German) meaning twice-baked, is one of the most palatable and easily digested foods. Thorough chewing and mixing with saliva assists digestion. Zwieback often eliminates mucous formation or allergies that may be a problem for some when eating fresh bread. Zwieback and fruit or zwieback with warm milk or soup, will satisfy for a nourishing, light supper.

To make zwieback, soup stars or croutons: Slice ordinary whole grain bread into desired shape (any kind may be used). Place slices on oven rack or cookie sheet-single layer. Bake in slow oven 225-250° for 1 hour or until thoroughly dry, crisp and golden in color. Store in a paper bag in cool dry place or a sealed container in refrigerator or freezer.

Herbed Focaccia

Simple Italian flatbread that is often served with seasoned olive oil for dipping. This version is made with whole grains and baked on a bread stone.

1½ cups whole wheat flour
1 Tbs. gluten flour
1½ cups barley, spelt or gold'n white flour
½ - ¾ tsp. sea salt
2 tsp. active dry yeast (1 pkg.)
1Tbs. dried rosemary
  or 2 Tbs. fresh leaves, cut
1 cup pure warm water (120°)
1 tsp. honey
1 Tbs. pure olive oil
2 onions, diced, sautéed
  or 8-10 cloves garlic, sliced

1. In a medium mixing bowl, mix 1cup of each flour, the salt, dry yeast and rosemary. Add the warm water mixed with honey and oil. Beat with mixer on medium speed for 5 minutes to form a sponge. Add the onions, and remaining flour as needed, until dough is soft and leaves sides of bowl.

2. Turn dough onto floured surface and knead 3-5 minutes until smooth and springy. Return to oiled bowl, cover and let rise in warm place until almost double.

3. Divide in half. Press into 10" rounds or squares on bread stone lightly sprinkled with cornmeal or floured baking sheet. Cover with plastic wrap, let rise about 30 minutes until nearly double.

4. Gently make ½" depressions with fingers, every 2" apart in dough. Lightly brush with olive oil, and sprinkle with garlic, onion powder or course sea salt if desired. Bake in 400° oven 25-30 minutes until golden brown. Cool on wire rack. Serve warmed or cold.

Variations: Add **Italian seasoning, sweet basil, dill weed, chopped kalamata olives** or **dried tomatoes.** Dough can be shaped into breadsticks, narrow baguette or round loaves.

Baking Stones: For a crisper crust carefully slide unbaked loaves from floured baking sheet onto pre-heated bread stone (pre-heat stone 20-30 minutes). Using a spray bottle, mist bread with cold water before baking and 1 or 2 times during baking.

Herbed Breadsticks

Our daughter Esther, now a young mother, and talented cook, loves to create her own recipes, and make tasty bread.

Follow recipe for **Herbed Focaccia** or your favorite bread dough. Divide in half; using your hands press the dough into a 12" x 9" rectangle. Cut into twelve 1" strips; roll lightly and shape each piece or twist if desired. Let rise in a warm place until almost double. Bake at 375° for 20 minutes or until golden brown. Yield: 12 breadsticks about 10" long.

Breadsticks

These savory breadsticks are delicious with soup or salad

1 cup warm water or potato water
½ tsp. onion or garlic powder
1 tsp. leaf sage, crumbled
2 tsp. caraway seed, crushed
1 ½ tsp. sea salt
1 pkg. dry active yeast
1 Tbs. honey
2 Tbs. olive or soy oil
3 cups flour, whole wheat, spelt, rye

Mix first 5 ingredients together; stir in next 4. Beat vigorously but do not knead. Cover and refrigerate at least 2 hours or overnight before forming into sticks. Divide chilled dough into 24 pieces. Roll into 8" rope-like strips and place 1" apart on floured non-stick baking sheet (or roll in sesame seeds, if desired. Let rise to almost double. Bake 12-15 min. at 425° until golden brown. Yield: 24 breadsticks.

"…..There is more religion in a good loaf of bread than many think." Diet & Foods p. 316

A Loaf of Bread

Do you want to make a difference
In someone's life today?
Just take a loaf of bread
'Cause it has so much to say.

It says, "I have the time for you."
t says, "I really care."
It says, "You can depend on me
To keep you in my prayers."

That little loaf of bread
With the blessing of the Lord
Can open up the distant heart
Where hurts and fears are stored.

Don't leave it for tomorrow
The chance may slip away
Let God use that little loaf of bread
To reach someone today!
-Linda Shelton

Breads (quick)

Index - CHAPTER 5

Breads, Yeast

142

Ten Talents

Feed the Soul

Man shall not live by bread alone,
Our Lord and Master said,
But by the living Word of God,
Our souls must daily be fed.
So as I cook and serve the meals,
I will sincerely pray,
That I shall give, along with food,
Some Christ-like love today.
And as I clear the meal away,
And wash the pots and pans,
Dear God, please cleanse
my thoughts and heart
With Thine own loving hands.
Man shall not live by bread alone,
So we now pray, Dear Lord,
"Please make us very hungry
For a knowledge of Thy Word."

Chapter cover photo: *Crusty Corn Bread, page 151*

Quick Breads

Quick Breads refer to types of bread that do not rely on yeast to rise. These include flat bread, crackers, crepes, tortillas, biscuits, pancakes, some muffins and waffles.

The unleavened crackers and quick bread recipes given in this section are made with whole grain flours, pure soft water and other natural ingredients. They have a good flavor and require thorough mastication, which is good for the teeth, and the chewing aids in proper digestion. Crackers made with a variety of whole grain flours and seeds, will give nourishment not found in many crackers made with harmful soda or baking powder, white flour, sugar, and hydrogenated fats.

To make uniform crackers or wafers that are extra thin, use a tortilla press, it's easy! Crackers can be wrapped and frozen for later use, to serve with soup, salad, or fruit.

To refresh second-day muffins, biscuits, corn bread or waffles, warm in a toaster or oven. Serve with your favorite spread, homemade butter, or fruit topping.

Whole Grain Crackers

Oatmeal Crackers

2 cups quick oats
½ cup whole wheat flour
½ cup gold'n white flour
½ cup corn meal
¾ cup soy flour
¾ tsp. sea salt
¼ cup cashew meal or 2 Tbs. oil
½ cup honey or raw sugar
½ tsp. pure vanilla or coriander

Mix dry ingredients together. Add oil and honey and enough water to make a stiff dough. Knead until smooth. Roll out ⅛" thick, directly on bottom side of baking sheet. Prick with fork and mark off squares. Bake in moderate 350° oven, until golden brown, approximately 15-20 minutes, being careful not to burn edges.

Variation: Sprinkle and roll in a few sesame seeds before marking squares or cutting into shapes. Delicious flavor!

A diet high in Fiber has been shown to lower cholesterol levels and reduce the risk of heart disease.

Breakfast Oatmeal Squares
Simple and delicious

1 cup pure water or soy milk
1 Tbs. honey
¼ cup applesauce or soy oil
1 tsp. sea salt
1 tsp. pure vanilla
4 cups quick oats, approx.

Mix in order given. Knead lightly; roll out ¼" thick on a non-stick baking sheet or between wax paper; cut in squares. Bake at 350° for 10-15 min.

Optional: Add ⅓ cup finely chopped dates to mixture, knead. Roll out very thin.

Corn Crackers

½ cup dry soy beans (soak overnight – will yield 1 ¼ cups).

In the morning rinse beans and blend with:

**2 cups water
2 Tbs. oil or nut butter
1 Tbs. honey
2 Tbs. sesame seed
2 Tbs. shredded coconut
1 tsp. sea salt**

Blend to very smooth. Add 1½ cups cornmeal and whiz again. Pour into non-stick or treated pans ¼" thick. Bake at 375° for 45 minutes or until done. Cut while still hot.

Note: This thick batter may be dropped from a spoon into oblong shapes. Good with soup!

Graham Crackers

**2 cups whole wheat graham flour
1 ½ cups golden white flour
½ tsp. sea salt
1 ½ tsp. cinnamon substitute
2 Tbs. arrowroot, optional
⅓ cup soy oil
½ cup water or soy milk
¼ cup honey or maple syrup
⅓ cup molasses
½ tsp. pure vanilla**

In a mixing bowl, stir dry ingredients together; add oil working into flour to crumble together. Blend liquid ingredients; pour over flour mixture. Round up and knead a little. Roll or press to about ⅛" thin. Score into squares, and prick with a fork. Bake at 275-300° for 20-25 minutes or until done.

Date Graham Crackers: add ½ cup chopped dates and nuts to flour mixture.

Hi-Fiber Dinner Wafers

The simple combination of ingredients in these thin wafers is surprisingly delicious! Add your choice of herbs and seasonings or dried tomatoes for a variety of flavors.

**1½ cups oat flour or part barley flour
1 cup cashew meal,
    or part Brazil nut meal
¼ cup sesame seed
    or part flaxseed meal
½ tsp. sea salt
½ cup pure water, approx.**

In a mixing bowl, combine dry ingredients together. Stir in water sufficient to make a stiff dough. Mix well, form a roll 8" long x 1½" in diameter. Cut into 24 ¼" slices. Press slices into 3½" circles. Place on non-stick cookie sheets. Bake at 350° 10-12 min, being careful not to burn (wafers are very thin).

Note: I use a tortilla press (eliminates hi-low spots). to form thin wafers that bake evenly.

Corn Dodgers

So simple- a child or helpful husband can make these chewy gems. Take along, pack for a picnic or lunch.

2 cups yellow cornmeal, finely ground
1 Tbs. honey or other sweetener
1 Tbs. soy oil or 2 Tbs. ground cashews
1 tsp. sea salt, scant
½ tsp. vanilla, opt.
2 cups boiling water

Mix together in order given; adding boiling water last. Stir to combine; allow to set *5 minutes. Pre-heat oven to 400°. Spoon dodgers 1" apart, side by side, onto a non-stick baking sheet in oblong shapes approx. 1½" x 2". Bake 30 min. or until nicely browned.*

Sesame Bread Sticks

2 cups flour (whole wheat, gold'n
   white, soy, barley)
½ cup sesame seeds
1 Tbs. sucanat or date sugar
½ tsp. sea salt
½ tsp. cinnamon substitute
3 Tbs. soy or olive oil
¾ cup pure cold water

In mixing bowl sift and stir flour together. Add sesame seeds, sweetening, salt and cinnamon substitute. Mix oil and water together, add to dry mixture. Round into ball; knead a little. Roll into pencil-strips ½" around; cut into sticks 6- 8" long. Place on non-stick baking sheet. Bake 30 minutes at 350° or until golden brown.

Spelt Sticks

Spelt is used in these crackers, especially for those on a wheat-free diet

2 cups spelt flour
½ cup sesame seeds
2 Tbs. flax meal
½ cup pure water
2 Tbs. virgin olive oil
½ tsp. sea salt

In a mixing bowl stir together the flour, sesame seeds and flax meal. Blend together the water, oil and salt. Pour over dry ingredients, mix and knead lightly to combine. Roll out ⅛" thick between wax paper or plastic wrap on moistened countertop. Score into pencil wide sticks 1¼" long, or cut into desired shapes. Bake in 350° oven, 15 minutes or until golden brown.

Sesame Crackers

1 ¼ cups whole wheat or spelt flour
1 ½ cups quick oats
1 cup sesame seed
¼ cup soy or barley flour
½ cup coconut
⅓ cup raw or date sugar
1½ tsp. sea salt
2 Tbs. soy or olive oil + 2 Tbs. soy milk

Mix ingredients together adding water as needed to make a moderately firm dough. Roll thin; cut into desired shapes. Bake at 250° for 25-35 min.

Sesame Soup Thins

*A favorite soup cracker. The addition of
olive oil gives an earthy flavor.*

Into blender put:

**½ cup pure water or broth
½ tsp. sea salt
2 Tbs. soy oil + 2 tsp. olive oil**

Blend at medium speed till well blended.

Remove from blender and add:
**2 cups whole wheat or barley flour
½ cup sesame seeds**

Mix well and knead a little. Let rest
10 min. Divide into 2 parts and roll
between waxed paper or plastic wrap.
Moisten countertop to prevent paper
from slipping. Sprinkle with salt and
a generous amount of sesame seeds;
continue rolling to thickness of thin
wafers (sesame seeds rolled in will not
fall off). Prick and mark squares. Bake
at 350° for about 15 minutes.

Oatmeal Sticks

**2 cups quick oats
¼ cup shredded coconut
¼ cup whole wheat flour
2 Tbs. date sugar or sucanat
¼ tsp. sea salt
½ tsp. pure vanilla
1 cup nut milk or water
2 Tbs. soy oil + ½ tsp. lecithin**

Mix dry ingredients together in mixing

bowl. Blend liquid ingredients, add to
mixing bowl. Mix and combine with
hands until it stays together like pie
crust. Grease pans with oil and sprinkle
with oats. Press into non-stick pan. ¼"
thick. Cut or score into desired shape.
Bake in 350° oven for 5 minutes, then at
250° until crisp or golden brown.

Whole Wheat Walnut Sticks

**1 ½ cups whole wheat flour
½ tsp. sea salt
½ tsp. coriander or anise, opt.
2 Tbs. soy or coconut oil
2 Tbs. honey + 1 Tbs. sucanat
½ cup walnuts, finely chopped
½ cup cold water or soy milk**

Mix ingredients in order given, adding
liquid gradually to make a stiff dough.
Knead thoroughly until smooth. Roll
pieces of dough into a 12" long rope. Cut
into 3" sticks or roll out to ¼" thick and
cut into 1 x 3" strips. Bake round sticks
30-35 minutes in moderate (325-350°)
oven; roll or turn once or twice during
baking. Bake flat sticks 20-25 min. or
until golden brown.

Sesame Wheat Germ Wafers

In a mixing bowl stir:

**2 cups mixed whole wheat + oat flour
¼ cup wheat germ
¼ cup sesame seeds
1 tsp. cinnamon substitute
½ tsp. sea salt
2 Tbs. honey or sucanat**

Combine together then add:

**¾ cup water or soy milk
⅓ cup soy or olive oil**

Toss together with a fork until all dry
ingredients are wet. Knead a little;
form a 1½" roll; then cut into ¼" slices
(sprinkle with more sesame seeds if
desired). Roll or press into thin wafers.
Bake at 325° until golden brown.

Quick Breads – Misc.

"Hot biscuits raised with soda or baking powder should never appear upon our tables. Such compounds are unfit to enter the stomach." **Diet and Foods pg. 319**

Some recipes may contain leavening comprised of ingredients which when used in moderation are not harmful. (See Glossary of Foods - Ener-G products)
Baking Tip: Mix leavening with a little flour. Add as last ingredient to recipe just before baking in hot oven to maximize leavening action and minimize absorbtion or taste in finished product.

Boston Brown Bread

1 cup whole wheat or graham flour
2 cups fine yellow corn meal
1 cup rye flour or meal
1 tsp. sea salt
2 cups sweet or sour milk
  (add 2 T. lemon to soy milk)
⅔ cup dark molasses
1 cup chopped dates or raisins
1 Tbs. grated orange or lemon rind
½ cup chopped walnuts or pecans

Sift together flour and salt. Mix molasses and milk, add to flour. Beat thoroughly; add fruit and nuts. Pour in prepared molds (brush or spray juice cans with non-stick coating). Cover cans; place on rack in pan with water; steam 3 hours. Cool thoroughly; open end of can, and pushing on lid, slide loaf out. Slice thin.

Presto Pancake Mix

Combine your own freshly ground whole grains for this make-ahead mix. Use for pancakes, muffins, waffles, crepes or quick breads.

3½ cups whole wheat pastry flour
1½ cups barley flour
¼ cup buckwheat flour or quick oats
1 cup soy milk powder
¼ cup fructose or sucanat
2 Tbs. non-aluminum baking powder
2 tsp. sea salt

In a mixing bowl, stir all ingredients together. Place mix in a tightly covered wide-mouth jar. Store in a cool, dry place up to 6 months, and use as needed. Yield: 6½ cups mix.

Presto Pancakes

Pancakes are fun to flip, and a nice alternative to waffles, especially when camping or cooking without electricity!

1½ cups Pancake Mix
1 cup water or soy milk
2 Tbs. soy or corn oil
1 Tbs. tapioca
    or potato flour, opt.

Blend together thoroughly, adding more water for thinner pancakes. Let stand 5 minutes. Bake on hot oiled griddle or heavy non-stick skillet, 3-4 minutes until browned on both sides. Makes: 10-12, 4" pancakes. Serve with fresh berries, or other favorite fruit topping.

Just Like Cinnamon Toast

Toast whole grain bread – spread with **homemade butter** and **honey**. Sprinkle with **Cinnamon Substitute #1** (**2 parts coriander + 1 part anise seed.**)

Stir-N-Roll Biscuits
(Tender and flaky)

2 cups sifted whole wheat pastry, barley, or white wheat flour
3 tsp. non-aluminum baking powder
¼ tsp. sea salt
1-2 Tbs. honey or fructose
¼ cup soy or canola oil
¾ cup soy, rice or nut milk

Heat oven to 425°. In a bowl, stir flour, baking powder and salt together. Blend oil, milk and honey. Make a well in the center of the flour mixture; add liquid mixture all at once. Using a fork, stir just until moistened, forming a ball. Turn out onto a lightly floured surface. Gently knead 3-5 strokes. Press or roll dough to ⅝" between wax paper. Cut with floured 2½" biscuit cutter. Place 1" apart on non-stick cookie sheet. Bake 15 min. or until golden. Good served with fresh strawberries and cream. Yield: 12 -16 biscuits.

Simple Sesame French Toast

*Start with whole grain bread and a few simple ingredients. Serve with applesauce, berries, molasses, **fig sryup** (pictured), or your favorite topping.*

¾ cup almond or soy milk
½ cup orange juice concentrate or water
¼ cup cashews
    4 Tbs. flour or quick oats
    2-3 tsp. honey, optional
    ½ tsp. pure vanilla
    pinch of sea salt
    2 Tbs. sesame seeds

Blend all ingredients except sesame seeds until smooth, adding milk as needed to make a thin batter. Pour cashew mixture into a shallow dish, stir in sesame seeds. Dip bread slices into mixture, allowing bread to soak for about 30 seconds. Place slices on hot oiled griddle and brown on each side 2-3 minutes, or bake on non-stick baking sheet until golden brown. Makes 4-6 slices.

brown. Delicious served with a**lmond butter, Orange Sauce, fresh berries,** or **syrup**.

Oven French Toast

Transform ordinary day-old bread into egg-free French toast, rich in protein, calcium, iron, and essential omega 3. Serve plain, with almond butter, molasses, or fig syrup.

**1½ cups (12oz.) silken firm tofu
2-3 cups creamy soy or nut milk
3 Tbs. flour or arrowroot
2 Tbs. flaxseed meal
1 Tbs. honey, or other sweetener
2 tsp. pure vanilla
½ tsp. cinnamon substitute, opt.
pinch of sea salt
¼ cup sesame seeds**

1. Pre-heat oven to 475°. Apply non-stick spray on baking sheet, heat pan in oven 5 minutes.
2. Place all ingredients (except sesame) in blender and puree until smooth adding soymilk sufficient for medium-thin batter. Pour into a shallow pan, add the sesame seeds. Dip your favorite day-old bread slices in mixture to coat both sides, allowing the liquid to soak in for about 15-20 seconds.
3. Place the dipped bread in hot pan. Drizzle some of the batter on slices. Bake 5-7 minutes until bottoms are golden brown. Turn slices over bake 2-3 minutes. Serve with maple syrup, nut butter, or fresh berries.

Sesame-Flax French Toast

Top with your favorite nut butter, fresh fruit, or fruit sauce, for a special breakfast treat

**1½ cups soy, cashew
    or almond milk
2 Tbs. sesame and/
    or flax meal
3-4 pitted dates, cut
2 Tbs. w.w. pastry flour
    or arrowroot
½ tsp. pure vanilla
½ tsp. orange zest, opt.
¼ tsp. cinnamon substitute
½ tsp. lecithin granules, opt.
6 slices day-old whole grain
    or raisin bread**

1. Blend first 5 ingredients until very smooth adding milk as needed. Add seasonings and blend briefly. Pour into a shallow bowl.

2. Dip slices of your favorite bread into the milk mixture, turning slices over to coat both sides and allowing the bread to soak, about 10-15 seconds.

3. Brown both sides on pre-heated non-stick skillet, or bake until golden

What is a Crêpe?

Crêpe is French for "*pancake*," actually much thinner than a pancake. A versatile quick bread that can be sweet or savory, made with a thin batter that is poured and spread very sparingly into a heated oiled skillet. The crepe is quickly cooked on both sides to golden brown, then folded over a variety of fillings, i.e. warm canned fruit, crisp tender seasoned vegetables with browned tofu cubes or juicy fresh fruit, jam and berries, topped with maple syrup, honey or cream. Crepes are used in a variety of ways for breakfast, dinner or supper, and make exciting choices for the vegetarian. With a little practice, perfect crepes can be made, even without eggs, and they are always delicious! (see Index for recipes)

Fruit Crêpes

For that special weekend breakfast spread crêpes with nut butter and apple-sauce, cover with fresh fruit; fold or roll and top with strawberries, blueberries, bananas, or your favorite syrup.

**1 cup sifted whole wheat
    pastry flour
1 Tbs. arrowroot powder
¼ tsp. sea salt
1 Tbs. honey or fructose
½ tsp. pure vanilla
1 Tbs. soy oil
    or ½ tsp. lecithin
½ cup soy milk
½ cup water, approx.**

1. In a mixing bowl combine dry ingredients. Combine liquid ingredients in a blender or measuring cup; add to dry mixture, while stirring with a whisk until smooth. Batter should resemble thin cream.

2. Heat non-stick skillet over medium heat or use cooking spray on the pan. (Heat is just right, when a few drops of water jump around, when sprinkled on pan) Pour 3-4 Tbs. batter (scant ¼ cup) into the pan. Immediately rotate the pan from side to side to cover the bottom with a thin and even layer of batter.
3. Cook the crêpe until golden brown on each side. Flip the crêpe with tongs or carefully grab the edge with your fingers, or run a wide spatula around edge to loosen. Stack cooked crêpes on a plate, cover to keep warm. Repeat steps for cooking the batter until finished. Yield: 12- 6" crêpes.

Note: See recipe **Savory Vegetable Rice Crepes** in Meatless Main Dishes chapter

Crusty Corn Bread

There are many versions of cornbread. This one a bit sweeter, and made often by our daughter was adapted for dad who loves corn bread and enjoys is at any meal.

**¾ cup yellow cornmeal
¾ cup barley flour;
    whole wheat pastry, mixed
2 Tbs. fructose or Sucanat®
¼ tsp. sea salt
¾ cup soy milk
2 Tbs. soy oil
½ tsp. pure vanilla
1½ tsp. non-aluminum baking powder**

Cornmeal: To make fresh cornmeal or any kind of flour I use a flour mill, as shown on right. Dried popcorn kernels are ground into a coarse, medium or fine texture which makes a beautiful bright yellow cornmeal. Home ground or stone-ground cornmeal which retains the wholesome outer hull and essential germ of the corn is more nutritious than commercial de-germinated cornmeal which has the hull and germ completely removed.
Inquiries: Contact authors.

1. Pre-heat oven to 400°. Prepare pan (iron skillet, muffin cups, or 8"x 8"square pan) with non-stick coating.

2. In a mixing bowl, combine dry ingredients together (except baking powder). In a measuring cup stir liquid ingredients together. Add to dry ingredients. Mix thoroughly. Last, sprinkle on baking powder and stir briefly to mix in.

3. Pour batter into a non-stick pan, hot skillet, or muffin cups about ¾ full. Bake 35 minutes or until a toothpick inserted near center, comes out clean.

*Note: I use Popcorn for milling, which yields a bright yellow cornmeal containing the germ and all the nutrients of whole kernel corn.

Corn Muffins

Good served with molasses or as a base for strawberry shortcake with fruit topping. These muffins can also be frozen and re-heated.

Combine and mix ingredients in order given for **Crusty Corn Bread**. Fill prepared muffin cups ¾ full. Bake at 400° for 20-25 minutes. Yield: 15 small muffins.

Corn and Soy Muffins

Enjoy the old-fashioned appeal of corn bread with chili beans or soup. This version made with heart-healthy ingredients, is hearty as well as tasty.

Mix in blender till very smooth:

2 cups soaked soy beans, rinsed
2 cups pure water
1 Tbs. olive oil + ½ tsp. lecithin
2 tsp. sea salt
2 Tbs. honey or molasses
¼ cup quick oats or flax meal

Add and mix with a spoon:

2 cups corn meal, fine

Fill small, hot, prepared muffin cups. Bake at 375-400° for 35-45 min. May also be baked in a shallow baking pan, but I think you'll like the muffins better. Serve with a little honey. Good warmed the next day.

Variations: In place of oats use:
2 Tbs. sesame seed + 2 Tbs. coconut
4 Tbs. wheat germ flakes

Crunchy Unleavened Gems

2 ½ cups whole wheat or mixed flours
½ tsp. sea salt
¼ cup oil + 1 tsp. lecithin
1 cup pure soft water
2 tsp. lemon juice

Sift flour into bowl with salt. Add oil

mixture slowly while stirring. Add water and mix well until smooth. If sticky add a little more flour – but not too much. Shape small biscuits, quite flat. Bake in hot oven 375-400° about 10 minutes then reduce heat to 275-300° for 30 minutes or until baked through.

Dr. B's Good Gems

A retired O.B. specialist who lived in our home made these gems frequently. Although they are not as light as some raised breads, we enjoyed their good flavor, topped with a little honeycomb. Here is the doctor's original recipe:

1 ⅓ cups whole wheat flour
1 ¾ cups water or part soy milk
1 ½ Tbs. olive or soy oil
¼ tsp. sea salt
¼ cup raisins, optional

Mix well all together; should resemble pancake batter. Pout into sizzling hot prepared gem pans. Bake at 400° for 35-40 minutes. Yield: 18 gems.

Note: occasionally he would add 1 farm fresh organic egg to enhance texture.

Lemon Honey Glaze
(for Zucchini Quick Bread, opposite)

2 Tbs. fresh lemon juice
1 Tbs. lemon zest
¼ cup creamed honey
  or powdered fructose
2-3 Tbs. soy milk powder

In a small bowl, stir lemon zest into lemon juice; whip in honey or fructose. Add soy milk powder sufficient to make consistency for glaze. Drizzle over loaf, if desired.

Carrot Cake or Muffins

Substitute **1 ½ cups shredded carrots** for the zucchini in **Zucchini Quick Bread**, opposite. Spoon batter into prepared muffin cups ¾ full. Bake 30-35 min. Cool on wire rack; drizzle with lemon glaze if desired.

Zucchini Quick Bread

*Quick bread with **Lemon Honey Glaze** (opposite)*

**2⅓ cups golden white
   or whole wheat pastry flour
¾ cup Sucanat® or other sweetening
2 tsp. baking powder, non-aluminum
1½ tsp. cinnamon substitute #3
1 tsp. EnerG® baking soda
½ tsp. sea salt
1 ½ cups shredded zucchini or carrots**

**½ cup soy milk
¼ cup soy oil
2 Tbs. grated lemon zest
1 tsp. pure vanilla
1½ tsp. EnerG® Egg Replacer + 2 Tbs. water
⅓ cup chopped walnuts, optional**

Preheat oven to 350°. Sift flour before measuring. Combine sifted flour with dry ingredients in a mixing bowl. Combine the zucchini, milk, oil, lemon rind and vanilla in a bowl. Whip the egg replacer with water until frothy; add to zucchini mixture. Make a well in the center of flour mixture. Add liquid mixture all at once; stir just until moist. Spoon batter into an 8" x 4" non-stick loaf pan or apply cooking spray. Bake at 350° for 55 minutes or until a wooden pick inserted in center comes out clean. Cool loaf in pan 10 minutes, then remove loaf and cool completely. Drizzle with **Lemon Honey Glaze**, if desired.

Sweet Raspberry Flax Muffins

Made with dried raspberries and flaxseed- rich in anti-oxidants and omega-3

2 large baking apples, peeled
½ cup pure water or juice
3 Tbs. fructose or sucanat
¾ cup 100% frozen raspberry
   juice concentrate
4 Tbs. flaxseed meal
½ cup golden white or barley flour
¼ cup quick oats
¼ tsp. sea salt
1 cup dried raspberries

Coarsely chop apples and cook with the water, and sweetening until soft. Remove from heat; add the raspberry juice concentrate and dried raspberries. In a bowl mix dry ingredients together. Add the raspberry mixture and combine gently; it's fine for it to be a little lumpy. Spoon into 12 lined or non-stick muffin cups, three-fourths full. Bake at 375° for 25 - 30 min. or until toothpick inserted in muffin comes out clean.

Apple Oat Bran Muffins

Rich in fiber - naturally moist and tender

1 ½ cups golden delicious apple chunks
¼ cup apple juice concentrate or water
1 cup smashed banana
¼ cup light honey or maple syrup
1 tsp. orange zest
¼ cup almond or cashew butter
1 cup quick oats + 1 cup oat bran
⅓ cup shredded coconut,
   unsweetened
⅓ cup chopped walnuts or pecans
1 cup finely chopped dates

In a saucepan cook chopped apples with apple juice until just wilted; transfer to mixing bowl. Stir in next 4 ingredients and mix together. Add the oats, bran, coconut, nuts and dates; stir to combine. Spoon into paper-lined or prepared muffin cups ¾ full. Bake at 375° for 25-30 minutes or until toothpick inserted in center of muffin comes out clean.

Hi-Energy Carob Walnut Muffins

Dark and delicious - these muffins look like chocolate- but are better for you!

1 ½ cups whole wheat pastry flour
1 cup carob powder
2 tsp. non-aluminum baking powder
¼ tsp. sea salt
1 cup date sugar or sucanat
1 cup soy milk, vanilla flavor
1 ½ tsp. pure vanilla
2 Tbs. light molasses
1 cup soy yogurt
⅔ cup chopped walnuts
⅓ cup shredded coconut
⅓ cup carob chips, optional

In a mixing bowl sift the first 4 ingredients together. Blend the next 4 ingredients, pour into mixing bowl, add the yogurt, walnuts, coconut and carob chips. Stir just to combine ingredients together. Spoon into 12 prepared muffin cups ¾ full. Bake at 375° for 25 min. or until toothpick inserted in center of muffin comes out clean.

Banana Orange Date Muffins

*If you like bananas you'll love the taste
of these fruity breakfast muffins*

1 ½ cups cooked spelt or kamut grain
½ cup soy milk
1 tsp. pure vanilla
½ tsp. sea salt
¾ cup banana, sliced and mashed
⅔ cup quick oats
1 cup pitted chopped dates
½ cup orange juice
1 ½ tsp. orange zest
1 cup golden white or w. w. pastry flour
2 tsp. non-aluminum baking powder

Blend the first 4 ingredients in a blender until combined and fairly smooth. Transfer to a large mixing bowl; add the smashed banana and oats. Blend the dates, orange juice and orange zest to chunky smooth; add to mixing bowl. In a separate bowl sift the flour and baking powder together. Add to blended mixture, lightly stir just to combine ingredients together; it is fine for it to be a little lumpy. Spoon into 12 lined or non-stick muffin cups ¾ full. Bake at 375° for 25 min. or until toothpick inserted in center of muffin comes out clean.

Communion Wafers

(serves 150 people)

2 cups 100% whole wheat flour
6 Tbs. pure virgin olive oil
½ cup pure soft water
½ tsp. sea salt

Sift flour with salt. Blend oil and water. Pour over flour; mix and knead lightly. Roll out very thin (approx. ⅛"). Score with a dull knife into 1"squares. Bake in a slow-moderate oven (325-350° F) until golden brown; being careful not to burn edges.

Sicilian Bruschetta

*A fancy name given to a simple appetizer,
The Italian name 'bruschetta' meaning to toast or
grill thick slices of bread, which have been rubbed
with garlic and olive oil, and often topped with tomatoes and herbs. Topping tips: Fresh Tomatoes, Sweet
Basil, Garlic, Sliced Olives, Tomato Salsa*

Whole Grain Flour Tortillas

*Enjoy healthy unleavened tortillas - high in fiber, rich in complex carbohydrates and B vitamins without hydrogenated fats, dough conditioners or preservatives. The **Latin American** version of this quick bread is the **tortilla**; in **India** the **chapati**; in **Afghanistan** the **nan**; in **Norway** similar to the **lefse** spread with a sweet filling and rolled.*

**3 cups fine flour mix (soft whole
     wheat, barley, oat)
3 Tbs. olive or soy oil
½ tsp. sea salt
1 cup pure water, more or less**

Mix the flours and measure. Blend the water, oil and salt; add to flour mixture. Mix; knead lightly 2-3 minutes until dough is smooth and firm. Form into long roll and divide into 12 portions; cover and let rest 5minutes. Roll or press into 6" thin circles. Bake on a hot ungreased skillet or griddle on each side for 20-30 seconds until golden brown.

Note: Amount of water will vary, depending on texture and moisture of flour used.

Corn Tortillas

**2 cups fine corn flour
½ cup whole wheat pastry flour
2 Tbs. soy flour (opt.)
½ tsp. sea salt
1 cup pure water, approx.**

1. Mix and sift the flour and salt together. Add the water to flour while mixing and kneading dough until smooth for 2-3 minutes, to form a firm (not sticky) ball.

2. Divide dough into 12 equal balls. Cover with damp cloth to keep dough moist. Flatten each ball between hands. Place on floured board or between 2 sheets of wax paper or plastic wrap. Roll out very thin to 6-8" circles or use a tortilla press.

3. Bake on a very hot ungreased skillet or griddle for 15-30 seconds. Flip over and cook other side 20-30 seconds until

golden brown. Cover cooked tortillas with a towel to keep soft and pliable. Serve while warm, plain, with soy butter, avocado spread or filling of beans, tomatoes, avocado, and chopped lettuce.

Suggested Uses for Flour and Corn Tortillas

Wraps: Heat tortillas to soften, over med-high heat on ungreased skillet, for 10-15 seconds. Place ½ cup desired filling on tortilla; roll up. Cut in half on diagonal.

Vegetable Pizzas: Lightly toast one side of tortilla; spread toasted side with oven-roasted veggies (sweet peppers, onions, mushrooms, zucchini, etc.). Top with soy cheese. Grill or broil 2-3 min. until cheese begins to melt and veggies are heated.

Tortilla Salad Cups: Lightly brush tortillas with water or cooking spray. Press coated side up in non-stick bowls. Bake at 350° 10 min. or until light brown. Let cool; remove from bowls. Fill with savory beans, chopped tomato, pepper, onion, avocado, olives, lettuce and soy cheese. Top with your favorite dressing. Serve.

Tortilla Crisps: Cut tortilla into wedges, bake at 350° until dry and crisp. Serve with soup or your favorite dip or spread. Store in sealed container 1 week or freeze.

Bean Burritos: Heat tortillas to soften. Spoon ⅓ cup mashed, seasoned or refried beans on tortilla, add chopped onion and grated soy cheese. Fold bottom up and over filling, fold top down, roll up. Place on baking sheet; bake at 350° 8-10 min. till heated through. Serve with salsa and salad, or cover with tomato sauce; bake.

Empanada: Spread tortilla with a sweet filling of dried fruits such as apricots and dates blended with pineapple juice, marmalade or conserves, then roll it up.

Croutons or Zwieback

Make your own homemade croutons, from wholesome grain bread, using oven, dehydrator or stovetop. Croutons add a finishing touch when served with soup or salad.

Plain croutons: Cut fresh or day old bread into cubes, stars, or other shapes.

Herb Seasoned Croutons: Cut sliced bread into ½"cubes or desired shape. Toss lightly with olive oil to coat. Sprinkle with onion or garlic powder, Italian seasoning or your favorite herbs. Spread single layer in shallow baking pan. Bake until crisp.

- **Oven method:** Spread evenly on baking sheet. Bake at 250° for 30-60 min. until thoroughly dry, crisp and golden, stirring croutons once or twice to brown evenly.

- **Dehydrator method:** Place croutons on drying trays, at medium temperature. Croutons will dry evenly, without burning, (in 1-2 hours); no need to stir when dehydrating.

- **On Stovetop:** Cook in heavy dry skillet, medium heat 5-7 minutes, stirring often, until golden brown (these croutons are semi-dry). Ready to use or store in freezer.

Note: For **Zwieback**, see **Yeast Breads, p. 138**.

Garlic Bread

No leftovers when serving healthy garlic bread. Delicious with vegetables, lentil or bean soup, or to compliment a salad. Everyone reaches for seconds!

Garlic Spread for bread:

¼ cup pure olive or soy oil
¼ cup pure water
2 Tbs. minced parsley
6-7 cloves minced fresh garlic
1 tsp. onion powder
¼ tsp. sea salt

Slice any favorite bread, leaving ½" attached at the bottom. Blend spread until smooth then brush on one or both sides of bread, making sure each slice is covered. Place the whole loaf in foil wrap or in a thoroughly wet paper bag (to avoid burning bag- saturate in water then squeeze out). Bake at 450° 10-12 minutes.

*For crusty brown garlic bread, unwrap and bake 5 minutes more. Delicious!

Grilled Sesame Bread

**12" long loaf Italian or Soy bread
⅓ cup soy butter or mayonnaise
⅓ cup finely chopped parsley
2 Tbs. finely chopped chives and/or
¼ tsp. garlic powder
sesame seeds**

Slice bread diagonally. Combine soft butter, parsley, chives, and garlic. Spread on cut surfaces of bread. Sprinkle generously with sesame seeds. Toast under broiler a few minutes till heated through, or bake in oven until crisp.

Crostini

Crostini is Italian for "little toasts".

Small ½" thick slices of Italian or French bread are brushed with olive oil, a topping (opt), and toasted in 400° oven 5-7 minutes, until crisp.

Topping tips: Olive Spread, Soy cheese, Roasted Pimentos, Roasted Garlic Spread

Desserts

Index - CHAPTER 6

Desserts

Ten Talents

160

Chapter cover photo: *Macadamia Pineapple Coconut Cheesecake, page 183*

Nature's Sweets

**Carob Cream Pie
or Pudding**
is good with any meal

We all desire something sweet – lemon pie, popcorn balls, pineapple cheesecake, ice cream or cookies - at some time. For enjoying at home or for giving gifts, nothing compares with homemade varieties packed with wholesome goodness and love.

Desserts should be prepared from the storehouse of natural foods such as fruits, seeds, nuts, whole grains, honey or other natural sweets. Then with careful planning you can include a healthy dessert that is compatible with the kinds of food served at the meal. There is no place for desserts made primarily with refined sugars, saturated fats, or devitalized grains, in the optimal diet. Americans today are guilty of consuming more than 150 lbs. of sugar per person per year, making the average still higher, considering those who do not use it.

The desserts in this chapter are designed to be served as part of the meal and help curb the desire for hi-fat, sugar laden, sweet desserts and dainties.

Note: In a few recipes listing oil, the amounts may be further reduced, omitted, or replaced with nut butter, tahini or applesauce, if desired, without greatly altering the finished product.

See **Glossary of Natural Foods** for information about natural foods used in this chapter (such as agar, arrowroot, carob, honey, sucanat, tapioca, etc.).

Seven Ways to Control Your Overgrown Sweet Tooth

1. Drink at least eight glasses of water daily. Start with a squeeze of fresh lemon in pure water every morning.

2. Enjoy an abundant supply of fresh and dried fruits (high in natural sugars).

3. Include in the diet an adequate variety of fresh vegetable, whole grains, and proteins (found in legumes, seeds, nuts, and grains). A lack of protein in the diet often manifests itself by a craving for sweets.

4. Avoid the sugar bowl at your table. Enjoy dates and raisins on your cereal instead.

5. Eliminate the sugar-coated cereals and eat the natural whole grain cereals which are so delicious! Top with fresh berries, other fruits, soy or nut cream, juice, or honey.

6. Learn to replace refined sugars with the richer flavor of more natural sweeteners as: date sugar, barley malt, rice syrup, agave, molasses, maple syrup, raw honey or carob.

7. Let desserts be a special treat – not served every day of the week.

"Sugar is not good for the stomach. It causes fermentation, and this clouds the brain and brings peevishness into the disposition." Counsels on Diet and Foods, p. 327

Benefits of Natural Raw Honey vs. White Sugar

"My son, eat thou honey, because it is good: and the honeycomb, which is sweet to thy taste." Proverbs 24:13 KJV

Long used as a culinary sweetener, honey is also valued for its many healing properties. Honey, the nectar of flowers, is basically the fruit sugar- fructose, which consists of varying amount of dextrose, levulose, maltose, and other simple sugars, water, small amounts of minerals, B vitamins, folic acid, and protein.

Natural raw, unclarified honey contains small amounts of minerals, traces of protein and B vitamins as well as vitamin K, which is known to inhibit tooth decay by halting the formation of acid bacteria in the mouth.

Honey has been used effectively in the treatment of nervous fatigue or exhaustion, respiratory ailments, throat irritations, healing of infected wounds, and burns. It has antiseptic properties, a gentle laxative action and a calming effect for relaxed sleep.

The numerous medicinal properties of honey, both for internal and external use, when used in moderation, make it a favorite sweetener, and a sweet medicine. (see **Honey** in Glossary of Natural Foods).

"If you find honey, eat just enough - too much of it, and you will vomit." Proverbs 25:16 NIV

"It is not good to eat too much honey.." Proverbs 25:27 NIV

Desserts

162

Ten Talents

What Shall We Have for Dessert?

No-Bake Pies

Cheery Cherry Pie

6 cups pitted tart cherries, fresh or frozen
6 Tbs. arrowroot or quick tapioca
   dissolved in:
6 Tbs. juice from cherries + 2 Tbs. water
¾ cup honey, to taste
¼ tsp. almond extract, opt.

Mix the juice, honey, almond extract and arrowroot together; cook until thickened. Add the pitted sour cherries; simmer 1-2 minutes. Cool. Pour into baked Pie Shell. Garnish with your favorite granola crumbs, if desired. Cool 2-3 hours until firm. Serve with homemade ice cream or fresh grated coconut. Colorful and delicious!

Date Nut Banana Pie
Easy – no bake!

1 cup dates, pitted
2 cups pure water
⅔ cashew nuts, raw or lightly toasted
2 Tbs. arrowroot powder
½ tsp. sea salt
1 tsp. grated orange zest
1 ½ tsp. vanilla, opt.
1-2 bananas

Blend all ingredients in blender (except banana) until smooth. Stir over heat until thick. Slice bananas into pre-baked or favorite no-bake pie shell (see recipes). Pour over cooled filling. Garnish with finely ground nuts or shredded coconut. Refrigerate to chill and set.

No-Bake Apple Pie

No-Bake Pie Crust
or pre-baked shell
**8 cups sliced apples,
Golden Delicious,
Jonathan, etc.**

1. Steam 8 cups sliced pie apples just until tender, about 5 min.

2. Drain juice, thicken with **3 Tbs. arrowroot**, dissolved in **¼ cup frozen apple juice concentrate**. Add: **½ cup honey, 2 Tbs. lemon juice, ⅛ tsp. salt, 1 tsp. cinammon substitute**

3. Cook juice until clear and thick. Pour thickened juice over apples and stir lightly to combine.

4. Fill prepared pie shell. Sprinkle on **chopped nuts** or **coconut**.

Fresh Raspberry Pie

I made this pie especially for my husband who loves raspberries and enjoys caring for the plants in our garden. He shared it with the rest of our family who cheers him on, to keep growing more!

**½ cup pure water
⅓ cup tapioca granules
8 oz. white grape/
   raspberry, 100% frozen
   juice concentrate
6 cups fresh raspberries, divided**

In a saucepan over low heat, combine the water and tapioca granules to soften.Add the juice and slowly heat to boiling; add 2 cups raspberries; cook and stir 2-3 minutes or until thickened and bubbly. Remove from heat. Stir in remaining berries. Cool 5-10 minutes. Pour into prepared 9" pie shell (**Barley-Nut Pie Crust** or other). Garnish top with more berries and cream, if desired. Refrigerate until serving. Yield: 6-8 servings

Cooking – Success?

Once upon a time I planned to be
  An artist of celebrity
A song I thought to write one day,
  And all the world would homage pay.
I longed to write a noted book
  But what I did was learn to cook.
For life with single tasks is filled
  And I have done not what I willed
Yet when I see boys' hungry eyes
  I'm glad I made fresh apple pies!

-Anonymous

Carob Banana Pie

Follow recipe given for **Carob Cream Pie** on next page. Add at least **1 cup mashed ripe banana** to the slightly cooled thickened mixture. Pour into baked pie shell lined with sliced bananas. Chill in refrigerator until firm. Delicious served plain or with **Soy Cream** or **fresh grated coconut**.

Fresh Blueberry Pie

6 cups fresh or frozen blueberries
¾ cup grape or apple frozen juice
**   concentrate**
¼ cup honey or maple syrup, opt.
⅓ cup tapioca fine granules
1½ Tbs. lemon juice + ½ tsp. zest

In saucepan combine juice, honey and tapioca; set aside 15 minutes. Add 4 cups berries then bring to a boil, stirring until thickened. Add lemon juice, zest, and remaining 2 cups berries. Pour into a **no-bake crust** or **prepared granola, graham cracker** or **simple toasted coconut crust**. Chill till firm. Serve with **soy whip cream** or favorite topping (see recipes).

Cherry Tarts

1 Stir-N-Roll Pie Crust recipe
3 cups Cheery Cherry pie filling

Roll out crust ⅛" thick; cut into 5"
circles. Press pastry into individual tart
or pie pans or fit pastry over back of
muffin cups; prick to prevent puffing.
Bake at 450° 8-10 min. until golden.
Cool. Fill baked pastry shells with fruit
filling. Serve with soy whipped cream.

No-Bake Winter Pie

1 cup apricots, dried unsulphured
1 cup raisins
½ cup dates, pitted
honey, to taste
2 tsp. orange or lemon zest

1. Coarsely chop fruit; combine and cover
with pure water; let soak few hours.

2. Pour off remaining liquid. Thicken
with **arrowroot** or **agar flakes**.
(1 c. liquid + 1 Tbs. agar-agar flakes
or 2 ½ Tbs. arrowroot starch)

Agar: Soak 2 min. Boil 2 min. Cool 2
min. Add fruit, honey, and zest.
Arrowroot: Cook arrowroot in liquid
until clear and thick, Stir in fruit and zest.

3. Pour into a single baked Pie Crust.
Sprinkle with chopped **pecans, walnuts,**
or **fresh grated coconut**. Chill and serve.

No-Bake Raisin Pie

Raisins, seeded Muscat best
Tapioca or agar flakes
Lemon juice and lemon zest
1 No-Bake Pie Crust or favorite crust

Stew raisins in small amount of water.
Thicken with tapioca or agar flakes. Add
a little lemon juice and zest of lemon.
Spoon into a prepared pie shell. Chill
2-3 hours until firm. Served with soy
cream or soy yogurt if desired.

Carob "Chocolate" Pudding

A simple dessert that looks and tastes like chocolate pudding
without the cocoa. Makes a delicious cake topping too!

1 qt. cashew nut milk or soy milk
¼ cup coconut, shredded
½ cup honey or date sugar
¼ cup carob powder
1½ tsp. Cafix, Pero or Postum
½ tsp. sea salt
1½ tsp. pure vanilla
6 Tbs. arrowroot starch

Blend 1 cup of the milk with coconut
until very smooth. Add 2 more cups of
milk, the sweetening, carob powder,
cafix, salt and vanilla. Blend again. Pour
into saucepan; heat on stove to boiling,
stir to prevent lumping. Blend remaining
cup of milk with the arrowroot, add to
hot mixture, stir constantly to keep from
sticking until it comes to boil and is thick.
Pour into dessert cups. Garnish with
coconut; chill to set. Yield: 8 servings.

Carob Cream Pie

*Looks and tastes much like chocolate, and better for you! (see **Carob** in Glossary of Natural Foods)*

1 cup cashews +
1 qt. pure water,
or 1 qt. nut milk
½ cup coconut,
shredded
⅓ cup carob powder
½ cup honey
1½ tsp. Cafix or Pero
1 tsp. pure vanilla
½ tsp. sea salt
6 Tbs. arrowroot pwd.
9"or 10" baked pie crust

Blend cashews and coconut with half the liquid until very smooth. Add carob, honey, cafix, vanilla and salt; blend again. Heat in saucepan on low, stirring to prevent sticking or lumps. Blend remaining 2 cups liquid with arrowroot; pour into hot mixture, stirring until mixture comes to a low boil. It will get very thick. Remove from stovetop. Pour into graham cracker crust or baked pie shell (see recipes). Garnish with fresh coconut. Refrigerate to chill and set. Serve with soy whipped cream or your favorite topping.

Banana Coconut Cream Pie

1 qt. nut or soy milk
1 cup coconut
½ cup honey
¼ tsp. sea salt
1 tsp. pure vanilla
6 Tbs. arrowroot powder
1 Tbs. agar flakes
½ cup pure cold water
3 bananas; 1 mashed + 2 sliced

Blend first 5 ingredients with half the milk until very smooth. Pour into saucepan, heat on stovetop. Blend remaining milk with arrowroot; add to mixture, stir until thickened. In a small saucepan combine water and agar flakes. Boil 1 minute to dissolve. Add agar to blended mixture, stir evenly to combine. Fold in mashed banana. Pour filling into favorite prepared pie shell, alternately with layers of sliced banana. Chill before serving. Tip: Soak or sprinkle pineapple juice over bananas to keep from darkening.

Note: Agar-agar flakes give a smooth creamy texture and better shape to the pie. However, if not available, simply add 1 more Tbs. of arrowroot powder to mixture while blending.

In a saucepan, stir agar into warm water; heat and boil 1 minute to dissolve. Pour into blender; add cashews, coconut, honey, salt, and lemon zest with 2 cups of the water or juice, added gradually while blending very smooth. Return mixture to saucepan, heat on low; stir to avoid sticking. Blend remaining 1 cup liquid with arrow-root; add to hot mixture. Stir const-antly until mixture comes to a boil and thickens. Remove from heat; stir in lemon juice. Pour into prepared or pre-baked pie shell (see recipes). Chill until firm. Garnish with thin slices of fresh lemon, grated coconut or soy whip cream. Delicious!

Lemon Pie

Refreshing lemon - tasty and nutritious! Lemon Pie was sometimes used in simple diet of Ellen White - Diet and Foods p. 491

½ cup pure warm water
1 Tbs. agar flakes
⅔ cup cashews, rinsed
⅓ cup coconut, fine, opt.
⅔ cup light honey, to taste
¼ tsp. sea salt
2-3 Tbs. finely grated lemon zest
3 cups mixed water / pineapple juice
**   or pineapple coconut juice**
6 Tbs. arrowroot powder
5-6 Tbs. fresh lemon juice

Lemon Bars

Press Graham Cracker Crust into 8" x 8" x 2" glass pan. Bake at 350° 10 min. Cool crust. Pour filling over crust. Chill to firm. Cut into bars. Top with soy cream.

*Lemon Zest and fresh lemon juice are used to enhance the flavor of many desserts in this chapter. 1 lemon yields approx. 1 Tbs. zest, and 2-3 Tbs. juice; 1 medium orange will yield almost double. For tips on freezing lemon juice and lemon or orange zest – see **Misc.** chapter.*

Baked Pies

Apple Pie

1 double Stir-N-Roll Pie Crust, or other
8 cups thinly sliced pie apples
3 Tbs. tapioca granules
dash of sea salt
2 tsp. coriander or cinnamon subtitute,
   see recipes
2 Tbs. lemon juice or 1 tsp. lemon zest
½ - ¾ cup sucanat or honey, adjust to
   tartness of fruit

Cook apples just to shrink with a few

spoonfuls of water (about 5 min.) Add tapioca, salt, coriander, lemon juice or rind, and sweetening; stir to combine with apples. Roll crust and line pie pan. Add filling. Cover with top crust. Seal, flute edges. Bake at 375° for 40 min. or until golden brown.

Note: see Pie Crust Pointers to prevent excessive browning.

French Apple Pie

Make pastry for **One Crust Pie**. Put apple pie mixture into pastry-lined pie plate. Cover filling with **Crumb Topping**. Bake at 375° 45 minutes until golden. Serve warm.

Apple Turnovers

Follow recipe above for **Apple Pie** filling and crust. Roll crust and cut into 6" squares. Place 3-4 spoon-fuls of filling in center of each square. Fold in half like a triangle. Seal edges with a fork, prick tops. Bake at 425° for 20 min. or until golden brown.

Cherry Turnovers

one double pie crust,
  see recipes
4-5 cups fresh or frozen
  pitted tart cherries
4 Tbs. arrowroot powder
  or quick tapioca
½ cup sucanat or fructose
¼ tsp. almond extract, opt.

In a large bowl stir together
the sweetening and arrowroot
or tapioca; add cherries
and almond flavor. Gently
toss until coated; set aside.
Meanwhile make and roll pie
crust ⅛" thick; cut into 5-6" circles or squares. Place 3-4 Tbs. cherry filling in center
of each circle. Fold in half; seal edges with tines of fork. Prick top or cut slits. Place
turnovers on non-stick baking sheet. Bake at 375° 25-30 min. or until golden.

Berry Pie or Crisp

8 cups mixed blueberries, blackberries,
  raspberries
½ cup sucanat or date sugar
1 Tbs. lemon juice
½ tsp. coriander, opt.
6 Tbs. arrowroot starch
Stir and Roll Pie Crust or Crumb Crust

Heat oven to 425°. Make crust. In mixing bowl
combine berries, lemon juice and zest; add sucanat
and arrowroot. Line pie plate or pan with crust; add filling. Cover with top crust or
lattice crust; flute edge, or cover with crumb topping. Bake 35-45 minutes until crust
is golden and filling begins to bubble through crust.

Mock "Mince Meat" Pie

Nuts are used with a mixture of finely chopped apples, dried fruit and spices, for this favorite pie filling

2 cups apples, chopped
½ cup prunes, chopped
1 cup raisins, cut
½ cup pitted dates, chopped
½ cup pecans, chopped
⅓ cup honey
⅓ cup orange juice
juice and rind of 1 small lemon
1 tsp. coriander or mace
3 Tbs. arrowroot or flour

Finely chop and mix all ingredients
together; allow flavors to marinate
while preparing a double pie crust.
Spoon filling into pie shell. Cover with
top crust; make several slits in crust.
Seal and flute edge. Bake at 375° 40-45
minutes. Serve with **lemon sauce**,
cream, or your favorite topping.

Creamy Tofu Pumpkin Pie

Follow recipe for **Perfect Pumpkin Pie**, omit nut butter and molasses, and add:

12 oz. Silken X-Firm Tofu
¼ cup maple syrup
2 Tbs. barley malt or malted soy milk pwd.
2 tsp. orange zest

Pour filling into unbaked pie crust. Decorate with pecan halves pressing gently in filling so they will not burn during baking, or garnish with long shred coconut, if desired. Bake at 425° for 15 min., then at 350º for 45 min. longer or until center is fairly firm. Delicious served with homemade **vanilla ice cream**.

Perfect Pumpkin Pie

2 cups creamy nut or soy milk
½ cup honey
½ cup sucanat or date sugar
1 ½ Tbs. molasses
¼ cup cashew or almond butter
¼ cup arrowroot or cornstarch
1 Tbs. pure vanilla
1 Tbs. coriander or cinnamon substitute
½ tsp. sea salt
3¼ cups pumpkin, mashed

Blend all ingredients together until smooth or use electric mixer. Pour into unbaked pie crust. Bake at 425° for 15 min., then at 250° for 60 minutes (cover edge of pie crust with 2" aluminum foil to prevent over- browning; remove foil during last 15 min. of baking). Cool on wire rack 1-2 hours to firm.
Yield: 2 - 9" pies.

Pie Crusts

*Recipes made without hydrogenated fats are more nutritious. Make tender, flaky pie crust in half the time! Use **Stir-n-Roll** method, or press into pan, so simple-beginners can't fail!*

Pie Crust Pointers

Double Crust Pie - Roll dough ⅛" thick between waxed paper or plastic wrap (moisten counter top to prevent sliding). Fit dough into pie pan. Add filling. Trim edge of pastry ½" from rim of pie plate. Roll top crust and place over filling; trim to 1" of plate. Roll top edge under lower edge of crust, pressing to seal, flute edge; cut slits in crust, bake.

To prevent excessive browning: Cover edge with 2 to 3 inch strip of aluminum foil. Remove foil during last 15 minutes of baking. (see picture below).

Lattice Pie Top – Make pastry for a two crust pie, rolling out bottom with a 1" overhang on crust. After rolling top crust, cut into ½" wide strips, using a straight edge or pastry wheel for decorative strips. Place 6-7 strips over filling in pie plate. Weave cross-strips, or, for a **quick lattice**, place cross-strips over tops of first strips. Fold edge of bottom crust over ends of strips; building a pastry edge, to prevent a juicy pie from bubbling over. Seal, flute, and bake as directed in pie recipe.

One Crust - baked pie shell (for pie with prepared, ready-to-eat filling such as lemon, fresh berry, carob pie, banana cream or date-nut). Roll dough ⅛" thick. Fit into pie pan (moisten rim of pan to prevent shrinking). Prick bottom and side of pastry with fork to prevent bubbles (if pastry persists in puffing up during baking – gently press bubbles down with back of spoon. Bake at 425° for 10 minutes. Cool thoroughly. Fill shell with desired pie filling.

One Crust - unbaked (for pies such as pumpkin pie, to be baked with filling, or pies to be baked, with a crumb crust topping). Fold and roll dough under, flute edges, fill and bake as directed in recipe.

To prevent crust from becoming soggy: Partially bake crust before adding the filling. Bake at 425° 10 min. Cover with foil first 8 min., then uncover and bake 2 min. longer, until pastry just begins to brown.

Pie Crust - Possible Problems

1. Tough crust: too much flour or water or over-mixing of dough.

2. Crust falls apart or crumbles: too little water or too much oil.

3. Crust does not brown evenly: baked in shiny pan instead of dull or glass pan.

4. Bottom crust soggy: oven temperature too low, baked in shiny pan.

No-bake Nutty Crust

1 cup almonds or pecans, finely ground
¾ cup fresh coconut shreds
2 Tbs. maple syrup
1 tsp. lemon zest, opt.

Mix well and press mixture into baking dish or pie pan. Pour in desired filling. Chill to set.

Very Good Pie Crust

(pictured, right)

2½ cups sifted flour, (1 c. w.w. pastry,
    1 c. gold'n white, ½ c. barley or oat)
1 tsp. sea salt
1 Tbs. fructose - for turnovers /tarts, opt.
½ cup + 3 Tbs. soy milk or water
⅓ cup soy oil + 1 tsp. liquid lecithin

1. Sift flours and salt together (add fructose, if making turnovers or tarts).

2. Mix water, oil and lecithin in measuring cup.

3. Add all at once to flour mixture; toss lightly with fork and gather into a ball. Divide, roll dough; bake as recipe indicates.

Note: For apple turnovers, or cherry tarts, cut crust into squares or circles.

Stir-N-Roll Pie Crust

(9" double crust)

2 cups sifted whole wheat pastry flour
    (or mix all purpose flour + 2 Tbs. soy)
½ cup water or cold soy milk
¼ cup oil + ½ tsp. liquid lecithin
    or ⅓ cup oil
¾ tsp. sea salt

Mix flour and salt. Pour oil and milk into measuring cup; add to flour, stir lightly. Form into a ball, divide in half. Place between waxed paper (moisten table top to prevent slipping). Roll out each half into large circle. Peel off top paper. Transfer, paper-side-up into 8 or 9" pie pan. Fit into pan, remove paper. Add filling to pie shell. Roll top crust, place over filling. Tuck edges under bottom crust. Flute to seal. Bake 40-45 minutes at 425° until golden brown. Cool on wire rack.

Note: The addition of 1-2 Tbs. more water may be needed for proper consistency.

1. Roll dough between plastic wrap; remove top plastic. Invert a pie plate over crust, flip crust over and press into pan.

2. Carefully peel off remaining plastic wrap.

3. Flute edge or cut 1" stars or desired shapes and decorate edge before baking.

Wheat Germ Crumble Crust

2 cups quick oats
⅓ cup wheat germ
⅓ cup fine shred coconut
½ cup soy milk powder
1¼ cup whole wheat pastry or barley flour
½ cup sucanat, date sugar or honey
1 Tbs. lemon or orange zest
½ tsp. sea salt
⅓ cup white grape
   or apple juice concentrate
¼ cup tahini or soy butter
2 tsp. pure vanilla

Mix dry ingredients. Stir liquid ingredients. Using a fork and fingers, combine all ingredients together, until mixture resembles coarse crumbs. Bake as directed in recipe.

Barley-Nut Pie Crust

1¼ cups barley flour
½ cup walnut or cashew meal
¼ cup apple or white grape juice
   concentrate
1-2 tsp. honey or maple syrup
¼ tsp. sea salt
½ tsp. pure vanilla, opt.

In a medium bowl combine the barley flour, ground nuts, and salt together. Stir the water, honey and vanilla together and add to flour mixture. Toss to mix well. Press onto the bottom and sides of 9" pie plate, or roll between wax paper or plastic wrap. Fit into pie pan. Roll top crust, cut slits or cut strips and weave a lattice top. Bake in a 350° oven about 12 minutes or until edge is golden brown. Cool and fill.

No-Bake Fruit Nut Pie Shell

¾ cup soft dates, pitted
¾ cup coconut, brazil, filbert or pine nuts
zest of ½ orange or lemon
pinch of sea salt

Put nuts and dates through fine food grinder or food processor; add orange or lemon zest and salt. Press into 9" pie pan to form crust. Fill with a cream pie filling, fresh fruit, or berries. Chill for 1-2 hours until firm. Top with **Tofu Vanilla Creme**, if desired.

Wheat Germ or Weetabix Pie Crust

1½ cups toasted wheat germ
   or Weetabix*
⅓ cup cashew or almond butter
¼ cup sucanat or date sugar
2 tsp. orange or lemon zest
½ tsp. pure vanilla

Mix together, adding 1-2 Tbs. water as needed. Press with fingers into pie pan, forming a small rim. Reserve a few crumbs for sprinkling on top of pie. Bake in preheated 350° oven for 8-10 min. Cool to set before filling. Yield: one 9" crust

*toasted whole grain biscuits or flakes

Granola or Graham Cracker Crust

Make a healthy "graham cracker" crust using your own home made granola or crackers.

1½ cups graham cracker
   or granola crumbs*
3 Tbs. apple frozen juice concentrate
3 Tbs. whipped butter* or cold-pressed
   Earth Balance® soy spread
½ tsp. pure vanilla extract
1 tsp. grated lemon zest, opt.

Mix all ingredients together using fork or fingers to mix evenly. Press mixture firmly against bottom and side of 9" pie plate or springform pan, to form an even crust. Bake at 350° for 8-10 minutes or until golden (baking the crust helps it hold together when cut) Cool crust before adding the filling. *see recipes

Note: Double recipe for cheesecake in 3"deep pan.

Cakes – No Bake

Pineapple Tofu Cheesecake

Crust:

**1½ cups graham cracker
or fine granola crumbs**
½ tsp. pure vanilla
**¼ cup applesauce or 3 Tbs.
apple juice concentrate**
**1 Tbs. cold-pressed Earth
Balance® spread, opt.**

Pineapple layer / Topping:

**1 20-oz. can crushed
pineapple with juice**
**2 Tbs. white grape frozen
juice concentrate**
2 Tbs. arrowroot powder

Tofu Filling:

**2 cups pineapple juice,
or part Silk Soy Creamer, divided**
¾ cup cashew halves, rinsed
4 Tbs. agar-agar flakes, heaping
1 cup light honey or agave
½ tsp. sea salt, scant
2 lbs. (4 cups) extra-firm or silken tofu
1 Tbs. lemon zest
3 tsp. fresh lemon juice
1 tsp. pure white vanilla, optional

For crust: Combine first 4 ingredients;
Press on bottom and sides of 8½"
springform pan. Bake at 375° 10-15
min. until light golden brown; cool.

Pineapple layer: Combine crushed pine-
apple, arrowroot and juice concentrate
Bring to a boil, stir until thickened. Cool.
Spread half in bottom of prepared crust.

Tofu Filling: Blend 1 cup pineapple juice
or creamer with cashews until smooth.
Add honey, sea salt and tofu, blend
again. In a saucepan, stir agar-agar in
remaining 1 cup juice. Boil 1 minute;
add to tofu mixture, add lemon zest and
lemon juice. Blend until very smooth.
Pour tofu filling over pineapple layer in
crust. Refrigerate 4-5 hours to chill and
firm. Spread remaining pineapple filling
on top of cheesecake. Decorate with
fresh fruit or flowers, if desired. Serve
with strawberry pineapple topping or
other favorite topping.

Note: Cover cake so top doesn't dry or pick up
odors. Carefully loosen removable side of pan
before serving. To cut cheesecake, dip clean
knife into water, or use a piece of dental floss.

Ice Box Fruit Cake

½ cup Sesame Seed Spread*
  or cold-pressed Earth Balance® spread
½ cup honey or part molasses
  for dark cake
⅓ cup white grape
  or apple juice concentrate
2 cups soft dates, pitted chopped
2 cups glazed fruit pineapple, cherries,
  apples (see Index for recipes)
1 cup soft raisins, soaked or steamed
1 Tbs. orange zest
1 tsp. ground coriander, opt.

Combine above ingredients; refrigerate 3-4 hours; then add:

2 cups chopped nuts: pecans, walnuts,
  almonds, filberts
4-5 cups graham cracker
  or fine granola crumbs*

Mix all together; pack firmly into small loaf pans. Cover; refrigerate at least 2 days to firm and marinate flavors.

Easy No-Bake Cheesecake

Crumb mixture:
6 Tbs. soft coconut butter
4 Tbs. date or raw sugar
1 ½ cups graham cracker crumbs
½ tsp. coriander + 1 tsp. orange rind

Filling:
2 rounding Tbs. agar flakes
1 cup cashew or soy milk
¾ cup honey
⅛ tsp. sea salt
1 tsp. pure vanilla
3 cups soft or silken firm tofu
2 tsp. lemon juice + 2 tsp. zest
1 cup soy whipped cream

1. Press crumb mixture into bottom of 8" springform cake or pie pan.

2. Stir agar into milk. Let stand 5 min. Add honey and salt. Place over low heat, stirring constantly until agar dissolves and mixture thickens slightly.

3. With electric mixer beat in vanilla, tofu, lemon juice and zest. Fold in soy cream. Turn into prepared pan. Chill to firm.

Clockwise from bottom left: **Ice Cream - low fat, Mango-Peach Sherbet, Festive Fruit Cake, Banana Split, Fresh Strawberry Ice Cream, Vanilla Ice Cream #2, Crreamy Carob Ice Cream, Perfect Cheese Cake, Health Candy, Homemade Carob Candy, Fruity Sticks, Apple Tarts, Avocado LIme Sherbet.** Center: **Cheery Cherry Pie**

Popcorn Cake or Balls

This light and easy, fun-to-make dessert, can be a family affair; children will love to make their own popcorn balls!

¾ cup honey
½ cup raw sugar
¼ cup light molasses
¼ cup water
2-3 tsp. vanilla
1 tsp. orange zest

1. Cook the first 4 ingredients over medium-high heat, stirring constantly until mixture boils. Reduce heat and simmer, stirring occasionally until 1-2 drops form a hard ball when dropped into water. Add vanilla and orange zest.

2. Quickly pour syrup over 10-12 qts. popped corn, lightly salted; add 2 cups broken pecans, pumpkin seeds, filberts or other nuts. With long spoons, stir gently to coat.

3. Firmly pack popcorn into lightly oiled cake or loaf pans, or shape into 3" balls. Decorate with pecan halves, if desired. Cool and slice. Delicious! Serves: 36

Cakes – To Bake

Many cake and dessert recipes found in modern cookbooks today, are largely made up of white sugar, white flour, butter, cream and eggs. These foods are unnecessary, and often detrimental to health.

As we learn and experience the blessings of a wholesome diet, we will shun the rich cakes and pastries and be willing to live on a more simple fare, using the vital foods that promote health and vitality.

Persimmon Cake or Bars with Lemon Glaze

The holidays wouldn't be complete without persimmons. If you delight in the taste of fruits and nuts, you will enjoy this dessert. Adapted from a recipe my sister often makes. Thanks Sis, for sharing!

1 cup fresh or frozen persimmon pulp
1½ tsp. lemon juice
1 tsp. EnerG® baking soda

1 cup sucanat or raw sugar
⅓ cup soy oil
1 cup chopped dates
1 cup raisins, cut
1¾ cups golden white, w.w.pastry, or
   barley flour
1 tsp. sea salt
1½ tsp. cinnamon substitute
1 tsp. cardamom or mace
1 cup walnuts or pecans

Combine lemon juice and persimmon pulp, add soda; set aside (it will become frothy). Combine sweetening, oil and dates. Mix flour, raisins, salt and spices together. Add flour mixture to date mixture alternately with persimmon pulp, just until blended. Stir in nuts. Spread evenly in a non-stick, oil and floured 15"x 10"x1" baking pan. Bake at 350° for 25-30 minutes until lightly browned. Cool 10 minutes, then spread with **Lemon Glaze**. Chill to set glaze before cutting. Yield 24 bars.

For Cake: Double the recipe; bake in a tube cake pan 50-60 minutes or until a toothpick inserted near the center comes out clean.

(above) Persimmon Bars with Lemon Glaze
(below) Persimmon Cake slices

Lemon Glaze

2 Tbs. lemon juice
zest of 1 lemon- grated rind
⅓ cup powdered fructose
2 tsp. Instant Clear Jel®

Add lemon rind to lemon juice. Mix powdered fructose with Instant Clear Jel- modified food starch. Slowly add just enough fructose mixture to lemon juice, while stirring until thick and smooth. Drizzle lemon glaze on persimmon bars or cake. Chill to set glaze.

Festive Fruit Cake

Use 1 lb. of your favorite yeast dough or the following:

1 cup hot soy milk or water
1 Tbs. dry active yeast
⅓ cup honey or sucanat
3 cups w.w. pastry or gold'n white flour
3 Tbs. soy oil
1 tsp. sea salt

Mix and knead dough. Let rise once, then with hands squeeze in the following fruits, etc. until dough is totally mixed with fruit and cannot be seen.

2 cups chopped soft dates
1 cup soft raisins, cut
½ cup chopped dried figs
½ cup dried or glazed pineapple tidbits

2 cups chopped walnuts or pecans
2 cups chopped apples
2 Tbs. orange zest + 2 Tbs. lemon zest
4 Tbs. honey
1 tsp. cinnamon substitute
½ tsp. pure vanilla

After dough and fruit is evenly mixed, place in oiled and floured tube cake pan or non-stick loaf pans and set in warm place to rise. It will take 1½ -2 hours to rise- the fruit is quite heavy – but the results are delicious. When it has risen double in size, bake at 325-350° for approx. 1¼ hours depending on size of pan. Remove from pans; cover with a clean cloth to retain moisture. Cool completely; wrap securely and store in cool place or freeze until ready to use.

Easy Holiday Fruit Cake

To 1 pound of **Sweet Dough** or favorite dough add:

2 cups chopped soft dates
1 ½ cups raisins, dark & golden
3 cups chopped apples, peeled
1 cup chopped walnuts or almonds
1 cup chopped pecans or filberts
¾ cup date sugar, sucanat or honey
1 Tbs. grated orange rind
1 Tbs. grated lemon rind
¼ tsp. almond extract or 1 tsp. vanilla
1 tsp. ground coriander, opt.

In a mixing bowl combine all ingredients. Work the dough and fruits together with fingers, until thoroughly combined, and the dough and fruit cannot be separated. Place dough in prepared non-stick loaf pans, ⅔ full. Let rise to almost double. Bake at 325° about 55 minutes depending on the size of pans. Yield: 2-2 lb. fruit cakes.

Note: The dough should rise once before adding the fruits, then rise again in the pans before baking.

Simple Raisin - Nut Cake

(Sure and easy to make, favorite yeast-raised cake)

In a mixing bowl, dissolve:

½ cup pure warm water
2 Tbs. dry active yeast
1 Tbs. honey or sweetener

Let set 5 min. to foam. Meanwhile whiz in blender:

1 cup pure warm water
1 cup sucanat, or date sugar
½ cup soy oil
1 Tbs. vanilla + 1 Tbs. lemon or orange zest
⅓ cup whole wheat pastry flour
1 tsp. sea salt

Add blended mixture to yeast mixture, stir as little as possible. Fold in:

1 cup whole wheat pastry
  or gold'n white flour

Allow to rise 15-20 min. not more. Fold in:

1 ½ cups gold'n white,
  or w.w. pastry flour
¼ cup chopped pecans or walnuts
¼ cup wheat germ, or ¼ cup barley flour
½ tsp. ground anise or coriander seed, opt.
1 cup soft raisins, soak 10 min./drain

Prepare angel food cake pan (tube pan) or loaf pans with non-stick coating, or oil and dust with flour. Fill pans about half full. Let set to rise 5-7 minutes, not more. Bake at 350° 35-40 minutes. Remove from pan, cool thoroughly. Cover with desired cake topping, **Lemon Sauce**, or enjoy plain.

Banana Nut Cake: omit raisins, add **1 cup mashed bananas.**

Fruity Fruit Cake

¼ cup almond butter
  or 2 Tbs. oil + 2 tsp. lecithin
¼ cup boiling water
1 ½ tsp. pure vanilla
½ cup honey + 1 Tbs. molasses
⅓ cup sucanat or date sugar
1 cup glazed pineapple or cherries*
1 ¼ cups grated apple or applesauce
2 cups pitted chopped dates
1 ½ cups diced dried figs or apricots
½ cup raisins, cut
1 Tbs. orange zest
1 ½ cups chopped walnuts or pecans
½ tsp. sea salt
1½ tsp. baking power, non-aluminum
2 cups w.w. pastry, barley or oat flour

Heat oven to 300°. Prepare small or mini-loaf pans with non-stick coating. Blend first 3 ingredients, pour into mixing bowl; add sweetening, fruits and nuts. Combine flour, salt, and baking powder; mix all together. Fill pans; bake 1hr. or until toothpick inserted in center comes out clean. Cover with foil last 20 min. to prevent over-browning. Cool completely. Wrap tightly, store in refrigerator.

Note: Fruitcake will develop flavor after long storage, so make 2-3 weeks ahead of holidays.

Just-a-Slice

Pineapple Square p 206

Fresh Blueberry Pie p 165

Fresh Raspberry Pie p 164

Cherry Turnovers p 170

Apple Pie p 169

Berry Pie p 170

Macadamia Pineapple
Coconut Cheesecake p 183

Carob Pie p 167

Pumpkin Pie p 171

Cheesecake
p 175

Popcorn Cake p 177

Polynesian Bars p 210

Lemon Pie
p 168

Strawberry Shortcake

2 cups w.w. pastry flour
   or mix white, soy
2 Tbs. fructose
   or honey
2 tsp. baking powder, non-aluminum
1 tsp. lemon
   or orange zest
½ tsp. sea salt
4 Tbs. Earth Balance® spread
   or almond butter
1 tsp. pure vanilla
¾ cup soy milk
   or orange juice
Strawberries, sweet ripe
Soy Whip Cream

Sift and measure flour, sweetening, baking powder, zest, and salt. Mix in soy spread using a pastry cutter or fork until mixture looks like fine crumbs. Stir in milk mixed with vanilla, just until dough leaves side of bowl (will be soft and sticky). Spoon onto cookie sheet or use a medium scoop. Pat ½" thick (or lightly roll dough; cut with biscuit cutter or cookie shapes). Bake at 400° 15-20 minutes or until golden brown. Yield: 12 biscuits. Serve cut layers with fresh sliced or crushed strawberries. Top with Soy Whip Cream.

Carob Marble Cake

½ cup honey + ½ cup maple syrup
⅓ cup soy oil
4 Tbs. almond or cashew butter
2 tsp. pure vanilla
½ tsp. sea salt
1 tsp. lemon or orange rind
1 cup rich nut or soy milk
1 ¼ cups whole wheat pastry flour
2 tsp. lecithin + 4 Tbs. lemon juice
   or 2½ tsp. baking powder, non-aluminum
1 cup chopped nuts, opt.

Prepare 2 - 8" layer cake pans with non-stick coating – or cut waxed paper to fit. In a mixing bowl, cream together first 6 ingredients. Slowly add the soy milk and flour alternately. Stir in the leavening and nuts. Divide batter in half. Add ½ cup carob + 1 Tbs. molasses to one part and ½ cup unbleached flour to other part. Drop by spoonfuls into cake or muffin pans – alternating dark and light batter like a checkerboard. Bake at 350° 45 min. or until toothpick inserted comes out clean.

Matrimonial Cake

¾ cup date or raw sugar
½ cup orange juice concentrate
¼ cup soy oil + 1 tsp. lecithin
1 tsp. pure vanilla
1 tsp. orange zest
3 ½ cups quick oats
¾ tsp. sea salt
1 ¼ cups w. w. pastry flour
½ tsp. ground anise seed, opt.
¼ cup wheat germ flakes

In mixing bowl, cream together first 5 ingredients. Add remaining ingredients. Mix for crumb mixture. Spread half of mixture on bottom of square baking dish. Cover with Date Butter or Apricot Date Filling (see recipe in Spreads). Top with remaining crumb mixture. Bake in 350° oven until golden brown. Cool and cut in squares. Serve with Vanilla Ice Cream.

Macadamia Pineapple Coconut Cheesecake

Add a touch of Hawaii to that special occasion, when serving this delectable dessert!
Just a slice of this delectable dessert adds a touch of Hawaii to that "special occasion".

Crust:

1½ cups coconut shreds or flakes

Filling:

**2-12 oz. Tofutti® Better than
Sour Cream**
**2- 8 oz. Tofutti® Better than
Cream Cheese**
**⅓ cup Silk® soy creamer,
french vanilla**
**1 cup fructose, light honey
or ½ cup agave sweetener**
2½ tsp. pure vanilla
6 Tbs. tapioca flour
**1 cup fresh or dry coconut
shreds**
**1 cup chopped macadamia
nuts, unsalted**
**1-20 oz. can pineapple tidbits or
chunks, with juice**

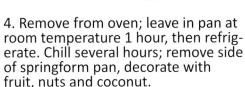

1. For crust: Lightly spray or butter 8" x 3" springform pan. Press coconut on the bottom and up sides at least 1". Set aside.

2. Heat oven to 425° while making filling.

3. Mix and spoon filling into coconut lined pan. Bake at 425° for 15 minutes, reduce heat to 350° and continue baking for 40-50 minutes.

4. Remove from oven; leave in pan at room temperature 1 hour, then refrigerate. Chill several hours; remove side of springform pan, decorate with fruit, nuts and coconut.

Traditional Creamy Cheesecake: Blend last 7 ingredients until creamy. Add 2 remaining ingredients and mix until smooth.

Note: **Tofutti Sour Cream** (blue label) and **Tofutti Cream Cheese** (yellow label) are made with non-hydrogenated, expeller-pressed oils.

Cake and Pie Toppings

1. **Carob "Chocolate" Pudding** - *Delicious on **carob brownies**, dark or light cake.*

2. **Homemade Ice Cream** - *Good on fruit cake, fruit or pumpkin pie, or bars.*

3. **Nut Butter mixed with Honey** - *spread on cooled cake. Sprinkle with coconut.*

4. **Carob Peanut Butter Frosting** - *good filling or topping for **Waffle Cake** or bars.*

5. **Thickened Cherries** - *good on **Banana Cream Pie, Lemon Pie**, and **Cheesecake**.*

6. **Lemon Sauce or Lemon Glaze** - *good on **fruit cake, carob** or **persimmon bars**.*

7. **Creamed Honey /honeycomb** – *add a bit of lemon or orange zest. Spread on cooled cake or waffles. Sprinkle on a mixture of chopped nuts and coconut.*

8. **Powdered Fructose and Coconut** - *place decorative doily over brownies or dark cake; sprinkle on fructose mixture. Carefully remove doily to reveal pretty design.*

9. **Fruit Marmalade, Jam, or Jello Topping** - *good on plain cake, bars, or pie.*

10. **Royal Coconut or Caramel Frosting** - *delicious on any cake, bars, or muffins.*

Yumedy Cake

¾ cup pure water, hot
½ cup honey or maple syrup
¼ cup soy oil
½ cup date or raw sugar
1 Tbs. lecithin
2 Tbs. barley malt, opt.
½ tsp. sea salt
2 cups flour, w.w. pastry or gold'n white
3 ½ tsp. baking powder, non-aluminum
2 Tbs. arrowroot powder
2 tsp. orange zest
½ cup nuts, chopped

Blend first 7 ingredients. Pour into mixing bowl. Sift next 3 ingredients; add to blended mixture in bowl, stirring just enough to combine. Fold in zest and nuts. Put into 2 layer cake pans treated with non-stick coating. Bake at 350° 35-45 min. or until toothpick inserted in center comes out clean. Fill layers, frost as desired.

Tropical Treasure or Waffle Cake

1. Make and bake two or more 8" cake or waffle layers

2. Make recipe **Royal Coconut Frosting.**

3. Cover top of cake plate with waxed paper (cut in 2 overlapping pieces). Place one cake layer on top.

4. Over cake layer spoon **½ cup fruit jam or crushed unsweetened pineapple** (drained). Spread a thin layer of frosting over all.

5. Place second layer – repeat steps. Spread frosting over entire cake. Sprinkle top and sides of cake with **1 cup shredded coconut**; decorate top with fresh strawberries, nuts or other fruit. Pull out strips of wax paper – leaving a clean plate and neatly decorated cake.

Favorite Desserts

Oatmeal Cookies p 201

Avocado Lime Sherbet p 198

Lemon Pie p 168

Pineapple Tofu Cheesecake

Carob Fudge p 189

Apple Pie p 169

Ice Cream p 194-195

Cherry Turnovers p 170

Popcorn Cake p 177

Biscotti p 203

Carob Cream Pie p 167

Fruit-filled Cookies p 208

Frostings & Jells

Royal Coconut Frosting

½ cup light raw honey
½ cup soymilk powder
¼ cup cold-pressed coconut oil
   or Earth Balance® spread
1-2 Tbs. nut milk or water
1 tsp. pure vanilla powder
1 tsp. orange zest
pinch of sea salt

Cream honey and soymilk powder together. Add coconut oil or soft spread, and rest of ingredients; whip until smooth. Spread on cooled cake. Sprinkle generously with fresh shredded coconut. Chill to set frosting.

Optional: To color coconut pink, just add a little **strawberry juice**.

Carob Coconut Frosting

Follow recipe for **Royal Coconut Frosting,** omit orange zest; add:

1-2 Tbs. carob powder
2 Tbs. chopped filberts, walnuts, or other

Mix together. Spread on cooled cake. Refrigerate to set.

Lemon Glaze

2 Tbs. lemon juice
grated rind - zest of 1 lemon
5-6 Tbs. powdered fructose or sugar*
2 tsp. Instant Clear Jel®

Add lemon rind to lemon juice. Mix powdered fructose with Instant Clear Jel (modified food starch). Slowly add just enough fructose powder mix to lemon juice, while stirring until thick and smooth. Drizzle lemon glaze on bars, cake or muffins. Chill to set glaze.

*Note: Fructose can be powdered with Instant Clear Jel® food starch, in a small nut and seed mill. If using powdered sugar (already contains corn starch), omit the Instant Clear Jel.

Carob Peanut Butter Frosting

2 Tbs. peanut butter
¼ cup raw honey
½ cup soymilk powder
½ cup carob powder
3 Tbs. thick soy milk or cream
1 tsp. pure vanilla
1-2 drops mint extract, opt.

Cream ingredients together. Add chopped nuts, if desired. Spread on muffins, brownies, or cake.

Caramel Frosting

⅔ cup maple syrup, raw honey
   or honeycomb
⅔ cup cashew meal
   or ½ cup cashew butter
2 Tbs. coconut oil or almond butter
1 tsp. pure vanilla; pinch of sea salt
¼ - ½ cup soy milk powder, coconut
   or flax meal

Cream together in order given until smooth. Good on **Swedish Tea Ring,** sweet rolls, etc.

Carob Frosting: add **2-3 Tbs. carob powder**

Jello Cake Topping

Make ½ recipe **Orange Agar Jell,** adding **1 cup finely chopped soaked dates** and **1 cup unsweetened crushed pineapple, drained.** Cool until slightly thick. Fold in **1 cup soy whipped cream**. Spread 1" thick over baked and cooled cake (use oblong pan with high sides). Chill until set - cut into squares. This is a good topping for a plain cake. Something different!

Fruit & Nut Candies

Vanishing Fruit-Nut Balls

Our daughter, at nine-year-old, made these for a picnic. Everyone liked them so much - we've used the recipe over and over again

¾ cup coarsely ground brazil nuts
¾ cup broken pecans
1 cup soft chopped dates
1 cup soft raisins, cut
2 Tbs. raw honey
2 tsp. orange or lemon zest

Put nuts and dried fruit through coarse food grinder, or finely chop. Add honey and zest; mix all together. Form 1" balls; roll in coconut, if desired. Refrigerate to harden; wrap in wax paper. Delicious!

Sprouted Wheat Candy

2 cups tender sprouted wheat
2 cups pitted dates
1 ½ cups coconut shreds
½ cup almonds or Brazil nuts
½ cup peanut butter
2 Tbs. orange peel, zest
1 Tbs. lemon peel, zest
½ tsp. sea salt

Put first 4 ingredients through a fine food grinder. Add the rest of ingredients. Mix well. Shape into 2 rolls and wrap in wax paper. Chill or freeze to firm. Slice.

Health Candy

1 cup walnuts, finely chopped
1 cup almonds, lightly toasted, finely chopped
¼ cup sesame tahini, or cashew butter
3 Tbs. flaxseed meal or carob powder
1 tsp. pure vanilla
½ cup raw honey
3 Tbs. soy milk powder
¾ cup fine unsweetened coconut

In food processor, or mixing bowl, combine ingredients in order given. Finish mixing by hand adjusting ingredients to make a stiff batter. Press into pan. Refrigerate until firm. Cut into bars or squares.

Carob Kisses

½ cup molasses
½ cup peanut or cashew butter
½ cup chopped pecans or filberts
½ cup fine shred coconut
¼ cup carob powder or melted carob chips
¼ cup soy milk powder or flaxseed meal

Mix all ingredients and knead a little. Add coconut or soy milk powder as needed for a stiff mixture. Cut into small squares or form balls. Pinch up a peak in center with fingers. Chill to harden.

Almond Florentine

Simply delicious, chock-full-of-nuts, a healthy dessert that can be made-ahead, and served at any occasion. For an extra decorative touch, or gift, individually wrap and tie with ribbon.

⅓ cup Silk® Soy Milk or Creamer
⅓ cup creamed honey
⅓ cup maple syrup
1 tsp. molasses
sprinkle of sea salt
2 cups sliced almonds, lightly toasted
⅓ cup fresh shredded coconut or other nuts

In a saucepan, bring first 5 ingredients to a low boil, while stirring. Simmer to soft ball stage. Stir in the sliced almonds and coconut, or other chopped nuts. Pour or spoon ¾" thick into small cups. Chill until firm and set. Remove from cups. Drizzle with melted carob chips, if desired. Store in refrigerator or freezer.

Peppermint Carob Candy

⅔ cup carob powder
½ cup raw honey
½ cup soy whipped cream
2 Tbs. soy milk powder
1 tsp. peppermint or vanilla flavor
1 cup mixed nuts, seeds, or coconut
flaxseed meal, or soy milk powder

Mix well all together. Add enough flaxmeal, milk powder or coconut to make stiff. Form into a roll, wrap in wax paper; chill to firm. Slice or cut into bars.

recipe below

Fruity Date Chews

Put through a food grinder or processor:

2 cup dates, pitted soft
½ cup raisins
½ cup dried apricots, unsulphured
1 cup brazil nuts or walnuts, chopped

Add and mix in:

1 cup coconut, fine shred
½ cup almonds, blanched chopped
2 Tbs. fresh lemon juice
1 Tbs. orange zest
garnish: almonds, whole blanched

Pack ½" thick into glass dish or pan lined with waxed paper. Garnish with blanched almonds. Chill and cut into squares or bars. May be rolled in fine coconut. Freezes well.

Homemade Dandy Carob Candy

½ cup raw honey
½ cup non-dairy carob chips
3 Tbs. soy milk powder
1 ½ tsp. pure vanilla
½ cup ground almonds
½ cup chopped pecans
½ cup chopped walnuts or pine nuts
½ cup unsweetened coconut, fine

In saucepan, stir honey and carob chips until melted. Add rest of ingredients. Mix all together. Spread mixture ½" thick in a glass pan. Set in refrigerator or freezer to harden. Cut into bars; wrap individually. Keep cold. Freezes well.

Carob-Nut Fudge

⅓ cup almond butter
⅓ cup carob powder
⅓ cup honey or maple syrup
¼ cup soya* or soy milk powder
1 tsp. pure vanilla
⅛ tsp. sea salt
¼ cup chopped walnuts, pecans, or coconut
1 tsp. soy milk or water, opt.
garnish: pecan halves, shredded coconut, opt.

Combine all ingredients, using gloved hands for final mixing if necessary. Press into pan ½" thick. Garnish with pecans and coconut if desired.

*see Fearn® Soya Powder in Glossary of

Easy Carob Walnut Fudge
(Pictured above)

½ cup carob powder + ½ cup soy milk powder or 1 cup carob powder
½ cup raw honey
¼ cup cashew or peanut butter
2 tsp. pure vanilla
pinch of sea salt
½ cup chopped walnuts
1-2 Tbs. almond, soymilk or water

Cream honey, nut butter, vanilla, and salt until smooth. Add carob or soymilk powder, and liquid as needed. Press flat in pan. Garnish with walnut haves. Chill to firm. Cut in squares.

Maple Nut Clusters

½ cup pure maple syrup
½ cup honey
1 Tbs. molasses
3 Tbs. pure water
2 tsp. pure maple
    or vanilla flavor
½ tsp. orange zest
3 cups broken mixed nuts
(filberts, brazil nuts, cashews, peanuts)

Heat first 4 ingredients over medium-high heat, stirring constantly until mixture comes to boil. Reduce heat, simmer until 1-2 drops form a hard ball when dropped into water. Add maple flavor, orange zest, and nuts. Stir evenly to combine. Immediately spoon clusters of nut mixture onto waxed paper. Refrigerate to chill and harden. Delicious!

Crunchy Sesame Fingers

Simple and delicious! High in phosphorus and calcium - Everyone reaches for seconds!

3 cups raw sesame seeds
1½ cups fine shred coconut
3-4 Tbs. almond or peanut butter
½ cup honey or maple syrup
½ cup raw or date sugar
1 tsp. grated orange rind
½ tsp. pure vanilla
½ tsp. sea salt
½ cup chopped nuts,
    optional

Mix all ingredients together thoroughly. Pat ½" thick into a non-stick pan. Bake at 300° for 25-30 min. Cool thoroughly. Slice in 3" long fingers or squares. Chill to harden.

Apricot Yummies

Apricots, sun dried unsulfured
Walnuts, chopped

Mix equal part of apricots and walnuts in coarse food grinder. Press flat; cut in squares, or make a roll and cut slices. Sprinkle on shredded coconut, if desired.

Peanut Butter Balls

Our youngest daughter originated this recipe:
a simple take-along treat, for picnic or potluck

½ cup crunchy peanut butter
½ cup raw honey
½ cup Fearn® Soya Powder
1 tsp. pure vanilla
⅛ tsp. sea salt

Mix all together. Form into small balls. Roll in nuts or coconut, if desired. Chill to firm.

Carob Peanut Butter Cups

1 cup crunchy peanut butter
⅓ cup honey or maple syrup
¼ tsp. pure vanilla
½ cup non-dairy carob chips

In a saucepan mix the peanut butter and sweetening, stirring constantly over medium heat until combined. Add the vanilla and carob chips, continue stirring until mixture is blended. Remove from heat; spoon mixture into miniature dessert paper cups. Chill to set. Store in refrigerator or freezer. Yield: approx. 24 small cups.

Ice Cream, Thickshakes & Sherbets

Vanilla Ice Cream #1
(light, soft, creamy texture)

1 Tbs. agar flakes
1 cup pure water
1 cup cashew nuts
2 cups pure water or Silk® creamer
3 Tbs. soy milk powder
¼ tsp. sea salt
½ cup light raw honey
1 Tbs. pure vanilla, preferably clear
¼ cup soy or cold-pressed coconut oil, opt.

Soak agar in 1 cup water, stir and bring to boil; simmer 1 minute, cool 1 minute. Meanwhile blend cashews with next 3 ingredients, until very smooth. Add agar, honey and vanilla; blend. Slowly add oil while blending; blend 1 minute more. Freeze. Serve before it gets too hard. The agar lends a smooth texture - keeps ice cream from melting.

Note: Freeze ice cream made with agar in a bowl or freezer tray; allow to freeze undisturbed.

Homemade Banana Split - *See recipe for this healthy treat*

The automatic Ice Cream Maker allows you to create a variety of soft custard-like desserts

The History of Ice Cream
News and Views

A long time before Dolly Madison first served ice cream in the White House, people were licking, spooning, and enjoying what has often been called the dessert of kings.

Nero, emperor of Rome, employed runners to dash off to nearby mountains and bring back snow! Honey and fruit juice were added to create what was really a first century A.D. form of sherbet. Nero was so jealous of the delicacy that he ordered it reserved exclusively for his use.

Marco Polo, who spent his life traveling, brought a recipe from 13th century China back to his native Venice. Milk was substituted for the snow Nero had enjoyed. Only the wealthy could enjoy it, since the freezing process was so difficult. Ice cream was a favorite in the 17th century English court of Charles I. By royal decree, the cook who knew the secret was sworn not to reveal it to anyone. The historical development of ice cream has given way to mechanical production. This year, Americans will eat their way through an astonishing 900+ million gallons of ice cream – a frozen flavored mountain 500 feet square and as tall as the Empire State Building. The average American will consume approximately 23 quarts of ice cream this year. What is our ice cream like today??

American Ice Cream

The ice cream industry of today has grown by leaps and bounds, and today ice cream is America's favorite dessert. The sweeping advance of ice cream from a rarity to common food has grown at a rapid rate. According to the International Association of Ice Cream Manufacturers in Washington, D.C., approximately 900 million gallons of ice cream were sold in 1983. To give you a picture of how much that would be, Prevention magazine stated that if all the ice cream were packaged in half-gallon containers and place in a line, the line would wrap around the world at the equator eight times.

In the olden days when ice cream was made of cream, milk, eggs, and sugar and laboriously cranked in the old farm freezer, a serving of ice cream was only an occasional family "treat" which didn't do much harm. Today in this mass-producing, synthetic age, it is another matter entirely.

According to Consumers Digest July-Aug. 1983: A gallon of ice cream from the supermarket may contain any of an estimated 1,200 ingredients including chemical additives, emulsifiers, stabilizers, artificial flavorings, artificial coloring, dairy by-products, and 16-50% air. Refined sugar is still the primary ingredient and less desirable than natural sweetening agents such as honey and fresh fruit.

More nutritious "homemade ice cream" (varieties can be made using natural ingredients without the chemicals, stabilizers, or preservatives, and can be delicious and as satisfying as the more expensive, exotic varieties sold on the market today).

Ice Cream Sandwich

Two Crisp Oatmeal, Molasses,
** or any favorite cookies**
Vanilla Ice Cream, frozen hard
Carob Fudge Syrup, hot - see recipe

Make 3" flat cookies (omit raisins) or use made-ahead or frozen cookies. Slice frozen ice cream ½" thick. Using a cookie cutter, cut 3"circles to match size of cookies.

Place slice of ice cream between 2 cookies to form a sandwich. Dip sandwich into hot **Carob Fudge Syrup**, to coat all sides. Place on tray lined with wax paper. Freeze immediately to harden.

Low-Fat Tutti-Fruity Ice Cream
(pictured above)

1½ cups frozen white grape juice
1 cup pineapple mango juice, unsweetened
½ cup pure water or pureed fruit
2 Tbs. lime juice, fresh
½ cup blanched almonds + ½ cup
   cashews, or 1 cup cashews
pinch of sea salt
⅓ cup light honey, to taste
2 ripe bananas, fresh or frozen
2 tsp. agar powder, or 2 Tbs. coconut oil
blueberries, diced mango, pineapple, opt.

Blend the above ingredients in a
blender until very smooth (boil agar in
½ cup juice or water before blending).
Freeze in bowl or freezer tray, blend
again; add fruit and serve or return to
freezer. Serve before it gets too hard.
Top with crushed pineapple, if desired.

Sesame Coconut Ice Cream

3 cups pure hot water, add gradually
1 cup fresh coconut shreds
¼ cup sesame tahini
⅓ cup raw honey or agave syrup
1 Tbs. pure vanilla
¼ tsp. sea salt
2 Tbs. cold-pressed coconut or soy oil

Blend first 2 ingredients 2-3 minutes;
pour through fine strainer. Add tahini,
honey, vanilla, salt; blend again while
adding oil slowly. Freeze and serve
before it gets too hard.

Variation: Add **3 Tbs. carob powder** for
Carob Coconut Ice Cream

Creamy Carob Ice Cream

Follow recipe for **Vanilla Ice Cream # 1** or **2**. Add:

1 Tbs. raw honey
3-4 Tbs. carob powder

Blend well. Freeze. Serve before it gets too hard.

Note: When agar is used, results are similar to soft-serve ice cream

Vanilla Ice Cream #2

1 cup cashews
1-2 Tbs. soy milk powder, opt.
3 cups pure water, add gradually
1 tsp. slippery elm powder,* opt.
1 Tbs. pure vanilla
¼ tsp. sea salt
½ cup light raw honey
⅓ cup cold-pressed coconut or soy oil

Blend first 7 ingredients until very smooth. Slowly add the oil while blending. Freeze. Whip again and return to freezer. Serve before it gets too hard, or freeze in ice cream maker, if using coconut oil.

*Slippery elm adds a creamy texture.

Variation: Fresh fruit, purees or juices may replace part of the water.

Pineapple Ice Cream

1 cup raw cashew nuts
1 ½ cups pure water or pineapple juice
3 Tbs. soy milk powder or coconut
⅓ cup light raw honey
1 cup crushed pineapple
1 tsp. slippery elm powder
¼ tsp. sea salt
1 tsp. fresh lemon juice
¼ cup cold-pressed coconut or soy oil

Blend until very smooth. Slowly add oil while blending. Freeze in bowl or tray. Whip again, freeze. Serve before it gets too hard with sliced bananas or coconut, if desired.

Fresh Strawberry Ice Cream

Follow recipe for **Vanilla Ice Cream No. 1** or **2** with changes: Omit vanilla. Fold or whip in **1 cup fresh or frozen strawberries**. Add **2 Tbs. honey** for each cup of berries. Freeze. Serve before it's too hard.

Banana Split
(pictured, left)

1. Line dish with **1 banana** sliced lengthwise

2. Top with **3 scoops home-made ice cream: carob, vanilla, strawberry**

3. Sprinkle with **chopped nuts, fruit, coconut,** or **soy whip cream**

Maple Peanut Ice Cream

1 cup peanuts, lightly toasted
3 cups coconut milk or part water
1 Tbs. soy milk powder, opt.
4-5 Tbs. pure maple syrup, to taste
¼ tsp. sea salt
½ tsp. pure vanilla
¼ cup cold-pressed coconut or soy oil

Whiz first 6 ingredients in blender until very smooth. Slowly add the oil while blending. Freeze in ice cream machine or freezer try. Serve before it gets too hard.

Milkless Date Ice Cream

2 cups pure water
15 almonds or cashews
25 small pitted dates
2 Tbs. carob powder
2 Tbs. honey
2 Tbs. coconut or soy oil, opt.
1 tsp. pure vanilla
¼ tsp. sea salt
1 Tbs. agar dissolved in 1 cup water

Soak agar 1 min., boil 1 min., cool 1 min. Meanwhile, blend rest of ingredients until smooth; add agar, blend again. Freeze. Serve before it gets too hard.

Banana Soya Ice Cream

2 cups rich soy or almond milk
12 soft dates, pitted
½ cup cashews
1 Tbs. maple syrup or honey, opt.
2 large bananas
1 tsp. slippery elm, opt.

Whiz in blender. Freeze. Serve before it gets too hard.

Banana Ice Cream

Follow recipe for **Vanilla Ice Cream #1** or **2**. Freeze. Add **2 ripe bananas**. Whip again and return to freezer, or freeze in ice cream freezer. Serve before it gets too hard. Serve with **fresh berries**, if desired.

Strawberry Thickshake

2 cups Strawberries frozen or fresh
1 cup orange juice
   or ½ juice conc. + ½ water
1-2 bananas, frozen or fresh

Puree strawberries in blender with orange juice. Add bananas, blend until smooth. Spoon into tall glass, top with whole strawberry for garnish. Serve immediately.

Optional: Add a spoonful of **soy milk powder**, your favorite **ice cream** or **yogurt.**

Persimmon Thickshake

3 ripe persimmons, frozen
   or fresh chilled
1 cup pineapple juice, chilled
½ cup frozen soy yogurt or ice cream

Wash persimmons, remove stem; slip skin off frozen persimmons while holding under hot water. Blend with juice and yogurt until smooth and creamy. Serve in sherbet glass.

Variation: Use other fruits such as **Peaches, Apricots, Mango**

Ice Cream Toppings (above) Choose from: **Fruit Sauces, Chopped Nuts, Fruit Juice Toppings, Carob Fudge Syrup, Caramel Sauce,** *(see recipes in* **Sweet Creams & Toppings** *- Main Index*

Orange Sherbet

Follow recipe for **Mango-Peach Sherbet**. Omit mango and peaches, replace liquid with:

**½ cup water + agar
1 cup orange juice
½ cup pineapple juice
1 orange, with part zest**

Blend until smooth. Freeze. Serve before it gets too hard.

Peach Sherbet

Simply delicious and easy to prepare – serve with a bowl of fresh, just- popped corn, for a light summer supper

**½ cup Silk® creamer, soy milk
  or cold water
3 cups sliced peaches, fresh or frozen
1 cup frozen white grape juice
  concentrate
1 Tbs. fresh lemon juice
  or frozen juice cube
lemon zest, opt.**

Blend creamer, milk or water, peaches, grape juice and lemon juice until smooth. Pour into shallow square dish; freeze approximately 4 hours, stirring occasionally until set. Re-blend or process briefly until smooth. Garnish with fresh peach slices, if desired. Yield: 4 servings.

Avocado Lime Sherbet

**1 cup water + 1 scant Tbs. agar flakes
1 ¼ cups pineapple juice
¼ cup cashew nuts and/or coconut
¼ cup fresh lime or lemon juice
½ cup light raw honey, to taste
1 tsp. slippery elm powder, opt.
¼ tsp. sea salt
1 medium ripe
  avocado**

Soak agar 1 min. Boil 1 min. Cool 1 min. Meanwhile, blend cashews and coconut with pineapple juice. Add the agar mixture, lime juice, honey, salt, slippery elm. Blend well. Last add avocado. Blend and freeze. Serve before it gets too hard.

Mango or Peach Sherbet

**1 cup water + 1 Tbs. agar flakes
1 cup pineapple or white grape juice
½ cup coconut shreds or cashew nuts
1 tsp. lemon juice
⅓ cup honey, to taste
pinch of sea salt
½ tsp. slippery elm powder, opt.
1 mango or 2 cups fresh peaches**

Soak agar 1 min. Boil 1 min. Cool 1 min. Meanwhile, blend pineapple juice and coconut or cashews until smooth. Add agar mixture, and rest of ingredients. Whip again until smooth. Freeze and serve before it gets too hard.

Optional: *½ cup soy whipped cream may be folded in before freezing.*

Fruit Parfaits

7-Layer Fruit and Granola Parfait

An excellent way to include a variety of fresh fruit in the diet, with plenty of eye appeal.

Vanilla Ice Cream or Soy Yogurt
Bananas, sliced or diced
Peaches, sliced
Raspberries
Granola (see recipes)
Mango slices
Strawberries, sliced
Blueberries

Layer fresh fruit, granola, and ice cream or yogurt into parfait glasses, alternating colors, kinds, and shapes of fruit for maximum nutrition and eye appeal. Start with 1/4 cup yogurt or ice cream (mixed with sliced or diced bananas). Layer with fresh cut peaches, raspberries, or blueberries, more yogurt or cream, banana, healthy granola, sliced mango or strawberries. Top with a layer of yogurt or cream covered with choice raspberries, or other fresh fruit favorites. A winner at breakfast or supper!

Parfait varieties shown above include:

Kiwi slices, Boysenberries, Bing Cherries, Pineapple Chunks, Raspberry and Orange Jel, Sliced Almonds, Crushed Filberts (lightly toasting will enhance flavor of nuts).

Note: For more Parfait recipes, see chapter Fruit & Fruit Salads

Cookies – Bars

No-Bake Brazil Nut Cookies

¾ cup honey or honeycomb
¼ cup almond or cashew butter or tahini
1 cup chopped brazil nuts
1 cup wheat germ, toasted
¾ cup coconut, shredded
½ cup chopped dates or raisins
½ tsp. pure vanilla

Cream together first two ingredients. Add remaining ingredients. Form into a roll; wrap in wax paper. Chill 1 hour. Slice thin, roll in finely ground brazil nuts.

Haystack Cookies

1½ cups chopped dates, soft
¼ cup dried chopped apricots or raisins
¼ cup orange juice concentrate
¼ cup pure water
⅓ cup whole wheat pastry or barley flour
¼ cup quick oats
1 tsp. orange zest
¼ tsp. sea salt
1 Tbs. flaxseed, ground, optional
¾ cup chopped walnuts or pecans
2 cups coconut, long shred unsweetened

1. Process dates, apricots or raisins with orange juice and water in blender or food processor until coarse and chunky.

2. Add to remaining ingredients in a mixing bowl; stir lightly to combine.

3. Using a small or medium scoop, mound onto non-stick cookie sheet.

4. Bake at 375° for 15-20 min. or until golden brown. Yield: 12 - 24 cookies.

Peanut Butter Cookies

½ cup crunchy peanut butter
½ cup honey
¼ cup date sugar or sucanat
¼ cup pure water
¼ tsp. sea salt
1 tsp. pure vanilla
½ tsp. lemon zest
1 cup whole wheat pastry flour
4 Tbs. oat flour or wheat germ

Cream and mix together in order given. Add raisins or nuts if desired. Form into flat cookies by using a fork. Bake at 350° for 20 min.

Cashew Cookies

1 cup sucanat or honey
1 cup cashew nuts, ground
¼ cup soy oil + 1 tsp. lecithin
2 cups quick oats
1 cup shredded coconut
½ cup w. w. pastry flour
2 Tbs. soya powder or barley flour
½ tsp. sea salt
½ tsp. pure vanilla
½ cup water, soy or nut milk

Cream together first 3 ingredients. Add and mix in rest of ingredients. Shape into cookies and place on non-stick cookie sheet. Bake at 350° for 20-25 minutes until golden color.

Note: omit ¼ cup liquid when using honey.

Anise Cashew Crumbles

(melt in your mouth morsels!)

½ cup cashews, ground
¾ cup honey
¼ cup tahini or soy oil
½ tsp. sea salt
½ tsp. pure vanilla
1 tsp. anise seed, finely crushed
3 cups whole wheat pastry flour

Cream together first 6 ingredients; add flour, mix well. Drop by teaspoonful on cookie sheet; bake at 350° 10-15 min.

Oatmeal Raisin Cookies

1 cup honey or sucanat
½ cup oil + 1 tsp. lecithin
2-3 tsp. lemon zest
1 tsp. sea salt
1 ½ tsp. pure vanilla
¼ cup soya powder or barley flour
1 cup cold water
or ½ c. when using honey
5 cups regular or quick oats
1 cup w. w. pastry flour
½ cup raisins or coconut, opt.
¾ cup chopped nuts
or carob chips

In a large bowl, combine all ingredients except flour, oats, raisins and nuts, with electric mixer or mix with spoon. Stir in oats, flour, raisins and nuts. Mix well. Drop by spoonfuls on non-stick cookie sheet. Flatten with fork. Bake at 350° for 15-20 minutes or until golden brown.

Note: Instant oats are not the same as quick oats; if used in baking, results are gummy/ mushy.

*Non-stick food grade **silicone bakeware** requires no greasing. Bake cookies, muffins, roll dough, etc. Cookie sheets, muffin and bread pans, available at kitchen stores.*

Simple Molasses Cookies

½ cup molasses
¼ cup safflower or soy oil
½ tsp. pure vanilla
½ tsp. sea salt
½ tsp. ground ginger or cinnamon sub.
1 cup w. w. pastry flour
½ cup regular or quick oats

Combine all ingredients in order given. Drop by spoonfuls onto non-stick cookie sheet. Bake at 325° for 15-20 min. being careful not to overbake.

Wheat Germ Drop Cookies

⅔ cup honey or date sugar
2 Tbs. cashew, almond or peanut butter
1 Tbs. lemon juice
⅓ cup fruit juice or part soy oil
1 cup wheat germ, toasted
½ cup quick oats
½ cup whole wheat pastry flour
¼ cup chopped walnuts
2 Tbs. soya powder, opt.
½ cup soy or nut milk
2 tsp. pure vanilla
½ tsp. sea salt

Cream together the first 4 ingredients. Add rest of ingredients; mix well. Drop by spoonfuls onto non-stick baking sheet. Bake 350° until golden brown.

Grandma's Simple Sesame Fingers

Memories still linger, of my mother (who lived nearly 105 yrs.), lovingly rolling these little biscotti in her hands and coating them with sesame seeds. She enjoyed making them, everyone enjoyed eating them!

¾ cup whole wheat pastry flour
¾ cup barley or unbleached flour
1 Tbs. soya flour
½ cup sucanat, date or raw sugar
½ tsp. sea salt
1 tsp. baking powder, aluminum free
4 Tbs. soy oil or
   soft cold-pressed soy spread
1 tsp. pure vanilla
½ cup pure water, approx.

Coating:

1½ cups sesame seeds, unhulled

Mix dry ingredients together in mixing bowl. Add vanilla to soy oil and mix with dry ingredients. Slowly add water, working dough into a soft, but not sticky consistency. Put sesame seeds into a pan with high sides. Cut dough and hand roll into small 3"sticks. Dip sticks into flaxseed jel (to replace eggwhite), lift with fork, and roll in sesame seeds to coat. Arrange on dry cookie sheets. Bake in slow oven 250° for 1 hour; reduce heat and continue drying until crisp (like zwieback). Store in covered container to keep crisp.

Note: The baking is the most important step. When the sticks have baked sufficiently to hold their shape (about 1 hour) they may be transferred to one baking sheet for the final slow drying process which may take another hour, or complete the drying process in a dehydrator.

Aunt Joan's Anise Biscotti

These crunchy Italian biscotti (recipe adapted) are a favorite family tradition.
The perfect homemade gift. Eat them plain or dunk them in hot soymilk. Enjoy!

1 cup soymilk or use part soy yogurt
½ cup raw cashews or ¼ cup cashew butter
1 cup sucanat or raw sugar
2 Tbs. soft soy spread or Earth Balance®
1 tsp. anise seed, crushed
1 tsp. pure anise extract flavor
zest of 1 orange - grated rind
2 Tbs. Fearn® Soya Powder
½ tsp. sea salt
1 cup chopped almonds or filberts
2¾ cups mixed flour, unbleached, barley,
or w.w. pastry flour
1 Tbs. EnerG® Egg Replacer + 1 Tbs. water
1 tsp. baking powder, aluminum free

1. Blend milk and cashews until smooth. Pour into bowl, cream with next 7 ingredients. Add nuts, 2½ cups of flour, and egg replacer mixed with water. Combine remaining ¼ cup flour with baking powder. Add last, mixing just enough to combine before baking.

2. Lightly spray 1 large 11½"x17" baking sheet with non-stick spray. Quickly mound the thick batter into three 2"wide strips down length of baking sheet, leaving at least 1½" for expansion, between each row, and sides of pan (or form 2 strips on 2 smaller cookie sheets).

3. Bake in pre-heated 350° oven for 15-18 minutes (do not overbake). Remove to cutting board. When cool, cut into diagonal slices ½"- ⅝" wide. Lay slices, cut-side down, on cookie sheet. Bake at 140° lowest oven setting, until completely dry or finish drying in dehydrator.

Cranberry Pistachio Biscotti- Omit almonds, orange zest, and anise. Add **1 cup dried cranberries** and **1 cup shelled whole pistachio nuts.** Use zest of **1 lemon and lemon extract**.

Apricot Pecan Biscotti - Omit almonds, orange zest, and anise. Add **1 cup diced dried apricots** and **1 cup chopped pecans**. Use zest of **1 lemon** and **lemon extract**.

Apricot Crumble

1 cup apple juice or apricot nectar
2 Tbs. tapioca granules
⅓ cup honey or maple syrup
2 Tbs. fresh lemon juice
1 tsp. orange zest
½ tsp. ground cardamom
½ tsp. minced fresh gingerroot, opt.
8 cups apricot halves, fresh or canned
Crumb Crust, see recipes

In a bowl combine the first seven ingredients; stir into apricots. Set aside while making crumb crust. Spread a thin layer of crumb mixture in a 9" x 13" glass baking dish. Spoon apricot mixture into dish. Sprinkle crumb crust over fruit. Bake at 350° for 45-55 minutes or until topping is golden brown and fruit is tender. Yield: 10-12 servings

Key Lime or Lemon Squares

⅓ cup white grape juice concentrate
3 Tbs. Kojel®, plain or agar flakes
2-12 oz. pkgs. soft or silken firm tofu
8- oz. Tofutti Better than Cream Cheese
⅓ cup fresh lime or lemon juice
½ cup light honey or maple syrup
2 tsp. lime or lemon zest
¼ tsp. sea salt

In saucepan dissolve Kojel in white grape juice. Bring to boil. Pour into blender; add remaining ingredients and blend until smooth. Pour into square dish lined with Granola or Graham Cracker Crust (see recipe). Chill to firm. Cut into squares or use 10" pie pan.

Apple Crisp

A favorite special occasion breakfast dish or dessert that's quick and easy to prepare - freezes well

Fill a 9" x 13" baking dish with sliced sweet apples (see chart - Apple varieties):
Honeycrisp, Golden Delicious, Braeburn, etc

Add to apples, a mixture of:
½ cup apple juice concentrate
3 Tbs. tapioca granules
1 Tbs. lemon juice; pinch of sea salt
1 tsp. cinnamon substitute
honey to taste, opt.

Topping – Mix together:

2½ cups quick oats
½ cup whole wheat pastry
  or barley flour
1 Tbs. soy flour
⅓ cup chopped walnuts
⅓ cup honey or date sugar
⅓ cup fruit juice
  or 3 Tbs. oil + 2 Tbs. juice
1-2 tsp. pure vanilla

Cover with crumb crust topping. Bake at 375° 35-40 min. until apples are tender. Delicious served warm or cold with **Cashew Cream** or homemade ice cream. (see recipes)

Apple - Berry Crisp

Follow recipe for **Apple Crisp**, replacing ⅓ of the apples with **fresh or dried raspberries.**

Cashew-Orange Thumbprint Cookies

3 Tbs. cashew butter
½ cup honey or agave syrup
1 tsp. vanilla extract
1½ tsp. orange zest
½ cup orange juice
  or soy milk
2 Tbs. ground flaxseed
  or soymilk powder
1½ cups flour, barley
  and/or w.w. pastry
2 tsp. Ener-G® baking
  powder

In a medium bowl combine the cashew butter, honey, vanilla and orange zest, until creamy. Add orange juice, ground flax, and rest of ingredients. Mix well. Shape dough into 1" balls. Place 1½" apart on floured, non-stick cookie sheet. Press thumb halfway down into center of each cookie, making indentation. Bake at 350° for 12-15 minutes until golden brown. Remove from oven to cooling rack. Fill each thumbprint with 1 tsp. of your favorite fruit jam.

Carob Nut Brownies or Muffins

½ cup raw honey
  or honeycomb
4 Tbs. soy oil
  + 1 tsp. lecithin
2 Tbs. cashew butter
  or soy milk powder
1 tsp. grated orange
  or lemon zest
2 tsp. pure vanilla
2 tsp. lemon juice
¼ tsp. sea salt
⅔ cup carob powder
1 cup chopped walnuts
  or pecans
1 ⅛ cups sifted w.w.
  pastry flour

Cream together first 7 ingredients. Stir in remaining ingredients. Spread in prepared non-stick 8"x 8" pan. Bake at 350° for 35-40 min. or just until brownies begin to pull away from sides of pan. Cool completely in pan on wire rack. Top with carob frosting if desired.

Carob Cake: Add ⅔ cup soy milk + 2 tsp. non-aluminum baking powder

Orange Molasses Cookies

½ cup molasses
¼ cup honey
2 Tbs. oil + 1 tsp. lecithin
½ cup oats, finely ground
½ cup coconut, fine shred
½ tsp. sea salt
1 tsp. pure vanilla
1 ½ Tbs. orange zest
1 cup whole wheat or pastry flour
¼ cup soya powder or flour

Mix well in order given. Drop by spoonfuls onto non-stick cookie sheet. Bake at 350° 20 min. or until almost no indentation remains when touched in center.

Pineapple Squares

1 cup pineapple juice
1 cup cashews
½ cup maple syrup or ¼ cup honey
¼ cup pure water
1 tsp. pure vanilla
4 Tbs. arrowroot or cornstarch
½ tsp. sea salt
1-15 oz. can crushed pineapple

Blend juice and cashews until smooth and creamy. Add the sweetening, vanilla, salt and pineapple, blend again. Pour into saucepan, bring to boil. Blend the water and arrowroot together and pour into hot mixture. Heat and stir until thick. Pour into a no-bake crust, crumb crust, or pre-baked shell. **Topping:** Thickened crushed pineapple or granola crumb crust.

Coconut Cashew Bars

1 cup honey or date sugar
1 cup ground cashews
¼ cup tahini or oil + 1 tsp. lecithin
¼ cup water, or more if date sugar is used
2 Tbs. lemon juice
½ tsp. pure vanilla
½ tsp. sea salt
½ cup soya powder or wheat germ flakes
2 cups quick oats
½ cup chopped pecans, opt.
1 cup shredded coconut

Combine all ingredients. Press ¼" thick onto non-stick cookie sheet. Bake 15-20 min. at 350°. Cut in squares while still hot.

Note: The honey gives a softer, lighter, cookie.

Baked Fruity Squares

1 ½ cups dates, chopped
1 ½ cups raisins, soft
1 Tbs. lemon zest
1 cup whole wheat flour
1 cup quick oats
1 cup gold 'n white flour
½ cup soy or barley flour
½ cup millet, fine meal
1 cup coconut, fine shred
1 ½ tsp. orange zest
1 tsp. sea salt
1 ½ cups fruit juice or water
⅓ cup tahini or soy oil
½ cup honey
1 Tbs. lemon juice
1 ½ tsp. pure vanilla

For filling, combine first 3 ingredients in food processor with a little orange juice. Set aside. In bowl, mix dry ingredients. Blend liquid ingredients. Combine the 2 mixtures, adjusting liquid as needed; form into a ball. Roll half the dough ⅛" thick in a non-stick pan. Spread with filling. Cover with more dough. Bake at 375° 15 min. or until golden. Remove from oven and cut immediately into squares or strips 1"x 4". Cool completely.

Variation – cut dough with any desired shape cookie cutter. Place a spoonful of filling in center. Cover with a top piece of the same shape. Press edges together with fork to seal

Coconut Apple Macaroons

1½ cups fine shred
  or flake coconut
1 cup grated golden
  delicious apple
¼ - ⅓ cup fine oat*
  or w.w. pastry flour
2 Tbs. fructose, agave
  or light honey
½ tsp. pure vanilla
1 ½ tsp. finely grated
  lemon peel - zest
2 Tbs. creamy soy
  or coconut milk

In a mixing bowl, combine the
grated apple, sweetening and oat
flour (amount depends on sweetening
used). Mix the vanilla, lemon and soy milk together, add to apple mixture in bowl.
Fold in coconut. Using a small scoop, press and drop rounded teaspoons on a non-stick cookie sheet. Bake in 325° oven for 20 minutes until golden brown. Transfer to wire rack; cool completely. Yield: approx. 24 macaroons.

*Oat flour can be made by grinding quick oats in a small nut and seed mill.

Banana Date-Nut Cookies

A perfect breakfast cookie made with fruits, nuts and grains - naturally sweet with no added sweetening.

2 bananas, medium size
½ cup soft dates,
  pitted chopped
⅓ cup walnuts, chopped
¼ cup coconut shreds
  or 1 Tbs. tahini
1 tsp. pure vanilla
½ tsp. sea salt
2 Tbs. toasted wheat germ
  or flour
1 cup quick rolled oats

Heat oven to 375°. Chop
or coarsely smash bananas.
In a mixing bowl, combine
bananas, dates, walnuts, oil,
vanilla and salt. Beat with fork
to combine. Stir in wheat germ and
oats; let rest 2-3 min. to absorb. Drop
by spoonfuls onto prepared non-stick
baking sheet or press flat. Bake 25 min. or
until golden brown. Yield: approx. 12-15 cookies..

Fig-Filled Cookies

Filling: (or see Fig Conserves)

1½ cups dried figs, chopped
½ cup apple juice
    concentrate
¼ tsp. cardamon or mace
1 tsp. lemon zest
honey to taste

Cookie Dough: (or favorite crust)

2 cups barley or pastry flour
½ tsp. salt; + ½ tsp. vanilla
⅓ cup cashew nuts + 2 Tbs. oil
½ cup water + 1 Tbs. fructose

1. Combine filling in a saucepan, cover and simmer until figs are soft. Set aside.

2. Sift flour in a bowl. Process rest of ingredients in a blender until very smooth.

3. Pour over flour, tossing with a fork, until all flour is moistened. Sprinkle on more water if needed. Gather pastry into a ball. Shape into flattened rectangle. Divide in half.

4. Roll pastry on lightly floured board, in a 10" x 15" rectangle shape, ⅛ " - ¼ " thick. Spoon on 1 Tbs.of filling for each cookie, spacing the filling 2" apart on the dough. Roll the remaining cookie dough and place on top of the filling. Cut into squares or circles using a cookie cutter or glass. Seal edges with the tines of a fork. Prick tops. Gather up remaining scraps of pastry dough; roll out again, add filling, cut in desired shape.

5. Place cookies on floured non-stick cookie sheet. Bake at 375° for 15 min. Yield: 20-24

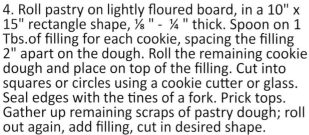

Fillings: Dates, raisins, prunes, apricots, cherries or other dried fruit may be used instead of figs.

Fruit-Filled Bars

Crumb Crust #1

½ cup honey
¼ cup almond or cashew butter
¼ cup date or raw sugar
1½ tsp. vanilla
¼ cup oil, or creamy soymilk
1 tsp. sea salt
¼ cup barley or soy flour
2½ cups quick or rolled oats
1½ cups whole wheat pastry flour

In a mixing bowl, combine ingredients in order given. Mix thoroughly with fingers until mixture resembles coarse crumbs. Press one-half of crumb mixture into bottom of 7½" x 12" baking dish. Spread with desired fruit filling. Cover with remaining crumb crust, patting lightly. Bake in a 350° oven 30-35 minutes, until top is light golden brown. Cool and cut into bars. Remove from pan.

Optional: For delicious crumb crust, add **1 Tbs.** grated lemon or orange zest

Crumb Crust #2

2 cups quick cooking oats
2 cups whole wheat pastry flour
½ cup shredded coconut
½ cup walnuts, chopped
6 - 8 Tbs. frozen apple juice concentrate
2 tsp. lemon zest
½ tsp. sea salt

In a bowl combine all dry ingredients together. Add just enough frozen (thawed) apple juice concentrate to dry mixture, to resemble coarse crumbs.

Date Bars

Crumb Crust: see recipes

Filling: Mix together in saucepan:

4 cups pitted dates, cut
2 cups pure water
2 Tbs. lemon juice
1 Tbs. lemon or orange zest

Slowly bring to a low boil. Stir and simmer until thickened. Spread filling between your favorite crumb crust. Bake at 350° 30-35 min. Cool; cut into bars.

Apricot-Date Bars

Crumb Crust: see recipes

Filling:

2 cups dried apricots, natural unsulfured
2 cups pitted dates, cut
2 Tbs. honey
2 tsp. orange zest
4 Tbs. apricot or pineapple juice

Soak 2 cups cut, dried apricots in 1 cup pure water until plump, and water is absorbed. Coarsely chop apricots in a food processor. Mix together in saucepan with dates and rest of ingredients. Stir over low heat 5-8 minutes until combined and thickened. Cool; spread filling between layers of your favorite crumb crust (see recipes). Bake at 350° 30-35 min.

Polynesian Bars

Crumb Crust: see recipes

Filling:

1½ cups dates, pitted chopped
¼ cup dried apricots, chopped
2 cups (1-20 oz can) crushed pineapple
¼ cup orange juice
1 Tbs. tapioca, fine granules

In a saucepan stir pineapple, orange juice and tapioca together. Heat to simmer; add finely chopped dates and apricots. Cover and simmer 2-3 minutes. Set aside while preparing crumb crust. Press half of crumb crust into 7½" x 12" glass baking dish. Spread with filling. Top with remaining crumb mixture; press lightly. Bake at 350° for 25 - 30 minutes or until light brown. Cool before cutting into 36 bars.

Prune-Orange Bars

Crumb Crust: see recipes

Filling - combine in saucepan:

3 cups prunes, pitted, cut in pieces
½ cup prune or orange juice + 1 Tbs. zest
1 Tbs. tapioca granules
1-2 Tbs. honey
1 Tbs. lemon juice + 1 Tbs. zest

Add pure water to prunes in saucepan (just enough to cover). Slowly bring to boil, simmer 2-3 minutes. Let set 15-20 minutes, drain juice into cup. Measure prune juice or add orange juice to make ½ cup. Pour back into saucepan; add tapioca, honey, lemon juice and zest. Simmer over low heat until thickened. Cool. Spread between your favorite Crumb Crust. Bake at 350° 30-35 min. Cool; cut into bars.

Recipe For A Happy Home

Half a cup of friendship
And a cup of thoughtfulness
Creamed together with a pinch
Of powdered tenderness.

Very lightly beaten
In a bowl of loyalty
With a cup of faith, and one of hope,
And one of charity.

Be sure to add a spoonful
Of gaiety that sings
And also the ability
To laugh at little things.

Moisten with the sudden tears
Of heartfelt sympathy:
Bake in good-natured pan
And serve repeatedly.

-author unknown

Fruits &
Fruit Salads

Index - CHAPTER 7

Fruits & Fruit Salads

Ten Talents

212

Dishes or Banana Leaves

Dishes to wash
then put on the shelf
And no one to do it
except myself.
Pots and pans
and a stack of plates
The very thought
exasperates!
I must put my hands
in the hot soapy water,
The work they say
belongs to a daughter.
I'll hurry and finish
and sweep the floor
But I needn't bother –
there'll soon be more.
When I grow up
I'll have a machine,
I'll put them all in
and they'll be clean.
One other solution
that I know,
Is to live in a land
where banana leaves grow.
I'd use them as plates
and throw them away,
And do as I please
the rest of the day!!

Chapter cover photo: *Colorful Fresh Fruits in Abundance*

"The more we depend upon the fresh fruit just as it is plucked from the tree, the greater will be the blessing...It would be well for us to do less cooking and to eat more fruit in its natural state." E.G. White, **Diet and Foods**, pg. 309

Fruit and Fruit Salads

The Beauty and Blessing of Fresh Fruit

Tree ripened fruit, is without a doubt, a blessing to health and vitality. It is artistic in form, naturally full of color and flavor, appetizing, and easy to digest. Fruits contain an abundance of fiber, and natural unrefined sugars, as well as vitamins, minerals, trace elements, antioxidants, and numerous phytochemicals that protect against disease. The fiber in fruit assists in lowering cholesterol, maintaining bowel regularity and proper blood sugar levels.

And what could be more appetizing than a cluster of blue grapes, a handful of tree ripened red cherries, or a perfectly formed fragrant peach, dripping with juice, just waiting to be eaten! All these are beautiful gifts from the bountiful hand of our Creator.

A simple diet of fresh fruit, for a few days, often brings relief to the overworked digestive system and to those who do a great amount of mental labor. Fruits are cleansing, vegetables are builders.

Fresh fruits and fruit salad, are excellent for those who want to keep slim and fit. Learn to cultivate a taste for fresh ripe fruit, part of the original diet created by God, for man.

Wonderful Fresh Fruits
many varieties

Apples*
- *Braeburn*
- *Cortland*
- *Delicious, Red & Yellow*
- *Fuji*
- *Granny Smith*
- *Honey Crisp*
- *McIntosh*

Apricots
Avocado
Bananas
Berries*
- *Blueberry/Huckleberry*
- *Blackberry/Marionberry*
- *Boysenberry*
- *Cranberry*
- *Currants-Red, White, Black*
- *Elderberry*
- *Gooseberry*
- *Loganberry/Dewberry*
- *Raspberries-Black, Red*
- *Strawberry*

Carob
Cherimoya
Cherries*
Coconut
Dates
Figs*
- *Calimyrna*
- *Mission, Black*
- *Kadota, White*
- *Adriatic*
- *Brown Turkey*
- *Desert King*

Grapes/Raisins*
- *Black, Purple, Red Grapes*
- *Champagne*
- *Concord*
- *Seedless Grapes-Green, White*
- *Zante Grapes (Dried Currants)*

Grapefruit-white, pink
Guava
Kiwifruit-green, gold
Kumquat
Lemon
Lime
Mangos
Melons*
- *Banana Melon*
- *Cantaloupe*
- *Casaba*
- *Christmas Melon*
- *Crenshaw*
- *Honeydew*
- *Juan Canary*
- *Muskmelon*
- *Nutmeg Melon*
- *Pepino*
- *Persian*
- *Watermelon*

Nectarine
Oranges*
Papaya
Passion Fruit
Peaches*
Pears*
- *Bartlett*
- *Bosc*
- *Comice*

Persimmon
Pineapple
Plums*/ Prunes
Pomegranate
Prickly Pear/Cactus Pear
Pummelo
Quince
Sapote
Star Fruit/Carambola
Tangerine/Mandarin
Ugli Fruit

Fruit Uses

Fresh Picked - as is
Fruit Topping
Fruit Parfaits
Fruit Sherbet
Fruit Juices, Drinks
Fruit Candy
Fruit Salads
Fruit Cake
Fruit Pies, Tarts

Fruit "Smoothies"
Frozen Fruit Cream
Fruit Jello Mold
Fruit Sauces, Pudding
Fruit Whip, Purée
Jam, Jellies, Preserves
Infant, Baby Feeding
Cleansing Diet
Convalescent Diet

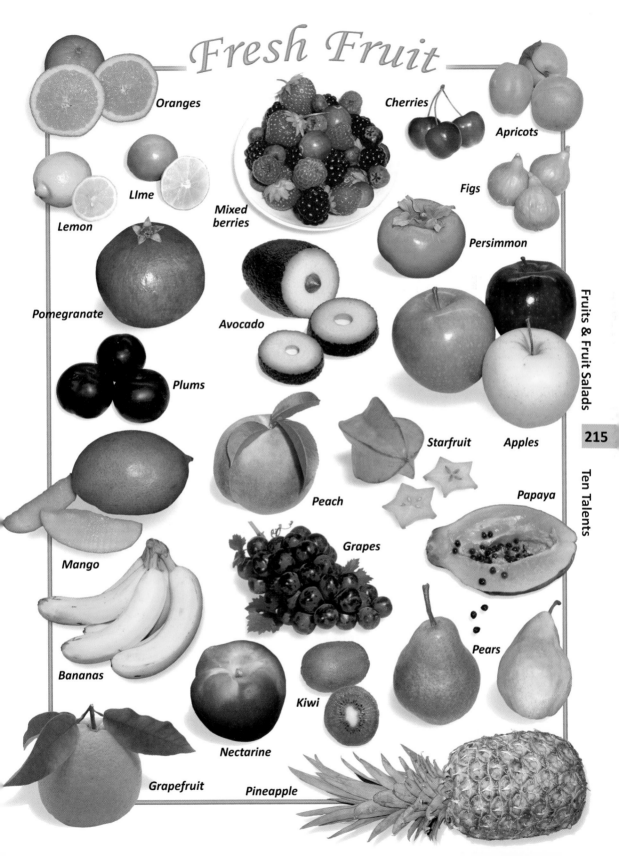

Fresh Fruit

Oranges

Cherries

Apricots

Lime

Figs

Lemon

Mixed berries

Persimmon

Pomegranate

Avocado

Plums

Starfruit

Apples

Peach

Papaya

Mango

Grapes

Bananas

Pears

Kiwi

Nectarine

Grapefruit

Pineapple

Fruits rich in antioxidants include blueberries, grapes, raspberries, cranberries, strawberries, kiwi and citrus fruits. Foods rich in antioxidants and phytochemicals, boost the immune system, help to improve circulation, enhance memory, and slow down the aging process.

What are Antioxidants?

A substance or vitamin that inhibits oxidation and helps protect our body from the destructive activity of free radicals. Free radicals are molecules or groups of atoms that can cause damage to our cells, impairing our immune system and leading to infections and various degenerative diseases. Listed are a few of the more common antioxidants known, and their plant sources to include in our dietary.

Carotenoids

Beta-carotene: (orange, dark green, yellow fruits and vegetables) yams, carrots, spinach, kale, broccoli, apricots, cantaloupe, mango, papaya, etc.

Lycopene: (red fruits, & vegetables) tomatoes, red pepper, watermelon, strawberries, etc.

Lutein: Citrus fruits, corn, dark leafy greens, romaine

Flavonoids or Bioflavonoids

Anthocyanidins: (purple or reddish pigment) grapes, blueberries, mulberries, currants, etc.

Quercetin: apples, grapes, red grape juice, citrus fruits, onions

Rutin, Hesperidin: buckwheat, currants; grapes, citrus fruits and peel

Isoflavones – Phytoestrogens: soybeans, tofu, legumes, flaxseed, whole wheat

Vitamin C

Fruits: Citrus fruits, acerola, currants, kiwi, strawberries, etc.

Vegetables: Sweet red peppers, broccoli, tomatoes, sprouts, etc.

Vitamin E; Selenium

Vitamin E: Wheat Germ and oil, sunflower seeds, almonds, avocado, whole grains, etc.

Selenium: Brazil nuts, wheat germ, nutritional yeast, molasses, legumes, grains.

Organosulfurs; Sulfides

Cruciferous vegetables: Brussels sprouts, cabbage, broccoli, bok choy, cauliflower, turnip, watercress, etc.;

Sulfides: Onions, garlic, leeks, chives

Citrus fruits (Grapefruit, Lemon, Lime, Orange, Kumquat, Tangerine, etc.) contain many beneficial properties and are rich in the antioxidant vitamin C, important in the promotion of health and prevention of disease.

APPLE - This versatile "queen of fruits" is rich in boron, increasing mental alertness. Rich in phytochemicals and flavonoids, such as quercetin a powerful antioxidant. Apples contain pectin, an insoluble fiber, that helps eliminate toxins; and properties which aid in reducing cholesterol levels. Apples contain medicinal properties and are well tolerated by diabetics. A good source of vitamin C, E, potassium, iron and fiber.

AVOCADOS contain heart-healthy monounsaturated fats, that help lower LDL (bad) cholesterol, and boost HDL (good) cholesterol. In addition avocados are rich in protein, contain vitamins A, C, and E, B6, folate, iron, potassium, magnesium, and fiber. The avocado is the richest fresh fruit in vitamin E; plant foods that surpass are oil-bearing nuts, wheat germ, and olives. Vitamin E, a powerful antioxidant, may protect against cancer, cellular aging, and infertility. Like olives, avocados can be eaten at any meal.

Hass avocado – dark, pebbly skin, rich and buttery, with a sweet nutty flavor. Smaller and creamier than many varieties.

Florida avocado – smooth green skin, lighter and moister, contain less fat, generally has a larger pit, also known as "alligator pear."

To Ripen Avocado – keep at room temperature. The skin of a Haas avocado will turn from green to black when ripe. The skin of Bacon, Fuerte, Gwen, Pinkerton and Zutano avocados remain green when ripe. All varieties when ripe, will yield to gentle pressure.

BLUEBERRIES – One of the top 20 nutrient-rich healing foods. These small berries are rich in vitamin C, and packed with antioxidants that can help prevent heart disease, cancer, eye disease, memory loss, and a host of other maladies. The plant pigments that make blueberries blue- flavonoids called anthocyanins- guard against age-related blindness. Like cranberries, blueberries (and blueberry juice) aid in preventing urinary tract infections. Blueberries are a rich source of fiber (antidote to constipation); ½ cup contains almost the same as a slice of whole-grain bread. Blueberries are delicious just plain, blended into fruit smoothies, as topping for breakfast cereal or waffles, added to yogurt, or mixed into muffins. Blueberries freeze well. When using fresh berries in a batter, it's a good idea to freeze them for at least 1 hour before mixing them in. This helps prevent the delicate fruit from breaking during stirring, which will streak the batter.

CRANBERRIES belong to a group of shrubs that produce some of the world's favorite berries including blueberries, bilberries, and huckleberries.The fruit and juice is effective in cases of urinary infection, and to help improve venous circulation. Rich in antioxidants, flavonoids, fiber, and vitamin C. Cranberries are enjoyed during the fall and winter months and especially at Thanksgiving meals. Cranberries are naturally tart, or sour. Commercial cranberry cocktail often contains limited amounts of cranberry juice and lots of sweetener. Pure cranberry juice when mixed with pure grape juice (no added sugar) is healthful and very palatable. Cranberries when combined with sweet apples are wholesome and surprisingly delicious.

FIGS – vary in color from green to yellow, purple, brown or black. Figs are an excellent source of fiber, natural sugars, and other nutrients. Fresh ripe figs are highly perishable and should be refrigerated. For drying figs see chapter **Miscellaneous**.

GRAPES – Rich in antioxidants, phytochemicals, and flavonoids (especially quercetin and resveratrol) associated with a decrease in LDL (bad) cholesterol, and heart disease. Grapes freeze well. Just wash, put in plastic bags in your freezer. Delicious in fruit salad.

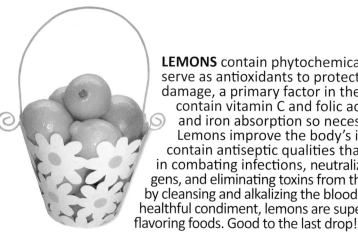

LEMONS contain phytochemicals including flavonoids that serve as antioxidants to protect the cells against free radical damage, a primary factor in the aging process. Lemons also contain vitamin C and folic acid, aiding in blood production and iron absorption so necessary for those with anemia. Lemons improve the body's immune system and contain antiseptic qualities that are useful in combating infections, neutralizing carcinogens, and eliminating toxins from the body by cleansing and alkalizing the blood. As a healthful condiment, lemons are superior for flavoring foods. Good to the last drop!

The **Meyer** variety of lemon is sweeter, with brighter flesh than the common **Eureka** lemon. The Meyer skin is thinner and smoother, and not as suitable for zesting the rind.

Note: The entire (pesticide-free) lemon may be used fresh or frozen: the juice, pulp and peel. (See chapter Miscellaneous).

Fruity Fact: One medium juicy lemon will yield 2-4 Tablespoons of juice and 1-2 Tablespoon of grated lemon zest. (Grate the peel before juicing the lemon. Freeze zest to use in recipes).

LIMES are similar to lemons in size and shape, but are slightly sweeter in flavor and more acid than lemons. Used in guacamole, dips and sauces. Its pleasant aroma makes it ideal for a refreshing beverage.

MANGO – The finest of tropical fruits, sweet and juicy. A favorite fruit of the Orient. Mangos have a smooth aromatic pulp reminiscent of a peach. When ripe, a mango yields to gentle pressure like a ripe avocado, and the stem end has a sweet fragrance. The mango is riper near the seed. The **Haden** and **Manila** mangos are two of the best varieties.

Peel a mango downward, starting at the top or stem end. When slicing use a slight sawing motion following contour of the flat seed. Mango enthusiasts claim the only way to eat a mango is over a sink- they are so juicy, and nibble the last bits that cling to the hairy seed.

To ripen, place at room temperature, uncovered, out of direct sunlight. Delicious served in fruit salad with peaches or pineapple, sliced or diced, in jells, ice cream, or smoothies. Freeze well. Good source of vitamin A, C, E, and folate.

MELONS contain a high percentage of water (90-95% depending on the variety). The sweet water of melons contains mineral salts, balanced to quench the thirst on a hot summer day. Melons are alkalizing, diuretic, and laxative, and contain properties beneficial in kidney and urinary disorders. They are virtually fat-free, but provide a well-balanced supply of vitamins and minerals. Similiar to drinking water at mealtime (a practice not recommended), melons tend to interfere with digestion by diluting gastric juices. Melons make a good supper meal, eaten alone or with other juicy fruits.

Cantaloupe – The cantaloupe, actually a muskmelon, with its characteristic aroma and flavor, has a raised netting on a pale gold or gray-green rind. The flesh is bright orange, sweet and juicy. Cantaloupe is a smaller variety of melon, but the richest in beta-carotene, which converts in the body to vitamin A. Delicious on it own, or add to fruit salads or smoothies. Blossom end will yield to slight pressure when ripe.

Casaba – The cream-colored flesh of this winter melon is sweet and juicy, with a distinctive mild taste likened to cucumber. A squeeze of lime enhances its flavor.

Crenshaw – Melon connoisseurs have labeled the crenshaw the most sweetly succulent of all melons. This melon has a golden pink flesh that is tender and juicy; a hybrid cross of the casaba and cantaloupe. Ripe crenshaws give off a spicy fragrance.

Honeydew – A sweet, delicious, succulent melon. A perfectly ripe honeydew has pale-green flesh, and pale-greenish white skin with a subtle velvety surface or slight wrinkling that can be felt. A good melon is symmetrical; the blossom end gives with slight pressure. Avoid rock-hard, shiny smooth melons; honeydew melons picked before maturity never reach full flavor.

Persian – A large, grayish-green variety of muskmelon with delicate netting on the rind. The flesh is deep reddish-orange, and is sweet and delectable; larger and richer than cantaloupe in color, flavor, and nutrition, especially vitamin A. When ripe, the skin turns slightly golden, the blossom end gives with slight pressure, and the fragrance becomes more pronounced. Best eaten when just ripened.

Watermelon – A round or large elongated, oval-shape melon weighing up to thiry-five pounds. The thick rind ranges from pale to dark-green in color and can be solid or striped. The flesh is red or deep pink (although there are also white, yellow or pale pink watermelons). The watermelon is a refreshing, juicy fruit (about 90% water) and a great thirst quencher. Watermelon is diuretic and beneficial for kidney disorders, and as a depurant to remove toxins from the blood. Uncut melon can be stored at room temperature for 7-10 days. Refrigerate after cutting.

Melon Varieties

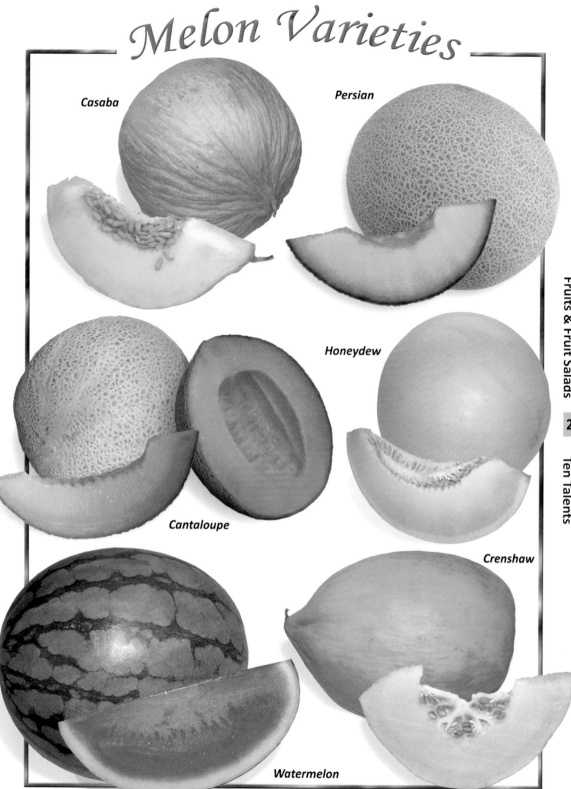

Casaba

Persian

Honeydew

Cantaloupe

Crenshaw

Watermelon

PAPAYA – A rich source of papain, a proteolytic enzyme which activates digestion. Papaya is a source of vitamin C, A, folate, and powerful antioxidants such as beta carotene.

PINEAPPLE – A rich source of bromelain, an enzyme which aids digestion by "breaking down" proteins. Pineapples contain vitamin C, B1, B6, folate, manganese, potassium and fiber.

PERSIMMON –
Hachiya and Fuyu

The **Hachiya** persimmon, an Oriental variety (also called Japanese persimmon). A most delicious and exotic tree fruit, shaped like a large acorn, with smooth, deep-orange skin. Best eaten when fully ripe, very soft, like a baby's cheek, and almost mushy. Unless fully ripened, its bitter tannin will "pucker" the taste. Persimmons are generally picked when hard. Place in paper bag, at room temperature, to hasten ripening. Refrigerate ripe fruit, or freeze whole to retain delicious flavor. If desired, remove the skin by holding fruit under hot water while slipping skin off. Eat plain, in combination with other fruits, or cut and blend the frozen fruit for delicious smoothies or desserts. Excellent source of Vitamin A.

The **Fuyu** persimmon is flat and sweet (see picture below), with a smooth yellow to orange-red skin. The Fuyu remains firm when ripe. It has a sweet spicy flavor, and can be eaten with the skin, when crisp to hard, and yields to gentle pressure. Best choice for fruit salad because of its firm slicing texture.

Persimmons are available from November to February, a colorful holiday fruit with good keeping quality.

Christmas Pineapple

Sliced pineapple rings
Strawberries, fresh or frozen
Avocado, cut in rings

Peel and cut pineapple in ½" slices. Chop fresh strawberries, sweeten with honey, (juice will flow from berries). Place pineapple slices under berries in bowl to absorb berry juice, until slices are light red in color. Arrange individual breakfast plates with green avocado slices, red pineapple and strawberries. Top with **Soy Whipped Cream.**

Hawaiian Tidbits

¼ cup honey or agave
1 Tbs. pineapple juice
2 bananas, sweet speckled
½ cup finely chopped macadamia nuts or coconut shreds

Mix honey with juice. Peel, cut bananas into 1" slices. Dip each piece in honey

Easy Way to Cut and Serve Pineapple

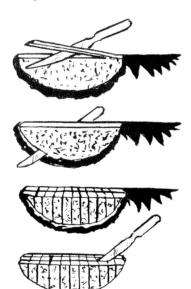

Tropical Treat

Pineapple, crushed: fresh, frozen or canned
Persimmons, ripe, very soft

Cut persimmons in half. Scoop out pulp and mix lightly with pineapple until colors are blended. Serve in sherbet cups or fill cantaloupe halves. Garnish with fresh mint.

Persimmon Coconut Cup

2 cups ripe persimmon pulp
½ cup whipped soy cream, see recipes
fresh coconut shreds

Combine the persimmon pulp and cream. Fill fruit cups – Garnish with grated coconut. Chill and serve.

Fruit Kabobs

(see Fruit Salad chapter)

A is for Apples

Apples are a superior fruit and should be considered as a staple fruit. If a variety of fruit is not available, apples eaten fresh and prepared for winter use, are a good standby. There are many varieties to chose from for different purposes:

For fresh eating out of hand, choose apples that are juicy, sweet and attractive.

For applesauce, and desserts, choose tart, firm apples that cook quickly.

For baking whole or sliced for pies, choose apples that will hold their shape.

Remember?
"An Apple a Day Keeps The Doctor Away".

Maple Baked Apples
Delicious with cashew cream for a special breakfast or supper

½ cup mixed dried fruit bits, raisins
   or chopped dates
4 large tart baking apples,
   (Rome, Jonagold, Cortland, etc.)
¼ cup apple juice or water
2 Tbs. maple syrup or honey, opt.
½ tsp. lemon zest
cashew cream; walnuts, opt.

Combine the dried fruit, with 2 Tbs. water; set aside to soak while preparing apples. Wash and core the apples. Peel a thin strip off the top (to prevent splitting) and place apples in a baking dish. Fill centers with the dried fruit mixture. Pour the apple juice mixed with honey and lemon zest, over apples. Bake in a 375° oven for 40-45 min. or until apples are tender, basting occasionally. If desired, top with cashew cream or chopped walnuts. Serve warm or cold.

Apples

VARIETIES	CHARACTERISTICS	USES OF / TIPS
Braeburn	Developed in New Zealand. Red-flushed and stiped over greenish-gold skin. Juicy flesh and sweet tart flavor. U.S. Braeburn are available year round.	Good eating apple. Excellent choice for fruit salads, and a good choice for applesauce or pies. Cut apples will discolor. To keep from browning, dip in citrus or apple juice.
Cameo	A crisp, juicy sweet-tart variety is recognized by its red and yellow bi-coloring, with white speckles on the skin. The flesh is white to cream color. Available late autumn.	Good salad apple. Slow to brown when cut. Cameos hold their shape and flavor when baked. The extra dense flesh may require a little longer cooking time. Good for baking.
Crispin Mutsu	Re-named Crispen (originally Mutsu in Japan). A large greenish russet apple with golden bush. The flesh is crisp, creamy colored, and when ripe has a sweet, light honey flavor.	Excellent eating & cooking apple. Crispens retain their shape when sliced & cooked. Good choice for apple crisp, pie, or sauce. Use the same as Granny Smith for pies.
Fuji & Honeycrisp	Fuji & Honeycrisp (our favorites) the do-it-all apples. Fuji originally developed in Japan. Fuji apples have a pretty red-orange blush, and firm flesh. Available year round. Honeycrisp are a crisp eating apple., good in salad, sauce, or baking. Sweet honey flavored.	Both are exellent eating apples. You can depend on them to be crisp, juicy, and sweet flavored. A good choice for eating out-of-hand, fruit salads, apple crisp, pie, sauce, etc.
Gala	Gala apples come from New Zealand. A hpbrid cross of the Orange Pippen with Delicious. The skin is creamy yellow, striped with pink, with a honey perfume flavor.	Texture will disintegrate with heat, so these are best eaten raw. Store in the refrigerator.
Golden & Red Delicious	Golden Delicious is an older variety. Color: dull gold with pink blush. Flowery sweet, even when slightly wrinkled. Moderately juicy. Good keeper. Store: high humidity. Red Delicious: Large, bright red, elongated shape with five knobs at base. Sweet, juicy.	Good eating & cooking apple. Will retain their shape when cooked. A good choice for apple pies, tarts, & applesauce. Red Delicious are one of the best eating apples. Texture disintegrates with heat. Store in a plastic bag in the refrigerator. To keep from browning, toss with citrus or apple juice. Available year round.
Jonagold	A cross between Golden Delicious and Jonathan apples. Jonagolds are large, golden-skinned, stiped ad blushed with red. Avaialable late autumn through spring.	Excellent eating apple with a rich, juiy, spicy flesh. Good in fruit salads & cooking.
Lady Pink Lady	Lady: Petite lady is the oldest apple, small and flattened on both ends. Skin is shiny, pale green with a red blush. Delectably crisp and tart. Pink Lady: True pink coloring, smooth texture, and crisp crunch. Sweet-tart flavor similar to the Granny Smith. Available late fall through spring.	Lady - Excellent eating and cooking apple. Small size is perfect for children or decorating. Pink Lady: An excellent eating fresh dessert apple. Ideal for salads, resists browning.
McIntosh	A most popular apple in America, with bright-red skin, tinged with green. The McIntosh is crisp, with a strawberry sweet flesh. Available year round.	Best eaten out-of-hand. Texture will disintegrate with heat. Store wrapped, in refrigerator.
Rome	Large deep-red with yellow speckling. Coarse skin. Taste ranges from sweet to mildly tart. stores well - considered one of the best stored by the bushel apple.	Excellent as baking or cooking apple. Good for pies, apple crisp, and applesauce.

Fresh Raw Applesauce

6 apples, golden delicious or other sweet
2-3 Tbs. lemon juice, fresh
1-2 Tbs. raw honey, to taste
pinch of sea salt

Core and slice apples (peeling is optional). Combine lemon, honey, and salt with apples. Process in blender just until smooth. Serve immediately or chill. Freezes well. Servings: 4

Cranberry Fruit Relish

Rich in fiber, Vitamin C and Antioxidants

1 lb. cranberries, washed
4-5 sweet apples, with peel
1 orange + part of rind
¼ cup frozen orange juice concentrate,
**   or honey to taste, opt.**

Process the cranberries through a food processor alternately with oranges and apples or process in blender until finely chopped. Add juice concentrate or honey if desired. Top with walnuts or pecans. Chill to blend flavors. Keeps well in refrigerator 1- 2 weeks or freeze. Servings 6-8

Coconut Apple Betty

4 large tart apples, sliced, peeled, opt.
1½ cups soft bread crumbs
½ cup flaked coconut
⅓ cup honey or maple syrup
4 Tbs. apple juice concentrate
**   + 2 Tbs. water**
½ tsp. coriander or mace
½ tsp. orange zest
12 almonds, slivered

Arrange a layer of apple slices in shallow baking dish. Cover with breadcrumbs and coconut. Dot with honey; sprinkle on apple juice mixture, (mix apple juice, coriander, and orange zest) Repeat layers until all ingredients are used. Top with coconut and almonds. Bake covered 350° for 35 min., then bake uncovered 10 min.

Dried Fruit Compote

(Rich source of Iron)

Golden Fruit Compote

Apricots, dry unsulphured
Dates, pitted
Figs, dried
Raisins
Prunes

Use **2 cups** each dried unsulphured **pears, peaches, apricots,** and **pineapple,** and **4 cups dried tart apples.**

Cut equal amounts of the dried fruits. Place in large saucepan, cover with 2" of water. Let soak ½ hour, slowly bring to a boil. Simmer for 3 minutes. The fruit will be soft. Stir in grated zest of ½ orange or lemon unsprayed. Stir a little arrowroot or tapioca starch in orange juice or cold water; add to simmering fruit to thicken slightly. Remove from heat.

Cut fruit into bite-size pieces. Place fruit in kettle big enough to allow fruit to swell. Cover with water, 2-3". Let soak 30-60 minutes. Add **orange** and/or **lemon zest** and **2 Tbs. arrowroot** or **tapioca** mixed with water. Follow same procedure as given above. Simple and delicious!

Apricots n' Cream

Use fresh or soak **unsulfured dried apricots** in **pineapple juice** to soften. Whiz in blender until smooth. Mix with ¼ as much **Soy Whipped Cream**. Serve in sherbet cups topped with fresh moist **shredded coconut.**

Add a little honey if desired (about 1 Tbs. for each 3 quarts of fruit). Last add **1 quart of home canned peaches or pears**. The finished compote should be quite thick. Best served cold or at room temperature. Delicious on toast, zwieback cubes or waffles spread with nut butter. Add a few nuts to the menu for a complete and satisfying meal.

Note: Simple to make - large quantities can be stored in refrigerator. Keeps well.

Fluffy Fig Whip
(rich in iron and calcium)

3 cups dried figs, chopped
1 cup coconut milk
1 Tbs. honey, opt.
1 Tbs. carob powder
1 Tbs. flax or toasted sesame seed

Whiz in blender until smooth. Spoon into fruit cups. Chill before serving. Sprinkle with **fresh grated coconut** or top with **Soy Cream** if desired.

Stuffed Figs or Dates

Simply pull dry **figs** or **dates** apart to form a nest. Fill with nut meats (whole **almonds, pecan halves, walnut halves, filberts** or your favorite nut. Better than candy; sweet, simple and delicious!

Stewed Prunes or Prune Whip

1 lb. prunes, unsulphured
3-4 lemon slices or wedges
pure cold water

In a 2 qt. saucepan soak prunes and lemon in sufficient water to cover about 1". Bring to slow boil, simmer 2-3 minutes, stir. Set aside few hours or refrigerate overnight. Prunes will puff up, juice will become thick like syrup. Store prunes in glass jars in refrigerator. **Prune Whip:** Remove prune pits (leave lemon if desired); blend prunes and lemon until smooth, adding juice as needed. Spoon purée into small *fruit cups. Delicious for breakfast or simple supper with zwieback.

*To decorate fruit cups: Dip rim of empty fruit cup in honey, then dip in fine coconut. This makes a simple but attractive border. Fill with fruit, chill before serving.

Raisin Breakfast Treat

Soak **raisins** in hot water for a few minutes to soften. Put into blender and puree using the liquid the raisins were soaked in; blend until smooth. A few **sunflower seeds** or **pumpkin seeds** may be blended with the raisins, also some **lemon juice** or **orange zest**. Serve cold with thick **cashew cream** or **coconut milk**.

Dried fruits (facing page) such as raisins, prunes, apples, pears, peaches, and apricots, contain protective health benefits, much like fresh fruit, and can be used as a staple article of diet.

Dried Fruits

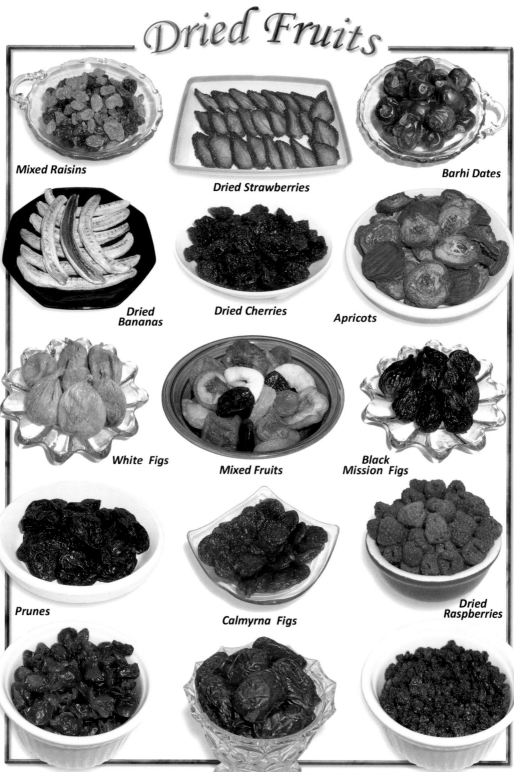

Mixed Raisins

Dried Strawberries

Barhi Dates

Dried Bananas

Dried Cherries

Apricots

White Figs

Mixed Fruits

Black Mission Figs

Prunes

Calmyrna Figs

Dried Raspberries

Dried Cranberries

Medjool Dates

Currants

Fruit Juice Tapioca

Tapioca – a nutritious and easily digested granular starch from the cassava plant.

1 qt. fruit juice - apricot, pineapple, cherry, grape, berry (or favorite combination)
8 Tbs. tapioca granules

In medium saucepan, combine juice with tapioca. Let stand 10 minutes. Bring to a boil while stirring. Add honey and lemon juice to taste, if desired. Chill 15-20 min. Fresh cut fruit or berries may be added. Yield: 8- ½ cup servings

Wonderful Avocados

(*a perfect butter substitute*)

Ways To Serve Avocado:

Sandwich filling or spread, salads, dressing or dips, fruit cups, fruit smoothies, baby food, sherbet, molded salads, topping for waffles, garnish.

Ways To Cut Avocado:

January Fresh Fruit Whip

1 pear, juicy ripe
1 avocado, firm ripe
1 banana, fresh or frozen
pineapple juice or frozen concentrate

Blend just until smooth with juice as needed. A few pine nuts may be added (optional but delicious). Serve in sherbet glasses; garnish with a dollop of soy cream and a red berry, if desired.

Pears and Pineapple

Blend **home canned pears** (skins may be left on) with **unsweetened crushed pineapple. A**dd a little l**emon juice** and **honey**, if desired. Sprinkle on **chopped nuts** or **coconut.** Good on French toast, filled fruit crepes or waffles.

Avocado Fruit Blend

1 ripe avocado
2 ripe bananas
1 Tbs. honey or fruit juice, to taste
½ tsp. orange or lemon zest, opt.

Combine avocado and banana by mashing with fork, add zest and honey to desired consistency. Serve in fruit cups or as a topping for waffles, toast, or zwieback.

Pretty Peach Parfait

Fruit Jell, cut in cubes
Soy Yogurt or Tofu Vanilla Crême
Granola, see recipes
Strawberries, sliced
Bananas, sliced
Peaches, fresh or frozen

In chilled glasses, layer Orange or Cherry Jell (see recipes) with yogurt or crême, your favorite granola, sliced strawberries and bananas. Repeat layers to fill glass. Top with fresh or frozen peach slices, perfectly arranged side by side with an accent of strawberries and blueberries if desired. Delicious!

*Note: See the **7-Layer Fruit and Granola Parfait** recipe and other delicious Parfaits in chapter: Desserts.*

Raspberry Orange Jell Parfait

Red Raspberry Agar Jell
Orange Agar Jell
Pineapple chunks
Strawberries
Cream

Cut ¾" cubes of Red Raspberry Agar Jell and Orange Agar Jell, (see recipes). Gently layer ½ cup of each raspberry and orange jells with ½ cup pineapple chunks and cream, (see recipes). Top with sliced strawberries. Use your creativity to garnish this light, refreshing treat!

Frosty Fruit Parfait

So simple and fun, even children will love to assemble their own parfait, and eat it too!

⅓ cup Soy Yogurt or Tofu Vanilla Cream
⅓ cup Peach Chunks, fresh or frozen
⅓ cup Blueberries, fresh or frozen
⅓ cup sliced Strawberries
¼ cup sliced Bananas
¼ cup Granola, see recipes

Layer fresh or frozen fruits with granola and yogurt or cream (see recipes). Try different fruits (apricots, kiwi, oranges, pears, grapes, apples) creating your own design. A healthy way to introduce new fruits, even to the most finicky eater. Serving: 1-2

Fresh Berry Topping

A simply delicious, good-for-you topping, on waffles, French toast, crepes, pancakes, biscuits, etc. Use your favorite berries in season, alone, or combine 2 or 3 varieties for a colorful combination.

1½ cups unsweetened frozen juice concentrate (white grape, raspberry, or other)
1¼ cups pure water
1 Tbs. fresh lemon juice or ½ tsp. lemon zest
⅓ cup granulated tapioca
8 cups fresh berries (strawberries, blueberries, raspberries, or other)

Combine juice and water together in saucepan. Add tapioca granules, stir and set aside to soften (15 min). Bring to boil while stirring; reduce heat, simmer until thickened and clear. Remove from heat; add berries (sliced, whole, or chopped), and lemon juice or zest.

Berry-Good Fruit Topping

Rich in antioxidants, vitamin C, and nutrients that protect against cancer, aging and heart disease.

4 cups fresh or frozen blueberries, strawberries, raspberries, etc.
½ cup white grape juice concentrate + ½ cup pure water
2 Tbs. arrowroot starch
½ tsp. lemon zest or 1 tsp. lemon juice
2 Tbs. honey, optional

Wash berries; remove stems and leaves. Combine juice, water, arrowroot, and pinch of salt. Stir over low heat, until thickened. Add blueberries, lemon and honey. Heat but do not cook berries. This is delicious over whole grain toast, waffles, crepes or cereal.

Plum Cups

When a plum puckers up, it's a prune!

2 cups sliced pears, firm ripe
3 cups plum chunks, red and blue

Toss fruit together with a little **Mint Sauce** or **honey**. Fill sherbet cups. Top with **Soy Whipped Cream**, if desired. Serves 4.

Strawberry Pignolia Purée

2 cups strawberries, fresh or frozen, thawed
1 Tbs. raw honey or honeycomb
½ cup pignolia-pine nuts

Blend together until creamy smooth. Chill. Delicious over fruit filled crêpes or salad.

Cherries on Toast

1 cup apple juice or water
1 Tbs. arrowroot powder
pinch of sea salt
¼ cup honey
dash of fresh lemon juice
1 qt. pitted cherries

Thicken juice with arrowroot, stirring while bringing to boil to avoid lumps. Add honey, salt, lemon juice, and cherries. Heat till warmed through. Serve over nut-buttered toast, waffles or zwieback cubes.

Marionberry Cobbler

These large black, juicy sweet berries, originating in Oregon, are perfect for this deep dish fruit cobbler with thick crumb crust.

½ cup grape juice
3 Tbs. tapioca, granules
12 oz. white grape/raspberry juice
  concentrate
8 cups marionberries*
3 cups crumb crust or granola

In a large pan, combine grape juice and tapioca. Let stand 5 minutes. Bring to a boil, while stirring and adding the juice concentrate. Stir until blended. Gently fold in the marionberries (rinsed and drained), or other berry combination of your choice. Place berry mixture in glass baking dish. Cover with crumb crust or pie crust (See recipes). Bake in a 375° oven for 30-35 min. until berries are bubbly and crust is golden. Serve with **cashew cream** or **soy yogurt**.

* Blueberries, Blackberries, Boysenberries, Raspberries, can substitute.

Cherry Cobbler

5-6 cups pitted tart cherries
½ cup honey
¼ cup cherry-apple, frozen juice
  concentrate
1 Tbs. tapioca granules
Crumb Crust, (recipes in Dessert chapter)

In a large bowl combine the cherries (fresh, frozen or canned), with the honey, juice concentrate and tapioca. Let stand 10 minutes. Meanwhile, prepare the crumb crust. (can be made ahead and kept in the freezer for quick use). Transfer cherry mixture to a glass baking dish. Sprinkle with crumb crust. Bake at 350° uncovered for 30-35 minutes or until filling is bubbly and topping is golden brown. Good served warm or cold. Top with **Soy Cream** if desired.

Cantaloupe Cup

Cut cantaloupe cups as pictured. Scoop out seeds. Fill with mixed fresh fruit or berries sweetened with honey.

Jellied Cranberry Sauce

A holiday must! You can make this at home with naturally sweet juice – quick, easy, delicious!

3 cups pure cranberry grape juice
½ cup pure water
1 Tbs. agar powder
½ cup dried cranberries

Dissolve agar in the water, add 1 cup of the juice, bring to boil. Simmer 1 minute; add dried cranberries, simmer 1 more minute. Add remaining 2 cups juice. Pour in mold (a juice can works well), refrigerate. Allow 3-4 hours to set before slicing.

Slimmerboard

The perfect supper to serve on a hot summer day!

In the center of a large platter place half of a watermelon cut and filled with 1" melon cubes. Serve plain or arrange slices of cantaloupe, honeydew, and pineapple around watermelon.

Melon Fruit Bowl

Make melon balls using a small scoop. Toss lightly. Juice may be drained - a delicious drink! For color contrast use: Watermelon balls, Honeydew balls, Cantaloupe balls (red, green, and orange). Melon balls freeze well for later use. (see chapter - Misc.)

How to Cut and Serve Mango

Cut a thick slice from each side of flat mango pit

Using a sharp knife, score mango into small cubes

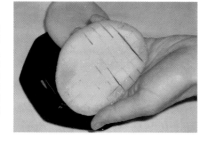

(be careful not to cut through skin).

Mango Peach Mousse

½ cups fresh cut mangos or peaches
½ cup soft or silken tofu, rinsed
¼ cup honey, agave or fructose
¼ tsp. coconut or vanilla extract
2 tsp. Instant Clear-Jel®

In a food processor or blender place 3 cups of fruit, tofu, sweetening and flavors. Blend until smooth, then slowly sprinkle in the instant Clear-Jel, while blending. Divide the mixture into 4 dishes. Top with remaining slices of fruit; sprinkle with **toasted coconut**, if desired. Cover and freeze 1 hour, or chill 1-2 hours until set.

Fold mango back, exposing cubes, "hedgehog style"

*Below: **The Manila variety of mango (also called Champagne) is creamy and sweet. Its intense yellow color indicates its richness in beta-caroten-provitamin A.***

Ready to serve and enjoy eating, or cut from skin for fruit salad

Creamy Tapioca Banana Pudding

½ cup tapioca granules
1 qt. soy vanilla or cashew nut milk
2 Tbs. agave or honey, to taste
1 tsp. pure vanilla, opt.
2-3 bananas, diced, sliced
½ cup pineapple chunks, optional

Mix tapioca and milk in medium sauce-pan. Let stand 10 minutes. Cook on medium heat, stirring constantly until mixture comes to a full boil. Add honey and vanilla; remove from heat. Pudding thickens as it cools. Add banana and/or pineapple chunks. Serve warm or chilled. Store leftover pudding in refrigerator. Yield: 8-½ cup servings.

Berry Tapioca Pudding

Follow recipe for **Creamy Tapioca Banana Pudding**. While pudding is warm, add ½ cup raspberries, boysenberries, or blackberries, instead of pineapple; omit vanilla.

Rainbow Fruit Layers

Colorful fresh fruit is layered with fruit jell to make a refreshing, satisfying breakfast or supper. One large glass is enough for two; serve with cornbread, muffins or crackers.

Tall glasses, 20 oz.
Tangerine sections
Lemon agar jell, cubed
Grape agar jell, cubed
Mashed avocados
Soy Whip Cream
Pomegranate
Sliced bananas
Strawberry on top

Agar Prune Preparation

(a simple and gentle laxative- aids peristalsis)

½ pound prunes, pitted
2 slices of lemon, unsprayed
3 cups pure cold water
2 Tbs. agar flakes
1 Tbs. lemon juice

Place prunes and lemon in cold water. Bring to a boil, stir, simmer 3-4 minutes. Let stand a few hours until juice is dark like syrup from prunes. Drain juice into a saucepan, add just enough water to make 3 cups, add agar, boil gently until dissolved. Add the lemon juice, a little honey to taste, if desired. Pit prunes, stuff with nut meats (opt.); arrange prunes and lemon slices in bottom of glass bowl or mold. Pour the warm juice over prunes. Refrigerate to cool and set.

Creamy Date Whip

Dates are high in complex carbohydrates-a good energy source. The sweet nuggets provide a healthy dose of potassium and iron, as well as fiber.

¾ cup cashew or almond milk
8-10 pitted dates, soft
2 tsp. flaxseed meal
½ tsp. orange or lemon zest
1 tsp. lemon juice

Blend all ingredients together until smooth. Add lemon juice last. Delicious on sprouted wheat, cooked hot cereal, toast or waffles.

Fruit Salads

*"Use simple wholesome food. Fruit in its natural state is excellent...
eat freely of the fresh grapes, apples, peaches, pears, berries, and all
other kinds of fruit."* E. G. White, **Diet and Foods,** pg. 309

Fruits rich in antioxidants include blueberries, grapes, raspberries,
cranberries, strawberries, kiwi, and citrus fruits. These foods may help
to improve circulation, enhance memory, and slow
down the aging process.

Florida Fruit Bowl

Citrus fruits, such as grapefruit and orange, are excellent served for breakfast

Grapefruit sections
Orange or tangerine sections
Grapes, green or red, cut in half
Apple, sweet diced, opt.

Combine cut orange and grapefruit sections with grapes and diced apple. Fill fruit cups; serve with **Orange Sauce** or **Lemon Sauce**, if desired.

Citrus - Avocado

Oranges, peeled, sliced in circles
Avocado, peeled, sliced in wedges

Alternate orange slices and avocado slices on plate. Good served for breakfast or light supper.

Apple Fruit Salad

2 quarts chopped sweet apples
2 cups grapes, seeded halves
3 tangerines, seeded sections
¾ cup pecans or walnuts, chopped
3 figs, fresh sliced or dried chopped
¼ cup frozen orange
   or apple juice concentrate

Combine all fruits. Add juice concentrate or honey to taste. Serve at breakfast with zwieback or toast and nut butter.

Variations:
Combine apples with grapefruit, orange, coconut, dates, banana

Filled Avocado Halves

Avocados*, firm and ripe
Bananas or berries, chopped
Apples or pineapple, diced
Nut meats, chopped

Cut and peel avocado halves; remove pit. Fill cavity* with combination of diced fruit and nuts, sweetened with honey or frozen orange juice concentrate. Arrange avocado halves on plate with crackers and clusters of grapes.

*Florida avocados work best – the larger pit, when removed, gives more filling space.

Kiwi Pomegranate Grapefruit Salad

These fruits are rich in vitamin C, potassium and folate, essential in maintaining a healthy immune system. Be sure to wear an apron when preparing the pomegranate, a squirt of juice can stain!

2 kiwi fruit, peeled and cut into slices
1 large pomegranate, peeled
1 large grapefruit, peeled
fruit juice dressing, opt.

Slice kiwi in circles; remove membrane from pomegranate seeds. Divide grapefruit into sections and remove thin skin. Arrange fruit on individual serving plates. Drizzle with your favorite fruit juice dressing, if desired. Servings: 2

Waldorf Salad

An old time favorite dating back to the Waldorf Astoria Hotel in N.Y. For a change, why not try fresh pears instead of apples?

2-3 red apples, or pears, coarsely chopped
1½ tsp. lemon or lime juice
½ cup green grapes, seeded halves
⅓ cup chopped walnuts or pecans, toasted
¼ cup snipped pitted dates
¼ cup raisins or dried cherries
⅓ cup Soy Yogurt or Palm Fruit Dressing

In a medium bowl toss apples or pears with lemon juice. Add the grapes, nuts, dates, raisins. Gently fold in **Yogur**t or **Palm Fruit Dressing** to coat mixture. Serve immediately or cover and chill for up to 6 hours.

Cranberry - Apple Pecan Cup

Naturally sweet, healthful, and delicious!

Follow recipe for **Cranberry Fruit Relish, (see Fruit chapter)** using **frozen cranberry/apple unsweetened juice concentrate** instead of orange juice concentrate. Add **⅓ cup chopped pecans**. Let stand to marinate flavors. Garnish with **pecans halves** or **toasted coconut shreds**, if desired. The perfect start for the special occasion breakfast!

Fun and Easy

Fruit Wagon

4 pineapple
  or apple circles
2 strips pineapple,
  4" long (use
  hard centers)
1 slice whole
  wheat toast
  with nut butter
and honey, or 1 waffle
2 bunches grapes, pineapple, apple,
  avocado chunks
dates, figs, stuffed with nuts

1. Fasten the pineapple or apple circles to the ends of each 4" long pineapple strip. (use toothpicks as needed)
2. Lay slice of bread (or waffle), with nut butter and honey, on top to form wagon bed.
3. Load wagon with fruit: pineapple, avocado chunks, apple, dates, figs, or grapes.
4. Use a shorter strip of pineapple or banana to form handle of wagon

Cherry Salad

Cherries, pitted
Pineapple, chunks
Banana, sliced or diced
frozen orange juice, opt.

Pit cherries. Mix with pineapple chunks. Add a little frozen (thawed) juice concentrate. Scoop into fruit cups on layer of sliced banana.

Note:
Soak banana in some pineapple juice to keep from darkening.

Banana Split Fruit Salad

Bananas - ripe speckled
Grapes - red, green or Blueberries
Pineapple - chunks

Peel 1 banana for each person; split in half lengthwise. Sprinkle with a lemon juice. Make 3 mounds of fruit (different colored grapes, blueberries or pineapple) on top of split banana. Serve with **Soy Whipped Cream**.

Frozen Banana Treats

Peel banana, cut in half. Roll **banana** in **lemon juice** mixed with **honey**, then roll in finely chopped **filberts** or **coconut**. Freeze.

Tropical Fuit Cup

1 orange, peeled
1 avocado or banana, peeled
1 cup pineapple chunks
fresh coconut shreds

Cut orange sections in half, remove seeds. Dice avocado and banana, add pineapple. Mix fruit in bowl with a little shredded coconut. Fill 2 fruit cups- enjoy!

Recipes for Kids

Fanny Fruit Doll Salad

½ **pear**
½ **peach**
1 banana
Berries
Soy Cream
Piece of apple

Arrange fruit on individual salad plate using:

Head – Pear half, small end down
Body – Peach half
    rounded side up
Arms – Banana sliced
    in half
Skirt – Triangular
    mound of berries
Hair – Berries set in
    soy whipped cream
Eyes – 2 blueberries
Mouth – piece of red
    apple
Feet – 2 dabs of soy
    cream

Painted Bunting Bird Salad

(Child's idea)

Use fruit to form the body of bird:

Purple plum – head
Banana mashed - stuffing for body
Apple strips – red breast
Avocado slices – wings and back
Pineapple pieces – beak, eyes, feet

Arrange **chopped nuts** or **shredded coconut** around bird to form nest.

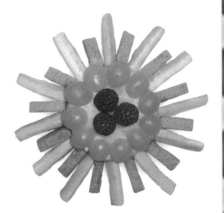

Fruit Petal Salads

A wonderful way to serve fresh or dried fruit and nuts. Children enjoy making and eating the flowers - try some simple combinations. Here are some suggestions:

For the center of each flower, use a **pineapple circle, fresh grated coconut, mound of berries, cherries or grapes.** Around the center form petals using a variety of fruits:

Apple wedges
Dates, stuffed with nuts
Banana slices
Avocado slices
Kiwi or mango slices
Melon balls or slices
Dried apricots, peaches, apples, walnuts

Blueberry Rice Salad

Blueberries are an excellent source of antioxidants, flavonoids, vitamin C, A, E, fiber, potassium, and folate. Blueberries contain medicinal properties that assist in improved circulation, memory, heart health, diabetes and cancer protection.

3 cups fresh blueberries
2 cups cooked cold rice
½ cup flaked coconut
¼ cup honey or agave, to taste
½ cup pecans, filberts or almonds
Soy Whip Cream Topping, to taste

Mix blueberries, cold brown rice, coconut, honey, and chopped nuts together. Fold in **Soy Whip Cream** (approx. 1 cup). Top with **toasted coconut**. Can be served as a dessert.

Blackberry - Coconut Salad

Wash fresh **blackberries**; fill fruit cup. Surround it with freshly grated **coconut**. Arrange **mango** or **peach slices** on top of coconut. Thread **honey** on berries.

Summer Fruit Salad

2 parts sliced peaches
2 parts fresh blueberries
1 part whole fresh raspberries
1 part strawberries, sliced
1 part kiwi, peeled and sliced
1 part bananas, sliced
½ part grapes, green, seeded
½ part orange sections, cut
½ part pineapple or cantaloupe chunks

Toss together with a little **orange juice concentrate, honey**, or **Sesame Seed Sauce**. Serve with toast or bagels and **Pineapple Cream Cheese** (see recipe).

Perfect Golden Salad

Golden Delicious apples
Peaches, fresh sliced
Pineapple, fresh chunks
Cantaloupe, cut in cubes

Mix 3 parts of cubed apples with 1 part each of other fruits, cut in pieces. Serve with **Soy Whipped Cream** or your favorite fruit dressing.

Note: After cutting the apples and peaches, toss the pieces with a mixture of lemon juice and water to prevent the fruit from darkening.

Pineapple Boats

**1 ripe pineapple
with top
2 kiwi, fresh sliced
2 cups strawberries
and/or grapes, sliced
2 cups pineapple,
cut in chunks
2 red apples, diced
1 orange, cut sections
1 banana, sliced**

1. Leave top on fresh pineapple, *or* twist off. Cut pineapple in half lengthwise.

2. Score pineapple as illustrated (page 223), remove from shell, cut into chunks.

3. Toss pineapple chunks with other fresh fruits; add your favorite **fruit dressing**, then refill shells with fruit mixture. Garnish with **fresh shredded coconut**, if desired. Serve for breakfast with whole grain bread, as part of a fruit dinner, or supper.

Pineapple Tofu Salad

Pineapples contain bromelain, a protease with anti-inflammatory, anti-edema properties; pineapple also contain manganese for bone health.

**2 cups fresh tofu
¼ cup chopped walnuts
½ cup chopped dates
1 pineapple, cut in 6 slices**

Lightly mix mashed tofu with walnuts and chopped dates. Fold in **¼ cup Pineapple Fruit Dressing** or your favorite. Place a large scoop of mixed tofu on each slice of pineapple. Servings: 6

Persimmon – Pineapple Salad

Peel and puree **3 large very ripe persimmons**. Add **1 cup crushed pineapple, drained**, and the **juice of ½ lemon**. To the drained pineapple juice add **2 Tbs. honey** and water to make one cup. Add **½ Tbs. agar flakes**. Let set 1 minute, boil 1 minute, cool 1 minute. Fold into fruit; pour into a mold and chill until set. Serve with **Soy Cream**.

Gingered Fruit Salad

2 cups fresh pineapple chunks
2 cups peaches, peeled,
   sliced or chunks
2 cups cubed cantaloupe
2 cups blue and or green grapes,
   (remove seeds) or seedless
1 cup fresh strawberries, sliced
1 orange, peeled and sectioned
1 cup fresh or frozen blueberries

Grape Salad

Red, blue, or green grapes
Strawberries, sliced
Apple, diced
Pineapple chunks
Banana, sliced
Orange sections
Avocado
Walnut or pecan halves or pieces

Make a fruit salad mostly of red, blue
or green grapes, (cut and seeded). Add
some apple, strawberries, fresh pineapple, banana, orange, avocado, and
nuts. Toss with **Sesame Seed Sauce** or
Palm Fruit Dressing. Fill fruit cups.

Dressing:

1 cup soy yogurt, vanilla
2 Tbs. soy mayonnaise
2 tsp. sucanat
1 tsp. fresh grated ginger

In a large bowl combine the pineapple, cantaloupe, grapes, orange,
strawberries, and blueberries. For the
dressing: stir together yogurt, mayonnaise, sucanat and ginger. Serve
in fruit bowls or on salad plates. Top
each serving with dressing.

Avocado - Mango or Peach Salad

When **mangos** are not available, **peaches** may be used in their place. Peel mango, dice, or cut in slices; drizzle on lime juice. Arrange in circle for a border. Fill center with **avocado rings** dipped in **lime juice** mixed with **honey**. Garnish with **berries**, if desired.

Gelatin Salads

Animal gelatin is a protein processed from beef bones and cartilage, or the skin of pigs.

*Fresh or frozen pineapple, papaya, and kiwi juice contain an enzyme that breaks down the animal gelatin so it will not set. However, when using vegetable gelatin (such as **Agar** or **Kojel®**) these fresh fruits or juices can be used with no adverse effects. For vegetable gelatin to 'set up' it must be dissolved completely in boiling liquid. Lightly spray mold with cooking spray before filling.*

To Unmold a Gelatin Salad:

Quickly dip mold (for 5 seconds) into a pan or sink of hot water up to line of gelatin. Loosen an edge of the salad with the tip of a knife. Tilt the mold slightly to allow air in, and to break the vacuum. Rotate the mold to loosen all sides. Place a serving platter on top of the mold, and while holding the mold and the plate firmly, turn the mold upside down. Gently shake mold, carefully lifting it up and off salad on platter.

Strawberry Star

Serve as a summer salad, for holidays or special occasions. It's as pretty as it is good!

Follow recipe for **Red Raspberry Jell**, using **3-4 cups fresh or frozen Strawberries** instead of raspberries. **Kojel® or Gefen®** may substitute for **agar flakes.** Decorate bowl before filling, by spreading a thin layer of **honey** on rim of bowl, then turn bowl onto a plate of **shredded coconut** and press firmly.

Royal Cranberry Mold

1 cup fresh or frozen cranberries,
 coarsely ground or chopped
1 cup grated or chopped apples
1 20-oz. can pineapple tidbits,
 drain and reserve juice
¾ cup raw honey
½ cup chopped nuts, pecans or walnuts
½ cup seeded grape halves, red or green
1 Tbs. agar, granulated or 2 Tbs. flakes
1½ cups pineapple juice
 or cranberry apple juice

Combine first 4 ingredients in a bowl and set aside. In a saucepan sprinkle the agar into ½ cup water.Let stand 1 min. to soften. Add ½ cup hot water. Boil 1 minute until agar is dissolved. Stir in the 1½ cups pineapple or cranberry apple juice. Transfer to a mixing bowl. Chill about 30 minutes or until partially set. Fold the cranberry mixture and nuts into the partially set agar mixture. Spoon into a ring mold. Cover and refrigerate 3-4 hours or overnight until firm. Serve plain, with your favorite topping or **Soy Whipped Cream**. Delicious!

Cranberry Orange Gel Salad

This salad has been a "must" at holidays and special occasions. It's as pretty as it is good- for- you!

3 cups (1 pkg.) cranberries
2-3 apples (Fuji, Delicious)
2 navel oranges with skins
½ cup chopped pecans
 or walnuts
1-20 oz. can crushed pineapple in juice
5 Tbs. Kojel® or agar flakes
½ cup pure boiling water
1½ cups raspberry /apple frozen
 juice concentrate

Wash cranberries, apples, and oranges. Process through a food/meat grinder that has ¼ " round holes. Let set 2-3 hours to combine flavors. Dissolve gelatin in boiling water, add juice, fruit mixture, nuts and pineapple. Pour into a ring mold. Chill until set.

To unmold salad: Fill sink or pan with very hot water. Dip mold in water 2-3 seconds (in-out). Turn upside down onto crystal platter. Servings: 8-10

Orange Agar Fruit Jell

Mix:

2½ Tbs. agar flakes with **1 cup cold water**

Let set 1 minute. Add:

1 cup hot water

Boil 2 minutes. Add:

1-12 oz. can frozen orange juice
2 Tbs. fresh lemon juice
¼ cup raw honey
4 cups mixed fruit, fresh, frozen or canned

Add **2-3 sliced bananas** and the mixed fruit (grapes, diced peaches, pears, pineapple, blueberries, etc.) Pour into a mold, let set in refrigerator, undisturbed. Fruit jell will set in 3-4 hrs.

Cherry - Grape Agar Jell

(pictured - below)

Fresh grapes and pure natural grape juice contain a wide spectrum of nutrients including simple sugars (glucose and fructose), B-complex vitamins, vitamin C, iron, potassium, selenium, and fiber (pectin).

**2½ cups pure grape
    or cherry juice
½ cup pure water
2 Tbs. agar flakes**

Stir water and agar together, let stand 2 minutes. Bring water to boil, simmer 1 minute. Add juice; pour into glass bowl or fruit mold. Refrigerate to chill and set.

Note: Blue and red seeded grapes or cherries may be added to Jell before setting. Unmold onto plate and decorate with fresh fruit or flowers, if desired.

Red Raspberry Jell

Mix:

2 Tbs. agar flakes with 1 cup cold water

Let set 1 minute. Add:

½ cup hot water or juice

Boil 2 minutes. Add:

**1 cup white grape or raspberry juice
⅓ cup raw honey
3 Tbs. white grape /raspberry frozen
    juice concentrate
½ Tbs. fresh lemon juice
1 tsp. grated orange zest
¼ cup chopped pecans, opt.
fresh ripe raspberries**

Cover bottom of glass mold with a layer of fresh raspberries. Pour jell over fruit. Chill to set. Repeat process to form layers of fruit and jell. When firm and set, unmold onto salad plate. Top with fresh raspberries and **Soy Whipped Cream.**

Avocado Salad Mold

2 level Tbs. agar flakes
1 ¼ cups pure water
1 cup hot pear or apricot juice
1 cup more cold juice
¼ cup light raw honey
1 Tbs. fresh lemon juice
Avocado and Mango slices

In saucepan, stir agar into water, let set 1 minute. Bring to boil, add the hot juice, boil 1-2 minutes to dissolve agar. Add remaining cup of cold juice, honey and lemon. Set in refrigerator to cool and slightly jell (15-20 minutes). Meanwhile, lightly spray 1-quart mold with cooking spray. Decorate with slices of mango and avocado. Pour agar jell slowly over fruit in mold. Cover and refrigerate undisturbed at least 3 hours until firm.
To unmold salad: Set the mold in a bowl or sink filled with very warm water for several seconds until the salad edges appear to pull away from the mold. Unmold salad by turning upside down onto serving plate. Fill center with **sliced bananas /soy whip cream.**

Optional: Garnish platter with clusters of red, blue, and green grapes, or other fresh fruits.

Pineapple Cream Cheese

Recipe in chapter,
Page 453,
Sandwiches
& Spreads

Fruit Pizza: Berry

Choose a variety of fresh fruits in season to make a sweet pizza. Use your artistic skills to create a topping that is healthy and attractive. Remember "We eat with our eyes"

Make a Crust - See recipes in *Desserts*:
Sweet Dough, Barley Nut Pie Crust,
  No-bake Nutty Crust, or your favorite

Topping:
Pineapple Cream Cheese
  or Tofu "Cream Cheese" (see recipes)
Fresh Fruit: (peeled, sliced, halved,
  diced, whole) Apples, Blueberries,
Pineapple, Grapes, toasted Cashew halves,
Strawberries, Bananas, Kiwi fruit,
  Blackberries, toasted Coconut, etc*

1. Pat your favorite cookie dough or pie crust into a 12" non-stick pizza pan.
2. Bake at 375° for 10-12 minutes until golden brown; cool crust.
3. Spread with a thick layer of plain or **Pineapple Tofu "Cream Cheese"**.
4. Arrange the fruit on top alternating colors to form a design with eye appeal.
5. Brush fruit with cooled **Orange Sauce**, if desired (see recipe). Chill pizza.

More Fruit Pizza Combinations:

1. apples, strawberries, green grapes, peaches, blueberries, crushed filberts
2. raspberries, star fruit, bananas, blue grapes or bing cherries, slivered almonds
3. apricot halves, pitted dates, apple slices, pineapple rings, toasted coconut shreds
4. mandarin orange, avocado wedges, pineapple chunks, apple slices, pecans
5. dried apricots, dried pears, dried banana chips, golden raisins, toasted almonds

Fruit Pizza: Pineapple Peach

Use your culinary skills and create a beautiful, colorful arrangement that is sure to awaken the appetite for nourishing fresh fruit.

Pineapple Cream Cheese
  or Tofu "Cream Cheese" (see recipes)
Peaches or strawberries, sliced lengthwise
1-30 oz. can pineapple chunks
  or tidbits, drained
2-3 bananas, sliced, dipped in pine-
  apple juice
2-3 kiwi fruit, peeled, sliced in circles
  or wedges
Pecan or walnut halves
Sweet Dough, Pizza Dough, Stir-N-Roll
  Pie Crust, or favorite crust
  (see recipes in Breads
  or Desserts)

Make the crust, press into a pizza pan, bake at 375° for 10-12 min. until golden brown. Cool crust. Spread with a generous amount of **Pineapple Cream Cheese** (see recipe). Arrange the fruit, alternating colors, textures and shapes to form a pleasing design. Garnish with nuts, if desired, and enjoy a little extra protein besides! Get the children involved in making a miniature fruit pizza- a class in artistic design! The variety of fruit and combinations are endless!
Yield: 1 extra-large or 2 medium pizzas.

Fruit Kabobs

*Lots of eye appeal! Simple,
Colorful and Delicious!*

**Fruits: Apricot halves, kiwi
slices, whole strawberries, pineapple
chunks, cherries, banana logs, papaya,
starfruit, or peach pieces.**

Assemble fresh ripe fruit pieces on
bamboo skewers for a ready-to eat-
appetizer, special breakfast or supper
occasion. Serve with **Creamy Lemon
Fruit Topping** or your favorite **yogurt**
(see recipes).

Lesson From Nature

The horse is big and fat and round,
But eats the grains that do abound.

The camel who bears his burden long,
On natural food he is made strong.

The ox is wide and thick and stout,
And lives on grasses grown about.

The elephant, so great and strong,
With hay and grain his days prolong.

The dinosaur – his years amaze,
Yet vegetation stretched his days.

A baboon's strength is not from meats,
For fruits and vegetables he eats.

If fruits and grains, and grass and hay,
Give animals such strength each day –

Then give me, too, that simple fare
That Mother Nature does prepare.

If we would have endurance at last –
To finish each small important task –

Than we should follow God's simple plan
And eat the good fruits of the land.

G.C. Hoskin (Adapted – R.H.)

Grains

Index - CHAPTER 8

Grains

252

Ten Talents

Chapter cover photo: ***Wholesome Whole Grains Included in this Chapter***

Grains and Cereals

GRAINS are one of nature's abundant luxuries, and have been a staple super food in each generation for all mankind. As part of the original diet provided for man, whole grains and the products made from them, are the foods that furnish the foundation on which to build a healthy body. Simply prepared and properly combined with fruits, nuts and vegetables, make the most healthful diet. Grains and cereals cost little and are fundamental in planning nutritious menus for the optimal plant-based diet. Grains are a source of complex carbohydrates, proteins, vitamins and minerals, and an essential ingredient in many of the healthy recipes found in TEN TALENTS.

"It is a mistake to suppose that muscular strength depends on the use of animal food. The needs of the system can be better supplied, and more vigorous health can be enjoyed, without its use. The GRAINS, with fruits, nuts, and vegetables, contain all the nutritive properties necessary to make good blood." **Diet and Foods** p. 313

1. Grains should be *thoroughly cooked*. (sprouted grains are the exception).
2. Grains should be *thoroughly chewed* – digestion begins in the mouth.
3. Sweeten grains with fresh or dried fruit, date sugar, or raw honey (avoid refined sugar). For added nutrition top with ground seeds, malted nuts, nut cream or milk.

Note: Most cereal grains, except those that are sprouted, require 1 hour or more of cooking or steaming. This is necessary in order to properly change the starch so it can be easily digested. Sprouting grains not only changes the starch but adds to the nutritional value. *Sprouted grains*, such as wheat, can be eaten raw in a variety of healthy treats, lightly steamed for cereal, or added to bread recipes. (see chapter on sprouting and recipes using sprouts).

The soluble and insoluble fiber found in plant foods (grains, legumes, vegetable and fruits) is essential in maintaining proper weight, low cholesterol levels and a healthy digestive system. On the contrary, animal foods are high in fat and cholesterol, contain no fiber, and are detrimental to health.

Rice Polish or Bran – Layers of bran are removed during process of polishing brown rice into white rice. Rice polish contains valuable vitamins and minerals which are lost in the refining process. High in B1, Niacin, and Phosphorus. Also contains Iron, Potassium, and Calcium in lesser amounts. Use much like wheat germ, in breads, on cereal, granola or fruit.

Fiber – Whole grain cereals and whole-wheat breads are excellent sources of fiber. Fiber is extremely important. Research evidence links inadequate fiber intake with conditions such as constipation, heart disease, diabetes, and some types of cancer.

Soluble fiber – slows digestion and helps the body absorb vital nutrients.

Insoluble fiber – adds bulk to the stool, helping foods pass through the stomach and intestines.

"Grains used for porridge or 'mush' should have several hours' cooking..."
Diet & Foods, pg. 314

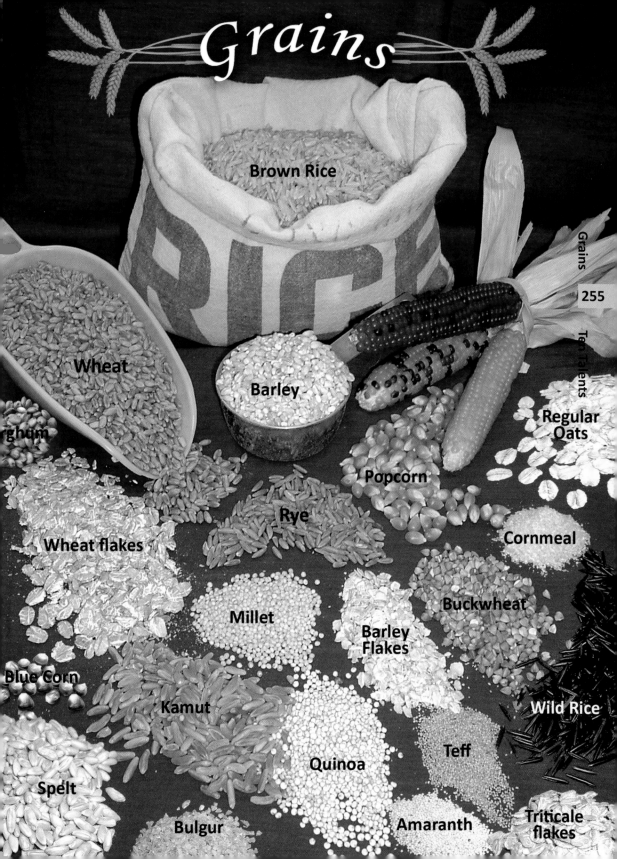

Grains

Brown Rice

Wheat

Barley

Regular Oats

rghum

Popcorn

Rye

Cornmeal

Wheat flakes

Buckwheat

Millet

Barley Flakes

Blue Corn

Wild Rice

Kamut

Teff

Quinoa

Spelt

Bulgur

Amaranth

Triticale flakes

Grain Glossary

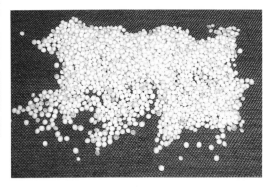

Amaranth – These tiny ancient seeds of the Aztecs empire now making a comeback in American cuisine. Amaranth is a complete protein, supplying all the essential amino acids. It is ground into flour and used in baking, or toasted and cooked with other grains.

Barley – One of the oldest cultivated cereals; a staple food in Egyptian culture. Barley is lower in fiber than most grains, (excellent for those with fiber intolerance or allergies to other grains). Barley is mild in flavor and easily digested; can be used in baking, soups, meatless dishes, or breakfast cereal. Hulled barley is more nutritious than pearled barley.

Bran – Outer layers of whole grain. Rich in fiber, vitamins and minerals. Wheat bran is mostly used for its laxative action. Oat bran is widely used for its cholesterol lowering properties. It is preferable to consume bran in its natural state, with the rest of the kernel.

Buckwheat – The triangular seed of the buckwheat plant (not a true grain) cooked as a cereal. Native to central Asia; a staple food in Russia. Buckwheat groats also known as Kasha, is a good source of rutin (for healthy capillaries, arteries and gums), and other nutrients including protein (lysine-rich, an amino acid lacking in wheat and other grains), magnesium, phosphorus, iron, B-vitamins, vitamin E and fiber. Buckwheat is very nutritious and has a distinctive nutty flavor. Buckwheat flour is used in pancakes, and crepes.

Bulgur – Parched cracked wheat with the same nutritional value as whole wheat. The baking (toasting) process produces a sweet-nutty flavor and shortens the cooking time. Bulgar is the result of soaking, cooking, drying, and cracking whole wheat kernels.

Corn – A broad term for cereal grains including wheat and oats. Corn is a major food source in Central America and Mexico, and widely used in the U.S. Whole corn in many forms (sweet corn, popcorn, cornmeal, grits, corn flour) contains magnesium, calcium, B-vitamins, iron, vitamin A, protein, complex carbohydrates and fat.
Blue Corn – Provides more nutrition than yellow corn; being higher in protein, complex carbohydrates, and trace minerals. Hopi Indians used it to prepare for long journeys and strenuous activities.

Couscous – The most tiny of pasta; made from hard wheat middling; yields a glutenous durum semolina wheat flour. Often used in place of rice, mistakenly thought of as a grain. The common form is pre-cooked; the traditional brown couscous requires longer cooking.

Kamut – An ancient grain thought to have originated in the Nile valley of Egypt. One of the largest grains; a kernel, when cooked is two-three times the size and softer than common wheat. Kamut contains higher levels of protein; and other nutrients. A chewy textured grain with a rich buttery flavor.

Millet – A small but valuable seed grain of the world. The principle source of protein for millions in Africa, China, India and used widely by the healthy Hunzas. Millet contains 11 % protein, (a little more than wheat, rice and corn), all the essential amino acids, iron, B-vitamins, calcium, and other minerals. A nutritious, alkaline, virtually gluten-free, golden colored grain suitable for infant feeding, cereal, and flour for flatbread.

Oats – A popular grain grown in the U.S. and cool moist regions of Scotland, Russia, and Canada. The nutritional value of oats remains intact during processing; the germ and bran and not removed. In addition to its lowering cholesterol properties, oats are a good source of protein,fiber and many essential nutrients including the B-vitamins, vitamin E, calcium and silicon. Oats, in various forms- oat groats, steel-cut oats, rolled oats, quick oats, and oat flour, are used in heart-healthy breakfast cereals, in baking, bread, and baby foods.

Quinoa – The mother grain of the Incas; known as the "supergrain". A complete protein, containing all the amino acids. Native to the Andean highlands, quinoa comes closer than any food in supplying all life-sustaining nutrients. Its small starchy seeds are cultivated for food, or ground into flour. Quinoa is tasty as breakfast cereal or added to other dishes.

Rice, Brown – The grain highest in B-complex vitamins. It is the staple crop for over half of the world's population; it has a balance of nutrients that make it a superior food. There are numerous different kinds of rice, ranging from long to medium and short grain. Rice in its various forms is boiled or steamed; and used in a variety of vegetarian dishes.

Rice, Wild – Minnesota state grain- the only grain native to North America. A tall aquatic perennial grass yielding an edible grain that is an entirely different species than domesticated rice. For centuries wild rice has been cultivated by Native Americans of the Minnesota lake region. Wild rice is high in protein, twice as much as white rice, and contains iron phosphorus, calcium, potassium, and B vitamins. Wild rice has its own distinctive flavor, and may be served as a side dish, in soups, stuffing, crepes, or your favorite casserole. Cooked wild rice freezes well, and is convenient to have on hand! Wild rice will keep indefinitely if stored in a closed container in a cool dry place.

Rye – A hearty nutritious grain, with a strong flavor, used in much of northern Europe and Russia. Rye often grows in adverse soil conditions and has the greatest winter hardiness of all grains. Rye flour is mostly used in combination with wheat in making wholesome dark bread. Sprouted, cracked, or whole rye, is great as a cereal, in casseroles, or pilafs.

Sorghum – Several types of Old World tropical grasses cultivated for its many uses. Grain sorghums include milo, maize, etc; ranging in color from white, yellow, red, or brown. In some countries the grain is used as a cereal food or ground into flour for flatbreads; its nutritive value similar to white corn. The juice from sweet sorghum is made into syrup.

Spelt – In the Bible Spelt is also referred to as fitches (Ezekiel 4:9) Spelt is among the original grains known to man. Spelt contains more protein, fats and crude fiber than wheat, and is a good alternative for wheat-free diets. Can be sprouted and used in making bread, in place of wheat, in the same proportions, with good results, or cooked as cereal.

Teff – An important staple Ethiopian crop. A very small nutritious grain, rich in protein, iron, and calcium which yields a gluten-free flour used in making flatbread. Teff varies in color from brown to red, or natural. Best when combined and cooked with other grains.

Triticale – A hybrid of wheat and rye with nut-like flavor. Triticale contains more gluten than rye and a higher protein content and balance of essential amino acids than wheat or rye. Sprouted, whole or flaked triticale is tasty as a breakfast cereal, in pilafs, or bread.

Wheat – The world's most important grain crop dates back to ancient Egypt. The whole wheat berry is a powerhouse of nutrition, containing over 25 vitamins and minerals, protein, fiber, and fat. Wheat gluten is in proper balance to facilitate the rising of bread when kneaded. In addition to bread 'the staff of life' wheat provides wheat germ, wheat bran, wheat germ oil, etc. The kinds of wheat grown– hard winter wheat, hard spring wheat, soft spring wheat, white wheat and durum wheat, are milled to produce a variety of flour including whole wheat, graham flour, pastry flour, gluten flour. Whole kernel wheat can be sprouted.

A Kernel of Wheat

A kernel of wheat, sometimes called the wheat berry, shows the 3 main components of all grains *(bran layers, germ, endosperm)* plus protein, vitamins and minerals, perfectly balanced by the Creator to form a complete unit. The nutritional value derived from the entire kernel (as provided in nature) surpasses the total value of the bran, endosperm, or germ when separated.

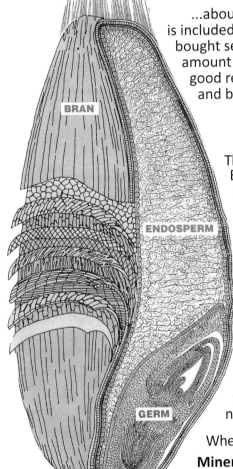

Bran

...about 14 ½ percent of the kernel weight. Bran is included in whole wheat flour and can also be bought separately. The bran layers contain a large amount of fiber, VITAMINS, MINERALS (iron to make good red blood cells and phosphorus for nerves and bones), and a very good quality of PROTEIN.

Endosperm

The inner part of the wheat kernel, called the Endosperm, consists mostly of starch and a small amount of protein. The Endosperm contains almost no vitamins or minerals. White flour is made from this part of the kernel, which is low in those nutrients upon which we depend for our health.

Germ

The embryo, or "wheat germ", is the life giving part from which the wheat plant sprouts, and is one of the richest known sources of B and E vitamins. It also contains valuable protein and fat. In white flour about one-half of the fat is lost. This fat has a high food value, since it contains unsaturated fatty acids and vitamin B1, all of which are nutritionally very important.

Wheat contains these essential minerals and vitamins:

Minerals: Calcium, Iron, Phosphorus, Magnesium, Potassium, Manganese, Copper, Sulphur, Iodine, Fluorine, Chlorine, Sodium, Silicon, Iron, Barium, Silver, and other Trace Minerals.

Vitamins: Thiamine (B_1), Riboflavin (B_2), Niacin, Pantothenic Acid, Pyridoxine (B_6), Biotin (H), Inositol, Choline, Vitamin E, plus at least four other vitamin factors generally found in Bran and Wheat Germ.

Barley Flakes

Mixed Rice

Spelt

Millet

Great Grain Cooking Guide

WHOLE GRAIN, BERRY, or GROAT

Least processed: only inedible outer hull is removed. Cook slowly for several hours or overnight.

Barley, whole (hulled)
Kamut berries, whole
Rye berries, whole
Triticale berries, whole

Buckwheat groats
Oat groats, whole
Spelt berries, whole
Wheat berries, whole

Basic proportions: 1 cup grain + 4 cups (1 qt.) water + ½ tsp. sea salt
Cooking Method: Crock pot, Oven, or Vapor unit.
Yield: 1 cup dry berries = 3-4 cups cooked berries

SMALLER WHOLE GRAINS: CUT, CRACKED, or PROCESSED

Cook slowly 45 minutes- 1 hour or more, depending on size of grain.

Barley, pearled
Cornmeal, coarse
Kasha - toasted buckwheat
Oats, steel cut
Rice, brown: whole, varieties
Wheat, whole cracked

Bulgur, whole, parched
Hominy, hulled corn kernels
Millet, whole
Quinoa, whole (20-30 min)
Teff, whole
Wild Rice, parched

Basic Proportions: 1 cup grain + 3- 4 cups water + ½ tsp. sea salt
Cooking Method: Crock pot, Double boiler, Oven, Skillet Method

PRE-COOKED, CRACKED, STEAMED or ROLLED FLAKES
Steamed to speed-up cooking time: Cook 15-30 min., let set 10 min.

Barley flakes
*Bulgur, coarse cracked
Oats, old-fashioned rolled
Rye flakes
Triticale flakes

Buckwheat, grits cereal
Kamut Flakes
Rice, converted, parboiled
Spelt flakes
Wheat flakes

Basic Proportions: 1 cup grain + 2 - 3 cups water + salt, to taste
(Proportions of grain + water vary with variety of grain and method of cooking)
Cooking Method: Stovetop, Oven, Crock pot

Bulgur wheat (bulgar, bulghur) To make your own: Soak 1 part wheat berries in 3 parts water for 1 hour. Bring to a boil, then simmer berries until tender (all water should be absorbed), or cook on low heat in crock pot overnight. Spread berries on a cookie sheet, bake in 225° oven, stirring occasionally, until dry (about 1 hour). Grind in blender or crush with a rolling pin. **Yield:** 1 cup dry bulgur= about 3 cups cooked.

INSTANT GRAINS, FINE GRITS, STONE GROUND MEAL, FLOUR

Granola
Popped corn
Wheat germ

Oat bran, wheat bran
Sprouted grains (wheat, etc.)
Flour, varieties

Method: Ready to eat granola, whole grain cereal, popped corn, or instant hot cereals requiring little or no cooking. Flour is used in bread, cooking, or breading meal.

Cooking Methods for Grains

Listed are 7 methods for properly cooking grains. Generally, slow cooking is best. Allow enough time for grains to cook thoroughly. They will be fuller, softer, chewy, rather than crunchy and have a sweeter nutty flavor. Grains that are undercooked are hard and tend to taste starchy.

Double Boiler: Put grain and water in upper part of double boiler; bring to a boil on stovetop, then place over bottom part of double boiler containing 2-3" of hot water. Cover. Cook on low-medium heat 1 hour, or until grain has absorbed all the water.

Oven Method: Bring water and grain to a boil on stovetop; transfer to a covered oven-proof baking dish. Bake several hours or overnight in a moderately-slow oven. Oven baking is best for grain-based casseroles, pilafs and grains with dried fruit combinations.

To Bake Granola: Mix cereal grains and ingredients according to recipe, spread on baking sheet. Bake in slow oven, stirring occasionally, until totally dry, .

Thermos Method: Soak very small grains i.e. quinoa or cereal flakes with half the water in a pan, until grains are double in volume. Add remaining water, bring to boil, simmer 5 min. Pour into a pre-heated wide-mouth thermos. Apply cap. Turn thermos on its side for several hours or overnight. Convenient method when packing a hearty lunch or to take along when traveling.

Skillet Method: (pictured below) Toast grains by stirring in dry skillet until golden brown; add water, stir once. Cover, then cook, without stirring, on low heat, until grain has absorbed all the water. Excellent method for cooking whole grain brown rice. (1 cup brown rice = 3- 4 cups cooked)

Stovetop Method: In a medium saucepan, bring water to a boil. Slowly add cereal while stirring. Cover, cook on low heat to desired consistency. Let set covered 10 minutes. This method is best for quick cooking cereals such as barley flakes, wheat and rye flakes, quinoa, bulgur, and oatmeal, (stir occasionally).

Vapor Unit: You will need a large kettle and one smaller pan that will set inside the large kettle, and a rack with legs. Put water in bottom of large kettle (up to rack). Set rack inside kettle with smaller pan containing whole grains + hot water, on top of rack (cover pan with a plate or cover that fits). Cover the large kettle with a tight fitting lid so the steam will not escape. Cook whole grains (such as wheat or kamut) overnight; cracked grains (such as steel cut oats) and smaller grains (like millet or kasha) require less cooking. No stirring is needed.

Crock Pot/Slow Cooker: (pictured below) Pour boiling water over grain in crock pot, or for large whole grains, boil water + grain on stovetop 3-4 minutes, then transfer to crock pot. Cook several hours or overnight until water is completely absorbed.

Millet

Millet is one of the most nutritious grains; gluten-free, alkaline, a good source of calcium, iron, and protein; a wonderful breakfast food and base for many meatless dishes.

1 cup millet, whole
4 cups pure water
½ tsp. sea salt

In a saucepan, bring millet, water and salt to a boil; simmer 2- 3 minutes. Pour into a crock pot; slow cook several hours, overnight or until water is absorbed or cook millet in a double boiler 1 hour or until tender. Remove from heat. Allow to steam 5-10 minutes before serving. Use leftovers in patties, etc. (see Cooking Methods for Grains)

Millet - Date Pudding

In saucepan bring to boil and simmer for 3 minutes:

¾ cup millet, whole
4 cups pure water

Pour off water and blend into milk with:

½ cup cashew nuts
2 Tbs. soy milk powder
4 Tbs. honey
½ tsp. lemon zest; ¼ tsp. coriander

1 tsp. pure vanilla
¼ tsp. sea salt

Pour mixture over millet in baking dish; add:

½ cup grated coconut
½ cup chopped dates or raisins

Cover, bake at 350° 1 hour, stirring occasionally. Good served with **Lemon Sauce**.

Dried Sweet Corn

1. In season, select full ears of Sweet Corn. Husk, and remove all silk; wash clean.
2. Scald corn in boiling water for 3 minutes. Cool quickly in ice water; cut off cob.
3. Place on trays in dehydrator, the sun, or oven at 250° - 300° until thoroughly dry. Eat dry, chewing well, or soak/cook in a little soy milk. Serve as a cereal. Delicious!

Buckwheat Cereal

Toasted buckwheat or Kasha has a sweet, earthy flavor and is packed with nutrients (see Grain Glossary). Buckwheat tends to absorb more water than most grains.

1 cup buckwheat groats
5 cups pure water
½ tsp. sea salt, to taste

Cook in crock pot overnight or double boiler, 1 hour on low heat until water is absorbed. Add diced dates, figs or raisins; top with cashew cream. Delicious! (one of my favorites!)

Old-Fashioned Oatmeal and Fruit

Reduce cholesterol by eating a heart-healthy breakfast. Start the day with a bowl of fiber-filled cereal and sweet berries or other fruits. Here's a simple stand-by that never grows old!

One serving:
1 cup pure water
½ cup rolled oats
dash of salt, optional

Four servings:
3 ½ cups pure water
2 cups rolled oats
¼ tsp. salt

Bring water to a boil, with salt if desired. Add old-fashioned regular oats, or quick oats while stirring. Cover and cook on low heat 5 minutes; stir occasionally. Delicious served with fresh peaches, blueberries, dates or raisins; and your favorite nut milk or cream.

Rye Cereal

1 cup rye flakes
3 cups boiling water
½ tsp. sea salt

Put cereal, water, and salt in the top pan of a stainless steel double boiler. Add water to the lower part of pan and let steam for 45 minutes or cook 30 minutes on stovetop, in a 2 qt. saucepan, stirring occasionally. Good combined with wheat flakes.

Note: Cereal can be prepared in the evening and warmed in the morning by re-heating the water in lower part of double boiler.

Steamed Whole Barley

Barley (pearl) is mostly used in soups and stews as a thickener. Whole hulled barley, richer in fiber, makes a chewy breakfast cereal that is really good for you.

1 cup whole barley
4 cups pure water
½ tsp. sea salt, to taste

Cook whole hulled barley in a double boiler for 2 hours or more until all the water is absorbed; or cook overnight in a crock pot or slow cooker. For other forms of barley, such as: barley flakes, barley grits, pearl barley (see Cooking Methods for Grains).
Note: Use leftover Barley to make delicious **Barley Burgers or Barley Buns.**

Steel Cut Oats

A good source of protein, fiber and minerals. Oats can be used as a base for savory patties.

1 cup oats, whole or cut
1 qt. pure boiling water
½ tsp. sea salt, to taste

Put oats, water, and salt in top of stainless steel double boiler; and enough water in bottom pan to prevent boiling dry. Cook oats over low heat 1½ hrs. or more. Add chopped dates if desired. let stand to soften. Tip: soak grain 1 hr. to reduce cooking time.

Triticale or Wheat Cereal
cross between wheat and rye- see Grain Glossary

2 cups triticale* or wheat flakes
1 qt. boiling water
½ tsp. sea salt

　　Put cereal, water, and salt in the top part of a stainless steel double boiler. Place water in lower part. Steam for 45 minutes, or cook covered on stovetop; stir occasionally. Turn off heat; add a few chopped dates, if desired, let steam until serving time.
　　Whole Kernel Wheat or **Triticale** – Soak 2 hours then steam in a vapor unit or a double boiler over low heat 8-10 hours.
　　Sprouted Wheat Cereal – Sprout wheat (see sprouting). Steam lightly to warm.

Sprouted Grain Cereal

1. Sprout grains: wheat, barley, millet, spelt, etc. (see chapter- Sprouting).
2. Wheat sprouts can be eaten raw, or lightly steamed for a hot cereal.
3. Other sprouts may require a short amount of cooking. Cover pan with tight fitting lid and steam till just tender. Serve with chopped dried fruit, nut milk or cream.

Basic Preparation for Wild Rice
(Wild rice is a marsh grass with a nutlike flavor and chewy texture)

1 cup uncooked wild rice
½ tsp. sea salt (omit salt if using broth)
3-4 cups water or broth (see recipes)

Place wild rice in heavy saucepan with salted water or broth (chicken-style or vegetable). Bring to a boil, reduce heat and simmer covered for 50 min. or until rice is tender and most of the grains have split slightly. Uncover. Fluff with a fork. Simmer 5 min. more. Drain excess liquid if any. Avoid overcooking wild rice or it will lose its unique texture. Yield: 3-4 cups cooked wild rice.

Note: Toasting rice (lightly) in a dry skillet, before adding water, helps kernels to fully open.

Helpful Hints for Wild Rice

● Prepare 1 lb. of wild rice at a time and refrigerate or freeze some for use later.
　One pound of wild rice provides 20 (½ cup) servings
● To reheat wild rice, warm in a covered skillet, with a little water or broth for moisture, if needed.
● Wild rice may be combined with brown rice, wehani, basmati, jasmine or other varieties of rice when cooking.
● Use cooked wild rice in place of pasta in casseroles or in place of bulgur in tabouleh salads.
● Serve wild rice as a base for your favorite vegetable stir-fry topping.
● Add cooked wild rice to cream or clear soups; or add to batters for muffins, crêpes or waffles.
● Wild rice, mixed with onion, parsley and/or tomatoes, makes a good filling for squash or peppers.
● Mix cooked wild rice into your favorite breakfast cereal, or try wild rice as a breakfast cereal by itself.
● For a simple colorful side dish, combine cooked wild rice with your favorite frozen mixed vegetables. Add browned tofu for a complete one-dish meal.

Toasted Natural Brown Rice

1 cups brown rice
4 cups hot water or broth
½ tsp. sea salt

Place rice in a large, dry heavy skillet; stir over medium heat until lightly toasted. Slowly add water and salt, stir only once. Cover, do not remove lid while cooking Cook on low heat 55-60 min. until all liquid is absorbed. Let stand 10 minutes. Using a fork, lift grains to separate before serving.

Note: Toasted rice absorbs more liquid. Kernels are fluffy and tender, if given time to cook slowly.

Note: Rice may be toasted in advance; store in covered jar; refrigerate and use as needed.

Garden Trio* Rice

Lightly toast and cook **1 cup brown rice** with **1 qt. water + ½ tsp. sea salt** then add:

for Green Rice:

Add **1 Tbs. *BarleyLife***, mixed with **1 Tbs. water**; stir into rice, or add c**hopped chives, parsley, watercress, green peppers**, or **green onion tops**.

for Red Rice:

Mix **1 Tbs. *RediBeets* + 1 Tbs. water**; stir into rice, or add a little **beet juice** to cooking water. Serve with **diced red pepper** or **pimento**, sprinkle on **olive oil**, if desired.

*****Garden Trio** information: contact authors

for Yellow Rice:

Prepare rice; add **1 Tbs. *Just Carrots* + 1 Tbs. water**; stir into rice, or add **⅛ tsp. saffron** or **½ tsp. turmeric** to cooking water.

Brown Rice for Breakfast or Dinner

1 cup natural brown rice
3-4 cups* pure water
½ tsp. sea salt

In a sauce-pan, bring water and salt to full boil. Add rice, stir 1 time (more stirring will cause rice to stick). Cover, simmer gently about 1 hour, turn off heat. Let steam until ready to serve.

Note: Rice for breakfast can be prepared the night before. Serve warm or cold with chopped dates or raisins; top with nut cream or soymilk.
*Use 3 cups water for a firm stuffing rice.
*Use 4 cups water for softer tender rice.

Rice Crème Pudding

1 cup fruit juice (pear is good)
4 Tbs. almond or cashew butter
4 cups cooked brown rice
1 tsp. each, orange and lemon zest
1 cup chopped dates or raisins
½ cup chopped pecans or filberts

Blend fruit juice, nut butter, grated lemon and orange zest, and 1 cup cooked rice, to partly smooth. Pour in non-stick baking dish. Add remaining rice, fruit and nuts. Bake at 375° for 30-45 min. Good served with sesame sauce, mint sauce, or your favorite nut cream. Servings: 6- 8

Swiss Muesli

Bircher-Benner, the famous Swiss doctor, was first to popularize the traditional robust Swiss country breakfast. Made of toasted whole-grain cereal flakes, nuts, and fruits, providing nutrition for the heart, and fiber to help lower cholesterol levels in the blood.

1½ cups toasted* rolled oats
½ cup walnuts, chopped
¼ cup hazelnuts, chopped
¼ cup raisins
¼ cup dried apricots,figs or prunes, chopped
2 Tbs. sliced almonds
fresh fruit: apples, pineapple, banana, pear, pomegranate, etc.
juice of ½ lemon +1 tsp. honey, opt.

*To toast oats: heat oven to 325°. Spread oats on baking sheet. Toast for 15-20 minutes, stirring often, until golden brown.

Soak oaks in warm water; add the chopped dried fruit and nuts; let rest until softened. Cut the fresh fruit (dip apples, banana, in lemon juice and honey). Add to oats, dried fruit and nut mixture. Serve with soymilk, cream or yogurt or eliminate soaking and just serve with hot soymilk or fruit juice.

Grapenuts

Have you ever wanted to make Grapenuts? I have. This original recipe handed down from college days is one I remember making in Home Ec. Lab many (over 50) years ago. The ingredients only have been modified. As I read the recipe it brought on a smile, - maybe the procedure needs some attention too? Anyway, if you have nothing better to do- give it a try!

1 ¾ C whole wheat flour   *(1½ cup w.w.flour + ¼ cup barley malt)*
2 Tbs. to ½ C brown sugar   *(or sucanat)*
½ tsp. salt   *(or sea salt)*
½ tsp. soda   *(omit or use ½ tsp. baking yeast)*
½ scant C buttermilk or sour milk   *(or warm soymilk + 1 tsp. lemon juice)*

1. Combine dry ingredients and mix well.
2. Add liquid gradually and mix in (after liquid is added the dough should look crumbly like pie dough does before liquid is added). All flour should come in contact with liquid.
3. Spread out on greased baking dish and bake. Dough may be kneaded and rolled out very thin, and marked off into small squares. *(with fingers make a coarse crumb mixture)*
4. Watch the oven closely as it will burn easily. *(bake at 275-300° until thoroughly dry)*
5. At the end of 10 to 15 minutes remove from oven and break up into smaller pieces if necessary. *(to make uniform size pieces run through a coarse food or meat grinder).*

Baked Barley Fruit & Nut Breakfast

Tender whole grain flakes, apples, dates and nuts make this one-dish simple breakfast especially good served with rich nut milk or cream, and topped with berries.

1 cup barley flakes
1 cup regular rolled oats
7 cups liquid (5 cups water + 2 cups
    apple juice concentrate)
½ tsp. sea salt, to taste
1 cup dried apple rings, diced or
chopped
1 cup chopped dates
¾ cup chopped pecans, almonds
    or Brazil nuts
1 tsp. pure maple or vanilla flavor
½ tsp. lemon zest + ½ tsp. coriander

Heat liquid to boiling and pour into a baking dish, slow-cooker or crock pot. Add grains, salt and dried apples. Cover and cook until liquid is mostly absorbed. Lightly toast nuts (see chapter Nuts). Add dates, nuts, and rest of ingredients to grains. Cover and continue to cook until all the liquid is absorbed. Serve warm with nut milk or cream. Yield: 8 servings.

Oven Method: Bake at 250° overnight, repare day ahead and reheat for breakfast.

Wheat Germ Granola

The germ is the portion of the grain richest in nutrients. Wheat germ contains essential fatty acids, proteins, B-vitamins and vitamin E, a powerful antioxidant.

4 cups quick oats
½ cup wheat germ, toasted
¼ cup wheat bran or oat bran
½ cup date or raw sugar
½ cup slivered or sliced almonds
½ cup shredded unsweetened coconut
¼ cup pumpkin seed or sunflower seeds
½ cup white grape juice concentrate
2 tsp. pure vanilla
½ tsp. sea salt
2 tsp. orange or lemon zest

Mix dry ingredients together. Stir vanilla, salt and zest with frozen, thawed juice concentrate. Mix well with dry mixture. Crumble and spread out on baking sheets. Bake at 300° for 30 minutes, reduce temperature to 250° and continue baking until dry, stirring occasionally. Chopped nuts may be added last. Cool completely. Store in glass jar.

Good Morning Muesli

This simple-to-make delicious all-in-one breakfast is packed with energy; a family favorite!

2-3 apples, grated with skin
1 ½ cups orange, or peach, frozen juice concentrate (diluted 1:1)
3 cups oats, quick
1 20-oz. can pineapple chunks with juice
½ cup sunflower seeds
½ cup raisins
1 Tbs. honey, opt.
½ cup chopped almonds
¼ tsp. sea salt
½ tsp. pure vanilla
¼ cup shredded coconut
fresh or dried berries, opt.

In bowl, combine apples with 1 ½ cup juice. Add rest of ingredients (lightly toasting oats and almonds in oven adds a nutty flavor). Pour on more juice or water just enough to moisten (about 1 cup). Stir lightly. Cover, marinate in refrigerator 4-6 hrs. Serve with fresh, frozen or dried berries. Top with almond milk or cream. A delicious and satisfying breakfast! Yield: approx. 8 cups.

Easy Granola

4 cups rolled oats
¾ cup date, raw sugar or honey
½ cup hot water + 2 Tbs. soy oil
1 Tbs. pure vanilla
1 tsp. sea salt
1 cup whole wheat or barley flour
½ cup shredded coconut
½ cup sunflower seeds or nuts, opt.
½ cup soya powder

Blend the sweetening, water, oil, vanilla and salt. Stir into dry ingredients. Crumble and spread on cookie sheets. Bake at 300° for 30 minutes, reduce temperature to 225° and continue baking until dry. Stir occasionally while baking to prevent edges from darkening. Cool. Store in covered jars, or freeze. Yield: approx. 8 cups. Serve with applesauce, soy milk, or fresh fruit topping.

Tropical Maple Nut Granola

2½ cups rolled oats
½ cup barley or rice flour
1 cup sliced almonds
½ cup chopped brazil nuts
½ cup coconut, shredded
½ cup maple syrup or honey
3 Tbs. pineapple juice concentrate
¼ tsp. sea salt
½ cup dried banana slices, dates or pineapple chunks*

In a mixing bowl, combine the first 5 ingredients. Stir the maple syrup or honey, and salt with pineapple juice concentrate; stir into the oat mixture. Spread evenly on a large baking pan. Bake in a 300° oven for 30 minutes or until lightly browned; reduce temperature to 225° and bake until dry, stirring occasionally.

*Remove from oven, stir in dried fruit, if desired. Freeze to store. Yield: 6 cups.

7 Grain Granola

3 ½ cups quick or rolled oats
2 ½ whole wheat flour
1 ½ cups barley flakes
1 cup chopped almonds or hazelnuts
1 cup wheat germ, toasted
1 cup coconut, shredded
½ cup soya powder
¼ cup cornmeal, fine
¼ cup rye flour
1½ tsp. sea salt
¾ cup hot water + ¼ cup soy oil
2 Tbs. pure vanilla extract
1 cup honey, sorghum or agave
1 Tbs. pure hazelnut extract,* opt.

Mix dry ingredients together in mixing bowl. Blend liquid ingredients. Slowly pour mixture over dry ingredients while stirring to moisten grains. Mix well with hands. Spread ½" thick on cookie sheets, bake at 250-275° for 1 hour, stirring and rotating pans often. Reduce temperature to 200° and continue baking overnight or until thoroughly dry and golden in color (or finish drying in dehydrator). Cool, store in jars or freeze. Yield: approx. 4 lbs or 12 cups. Delicious served with fresh or dried fruit such as raisins or dates and your favorite nut milk or cream.

* If using hazelnuts (filberts), the addition of pure hazelnut extract enhances the flavor.

Rosalie's Raw Granola
(Ready-to-eat; chock-full of nutrition)

6 cups quick oats
  (lightly oven toast if desired)
1 cup sliced almonds
  or chopped pecans
1 cup sesame seeds, ground
1 cup sunflower seeds, chopped
1 cup medium shred coconut
1 cup pumpkin seeds, chopped
1 cup flax seed meal
1 cup date sugar, to taste
1 cup raisins
½ tsp. sea salt
½ tsp. ground anise seed
  and/or 1 tsp. orange zest

Mix together. Store in glass jar. Keep cool or freeze. Eat as is, chewing thoroughly. Serve with **dried apricots**, **sliced fresh fruit**, or **molasses**. If desired top with **nut milk** or **soy cream**. Good survival food or breakfast food for backpacking trips, camping and hiking. Yield: approx. 3½ qts.

Mixed Grain Cereal

Combining grains together is more nutritious than a single grain, and tends to balance the amino acids to enhance total food value.

1¾ cups mixed grains
2 qts. pure water
½ tsp. sea salt, to taste

Cook as other cereals, one hour or more depending on combination of grains, and method of cooking. Whole grains require longer cooking than cracked or rolled grains.

Polenta - Corn Meal

Polenta-is made from various meals such as corn, barley and chestnut. A versatile dish that can be served as a breakfast cereal with sweet toppings or a savory side dish with vegetables and beans.

1 cup yellow corn meal
4½ cups pure water
¾ tsp. sea salt, to taste

Heat 3 cups of water to boiling. Add the corn meal and salt to the remaining 1½ cups of cold water. Add mix to the boiling water stirring until smooth. Cook in a covered double boiler pan for 50-60 minutes or simmer in a heavy covered saucepan, stirring often to prevent lumping. Serve warm or spoon into a glass pan or a loaf pan lined with plastic wrap. Refrigerate until firm. Cut into ½" slices, brown each side in a non-stick skillet, lightly oiled pan, or hot oven.

Note: Serve with fruit sauce, molasses, jam, or agave sryup for breakfast or as a savory side dish for dinner, with added herbs, tomato sauce, vegetables, salad or beans. (See **Savory Herbed Polenta** in chapter *Vegetables and Side Dishes*).

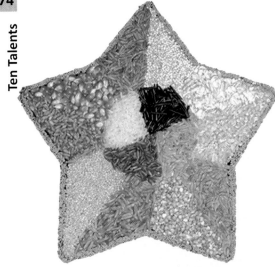

3-Grain Combinations

Oats, rolled	Millet
Barley flakes	Quinoa
Triticale flakes	Corn meal
Spelt, whole	Barley, cracked
Barley grits	Corn, cracked
Buckwheat groats	Wheat, cracked
Kamut, cracked	Bulgur wheat
Brown rice, cracked	Teff, whole
Rye, cracked	Kasha - toasted
	Buckwheat

Waffles

Waffles add that extra special touch that can make breakfast a memorable meal.
The variety of fresh fruits, nut butters, fruit sauce and syrup toppings are endless and when combined with the grains and ingredients in waffles make a satisfying all-in-one dish fit for a king!

We mix the batter and let it set a few hours or mix it the night before and let it set in the refrigerator. In the morning the batter is very thick (oats have soaked up the milk).

To Blend: Start with **¼ cup water** in blender, add **1-2 cups oat mixture** and blend to a smooth semi- thick batter.

The **sesame seeds** are sprinkled on hot prepared (lightly apply non-stick coating) waffle baker, and on top of batter for extra nutrition and to keep the waffles from sticking.

Close lid and allow waffles to steam bake until golden brown 7-10 minutes depending on your appliance (no peeking for at least 7 minutes). When done, use a fork to lift waffle off grid. These waffles are quite light, and very filling.

Sometimes I'll make a double batch of waffles to freeze, for later use. To re-heat: Just pop in toaster.

 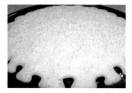  

Note: Waffles without leavening bake better than pancakes, due to the simultaneous heat applied to both top and bottom. During the steam-baking process you will see the lid rise, then settle again. Most of the healthy ingredients in these recipes are either pre-cooked, or require little or no cooking. The prepared batter can be used in regular or deep Belgian waffle bakers. Waffles given proper time, will be sufficiently baked and ready to eat, refrigerate, or freeze; then re-heat when ready to use. Waffles freeze well.

Basic Oatmeal Waffles

This simple-to-make, basic waffle recipe, is foolproof and delicious. Top with your favorite nut butter and fruit sauce for a healthy, hearty breakfast

Note: Waffle cake and toppings
See page 184

7 cups quick oats
7 cups soy or nut milk
¼ cup seeds, nuts or flaxmeal or 1 Tbs. oil
** + ½ tsp. lecithin, opt.**
1½ tsp. sea salt
1 tsp. pure vanilla, opt.
1 Tbs. honey or other sweetening, opt.

In a large mixing bowl, mix ingredients together. Let stand for 2-3 hours or overnight until oats have absorbed all the milk. Have waffle iron piping hot. Whiz 2-3 cups at a time in blender until smooth, diluting with water as needed to make a medium-thick batter. Prepare waffle baker with non-stick coating or spray. Sprinkle on sesame seeds. Pour batter onto hot waffle iron. Sprinkle on more sesame seeds. Bake 7-10 min. depending on your waffle baker. (no peeking!) Serve with your favorite fruit topping. Yield: approx. seven 9" x 9" waffles.

Variation: Add 1 cup cooked grain such as: barley, bulgur, buckwheat, millet, rice, spelt, etc. before blending.

Note: To keep waffles from sticking, simply sprinkle a generous amount of sesame seeds onto pre-heated waffle iron. Pour on batter, then sprinkle on more sesame seeds. Close lid and bake. This simple step will also add a rich nutty flavor to baked waffles.

Best Blueberry Waffles

4 cups quick oats
¼ cup cooked corn meal
4 cups milk, soy or nut
1 tsp. sea salt
2 tsp. oil + ½ tsp. lecithin, opt.

1 Tbs. lemon juice
2 tsp. pure vanilla
2 Tbs. sesame seeds, opt.
1 Tbs. honey or sweetener, opt.
1 cup fresh or frozen blueberries

Blend all ingredients (except blueberries) until smooth. Fold in berries. Let stand at least 2 hours, or in refrigerator overnight. Bake in a hot prepared nonstick waffle iron 7-10 minutes. Serve with fresh blueberry topping.

Wheat Germ or Flax Waffles

Follow recipe for **Oatmeal Waffles**. Replace 1 cup oats with **1/2 cup flax meal or toasted wheat germ**. Adjust amount of water when blending. Follow directions for baking batter.

Millet Waffles

Follow recipe for **Oatmeal Waffles**. Replace 2 cups oats with **2 cups millet meal**. Bake in non-stick waffle iron a little longer. Follow directions given for baking, using sesame seeds. Serve with nut butter, stewed peaches, warm pear sauce, or your favorite **fruit topping**.

Quinoa Oat Waffles

Quinoa has more protein than other grains, and contains all 8 essential amino acids, making it a complete protein, ideal for vegetarians.

3 cups milk, soy or nut
1 cup cooked quinoa or corn meal
½ cup coconut, fine shred
1 Tbs. honey or sweetener, opt.
½ tsp. sea salt
1 tsp. orange zest, opt.
½ tsp. lecithin granules, opt.
3 cups quick oats, raw

Blend quinoa or corn meal, milk, coconut and honey until smooth. Pour into a mixing bowl; stir in remaining ingredients. Let stand 1 hour or more in refrigerator. Bake on piping hot, prepared non-stick waffle iron 8-10 minutes until golden brown. Delicious served with applesauce and strawberries. Top with your favorite syrup.

Sesame-Oat Waffles

1 cup sesame seed
3½- 4 cups hot water
1½ cups quick oats
1½ cups cornmeal or rice flour
1 tsp. pure vanilla
½ tsp. sea salt

Blend seeds in blender with part of the water until smooth. Add remaining ingredients, blend again with just enough water to make a medium-thick batter. Bake in hot, non-stick, prepared waffle iron until browned and baked through, 8-10 minutes. Serve with nut butter, pear sauce and sliced banana, maple syrup or molasses.

A diet that contains whole grains and cereals, fruits, nuts, seeds, and vegetables, in proper combination, is more than adequate to provide the needed protein, essential amino acids, vitamins, and minerals, for a healthy vegetarian.

Herbs & Seasonings

Index - *Chapter 9*

Chapter cover photo: ***Organically Grown Garden Herbs and Vegetables***

Herbs & Seasonings

There is a vast variety of herbs, seeds, spices and condiments available today to improve the flavor of foods and enhance the desire to eat them. Whether you grow them in your herb garden, or purchase them fresh or dried, you will love getting to know more about the world of seasoning available to cooks.

The taste buds perceive 4 basic flavors: sweet, sour, bitter, salty. The art of combining the delicate aromatic herbs such as sweet basil or rosemary, and healthful condiments such as lemon and garlic, to enhance the flavor of food, rather than dominate or mask the primary ingredient, is unquestionably a culinary art.

This chapter includes some herbs used for their medicinal benefit, as well as the most common culinary herbs to add great flavor to your cooking!

"He causeth the grass to grow for the cattle, and herb for the service of man, that he may bring forth food out of the earth." Psalm 104:14

Some Herbs and Where to Use Them

For the Herb Cook

Salt is the universal seasoning; choose the best: **Celtic Sea Salt,** but use sparingly.

Herb Hint: 1 Tablespoon fresh minced herbs equals ¾ **teaspoon dried herbs.** (If cooking time is more than one hour, add herbs during the last half hour.)

BASIL

Tomatoes, Tomato sauce, Pesto, Salads, Pasta dishes, Soups and stew, Tofu scrambled eggs, Bruschetta.

Aromatic; pungent flavor: cross between licorice and cloves

ANISE

Salads, soups, stews, relish
Licorice-like flavor and aroma

Aniseed: Apple, Pumpkin pies, Cookies, cakes, Bread, Cinnamon substitute

Chinese Star Anise (pictured): very beautiful to behold, taste and aroma similar to common anise

BAY LEAVES (Laurel leaves)

Legumes (remove before serving)
Stews, Soups, Vegetable kabobs

Pleasant odor, bitter aromatic taste

Uses: Place in flour bin to deter weevils
Hang to freshen air; crumble in potpourri

BORAGE

Potato Salad, Tossed greens, Herbal Iced tea

ARUGULA

Salads
Pasta

CARAWAY SEED

Breads, Rye-pumpernickel, Cabbage, Salad, Beets, Cottage cheese, (tofu)

CARDAMOM (seed, ground)

Breads, Cookies, Pies, Baked goods,
Spicy-sweet, peppery, ginger-like flavor
Curried dishes, Bean dishes

CELERY SEED

Salads – Potato, other; Salad dressings,
Tomato juice, Soups, Stews, Stuffing

CHERVIL

Green salads, Garnish, Soups,
Stews, Vegetables
Flavor: similar to parsley/hint of tarragon

CHIVES

Salads, Seasoning,Garnish, Potatoes,
Potato soup and salads, Sandwiches,
Carrots, Green beans
Scrambled tofu (eggs), Soy cottage cheese

CILANTRO (coriander leaf)

Salsa, Sauces, Guacamole
Mexican, Thai, Chinese dishes

CORIANDER (seed, ground)

Flavoring: Apple & Pumpkin pies
Cinnamon substitute
Bread, Cookies, Rolls, Waffles

CUMIN (seed)

Chili, Stews, Kidney beans.
Pungent spicy flavor,
Mexican and Indian cuisine

DILL (leaves and seed)

Potato Salad, Peas, Carrots, Vegetables,
Cabbage, Coleslaw, Sauerkraut, Tofu egg
salad, Soups, Dressings, Gravy, Breads,
Herb Tea (Seeds: appetite, flatulence)

FENNEL

(Sweet anise: in Italy - **finocchio**)
Fleshy Bulb, whole-sliced, Salads,
Stalks and flowery green tops (aromatic)
Flavor soups, Salads, Tomato sauce.
Lentils, Beans, Rice, Pasta, many dishes
Chew - pleasant, mild licorice-like taste
Seeds- Breads, Herb tea (appetite, digestion)

GARLIC (bulb)
Soups, Salads, Dressings, Sauces
Roasted (nutty sweet), Spreads
Legumes, Stews, Stir-fry, Vegetables,
Potatoes, Tomatoes, Bread, Pasta, Pizza
Italian Garlic (mauve skin-mild)
American (white-pungent)

HYSSOP
Herb teas, Green salads

MARJORAM
Salads, Salad dressing, Sauces, Beans,
Pasta, Patties, Meatless loaf, Soups,
Stews, Roasted vegetables.
Flavor: similar to oregano; sweeter, milder

MINT – (Spearmint, Peppermint)
Beverages, Herb teas
Peas, Carrots, Potatoes,
Salads, Vegetables, Soups,
Carob fudge, Frosting, Desserts,
Garnish, Sauces, Marinades,
Mint honey

NASTURTIUMS
Salads, Flower garnish, Sandwich greens

ONIONS (bulb) – Shallots
Salads, Dressings, Sandwiches, Soups,
Stews, Stir-fries, Vegetables, Legumes,
Kabobs, Burgers, Roasts, Patties, Bread,
Rolls, Wraps, Pizza, Salsa, Pasta sauce, Dips
Shallots - mild, hint of onion & garlic flavor

OREGANO
Pizza, Pasta, Beans, Salad dressings,
Salads, Tomato dishes, Soups, Sauces,
Meatless loaf, Patties

PAPRIKA - (pepper, sweet)
Salad dressing, Soups, Cole slaw, Salads,
Potato salad, Potatoes, Roasted vegetables

PARSLEY

Soups, Salads, Vegetable dishes, Sauces,
Potatoes, Rice, Pasta, Dressings, Gravy
Compliments most foods/flavors
Garnish, Herb tea

SUMMER SAVORY (mint family)

Legumes, Bean dishes, Stews, Potato soup,
Mushrooms, Cabbage, Stuffing, Marinades

SORREL

Salad mix, Greens, Soups, Stews

TARRAGON

Salads, Sauces, Dressings,
French cuisine, Roasts,Stuffing,
Aromatic, warm, subtle licorice-like flavor

PEPPER, RED (cayenne)

Pungent condiment, many varieties,
(no heat standard) varying in degrees of
heat. Avoid hot sauces (irritating)

POPPY SEED

Breads, Rolls, Muffins, Salad dressings,
Cabbage, Topping, Flavoring

ROSEMARY (mint family)

Bread dressing, Herbed bread, Soups,
Stews,Seasoning, Potatoes, Peas, Turnips
Salad dressing, Marinades, Herb tea
(headache) used in potpourri, perfumery

SAFFRON

(A costly herb - orange stigmas of flower)
Aromatic, adds deep yellow color,
Pungent flavor, Rice dishes, Baked goods

THYME (mint family)

Soups, Stews, Stuffing, Gravy, Tomatoes, Onions, Corn, Carrots, Meatless
loaf, Garnish bouquet, (light minty-lemon)

TURMERIC

Salad dressings, Sandwich spreads,
Scrambled tofu, Potato salad,
Flavoring and coloring (yellow-golden)

WATERCRESS

SAGE

Stuffing, Meatless loaf, Patties, Legumes,
Soups, Vegetables, also see Herbal Remedies

WATERCRESS (perennial - aquatic)

Salads, raw, Garnish, Sandwich greens,
Flavor soups, Pasta and Potato dishes
Garnish; Medicinal: tonic, blood purifier

Aromatic Herbs such as sweet basil, oregano, rosemary, thyme, are excellent to replace irritating spices. The herbs contain essential oils, having medicinal properties as well.

Chives - a member of the onion family, contains vitamin A, C, folic acid, iron, calcium, potassium. Long used as a culinary herb, having medicinal properties as well. Snip chive leaves just before using to preserve aroma and delicate flavor. The purple flowers have a mild taste, and add a decorative touch to salads. Freeze chives to retain flavor. Snip chives, place in ice-cube tray, fill with water and freeze. To thaw, simply put a chive cube in soup or strainer; use in potato salad, tofu cottage cheese, carrots, green beans, or dressing.

Herb Hint - The flavor of garlic is 7 times stronger when put through a garlic press, than when mincing with a knife (more of the essential oils in the clove are released when pressed).

Parsley, a European garden herb of the carrot family, is one of the favorite four *fines* herbs used by chefs; also combined with bay leaves in *bouquet garni*, a French term for a bundle of herbs tied together with kitchen string or placed in cheesecloth for easy removal from a pot of soup or other cooked dish. Parsley grows easily in a garden container. It is available year-round, and can be preserved by freezing or drying (see **Misc. chapter**). Use it freely. Parsley is very nutritious; packed with vitamin A, C, some B vitamins, and containing calcium, iron, potassium, magnesium, and protein. The two varieties are: Italian flat-leaf parsley and common curly-leaf parsley.

Vinegar or Lemon ?

The flavor of salad dressing, green leafy vegetables and legumes is enhanced by adding fresh squeezed lemon juice. Lemons enhance digestion and increase the nutritional value of foods due to the vitamin C and other nutrients found in lemons.

Vinegar, a sour liquid, is a byproduct of fermentation. Through processing the alcohol from grapes, grains, apples, etc. is changed to acetic acid (4 -12%), a toxic substance that if taken in sufficient quantities, can potentially cause anemia, renal failure, and gastritis. Vinegar does not add to the nutritive properties of food, facilitate digestion, or improve the absorption of iron and other nutrients as do lemons.

The flavor and benefits of using lemon juice surpass vinegar; in addition - the entire lemon (pesticide-free), including the pulp and peel (zest), can be used which contains medicinal properties. So, squeeze away- safely season your food, enjoy fresh lemonade, but remember to grate and freeze the peel first; it's the secret ingredient for delicious date bars (see recipes and **Misc.** chapter).

Garden Herbs

Bay Leaves

Summer Savory

Parsley

Mint

Tarragon

Chives

Cilantro

Fennel

Garlic

Basil

Marjoram

Dill

Italian Parsley

Thyme

Sage

Rosemary

Oregano

Herb Blends

Many mixtures, or blends of herbs and spices have been developed by spice manufacturers to make the art of seasoning an easy task (commonly called condiments).

Some of these condiments are irritating to the stomach and exciting to the nerves. Those most injurious are: mustard, pepper spices, pickles, and those of like character. They seem to some, to aid in digestion, but this is questioned. They do irritate and inflame the delicate coatings of the stomach; leaving the system weakened and the blood contaminated. There are beneficial herb seasonings that we can use, but even those of less concentration may be harmful in large amounts.

Use a gentle hand when it comes to seasonings; an over-stimulated palate is often insensitive to the subtle flavors of whole, fresh food.

Definitions

HERB – *Webster's New Collegiate Dictionary*
　　1. *"A seed plant which does not develop woody persistent tissue, as that of a shrub or tree, but is more or less soft or succulent; spec., one used for medicinal purposes, or for its sweet scent or flavor".*
　　2. *"Grass, herbage."*
A modern dictionary definition for "Herb" is *"Any Plant used for flavoring, fragrant, or medicinal purposes".*

CONDIMENT - *Webster's New Collegiate Dictionary*
　　"Something, used to enhance the flavor of food, usually a pungent seasoning."
There are 5 classifications of condiments in *Taber's Cyclopedic Medical Dictionary:*

1. **Aromatic** – basil, dill, rosemary (herbs); vanilla (seed pod); cinnamon (spice-inner bark of tree); clove (spice-dried flower bud of Asian tree); the essential oil used in perfume and medicine.
2. **Acrid or Peppery** – pepper, allspice, ginger etc.
3. **Allylic or Alliaceous** (containing certain oils) – garlic (bulbous herb); onion (plant-bulb); mustard (pungent seed - irritant); horseradish (a pungent root of the mustard family).
4. **Acid** – vinegar (obtained by the fermentation of dilute alcoholic liquids, as wine, cider, beer, malt); capers (shrubs – greenish flower buds and young berries); citron (the fruit of a tree like the lemon but larger); gherkins (small prickly fruit – a species of cucumber).
5. **Animal Origin** – caviar (the eggs of fishes as lobster); anchovies (small herring like fishes – used for pickling and spices).

SPICES - *Webster's New Collegiate Dictionary*
　　"Any of various aromatic vegetable products, as pepper, nutmeg, cloves, etc, used in cooking to season or flavor foods, sauces, pickles, etc."
It would *not* be wise to make a blanket statement that all spices, condiments or herbs are harmful, stimulating, or toxic. We are told by inspiration *"our tables should be free from every irritating substance".* E.G. White, Counsels on Diet and Foods, p. 339.

According to Webster's definition, Spices and Condiments could indicate various kinds of flavorings and seasonings; concerning Herbs - some plants are very toxic. Therefore we need to study to know the difference.

Herb Culture and Use

Chives · Lemon Balm · Cilantro · Sage · Marjoram · Sweet Basil

Planting Your Herb Garden

Plant your herb garden near the kitchen. This will encourage their use more often. Some seed varieties may be started indoors and transplanted; but with proper attention any variety may be sown directly outside. Check seed packages for best sowing time. Choose a garden spot where soil is fertile. Work soil at least 7-8 inches deep. Make sure soil is pulverized for easier planting and better germination. Organic matter (such as compost or manure) should be added every year or two. Compost is made of leaves, grass clippings, waste hay, straw, and weeds. Sprinkle on a little limestone. Keep weeds out by cultivating, or by using a mulch of grass clippings, hay, or straw. For ways to preserve Sweet Basil, see chapter *Miscellaneous*.

Collecting and Preserving Wild Herbs

Take a good field identification book of the herbs with you (such as The Herbalist) as you go out. It is best to concentrate on a few local varieties until you become more skilled in gathering and drying. Lack of knowledge in the gathering and preserving of herbs may render them of little therapeutic value. Knowledge of soil is also necessary. Plants grown in virgin soil will be of better value than those grown on poor soil. There is also a difference between cultivated plants and those growing in their natural wild state. The dandelion is a good example of this. Wild herbs are much more effective than those grown in gardens. The time of the year in which they are gathered is also important. It is best to gather them in dry weather.

Collecting Leaves and Flowers

Flowers and leaves should be gathered when they are in their prime, gathering only the perfect ones. Collect in clear, dry weather, in the morning, after the dew is off. In collecting herbs, strip off the flowers, smaller leaves, and very small stems. Blossoms are their best the day they open. Spread out in a thin layer on a clean surface and dry in the shade, in dehydrator, or in a very slow oven (200°), with the oven door open.

Collecting and Drying Roots

Roots are lifted either in the spring when the sap is rising, or in late autumn, after the sap has gone down. Wash, Cut and dry thoroughly. If any moisture is left in the roots when stored away, they will mold.

Collecting and Drying Seeds

Seeds should be gathered as soon as they ripen. Heavy, fully developed seeds are of the most value. Spread out thin on screening. Cover with cheesecloth if necessary, to keep out dust. Dry them in the shade. As a rule, seeds, flowers, leaves, roots and bark, should all be dried in the shade, dehydrator, or an airy place. They may be dried in the sun for a short time, to hasten the drying process, but always complete the drying process in the shade. When thoroughly dried and kept dry, they will retain their therapeutic value for years. Store in a heavy brown paper bag, or glass mason jar, in a cool dark place.

Preparing Herb Teas

Finely Cut or Granulated Herbs

Steep – *never boil* – herbs. Bring water to a boil; turn off heat; add herbs and let set for 20 minutes. This is steeping. Strain, and drink warm, one-half hour before meals or retiring.

Flowers and Leaves

Flowers and leaves should never be boiled. Steep them in boiling water in a covered pan for twenty minutes. Boiling evaporates the aromatic properties.

Roots and Bark

Roots - Simmer 15 minutes or more in order to extract their medicinal value. Avoid boiling.

They are more easily prepared when they have been cut fine, or crushed.

Other Herbal Preparations

Herb Syrups
Dissolve two pounds of raw sugar or an equivalent amount of honey, molasses, etc., in a pint of boiling water. Boil until thick. To this, add a cup of granulated herb; boil to a syrupy consistency; strain through a double cheesecloth, and bottle.

Herb Salves
Use either fresh leaves, flowers, roots, bark, dried granulated, or powdered herbs. If freshly gathered, be sure that they have been cut up finely. Use one pound of herbs to one and a half pounds coconut oil or any pure vegetable oil, and four ounces of beeswax. In the warmer climates, a little more beeswax is necessary. Mix together, cover, and place in the hot sun or low oven, for three or four hours. Strain through a fine sieve or cloth. When cold, it will be firm and ready for use. It can be used, however, before it is cold.

Herb Poultices
It is best to have herbs in a powdered or granulated form. If powdered, mix with just enough water to make a thick paste; when granulated, mix with water, flax-seed meal, cornmeal, or flour to make a thick paste. If *fresh green leaves* are used, soak in very hot water (steep) and apply. Do not re-heat a poultice that has been used. To enhance effectiveness, do not allow poultice to become cold or dry. Have another poultice ready to apply, until results are achieved.

Flax or Charcoal Poultices
Wet flax meal and /or charcoal into consistency of a paste. Spread on either gauze, muslin, or other white cotton material. Can be heated. Apply to affected area.

Fig Poultice
In II Kings 20:7 we read of the experience of Hezekiah, *"Take a lump of figs. And they took and laid it on the boil, and he recovered."*

Cut fresh or dried figs in slices. Place directly on affected area. Cover with a clean cotton cloth, guaze, or plastic wrap. Change poultice daily until results are achieved.

"The Lord has given some simple herbs of the field that at times are beneficial; and if every family were educated in how to use these herbs in case of sickness, much suffering might be prevented, and no doctor need be called. These old-fashioned, simple herbs, used intelligently, would have recovered many sick, who have died under drug medication."
- E. G. White - Letter 82, 1897

"God has caused to grow out of the ground herbs for the use of man, and if we understand the nature of these roots and herbs, and make a right use of them, there would not be a necessity of running for the doctor so frequently, and people would be in much better health than they are today." E.G. White, Sel. Mess. 2:297

Glossary of Herb Terms

ANTIBACTERIAL – A substance that destroys bacteria or suppresses their growth or reproduction.

ANTIDOTE – A remedy to counteract or neutralize poisons and toxins.

ANTISEPTIC – A substance that inhibits the growth or action of microorganisms.

ANTISPASMOTIC – Any agent that relieves spasms.

AROMATIC – A medicinal substance yielding aroma, spicy, fragrant, sweet-smelling.

ASTRINGENT – An agent that has a constricting, drawing together, or binding effect.

CARMINATIVE – An agent that aids in relieving gas from the gastrointestinal tract – as in colic or gripe (spasmodic pain in the bowels).

DEMULCENT – An agent that will soothe and soften the part to which applied, usually acting on mucous membrane.

DEPURATIVE – Having cleansing properties, purifies blood.

DIAPHORETIC – A substance which increases perspiration.

DIURETIC – An agent which increases the secretion and discharge of urine.

EMOLLIENT – An agent that will soften and soothe surface of the body when applied locally to the skin.

EXPECTORANT – A medicinal substance that helps in the expulsion of mucous or phlegm from the throat or lungs.

HEMOSTATIC – Any substance that prevents bleeding or promotes clotting of blood.

NUTRITIVE – A nutritious substance providing nourishment.

PURGATIVE – Cleansing. An agent that will purge as a laxative.

STIMULANT – An agent that produces a temporary increase of functional activity.

STOMACHIC – An agent that is good for and strengthening to the stomach.

TONIC – An invigorating medicinal preparation that increases strength and healthy muscle tone.

VERMIFUGE – A substance for expelling intestinal worms.

VULNERARY – A remedy used to assist in healing wounds.

Helpful Herbal Remedies

Alfalfa
Nutritive, Stomachic, Tonic. High in chlorophyll. Good source of Vitamin A, B, C, E, K, and other minerals, and protein. Medicinally effective in treating anemia, controlling cholesterol, diabetes, stomach disorders, general health as a dietary supplement. No adverse effects. The leaves, flowering tops, seeds, and sprouts are used. Also available in powder, tablet or tea form.

Aloe Vera
Healing, Emollient, Demulcent, Purgative. Accelerates healing process and reduces sensitivity. Provides a natural soothing protection for the skin. Used effectively in healing burns, wounds, sores, ulcers, to reduce tissue inflammation, and as a purgative. Aloe gel and juice are used in cosmetic skin care.

Angelica
Carminative, Expectorant, Aromatic, Tonic. Used in relief of heartburn, gas, sour stomach, colic, coughs. Good general tonic. Leaves, root, and stalk may be used. Noted for its aromatic and some culinary uses.

Boneset
Diaphoretic, Tonic. Used as an antidote for fevers and colds. Stimulating effects of tonic produce perspiration. Large doses produce an emetic effect. Leaves and flowers used in tea.

Borage
Emollient, Diuretic, Exhilarating Tonic. Soothing for sore throat, catarrh. Leaves used as a culinary herb in salads, soups, seasonings, or steamed for greens. Externally a poultice of borage leaves has been applied to reduce swelling.

Catnip
Carminative, Diaphoretic, Aromatic. Used as an old-fashioned cold remedy, to settle upset stomachs, stimulate sweating and break up a fever. A weak infusion of the leaves (1 Tbs.to a pint of boiling water- steep 10-15 minutes) has been found helpful, given in small doses, to ease infant colic, has a calming, quieting effect.

Cayenne
(Capsicum) Stimulating, Pungent. Used effectively to increase circulation. Produces natural warmth when used as a poultice, as for pneumonia, pleurisy, and other acute congestions. A little capsicum sprinkled in the shoes will assist in warming cold feet. Effective gargle for sore throat; used to stimulate the appetite.

Chamomile
Aromatic, Tonic. Used medicinally as a general tonic. Home remedy for nervous headache, flatulence, colic, and sleep aid. As a poultice, used for swelling and pain. The flowers are dried and used in making tea for a soothing beverage, rinse for natural blonde highlights for hair, insect repellent, and as a aromatic addition to potpourris. Grows freely in any garden.

Charcoal

Antidote, Poultice. Effective remedy for intestinal flatulence and diarrhea. Antidote used for chemical poisons, intestinal bacteria, and toxins. Taken at the first feeling of queasiness, activated charcoal will often thwart the effects of toxins ingested from contaminated water or food. Charcoal poultices are very beneficial for insect and snake bites, pains, sores, bruises, inflammation of the eyes, and swellings. Charcoal may be obtained from eucalyptus, willow, pine, or other soft wood. Internal use: Mix with water or olive oil (healing). Poultices: Mix with water, smartweed herb, or flaxseed meal.

Comfrey

Demulcent, Emollient, Nutritive, Vulnerary, Astringent. Contains mucilage, a gelatinous substance and allantoin useful in healing wounds, burns, ulcers, and pain. Poultices made of the leaves and root are applied to swellings, bruises, and burns. A decoction made of the root is helpful in coughs, sore throat, and as a mouthwash or gargle.

Coriander

Aromatic, Carminative, Stomachic. Good to flavor other unpleasant herbs, and as a seasoning in breads, fruits, desserts. Stomach tonic, will help expel gas. Coriander is likened to the "Manna" provided by God for the Israelites during the forty years of wilderness journey. *"And the house of Israel called the name thereof Manna; and it was like coriander seed, white; and the taste thereof was like wafers made with honey."* Exodus 16:31

Cranberry

Astringent, Diuretic, Nutritive, Tonic. Low, mat-forming evergreen shrub that produces slightly oval-shaped, dark red fruits. Thrives in acidic bogs and wet sandy marshes. It belongs to the genus *Vaccinium,* which also includes blueberries, bilberries, and huckleberries. Cranberries are harvested in late summer. Some are pressed for juice, or dried for decoctions, liquid extracts, and capsules of powdered juice concentrate. Early settlers adopted cranberries both as a food and a source of medicine, particularly for bladder and kidney complaints. Cranberry's healing powers are well documented, and widely accepted for the treatment and prevention of urinary tract infections. Cranberry is rich in tannins, flavonoids, and powerful antioxidants.

Dandelion

Tonic, Stomachic, Diuretic. A lawn "weed" which spreads quickly and is difficult to eradicate. This bitter herb is an excellent source of Vitamin A. Also contains calcium, Vitamin C, and natural inulin. The tender leaves gathered in early spring are used in salad and cooked for table greens. The roots are dried and roasted, then ground and used like coffee. Good tonic, digestive aid, and blood purifier. The tea is used as a diuretic and remedy for anemia, and liver disorders.

Echinacea

Antibacterial, Antiseptic, Depurative, Tonic. A popular hardy perennial with large daisy-like flowers (also known as purple coneflower). Widely cultivated as a medicinal plant, available in extracts, tinctures, tablets, ointments, capsules or teas. Traditionally used to fight infections, and reduce the symptoms and duration of colds, flu, tonsillitis, and bronchitis. Echinacea may contain active substances that stimulate the immune system to counter bacterial, viral, and fungal infections.

Fennel

Aromatic, Carminative, Stomachic. A European herb of the carrot family often used for indigestion, bloating, upset stomach, and colic. A wonderful herb for flavoring foods and other medicinals. Chew the leaves, bulb, or seeds for a pleasant refreshing taste and breath sweetener. Fennel has been used to increase the flow of breast milk in nursing mothers by boiling the seeds in barley water. An old household remedy found in most Italian gardens. Also known as **finocchio**.

Garlic

Antibacterial, Antiseptic, Aromatic, Diaphoretic, Expectorant. Although unpopular with many because of its offensive odor, garlic has been used to help heal many ailments. An excellent remedy for coughs, colds, and bronchial conditions aiding in the removal of mucous from the throat and lungs. Several cloves may be blended with tomato juice and lemon for an appetizing drink. Garlic has a long list of positive benefits and has been used medicinally throughout history. Studies have shown garlic to raise beneficial HDL cholesterol and lower total and LDL cholesterol as well as triglycerides. Popular as a culinary herb, used in salads, breads, spreads, soups, stews, dressings, etc. Chew a little parsley or fennel seed, after eating fresh garlic, to sweeten breath.

Ginseng

Stimulant, Tonic, Nutritive. (Siberian, American) Ginseng is widely used to strengthen the immune system, for energy, strength, stamina and vigor. Helps to counteract male impotence, stimulate appetite and normalize blood pressure.

Golden Seal

Tonic, Stomachic, Hemostatic, Depurative. An extremely bitter herb noted for many remedial properties. It is considered a natural antibiotic, and is often mixed with Echinacea as an immune system tonic. Has been used to check internal hemorrhage, and as a bitter stomachic. Antiseptic and cleansing to wounds, sores, and ulcers. Useful as a mouthwash for canker sores, infected gums, and sore throat. Improved flavor when combined with other herbs.

Hyssop

Aromatic, Depurative, Antiseptic, Expectorant, Vermifuge. An old Bible remedy used for cleansing. *"Purge me with hyssop and I shall be clean..."* Psalm 51:7. A general cleansing tonic helpful in coughs, colds, fevers, to expel worms, and improve circulation. The leaves are used in making a pleasant tasting tea, and sometimes used as a culinary herb in salads, breads, and soups. The essential oil derived from hyssop is used in making perfume, soap, and candles.

Peppermint and Spearmint

Aromatic, Stimulant, Carminative, Antispasmodic. Popular, pleasant tasting herbs of the mint family. The tea is commonly used as a refreshing, invigorating beverage. Used also to improve digestion and relieve colic, cramps, nausea, chills, vomiting, headaches, fevers, and the flu. As a culinary herb, mint imparts a delightful flavor to jellies, sauces, fruits, spreads, and desserts. Used in cosmetics, shampoos, and lotions for its astringent, stimulating, and cooling effect. Also used as a natural fragrance. Peppermint leaves are broader, shorter, and a darker shade of green than spearmint.

Plantain

Antiseptic, Astringent, Vulnerary. A remedy useful in healing wounds. Fresh crushed leaves are used on stings and bites, and will give relief when rubbed on poison ivy. A poultice made of the ground leaves is good applied to wounds and sores and will often check bleeding. The ribbed ovate shaped leaf is easily identified and found growing most everywhere as a common weed.

Red Clover

Antispasmodic, Depurative. Everyone can gather and dry these pretty blossoms. They make a pleasant tea steeped alone, or combined with an aromatic herb. Red clover tea may be taken as freely as water. A good blood purifier, soothing the nerves and effective in coughs and bronchial conditions. Gather blossoms in summer when in full bloom. Dry in the shade. Store in clean jars. Red clover tea was one of E. G. White's simple home remedies.

Rosemary

Aromatic, Astringent, Tonic. A delightful culinary herb to season salads, soups, breads, etc. Also used externally in cosmetics, shampoos (to combat dandruff and thinning hair), in lotions for it's stimulating, toning effect. The tea is an old-fashioned remedy for colds, indigestion, headache, fatigue, depression, and as a mouthwash. Effective in treating arthritis, aching muscles, rheumatic pain.

Sage

Astringent, Expectorant, Tonic, Vermifuge. A common household herb used in many ways to flavor meatless dishes, soups, vegetables, etc. Useful in coughs, colds, fever, improved brain functions, gargle for sore throat, weak digestion, nervous exhaustion, headache, and tonic for hair and scalp. Sage tea has been used as an antiflatulent, an effective supplement to treat hot flashes, to expel worms, and when taken cold to help dry up milk in nursing mothers (if necessary).

Sorrel

Diuretic, Nutritive, Tonic. The fresh leaves add a lemony spark to salads and sandwiches, or lightly steamed, served much like spinach. Rich source of Vitamin A, C, Calcium, and Potassium. Very palatable. Chopped fine makes a wonderful addition to soybean curd (tofu) mixed with a little mayonnaise. Medicinally, sorrel has been used for skin disorders, as a preventive tonic against scurvy, and the tea given to reduce fevers and quench thirst. Also called sheep's sorrel, this herb is known for being one of four ingredients in Essiac, an herbal mixture promoted to have antioxidant, anti-inflammatory, anti-cancer activity.

Spearmint (see Peppermint above)

Thyme

Aromatic, Antiseptic, Carminative, Diaphoretic, Vulnerary. A popular household culinary herb widely used in seasoning. The oil is used as fragrance. A strong infusion made of the dried leaves, cooled, strained, and mixed with honey will yield a thyme syrup which is beneficial in coughing spells, sore throat, and colds. The tea is helpful in fevers, to expel gas and increase perspiration.

Wintergreen (berries)

Aromatic, Astringent, Stimulant (mild). The bright red berries are prized for their sweet and refreshing flavor. They can be eaten as a special treat, with fruit, or combined with honey to make a wintergreen honey spread (see recipe). The tea is beneficial as a gargle, and the oil from the leaves is used in liniment, salves, perfumes, and for flavoring.

Note: The herbal properties listed are a guide to the traditional use of herbs, not intended to be diagnostic or prescriptive for medical conditions. For additional Herbs see Medicinal Herbs of Yesterday for Today herbal chart set, a handy guide for the use of herbs, listed in the back of this book.

Homemade Seasonings

The use of healthful condiments such as aromatic herbs, garlic and lemon, help to stimulate the appetite, improve digestion, and reduce the need of salt in seasoning foods

Chicken-style Seasoning

2 cups food yeast flakes
1½ Tbs. garlic powder
¼ cup onion powder
1½ Tbs. sea salt
2 Tbs. Italian seasoning
1 tsp. celery seed, ground
2 Tbs. parsley flakes, dried
2 tsp. paprika or sweet pepper flakes

Put all ingredients in a food processor or blender. Process until fine and combined well. Store in glass jar. Delicious used as a soup stock, broth, in breading meal, or seasoning.

Chicken-style Broth:
add 1 Tbs. seasoning with 2 cups pure water.

Italian Seasoning

¼ cup oregano, dried leaves
3 Tbs. marjoram, dried leaves
¼ cup sweet basil, dried leaves
2 Tbs. thyme, dried leaves
¼ cup rosemary, dried leaves
1 Tbs. sage, dried leaves
1 tsp. garlic powder, opt.
½ tsp. paprika, opt.

Crush herbs in a bowl or use a mortar and pestle. Mix well all together to combine. Store in a covered container or glass jar, in a cool dry place. Use to flavor Italian dishes, pizza, pasta, sauces, and salad dressing.

Beef-style Seasoning

1 cup food yeast flakes
2 tsp. celery seed, ground
3 Tbs. onion powder
1 tsp. kelp or dulse powder
2 tsp. garlic and salt
1 tsp. thyme and sage

Put all ingredients into blender. Process until fine and blended together.
Store in covered container or glass jar in cool dry place. No need to refrigerate.

Poultry Seasoning

¼ cup dried sage
1 Tbs. dried thyme
1 tsp. fennel or coriander, ground
1 tsp. marjoram
1 tsp. dill seed
½ tsp. garlic salt
¼ tsp. paprika

Process all ingredients in a blender until fine and blended together. Store in small jar. Use in bread stuffing, gravy or recipes calling for poultry seasoning.

Chili-like Powder

¼ cup dried red pepper flakes
2 Tbs. onion powder
2 Tbs. garlic powder
2 Tbs. paprika
2 Tbs. parsley flakes
2 Tbs. coriander, ground
1 Tbs. oregano
2 tsp. cumin
1 tsp. turmeric
2 bay leaves (optional)

Put all ingredients together in a blender or food processor. Grind to a fine powder. Store in a glass jar in a cool dry place. Use to flavor Mexican dishes, chili, beans, soups, stews.

Curry-spice Powder

2 Tbs. coriander, ground
1 Tbs. cumin, ground
2 Tbs. fenugreek or fennel seed
1 Tbs. garlic powder
2 Tbs. onion powder
1 Tbs. paprika
1 Tbs. turmeric powder
1 Tbs. red pepper flakes
1 Tbs. celery seed powder
2 tsp. cardamom

Blend all together into a fine powder using a spice mill or blender. Store in a glass jar, in a cool dry place. Used in Indian cuisine, to flavor black beans, split pea soup, lentils, and vegetable sauces.

Sesame-Parsley Sprinkle

A simple, nourishing and tasty topping, for rice, stir-fry, vegetables, pasta and soup.

2 parts Sesame Seeds, hulled, toasted
1 part Fresh Parsley, chopped
Lemon juice, just a sprinkle

Toast sesame seeds (see recipe) to golden brown. Combine in food processor with fresh parsley and a sprinkle of lemon, pulsating until finely ground. Refrigerate in jar or freeze.

Parmesan "Cheese"

This substitute not only looks and tastes like real cheese, but also provides equal or greater amounts of protein, calcium, iron, B vitamins, and other nutrients.

1 cup almonds, blanched (opt.)
½ cup nutritional yeast flakes
⅓ cup sesame seeds, hulled, toasted
1 tsp. sea salt, to taste
¼ tsp. garlic powder

In a food processor, combine the almonds, yeast flakes, toasted sesame seeds, salt and garlic into powder. Cover, store in refrigerator. Use the same way as parmesan cheese.

Breading Meal - Hi B

2 cups fine bread crumbs
½ cup food yeast flakes
½ cup w.w. pastry flour
½ cup corn or soy flour
2 Tbs. onion + 2 tsp. garlic powder
2 Tbs. parsley flakes, dried, fine
1 tsp. paprika
1½ tsp. sea salt, to taste

Mix together. Store in covered jar, keep cool. Use breading meal for gluten steaks, not-meat balls, tofu, eggplant, squash, okra, etc.

Gomashio

Sesame salt: A popular seasoning with just 2 ingredients, used in Japan to season one's food.

1 cup unhulled sesame seeds, toasted
1 Tbs. sea salt, to taste

Grind toasted sesame seeds and add sea salt. An excellent garnish for any stir-fry, grain or vegetable dish. Sprinkle on gomashio *in place of* salt.

Au Gratin Topping

The perfect topping for Baked Chee Spaghetti casserole, potatoes, or green beans. Just sprinkle on and bake or broil for a crusty brown topping!

¾ cup dry bread crumbs or Grape-Nuts
¼ cup crumbled tofu
2 Tbs. ground almonds
1 Tbs. nutritional yeast flakes
¼ tsp. paprika, ¼ tsp. sea salt
1 tsp. olive oil

Combine all ingredients, using fingers to crumble together. Sprinkle over food. Bake uncovered, or place under broiler to brown.

Herb Salt

Dry the outer dark leaves of lettuce and other greens to make this vitamin and mineral rich seasoning salt.

⅓ cup finely ground
    dehydrated vegetables
2 Tbs. Celtic Sea Salt, fine
1 Tbs. onion and garlic powder, mixed
2 tsp. ground dried herbs
    (oregano, basil, paprika)

In a food processor or blender, process the dried vegetables (a variety of greens, parsley, chives, carrot, dill, fennel, sweet red pepper, etc.) to a fine powder. Mix with the sea salt and other ingredients. Use to season pasta, rice, potatoes, salad. broth, soup, and popcorn!

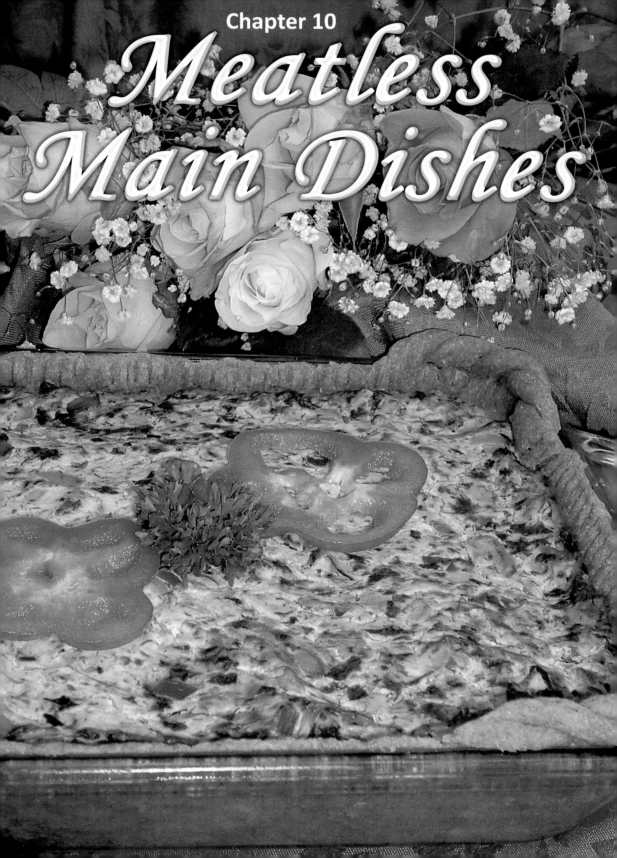

Meatless Main Dishes

Index - CHAPTER 10

Chapter cover photo: *Tofu Garden Quiche*, page 343

Meatless Main Dishes

Vegetarian dishes can include legumes, grains, vegetables, pasta, tofu, nuts, seeds, and herbs. These plant foods, simply and properly combined, will adequately supply an excellent source of protein in the diet. You will find a variety of recipes in this chapter that are wholesome, nutritious, and delicious, suitable for gluten-free diets.

Garden Veggie Patties

¼ cup chopped onion
¼ cup green bell pepper
2 cloves garlic, minced
2 slices whole grain bread
¼ cup shredded zucchini
½ cup shredded carrots
1 cup firm tofu, mashed
3 cups mashed potatoes
¼ cup parsley, minced
1 Tbs. onion powder
½ tsp. rosemary; ½ tsp. sage
½ tsp. sea salt; ½ tsp. paprika
1 Tbs. Vegenaise®, opt.

Lightly brown onion, chopped green pepper, and garlic, in a non-stick skillet, with little or no oil. In a mixing bowl, crumble the bread into med-fine crumbs; add the shredded zucchini, carrots, mashed tofu, potatoes, parsley, and seasonings. Mix and combine together. Using a jar ring and lid; form mixture into thin, 3½" patties. Brown on both sides, in a non-stick skillet or on a prepared baking sheet, in 350° oven. Yield: 12 patties.

Vegetable Pecan Nut Loaf

1¼ cups soy or nut milk
2 Tbs. flour
1 Tbs. soy or olive oil
1¼ tsp. sea salt or kelp
3 cups steamed brown rice
1½ cups chopped pecans, almonds
or walnuts
1 cup seasoned bread crumbs
1 cup finely chopped celery
¾ cup chopped green or red pepper
½ cup chopped onion, sautéed
2 Tbs. cashew or peanut butter

In a saucepan over medium heat, stir first 4 ingredients, until mixture comes to a boil. Place rest of ingredients in a mixing bowl. Add the cooked mixture, stirring to combine all ingredients together. Spoon into prepared loaf pan. Bake in 350° oven for 50-60 minutes. Turn out on platter, garnish with parsley. Serve with your favorite gravy.

Almond Rice Loaf

3 cups cubed whole grain bread
¼ cup dry quick oats
1 cup nut or soy milk
4 cups steamed brown rice
¼ cup cashew or peanut butter
2 cups chopped almonds
2 cups tofu, cut in cubes
¼ cup diced onion or 1 Tbs. powder
2 Tbs. finely chopped parsley
1 Tbs. soy sauce or sea salt, to taste

Soak bread and oats in milk. Combine the rice, nut butter and almonds. Add and mix with the rest of ingredients. Bake in a square baking dish or loaf pan at 350° for 40 minutes. Serve with **Almond Milk Gravy**, **Parsley Gravy**, or your favorite. Yield: 8 servings

Soy-Millet Patties or Loaf

2 cups soaked soybeans
½ cup pure water
1 Tbs. onion powder
1½ tsp. celery seed
1½ tsp. oregano
1 tsp. vegetable salt
3Tbs. soy sauce
1 Tbs. soy or olive oil, opt.

Blend above ingredients until beans are smooth, put into mixing bowl and add:

1½ cups cooked millet, firm
¼ cup raw ground cashews
¼ cup raw ground sunflower seeds
3 slices bread, crumbled
2 Tbs. nut butter, opt.

Mix well all together. Form patties or spoon into prepared casserole dish. Brown patties on both sides or bake dish at 350° for 1-1¼ hours. Serve with **Almond** or **Cashew Gravy.**

Note: Soaking beans removes objectionable characteristics (see Bean Basics).

Lentil-Nut Loaf

3 cups cooked lentils, soft purée
½ cup regular oats or 3 slices bread
1½ cups raw nuts, almonds, pecans
   or walnuts chopped
½ cup sunflower seeds, ground
½ cup chopped celery, sautéed
1 Tbs. onion powder
1 Tbs. soy sauce or Bragg Aminos®
1 tsp. sage, ½ tsp. thyme and garlic
1 tsp. sea salt, to taste
½ tsp. cumin or celery seed

Mix all ingredients together.

Bake in non-stick loaf pan for 1 hour at 350°. Good served with **Almond** or **Cashew Gravy.** Yield: 6 servings

Carrot-Rice Loaf

4 cups steamed brown rice
   or mashed garbanzos
½ cup peanut butter, crunchy
4 cups grated raw carrots
1 cup tofu, crumbled
2 Tbs. onion powder
   or ½ cup sautéed onions
1 cup coarse bread crumbs
thyme and sea salt, to taste

Mix brown rice with nut butter. Add carrots, tofu, onion, etc., using crumbled bread as necessary to make right consistency. Spoon into prepared casserole or loaf pan. Bake 45-55 minutes at 350°. Serve with your favorite gravy. **Yield: 8 servings.**

Cashew Brown Rice Loaf

1 cup raw cashews, finely chopped
2 cups steamed brown rice
2 cups rich nut or soy milk, plain
2 large onions, chopped, sautéed
1 cup finely chopped celery
4 slices bread, crumbled
2 Tbs. Bragg Aminos® or soy sauce
4 Tbs. minced parsley
½ tsp. thyme, sage, celery seed,
   to taste
veggie salt, to taste

Chop the nuts or run through a food grinder. Add the remaining ingredients and mix well. Spoon into prepared baking dish. Cover and place dish in pan of water. Bake 1 hour at 350°. Serve with **Cashew Gravy** or your favorite sauce. Yield: 6 servings

Mix well all together, (for uniform texture, cereal may be coarsely blended with water). Put into an oiled loaf pan and bake 350° for 45-60 minutes until set. Can be made ahead and re-heated. Slice and serve with **Cashew** or **Parsley Gravy**. Yield: 4 servings.

Harvest Nut Loaf

3 cups cooked brown rice, dry
1¼ cups finely shredded carrots
1¼ cups finely diced celery
¼ cup finely chopped parsley
⅓ cup chopped walnuts
1-2 slices soft bread, crumbled
1¼ cups plain soy or cashew milk
4 Tbs. almond or peanut butter
2 Tbs. soy flour
1 Tbs. Bragg Liquid Aminos®,
**   soy sauce or ½ tsp. sea salt**
1 Tbs. onion powder
**   or ¼ cup chopped sautéed onion**

In a large mixing bowl, combine the rice, carrots, celery, parsley, walnuts and bread together. Blend milk, nut butter, soy flour, soy sauce, and onion powder together. Add liquid mixture to ingredients in mixing bowl. Stir and combine thoroughly. Spoon into non-stick loaf pan or casserole. Bake 1 hour at 350°, until golden brown. Serve with your favorite gravy. Yield: 6-8 servings

Lentil-Tomato Loaf

4 slices bread, crumbled
2 cups tomato purée or soup
2½ cups (1 lb.) dry lentils, cooked
½ cup almonds, finely chopped
½ cup onions, sautéed
½ cup celery, sautéed
2 cloves garlic, minced
½ tsp. thyme, savory or sage
1 Tbs. olive oil, optional
2 tsp. sea salt, to taste
¼ tsp. cayenne, to taste, opt.

Mix bread with tomato soup. Add lentils (cooked almost dry), onions, celery, and rest of ingredients. Mix well and bake in non-stick loaf pan at 350° for 45 minutes, or until set. Serve with **Tomato Sauce** or gravy. Yield: 8 servings.

Millet-Barley Loaf

1 cup cooked millet
1 cup cooked barley
½ cup pure water
½ cup quick oats
½ cup ground cashews
1 Tbs. onion powder
2 Tbs. peanut or other nut butter
¼ tsp. thyme
⅛ tsp. cumin or cayenne
sea salt, to taste

Favorite Main Dishes

Savory Stir Fry with Bean Sprouts
page 345

**Three Grain Oven Pilaf
w/ Mushrooms**
page 315

Turkey Loaf
page 306-307

Eggplant Parmigiana
page 326

Tofu Quiche
page 345

Mini Layered Lasagna
page 332

Tofu Veggie Scramble
page 353, 466

Sprouted Lentil Casserole
page 320

Skillet Rice & Sugar Snap Peas
page 541

Tofu-Veggie Kabobs
page 349

Baked Chee Spagetti Casserole
page 323

One Dish Italian Meal
page 335

4. Spoon mixture and press firmly into a prepared 9"x 5"x 3½" loaf pan. (brush or spray with a non-stick spray, then sprinkle with sesame seeds). Cover with foil.

Baking method: Place loaf pan in a larger pan with 1" of water. Bake at 350° for 1½ hours. Remove from water pan and bake uncovered for another 45-60 minutes or until golden brown. Remove from oven; let set for 10 minutes.

To remove from pan, gently slide dull knife around edge of pan to loosen loaf.

Thanksgiving "Turkey" Loaf

A family favorite for that special holiday feast. This meatless loaf has a wonderful flavor, texture and lots of eye appeal for an exquisite presentation. Even the cold leftovers taste great!

4 cups light bread, day-old, crumbled
2 cups cooked brown rice
14-oz tofu, medium/soft
1½ cups soy, millet or rice milk, plain
3 Tbs. arrowroot, cornstarch or flour
**1-lb (3 cups) Cedar Lake frozen
   turkey roll***
2 cups finely chopped celery
2 Tbs. chicken-style seasoning
1 Tbs. Italian or poultry seasoning
2 tsp. sage, onion pwd, sea salt to taste

1. In a large mixing bowl place the crumbled bread and warm cooked rice.

2. Blend the tofu and soy milk with 3 Tbs. arrowroot, cornstarch or flour. Pour the blended mixture over the bread and rice. Stir well to combine.

3. Shred 1# (3 cups) of the turkey

roll (thaw the day before) by pulling off small pieces at a time. Add to mixing bowl. Add chopped celery and seasonings. Stir all ingredients together.

Place large platter on top of loaf, hold securely and turn upside-down onto platter. Cut loaf in half lengthwise. Pour **Holiday Gravy** over loaf. Garnish with **chopped parsley, pimento, and sliced or slivered almonds, lightly toasted**.

* Other frozen vegetarian products of your choice, can be substituted for the turkey.

1 Tbs. arrowroot or tapioca flour
1 tsp. chicken-style seasoning
1 tsp. soy margarine, opt.
*garnish: parsley, pimento, almonds

Holiday Gravy

The finishing touch to "Thanksgiving Turkey Loaf" or your favorite meatless entrée.

2 cups finely diced celery, steamed
1 cup pure water or cooking liquid
⅓ cup cashew nuts
½ cup soy milk, plain
1½ tsp. onion powder + ½ tsp. salt

In a medium saucepan, steam or cook diced celery 2-3 min. until crisp-tender. Drain off liquid into a measuring cup. Blend cashews and seasonings, adding the water gradually, while blending smooth. (use leftover liquid from cooking celery as part of the water). Add soymilk, arrowroot. Blend again. Pour over the cooked celery in saucepan. Bring to a boil, stirring constantly until thick. Serve over your favorite entrée.

Garnish with chopped pimento, parsley, and toasted almonds.

Millet-Pumpkin Seed Patties

Looking for a way to use that leftover cereal? These simple patties, any size, are good served in a sandwich, pita pocket, or casserole with your favorite gravy.

4 cups steamed millet cereal
1 cup steamed brown rice
1 cup ground pumpkin seeds, raw
¼ cup ground cashew nuts
**   or nut butter**
1 Tbs. onion powder
**   or ¼ cup chopped sautéed onion**
1 tsp. sage, leaf
1 tsp. sea salt or liquid aminos, to taste
1-2 tsp. minced garlic
1 Tbs. olive oil, opt.

Mix all together in a mixing bowl. Form into patties. Sprinkle with paprika and brown on both sides in non-stick pan or bake in 375° oven until golden brown.

Thanksgiving Roast

(For a large family)

3 cups cooked lentils
3 cups cooked millet
3 cups steamed brown rice
3 cups ground wheat gluten
1 cup chopped onion,
**   and/or 3 Tbs. onion powder**
1 Tbs. virgin olive oil
½ cup almonds or cashews
¼ cup sunflower seeds, chopped
1½ Tbs. sage, ground
½ tsp. celery seed, ground
½ tsp. garlic powder
sea salt, to taste
½ cup quick oats or grape nuts cereal
1 cup (3 slices) bread, crumbled

Combine the lentils, millet, brown rice, and ground gluten (see recipe). Brown onions in olive oil; lightly toast chopped almonds and sunflower seeds. Add to lentil mixture, add seasonings, quick oats, and crumbled bread, enough to make a firm mix. Place in non-stick loaf pans or prepared baking dish. Bake at 350° for 1 hr. Cover with towel to keep moist. Serve with your favorite holiday gravy.

Hi-Protein Millet Patties

Millet, is a favorite food in our family - often combined with other grains, legumes, nuts, herbs or seasonings, for a savory meatless dish. This super-easy patty recipe provides a good source of protein, vitamins and minerals, and again makes millet a winner!

4 cups cooked millet
½ cup almond, cashew
**   or peanut butter**
1 Tbs. soy sauce or Bragg Aminos®
2 Tbs. onion powder
1 tsp. veggie salt or garlic powder
celery seed, rosemary, thyme, to taste

Cook millet until fluffy and dry (see Cooking Methods for Grains). Combine with remaining ingredients. Form into patties and brown on both sides in non-stick or lightly oiled skillet. Simple and delicious served with **Parsley Gravy** or **Country-Style Gravy**. Yield: 12-16 patties.

Garden Burgers

1 large red potato, grated
¾ cup quick oats, raw
¼ cup soy milk, plain unsweetened
½ cup grated zucchini or summer squash
½ cup walnuts or pecans, finely chopped
⅓ cup green onion, finely chopped
1-2 cloves garlic, minced
1 Tbs. soy sauce or Bragg® Liquid Aminos
1 tsp. *Italian seasoning; 1 tsp. sea salt
1-2 slices whole grain bread, crumbled
*1-2 Tbs. Fresh chopped herbs (basil,
  rosemary, sage, oregano, thyme),
  can be used in place of dried herbs.

Scrub and grate raw potato. In mixing bowl, soak oats in milk; add grated potatoes, squash, nuts, onion, garlic and seasonings. Add crumbled day old bread sufficient to make a stiff mixture. Form into uniform 3½" patties using wide mouth jar ring and lid. Bake both sides at 375° on non-stick baking sheet or brown in skillet. Delicious served with whole-grain bun and trimmings (tomato, avocado, onion, sprouts); or in a casserole dish with your favorite sauce or gravy.

Multi-Grain Cereal Patties

1 cup diced celery
1 onion, chopped
  or 1 Tbs. onion powder
4 cups cooked multi-grain cereal
¾ cup cashews, finely ground
½ cup pumpkin or sunflower
  seeds, coarsely ground
2 Tbs. soy vegenaise
1 tsp. sage, sea salt, to taste
2 Tbs. soy sauce or Bragg Aminos®

Brown celery and onions in a non-stick skillet. Add the warm cooked cereal and rest of ingredients. Mix well. Form into 3 ½" flat patties. Brown in skillet on both sides, or in the oven on a prepared baking sheet, at 350° until crisp. Makes 10-12 patties.

Walnut Oat Burgers

1 cup quick oats
1 cup seasoned bread crumbs
1 cup finely chopped, sautéed, onion
1 cup walnuts, finely chopped
¼ cup soy flour
2 Tbs. cashew nut butter, opt.
savory, sage, sea salt, to taste

In a mixing bowl, combine all ingredients. Add just enough hot water to hold together. Mix well. Form into flat burgers. Brown on both sides in a non-stick or oiled skillet. Serve with burger buns and trimmings, or with gravy as a main dish.

Barley Burgers for Barley Buns

2 cups cooked whole barley or sprouted-steamed
1 Tbs. onion powder or 1 chopped onion
½ cup ground walnuts, pecans or pumpkin seeds
¼ cup grated raw potato
¼ cup minced green pepper
½ tsp. each thyme, sage, sea salt
1 Tbs. olive oil, optional
seasoned bread crumbs

Put barley through coarse food grinder or food processor. Add rest of ingredients, and sufficient bread crumbs to make firm. Mix well and shape into flat burgers. Brown on both sides in heavy skillet or broiler. Serve between **Barley Buns** with **Soya Spread** or **Health Ketchup**, onions and sprouts.

Sprouted Wheat Burgers

2 cups sprouted wheat (shown at right)
½ cup sunflower seeds
¼ cup walnuts
2 cups steamed barley or millet
2 Tbs. soy sauce
1 Tbs. onion powder
    or ¼ cup sautéed onion
½ tsp. each thyme, sage, sea salt
2 Tbs. peanut or cashew butter
½ cup soft bread crumbs
1-2 Tbs. olive or soy oil, opt.

Chop or coarse grind first 4 ingredients. Add rest of ingredients. Form into 3 ½" flat burgers. Brown quickly in a skillet on both sides. Place in burger buns and serve with **Health Ketchup**, sliced onion, lettuce or alfalfa sprouts (see recipe).

Note: Serve in casserole with **Almond** or **Cashew Gravy** as a meatless main dish.

Almond Lentil Patties

2 cups mashed lentils, cooked
½ cup ground sunflower seeds
2 cups tofu, cut in cubes
½ cup finely ground almonds
1 cup cereal flakes
sea salt and seasonings, to taste

Form into patties. Bake in 350° oven on both sides or in oiled skillet. Serve with your favorite gravy. Yield: 4 servings

Super Sunburgers

Finally, the secret's out for the recipe so often requested. Excellent served as a main dish, a hearty sandwich, for a picnic, potluck, or pack-it lunch. Super nutritious, supersedes the hamburger; low in fat, high in fiber, and super delicious!

4½ cups pure water
½ cup soy sauce or Bragg Aminos®
1½ tsp. Italian Seasoning
1½ tsp. sweet basil
1½ tsp. garlic powder
½ tsp. thyme; ½ tsp. oregano
¼ tsp. cayenne, to taste, opt.
½ cup chopped walnuts
⅓ cup raw sunflower seeds
½ cup finely chopped celery
1 medium onion, chopped, sautéed
½ cup finely grated carrot, opt.
⅓ cup nutritional yeast flakes
2 Tbs. Fearn soya powder, or granules, opt.
4½ cups regular oats

In a large kettle, bring water, soy sauce and seasonings to a boil. Add walnuts, sunflower seeds, celery, onion, carrot, food yeast and soya powder; bring to a boil again. Add the regular oats, stirring just enough to mix evenly. Turn off heat; cover, allow to cool 5-10 minutes. Form into 3" burger patties, using a wide mouth jar ring and lid. Place on non-stick or oiled baking sheets. Bake burgers in 400° oven, 15 minutes on each side, or until lightly browned and crisp.
Yield: approx. 18 - 3" burgers, or double the recipe; cool, stack, freeze for later use.

Stuffed Peppers with Brown Rice

1. Wash 6 bell peppers (any color). Cut peppers in half lengthwise, or if not too big, cut a thin slice off from stem end of pepper. Remove seeds; rinse peppers. Parboil or steam peppers for 5 minutes. Drain.

2. Fill peppers with rice stuffing (see recipes). Sprinkle with paprika. Bake covered 45 minutes at 350°, then uncover and bake 15 minutes longer or until peppers are tender.

3. Garnish with parsley and serve with tomato sauce if desired.

Brown Rice Stuffing #1

2½ cups cooked brown rice
½ cup ground cashews or tofu
½ cup tomato sauce
2 Tbs. onion powder or ½ cup fresh
2 cloves garlic, minced
1 tsp. olive or soy oil, optional
3-4 slices whole grain bread
1 tsp. sweet basil, dried
½ tsp. oregano, dried
½ tsp. sea salt, to taste

In a mixing bowl, combine the cooked brown rice, cashews, tofu, tomato sauce and herbs. Sauté the fresh chopped onions and minced garlic in olive oil; add to the rice mixture. Crumble the bread and combine with rest of ingredients; add salt to taste.

Brown Rice Stuffing or Loaf #2

1 cup diced celery
¼ cup diced red peppers
¼ cup minced onion
3 cloves garlic, minced
½ cup sliced mushrooms
    and /or chopped walnuts
½ tsp. salt or 1 Tbs. Bragg Liquid Aminos®
½ tsp. ground sage and/or thyme
3 cups cooked brown rice
3 Tbs. almond or peanut butter
½ cup fresh parsley, chopped
seasoned bread crumbs, coarse

Sauté celery, peppers onion and garlic in heated skillet with 1 Tbs. olive oil until crisp tender. Add mushrooms, salt and seasonings. Simmer 2-3 minutes. Combine with cooked rice. Stir in nut butter, parsley, and seasoned bread crumbs to right consistency; mix well. Good for stuffed peppers, squash, eggplant, cabbage rolls, or baked as a loaf.

Cashew Oriental Rice

Capture the full nutty-flavor and aroma of this dish with long grain finely textured basmati rice.

2 cups Tofu, cut in cubes, browned
½ cup sliced mushrooms, sautéed
½ cup cashew halves, lightly toasted
1-2 Tbs. chicken-style seasoning,
    or sea salt, to taste
4 cups cooked basmati or brown rice
1 cup frozen mixed vegetables, cooked

In a large skillet brown the tofu and mushrooms with a little canola or sesame oil. Add the cashew nuts, seasoning and cooked rice. Stir in the mixed vegetables. Serve in a casserole dish; top with gravy if desired. Serves 6.

Soy Peanut Patties

½ cup soaked or sprouted soybeans
1 stalk celery, chopped
1 cup peanuts, oven-toasted
   finely ground
1 cup cooked cornmeal
½ cup shredded carrots
2 Tbs. whole wheat flour
1 onion finely chopped, sautéed
1 clove garlic or ¼ tsp. garlic powder
1 Tbs. olive oil
¼ tsp. sea salt or liquid aminos, to taste

Blend soybeans with ½ cup water until smooth; add celery, blend again. Pour into mixing bowl; add peanuts, cooked cornmeal, carrots and flour. Sauté onion and garlic in olive oil, add to mixture; add sea salt or liquid aminos to taste. Form patties. Bake in 375° oven 35-45 minutes or brown on both sides in non-stick skillet.

Tofu Brown Rice Croquettes

3 cups steamed natural brown rice
4 Tbs. peanut or cashew butter
½ cup chopped pecans or walnuts
2 cups tofu, mashed
½ cup chopped fresh parsley
1 Tbs. onion powder
   or ¼ cup chopped onion
1 cup soft whole grain bread crumbs
1 tsp. crushed basil, rosemary,
   and fennel seed
1-2 Tbs. soy sauce or Bragg Aminos

Mix all ingredients in order listed. Form into croquettes or patties. Sprinkle with paprika or roll in favorite breading meal. Bake at 350-375° turning to brown on all sides, or brown in lightly oiled skillet. Serve with **Parsley Gravy.** Yield: 15 croquettes or patties

Thanksgiving Chestnut Croquettes

1 cup finely chopped celery stalks
   and leaves
½ cup finely minced onion
bread crumbs, seasoned or soft bread
2 cups boiled chestnuts or garbanzos
4 cups cooked mashed potato
   or cooked brown rice
¼ cup almond, cashew
   or peanut butter
½ cup minced fresh parsley
1 tsp. oregano; ½ tsp. savory
1 tsp. chicken style seasoning
sea salt, to taste

Sauté celery and onions until soft in a little water or olive oil. Add some bread crumbs (about ¼ cup), stirring to prevent excessive browning. Finely chop or purée boiled chestnuts or garbanzo beans. Turn mixture into a deep bowl. Add remaining ingredients, mixing well with clean hands or spoon. Add soft bread crumbs as needed, to make a firm consistency. Shape croquettes and sprinkle with paprika. Brown in a non-stick skillet or bake in a 350° oven, turning to brown evenly. Delicious served with **Health Ketchup, Parsley Gravy or Holiday Gravy.** (see recipes).
Yield: approx. 24 -3½" croquettes.

Spicy Wehani with Cashews

A nutritious, russet color, aromatic, long grain brown rice, with bran and germ layers intact.

1 cup Lundberg Wehini rice, uncooked
⅓ cup toasted cashews, chopped
1 Tbs. olive oil or soy butter
6 green onions with tops, sliced
2 cloves garlic, minced
½ tsp. ground cumin; ½ tsp. sea salt
½ tsp. onion powder
¼ tsp. coriander
1 bay leaf; pinch cayenne, opt.
2½ cups pure hot water

Lightly toast cashews in 350° oven, or in a dry skillet on stovetop. In heavy saucepan, with tight fitting lid, heat oil, onion, garlic, and seasonings. Stir and cook until onion is soft. Add rice, stir to mix thoroughly. Add the hot water. Bring to boil; reduce heat, stir once, cover and simmer 45 minutes. Do not remove lid. Remove pan from heat, let stand covered 10-15 minutes. Remove bay leaf. Stir in toasted cashews and serve. Yield: 4 cups

Variation: Add ½ cup crumbled tofu. Use as a filling for stuffed peppers or squash.

Savory Rice with Pecans

4 cups cooked brown & wild rice
1 cup toasted pecans or almonds
1½ cups celery, thinly sliced
1 tsp. onion powder
1 tsp. garlic salt
¼ cup fresh snipped parsley

Prepare the rice (see chapter - **Grains**). Lightly toast pecans or almonds. Sauté celery in 1 tsp. olive oil or a little water, until crisp tender. Add the seasonings, toasted nuts, mixed rice and parsley, stirring occasionally until heated through.

Variations: Sliced mushrooms, sliced green onion, or chopped red pepper, can be used in place of celery. For a main dish, add tofu, cut in small cubes and browned.

Wild Rice & Mushroom Pilaf

½ cup sliced green onion
½ cup chopped celery
3 cups sliced mushrooms, shiitake, chanterelle, portobella
1 cup wild rice*
1 cup sliced almonds, lightly toasted
1½ tsp. "chicken-style" seasoning
3 cups pure water or broth

In a medium covered pan, sauté the onions and celery in a little olive oil until tender. Stir in mushrooms, wild rice, almonds, and seasoning; saute' 2-3 minutes. Carefully add the water or broth; bring to a boil. Reduce heat, simmer covered, about 50 minutes until rice is tender and liquid is absorbed. Leave covered 10 minutes. Fluff with a fork before serving and garnish with more almonds if desired.

*Wild Rice: see Grains chapter for more information

Three Grain Oven Pilaf with Mushrooms & Peppers

Transform simple ordinary grains into an elegant entrée by smothering pilaf with sweet peppers & mushrooms. Lots of texture, taste, eye appeal & nutrition!

1½ cups mixed cracked grain,*(barley,
**   brown rice, quinoa, or wheat)**
1 cup diced celery
½ cup chopped onion
2 cloves garlic, minced
1 Tbs. pure olive oil
½ tsp. sea salt; ½ tsp. ground celery seed
½ cup sliced almonds, lightly toasted
4 cups veggie broth, boiling
roasted peppers, mushrooms
**   (See chapter-Vegetables)**

In a medium skillet or saucepan, sauté the celery, onion and garlic in olive oil until tender. Add the seasonings, almonds and cracked grain; stir to combine. Transfer to 3 qt. casserole dish. Carefully pour boiling veggie broth over grain mixture. Bake covered in a 350° oven for approximately 2 hours or until grains are tender and broth is absorbed. Serve pilaf smothered with roasted sweet peppers and mushrooms. Garnish with parsley. Yield: 8 servings

*Crack barley, rice and wheat in blender on high speed.

Brown Rice with Parsley

4 cups cooked brown rice
¼ cup chopped white or green onion
1-2 cloves garlic, sliced thin
1 tsp. pure olive oil, opt.
⅓ cup fresh minced flat leaf parsley
1 Tbs. light soy sauce or Bragg Aminos®

Cook whole grain brown rice until fluffy and dry, using 1 cup rice + 4 cups water + ½ tsp. salt (see skillet method for cooking rice in chapter **Grains**). Sauté onions, garlic and olive oil in skillet. Add the cooked rice, parsley and soy sauce; heat until warmed. Serve with parsley gravy or sprinkle on toasted sesame seeds if desired.

Bean Basics

- Beans of all kinds are virtually fat-free, and cholesterol-free. The colorful array of beans available (dried, canned, or frozen) are packed with protein, iron, calcium, vitamins, minerals and soluble fiber. Beans are a satisfying substitute for meat.

- Beans are inexpensive, mild flavored, and extremely versatile. When combined with grains, beans supply our body with adequate protein of high biological value. The nutrition derived from legumes (a plant source), far surpasses that of animal origin. *(to use as a replacement for eggs (binder) see **Egg Substitutes - Miscellaneous chapter**)*

- Beans are best stored in a cool dry place, in their original package or air tight container. Most legumes will keep for long periods of time, however beans are best if used within 1 year; beans may require longer cooking time if stored over 2 years.

- Beans / legumes- Soaking and Freezing: With exception of split peas and lentils, beans should be soaked 10-12 hours to soften and plump before cooking (1 cup dry beans = 2½ cups soaked). Soaking beans and changing the water removes most of the gas producing oligosaccharides (simple sugars), found particularly in the skin covering the bean. Soaking is most effective when boiling water is poured over the beans, allow to cool, then discard water and change at least twice during the soaking process. Beans are then frozen overnight and cooked to further aid digestion.

- Beans in their raw state contain toxic properties. Proper soaking, and several hours of cooking or sprouting legumes, is necessary for the proper digestion and assimilation of nutrients. An important fact to consider for the optimal digestion of legumes is **proper food combining.** Keep combinations simple i.e. legumes / beans with grains, green salads, vegetables and nuts. (see **Simple Food Combining Chart** pgs. 64-65, 673)

- Beans and legumes: Cooking methods include boiling /simmering on stovetop; slow– cooker method (pre-cook then transfer to slow-cooker or crock pot); baked in the oven; or cooked in a pressure cooker, (add 2-3 drops of oil to cooker, to prevent foam or skins from clogging the escape valve).

- Beans can also be pre-soaked, then frozen, ready to be used at a later time. Freezing beans often improves the flavor of the recipe, particularly soybeans when used in making soybean milk. Cooking time for beans will vary, depending on the kind, dryness, size, and age of the beans.

- Beans and Seasoning: Herbs may be added **(summer savory may help prevent flatulence)** while cooking beans however, salt or acidic foods, such as tomato paste, juice or sauce, should be added at the end of cooking cycle. Salt and acid toughens the beans.

Savory Mixed Beans, Recipe, pg 318

Legumes

E. Remelo

Kidney Beans

Soybeans

Garbanzos

Mung Beans

Lentils

Red Lentils

Navy Beans

Lima Beans

Black Beans

Pinto Beans

Adzuki Beans

Green Split Peas

Red Beans

Fava Beans

Anasazi Beans

Yellow Split Peas

Fresh Fava Beans

Green Soybeans

Black-Eyed Peas

Savory Mixed Beans

This hearty mixture of beans will satisfy even the healthiest appetite and when prepared in a slow-cooker overnight, will enhance flavors. Enjoy with your favorite cornbread or cornmeal polenta. Rich in protein, calcium, iron, B-vitamins and fiber.

1 cup dry pinto beans
1 cup dry Great Northern or red beans
½ cup dry black beans
4 cups pure water or vegetable broth
2 stalks celery, chopped
1 medium carrot, chopped
1 medium onion, chopped
3 cloves garlic, minced
½ cup dried cut tomatoes or tomato paste
½ tsp. each savory, thyme, oregano
½ tsp. sea salt, dash of cayenne
1 Tbs. olive oil, opt.

1. Sort and rinse beans. Place in large kettle and cover with water. Allow to soak several hours. Drain, cover with boiling water; when cool, drain and discard water. Add 4 cups fresh water or vegetable broth; bring to boil, simmer 30-45 minutes, set aside while preparing vegetables.

2. Lightly tenderize the chopped celery, carrots, onions and garlic in olive oil 3-5 minutes. Add to beans, simmer covered 1½ hours or overnight in a slow-cooker. Stir in tomato, herb seasonings and sea salt. Cover, continue to cook for 1 hour or more, until beans are tender and liquid is absorbed, or transfer beans to a casserole dish, top with soft seasoned breadcrumbs or onion rings and bake at 350° until tender and browned. Good served with steamed rice, a green salad and garlic toast. Yield: 8 main servings.

Baked Bean Loaf or Patties

½ cup minced onion, sautéed
2 cups cooked garbanzo or soybeans, mashed
2 Tbs. soy flour
1 cup steamed brown rice
2 Tbs. nutritional yeast flakes
1 cup soy milk, plain

1 Tbs. Italian seasoning
½ cup quick or rolled oats
salt or Bragg Aminos®, to taste

Sauté minced onions in a little olive oil. Mix all ingredients together in a bowl; let stand ½ hour. Bake in prepared loaf or casserole dish in 350° oven for 45 minutes, or form into patties and brown in a non-stick skillet 5-10 minutes on each side.

Boston Baked Beans

2 cups dry navy beans or *soybeans

Soak beans overnight; drain. In the morning cover beans with 2" fresh water. Cook until almost tender, (*soybeans require several hours or use a pressure-cooker). Add the following ingredients and place in a baking dish:

⅓ cup molasses
1 medium onion, chopped
1 tsp. honey
1 ¼ cup tomato purée
1 Tbs. lemon juice
1-2 Tbs. olive or soy oil, opt.
2-3 tsp. onion powder
2-3 tsp. sea salt, to taste
dash garlic powder or cayenne

Bake covered at 325° 3-4 hours, uncover last hour; or cook in a crock-pot or slow cooker, until beans are tender and liquid is absorbed.

Garbanzo Purée - Hummus

3 cups cooked garbanzos
⅓ cup lightly toasted sesame seed
   or 3 Tbs. sesame tahini
1 Tbs. olive or soy oil, opt.
1 Tbs. dried parsley
1-2 cloves garlic or garlic salt to taste
¼ cup chopped fresh parsley
1½ - 2 Tbs. fresh lemon juice

Blend first 5 ingredients to a smooth
consistency; may heat until warmed
through. Fold in fresh parsley and
lemon juice. Serve in deep bowl.
Delicious over pasta or rice dishes.

Lima Bean Casserole

1½ cups dried lima beans
1 cup tomato puree or soup
2 cups diced celery, sautéed
½ cup diced onion, sautéed
¼ cup chopped green pepper
1 tsp. sea salt
garlic powder and savory to taste
3-4 slices soft bread, crumbled

Soak dried lima beans and cook to
nearly tender, and most liquid is
absorbed.
Mix all ingredients together. Place in
prepared loaf pan or casserole dish;
cover with seasoned breadcrumbs.
Bake at 375° for 45-55 minutes.

Note: A little **corn
meal, grape nuts** or
**2 Tbs.garbanzo
flour** can be
used to
thicken
casserole.

Sprouted Lentil Casserole
(Tender sprouts – a powerhouse of nutrition)

To sprout lentils:
Soak 1-2 cups of dry lentils overnight in a 2 qt. jar. In the morning rinse lentils and drain well (use wire screen to fit wide mouth jar). Divide soaked lentils into 2-4 jars. Keep sprouts in a dark cool place and rinse 2 times a day. Drain well after each rinsing. Sprouts are ready to use in 3- 4 days, when they are ½-1" long. (see Sprouting) Sprouted lentils not used in this recipe, can be covered and stored in refrigerator 1 week. Yield: 1 cup dry lentils = 2½ cups soaked = 8-10 cups sprouted.

In a skillet, sauté vegetables to crisp tender, with 1-2 Tbs. olive or canola oil:

2 cups diced celery
2 cups sliced mushrooms
1 cup chopped onions
½ cup red bell pepper, diced
8-10 cups sprouted lentils
3 Tbs. Bragg Liquid Aminos®
or soy sauce.

Toss to combine sprouts and vegetables. Cover, steam 3-4 minutes just to tenderize and blend flavors. Add a dash of garlic powder or cayenne, if desired. Just before serving add **¼ cup minced parsley** for garnish.

Note: Sprouts prepared in this way are nutritious, crisp and tender. Served with a green salad, soup and bread – would make a complete meal. Serves 8

Chickpeas, (ceci) also known as ***garbanzo beans,*** are the main ingredient in hummus and falafels. These versatile beans have a mild nutty flavor, are rich in nutrients, and when combined with whole grains, provide protein comparable to that of meat. An excellent source of folate and other B vitamins, protein, iron, calcium, magnesium, phosphorus, and fiber. The heart healthy garbanzo bean (chickpea) is noted to contain properties that reduce cholesterol and promote normal bowel function.

Garbanzo "Chick" Patties

2 slices of bread, crumbled
¼ cup garbanzo broth
1½ cups chopped garbanzo beans
2½ cups steamed brown rice
½ cup pecans, finely chopped
2 Tbs. peanut or nut butter
¼ cup onion, diced or 1 Tbs. powder
2 Tbs. soy sauce or Bragg Aminos®
½ tsp. fennel seed, ground or poultry seas.
½ tsp. sea salt; ½ tsp. thyme
bread crumbs, as needed

In a medium bowl, soak 2 slices of bread in the garbanzo broth drained off beans. Add the rest of ingredients; use bread crumbs as needed for desired consistency. Mix well with hands and form into balls or patties; roll in breading meal;. Bake on prepared baking sheet at 375° for 45 minutes. Serve in pita bread or with gravy.

Lima Bean Loaf or Patties

3 cups mashed lima beans
2 tsp. onion pwd or 3 Tbs. sautéed onion
2 cups soft crumbled bread
2 Tbs. garbanzo or soy flour
1 Tbs. lemon juice
1 Tbs. chopped fresh Italian parsley
sea salt, to taste

Mix all ingredients together. Place in oiled loaf pan or shape into patties. Roll patties in seasoned bread crumbs. Bake at 375° 45 min.

Savory Sprouts

In a hurry? This protein-rich main dish is ready in just 2-3 minutes. Simple and delicious!

8 cups sprouted lentils or mung beans
2-3 Tbs. lemon juice
2 Tbs. Bragg Liquid Aminos®,
**   soy sauce or sea salt, to taste**
1 Tbs. onion powder
2 cloves garlic, minced
2-3 tsp. olive or soy oil, opt.

In a large skillet over medium heat, sauté the garlic with a little oil. Stir in the rest of seasonings, then add the rinsed / drained sprouts. Cover and steam 2-3 minutes, stirring once. They are ready! Sprouts should be **just wilted**, yet tender. Avoid overcooking!

Optional: Crisp sauté diced celery, red peppers, and sliced mushrooms. Add to tenderized sprouts.

Note: This simple method may be used for many sprouts. The cooking time may vary up to 15-20 minutes for larger legumes such as peas, garbanzo, and soybeans. To sprout lentils, etc. see the **Sprouting** chapter.

Sprouted Garbanzo Sauté

3 cups sprouted* garbanzo beans
½ cup water
½ tsp. sea salt
1 tsp. onion powder or ½ tsp. garlic powder
2 cups chopped onions
2 cups fresh chopped celery
1 Tbs. olive or canola oil
Chicken Style Seasoning or sea salt, to taste
fresh parsley, for garnish

Chop sprouted garbanzo beans. Place in a covered pan, lightly steam beans with next 4 ingredients, 10-15 minutes until tender. In a skillet lightly sauté the onions and celery in olive oil. Combine all ingredients together; add Chicken Style Seasoning or salt, to taste. Garnish with fresh parsley. Yield: Approx. 6 servings. Serve as a meatless main dish with steamed brown rice, and tossed green salad.

Simple Sprouted Lentils

Stir together in skillet:
2 Tbs. lemon juice
2 Tbs. soy sauce
1 Tbs. olive or soy oil
1 Tbs. onion powder
8 cups sprouted lentils

Cover; steam 3-4 min until just crisp tender. Good served hot or cold.

Sprouted Mung Beans

A favorite Chinese dish is to stir-fry **mung bean sprouts** by reducing 1-3 pounds of fresh mung bean sprouts to one serving. Other simple methods require less cooking. If you are serving them as a vegetable or side dish, try the **Savory Sprouts** recipe, using mung beans. These are quick and easy to prepare. You may have an endless variety of dishes by adding sautéed onion, celery, bell peppers, tofu, rice, parsley, tomatoes, etc. Adjust seasonings as desired.

* see chapter on Sprouting
Yield: 1 cup dry mung beans = 2½ cups soaked = approx. 8 cups sprouted.

GARLIC BASIL
FETTUCCINE
100% fancy durum flour with Jasmin
garlic, basil
NET WT. 8 OZ.
Mendocino Pasta Co. • Cotati, CA 94831

SPINACH & CHIVE
FETTUCCINE
100% fancy durum flour with
spinach, chive
NET WT. 8 OZ.
Mendocino Pasta Co. • Cotati, CA 9

TOMATO BASIL
FETTUCCINE
100% fancy durum flour with
tomato, basil
NET WT. 8 OZ.
Mendocino Pasta Co. • Cotati, CA 9485

LEMON PEPPER
FETTUCCINE
100% fancy durum flour with
lemon, pepper
NET WT. 8 OZ.
Mendocino Pasta Co. • Cotati, CA

Spelt, Soy, Soba (buckwheat), Whole Wheat Spaghetti

(how to cook)

Various kinds of macaroni, spaghetti, and noodles provide a base for many pasta dishes. We recommend the use of whole grain products – such as pasta and noodles made from whole wheat, artichoke, buckwheat (soba), spelt, soy, corn, brown rice, etc. These are available at health food stores, nutrition centers and markets where bulk foods are sold. For those who would venture to make their own – see recipe given.

1. In a large kettle, bring **4 qts. water** and **1 tsp. sea salt** to boiling (opt: Add **1-2 drops of oil** to the water to prevent pasta from sticking together).

2. Add **1 lb. spaghetti** to boiling water, while stirring. Return to boil, cook uncovered, for 8-12 minutes, until tender (al dente); do not overcook. Stir occasionally.

3. Drain in colander. Add your favorite sauce. Sprinkle on Parmesan Cheese (see recipe **Herbs & Seasonings**) Serve immediately, or (for salad dishes) rinse in cold water and drain.

Pasta Medley (right)

Left side: Cook soy spaghetti or the pasta of your choice according to package directions. Stir-fry asparagus, zucchini, mushrooms and garlic to crisp-tender; toss with pasta. Garnish with chopped fennel tops and a sprinkle of olive oil if desired.

Right side: Cook your favorite pasta according to package directions. Stir-fry broccoli florets, tofu cubes and diced sweet red pepper until crisp-tender; toss with pasta and a drizzle of olive oil. Add fresh sautéed minced garlic, if desired.

Note: Serve with **Parmesan "Cheese"** (see recipe in Herbs and Seasonings)

Baked Chee Spaghetti Casserole

A family favorite, and for the past 44 years one of the top-rated casseroles at our cooking schools and nutrition seminars. (minor changes have been made to the recipe, since first printed in 1968)

Cook **1 lb. of buckwheat, soy, or whole wheat spaghetti** in **4 quarts of boiling water** to which has been added **1 tsp. sea salt**. Cook till firm but tender (al dente) about 10 minutes.

Drain in colander; mix with the **Pimento Cheese Sauce:**

Cashew Pimento Cheese Sauce

Whiz in blender:

1 cup cashews
1 cup pure water
3 Tbs. sesame seeds
4 Tbs. nutritional yeast flakes
1¼ tsp. sea salt
1½ tsp. onion powder
⅛ tsp. celery seed and garlic powder
⅓ cup fresh lemon juice
2 Tbs. virgin olive or soy oil, opt.

Then add and blend until very smooth:
1 jar (4 oz.) pimentos or 1 cup tomatoes

Mix drained macaroni or spaghetti with the **Cheese Sauce.** Place in prepared baking dish. Top with seasoned bread crumbs. Bake in 350° oven for 30-40 minutes, or until heated through. Garnish with fresh parsley if desired. Serve with a large leafy green salad and a few ripe olives for a satisfying meal.

Variation:
Tofu Pimento Cheese Sauce: add **1 cup crumbled tofu** to sauce.

Pasta Varieties

1. Jumbo Shells – *Great for stuffing . fill with Ricotta Filling (see receipe)*
2. Vegetable Fusilli – *Short or long, spring-shaped, plain or veggie - good with sauce.*
3. Whole Wheat Spaghetti – *long thin strands of pasta, high in fiber- many other flavors- excellent with tomato sauce or pimento cheese sauce baked in casserole.*
4. Ditalini (tiny thimbles) – *tiny short tubes- good with sauce, in soup, or casserole dish.*
5. Penne ("feather") – *short tubular grooved or smooth pasta, slanted cut ends – good with tomato and vegetable sauces.*
6. Rigatoni – *Wide tubular, 1" long pasta - good with chunky garden tomato sauce.*
7. Farfalle (bow ties or butterfly) – *pretty shape for pasta salad, good with pesto sauces.*
8. Wagon Wheels (ruote) – *plain or flavored- a fun pasta for salad, soup or casserole.*
9. Vegetable Shells (conchiglie) - *medium size - suited to chunky tomato sauce.*
10. Elbow Macaroni – *short, curved, hollow – perfect for minestrone soup, salads, and baked macaroni with cashew pimento cheese sauce.*
11. Lasagna – *flat noodles about 2" wide with ruffled or straight edges - perfect for layering with tomato or pimento sauce and vegetables.*
12. Mafalda (bite-size lasagna noodles) – *short, flat with ruffled edge; use for casseroles and quick lasagna.*
13. Small Shells – *plain or vegetable flavors- perfect for soups, salads and thick sauces.*
14. Soup stars – *mini circles with star shaped edge- stars or alphabet -excellent in soups.*
15. Rotini – *thinner than rotelle – Rotini is preferred for pasta salad or with tomato sauce.*

Topping Variaties for Pasta Dishes

Buckwheat Soba with Tofu, Parsley, & Tomato Sauce

Pasta Bows, Tofu, Pine Nuts, Garlic, Basil, Tomato Sauce

Spelt Spaghetti, Broccoli, Tofu, Sun-Dried Tomatoes, & Peppers

Soy Spaghetti, Asparagus, Zucchini, Mushrooms, Fennel

Penne, Mushrooms, Sprouted Peas, and Tomato Sauce

Whole Wheat Spaghetti, Tofu, Mushrooms, Tomato Sauce

Favorite Italian Dishes

*Mushrooms or peas may be added to the Tomato Sauce.

For a savory touch, garnish with **Cashew Pimento Cheese Sauce (see recipe).

Note: Eggplant Parmigiana is a perfect make-ahead dish. Bake and serve or re-heat the next day and serve.

For the best digestion - eat a large raw salad before the main cooked dish.

Eggplant Parmigiana

Traditionally this Italian dish is made with mozzarella and parmesan cheese, however tofu, and non-dairy Parmesan "Cheese" may substitute. The tofu contains a good quality of easily digested protein. The addition of mushrooms and / or Cashew Pimento Cheese Sauce add a delicious flavor to this vegetarian dish.

1 large or 2 med. eggplant, ripe
2-3 cups tofu, cubed, diced or crumbled
2 ½ cups Italian Tomato Sauce*
Cashew Pimento Cheese Sauce, optional**

Wash whole un-peeled eggplant; cut in ⅜"- ½" round or lengthwise slices. Brush slices lightly with olive oil then coat with seasoned breading meal.
Place on baking sheet; broil or bake at 400° 5-10 min. on each side until tender. Spoon a little tomato sauce into square or rectangular baking dish. Arrange half of the eggplant slices, side by side and cover with sauce and crumbled tofu or non-dairy cheese. Repeat with remaining eggplant, tomato sauce and cheese. Bake, uncovered, in 350° oven, 25 min. or until lightly browned and sauce is bubbly. (see Cheese)

Tofu Eggplant Roll-Ups

2 medium-large eggplant, ripe
2½ cups tomato sauce

FILLING:
3 cups tofu, med-firm, mashed
1½ cups dry seasoned bread crumbs
⅓ cup minced Italian flat-leaf parsley
2 Tbs. soy mayonnaise or Vegenaise®
1 medium onion, chopped, sautéed
3 large cloves garlic, minced
2 cups chopped fresh spinach, packed
1 Tbs. olive or soy oil

1. Wash and cut fully ripe eggplant lengthwise in ¼"- ⅜" slices. Brush lightly with oil; place slices on baking sheet single layer. Bake or broil in 400° oven turning once to lightly brown on both sides.

2. Meanwhile prepare filling: In a large skillet, sauté onion and garlic in olive oil until transparent; add spinach, and sauté until wilted. Turn off heat. Stir in tofu, bread crumbs, parsley and mayonnaise.

3. Spoon ½ cup tomato sauce in bottom of baking dish. Place ¼ cup prepared filling on each slice of eggplant. Starting at narrow end, roll up tightly. Arrange rolls side-by-side in prepared pan, seam side down. Spoon remaining sauce over rolls.

4. Bake uncovered in 350° oven, 35-40 minutes until sauce is bubbly.

Note: Sprinke on Parmesan Cheese if desired.

Artichokes, Stuffed

Simply delicious served with angel hair spaghetti and Italian Tomato Sauce!

6 very small, tender globe artichokes
1½ cups seasoned bread crumbs
½ cup soft soy cheese (tofu)
3 Tbs. chopped fresh parsley
2 cloves minced garlic or ¼ tsp. powder

1. Clean the artichokes. Remove the stem. Cut ½"off top (use tender 2 ½- 3" artichokes). Mix ingredients for filling. Spread leaves to expose the heart; stuff with filling. Tie artichokes with a string. Dip cut end in a pasty mixture of flour and soy milk (or beaten egg). Brown cut end of stuffed artichokes in hot oiled skillet. This will seal the filling, so it will not come out while cooking in sauce). Have *uncooked* **Italian Tomato Sauce** (see recipe) all ready to cook.

2. Carefully place artichokes in tomato sauce, cut side up, and simmer very slowly (so the stuffing does not come out – the string will help hold stuffing). Have enough sauce in kettle to almost cover the artichokes. Cook until artichokes are tender and sauce is thick (test for tenderness by inserting toothpick near stem end). Serve artichokes hot or cold with spaghetti and warmed tomato sauce.

Note: Tomato sauce in which artichokes have been cooked, is extra special. Delicious served with angel hair, whole wheat, soy, or buckwheat spaghetti, with a few added peas if desired; or serve extra sauce over stuffed peppers, eggplant, or on pizza.

Tomato Sauce Tips and Variations

●**Sweet Basil** is the secret ingredient in making a flavorful sauce; measure generously.

●**Roma** or other *meaty* tomatoes are best. If juicy, blend tomatoes, let stand awhile, then pour off liquid that comes to the top (save for soup). Use the thicker pulp that settles to the bottom to make the best sauce. The same can be done with home-canned tomatoes.

●**Italian Tomato Sauce** can be canned and sealed in sterile jars, to be used on spaghetti, noodles, lasagna, ravioli, pizza, eggplant, stuffed peppers, artichokes, brown rice, and other dishes. If sauce is too thin, add cut dried tomatoes or tomato paste to thicken.

●When you have extra thick sauce, the cooking liquid from vegetables such as globe artichokes, and the sliced cooked stems, can be added to the sauce, for a delicious sweet flavor.

●**Pizza Sauce:** Add **dried or fresh cut oregano** to sauce before spreading on pizza crust.

●**Tomato Sauce with Peas:** Add **2 cups fresh or frozen peas** during last 5 min. of cooking.

●**Mushroom Tomato Sauce:** Add **1 cup sliced sautéed mushrooms** to sauce.

Italian Tomato Sauce

Savory- Sweet- Delicious! Garden fresh, or canned tomatoes with added herbs and vegetables provide a myriad of ways to use this basic sauce for pasta, pizza, casseroles, topping, stews, and a variety of other dishes.

**2 qts. vine ripened tomatoes
 (fresh or solid pack)
1 lg. onion, chopped or sliced
¼ cup basil leaves, fresh snipped or
 2 Tbs. dried sweet basil
1-2 Tbs. honey, to taste
1-2 cloves fresh garlic, minced
1 Tbs. pure olive oil
1-2 tsp. sea salt, to taste
1 small can tomato paste, opt.**

Blend tomatoes to a chunky consistency or until smooth. Pour into stainless steel kettle; bring to a boil; add remainder of ingredients. Reduce heat, simmer uncovered 30-45 minutes, stirring occasionally, to desired consistency. The sauce should be quite thick if the tomatoes used are meaty, or add tomato paste if needed. When using fresh tomatoes, blend, bring to a boil, then run through colander to remove skins and seeds if desired. Return to kettle, add remainder of ingredients and simmer to desired consistency.

Italian Ravioli

**Dough (see recipe for lasagna noodles)
Soybean curd (tofu), seasoned
Italian Tomato Sauce**

1. Make dough as given for lasagna. Roll out; cut in 3" squares or circles.

2. On each square or circle, put a spoonful of seasoned tofu (use recipe for **Scrambled Tofu**-omit turmeric and season to taste; filling should resemble mild Italian ricotta, or use **Ricotta filling** recipe on next page.

3. Cover with another square or circle. Seal around edges to keep filling inside.

4. Drop in lightly salted boiling water and cook 8-10 minutes, until tender. Remove with slotted spoon. Serve with **Italian Tomato Sauce** or **Garden Vegetable Pasta Sauce**.

Homemade Lasagna or Noodles

(for those who have the time – or shop for healthy varieties)

**1 cup whole wheat flour
(for noodles: replace 3 Tbs. w.w.
flour with 3 Tbs. soy flour)
1 cup golden white or w.w. pastry flour
1 cup pure warm water**

To make Dough:

1. Mix all ingredients together. Gather into a ball with fingers, kneading lightly.

2. Flour board and roll out dough ⅛" thick with rolling pin, in a rectangle shape, using more flour as necessary so it will not stick. When rolled out to proper thickness and shape, sprinkle top and bottom with a thin layer of flour, spreading evenly on dough.

3. Starting at wide end, fold floured dough over 3" and fold over again on itself 3" more. Fold again and again until folded to one 3" piece of several thickness.

4. Cut in1 ½" strips for lasagna or ¼" strips for noodles. Hang lasagna noodles to dry or:

5. Boil 4 qts. water and 2 tsp. sea salt, add ¼ tsp. oil to water. Open lasagna and drop into boiling water very slowly – one by one to avoid sticking together; water should be kept boiling. Stir occasionally. Cook till firm (al dente) approx. 7 min. Drain in colander and you are ready to make a dish of Lasagna.

To assemble Lasagna:

Italian Tomato Sauce (see recipe)
**12 cooked or dry lasagna noodles
Tofu soy cheese, seasoned to taste
mushrooms, peas, and/or
fresh spinach, opt.**

1. Spread thin layer of sauce in bottom of oblong baking dish.(use more tomato sauce if noodles are dry). On top of that, lay 3 strips of lasagna - side by side.

2. Cover with generous amount of Tofu (soy cheese), mushrooms, spinach, etc., if desired. Cover with **Italian Tomato Sauce**.

3. Repeat – alternating layers

of lasagna, soy cheese, spinach, mushrooms, and tomato sauce until pan is filled; end with tomato sauce on top (be generous with sauce when using dry noodles). Sprinkle with seasoned breadcrumbs, and thread with olive oil, if desired.

4. Bake in 375° oven for 1 hour. Cut in squares and serve.

Plain sauce or sauce with peas can be used in this recipe. Both are delicious!

For **Noodles**: Cut into ¼" strips and boil as above. Drain and serve with **Italian Tomato Sauce**, sauce with peas, or cooked artichokes, and **Soy Cheese**.

Note: The family can have lots of fun making noodles and lasagna and hanging them on a line to dry. They can be stored in paper bags, and cooked when needed. Allow 2-3 minutes more cooking time when noodles are dry.

Chunky Veggie Pasta Sauce

Follow recipe given for **Italian Tomato Sauce**. Add diced, sliced, or chopped sautéed peppers, onions, zucchini, carrots, and mushrooms to tomato sauce during last 10 minutes of cooking. Delicious on whole grain spaghetti, soy noodles, pizza, rice, or casserole dishes.

Ricotta Filling for Ravioli, Shells, or Manicotti

3 cups (1½ lbs.) firm tofu, mashed
1-10 oz. pkg. fresh or frozen chopped spinach
2 Tbs. soy mayonaise
1 Tbs. fresh lemon juice
1 tsp. sea salt
¼ tsp. garlic powder
14 manicotti or shells, cooked al dente
1 qt. tomato sauce with mushrooms

Lightly steam fresh chopped spinach or squeeze frozen spinach to drain. Mix with tofu, lemon juice, mayonnaise, and seasoning. Fill cooked manicotti or shells with spinach mixture. Spread 1 cup of sauce in 9" x 13" baking dish. Place shells on sauce in dish. Pour on remaining sauce covering shells. Sprinkle with **1-2 Tbs. Parmesan Cheese,** if desired (see recipe). Bake uncovered in 350° oven for 30 - 40 minutes or until heated through and bubbly. Servings: 6-7

Panelle al Forno

Once you have tasted this simple peasant's dish you'll want to make it again. In Palermo, Italy, these Chickpea fritters are served with crusty bread. Here is a healthy baked version of these savory flat pancakes.. The recipe is simple, harder to perfect, but definitely worth trying.

6 cups pure water (1½ qts.), divided
1 tsp. sea salt
2 Tbs. minced Italian flat leaf parsley
1 tsp. fennel seed, coarsely ground
½ lb. (2¼ cups) garbanzo flour
1 tsp. olive oil, opt.

1. Boil 3 cups water in a large saucepan. Add the salt, parsley, and fennel seeds.

2. Mix garbanzo flour with remaining 3 cups water in a bowl. Add to boiling water.

3. Cook on medium heat, beating with a wire whisk to prevent lumps forming. As it thickens, change to a wooden spoon and continue to cook 8-10 minutes more **stirring constantly**, until mixture begins to pull away from the sides of the kettle.

4. Quickly pour mixture into a 10" x 14" low-sided pan; spread into a layer ¼"- ½" thick (or pour into a glass loaf pan). Refrigerate or cool completely until firm.

5. Cut into thin slices, circles, or 2" x 3" rectangles. Lay pieces on a baking sheet; brush with olive oil. Bake in pre-heated 400° oven for 15 minutes, turning once, or brown in skillet or on heavy griddle. Serve warm, plain, or with **Gremolata**: a combination of parsley, lemon rind, and garlic - see recipe.

Fettuccine with Roasted Garlic Sauce and Parsley

(This variation is especially for garlic lovers)

½-lb. (8 oz.) cooked Fettuccine, al dente
2 cups water, divided
½ cup cashew nuts
1-2 whole garlic bulbs, roasted*
1 Tbs. onion powder
1 Tbs. nutritional food yeast
½ cup silken firm tofu
1 tsp. olive oil, opt.
½ tsp. sea salt + 1 Tbs. Bragg Aminos®
1 Tbs. fresh lemon juice
1½ Tbs. arrowroot powder
garnish- fresh parsley, fennel

Squeeze the roasted garlic cloves to release the garlic. In blender or food processor blend all sauce ingredients until very smooth (reserving ½ cup of water and the arrowroot until last). Pour into a saucepan, heat on stovetop to a low boil, stirring occasionally. Last add the remaining ½ cup water blended with the arrowroot starch. Pour into saucepan, stir until sauce is bubbly and thickened. Pour over cooked noodles. Toss lightly and quickly to coat well. Pile noodles on warm serving plate. Garnish with fresh parsley and paprika. Good served as a main dish with a large green salad and steamed artichokes.
*see **Roasted Garlic** recipe in chapter **Sandwiches and Spreads**

Note: For an extra cheesy Romano flavor, toss and sprinkle on **toasted ground sesame seed** or **Parmesan Cheese.**

Variation: Add finely chopped arugula, and/or sweet basil, slivered almonds, or pine nuts.

Fettuccine Alfredo

A rich creamy Italian sauce to toss with fettuccine or other cooked noodles. This heart-healthy version is minus the cholesterol, butter, whipping cream, and cheese.

12 oz. cooked Fettuccine, al dente
1 cup hot soy, almond, or tofu
milk, unsweetened
⅔ cup blanched almonds
or cashews
1 Tbs. sesame tahini
1 Tbs. nutritional yeast flakes
1½ tsp. onion powder
1 tsp. sea salt, to taste
2-3 tsp. fresh lemon juice
1 cup (8 oz.) soft tofu, rinsed, opt.
dash of garlic powder and cayenne
1 tsp. Instant Clear Jel®, opt.

Cook fettuccine according to package directions, drain. Blend milk and almonds until smooth and creamy; add the rest of ingredients except lemon juice. While blending, sprinkle on Clear Jel, to make desired consistency (omit, if tofu is used). Last, add lemon juice; blend briefly.

Note: Pour sauce over cooked noodles and toss; sprinkle with **fresh chopped Italian flat-leaf parsley** and **"Parmesan Cheese"** if desired. (see recipe)

Pasta Tip:

Did you know that 8 oz. of dry uncooked pasta = 4 cups when cooked? That's enough for 4 average servings of 1 cup each.

Hot Pasta Salad with Veggies

Chock-full of vegetables, this hearty pasta salad can serve as a main dish. Colorful and nutritious; good cold or hot.

8 oz. thin multigrain angel hair pasta
¾ cup Tomato Pesto, (see recipe)
2 ½ cups broccoli florets or asparagus tips
1 cup yellow summer squash, shredded
2 cups sweet red pepper, cut in strips
1½ cups black ripe olives, broken pieces
1-6 oz. jar whole mushrooms, drained

Break pasta (multigrain or whole wheat angel hair) in half; cook according to package directions, being careful not to overcook. Drain; add pesto to warm pasta and carefully toss with 2 forks to combine. Blanch the broccoli or asparagus in boiling water (briefly 1 minute). Add to pasta; add the squash, peppers, olives and mushrooms; toss lightly. Yield: 6-8 servings

Mini Layered Lasagna

(pictured on left)

Follow recipe for T**ofu Spinach Lasagna** using **12 oz. Mini Lasagna noodles** (Mafalda bite-size). Cook 10 minutes, drain. Reverse the amounts of sauce. (Use 4 cups of **Cashew Pimento Cheese Sauce** and 2½ cups of **Tomato Sauce**). For quick assembling, combine the spinach, tofu, onions and rest of ingredients (except tomato sauce) with the **Cashew Pimento Sauce**. To assemble casserole: Start and end with tomato sauce. Alternate layers of cooked mini- noodles and pimento/spinach/cheese mixture in between. Bake in 350° oven 35-45 minutes until bubbly. Servings: 8

Tofu Spinach Lasagna

Enjoy Italian cuisine with this non-dairy version of lasagna. This popular dish can be made with a variety of vegetables. Here is a healthy low-fat version that looks and tastes really good!

12 lasagna noodles, (12 oz.) uncooked
1-lb. chopped spinach, frozen or fresh
2½ cups Cashew Pimento Cheese Sauce*
1-lb. firm tofu, mashed
2 onions, (1½ cups chopped and sautéed)
2 tsp. sweet basil, crushed
½ tsp. garlic powder
½ tsp. sea salt, to taste
2-3 Tbs. Soy mayonnaise or Tofu Vegenaise
1 Tbs. fresh lemon juice
Tomato Sauce (approx. 1 qt.)

Cook lasagna al dente (tender-firm 12-15 min). Drain; rinse with cold water, drain. Lightly steam spinach; drain well. Mix spinach with **2½ cups of Cashew Pimento Cheese Sauce** (see recipe). Combine the tofu with onions and next 5 ingredients.

To assemble: Spread approx. ½ cup Tomato Sauce in the bottom of a 9" x 13" baking dish. Place 3 noodles in pan, top with one-fourth of the spinach and **Cashew Pimento Cheese Sauce**, the tofu mixture, and tomato sauce. Repeat the layers 3x, ending with tomato sauce and dabs of **Pimento Cheese Sauce**. Bake covered in a 350° oven for 30 min. Uncover and bake 20 min. until bubbly and lightly browned. Let stand 10 min. before serving.

Optional: Can add more layers of veggies: mushrooms, sliced raw zuccini, shredded carrots.

Garnish with minced **Italian flat-leaf parsley,** if desired. Servings: 8

***Cashew Pimento Cheese Sauce** pg. 323 (or see chapter: **Sauces, Creams, Gravy, pg. 474**)

Note: For a quick version, make this dish with *uncooked* **No-boil Lasagna Noodles,** and use a little extra tomato sauce.

Creamy Vegetable Lasagna

Chock-full of vegetables, colorful and creamy, without cheese, fat or cholesterol.

12 oz. lasagna noodles (about 12)
1 recipe Tofu Filling and/or Basil Pesto
1 recipe Cashew Milk Gravy (sauce)
4 cloves garlic, minced
3 cups frozen chopped broccoli
2 cups diced red or orange bell pepper
½ cup diced green bell pepper or strips
2 cups sliced mushrooms
2 cups grated carrots or zucchini
seasoned bread crumbs, opt.

Cook lasagna noodles according to package directions. Drain. Set aside. In the meantime make ready the **Pesto**, **Tofu Filling**, and **Cashew Milk Gravy**. In a non-stick skillet, quickly stir-fry the garlic, broccoli, peppers, and mushrooms to crisp-tender. Remove from heat; Stir in the carrots, pesto and ½ cup of the **Cashew Sauce**.

To assemble: Place 3 noodles in a 9" x 13" prepared baking dish. Spread with one-fourth of the tofu filling, then one-fourth of the vegetable mixture. Repeat the layers three times, until all the noodles and vegetables are used. Pour remaining **Cashew Milk Sauce** evenly over the vegetables. Sprinkle top with breadcrumbs if desired. Bake uncovered in a 350° oven for 40-45 min. or until heated through. Let stand 10 minutes before cutting. Servings: 8

Note: Lasagna can be baked ahead, and re-heated before serving.

Tofu Stuffed Manicotti Shells

1-8 oz. box Manicotti
or Jumbo Pasta Shells
3-4 cups chunky Tomato Sauce

TOFU FILLING:
1½ -lb. firm tofu, mashed
1 large onion, chopped,
sautéed
2 cloves garlic, minced,
sautéed
1 Tbs. chicken style seasoning
1 Tbs. minced sweet basil
or 1 tsp. dried
½ tsp. fennel seeds,
crushed
¼ cup minced fresh parsley
1 Tbs. lemon juice,
fresh squeezed
¼ cup Creamy Cashew
Mayonnaise,
Tofu Sour Cream or
Tofu Vegenaise

1. Cook Manicotti or Jumbo Shells according to package directions. Drain. Cool.

2. In the meantime, make **Tofu Filling**. Combine and mix ingredients together.

3. Fill manicotti or jumbo shells. Spread tomato sauce over the bottom of baking dish. Place pasta shells on top. Top with more tomato sauce. Cover and bake at 350° for 30-35 min. then uncover and bake another 15-20 min. Servings: 6-8

Make ahead directions: Prepare pasta shells. Cover and refrigerate up to 48 hours or freeze. Bake uncovered for about 1 hour until heated through. Enjoy.

Lasagna Roll-Ups

1. Cook 12 extra-wide (2½") lasagna according to package directions. Drain.

2. Spread the mixed **Pimento Cheese Sauce** and chopped spinach on lasagna strips; top with the seasoned Tofu filling; then roll each strip.

3. Cover the bottom of a 9" x 12" glass baking pan with a layer of Tomato Sauce. Lay lasagna roll-ups seam-side-down in pan. Pour tomato sauce over roll-ups. Cover. Bake in 350° oven 35 min. Uncover; bake another 25 min. Serves 4-6.

"Flesh was never the best food; but its use is now doubly objectionable, since disease in animals is so rapidly increasing." - E. G. White, **Ministry of Healing,** pg. 313

One Dish Italian Meal

A colorful combination of vegetables that is both satisfying and nutritious.

Potatoes, steamed whole
Green beans, cut, lightly steamed
Tomatoes or Pimentos, sliced
Olives, black, sliced
Oregano, garlic powder, sea salt
Olive oil

Peel thin skin off potatoes after steaming, reserving any liquid for soup or gravy. Cut potatoes in bit-size pieces. Arrange foods on one large platter or individual plates. Begin with potatoes, steamed green beans, tomatoes sliced in wedges, and olives. Sprinkle generously with oregano, garlic powder, sea salt and olive oil.

Note: **Sliced avocado** and **diced red bell pepper** may be added or used in place of olives or pimentos.

Italian Arancini (Rice Balls)

Traditionally Arancini are eaten out-of-hand, served either hot or cold on a paper napkin. Everyone wants seconds! A tossed green salad with Italian dressing would complete the meal.

Simple to make - detailed directions are given on right. These are delicious rice balls with a surprise filling inside. This dish has received many compliments. Usually the rice balls are browned in vegetable oil, which makes a nice brown crust, then drained on paper towels. The rice balls absorb very little oil because all the ingredients are already cooked (we have measured the oil before and after). * However, if you prefer not to brown them in oil, try baking or broiling them in the oven. Before baking or broiling, spray balls with cooking spray (Ariel® spray is made with canola oil, lecithin and water). Recipe makes **12 Arancini** (size of medium orange).

2 cups natural brown rice
6 cups boiling water
1 tsp. sea salt

Stir rice in boiling salted water. Cook until tender and dry. Allow rice to cool thoroughly, or use leftover cold rice. With hands, mix **2 Tbs. nut butter or garbanzo flour**, into rice to hold it together.

Fresh or Dry Fava Beans

One of the largest beans, also known as horse-bean or broad bean. Fava beans are a rich source of iron, protein, B vitamins, folate, and fiber.

Soak dry **Fava beans** overnight. Cut skin at top with a knife or just pinch between teeth. Cover with fresh water 1" over beans. Add **2-3 garlic cloves,** un-peeled. Cook over low heat 1 hour or until tender; add **sea salt** to taste. Serve with a drizzle of **olive oil** on top. **Fresh green fava beans** may be cooked with soy or buckwheat spaghetti until tender. Season with a little **garlic** and **olive oil** before serving. Delicious!

Note: Eat dry cooked fava beans one by one, squeezing bean into mouth and discarding the skin or benefit from all the fiber by thoroughly chewing skin and all, or blending beans into a purée.

Filling for Rice Balls

(see Italian Arancini, left)

⅓ cup thick tomato sauce
1 cup firm crumbled tofu
   or diced not-meat
1 cup frozen cooked peas
2 Tbs. toasted sesame seeds, ground

How to Put Together:

Step 1 Open palm of hand –place some cooked rice in palm and shape like a half ball. Put a spoonful of filling sauce in center. With free hand, add more rice to cover, forming a solid round ball, sealing in all the sauce. Shape firmly to be sure sauce will not leak out, and to prevent Rice Balls from falling apart when browning.

Step 2 Place seasoned breadcrumbs (about 3 cups) on a paper towel. Place rice ball on top of crumbs one at a time, do not roll, but by lifting edges of paper, generously cover rice balls with crumbs. Now take the balls one by one and firmly shape with your hands (like you would a snowball) until crumbs are firmly packed.

Step 3 In a small deep pan, heat vegetable oil (just enough to cover 1-2 balls). Brown rice balls in hot oil, one or two at a time, for 1-2 minutes until golden brown, gently lowering and lifting out. Remove onto paper towels. Repeat till all rice balls are browned (keep oil temperature constant to avoid absorption), or bake at 375° (see* above left).

Note: Rice balls can be made plain - with no surprise filling inside - however, they are not as tasty.

Fava Beans, recipe on left

Holiday Chestnut Stuffing

1 lb. fresh chestnuts (3 cups)
2 cups cooked millet or barley
½ cup firm tofu, crumbled
1 cup finely chopped celery
½ cup onion, chopped, sautéed
¼ cup cashew, coarsely ground
1 Tbs. fresh cut sage or 1 tsp.dried
1 Tbs. onion powder + ¼ tsp. garlic
4 cups dry bread cubes
¼ -½ cup vegetable broth or water

Prepare firm chestnuts for baking. (see page 386, #2). Spread on a large baking sheet. Roast chestnuts in a 400° oven for 15 minutes. Cool enough to handle, peel and coarsely chop chestnuts. Sauté the celery and onions until tender, but not brown. Stir in nuts and seasonings. Place dry bread cubes in a large bowl; add the celery, onion, nut mixture, cooked millet, tofu, and salt to taste. Drizzle on broth to moisten, toss lightly to combine. Good stuffing for peppers, acorn squash, pumpkin, etc. or place in a prepared non-stick casserole dish. Bake covered, in a 350° oven for 45 min. Serve with your favorite gravy.

Italian Tofu Mushroom Frittata

Seasoned Tofu and vegetables are used instead of eggs in this cholesterol- free frittata. Serve hot or cold, for a light lunch, open face sandwich, or main dish for dinner.

12 oz. firm tofu, seasoned or plain
1 cup sliced zucchini or broccoli
½ cup mushrooms, sliced

¼ cup carrots, thin slices or shreds
¼ cup green onions, thinly sliced
¼ cup red bell pepper, chopped
2-3 cloves minced garlic, or ½ tsp powder
½ cup pure water + 3 Tbs. all-purpose
   or potato flour
3 Tbs. golden flaxseed meal
2 tsp. onion powder; ¼ tsp. turmeric
½ tsp. sea salt, to taste
1 tsp. chicken-style seasoning
garnish: Italian parsley, chopped

1. Stir-fry vegetables in a large non-stick oiled skillet until crisp tender. Set aside.

2. Combine water, flaxseed meal, flour, seasonings, and approx. 8 oz. tofu in a food processor until smooth. Add remaining tofu; blend to a chunky purée. Pour tofu mixture into a bowl, add the vegetables, and lightly combine.

3. Spread approximately 3/4 cup of the tofu / vegetable mixture in center of heated non-stick heavy skillet.

4. Cook, uncovered, over medium heat, 5-10 minutes, without disturbing, until frittata can be lifted (test with a wide turner). Flip over; brown other side. or bake in 400° oven, 15 min on each side to golden brown. Servings: 3-4

Pizza Toppings

Combine your favorite toppings to make an endless variety of healthy pizza!

Tomato Pizza Sauce
Pesto Sauce, tomato, spinach
Soy Cheese, grated or crumbled
Broccoli, chopped, steamed
Onions, sliced, sautéed
Peppers, red and green, chopped
Mushrooms, sautéed
Olives, sliced, chopped
Spinach, fresh chopped
Artichoke hearts, cut, cooked
Sauerkraut, drained
Carrots, fresh grated
Tofu slices, cubes, strips; browned
Tomatoes, sliced, diced
Pimento Cheese Sauce
Super Sunburger, crumbles
Non-dairy Cheese-recipes pg. 454-457
Pizza Dough-see recipe page 128
Seasoning: Oregano, Basil, Olive oil

Use a pre-baked and, or frozen pizza crust. Spread with sauce and toppings of your choice.

or:

Make pizza or your favorite bread dough (may use less yeast when making bread dough), and roll out ⅜"- ½" thick (after 1st rising). Place on a baking stone, or non-stick pizza pan. Let rise to almost double. Pre-bake at 350° 10-15 minutes depending on dough used, thickness and size. Remove from oven,

cool and wrap for freezer. When ready to use, spread sauce on frozen pizza shell and cover with desired toppings. Bake at 425° for 10-15 minutes until crust is well baked and pizza topping is bubbly and heated through. Remove from oven, slice and enjoy!

A pizza crust made with yeast is better re-heated the next day. This is more healthful than eating fresh yeast dough, hot, out of the oven.

or:

Use slices of **day-old bread**; works great! Lay slices side-by-side in rectangular pan. Spread with tomato sauce, top with seasoned tofu cheese and other toppings of your choice. Finish with **Pimento Cheese Sauce**, thread on olive oil and sprinkle with oregano (the secret ingredient for making delicious pizza). Bake until toasted and bubbly. Just loosen from edges of pan, and serve (bread is already pre-cut in slices). Be generous with ingredients if you want a hearty Italian-style pizza. Pizza made in this way is nutritious and delicious!

Pizza pizza pizza

Tofu Mushroom Broccoli

Roasted Veggie & Basil

Roasted Veggie

Artichoke Pepper

Mushroom Gourmet

Tomato Olive with Pimento Cheese Sauce

Quick Miniature Pizzas

Stir-N-Roll Pie Crust, see recipe
   or use w.w. English Muffin halves
Italian Tomato or Pizza Sauce
soy cheese or tofu, seasoned
mushrooms or see other toppings
oregano, sea salt

Roll **Stir-N-Roll Pie Crust** ⅛" thick. Peel
off top wax paper. Cut into 5" rounds.
Place on un-greased cookie sheet.
Remove bottom paper. Spread rounds
with tomato sauce, top with soy cheese
and other toppings. Sprinkle with a
generous amount of oregano, thread
on olive oil and sprinkle with sea salt, if
desired. Bake at 425° (hot oven) about
10 minutes or until crust is light brown.
Serve hot.

Make a healthy pizza for supper tonight!

Bread Dressing or Loaf

8 cups dry whole grain bread cubes
1½ cup diced celery (2 large stalks)
1 cup diced onion (1 large onion)
4-6 garlic cloves, minced
½ lb. mushrooms, fresh sliced
   (button, shiitake, cremini)
½ cup minced parsley
1 tsp. poultry seasoning
1 tsp. sage, ground
½ tsp. thyme, dried leaves
½ tsp. rosemary, dried
½ tsp. garlic powder, and salt, to taste
2 cups chicken-style broth, soup stock
   or veggie broth, see recipes

In a large mixing bowl place the bread
cubes. In a non-stick skillet, lightly sauté
celery, onions, and garlic in 1 Tbs. olive
oil until crisp-tender; add mushrooms,
simmer 2-3 minutes. Toss celery, onion,
mushroom mixture with bread cubes and
seasonings. Add broth until all bread
cubes are moist (use more or less broth,
the amount varies with bread used).
Spoon into prepared 13"x 9"x 2" baking
dish. Cover and bake at 350° 40-45
min.; uncover, bake another 15 min., if
desired, until crusty and brown. Serve
with **Mushroom** or **Holiday Gravy**.

Roasted Veggie Pizza

For a change of pace, spread crust with Tomato Pesto or Basil Pesto Sauce or add fresh garlic and sweet basil to the tomato-based sauce, then top with a variety of roasted veggies and browned tofu strips; fantastic pizzas everyone reaches for!

12 medium mushrooms, sliced
1 large onion, sliced
1 cup sliced green pepper
1 cup sliced red sweet pepper
1 Tbs. pure olive oil
3 garlic cloves, minced
½ tsp. each dried oregano, thyme, rosemary
1 cup sweet basil, fresh chopped packed
2 cups firm crumbled tofu, or Tofu strips
Tomato Sauce or Tomato or Basil Pesto (see recipes)
2 ripe tomatoes, thinly sliced, optional
1- 12" Pizza Crust, pre-baked

1. Place mushrooms, onions and peppers in a roasting pan. Add 1 cup fresh chopped, packed, basil. Combine oil, garlic, oregano, rosemary, and thyme; drizzle over vegetables and toss to coat. Cover and bake at 400° for 15-20 minutes, stirring once.

2. Place pre-baked pizza crust on a baking stone or ungreased 12" pizza pan. Spread with **Pesto** or **Tomato Sauce** and the tomato slices, if desired. Top with tofu and the roasted vegetables. Bake 15 minutes at 400° until crust is golden brown. Yield: 8 slices.

Onion Pizza: In a covered skillet, cook 1 lb. sliced onions in ½ tsp. olive oil and sea salt till tender. Spread on pizza over tomato or pesto sauce. Top with sliced olives.

Mushroom Pizza: Sauté 1 lb. fresh mushrooms in a little olive oil until tender. Sprinkle on onion or garlic powder and sea salt. Use mushrooms over tomato sauce and soy cheese for a deluxe pizza.

Baked Walnut Balls

3 cups steamed brown rice
2 Tbs. nut butter
   (cashew, almond, peanut)
1 Tbs. soy flour (may be dextrinized)
1 Tbs. olive or soy oil
2 tsp. flour + 1 tsp. onion powder
¼ cup soy or nut milk, plain
½ cup walnuts or pecans, chopped
1 Tbs. each, chopped onion,
   parsley, pimento
½ cup crumbled tofu
¼ cup diced celery
½ tsp. sea salt, to taste

In a mixing bowl combine the first
3 ingredients. In a small pan, over
medium heat stir the oil, flour, onion
powder and milk until thick and bubbly.
Add to mixture in bowl. Add remaining
ingredients mixing well. Chill until
firm enough to hold shape. Using a
medium scoop, form balls by packing
and rounding mixture in the scoop.
Roll each ball in fine ground seasoned
bread or cracker crumbs. Place in
shallow baking pans. Bake at 375°
for 45 minutes. Serve in a casserole
dish with **Parsley** or **Cashew Gravy** or
your favorite sauce. Yield: approx. 8
servings.

Tofu Spinach Balls

*You'll be surprised at the taste of these moist tofu balls.
Serve with a crisp vegetable salad, garlic bread and a
simple or hearty vegetable soup.*

1 lb. firm tofu, (frozen, thawed,
   crumbled)
¾ cup dry bread crumbs or Grape-Nuts
½ lb. (8 oz. pkg.) frozen chopped spinach,
   (thawed, squeezed)
1 Tbs. onion powder
2 tsp. garlic powder
2 tsp. Italian Seasoning Herbs
1½ tsp. paprika
Tofu Mayonnaise or other

In a mixing bowl combine all ingredients.
Add Tofu Mayonnaise enough to moisten
ingredients to form balls and hold shape.
Brown in non-stick skillet or pan with
small amount of olive oil, or bake in 325°
oven, 25-30 min., turning often to brown.

Sweet-Savory "Meatballs"

*Meatballs that are tasty and good for you
without the fat or cholesterol.*

1 lb. tofu, firm
1¾ cups fine bread crumbs
1 small carrot, finely grated
1 medium onion, minced
1 cup pecan meal
2 cloves garlic, minced
2 Tbs. Bragg Liquid Aminos®
2 tsp. onion powder
½ tsp. celery salt
½ tsp. veggie salt
Barbecue Sauce, see recipe

Mash tofu with a fork. Combine all
ingredients together, mixing thoroughly
to make a consistency that hold together.
Form into balls using a small scoop. Place
on baking sheet that is treated with a
non-stick coating. Bake in 350° for 30-40
minutes turning 1 or 2 times to brown
evenly. Arrange baked meatballs in a
casserole dish. Spread on layer of sauce,
bake until hot. Serve with additional
sauce.

Tofu Garden Quiche

A savory and nutritious vegetable entrée

1 cup diced zucchini
1 cup diced orange, red, green peppers
1 medium onion, chopped
1 green onion, finely chopped
1½ cups sliced mushrooms
1 cup chopped steamed spinach or broccoli
1¼ lbs. (20 oz.) firm tofu, rinsed & drained
1¼ cups soy or nut milk, unflavored
2 Tbs. arrowroot powder or ¼ cup flour
2 Tbs. ground golden flax seed, opt.
2 tsp. onion powder
½ tsp. each garlic powder, marjoram,
   rosemary
1 tsp. sea salt, 1 tsp. dried basil
   or 1 Tbs. minced fresh
2 Tbs. minced fennel tops
   or 1 tsp. dried dill weed
¼ tsp. celery seed
1 cup grated non-dairy cheese,
   opional , see recipes

1. Prepare one double whole grain pie crust for a 9"x12" casserole dish or 10" quiche pan.

2. Lightly sauté the zucchini, peppers, onions and mushrooms in 1 Tbs. olive oil or water until crisp tender; add the spinach or broccoli; set aside.

3. In a blender or food processor, combine the tofu, milk, arrowroot, flax seed and seasonings. Blend until smooth using a spatula to scrape down sides.

4. In a mixing bowl, combine the blended tofu mixture with sautéed vegetables. Stir in grated cheese (opt.) and mix thoroughly.

5. Pour quiche mixture into pie crust in casserole or quiche dish. Bake at 400° for 15 minutes, then reduce heat to 325° and bake an additional 45 minutes or until done.
Servings: 10-12

Note: To prevent excessive browning, cover edge of crust with 2" strip of foil during last 30 minutes of baking. Quiche can be baked in advance, then re-heated.

Fluffy Eggless Soufflé

Tomatoes, canned or fresh
Soy flour
1-2 Tbs. soy oil (for each quart of mixture)
Water or tomato juice, as needed
Onions, fresh, dried flake or powdered
Seasonings:
    sea salt, sweet basil, onion powder,
    parsley, rosemary, garlic, oregano

Start in blender with tomatoes. Add soy flour gradually sufficient to make a thick batter. Add oil, onions, seasonings to taste. Pour into ungreased baking dish. Repeat if necessary to make 1½" thick. Bake in hot 425° oven for 10 minutes. Reduce heat to low, 300°- 325° continue baking 50 minutes. Remove from oven and cover with towel to set. When cooled cut into squares, and serve with a green salad. Cold soufflé is delicious mixed with diced celery and mayonnaise for a sandwich filling.

Corn Soufflé

¾ cup soy flour
¾ cup water or plain soy milk
1 cup canned tomatoes
2 Tbs. ground peanuts or peanut butter
dash of basil, paprika, and cumin
½ tsp. sea salt + 1 tsp. onion powder
1 cup cooked corn, drained
½ cup soft bread crumbs

Smoothly blend all ingredients except last two. Fold the corn and bread crumbs into the mixture. Pour into shallow ungreased baking dish. Set in pan of water 1" deep. Bake at 350° about 1 hour.

Soybean Soufflé

Be ready to eat when you take the soufflé out of the oven. It will loose its puffiness once it is on the table, but it still tastes good.

1 cup dried soybeans
1 qt. boiling water

Soak beans overnight, drain and rinse. Pour on boiling water; let stand 15 minutes. Drain; you should have 2½ cups soaked soybeans. Liquify the beans in blender with 2 cups hot water while adding:

½ cup tomato purée
½ tsp. celery salt and garlic powder,
    to taste
1 fresh onion or 2 Tbs. onion powder
2 Tbs. soy sauce or Bragg Aminos®
2 Tbs. oil, optional
2 Tbs. nutritional food yeast
1 tsp. sea salt, to taste
3-4 Tbs. peanut butter

Pour into a shallow non-stick or oiled baking dish. Bake at 400° for the first 15 minutes; reduce heat, bake for 1¼ hours at 325°. Let set 15 min. before serving.

Note: If you have soaked soybeans on hand, blend 2½ cups soaked beans with 2 cups water plus the rest of ingredients.

Savory Stir-Fry with Fresh Bean Sprouts

The variety of colors, shapes, and textures is sure to capture the attention and satisfy the appetite when serving this nourishing and savory main dish

2 cups fresh bean sprouts
1½ cups carrots, julienne slices
1 cup celery (2 stalks) ¼"slices
1 cup bok choy or napa cabbage, sliced
1 small yellow squash, thin slices
2 cups broccoli florets
1 red bell pepper, cut in 1"pieces
½ cup sliced fresh mushrooms
1 onion + 3 cloves garlic, chopped
1 tsp. olive oil + ½ tsp. sesame oil
1 tsp. grated fresh ginger, opt.
1 recipe Stir-Fry Sauce

1. Stir ingredients together for **Stir-Fry Sauce** (recipe next page) and set aside.

2. Pre-heat a large skillet or wok over medium-high heat. Quickly stir-fry the garlic and onion in the olive and sesame oil for 1 minute. Add the vegetables   starting with the carrots, celery, bok choy, squash, broccoli, red pepper, mushrooms, and bean sprouts. Continue to stir-fry, stirring constantly, just until crisp- tender, 3-5 minutes, adding a little water (¼- ½ cup) as needed. Push vegetables aside.

3. Stir sauce, add to wok. Cook and stir until thickened and bubbly. Stir all ingredients together to coat with sauce.

Note: **Crusty browned Tofu cubes** may be added for extra protein.

Delicious served over steamed wild rice. Garnish with **toasted sesame seeds** or **sliced almonds.**

Zucchini Summer Stir Fry

Overrun with zucchini? Try using twice the amount in this simple-to-make dish.

2 cups edible pod sugar snap
   or snow peas
1 cup zucchini squash, halved, ¼"slices
1 cup yellow summer squash,
   thin circles
1 cup sliced mushrooms
½ cup red bell pepper, large pieces
1 onion, cut into thin wedges
1 stalk celery, cut diagonally
1-2 gloves garlic, minced, opt.
Stir-fry Sauce, see recipe

Stir together ingredients for sauce and set aside. In a large skillet, pre-heat **1 tsp. olive** or **soy oil**. Add the onion, garlic and celery; stir-fry over medium-high heat 1-2 minutes. Add the squash, pea pods, mushrooms and bell pepper. Stir-fry 3-4 minutes, until vegetables are crisp tender, adding 3-4 Tbs. of water as needed. Push vegetables to side of skillet; stir sauce, add to center of skillet. Cook until thickened and bubbly. Quickly stir all ingredients together to coat with sauce.

Stir-fry Sauce

1 cup vegetable broth,
   reserved liquid or water
1-2 Tbs. Bragg Liquid Aminos,
   to taste
1 Tbs. arrowroot, or cornstarch
1 tsp. onion powder
⅛ tsp. garlic powder
optional but adds good flavor:
   •**Toasted sesame oil, few drops**
   •**Fresh grated ginger root, ½ tsp.**
   •**Paprika or cayenne, sprinkle**

Tofu Pepper Stir-Fry

1 lb. Tofu, extra firm, cut into strips*
½ sweet red bell pepper, cut into strips
½ orange bell pepper, cut into strips
½ green bell pepper, cut into strips
1 medium onion, cut in thin slices
1 tsp. pure olive oil
1 Tbs. Bragg liquid aminos®
   or lite soy sauce
chicken-style seasoning & sea salt, to taste

Brown tofu in a heavy non-stick skillet with olive oil, liquid aminos and chicken-style seasoning; remove and set aside. Add pepper strips and onion to skillet; sprinkle on sea salt to taste. Stir-fry to crisp-tender; add browned tofu strips. Servings: 4

*To make tofu strips: Cut tofu block lengthwise into ½" slices; turn to **stack slices**, and cut again into ½" strips.

Stir-fry Tips

Stir-frying is an Asian method of quickly cooking foods over high heat, in a lightly oiled pan, while stirring continuously, resulting in a crisp-tender texture, sealing in nutrients and flavors often lost with longer cooking.

● Use a large, non-stick, deep skillet, wok, or heavy sauté pan.

● Avoid overloading wok or skillet. (Too much food in the pan may result in stewing food, rather than stir-frying).

● Prepare ingredients before starting to stir-fry. Some ingredients may need to be pre-cooked, such as green beans, cauliflower, and larger sprouted beans, such as garbanzo and soybeans.

● Baby vegetables cook faster. A few including carrots, corn, bok choy, baby patty pan, summer and zucchini squashes, are available in markets as "tiny", "small", "baby" or "new". They are miniature versions of the larger ones, with thinner skin, and more delicate flesh. These are ideal for stir-fry dishes.

● To save prep time, fresh vegetables left from your salad bar, can be combined in some recipes. Allow at least 1 cup of vegetables per person

● Stir-Fry recipes are endlessly adaptable. Create your own vegetable combinations, using different colors and textures, to create an attractive dish. Add tender sprouts such as mung beans and sprouted lentils.

● Vary the cuts and shapes, when preparing the vegetables (thinly sliced, whole, bias-sliced, bite-size strips, wedges, shredded, large pieces, and florets).

Asian Secret: Just a few drops of **toasted sesame oil**, will enhance the flavor of vegetable stir-fry.

Oriental Stir-Fry

Enjoy your garden harvest while preparing this hearty main dish. Serve over rice or noodles; add dinner rolls or breadsticks to complete a meal

2 cups asparagus spears, fresh or frozen, 2" pieces
2 cups sugar snap pea pods, whole
1 cup green beans, bias-sliced, 1" pieces
1 cup baby carrots, 1½" thin strips
1 small zucchini
1 yellow summer squash, halved, cut in ¼" slices
1 cup cauliflower florets
1 cup celery, bias-sliced, ¼"pieces
½ red and orange sweet pepper slices
½ cup onions, sliced
½ tsp. olive or sesame oil
½ cup vegetable broth or water
optional: baby corn, water chestnuts, mushrooms,
**   sprouted mung beans (for color, texture, & nutrition)**

1. Pre-cook the green beans and cauliflower for 1-2 minutes, by lightly steaming, or blanch in boiling water. Drain and set aside. (reserve liquid for the sauce).

2. In a small bowl, stir ingredients together for **Stir-Fry Sauce** (see recipe p.346); set aside.

3. Pre-heat a lightly oiled wok, or large skillet, over med-high heat. Stir-fry the onions and celery in the olive oil until crisp tender.

4. Add green beans, cauliflower, sugar snap peas, asparagus, carrots, zucchini, summer squash, and sweet pepper slices. Stir-fry continuously, adding broth or water as needed, until vegetables are crisp-tender.

5. Pour **Stir-Fry Sauce** over vegetables. Stir lightly until sauce is thick and vegetables are glossy. Good served over rice, potatoes, or pasta. Sprinkle with **Gomashio** if desired (see recipe).

Garden Stir Fry

½ cup vegetable broth
  or water
3 cups broccoli florets
2 cups sugar snap peas,
  fresh or frozen
Red, Orange, Yellow, sweet
  bell peppers - ½ of each,
  cut in large pieces
1 cup baby carrots,
  cut in thin strips
1 medium onion,
  cut into thin wedges
2 cloves garlic, minced
½ teaspoon olive oil
few drops sesame oil
1 recipe Stir-Fry Sauce
*1 can sliced mushrooms, reserve liquid
*1 can sliced water chestnuts, reserve liquid

1. Preheat a lightly oiled wok or large skillet, over medium /high heat. Stir-fry the onions and garlic for 30 seconds, in the olive oil.

2. Add the broccoli flowerets and sugar snap peas; stir fry for 3-4 minutes, adding the broth, or water, as needed. Add the carrots, and sweet bell peppers, while continuing to stir fry, until vegetables are crisp-tender. Last, add the drained water chestnuts and mushrooms, if desired.

3. Push vegetables to one side of skillet or wok. Mix sauce; add to skillet, stirring until thickened. Gently stir, until all vegetables are coated with sauce, and flavors are blended. Serve over rice. Sprinkle with toasted sesame seeds, walnuts, or slivered almonds.

*Optional: adds texture and enhanced flavor

Savory Oven-Roasted Peppers

4 stuffing peppers
  (Anaheim, Bell, Poblano)
2 cups cooked rice*
  (wehani, basmati, jasmine)
1 cup crumbled tofu, firm
1 small onion, 1 clove garlic,
  diced, sautéed
seasonings to taste: sea salt
  basil, celery seed, thyme
2 cups chunky tomato
  mushroom sauce, divided

Cut thin slice from stem end of pepper, remove seeds, parboil or steam 5 min; drain. Mix rice, tofu, onion and seasonings together. Add ¼ cup tomato sauce. Fill peppers. Place in casserole dish, cover and bake at 400° about 45 minutes until peppers are tender. Uncover, and bake another 15-20 minutes until peppers are wrinkled and well roasted. Pour on remaining tomato mushroom sauce and bake another 5 minutes to heat sauce. Garnish with parsley, and serve.

*Aromatic rice contains a natural ingredient that gives it a nutty taste and aroma.

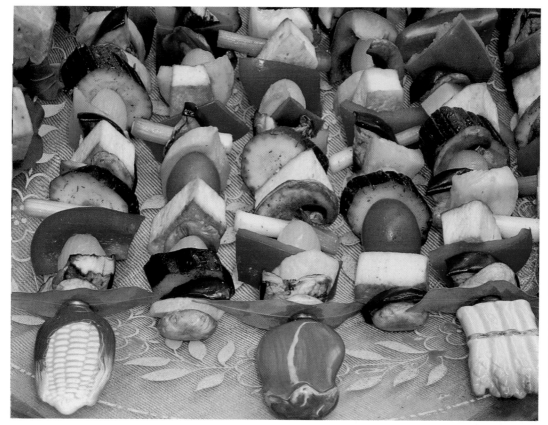

Tofu-Veggie Kabobs

Sweet and sour with lots of eye appeal. Serve kabobs as a main dish with a casserole of fluffy brown rice, and a tossed green salad. Savory as well as nutritious!

Vegetables: mushrooms, eggplant, tofu, red and green sweet peppers, pearl onions, asparagus or green onions, zucchini squash, yellow summer squash, cherry tomatoes.
Marinade: Sweet–and-Sour-Sauce

1. Cut mushrooms in ¼" slices, eggplant in ½" pieces, Tofu in 1 ¼" cubes. Place in bowl or zip-lock plastic bag. Cover with **Sweet-and-Sour-Sauce**, or **Lemon-Herb Marinade** (see recipes) Allow to marinate 25 - 45 minutes, turning occasionally.

2. In a covered saucepan, steam or cook onions in a little water for 3 minutes; drain, set aside. Drain the mushrooms, eggplant and tofu, reserving the marinade. Lightly brown vegetables in a heated non-stick skillet or pre-heated oven.

3. Cut zucchini and summer squash in thin slices, cut peppers in 2½"strips, cut asparagus or green onions in pieces.

4. On metal skewers, alternately thread the tofu and vegetables, to fill skewer. End with a whole mushroom. Place kabobs on non-stick or oiled baking sheet Brush with some of the marinade. Place under a broiler, or Bake in 400° oven until vegetables are crispy tender, turning and brushing with marinade, halfway through baking. To avoid burning vegetables, watch carefully, or cover pan with another baking sheet during part of the cooking cycle.

Note: Serve kabobs with steamed brown rice or couscous, and a green salad for a complete meal.

Tofu - Soybean Curd #1

Tofu is now available in most markets. Making it at home, may be a task of the past; however, if you enjoy the culinary art... like I do, try it- at least once. You may be surprised; quite easy to make, not too messy, and definitely less expensive - 1 lb. dry beans (2½ cups) yield = approx. 2 lbs. curd) Cost? Just pennies + a little time!

1. Rinse **2½ cups dry organic soybeans**. Soak in pure cold water 6-8 hrs. or overnight. Drain and rinse. (select large edible soybeans for the best yield of Tofu)

2. Blend beans until very smooth with no gritty feeling (1 cup soaked beans to 1 quart water). Blend pulp with more water. Squeeze out all milk using clean cloth or flour sack. Pulp can be used in bread or patties.

3. Bring milk to boiling point. Simmer 3 minutes; remove from heat; cool 5 minutes. Slowly add **1 heaping Tbs. Epsom salt** (dissolve in ½ cup warm water) to milk while stirring evenly, but not too much. Let milk set undisturbed 5-10 min. while it curdles.

4. Gently lift the curds into a towel or cheese cloth. Rinse with cold water to remove any trace of salt. Apply pressure or a weight to mold the curd. Let drain well (2-3 hours).

To mold a beautiful curd: Make a small wooden box 5 x 5" with removable top and bottom. Put cheese cloth in box. Lift curd into cheese cloth. Fold cheese cloth over soybean curd. Apply a weight. (a 2-qt. jar filled with water works fine- see illustrations).

5. Soybean curd will be firm enough to slice in 1 hour. Refrigerate up to 7 days in a jar filled with water, rinse daily.

To serve: Season tofu to taste with **onion powder, soy sauce, tomato puree, olives, chopped veggies** or **mayonnaise**; or try sweetening with **agave syrup** or **honey** for a creamy cheese. Also see **Scrambled Tofu "Eggs"**, and other recipes using Tofu.

Soy Cheese Curd #2

This recipe using soy flour and lemon juice as the coagulant yields a softer curd, suitable for dressings, dips, and sandwich filling.

1 quart pure water
1 cup soy flour
3-4 Tbs. fresh lemon juice
½ tsp. sea salt

Whiz in blender until very smooth. Pour into a double boiler pan, cook 20 min. Remove pan from lower part of double boiler. Add immediately 3-4 Tbs. fresh lemon juice and ½ tsp. salt. Stir once. Let cool. Do not disturb. In about 20 minutes the cheese will have formed a soft curd. Strain in a colander lined with a thin clean cloth or layer of cheese cloth. If firmer cheese is desired, place a weight on top. Hint: Do not be too generous with the soy flour, thinking you will get a better curd. Milk that is too thick will not coagulate. Add more water if needed, to thin milk.

Tofu (Dòufu) Types

Tofu (bean curd) is one of many products of the soybean. Packed with protein and B-vitamins and naturally low in sodium, tofu is a popular protein staple or alternative for the growing population of vegetarians. Tofu, known to the Chinese for many years, is readily available today, in the produce section of your grocery store. If purchasing tofu, rather than making it at home, check the "sell by" date on the package to ensure freshness. Store tofu in the refrigerator. Use before expiration

date on label. Once opened, change water daily, use within 1 week or freeze up to 6 months. Throw out tofu that smells sour. Tofu is sold in bulk form, in water filled tubs, individually vacuum packed, or in aseptic packages which can be stored in your pantry. Know the different types and uses:

Extra-Firm or Firm: The most versatile because of its sturdy, dense texture. Great for shredding, slicing thin or thick, for sandwiches, cut in cubes, for stir fries, scrambled tofu, or any dish where you want the tofu to keep its shape. This type is also the best for freezing. Although the texture will be spongy when thawed, it works great for marinating, for kabobs, or used when making tofu "chicken" salad. (see recipes)

Soft tofu: Can be used in recipes such as meatless loaf, patties, for blending or crumbling (such as for soft, scrambled tofu eggs). This type can also be used for dips, dressings, and cheesecake. Its delicate texture allows it to be prepared in many ways.

Silken Tofu comes in Silken Soft, Silken Firm, Silken X-Firm. These varieties are very creamy and smooth, with a custard-like appearance. Processed in airtight, shelf-stable small packages, it can be stored on the shelf, needs no refrigeration. Silken tofu is best used in blended or pureed dishes, such as dips, soups, salad dressings, soy sour cream, tofu quiche, smoothies and cheesecake (see recipes).

Tofu Strips or Cubes

To cut Tofu into uniform smaller pieces, first cut it lengthwise into even ½ - ⅝" slices; then turn, stacking slices, and cut again - into even ½ - ⅝" strips. To cube evenly, line up several strips and cut across.

Tofu Vegetable Pot Pie

2 cups tofu (1-lb), cubed, browned
⅓ cup chopped onion
2 cups cooked diced potatoes
1½ cups soy milk, plain
¼ cup arrowroot or flour
1 Tbs. chicken-style seasoning
¼ tsp. sea salt; pinch cayenne, opt.
1-lb. pkg. frozen mixed vegetables
1-10"double pie crust, see recipes

In a large saucepan, sauté onion and tofu in 2 tsp. olive oil until browned; add potatoes. Blend soymilk, arrowroot and seasonings; add to mixture in saucepan, cook, stirring constantly until mixture is thickened and bubbly. Stir in frozen mixed vegetables (first rinse in cold water to separate, drain); remove from heat. Make pie crust; divide into ⅔ and ⅓. Roll larger piece into a 13" square and ease into a 9"x 9" x 2" square pan. Pour vegetable tofu filling into pastry lined pan. Roll remaining crust into 11"square. Place over filling. Turn edges of pie crust under and flute. Cut design in top of crust. Bake in pre-heated 400° oven 30 minutes or until golden brown.

The hulls of beans and grains, contain enzyme inhibitors, which are neutralized by soaking, cooking or sprouting, aiding the body in the utilization of these foods during the digestive process.

Cremini Mushrooms, Crusty Tofu & Rice

Italian Brown/Cremini mushrooms are firmer with meatier flavor than the common white button mushroom. Sautéing intensifies the flavor, and when combined with crusty browned tofu cubes, makes a delicious base for this casserole dish.

4 cups cooked whole grain rice
1 lb. firm tofu, cubed and browned
1½ lbs. Cremini / Italian Brown mushrooms
⅓ cup diced sweet red bell pepper
⅓ cup minced parsley, curly or flat-leaf
1 Tbs. pure virgin olive oil
2 cloves garlic, finely minced
½ tsp. sea salt, dash of cayenne, to taste

Cook 1 cup rice in 3½ cups water or broth 45-55 min. until tender. Fluff with fork. Brown tofu cubes in non-stick skillet or oven with a sprinkle of liquid aminos until crusty. In a large 12" skillet heat last 3 ingredients; stir in clean whole mushrooms. Cook 4-6 minutes, stirring frequently until mushrooms are tender. Add diced red pepper, stir briefly; add tofu cubes and fresh minced parsley. Stir to combine ingredients and flavors. Transfer to casserole dish. Servings: 8

Freezing Tofu: Tofu can be frozen in the original container, or the tofu blocks wrapped individually in plastic wrap and put in a freezer bag. Tofu that has been frozen changes in texture to a more "chewy" or "spongy" consistency that will absorb flavors easily, making it ideal for marinating. It will naturally change in color to a light beige when frozen, however when thawed, will lighten in color again. Thaw in refrigerator. Press or squeeze out excess liquid before using. (see recipes for marinated tofu)

Extra firm (not Silken) tofu is used in these nutritious kabobs. A nice appetizer for a special dinner or banquet.

Tofu – Soybean Curd
(7 Ways to serve)

1. Sandwiches: slice plain firm tofu; brown or bake in oven; serve in sandwiches.

2. Stir-Fry: dice or cube Tofu; quick sauté in skillet with vegetables or bean sprouts.

3. Crumble and scramble like eggs (see recipe "Scrambled Tofu Eggs")

4. Cheesecake and Pies: Sweeten and use in place of dairy cream or cottage cheese.

5. Soups and Stews: Cut in cubes, brown, add to soups, stews, or Chinese chop suey

6. Meatless Entrées: Use as a base for patties, roasts, kabobs, a variety of vegetarian dishes.

7. Filling or Stuffing: Mash, mix with seasonings; use for stuffing pita sandwiches.

Chinese Tofu Loaf

1½ cups bean curd (tofu)
1 cup seasoned breadcrumbs
    or 2 cups crumbled soft bread
¼ cup finely chopped green onion
¼ cup chopped green pepper or celery
1 clove garlic, minced
1 tsp. sesame oil
1 Tbs. toasted sesame seeds, ground
1½ cups cashew white sauce, see recipe
veggie salt or sea salt, to taste

Mix well all together. Pack into well-oiled baking dish. Place dish in a pan of water; bake at 375° for 50 minutes.

Scrambled Tofu "Eggs"

A cooking school favorite with comments, "It looks and tastes like eggs".

Into a skillet put:

1 Tbs. olive or soy oil
1 Tbs. onion powder
    or ½ cup fresh sautéed onion
1 Tbs. soy sauce or Bragg Aminos®
¼ tsp. turmeric powder
1 drop liquid smoke, opt.
¼ tsp. sea salt, opt.

Stir well and add:

2 cups (1 lb.) firm tofu, mashed/cubed

Mix well with a fork, until seasonings are evenly distributed. Serve as scrambled eggs, with toast or pita pockets.

Variations: Tofu Veggie Scramble - Add **green onions, sweet red peppers, food yeast,** or **chicken style seasoning** (omit salt).

Vegetable Chop Suey with Toasted Almonds

This dish is prepared chiefly from bean sprouts. Virtually fat-free, makes a great accompaniment with rice. Almonds add the finishing touch!

**4-6 cups fresh mung bean sprouts
1 large onion, thinly sliced
1 cup celery, sliced diagonally
1 cup sliced mushrooms
1 red bell pepper, ¼"slices
¾ cup sliced almonds, toasted
Chicken-Style Seasoning, optional**

Steam-stir vegetables (except sprouts) in large skillet with a little olive oil and seasoning. When crisp-tender add rinsed and drained mung bean sprouts. Tenderize until almost soft. Add soy sauce, Bragg Aminos® or sea salt to taste. Serve over steamed brown rice, or buckwheat noodles. Top with toasted sliced almonds. Yield: 6 servings.

To Rinse Sprouts: Place sprouts in a colander, set in a large bowl of water. Gently rinse sprouts, discarding hulls that float to the top. Drain thoroughly.

Vegetarian Chow Mein

These saucy seasoned vegetables combined with tofu, make a colorful satisfying low-fat main dish we enjoy often - a family favorite!

**3 cups fresh broccoli florets
2 cups fresh celery, sliced diagonally
1 cup baby carrots, cut in strips
1 large onion, thinly sliced
2 cups fresh mushrooms, sliced
1 cups edible pod peas, fresh or frozen
1 cup water chestnuts or bamboo shoots
½ cup sweet red pepper strips or diced
2 cups tofu, cubed, browned, opt.**

In a covered skillet, stir and steam the broccoli, celery, carrots, onions and mushrooms until tender. Add the edible pod peas, sweet red pepper and water chestnuts (reserve liquid), stir until crisp-tender. Last, add tofu cubes, opt. Pour the following sauce over steaming vegetables and lightly stir until thickened:

**1¼ cups pure water
    or liquid from vegetables
1¼ Tbs. arrowroot starch
½ tsp. sea salt
¼ tsp. garlic powder
fresh grated ginger root
cayenne, to taste, opt.**

Delicious served over **steamed wehani, basmati or natural brown rice**, with a shaker of **soy sauce** or **Bragg Liquid Aminos**.

Soybeans are an excellent source of nutrition- with high quality protein containing all the essential amino acids, iron, calcium, phosphorus, magnesium, B vitamins including folic acid, and valuable phytochemicals. Soybeans contain properties beneficial in regulating hormones, improving heart health, reducing cholesterol, and preventing cancer.

Green Soy Beans

Softer in texture and rich in flavor; green soybeans are an excellent source of nutrition.

6 cups cooked green soy beans
1 tsp. onion powder
¼ tsp. garlic powder or 2 cloves, minced
¼ tsp. celery seed
1 Tbs. Bakon Yeast, opt.
sea salt and summer savory, to taste
sweet red pepper, parsley, olive oil, opt.

Soak 2¼ cups dry, green soy beans overnight in refrigerator. In the morning drain and cover with fresh water. Add onion, garlic, celery seed and Bakon Yeast, if desired. Simmer until tender (or cook in a crock pot or stainless steel pressure cooker). Add salt and summer savory to taste. Garnish with diced sweet red bell pepper and parsley. Drizzle with olive oil, if desired. Yield: 8-10 servings

Edamame Soybeans in Pod

1 lb. fresh or frozen edamame in shell
1 clove sliced fresh garlic, optional
¼ tsp. sea salt, to taste
garnish: diced pimento, chopped parsley

Place soybeans in kettle with garlic and salt. Pour ¼ cup boiling water over soybeans. Bring to boil, reduce heat, cook 5-10 minutes until tender. Add pimento and parsley. Drizzle on olive oil if desired. Yield: 4 servings

Moderate cooking of most protein foods increases their digestibility, particularly in the case of beans and grains. Beans and other legumes contain strong toxins that inhibit digestion, but they become harmless when neutralized by heat or sprouted.

Green Bean Chow Mein

1 cup celery, sliced diagonially
1 onion, cut in rings or sliced
1 tsp. olive or canola oil
¼ cup peanuts, lightly toasted
1½ cups cut green beans, steamed
(reserve liquid)
1 cup bean sprouts

In heavy skillet, stir-fry celery and onions over medium heat 5-6 min. with small amount of oil or water, just until celery is crisp-tender. Add the peanuts, green beans, and ¼ cup water; cover and cook 3 min., add the bean sprouts; stir until crisp- tender. Pour over the vegetables a medium sauce made with: **¾ cup water or liquid from cooking beans, 2 tsp. arrowroot, 1 tsp. soy sauce** or **Bragg's Aminos, garlic powder, and chicken-style seasoning to taste**. Stir sauce until thick. Serve over rice or noodles.

Spaghetti Crust

Here's another way to use leftover spaghetti- just press in pan, fill and bake or bake and fill.

1. Cook 4 oz. of your favorite spaghetti (artichoke, soy, whole wheat, etc.) al dente or according to package directions. Drain.

2. Return to warm pan; toss with **½ tsp. olive oil** and **1-2 Tbs. finely ground toasted sesame seed** (binds, adds flavor and nutrition).

3. Form crust by pressing spaghetti onto the bottom and up the sides of a 9"pie plate, coated with non-stick cooking spray. Bake in a 400° oven to lightly brown.

Veggie Spaghetti Pie

Use your favorite mixed vegetables or filling, for this simple spaghetti pie.

1-9" Spaghetti Crust, baked, see recipe
4 cups frozen mixed vegetables
1 onion, chopped, sautéed
½ red pepper, diced, sautéed
4-oz. can sliced mushrooms
½ cup firm diced tofu, opt.
clear sauce* or gravy,* season to taste

1. Cook spaghetti according to package directions. Drain (or use leftover spaghetti). Form crust by pressing spaghetti onto the bottom and up the sides of a 9"pie plate. Bake in 400° oven until heated, lightly browned, or crusty. In the meantime:

2. Steam frozen mixed vegetables until tender. Drain any liquid and use in blending the **Clear Sauce*** or **Cashew Gravy***. Pour sauce into a pan; bring to boil, stirring constantly.

3. Add mixed vegetables, onion, peppers, tofu and mushrooms. Stir to blend flavors. Spoon into baked spaghetti crust. Let set to firm, if desired. Serve with salad and bread.

*Clear Sauce: 1 ¼ cups chicken-style broth + 1 Tbs. agar or 2 Tbs. Instant Clear jel

*Gravy: make 1 recipe **Cashew Gravy** (reduce water to 1¼ cups; add 1 tsp. Chicken Style Seasoning)

Artichoke Mushroom Spinach Pie

*Crusty whole grain spaghetti with creamy filling
makes this a favorite main dish*

1- 9" Spaghetti Crust*
14 oz. can artichoke quarters or pieces
10 oz jar sliced mushrooms
1 cup cooked chopped spinach, drained
1 cup tofu, silken firm, diced
½ cup cashew nut pieces
1 Tbs. onion powder
1 tsp. minced garlic
1 tsp. dried sweet basil
½ tsp. rosemary, dried
2 Tbs. arrowroot starch
1 tsp. pure olive oil
½ tsp. salt; pinch of cayenne
1¼ cups liquid from vegetables

1. Cook 4 oz.of your favorite spaghetti al dente. Drain, return spaghetti to saucepan and toss with a little olive oil and 1-2 Tbs. toasted ground sesame seeds, if desired. Set aside.

2. Drain liquid from water packed artichokes and mushrooms (you should have approx. 1¼ cups). Put liquid into blender; add cashew nuts, arrowroot, olive oil and seasonings; blend until very smooth.

3. Pour into a large saucepan; bring to a boil over medium heat, stirring constantly until thick. Quickly add prepared vegetables (artichokes, mushrooms, spinach, tofu). Pour into spaghetti crust*. Bake at 350° for 20 min. or until crust is toasted. Remove from oven; let set covered, 5-10 min. before cutting into 6-8 pie pieces.

***Form crust by pressing spaghetti onto the bottom and up the sides of a 9" pie plate, that has been coated with a non-stick cooking spray.**

Savory Vegetable Rice Crêpes

Try filling crepes with crisp-tender stir-fry, roasted vegetables, creamy mushroom, garlic and spinach, or wrap around seasoned scrambled tofu. Serve with a salad for a delicious meal!

1 cup w.w. pastry flour
½ cup cooked brown or wild rice
1 tsp. olive oil and/or lecithin granules
¼ tsp. sea salt
¼ tsp. onion and/or garlic powder
1 cup plain soymilk
½ cup water, approx.
1½ tsp. Ener-G® egg replacer, opt.

1. Blend all ingredients together until smooth, adjust batter with water or flour as needed to resemble light cream. Allow to set 5-10 minutes while preparing skillet.

(If using egg replacer, beat 1½ tsp. with 1 Tbs. water until frothy, then fold into mixture)

2. Heat skillet over medium heat; lightly cover with cooking spray. *(Heat is just right, when a few drops of water jump around, when sprinkled on pan).* For each crepe, pour scant ¼ cup batter into skillet. Quickly rotate skillet to cover the bottom with a thin, even layer of batter.

3. Cook the crêpe for approximately 1½ minutes on each side. Flip the crêpe by carefully grabbing the edge with your fingers, or run a wide spatula around edge to loosen and flip. Stack warm cooked crêpes on a plate. Repeat steps for cooking the batter until finished. Yield: approx. 12- 6" crêpes.

Main dish Sandwiches

Super Pita

Calzone

Bun

Sliced Wraps

Open Face

Crepe

Burrito

Wrap

Tofu Stuffed Pita Pockets

Make a meal-in-minutes with these protein-rich filled pitas served alone or with a bowl of your favorite soup.

**Tofu slices, baked or browned
fresh ripe tomato, sliced
cucumber, sliced unpeeled
arugula, spinach,
     or garden lettuce leaves
Tofu Mayonnaise or other choice
whole wheat Pita Bread**

Slice tofu ¼" thick. Brown both sides in oiled skillet, or bake in hot oven.
Cut pita bread rounds in half crosswise; spread with your favorite mayonnaise. Fill pockets generously with tofu slices, tomato, cucumber, and salad greens. Serve 1-2 halves per person, or have each one fill their own pita pockets.

*Note: Tofu slices can be made ahead (refrigerate or freeze and thaw). I like to brown the slices in a non-stick skillet with a little **Bragg Liquid Aminos** and sprinkle on seasoning (**onion, garlic powder,** or **Chicken-Style Seasoning**).*

Falafel

A very tasty well-known Middle Eastern dish made with garbanzo beans. These small savory bean balls are ideal for stuffing in pita pockets or served with a tomato and cucumber salad and lemon wedges.

**5 cups cooked garbanzo beans,
     (2 cups dry)
3 cloves garlic, chopped
3 slices whole-grain bread, crumbled
¼ cup sesame tahini or soy starter
     (see recipe)
1 medium red onion, chopped
2 Tbs. chopped fresh cilantro
1 tsp. ground cumin
1 tsp. ground coriander
½ tsp. turmeric powder
½ tsp. fennel seed, crushed
¼ tsp. red pepper flakes or cayenne, opt.
sea salt, to taste**

1. In a food processor, put the cooked, drained garbanzo beans, garlic, bread, tahini, onion, cilantro and herb seasonings. Process for about 30-60 seconds, scraping down sides as needed to make a medium smooth consistency; stir and add sea salt to taste. Remove mixture from food processor to a shallow bowl.

2. Shape with your hands or small scoop into walnut-size balls. Roll in seasoned bread crumbs, if desired. Brown on stove-top in oiled skillet or place on non-stick baking sheet and brown in 375° oven, rolling to brown all sides. Yield: approx. 6 servings

Photo, left: Rolling **Garden Veggie Wraps** (see next page)

- Guacamole, steamed rice, sliced green onion, shredded carrots.

- Beans, Tofu Vegenaise, lettuce, olives, red pepper, non-dairy cheese.

- Edamame pesto, sliced olives, mushrooms, carrot/cabbage shreds.

- Tofu, salad dressing, baby greens, red onion, shredded yellow squash.

Garden Veggie Wraps

A variety of tortilla flavors are available in natural food markets. Some ready-to-eat selections include: whole wheat, fresh herb, spinach, tomato-basil, etc. Wholesome wraps can be made with a variety of fillings. They are fun and easy to make, portable, and have endless possibilities for serving.

(See step-by-step illustrated recipe in chapter **Sandwiches & Spreads p.465**)

1. Top tortilla with filling ingredients to within 1" of edge.

2. Roll up tortillas, gently pulling toward you, as you roll (see photo, prev. page).

3. Slice in 1½" pieces, or for a main-dish serving, cut rolls in half. Serve on bed of lettuce leaves.

To store: Wrap securely and refrigerate.

Filling Suggestions:

- Seasoned tofu, sliced olives, shredded zucchini, carrots, spinach leaves.

- Hummus, red onion, cucumber, diced tomato, broccoli, sprouts.

- Basil pesto, steamed rice, diced tomato, cucumber, toasted sesame.

Spicy Meatless Chili

Quick and easy! This hearty stew is perfect for warming you on those chilly days.Serve with cornmeal muffins steamed rice and a crisp salad for a filling and satisfying meal.

1 cup chopped onion
1 chopped green pepper
1 cup sliced celery
2 cups firm tofu, cube or crumble, opt.
1 Tbs. olive or soy oil, opt.
1 tsp. ground cumin, to taste
1-2 tsp. veggie salt, to taste
½ tsp. each celery seed and turmeric
onion, garlic powder, cayenne, to taste
2 ½ cups tomatoes, chopped
4 cups pinto or kidney beans, cooked

Lightly brown onion, pepper, celery and tofu in skillet, with 1 Tbs. olive oil, if desired. Add seasonings and a little water; cover and cook 2-3 minutes until tender. Add tomatoes and tender cooked kidney beans. Complement with a dish of steamed brown rice. Servings: 6

Enchiladas

12 corn tortillas
Filling:
3 cups pinto beans, cooked
1 cup chopped green pepper, sautéed
½ cup chopped onion, sautéed
1 cup black olives
½ cup Enchilada sauce
Sauce:
2½ cups tomato sauce
2 med. onions
1 green pepper
½ cup mushrooms, opt.
1 clove garlic
1 cup tofu, mashed
1 Tbs. lemon juice
1 tsp. cumin
¼ tsp. sea salt, celery seed, to taste

Chop and sauté the vegetables for Enchilada sauce in a little olive oil. Add tofu and seasonings. Simmer a few minutes and set aside. Combine ingredients for filling. Soften tortillas by steaming or heating just until soft. Fill softened tortillas with 2-3 Tbs. of filling. Roll and place them side by side in a casserole dish spread with tomato sauce. Cover with remaining sauce. Bake at 350° for 30 min. Yield: 6 servings

Re-fried Beans

The full bodied, earthy flavor of speckled pink and brown pinto beans makes them a staple of southwestern and Mexican cooking.

Pinto Beans
Sea salt
Garlic powder and seasonings, to taste
Olive or canola oil, opt.

Cook pinto beans until tender, or use canned, drained beans. Blend beans with seasonings in a food processor until smooth. Spoon into non-stick skillet; stir until heated through and bubbly. Ideal filling for bean burritos, wraps or pita bread.

Bean Burritos

Whole grain tortillas
Refried beans
 or mashed cooked pinto beans
Salsa - Fresh Tomato or Health Ketchup
Avocado slices
Cucumber slices
Green Leaf Lettuce

Warm tortillas in oven or skillet
to soften. Spread lightly with **Tofu
Vegenaise** or other soy mayonnaise.
Spoon ⅓ - ½ cup filling onto each
tortilla. Top with **Salsa**, sliced avocado,
cucumber, and green leaf lettuce.
Garnish with parsley and green onion
curls. Serve with crisp coleslaw, and
your favorite soup, for a complete meal.

Corn Tamale Bake

1 large onion, chopped
1 green pepper, chopped
3 cloves garlic, minced
3 cups tomatoes, canned crushed
¾ cup corn meal, fine
2 cups frozen, canned or fresh cut corn
¼ cup chopped olives
½ tsp. cumin and sea salt, to taste
¼ tsp. cayenne or paprika

In a skillet, sauté the chopped onion,
pepper and garlic, in a small amount
of olive oil until crisp-tender. Add the
tomatoes, cornmeal, rest of ingredients
and seasonings. Simmer in covered
skillet for 1 hour. Stir occasionally
adding a little water (up to ¾ cup) if
it gets too thick. Serve hot or place in
baking dish to re-heat. Serves: 6

Why Vegetarianism?

Note These Headlines:

MEAT – DIETARY LINK TO CANCER? HEART DISEASE?

GLOBAL HUNGER, DISEASE LINKED WITH FLESH DIET

FISH – LIVING REPOSITORIES OF MANY DANGEROUS CHEMICALS DUMPED INTO OCEANS

Vegetarianism is the oldest diet known to the human race (Gen. 1:29). It is the most economical and wholesome diet for human beings. There is sufficient evidence to be found in books and periodicals to support vegetarianism without a question. Humans are not biochemically suited to eat meat. We possess the features for a vegetarian fare. Our flat teeth are not sharp enough to tear through flesh or bone. Our lengthy digestive tract resembles that of the herbivore. Our digestion begins in the mouth as the salivary glands secrete an enzyme designed to break down complex carbohydrates. Conversely, carnivores secrete an enzyme that breaks down the uric acid in meat. Although designed to subsist on plant based foods, man has changed his dietary habits to accept the food of the carnivore and the resulting risk, an increase of disease. Vegetarians can have a nutritionally adequate diet; however, some find room to doubt and disbelieve. Here are just a few reasons why meat should be discarded:

1. Meat is high in saturated fat and cholesterol, a leading cause of hardening of the arteries and coronary heart disease.

2. Liability to take disease is increased tenfold by eating meat.

3. As a source of protein a meat-centered diet is the most expensive.

4. Meat is not essential to good health, strength, or endurance.

5. Meat is a carrier of diseases which are readily transmitted to man when flesh is eaten.

6. Meat is wasteful of our country's resources: A cow requires about 21 pounds of protein (grains) to produce 1 pound of meat for human consumption.

7. Animal flesh is stimulating and unsuitable as food for the human digestive system. Those who eat it are eating grains and vegetables second hand.

8. The moral, intellectual, and physical capacities are depreciated by the habitual use of flesh meat; digestion is impared.

9. Vegetarians enjoy better health and a greater life expectancy.

10. A vegetarian diet chosen from nature's bountiful and healthful supply tends toward freedom of intellect and a sweetness and serenity of disposition, imparting strength to meet the challenges of life.

*"THE GRAINS, WITH FRUITS, NUTS, AND VEGETABLES, CONTAIN **ALL** THE NUTRITIVE PROPERTIES NECESSARY TO MAKE GOOD BLOOD."* E. G. White, Diet and Foods, p. 396

"When flesh food is discarded, its place should be supplied with a variety of grains, nuts, vegetables, and fruits, that will be both nourishing and appetizing." Ibid, 315

Wheat Gluten "Beef" Steaks

Gluten (the elastic protein substance found in wheat) can be easily transformed into juicy steaks at home- and it's fun! When using whole wheat flour, gluten steaks are more nutritious and tender, than those made from white flour. Gluten steaks can be breaded and browned, resembling a tender beef steak, or ground and combined with other grains, nuts, and legumes, to make nourishing and digestible meatless dishes, or vegetarian casseroles.

12 cups whole wheat flour
4-6 cups cold water or broth

In a large bowl, add 4 cups water to flour, adding more water as needed, mixing and kneading together to form a stiff dough. Cover dough ball with cold water and let stand a few hours or overnight. Wash starch away, by kneading until water is almost clear (about 5 times), rinsing and adding fresh water each time. Gluten will hold together and be spongy. Drain well. Cut gluten in thin slices or pieces; flatten to desired shape and drop in boiling broth. Simmer for 1 hour allowing steaks to absorb broth.

Note: Steaks freeze well. Make ahead, simmer, cool and freeze in remaining broth. When ready to use, thaw, remove from broth, press firmly into breading meal and brown in skillet on both sides. Serve in sandwiches, or with gravy.

Broth for Gluten

8 cups pure water
1 cup tomato juice
½ cup soy sauce or Bragg Aminos®
2 Tbs. onion powder
   or 2 fresh onions, diced
1 Tbs. food yeast
garlic, sea salt or Vegex, to taste
Beef or Chicken-style seasoning*

Add homemade gluten pieces to boiling broth and let simmer till most of liquid is absorbed. Allow to cool. Remove gluten. Dip in breading meal and brown in non-stick skillet or oven. Thicken remaining broth with a little flour and serve for a tasty gravy over gluten steaks. *recipes for Seasonings, p. 297

Note: For extra special gravy, add **sliced mushrooms** and **chopped parsley.**

Pea-Not Meat

1 cup yellow corn meal
1 cup whole wheat flour or part oats
¾ cup peanut butter, raw
   or lightly toasted
1 qt. tomato purée, juice, or part water
1½ tsp. sea salt
1½ cups pure warm water

In a dry, heavy skillet, dextrinize (lightly toast while stirring) the cornmeal and flour. Blend together the peanut butter, tomato juice, salt and water. Mix all together. Fill small greased cans. Cover. Bake or steam about 1½ hours. Cool. Better the next day. Good sliced in sandwiches or use for spread.

Gluten "Soy Meat"

1 cup soaked soybeans
1 cup water or tomato juice
2 cups homemade gluten, ground
1 cup peanuts, toasted, ground
1 tsp. sea salt, to taste
soy sauce, sage and thyme, to taste
1 Tbs. arrowroot, soy or gluten flour
1 Tbs. onion powder
   or ¼ cup sautéed onion
¼ tsp. garlic powder
2 Tbs. soy oil, opt.

Blend soy beans with water or juice. Coarsely grind gluten (boiled in broth), with peanuts. Add rest of ingredients. Mix all together. Fill greased cans. Cover. Steam in boiling water for 3 hours. Cool. Remove from cans using a dull knife.

Nutee Supreme & Mushrooms

A protein rich casserole, smothered with sautéed mushrooms and onions. This satisfying main course dish goes well with a garden green salad and soup.

1-19 oz.can Nutee Supreme, (Cedar Lake Foods)
2# mushrooms; button, shiitake, or cremini
3 large onions, sliced
1-2 cloves garlic, minced
2 cups Italian Tomato Sauce or other

1. Open and remove both ends of **Nutee Supreme** can; then with a dull knife go around loaf to loosen from can. Reposition lid, and remove loaf by pressing lid, to slide loaf out. Cut loaf in ¼" slices.

2. Sauté sliced mushrooms, onion and garlic, in 1 Tbs. olive oil or water, until crisp tender.

3. Spread ¼ cup tomato sauce in a casserole dish; layer the Nutee Supreme slices alternately with the mushrooms mixture and tomato sauce. Finish with mushrooms and onions on top. Bake in 350° oven 30 minutes or until heated through.

Note: **Nutee Supreme** replaces Loma Linda **Nuteena.**

Veggie "Turkey" Deli Cuts

1¼ cups gluten flour
¼ cup whole wheat flour
3 Tbs. food yeast flakes
½ cup walnuts
1 cup cold water
2 tsp. onion powder
½ tsp. garlic powder
1 tsp. soy sauce, opt.

In a bowl, place the flours and nutritional food yeast. In a blender, process nuts, water and seasonings until creamy. Pour over flour in bowl, mixing thoroughly with hands,* forming a ball of dough. Roll into a 2" log shape. Cut in ½" slices; pat to shape and drop into boiling broth (see Broth p.365). Simmer for 1 hr. until tender. Remove from broth and let cool. Use in desired recipe. Dice or cut in cubes for salad or stir-fry; slice for sandwiches, or soak in marinade sauce for kabobs. (see recipes).

*Wearing thin rubber gloves is helpful when mixing ingredients together with your hands. Note: The steps of soaking, washing, and rinsing are eliminated when using gluten flour.

Nuteena Smothered with Onions

1 can Nuteena (or Nutee Supreme)
   cut in ¼" slices
6 cups sliced onion, (red, white or yellow)
2 cups fresh sliced mushrooms
½ cup sweet red pepper
   cut in 1" long, thin strips
1-2 Tbs. olive oil
1 tsp. each dried oregano and sweet basil
1 tsp. each onion powder,
   chicken-style seasoning
½ tsp. each garlic powder and sea salt
2-3 lemons, fresh squeezed
Italian parsley (handful), chopped

Sauté onions, mushrooms, peppers and seasonings in pan with olive oil until soft and tender. Add chopped parsley, set aside. Dip **Nuteena** slices in flax jell, then breading meal. Lay on baking sheet and brown in 400° oven, turning once. Arrange slices in casserole dish, alternating layers with onion and mushroom mixture. Top with juice of freshly squeezed lemons. Serve warm.

Nuti-Loaf with Zucchini and Tomato Sauce

A healthy meat analog made with peanuts, soy, corn and rice, is used for this tasty and simple make-ahead main dish, suitable for potluck or picnic.

1-19 oz. can Nuti - Loaf, (Cedar Lake Foods)
1 or 2 fresh zucchini, thinly sliced
1 medium onion, thinly sliced
Italian Tomato Sauce (see recipe)

1. Open and remove both ends of Nuti-Loaf can; then with a dull knife go around loaf to loosen from can. Reposition 1 lid, and remove loaf by pressing on lid, to slide loaf out.

2. Cut loaf in ¼" slices. Cut zucchini and onions in ⅛" slices.

3. Spread ¼ cup tomato sauce in the bottom of a 6" x 9"x 2" baking dish.

4. Layer the **Nuti-Loaf** slices, zucchini and onion slices alternately with tomato sauce, in baking dish. Cover with tomato sauce.

5. Bake in 350° for 45 minutes or until baked and sauce is bubbly. Good served hot or cold with a fresh green tossed salad, whole grain bread, rice or pasta.

Tostados

For a simple family picnic or potluck - just take along the crisp tortillas and other prepared ingredients. Tostados are a breeze to assemble and put together.

Corn tortillas, crisp
Red beans, cooked and seasoned
Lemon or lime juice, opt.
Lettuce greens, chopped
Fresh tomatoes, cubed
Guacamole sauce
Green onions, chopped
Black olives, sliced or chopped

Heat tortillas in 400° oven 5-10 minutes until crisp. Mash the cooked seasoned beans; add a **squeeze of lemon or lime juice**, if desired; spread on crisp tortillas. Top with **salad greens, tomatoes, olives, guacamole sauce, and chopped onion.**

Variation: Use **tender dark greens (cilantro, spinach, watercress)** instead of lettuce.

Peanut Soymeat

1 cup tomatoes or puree'
1 ¼ cups soy flour
1 cup pure water
2 Tbs. nutritional yeast flakes
1 cup toasted peanuts or cashews
2 Tbs. onion powder
2 Tbs. soy sauce or Bragg Aminos®
2 Tbs. gluten flour or arrowroot
1 tsp. salt; dash of garlic powder
¼ cup finely chopped peanuts

Blend all ingredients (except peanuts) until smooth. Add the finely chopped peanuts (for crunchy texture). Fill medium sized cans (that have been oiled or treated with non-stick coating), ¾ full. Cover with foil or plastic wrap secured with rubber band. Steam in kettle of water for 2-3 hours until firm (set cans on a rack – keep water level 2" from top of cans). Remove from water; allow to cool.

To remove Soymeat from cans:
Use can opener to remove bottom of can. Loosen around edge with dull knife; firmly press on lid to slide and remove Soymeat. Slice and serve hot or cold. Makes a delicious sandwich filling with mayonnaise. Freezes well.

Soy Meatless Round

1 cup soaked ground soybeans,
   or soybean pulp
½ cup bread crumbs, grape nuts,
   or dry oatmeal
1 cup tomatoes or purée
4 Tbs. toasted peanut butter
1 Tbs. onion powder
3-4 Tbs. soy sauce or Bragg Aminos®
1-2 Tbs. soy oil, opt.
½ tsp. sea salt
¼ tsp. garlic powder, to taste

In a mixing bowl combine the ground soybeans and bread crumbs. Blend tomatoes, peanut butter, onion, soy sauce, and seasonings in blender. Add this to the ground soybeans and bread crumbs. Mix well; fill 2 medium size cans (spray or brush with non-stick coating). Cover cans and steam for 2 ½ hours. Allow to cool, remove from cans and slice. Good for sandwiches with mayonnaise and sprouts or slice and serve with your favorite gravy. Freezes well.

Note: The cans may be set on a rack in a kettle of water filled to 1" from the top of cans. Cover the kettle and let cans process in boiling water.

Nuts, Seeds, & Olives

Index - CHAPTER 11

Husband Helps

*"A husband who despises housework
But frequently must help his spouse work –
At times can win a quick acquittal
By getting in the way a little!"*

Chapter cover photo: ***"Nuts over Nuts"*** **Fresh in Shell**

Nuts, Seeds, & Olives
Vital Food in Small Packages

Nuts and Seeds are compact sources of essential nutrients, some of the oldest and best of nature's products: botanically one-seeded fruits, differing widely in appearance and composition from foods commonly called fruits, and placed in a class by themselves.

Studies have shown nuts to lower blood cholesterol levels and reduce the risk of heart disease.

Seeds whether eaten out-of-hand like sunflower or pumpkin, or sprouted like alfalfa, or as a dietary supplement like flax or fenugreek, hold concentrated nutrition, and are

virtually the container of life.

Nuts and Seeds are packed sources of Protein, Fat, and Carbohydrates. Most of them are good sources of B vitamins, and minerals such as Calcium, Phosphorus, Magnesium, Iron, Potassium, Copper, and Zinc.

Many nuts are also well supplied with Vitamin E, Folic Acid and fiber, and when used in moderation, thoroughly chewed, and combined with grains, are a good source of protein for vegetarians, and part of a well-balanced plant based diet.

"The science of cooking is not a small matter. The skillful preparation of food is one of the most essential arts. It should be regarded as among the most valuable of all the arts, because it is so closely connected with life. Both physical and mental strength depend to a great degree upon the food we eat; therefore the one who prepares the food occupies an important and elevated position."
Counsels on Diet and Foods, pg. 475

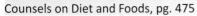

Nutrition in a Nutshell

Almonds: Nutrient-rich almonds deserve to be placed at the head of the list of edible nuts. It is the fruit (a drupe) of a small tree with edible kernel (the nut). Almonds are a good source of protein, B vitamins, magnesium, iron, calcium, phosphorus, potassium, and a rich source of the antioxidant Vitamin E. A very good source of mono-unsaturated fat and the essential omega 3 (linolenic acid). Almonds are preferable to peanuts, and can be eaten whole, made into nutritious nut butter, milk, or meal for baked goods. The "bitter almond" is not edible, but is grown for its oil, and is used in the base of many fine cosmetics. The extract is used in medicine and for flavoring.

Almonds are mentioned in the Bible many times. From Spain and other Mediterranean countries, almonds were imported to North America. Today, 85 percent of the world crop comes from almond orchards in western California.

Brazil Nuts: An oily, three-sided nut, with a rich white meat and dark brown, very hard, rippled shell. Brazil nuts are more than 65% fat, mostly unsaturated, and 20% being saturated similar to the palm and coconut. Brazil nuts are a rich source of thiamine (B1) which benefits the nervous system. They contain a high concentration of selenium (important in the treatment of irritability, depression and mental performance), and other nutrients such as protein, iron, magnesium, calcium, phosphorus, selenium, copper, zinc, and E. The creamy flesh tastes best in winter. They are good eaten alone or in baked goods. The Brazil nut is a vital crop of the Amazon region. It is grown mostly in Brazil, also Bolivia, Peru, Columbia and Venezuela.

Cashews: The cashew is not really a nut, but the seed of the cashew apple. Unlike other fruit seeds, it grows outside the apple on the lower end, and receives full benefit from the sun. This sweet-tasting nut is bean-shaped, eggshell colored, and contains protein, fat, and carbohydrates. The nuts are a source of magnesium, and contain moderate amounts of Vitamin B1, B2, B6, niacin, and zinc. Available shelled only, the kernels are treated before shipping to the U.S. Cashews are good dry roasted, eaten alone, in baked goods, beverages, casseroles, Chinese dishes, etc. The cashew is originally from Central and South America. Today 80 percent of the world's supply is imported from India and Brazil. Other countries include Kenya, Tanzania, Mozambique, Ceylon and Madagascar.

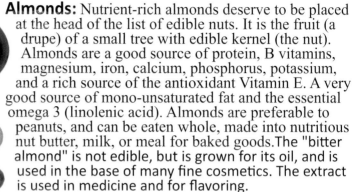

Chestnuts: Chestnuts are the edible nut of any tree of a genus (Castanae) of the beech family. The mound-shaped, smooth, thin, brown-skinned nut grows inside a hard prickly bur. Chestnuts are low in fat and protein, but high in carbohydrates, with more manganese and potassium than most nuts. They also contain B vitamins including folate, and small amounts of calcium, iron, magnesium, zinc and vitamin C. They have a satisfying sweetness adding a pleasant balance to a savory meal. Usually enjoyed roasted on an open fire, in the oven or boiled. Chestnuts are used widely in the northern provinces; in Italy, chestnut meal is used in bread and other dishes.

The majority of chestnuts imported from Europe to the United States are from Southern Italy, some are from Portugal and France. They are sold by the pound in many supermarkets. The chestnuts grown in North America are mostly in the eastern states.

Coconut: In Sanskrit, the language of ancient India, the coconut palm is called *kalpa vriksha*, meaning "the tree that provides everything necessary for life". The inhabitants of the islands of Polynesia have survived for generations using coconut liquid for drinking, and the pulp for solid food. The coconut fiber, trunk and fronds are used for everything from ropes, sandals, textiles, and toothbrushes to building homes.

The most abundant nutrient in coconut is fat. These are a type of saturated fatty acids -short and medium chain, which are absorbed and assimilated by the body and do not promote cholesterol production. Coconut contains good amounts of magnesium, calcium and phosphorus, which contributes to healthy bones, muscles, and joints.

Coconut can be combined with other ingredients in making tasty beverages, desserts and entrées, or used to garnish soup or salad. To extract "milk" from coconut: make a hole in soft "eye" on top of coconut, pour liquid into a glass. To remove pulp: break the shell with a hammer or place coconut in hot oven for 5 minutes. To extract oil: finely grind the pulp and catch the drippings in a bowl; it may be semi-solid in the refrigerator and return to liquid at room temperature. One medium fresh coconut yields 3-4 cups coconut shreds.

(More information: see **Glossary of Natural Foods**)

Filberts (Hazelnuts): Filberts are a genus of shrubs or small trees of the birch family. The nuts have smooth, hard, reddish-brown shells which are thin and brittle. The kernels are very tasty and among the most popular and favorite nuts. Filberts are rich in unsaturated fat, and are second to almonds in calcium content. They provide good amounts of protein, B vitamins, potassium, magnesium, manganese, iron, and Vitamin E. The sweet, buttery flavor of these nutmeats are delicious eaten alone, in baked goods, and desserts.

Filberts are grown primarily in the northwestern United States. The filbert and hazelnut are of the same family. The filbert is originally from Turkey, Italy, and Greece. The Barcelona hazelnut variety is extensively grown in the Pacific Northwest. Hazelnuts are grown commercially with 98 percent of the total U.S. crop produced in Oregon.

Flax Seeds: Flax as a plant or "linen" derived from it, was an important economic crop in all of Asia, mentioned over 75 times throughout Biblical history in contrast to the mention of "cotton" only once. Medicinally flax is used as a poultice for swelling and as a mild and effective laxative. Keep refrigerated after grinding. An excellent addition to Fruit Smoothies, resulting in a thick creamy texture. Flaxseed is good in bread, or ground and sprinkled on fruit or hot cereal, imparting a nutty flavor. (see recipes)

Hickory (Butternuts): A sweet edible nut from a species of North American hardwood trees of the walnut family. The shell of this nut is very thick and hard, making it difficult to crack. The sweet nutmeat is rich in oil, similar to the black walnut. Good eaten alone or in baked goods. Hickory nuts are grown primarily in the eastern United States.

Macadamia Nuts: Macadamia nuts are a hard, delicious, and expensive dessert nut. Sweet and buttery, high in monounsaturated fatty acids, low in protein, they are large and light beige in color, with an uneven, sphere-shaped nutmeat. The Macadamia nut is one of the most oil-rich of the oil-bearing nuts. The fats are similar in composition to olive oil, which lower cholesterol and improve blood circulation through the coronary arteries. Macadamia nuts are delicious eaten alone, in salads, or as a garnish for sweet dishes.

Available shelled only, they come primarily from Hawaii and Australia. Originally from Australia, the macadamia nut was developed into a commercial crop. Hawaii is now the largest producer of macadamia nuts, one of the main agricultural crops grown in Hawaii next to pineapple.

Peanuts: Technically not a nut, but a legume; the peanut is widely known and grown. Because of their high fat content, peanuts are often called nuts. They are the nut-like seeds of a Brazilian herb of the pea family. Unlike tree fruits, the pod of the peanut is ripened under ground. As the plant matures, the branch tips bury themselves into the ground where the pods mature and ripen. When the plant withers, the peanuts may be dug up. The soft, papery shell contains two or three bean-shaped nutmeats, which taste best when lightly roasted.

Peanuts are inexpensive and contain good nutritional value. They are a source of protein, rich in B vitamins (especially niacin), and contain magnesium, iron, and vitamin E. High in fat (approx. 50%), peanuts yield a rich oil used for salads, in cooking and margarines. Peanuts are commonly eaten alone, in baked goods, casseroles, and as peanut butter – another American favorite. Although not a complete protein (26%), ground peanut or peanut butter can be combined with grains, seeds, and legumes, to boost the total level of essential amino acids needed for proper nutrition. Peanuts are grown primarily in the southern and western United States.

Pecan Nuts: A native North American tree, a near relative of the hickory group, the pecan produces a rounded oblong nut with a semi-brittle shell which is easy to crack. The nutmeats have a sweet pulpy texture. Pecans are low in protein (10%), and one of the highest in unsaturated fat (approx. 70%). They are delicious eaten alone, erved with fruit, in baked goods, meatless patties, and desserts. The United States produces more than 80 percent of the world's pecans. Top production states include Georgia, Texas, New Mexico, Arizona, and Oklahoma.

Pignolia and Piñón Nuts (Pine Nuts):

Pignolia nuts are a sweet, buttery, thin white pellet-shaped nutmeat. Pignolia nuts are rich in protein, vitamin B1, and unsaturated fatty acids. They are difficult to shell, relatively scarce and expensive. The delicate pleasant taste and soft texture make them suitable for a variety of dishes; primarily used in pesto, baked goods, desserts, and fine cuisine. They are usually imported from Italy and Spain.

Many varieties of pine nuts are found in South America and Switzerland. About 200,000 pounds a year are brought to the USA from Italy, Spain, and Turkey. The most common in this country is the piñón nut which grows in the southwestern United States. They are very similar in taste and appearance to the pignolia nut. Pine Nuts are a delicacy, and will become rancid easily. Store in sealed refrigerator container or freezer.

Pistachio Nuts: Richest of all nuts in iron, and the lowest in fat. A small tree of the cashew family with hard seed shell, off white color with a pale green nutmeat. Mild flavor, rich in protein, iron, calcium, phosphorus, potassium, magnesium, B1, niacin, and vitamin E for heart-health. Noted for their color, eaten out-of-hand, in desserts and ice cream. Avoid pistachios with excess salt or covered with a red dye. Natural pistachios have a delightful flavor. A few nutmeats are very satisfying.

In early Bible times the patriarch Jacob living in Palestine, considered pistachio nuts as some of the best products of the land. (see Genesis 43:11, NIV). They are originally a staple of the Middle East of Iranian origin, and rumored to have been rooted in royalty (a favorite of the Queen of Sheba). Now large crops of these greenish colored nuts are grown in California.

Pumpkin Seeds: Also known as pepitas, these flat green seeds have a white outer shell. Pumpkin seeds are a very rich source of protein: 29%, and containing iron, phosphorus, calcium, niacin, and zinc. Good eaten alone, in granola, dried fruit and nut mixes, and on fruit and vegetable salads. Pumpkin and squash seeds can be dried, shelled, and lightly toasted. Good flavor!

Sesame Seeds: Sesame seeds are versatile and inexpensive, and can be used as a topping for fruit or cereal, granola, salad dressings, desserts, and in making tasty, nourishing milk, especially when combined with soy. When toasted, hulled or unhulled sesame seeds can be ground and sprinkled on salads, pasta, rice or stir-fry vegetables. The hulled sesame seeds are made into a smooth paste known as Tahini. (see recipes)

Sunflower Seeds: A powerhouse of nutrition, containing a broad spectrum of nutrients. Delicious on cereal, fruit, in granola, cookies, breads, meatless entrees, or just eaten out of the hand. Can be crushed, ground fine, or made into seed butter. Try sprouting them! (see recipes)

More information on Seeds: see Glossary of Natural Foods

Walnuts: Varieties include the English walnut, black walnut, and white walnut, also called butternut. The English walnut has a thin hard shell, with curly nutmeat halves. The black walnut resembles the English walnut, but with dark skin covering the white nutmeat. The shell of the Eastern black walnut is extremely hard and difficult to crack. Flavor is stronger than the English walnut and somewhat richer in nutrients. Walnuts contain high levels of essential fatty acids that reduce cholesterol and triglyceride levels in the blood. Walnuts contain a powerhouse of nutrients including phosphorus, potassium, mangesium, iron, zinc, manganese, vitamin E and vitamins B1 and B6 which strengthen the heart and enhance brain function. Black walnuts contain the essential arachidonic fatty acid, associated with alleviating symptoms of bursitis. Walnuts are rich in protein and combine well with grains in meatless dishes, bread, fruit and dessert.

Two major varieties grown in the United States - the English walnut and the Black walnut. The English walnut originated in Persia. English walnuts are grown in the western United States; California produces 99 percent of the nation's commercial crop. Black walnuts and white walnuts thrive in the eastern U.S.

Sesame Tahini is made in the Norwalk Juicer using whole or hulled sesame seed and screen #5.

"Eating nuts several times a week reduces the risk of heart attack by up to 50%."
-Adventist Health Study - 1

Nut Notes

• Nuts are best eaten in their raw, natural state, as nature provided, and chewed thoroughly, to assist proper digestion. Unfortunately, the common practice of some people is to snack on "roasted" nuts. Roasting nuts, which is usually done in coconut and peanut oil, is actually a form of deep frying, coating the nuts with oil, then heavily salting them, only to increase the amount of saturated fat (from the oil bath), and sodium (from salting the nuts).

• Nuts should be eaten in moderation because they are concentrated foods, rich in unsaturated fats. Nuts and seeds, however, have more to offer, being packed with protein (10-29% by weight), B vitamins, minerals, (calcium, iron, magnesium, phosphorus, potassium, copper and zinc), and Vitamin E.

• Roasting nuts makes them more difficult to digest, and can lower some vitamins, such as thiamine, as much as 75%. Dry-roasted nuts (pan or oven roasted) are better than regular roasted (deep frying in oil and salted). See method for toasting nuts and seeds.

• According to the United Stated Department of Agriculture, "mature dry legumes and nuts are the richest sources or protein among foods of plant origin". Nuts are good sources of thiamine and riboflavin, necessary for normal growth, healthy nerves and appetite, and contain magnesium, phosphorus, iron and beneficial unsaturated fatty acids.

• Nuts may be eaten whole, made into a meal or flour to be added to breads and baked goods, soaked, boiled or lightly toasted, as a topping for fruit or vegetables, made into nut and seed milks, or delicious butters to be used as a spread for crackers or bread.

• Almonds have approximately 3 times more calcium than walnuts or peanuts, 4 times more than pecans, and 6 times more than cashews. The iron content of almonds and cashews is approximately 2 times more than that in pecans, English walnuts, or peanuts. Try soaking them in water, overnight. They will be plump, milky, more digestible and most delicious!

• Peanuts (actually a legume; often referred to as 'nuts' because of their high fat content) are an excellent source of niacin, approximately 4-10 times more than most nuts. They are best combined with grains, legumes, and seeds, to obtain a complete protein.

• Nuts may easily become rancid. Unshelled nuts keep longer than those shelled. Shelled nuts should be refrigerated, and kept in covered containers to prevent rancidity. Nuts may also be frozen. Roasted and salted nuts become rancid more quickly.

• Seeds (sesame, sunflower, flax, and pumpkin) are packed with nutrients. Seeds that are ground into meal or butter are far easier to digest than eating whole. Their food value balanced by their low cost, make them a better buy than most nuts. The oil of sesame seed is used unrefined in salad and stir-fry; has a pleasant aroma.

• Seeds and Nuts contain certain amounts of oil with different types of essential fatty acids (monounsaturated, polyunsaturated, and saturated fatty acids). Flaxseed and walnuts are some of the richest in linolenic acid, an omega-3 polyunsaturated fatty acid that is known to reduce LDL (harmful) cholesterol and triglyceride levels (a form of fat) in the blood, as well as increase the HDL (good cholesterol) levels.

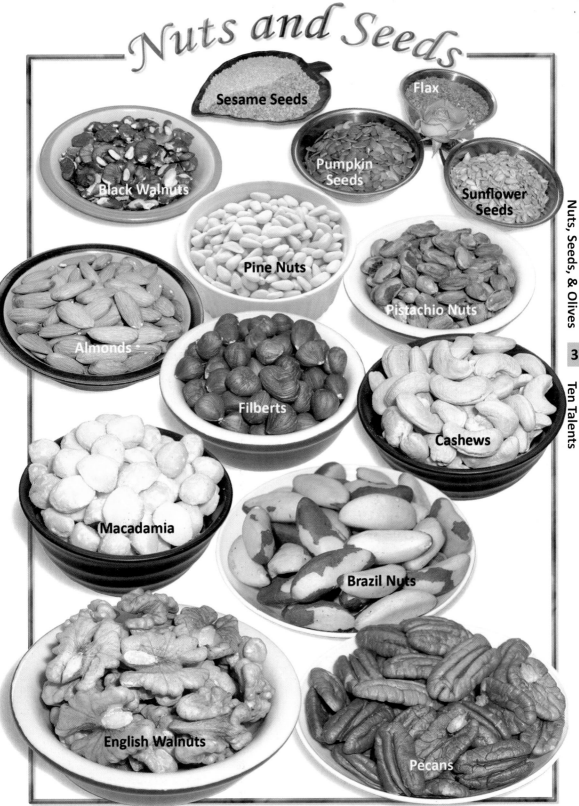

Nuts and Seeds

Sesame Seeds

Flax

Pumpkin Seeds

Sunflower Seeds

Black Walnuts

Pine Nuts

Pistachio Nuts

Almonds

Filberts

Cashews

Macadamia

Brazil Nuts

English Walnuts

Pecans

Blanching Nuts

To remove skin from Almonds, simply add nuts to boiling water in pan (do not boil) or pour boiling water over nuts in a bowl. Let set for 1-2 minutes. Drain off water. Rub nuts between fingers to loosen and remove skin. Presto! Nuts are blanched.

Soaking Nuts

Soaking nuts, particularly whole shelled almonds, makes them softer and easier to digest. You will find them easy to chew, more milky and tastier after soaking them overnight. Change the water daily, keep covered in the refrigerator. The hulls of nuts, beans and grains, contain enzyme inhibitors, which are neutralized by soaking, aiding the body in the breakdown of foods during the digestive process.

To prepare nuts: Simply put nuts in a jar, cover with pure water, refrigerate for several hours, until ready to use or eat. Change water daily. Soaking and rinsing some nuts and seeds releases enzyme inhibitors in the skin and may enhance the food value and digestibility. Try soaking other nuts, but almonds are best!

Toasting Nuts, Seeds and Coconut

Toasting enhances the flavor and aroma of nuts and seeds (for garnish; in some recipes)

Stovetop: Lightly toast slivered nuts, sesame seeds, pumpkin seeds, sunflower seeds or shredded coconut in a dry skillet, over med-high heat. Stir food 5-8 minutes until golden brown, and has a pleasant toasted aroma. Remove from hot skillet immediately; cool.

Oven method: Spread food single layer, in a shallow dry pan; bake 5-10 minutes at 350° until golden brown. Stir 2-3 times, watching so food doesn't burn. Remove food from hot pan to avoid getting too brown. Cool, store in refrigerator or freezer.

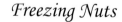

Freezing Nuts

Frozen nuts are easier to chop than nuts at room temperature. Try putting nuts in the freezer for 1 hour before chopping them.

Soaking Almonds enhances the flavor, and softens them, making them easier to chew and blend in recipes such as Almond Milk.

Almond Butter
(King of the nuts – see Glossary of Foods)

Almond butter can be easily made, simply by putting **whole almonds** (raw or very lightly toasted) through a *Champion or similiar juicer (with nothing added).

With a little patience, it can also be made in a Blender by following 3 steps.

Note: Almond butter is a little harder to make than most nut butters because almonds do not contain as much oil as some nuts.

Blender method:

1. Use whole or blanched almonds (To blanch: pour boiling water over nuts; let set one minute. Rub nuts between fingers to remove skins. Do not allow nuts to remain in the water – for they will become water-logged and be more difficult to make butter).

2. Grind nuts to fine powder (in a nut or seed mill). If blanching, dry nuts with towel before grinding.

3. Process in blender, adding oil first, then nuts, using spatula to guide nuts to center. Continue blending until nuts are smooth and creamy like butter. Store in a glass jar. Measurements:

2 cups Almonds, raw or lightly toasted
approximately 2 Tbs. oil
pinch of sea salt, opt.

Almond Butter can be used in the following ways:

- Delicious as a sandwich filling.
- Use as a binder for roasts and patties. Add water to make a smooth cream for cereal or fruit.
- Used with ½ the amount of lemon juice, will act as a natural leavening for cookies and some cakes (combine **4 Tbs. Almond Butter + 2 Tbs. lemon juice**).

Note: Juicers, Blenders, Nut & Seed Mills- are available from authors- call 1-877-442-4425 (see back of book for photos and description)

"Nuts and nut foods are coming largely into use to take the place of flesh meats. With nuts may be combined grains, fruits, and some roots, to make foods that are healthful and nourishing. Care should be taken, however, not to use too large a proportion of nuts." - E. G. White, **Counsels on Diet and Foods**, p. 363

Raw Nut Butters

Most nuts and seeds, or any combination of them (*with the exception of sesame seeds) can be made into nourishing and tasty butters, without added oil, by using a Champion or similar juicer. Simply install the *solid blank* in place of the juicing screen (provided with Champion juicer). Be sure nuts are fresh (shelled nuts may easily become rancid).

Feed whole shelled raw, or lightly toasted nuts through feeding hopper, and watch the nut butter flow out.

The following nuts and seeds are the more popular ones used in making butters: Almonds, Cashews, Filberts, Pistachio, Sesame Seeds, Sunflower Seeds and Peanuts.

Sesame Seed Butter (Tahini) is easily made in the *Norwalk juicer - p. 377.

Other nuts and seeds such as walnuts, pecans, brazil nuts, pumpkin and flax seed can also be made into butter. Nut butters are an excellent alternative to common peanut butter. Try making fresh nut butters in your blender, juicer, food processor or nut & seed mill.

Nut Butter Combinations

Try these combinations of nuts for delicious, rich, exotic flavors:

Cashew-Brazil-Nut Butter
Cashew-Pumpkin Seed-Butter
Cashew-Almond-Butter
Cashew-Hazelnut-Butter
Cashew-Macadamia-Nut Butter
Cashew-Pistachio-Nut Butter

Sesame Tahini

Also known as sesame butter, tahini is made by grinding seeds to a smooth paste. This concentrated food is rich in essential fatty acids and makes an excellent spread. (more information - see **Glossary of Natural Foods**)

Method: Warm **raw hulled sesame seeds** in 250° oven to encourage flow of oil. Feed through hopper of *Norwalk Juicer* using *fine screen #5* for making seed butter. That's all! (see photo in **Miscellaneous** chapter.)

Store in glass jars in refrigerator.

Natural Peanut Butter

A popular spread - commercially made by adding hydrogenated oils, sugar and salt. Here is a simple recipe for making wholesome peanut butter, without the hydrogenated fat and sugar.

3 cups oven-blanched peanuts,
lightly toasted
1-2 Tbs. peanut or soy oil
(for blender method only)
sea salt, to taste, opt.

Champion Juicer method: Simply install *solid blank* in place of the screen. Feed toasted peanuts through hopper (***no oil needed***). Have a jar ready to catch smooth peanut butter. Chopped peanuts may be added for crunchy peanut butter. Store in refrigerator.

Blender method: Put oil into blender first. Then add peanuts and salt, if desired. Cover and process at high speed, then low, to desired consistency. Use a rubber spatula to guide nut butter to center.

Yield: about 2 cups (1 lb.)

Note: It is important to use peanuts that are fresh *(with no trace of rancidity)* to make tasty, nutritious, homemade peanut butter. Natural oil separation may occur. Just stir in.

Flaxseed

An excellent source of soluble fiber, essential omega-3 (linolenic acid), valuable protein, and other vitamins and minerals. The mucilage and pectin in flax will soften the intestinal mucosa, regulate its flora, and assist in bowel regularity.

Flaxseed, golden or brown

Simply grind whole flax to a fine powder, in a nut and seed mill. Sprinkle on cereal or fruit. Whole or coarsely ground flaxseed may be added to bread. Flaxseed, ground to fine powder and blended into smoothies, adds a nutty flavor and rich creamy texture.

Sweet Sunnies

This simple combination is frequently enjoyed at our house for breakfast, lunch, supper, or a quick dessert. Tastes really good- and lots of nutrition!

Sunflower seeds, whole raw shelled, Molasses

For each serving: mix **¼ cup sunflower seeds** with **1 Tbs. molasses** (preferably light). Chew thoroughly - enjoy!

Four Seed Cereal Topping
(Omega-3, Vitamin-mineral rich)

4 Tbs. flaxseed meal, brown or golden
4 Tbs. ground sunflower seeds
4 Tbs. ground sesame seeds
4 Tbs. ground pumpkin seeds

Grind the seeds fresh daily in a *nut and seed mill, then mix together. Sprinkle on hot cereal or fruit. Store in covered container in refrigerator.

*Nut & Seed Mills are available - contact the authors- see Kitchen Appliances- back of book

Dr. Nedleys' Flax-Nut Butter
(rich in Omega-3 essential fatty acids)

Grind equal portions of **flaxseed** and **walnuts** together till smooth and creamy. A tasty topping or alternative spread, with texture similar to peanut butter.

Halvah

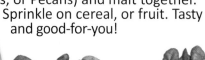

A flaky confection of crushed sesame seeds in a base of sweet syrup. Here's a simple healthy version with almonds that you can make at home.

1 cup tahini or crushed sesame seeds
½ cup honey, agave, or brown rice syrup
¼ cup chopped almonds or pistachio nuts
½ tsp. pure vanilla

In a saucepan heat ½ cup of sweetening and 1 Tbs. water to boiling, stirring constantly until 1-2 drops form a soft ball when dropped into cold water. Add vanilla, tahini and nuts, stir to combine. Remove from heat and press into shallow pan. Refrigerate to cool and set.
Carob Halvah: Add **¼ cup honey +**
2 Tbs. carob powder + ¼ tsp. vanilla.
Boil carob, honey and vanilla 1 minute. Lightly stir and swirl into plain Halvah. Press into shallow dish; refrigerate to cool and set before slicing.

Malted Nuts

¾ cup mixed nuts, finely chopped
¼ cup dry malt

Mix nuts (Brazil, Almonds, Walnuts, Filberts, or Pecans) and malt together. Sprinkle on cereal, or fruit. Tasty and good-for-you!

Peanuts — Oven Roasted

Spread natural **Virginia Peanuts** or **Spanish Peanuts**, with red skins, on a baking sheet. Bake in 450° oven for 10-15 minutes. Let cool, enough to handle. Rub between hands; skins will fall off. Peanuts prepared in this manner are not oily, only lightly toasted. Makes excellent peanut butter, or enjoy as they are.

Roasted Chick Peas or Soya Nuts

Crunchy, ready-to-eat, out of hand; similar to roasted Ceci - sold in Italian markets. Nutritious source of energy, protein, folate, B-vitamins, iron, and fiber.

1. Use **canned garbanzos** (or **soybeans**, for **Soya Nuts**); rinse, drain, dry with towel **or** soak beans in water 24- 48 hours. Change water daily. Cook until beans are tender.

2. Pre-heat oven to 400°. Spread chick peas on baking sheet. Bake 20 minutes (shake pan often to stir); reduce heat to 350° bake 10-15 minutes more, until lightly browned and crisp or place on dehydrator tray and dry until crisp. Either way, they are quite chewy.

3. In a plastic bag, mix **sea salt, garlic powder, paprika or other seasonings if desired**. Add roasted chickpeas (garbanzos) or soybeans and shake until coated.

The recipes for roasted legumes (peanuts, chick peas and soybeans) in this chapter, are often eaten at mealtime, out-of-hand like nuts.

Peanut Butter - Seed Spread

1 cup crunchy peanut butter, lightly toasted
1 cup sesame tahini
½ cup raw honey
2 Tbs. sunflower
or pumpkin seeds, finely ground

Mix thoroughly. Keep refrigerated. Delicious on crackers or bread. Good sandwich spread with chopped dates, and avocado.

Peanut Coconut Balls

½ cup crunchy peanut butter
2 cups moist shredded coconut
¼ cup finely chopped nuts
½ cup finely chopped raisins
1 tsp. lemon zest
½ tsp. pure vanilla

Mix all together. Form into 1" balls. Roll in coconut, if desired. Chill until firm.

Energy Nuggets

Almonds, Cashews, Brazil Nuts, Pumpkin seeds, finely ground coconut, Carob Powder, raw honey, peanut butter

Mix **1 part of chopped nuts, seeds, coconut**, with **2 parts peanut butter and raw honey.** Add enough **carob powder** to make stiff. Form into balls or press into a pan. Chill to set; cut into squares. A simple treat; can be made ahead and frozen.

Pistachi-Oh Balls

½ cup chopped pistachio nuts
2 cups shredded coconut, moist
¼ cup cashew butter
½ cup finely chopped dates
1 tsp. lemon zest
½ tsp. pure vanilla

Mix all together. Form into 1" balls. Roll in coconut, if desired. Chill until firm.

Heavenly Hazelnut Spread

A nutritious, simply delicious spread for toast, waffles, or crepes.

1 cup hazelnuts / filberts,
**   lightly toasted**
⅓ cup chopped apricots
¼ cup honey, your favorite
mashed banana or fruit juice, opt.

Spread nuts on baking sheet; toast at 350° for 10-12 min. Remove nuts from oven and rub in towel to remove skins. Place hazelnuts and apricots in food processor and puree until smooth. Blend in honey; and banana or fruit juice, (opt.) to desired consistency.

Roasted Chestnuts

Warm up on those cold winter holidays with some freshly roasted chestnuts. A nutritious, slightly sweet and tender treat, popular during Thanksgiving. Chestnuts can be roasted on an open fire, or in the oven.

1. Select large whole chestnuts with skins that have a healthy glow and beautiful brown shine. They should also be firm and feel solid, with no air space between the skin and the underlying flesh. If they look dim or mottled, they may have mold. The skins should be blemish free; small pinholes likely mean worms, pass them by. The darker *Italian Marroni* variety, are large, meaty, and richly flavored.

2. Wash thoroughly. With a knife cut an X into the shell of each chestnut to allow steam to escape while baking. This will keep them from exploding. Pour boiling water over chestnuts to cover. Let set for 20-30 minutes to soften before roasting. Drain. Spread the chestnuts single layer on a large baking sheet, cut side up.

3. Roast chestnuts in hot oven, 400°- 420° for 15 minutes or until skins have pulled back, can be easily removed and nutmeats are tender. Test with toothpick (avoid over-baking). Wrap in a towel for 5 minutes to loosen skin and cool enough to handle. Peel warm chestnuts by removing shell and inner skin. Delicious eaten as they are; or add to stuffing, casseroles, bread dressing, or gravy. Peeled chestnuts freeze well. Simply thaw and use.

Almond Fig Cakes

Dried Figs, cut
Almonds, chopped
Orange rind (zest)

In food processor or grinder, combine 2 parts dried figs with 1 part almonds and 1 tsp. orange zest for each cup of figs. Press together in a glass dish. Refrigerate until firm. Cut in squares or bars. These hi-energy bars are delicious!

Note: Dried figs are a rich source carbohydrates, vitamins and minerals. Figs medicinal properties include: mild laxative; relieve cough; help fight respiratory infections caused by colds and flu, and externally for skin disorders. (see chapter Miscellaneous on Home-Dried Figs)

Tree Chestnuts
The edible and delicious nut of the genus (Castanea) of the beech family.

Soak *dried* shelled tree chestnuts in enough water to cover them, for several hours until double in size. Bring to a slow boil. Simmer 10-15 minutes, or steam until soft. Serve with fruit and milk for breakfast, with a salad for dinner, mash and sweeten with honey, or use in bread dressing, savory stuffing, as an ingredient for grain dishes, pilaf, and other recipes. Delicious hot or cold. Boiled, steamed or roasted chestnuts freeze well. Dried chestnuts can be ground into flour and added to wheat when making bread.

Gomashio

A popular seasoning, also known as sesame salt (just 2 ingredients) used in Japan, to season one's food. (see chapter **Herbs & Seasonings**).

Sesame- Parsley- Sprinkle

A simple, nourishing and tasty topping, for rice, stir-fry, vegetables, pasta and soup. (see chapter **Herbs & Seasonings).**

Sprouted Sunflower Clusters

1. **Sprouted sunflower seeds, ¼" long** (see **Sprouting** chapter).
2. Chop, or coarse grind, in a food processor.
3. Mix with a combination of **peanut or almond butter** and **creamed honey,** just enough to hold together. Form into balls. Roll in **coconut**.

*Sesame Treats

A favorite healthy treat, rich in calcium, phosphorus, and protein.

2 cups sesame seeds, lightly toasted
½ cup honey and / or maple syrup
¼ cup pure water
1½ tsp. grated lemon peel
¼ tsp. pure vanilla; + ⅛ tsp. sea salt

In a non-stick saucepan combine honey or maple syrup (or some of both) with water and salt. Stir over medium-high heat until mixture boils. Reduce heat, stir occasionally, until 1-2 drops of the hot syrup, put into cold water, forms a hard ball (255°- 260° F).

Remove from heat, add vanilla and lemon zest. Pour syrup over sesame seeds. Mix well. Press into 8 x8 "glass pan (lightly oiled). Score while warm into 2" x ½" logs or squares. Can be individually wrapped for storing. Refrigerate to harden. Freezes very well.

*Resembles individually wrapped *Joyva Sesame Treats*.

Olives

The AHA (American Heart Association) recommends one half of the daily intake of fatty acids should be monounsaturated. Olive oil and avocado are a healthy source of oleic acid, the main monounsaturated fatty acid of diet.

Olive oil contains 77 percent monounsaturated fatty acids, 14 percent saturated fatty acids and 9 percent polyunsaturated fatty acids, plus vegetable mucilage and vitamin E.

"When properly prepared, olives, like nuts, supply the place of butter and flesh meats. The oil, as eaten in the olive, is far preferable to animal oil or fat. It serves as a laxative... and it is healing to an inflamed, irritated stomach. Olives may be so prepared as to be eaten with good results at every meal."
Counsels on Diet and Foods, pg. 359

"The oil in the olives relieves constipation,.....as a food it is better than any oil coming secondhand from animals." Counsels on Diet and Foods, pg. 349

Olive oil is considered to be the king of oils. Extra virgin, cold-pressed olive oil (unrefined), surpasses seed and nut oils in flavor, aroma, and dietary therapeutic values.

Olive oil provides the most medicinal properties and protection against arteriosclerosis and coronary disease. Studies indicate olive oil promotes heart health by raising beneficial HDL cholesterol levels, and is a rich source of monounsaturated fatty acids (primarily oleic), which safeguards the cardiovascular system.

In contrast to seed oils, olive oil is more stable and less likely to become rancid. Olive oil resists higher temperatures without decomposing; used in moderation is more suitable for cooking. Best if used raw on salads, and a seasoning for vegetables. The **oil from the olives** dates back to Bible times and was used in making bread even during times of famine (read 1 Kings 17: 11-14); and was sold as a precious commodity to pay one's debt (read 2 Kings 4:1-7).

Cured Black Ripe Olives
(Sun dried)

1. Select firm, **black olives** without blemish

2. Prick with flowerpot frog, and shake in colander with a generous amount of sea salt.

3. Lay on flat screen in the sun to dry.

4. Check olives every day, turning them; rub with salt occasionally (cover olives with a screen to keep clean).

5. When dry (wrinkled), put in a jar with a little olive oil; turn to wet each olive. Store in cool, dry place.

Note: *To obtain a copy of the Division of Agricultural Sciences, simple, concise working directions for curing, pickling and preserving olives at home, send a self-addressed stamped envelope + $1.00 to: Ten Talents - P. O. Box 5209, Grants Pass, Oregon 97527. You will receive a copy of the publication with complete directions for preparing a variety of olives at home.*

Some Plant Sources of Linolenic Acid - Omega 3

A dietary essential linked to optimal brain function

Flaxseed/Linseed oil	Almonds
Walnuts, English, black	Sunflower seeds
Wheat germ oil	Apples, Banana
Canola oil	Avocado
Green soybeans	Whole wheat bread
Spinach, turnips	Wheat germ, Barley

Olive Nut Spread

8 oz. pitted black ripe olives, drained
½ cup firm tofu, mashed
¼ cup tahini or cashew butter
3 whole green onions, chopped
3 cloves garlic, minced
juice of 1 lemon

Place all ingredients in a food processor or blender and puree until smooth.

Percentage % of Linoleic Acid in Fats & Oils

Safflower	70	Brazil Nut	
Sunflower		Almond	20
Rye germ	60	Pistachio	
Walnut		Filbert	
Corn		Olive	10
Soybean		Avacado	
Wheat germ	50	Cashew	
Cottonseed		Coconut	
Sorghum			
Sesame		*Animal Origin:*	
Oat	40	Eggs, Butter	0
Rice Bran		Lard, pork	0
Peanut	30	Shortening	0

Green Ripe Olives

Drain brine. Rinse olives. Ripe green olives are tastier when adding **¼ tsp. olive oil** and **1 clove minced garlic** to each cup olives. Stir and marinate for ½ hour before serving.

Brined Green Olives
(without lye)

1. Select **green olives** without blemish.
2. Put in jar with pure water for 3-4 days, changing water daily to remove bitterness.
3. After 3 days, add fresh solution of water and salt (**1 cup sea salt** to 1 gallon of olives).
4. Cure in jar for approx. 3 months or until ready to eat. Store in refrigerator. (olives may be pricked or crushed once with a quart jar before curing).

Stuffed Black Olives

Drain brine from **olives**. Stuff with whole **almonds**. Serve at any meal.

Chestnuts with Figs

Cover peeled chestnuts with water and cook to soften. Add 6-8 dried figs and simmer together until tender and flavors are blended. Good served for breakfast.

dried cherries

Happy Trail Mix

Going camping or hiking? This survival blend can supply the energy needed for your journey. An excellent breakfast mix to help start the day.

½ cup raisins
¼ cup almonds
¼ cup dried cherries or cranberries
¼ cup Brazil nuts, halved
¼ cup filberts
¼ cup pumpkin seeds
¼ cup diced dried pineapple or apple

Mix all ingredients together. Yield: 2 cups (4 servings)

Hiker's Fruit - Nut Medley

½ cup pineapple chunks, dried
½ cup walnuts, broken pieces
½ cup sliced banana chips, dried
½ cup cashews, whole or pieces
½ cup dates, pitted sliced

Mix all ingredients together. Yield: 2 ½ cups (4-5 servings)

Easy Trail Mix

1 # (3 ½ cups) mixed dry roasted nuts
1 cup raisins
½ cup dried apricot halves or pieces
½ cup dried pear pieces
½ cup dried flaked coconut

Mix all ingredients together. Yield: 6 cups (8-10 servings)

X-treme Survival Mix

¾ cup sunflower seeds, raw shelled
½ cup pumpkin seeds, raw shelled
½ cup raisins or currants
½ cup apricot halves, dried
½ cup almonds, raw whole
½ cup prunes, pitted pieces
½ cup apple slices, dried
¼ cup filberts, whole

Combine all ingredients and mix well. Yield: 4 cups

Salads, Vegetable

Index - CHAPTER 12

Salads, Vegetable

392

Ten Talents

Chapter cover photo: *Italian Fennel Salad, page 404*

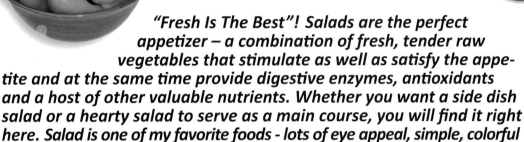

Salads
(Vegetable)

"Fresh Is The Best"! Salads are the perfect appetizer – a combination of fresh, tender raw vegetables that stimulate as well as satisfy the appetite and at the same time provide digestive enzymes, antioxidants and a host of other valuable nutrients. Whether you want a side dish salad or a hearty salad to serve as a main course, you will find it right here. Salad is one of my favorite foods - lots of eye appeal, simple, colorful crunchy and delicious! This chapter begins with some helpful information.

Selecting Greens

Keep in mind the words- fresh, crisp, bright, tender. Buy greens in a market where the vegetable area is properly refrigerated, and where the turnover is rapid. It is best to buy greens in quantities you can use within a week. When selecting a crisp-type lettuce, such as romaine, or iceberg, look for firm, hard, heads. Lift them in your hand and pick those heavy for their size. One exception: If they are to be used for lettuce cups (bib lettuce), choose loose heads. When buying green leaf, red tip, or escarole, endive, chicory type of greens, be sure you examine the heads carefully for bruises. These will be evident as browning on the outer leaves. Watch out for and avoid any brown, so-called "rust" edges. While this "rust" may not be harmful, it is unpalatable in appearance and may go deep enough to spoil the whole head.

Select those plants that have relatively few tough outer leaves, as the tender inside ones will have the best flavor and are more likely to stay crisp longer. Outside lettuce leaves may be washed and steamed lightly as any green vegetable, or dried and dried into powder for 'veggie green salt' (see recipe). Remember when choosing salad greens or vegetables: ***The more green, the more yellow, the more vitamin A!***

Washing and Storing Greens

Once you have arrived home from the market with your salad greens, they should be washed, blotted dry with a cloth, paper towels, or use a salad spinner. Drying off excess water from the greens will allow the dressing to cling to the leaves.

Store in the vegetable crisper drawer of your refrigerator, ready to use within a day or two, of making a salad. For longer storage, wait to wash before using, or for salad greens that are already pre-washed, refrigerate as quickly as possible, in their original wrap or plastic bag. This will insure the retaining of their crisp texture, pleasing color, and very best flavor. Here are some tips for handling certain greens:

Remove any bruised outer leaves from a head of lettuce. Remove the core of iceberg, by striking it against a counter top, then twisting and lifting the core out. Hold the head, core cavity up, under cold running water, to wash and refresh the leaves. Drain. For greens such as escarole, chicory, endive, and romaine, leave the core ends. Wash the leafy heads thoroughly under cold running water to remove sand, grit or soil. Drain greens after washing them. Shake off as much water as possible, then blot dry and store in plastic bags, or airtight containers in refrigerator. For small leaves such as spinach, cut off roots and remove any bruised leaves. Swish leaves in cold water, changing the water several times until clear and the leaves are clean. Blot them dry between towels.

Greens with small whole leaves like watercress and parsley are best stored standing in a glass of water, covered with plastic wrap in the refrigerator, or in a tightly covered container or jar.

Preparing Salad Greens for Serving

An hour or so before serving, remove crisped greens from the refrigerator. Tear into bite-size pieces, removing any tough stem portions if necessary. Torn greens make a more handsome salad and are less apt to develop browning edges, as do cut pieces. Use one, two, three, or more greens in your salads to give contrast in color, flavor, and texture. If serving a main-dish salad, add other filling foods and vegetables, such as broccoli, carrots, beans, tofu, or pasta. Top with avocado chunks or olives; be sparing of dressing! As a guide, use ¼ cup of dressing for each 2 quarts of greens. Toss lightly, till all the leaves are

just coated - not dripping. When the salad is served, there should be no more than a teaspoon of dressing in the bottom of the salad bowl. Toss chilled greens with dressing just before serving time, or serve the greens with dressing on the side.

When to Serve the Salad

Raw salads stimulate digestion and are best eaten before the main course. Salads can serve as a satisfying appetizer, or one dish meal, providing many valuable nutrients, as well as color, texture, and variety. Making salads can be exciting when experimenting with different greens. Iceberg is just the tip! Include a variety of other foods in your salad such as: avocado, olives, artichokes, broccoli, asparagus, beans, mushrooms and sprouts. Garnish with a lemon wedge or fresh herbs. Serve with your favorite salad dressing. For best digestion, serve vegetable salads at one meal and fruit salads at another. Fresh salads provide bulk, fiber and satiety, excellent for waistline watchers. (The recipes in this chapter will help you create and enjoy fresh, flavorful salads for every occasion throughout the year).

Salad Seasoning

Try a variety of salad dressing, to avoid the habit of using the same one each time. Ideally a simple dressing is all that is needed - preferably made with cold-pressed virgin olive oil, a little sea salt or aminos, and fresh squeezed lemon juice. Experiment with different herbs, to add flavor to your salads. A few suggestions: **Arugula, Sweet Basil, Chervil, Chives, Cilantro, Dill, Fennel, Garlic, Italian Parsley, Marjoram, Mint, Nasturtium, Oregano, Sorrel.**

Lemon juice on salad helps protect vitamins and minerals, replaces vinegar, improves the flavor, aids digestion, and reduces the need for salt. Vinegar vs. lemons: see Herbs & Seasonings.

Salad Greens to Know and Enjoy

ARUGULA or **GARDEN ROCKET** or **ROQUETTE** – of the mustard family, also goes by **RUGULA**. Cultivated for its foliage, which is used in salads. The leaves are small, dark green, with a distinct peppery, slightly bitter, pungent flavor. A lively addition to spice up other salad greens. Arugula is nutritious, digestive and diuretic.

BABY SPRING MIX (organic) – may contain all or some of the following: **baby red romaine, baby tango, baby arugula, baby red leaf, baby green romaine, baby lolla rosa, baby tatsoi, baby mizuna, baby green chard, baby red chard, baby red mustard, baby red oak, frisée, baby green oak, radicchio, baby green leaf, baby swiss chard, baby spinach, baby beet tops.**

BELGIAN or FRENCH ENDIVE – is a member of the chicory family. Grown in total darkness, resulting in a creamy white color, with tips of light yellow-green. The tightly tapered, compact, narrow heads, 4 - 6 inches long, have small leaves that are slightly bitter in taste. Usually served whole, or cut lengthwise, adding texture, color, distinctive taste, and shape to other torn greens in a salad.

BIBB LETTUCE – was generally unknown until rapid transportation took the tiny heads from their Kentucky homelands, where it was developed by Major John Bibb. It is a small cup-shaped lettuce with buttery, soft leaves and delicate crispness and flavor. The outer leaves are a rich green, blending to a whitish green toward the core. The leaves are prized for their dainty cups when making individual salads. Smaller than Boston lettuce.

BOSTON LETTUCE or **BUTTERHEAD** – a variety of butter lettuce, larger than the closely related Bibb lettuce. Loosely headed with leaves that have an oily feeling and more tender, rather than crisp. Outer leaves are a deep green, the inner leaves shade almost to a pale yellow. It is more perishable than crisphead types, and requires gentle handling. The leaves are prized for their sweet subtle taste. Combines well with other salad greens such as watercress.

CABBAGE – comes in many varieties – Green and Red head, Chinese (Napa), Salad Savoy- each with its own distinct flavor. Rich source of Vitamin C, and a member of the cruciferous vegetables. Red and green cabbage have solid heavy heads, and crisp waxy leaves. Savoy cabbage has crinkled leaves, Chinese cabbage is long and narrow and more tender than the round cabbage. Use in salads, finely sliced, or shred for coleslaw.

CURLY ENDIVE or **CHICORY** – is crisp with frilly, narrow, long ragged-edged leaves that have a slight bitter flavor. The leaves are dark green, with a pale, almost white heart. Endive adds a rich taste and interesting texture to tossed salads. Choose heads that are young, with no signs of decay. Along with escarole, curly endive is a "must" in Italian tossed salad. Mix with romaine, and other more mild salad greens.

CRISPHEAD or **ICEBERG** – though not as nutritious as the darker leafy lettuce greens, it is the best known and most available. Rich in water, about 94%, contains some B vitamins, primarily folic acid, protein, trace minerals and fiber. Lettuce has been noted to have a sedative, sleep-inducing effect. Heads are heavy, firm, and crisp-textured, and have a small core. Leaves are a medium green on the outside, shading to a pale green in the center. Iceberg is bland, mild flavored; best combined with other greens.

ESCAROLE – is actually another variety of endive. Its large, broad leaves shade from deep green on the outside to buttery yellow in the center, and have edges with a ruffled appearance. Sturdy and crisp, escarole adds a slightly bitter flavor to tossed salads and is particularly good in combination with sweeter leaves of lettuce and romaine. Rich in nutrients, an aid to digestion, alkalizing, useful in gallbladder disorders and obesity.

Broad-leaf escarole is crisp and chewy. An aid for weight-loss, stimulates digestion; has a slightly bitter taste. A handful of leaves add great flavor to fresh green salad.

Salad Greens

Arugula

Butterhead

Belgian Endive

Cabbage, red

Curly Endive

Cabbage, green

Celery

Escarole

Frisee

Napa Cabbage

Iceberg Lettuce

Radicchio

Italian Parsley

Savoy Cabbage

Romaine

Red Leaf Lettuce

Spinach

Watercress

LEAF LETTUCE – several varieties include Red leaf, Oak leaf, Green leaf, Salad Bowl, etc. Has tender crisp leaves but differing from other lettuce in that it does not form a tight head. This unheaded type of lettuce has loosely bunched leaves, that are generally mild and flavorful. Available year round. Grows easily in rich garden soil. The darker green varieties are richer in nutrients than the white or pale green.

MESCLUN (Field or Wild Greens) – A salad mix of tender greens with varieties that include some of the following: Arugula, Chickweed, Curled Cervil, Chicory, Dandelion, Frisée, Green Ice, Lollo Rosa, Mâche, Mizuma, Royal Oak Leaf, Paris White Cos, Radicchio, Ruby and Red Salad Bowl, Sorrel, Tat Soi, and Tango. Mesclun may be available in bulk or in pre-washed ready-to-eat packages. The Burpee Seed Company has a Mesclun gourmet summer salad mix, for planting in your garden.

PARSLEY – is more than a garnish. This nutrient-rich herb is used in salad, to flavor soups, vegetables, sauces, pasta, to balance garlic in a dish or as a natural breath- freshener. To keep fresh: Place standing in a glass of water. Cover with a plastic bag. Refrigerate. Parsley Varieties – **Flat-leaf (Italian) Parsley**: rich, more pronounced flavor, (left); **Common Curly Parsley**: slightly peppery, mild full flavored (right)

RADICCHIO – a member of the chicory family with burgundy-red leaves and broad white veins. The small bittersweet head has tender leaves that are smooth, satiny, and closely wrapped. Radicchio adds variety, texture and color to green salads. A type of endive very common in Italy and used today as a gourmet favorite.

ROMAINE or **COS** – is a lettuce with an elongated head and stiff leaves. The leaves are coarse though sweet, with good keeping quality. Dark green outer leaves shade to almost white at the root end. The lighter inner leaves are particularly tender and flavorful and are considered by many salad lovers a stand-by in tossed green salads.

SORREL or **DOCK** – (sour grass) leaves are dark green, shaped like spinach, and are from 2 - 10 inches long. Sorrel has a sharp, tart, lemony flavor, Just a few cut leaves adds a tasty touch to salads. Rich in Vitamin A, C, potassium, magnesium and iron. (Arugula or Watercress can substitute)

SPROUTS – are a wonderful addition to fresh green salads. Sprouts remain crisp and will not wilt. Alfalfa, clover, radish, and fenugreek sprouts are a few to try. Rinse thoroughly before adding to salad.

SPINACH – has dark green leaves which may be flat or curled, depending on the variety. Rich in nutrients, containing folate (folic acid), vitamin A, B, C, iron, calcium, potassium and iron. Raw spinach makes a wonderful salad by itself or mixed with other salad greens adds variety and color. Good in sandwiches too! Slightly tart, and tangy, spinach is gaining popularity, as a rich source of powerful antioxidants.

WATERCRESS – this member of the mustard family has small oval, crisp, dark green, mildly pungent, peppery leaves that are used as a salad ingredient. Perfect for sandwiches and soup, and delicious in scrambled tofu. Also used as a garnish. Found growing wild near fresh streams of water. Nutrient rich, watercress is a blood purifier, invigorating, stimulates the appetite and digestion. Watercress contains a phytochemical known to have cancer-protective benefits.Both leaves and stems are edible.

OTHER GREENS - Tender baby **kale, turnip greens, mustard greens, miners' lettuce, malva, beet greens**, and **dandelion greens** are regional favorites. Herbs, such as **fresh dill, chives, fennel, sweet basil**, are often available in produce markets, and many grow their own in herb gardens. Let's not forget the tender **celery leaves** – they are so common, and are often discarded, without a thought to their use as a tasty salad ingredient.

PEPPERS – Sweet bell peppers are not only pretty, but also power-packed with **antioxidant vitamins,** particularly **C** and provitamin **A** (beta-carotene). One red pepper provides more than 3x the daily requirement of vitamin C and half the needed amount of A. Raw sweet peppers (red, orange, yellow) are a superb addition to salads. Just cut in strips, circles, or anyway you like, and chew them well.

Italian Tossed Salad #1

Sometimes we make a meal of just salad and brown rice or pasta – or salad and beans with zwieback. Very Satisfying!

2 heads or equiv. lettuce (arugula, romaine, bib, red leaf)
2 small scallions, cut in strips or rounds
1 cucumber, cut in rounds or quarter slices
1 tomato, vine-ripe, sliced
artichoke quarters and,
   or baby sweet red peppers
2 cloves fresh garlic
   (more if you savor it as I do!)
handful flat-leaf Italian parsley

Wash greens, pat dry or combine chilled greens while preparing other ingredients. Cut the onions and cucumber, mince garlic and parsley. Toss ingredients together. Add tomato, artichoke and peppers. Drizzle on pure **olive oil**, the juice of **1-2 lemons, sea salt**, and a pinch of **Italian seasoning** or **oregano**, if desired. Toss lightly to blend flavors. Serve with **crusty garlic bread** or **zwieback**.

Italian Tossed Salad #2

arugula or radish tops,
(with no blemishes)
romaine lettuce
radicchio, chicory or curly endive
bibb lettuce
cucumber, sliced

Mix equal amounts of the above fresh, tender washed greens. Sliced radishes, red onion, or vine-ripened tomatoes may be added for more color, if desired. Toss; serve with your favorite dressing.

Italian Tossed Salad #3

2 carrots, shredded
or cut in narrow 2"pieces
2 Jerusalem artichokes* shredded

2 stalks celery, sliced or grated
2 garden cucumbers, with skins, sliced
1 head fennel (finocchio), bite-size pieces
6 cups lettuce
(butterhead, red leaf, bib, romaine)

Wash all vegetables thoroughly. Using fine cone of saladmaker, shred first 3 ingredients. Add cucumbers and fennel. Combine ingredients with mixed lettuce greens. Toss or serve with favorite salad dressing.

*useful in treatment of diabetes

Spring Mix #1 with Radishes

tender spring greens (arugula, chicory, oak leaf, radicchio, sorrel, tatsoi*)
fresh tender spinach leaves
6-8 radishes, sliced

Toss together with **pure virgin olive oil** and **fresh lemon juice**, adding a little **garlic powder, onion powder**, and **sea salt**.

*Tatsoi is a crisp baby Chinese leaf that looks like a mini bok choy leaf. It's good in stir-fry, but even better as a salad leaf.

Spring Mix #2 with Sweet Bell Pepper and Avocado

**tender spring greens
(arugula, chicory, oak leaf,
radicchio, sorrel, tatsoi*)
few leaves, firm green head lettuce
red bell pepper, cut in rings
avocado slices**

Toss greens together in salad bowl.

Garnish with avocado and red bell pepper rings. Serve with **Avocado Dressing** on the side, along with more **pepper rings**.

Fresh Escarole Salad

This salad includes a combination of flavors, textures and colors, for those who enjoy a bitter-sweet salad. One of my favorites!

**1 head fresh escarole*
few leaves of bibb or romaine lettuce
Haas avocado slices
crisp alfalfa sprouts
red onion, thin slices
black olives, sliced
tomatoes, whole cherry or cut
Italian Dressing (see recipe)**

Toss together lightly with just enough dressing to wet the leaves. Enjoy with crusty bread or **zwieback**.

Note: *Escarole contains a bitter substance that stimulates the digestive organs.

Italian Fennel Salad
Simply delicious as an appetizer or main dish!

green and red leaf lettuce
frisée, leaves seperated
radicchio leaves, torn in pieces
1 head fennel (finocchio), bite size pieces
¼ cup pine nuts
¼ cup diced sweet red pepper

Wash all vegetables thoroughly. Toss salad greens together. Arrange greens on 2-4 individual plates. Cut fennel bulbs in half, then in quarters and eights or smaller pieces; divide between plates. Sprinkle on pine nuts and diced red bell pepper. Serve with a simple **Italian Dressing** or **Lemon-Honey Dressing** (see recipes). Delicious!

Florence Fennel (Finocchio)

Fennel in Italy, is called **finocchio**. This is how my mother called it, and I remember looking forward with delight, to a refrigerator drawer full of these crispy, delicately sweet bulbs, especially during the holiday season, and without fail, every Thanksgiving Day. The pearly white bulb and pale green stems are eaten like celery. Feathery fern tops of dark green are a tasty addition to soups and salads, imparting a mild licorice-like aroma and flavor. When in season, the tops can be cut and dried as other herbs, or frozen for later use. Fresh finocchio is a real treat, cut in slices, just eaten raw. Delicious! Can be grown in rich soil or purchased at well-supplied produce markets.

Summer Salad Bowl

1 head butterhead (Boston) lettuce
½ lb. spinach, washed and crisped
1 bunch watercress, washed and crisped
¼ lb. zucchini, thinly sliced
2 chopped cucumbers
1 cup onion rings, cut ⅛" thin
1 cup celery, thinly sliced
5 fresh mushrooms or 4 oz. can,
   drained, sliced
Thousand Island, Italian,
   or Russian Dressing

Wash and crisp lettuce. Tear lettuce and spinach in bite-size pieces into bowl. Trim watercress; discard coarse stems. Add to lettuce with zucchini, cucumbers, onion, celery and mushrooms. Pour on about ¼ cup dressing; lightly tossing until leaves are coated. Serve with more dressing on the side, if desired.

Dandelion Spring Salad

Gather **dandelion greens** while young and tender, before flowers appear. Wash thoroughly; chop. Mix with **½ part mild sweeter salad greens, chopped sweet Maui, Vadalia, red onion, or scallions.** Toss with **Italian Dressing.** A good Spring   tonic!

Tossed Bouquet Salad

Lettuce, (red leaf, belgian endive,
   bib and frisee)
Onions, green sliced with tops
Cabbage, (green and red) finely sliced
Radishes, sliced

Tear lettuce into bite-size pieces. Add radishes, cabbage and onion. Toss with **Avocado Dressing** or **Creamy Italian Dressing**.

Stuffed Celery

Select **fresh tender celery stalks** having deep curves. Wash and fill with your choice of **spread, paté or dip**. Cut into 4" pieces, leaving on a few leaves.

Filled Cucumber Boats

Cut long, tender **cucumbers** in half lengthwise. Scoop out seeds and part of pulp. Mix with part of a **diced cucumber, chopped olives, chives, pimento.** Toss with **salad dressing**. Fill cucumbers. Serve on a bed of **leaf lettuce** or **romaine leaves**.

Onion Salad or Relish

The essential oil in onions softens and promotes the expulsion of mucus; their healing properties are suitable for coughs and bronchitis.

Slice sweet **Walla Walla, Vadalia or Red onions** in ⅛" slices. Separate rings. Cover with **Lemon-Herb Marinade**. Toss together and chill. The onions should not burn when you eat them, but have a mild flavor.   Serve on **watercress** or **lettuce leaves**. Good served as a relish with **Super Sunburgers** or other patties (see recipes).

A-B-C Salad

1 cup almonds,
blanched, shredded
2 cups beets, raw,
peeled and grated
3 cups carrot shreds
or finely chopped celery

Mix all together. Toss with your favorite **salad dressing**.

Raw Root Salad

"…He (God) is bringing them (His people) back to the diet originally given to man…(fruits, grains, and nuts) but various roots will also be used."
Diet and Foods, p. 270-271

1 part grated Jerusalem artichokes*
1 part grated carrots
½ part grated raw parsnips and, or beets
garnish: pumpkin seeds and parsley

Toss with **Creamy Italian Dressing**, or **French Dressing**. Sprinkle salad with coarsely ground **pumpkin seeds** and **parsley**.

Note: ***Jerusalem artichokes** (sunchokes) contain inulin- an aid for diabetes and gout.

Greens with Raw Beets

4 cups chopped watercress or frisee
2 beets, raw peeled
1 green onion with top

Scrub tender beets. Peel and finely grate. Chop watercress or endive, and green onion. Toss with beets. Serve with **Avocado or Lemon-Honey Dressing** on bed of crisp **lettuce**.

Sugar Snap Peas

Just eat raw - sweet and crunchy!
Add to salads or Stir-Fry;
Serve with your favorite dip.

Fresh Sugar Snap Pea & Jicama Salad

Sugar Snap Peas are sweet and crunchy. The thick round pods make delicious finger food, eaten raw or added to salad or stir-fry.

2 cups sugar snap peas, raw
2 cups peeled Jicama root,
cut in bite-size strips
2 tsp. pure olive oil
¼ tsp. sea salt,
to taste
1 Tbs. chopped
fresh mint

Combine all
ingredients;
chill and
serve.

Broccoli Jicama Salad

Jicama is sweet and crunchy; shred or slice raw in salad or steam like sweet potato. Rich in fiber.

1 large jicama root, peeled and cubed
2-3 cups fresh broccoli florets
½ cup shredded carrots

⅓ cup walnut pieces
3 Tbs. Vegenaise® or dressing of choice
2 Tbs. fresh lemon juice
1 tsp. honey
pinch of sea salt

Combine all ingredients; serve on a bed
of lettuce or warm brown rice.

Sweet-and-Sour Coleslaw

4 cups thinly shredded cabbage
½ cup thinly sliced radishes
⅓ cup carrots, thinly sliced
⅓ cup thinly sliced cucumber
¼ cup fresh minced Italian parsley
  ¼ cup minced green pepper
    or green onion
    ⅓ cup fresh lemon juice
    ¼ cup fructose or sweetening
    3 Tbs. canola or olive oil
    ½ tsp. each celery seed
      and sea salt
    2 tsp. dill weed, opt.

Place cabbage, radishes, carrots,
cucumber, parsley and peppers in salad
bowl. Shake remaining ingredients in
a covered jar or container. Pour over
vegetables and mix together. Cover
bowl, refrigerate several hours, stirring
several times, to marinate flavors and
chill. Garnish with dill weed. Serve with
slotted spoon. Servings: 6

Cabbage-Almond Salad

3 cups cabbage, shredded
1 cup almonds, slivered
¼ cup diced pimento
¼ cup chopped olives, black or green ripe

Toss all together with your favorite dressing. Garnish with **purple onion rings**, if desired.

Creamy Coleslaw

1 head fresh cabbage, shredded
½ cup carrots, shredded
½ cup diced avocado
3 radishes, thinly slivered
½ cup diced cucumbers
1 small onion or 3 green onions
    with tops, diced
½ tsp. celery seed
¼ tsp. sea salt
dash cayenne, to taste
garnish, minced parsley

Mix well all prepared ingredients. Toss with **Tofu Vegenaise**, **Tofu Sour Cream** or favorite dressing.

Red Cabbage Salad

2 cups finely sliced or grated red cabbage
1 cup minced endive or escarole
1 cup chopped cucumber or celery

Mix above ingredients together. Add **Low-Fat Salad Dressing** or your favorite (see recipes). Toss lightly; serve in salad bowl or on lettuce leaves.

Cabbage-Sesame Salad

½ medium head cabbage
2 medium carrots
2 stalks celery, thinly sliced

Finely shred the cabbage and carrots; mix with celery. Toss with **Sesame Seed Salad Dressing** and sprinkle with toasted sesame seeds.

Vegetables of the cabbage family are known to be rich in phytochemicals that act as antioxidants to stimulate the immune system and protect against cancer and other diseases.

Green Bean-Cabbage Slaw

Cabbage, shredded
Green beans, fresh, cut
Celery, fresh diced or seed celery
Onion, finely chopped

Toss together 1 part cabbage, ½ part green beans, diced celery and ⅛ part onion. Serve with your favorite mayonnaise.

Cabbage in Blossom

Cabbage, fresh garden
Bib lettuce leaves
Green Bell Pepper strips
Radishes, unpeeled
Dressing (see recipes)

On a large plate arrange leaves of bib lettuce (forming cups to hold salad). Fill leaves with scoop of cabbage slaw, mixed with dressing. Garnish with **radish roses** and **green pepper strips** to form leaves.

Chinese Snow Pea Pods are thin and crisp with tender sweet seeds. Both the pod and peas are eaten. When young and tender they are a tasty and colorful addition to salads.

Salad Garnishes

1. **Radish** roses or slices
2. **Carro**t roses (paper thin slices– arrange flower)
3. Flower leaves from **green pepper**, cut slits
4. **Coconut** - fresh grated or toasted shreds
5. **Olives** - green or black – stuffed, sliced, or whole
6. **Pimento** strips on cabbage or potato salad – sprinkle on paprika
7. Small **green onions** - feathered ends

8. Fresh **alfalfa spouts** in small bouquets
9. **Carrot** curls, **green pepper** rings or strips
10. **Cauliflower** florets- dip in dressing and grated carrot
11. **Red pepper** shells filled with salad dressing
12. Scoop out **carrot** - fill center with **nut butter**, cut carrots in thin slices.
13. **Avocado** balls rolled in grated **coconut**
14. **Celery** curls - tender 3" pieces - make close lengthwise slits at both ends. Leave ½" in middle uncut. Soak in cold water to curl.
15. Fringed slices - run fork prongs lengthwise down **cucumber** or **carrot,** then slice thin.
16. Pitted **olives** - fill center with a thin carrot stick.
17. **Parsley** and **watercress** - minced, springs, bouquets
18. **Onion** rings and/or **red, orange, green bell pepper** rings
19. Toasted **walnuts, sesame seeds**, slivered **almonds**
20. **Toast stars, seasoned croutons, garlic pop corn**
21. Sautéed whole or sliced **button mushrooms**
22. **Lemon** - thin slices or wedges
23. **Chives, dill weed**, **herbs** - fresh, dried, whole, chopped
24. **Tomatoes**, small - stuff with seasoned **tofu** or **guacamole**

Shredded Carrot & Coconut Salad

2 parts fresh shredded carrots
1 part shredded coconut
½ part chopped pecans or walnuts
½ part crushed pineapple, drained, opt.

Toss together with **Lemon-Honey Dressing** or your favorite.

Note: Unsweetened flake Coconut and moist Carrot pulp from which the juice has been extracted, may be substituted for fresh coconut and grated carrots.

Alfalfa Sprouts Salad

2 parts fresh green alfalfa sprouts
2 parts cubed avocado
1 part shredded carrots
1 green onion with top, chopped
dash of sea salt and lemon juice

Toss together; garnish with cherry tomatoes, serve with your favorite dressing.

Colorful Cauliflower Favorite

1 small grated cauliflower
½ cup grated carrots or butternut squash
1 small avocado, peeled and cubed
½ cup chopped green pepper or celery
2 Tbs. diced onion or 1 tsp. onion powder
4-5 radishes, sliced

Toss with your favorite salad dressing. Serve in lettuce cups.

Raw Cauliflower Salad

1 cup raw cauliflower, chopped or grated
1 cup raw tender garden peas
½ cup avocado, diced

Toss with your favorite salad dressing. Serve on lettuce leaves. Garnish with **red pimento** strips.

Green Soybean Salad

2 cups tender green soybeans
1 cup chopped celery
1 cup chopped cucumber
1 pimento, chopped
1 Tbs. chopped parsley
1 small green onion, diced

Mix all together with your favorite salad dressing or mayonnaise. Chill and serve on **romaine lettuce leaves** or other **salad greens**.

Confetti Rice Salad

3 cups cooked brown rice, cold
½ cup celery, chopped
1 cup cooked peas and diced carrots, cold
4 Tbs. dill pickles or cucumbers, diced

Toss ingredients together with your favorite mayonnaise. Serve on bed of **salad greens** or **alfalfa sprouts**.

Creamy Potato Salad

2 lbs. red skin potatoes, cooked with skins
1 cup diced celery
⅓ cup sliced green olives or dill pickles
⅓ cup sweet orange or red diced pepper
¼ cup finely chopped onion
1 Tbs. onion powder
½ tsp. celery seed and sea salt, to taste
¼ tsp. garlic powder, cayenne, to taste
⅓ cup Soy Vegenaise, more or less
dill weed and pepper strips for garnish

Scrub potatoes. Steam or boil potatoes in small amount of water, 25-30 minutes until tender. Peel off thin skin; cut into cubes, and place in large mixing bowl. Add the celery, olives, peppers, onions, and seasonings. Gently stir in mayonnaise, to taste, tossing lightly to coat vegetables. Transfer potato salad to bowl lined with lettuce leaves. Garnish with fresh or dried **dill weed** and **sweet pepper strips**. Serve warm or cover and chill in refrigerator. Yield: 6-8 servings

Sprouted Soybean Salad

1 head bibb lettuce, bite-size pieces
1 green or red bell pepper, chopped
2 cups tenderized soy sprouts, chilled
½ cup diced sweet onion
clove of garlic

Rub bowl with garlic. Toss together the rest of ingredients. Add your favorite dressing just before serving.

Zucchini-Radicchio Salad

2 cups radicchio, torn in pieces
¼ cup diced red bell pepper or pimento
2 cups shredded zucchini squash
¼ cup sliced black ripe olives
salad dressing

Toss the above together with your favorite dressing. Garnish with **fresh parsley** or **watercress**.

Potato Salad with Avocado

6 cups diced cooked potatoes
2 cups diced or cubed avocado
1½ cups chopped green or black ripe olives
2 Tbs. onion powder
   or chopped green onion
½ tsp. celery seed powder
½ tsp. dill powder
½ tsp. sea salt, to taste
salad dressing
garnish, chopped parsley

Steam potatoes with skins on. Peel; reserve any leftover water for soup or gravy. Mix potatoes together with rest of ingredients. Add your favorite salad dressing. Sprinkle with paprika and garnish with chopped parsley.

Surprise Salad

Even children who are reluctant to try new foods, come back for more!

fresh alfalfa or clover sprouts
½ tomato, small
½ avocado, small
¼ cup tofu, seasoned
1 salad lettuce leaf
celery or carrot strips
olives, black
soy mayonnaise

On bed of sprouts arrange foods to form a doll using:
Head – Tomato half rounded side up
Body – Avocado half cut lengthwise- small end for neck
Skirt – Mound of tofu hidden under lettuce leaf
Hair – Alfalfa sprouts/olives set in mayonnaise
Arms – Celery sticks or carrot strips
Eyes and mouth – Olives set into tomato
Feet – Olives or (almonds or brazil nuts)

Vegetable Petal Salad

Flower Petal salads are a wonderful way to serve all raw vegetables. The family will be surprised at the attractive and tasteful arrangements. There are many possible combinations. Use your imagination with various seasonal vegetables. Here are some suggestions (also see Kids Recipes pg 241)

In the center of each plate put a mound of **seasoned tofu** or **grated raw carrots** mixed with **chopped nuts** and **salad dressing**. Around the center, arrange **4 crisp lettuce leaves** with the stems toward the center and fill each leaf with one of the followihg:

Cubed avocado and tomato with dressing
Minced salad greens with dressing
Diced cucumber and radish with dressing
Scoop of coleslaw or potato salad

Optional: Place a **green bean** for stem of each flower.

Tofu Sun Face

Children will enjoy making and eating these faces

Tofu, seasoned
Stuffed olives
Red pepper strips
Parsley, fresh
Lettuce or salad greens
Carrot and Celery sticks

On a bed of lettuce leaves, place a flat mound of seasoned tofu (soy cheese). Make a face on tofu using stuffed olives for eyes, red pepper strip for mouth, parsley for hair, 2 small olive pieces for nose. From the face make alternate sunbeams of carrot and celery sticks.

Tomatoes - Fruit or Vegetable?

There are opposing views as to whether tomatoes are a fruit or a vegetable and how they best combine with other foods. Here is what Webster says about tomatoes:

*"A South American perennial **herb of the nightshade family**, widely cultivated as an annual for its fruit, with large rounded edible pulpy berry, which is red or yellow when ripe."* Webster defines **nightshade**: … *"as of herbs, shrubs… and some poisonous weeds… and crop plants, as the potato, **tomato** and eggplant (of the nightshade family, yielding edible **fruit**)."* **(fruit** meaning the end-product of the plant or vine).

It appears evident that the lowly tomato, we enjoy eating in so many dishes, fits perfectly into the **herb** (plant) **bearing seed** (and seed pod), or succulent food group cultivated as a **garden vegetable,** much like the squash, cucumber, eggplant, okra, and peppers (tomatoes would be a kind of **vegetable** or *"every herb bearing seed"*… not *"every tree with fruit…"* Genesis 1:29).

Let's look at the following quotes from ***Counsels on Diet and Foods by E. G. White:***

*"In their season we have grapes in abundance, also prunes and apples, and some cherries, peaches, pears, and olives, which we prepare ourselves. **We also grow a large quantity of tomatoes.**"* page 324

*"There is **no fresh fruit** at this season. **We have a good yield of tomatoes…**"* page 489

*"We raise our own loganberries, and use them freely. Strawberries do not grow well in this locality, but from our neighbors we purchase blackberries, raspberries, apples and pears. **We have also an abundance of tomatoes.**"* page 492

In all 3 quotes above, **tomatoes** were isolated from the fruits mentioned. In the chapter, ***Physiology of Digestion***, we find these noteworthy statements:

*"Disturbance is created by **improper combinations of food**; fermentation sets in; the blood is contaminated and the brain confused."*

*"You eat too great a variety at one meal. **Fruit and vegetables taken at one meal produce acidity of the stomach**; then impurity of the blood results, and the mind is not clear because the digestion is imperfect."* ***Counsels on Diet & Foods*** pgs. 110, 113

In summary, let's **keep the combinations simple**. When planning meals, it is best to combine tomatoes with beans, grains, nuts, olives, avocado and garden vegetables. If you still doubt whether tomatoes are a fruit or vegetable - here's a question:

Which would you rather have for dinner? a beautiful **Tossed Garden Green Salad** with **Tomato Wedges** and **Avocado Dressing** or a mixed **Apple/Banana/Peach Fresh Fruit Salad** layered with **Tomato Slices** and a dollop of cream on top? The choice is yours!

For more information see: **Natural Food Groups** and *Food Combining Made Easy* **Chart**.

Stuffed Tomatoes

The smaller ones make a perfect appetizer!
Attractive and delicious!

Tomatoes, ripe (cherry, roma or slicing)
Avocado, ripe mashed
Peas, tenderized
Squeeze of lemon
Sea salt, garlic powder, to taste

Wash tomatoes, cut off ¼" slice on top. Hold tomato firmly with one hand, spoon or scoop out center, being careful not to split edge of tomato (or cut wedge slices leaving bottom of tomato attached). Reserve scooped out tomato for sauce, soup, or add back to filling. Mash peas and avocado. Add the lemon and seasonings. Refill cavity. Serve tomatoes on a bed of tender salad greens, watercress or crisp sprouts. Garnish with a dollop of **salad dressing**, a sprinkle of **dill weed** or **paprika**.

*Hint: For easy filling of small cherry tomatoes, make a diagonal cut to remove 1 corner of a small plastic bag. Spoon filling into bag, hold bag over each tomato, squeeze to fill cavity.

Stuffed Tomato Fillings

Soy cheese, chopped olives, parsley, mayonnaise
Chopped cucumber, avocado, pimento, dressing
Cabbage slaw with celery, sprig of parsley
Mashed seasoned green lima beans, or peas, dill
Tofu-egg Sandwich filling, see recipe
Tofu with Herbs, see recipe
Guacamole or Avocado Butter, see recipes

Tofu Tomato Salad

Tomato – A rich source of lycopene a potent antioxidant and protector against cancer and other diseases. Ripe tomatoes contain significant amounts of vitamins and minerals including potassium, iron, folate, vitamins A, B, C, and E.

3 cups cherry or grape tomatoes, halved
1 lb. firm tofu, water pack
2-3 Tbs. lemon juice, fresh squeezed
1 Tbs. pure olive oil, to taste
3-4 Tbs. fresh chopped sweet basil
1 tsp. dried oregano
½ tsp. sea salt, to taste

Cube tofu, mix with lemon, olive oil, oregano and salt. Refrigerate 2-3 hours to marinate. Add cherry or grape tomatoes, and sweet basil. Serve with hearty bread. Delicious!

Vine-Ripe Tomato Salad

Tomatoes, med-large slicing
Lettuce leaves or Alfalfa sprouts
Tofu, mashed seasoned, and/or
Avocado, mashed seasoned
Black ripe olives, sliced

Instead of slicing the tomato in usual circles, cut through from top to bottom, being careful not to cut through the bottom (leave it attached). Spread open cut tomato on mound of alfalfa sprouts or lettuce leaves. Fill center with a scoop of seasoned tofu, or avocado or both (add sprinkle of lemon juice sea salt, onion, garlic powder). Garnish with olives, paprika, dill weed, or chives.

Avocado Tomato Salad

1 avocado, cubed
2 vine-ripe tomatoes, cut in chunks
watercress or alfalfa sprouts

Toss avocado and tomato with some of your favorite dressing. Put on a nest of mixed greens, watercress or crisp alfalfa sprouts. Simple, nutritious and delicious!

Italian-style Tomatoes

Tomatoes, vine ripened
Garlic, fresh
Olive Oil, pure virgin
Sea salt, to taste
Oregano, crushed dried

In a bowl, slice ripe, juicy tomatoes in ½" wedges. Thread on olive oil, sprinkle with sea salt and oregano herb. Add fresh sliced or minced garlic (1 clove for each tomato). Mix together to combine flavors. Eat with bread, dipping pieces of bread in the juice. Enjoy!

Dilly Cucumbers with Sour Cream

2 English or garden cucumbers, sliced*
1 small sweet onion, sliced or chopped
½ cup Tofu Sour Cream, see recipe
½ Tbs. lemon juice, fresh squeezed
¼ tsp. sea salt; dash of celery seed
1 tsp. dry dill weed or 1 Tbs.fresh minced

Slice onion and cucumbers (circles or halves) and place in a glass bowl. Add sour cream, lemon and salt, sprinkle with dill weed. Toss to coat. Cover and chill 1-2 hours before serving to blend flavors; stir occasionally. Store in refrigerator up to 3 days.

*For a scalloped look, run fork tines down the length of unpeeled or peeled cucumber before slicing.

Cucumber Avocado Salad

Lettuce or alfalfa sprouts
Tomato
Avocado
Cucumber

Slice tomatoes on lettuce leaves. Cube avocado and cucumber. Sprinkle with dill weed or celery seed; toss with mayonnaise. Cover tomato slices with a mound of the avocado and cucumber mixture. Sprinkle lightly with **paprika** and **sea salt**.

Marinated Garden Vegetables

A refreshing dish, served as a summer salad with pita or crusty garlic bread.

1-2 med. cucumbers, sliced or chopped
1 ripe tomato, cut in wedges or chopped
½ cup thinly sliced, red or sweet onion,
   (Maui, Vidalia or Walla Walla)
½ red and green bell pepper, cut in strips
2-3 Tbs. fresh chopped sweet basil
1-2 cloves garlic, minced

Wash and cut cucumber in slices or lengthwise in quarters and pieces. Slice tomatoes in wedges, onion in thin slices, peppers in strips. Add basil and garlic. Shake **Marinade** ingredients in tightly covered container. Pour over cucumbers, tomato, onion and peppers. Cover and refrigerate 30 minutes to blend flavors. Just before serving, drain or serve with bread to dip in juice. Garnish with **sweet basil** or **dill weed**. Delicious!

Marinade

3-4 Tbs. lemon juice, fresh squeezed
1-2 Tbs. fructose or light honey
½ tsp. sea salt, to taste
¼- ½ tsp. dill weed, or oregano
⅛ tsp. ground celery seed or paprika

¼ cup honey
½ tsp. sea salt
3 med. cucumbers, peeled, chopped
½ cup tofu vegenaise (see recipe)
½ cup diced celery
½ cup red and/or green pepper, chopped
2 cups diced or crumbled tofu
1 cup Soy Sour or Soy Whip Cream, plain
1 tsp. liquid aminos or soy sauce, opt.

Boil agar flakes and water 1-2 minutes; cool, add lemon, honey and salt. Refrigerate to partly chill; then fold in remaining ingredients. Pour into salad mold. Chill to firm; serve on **lettuce leaves**.

Haystacks - Veggie Salad

Perfect one dish meal for picnics. Set out bowls of ingredients in buffet style, for each person to layer their own plate.

Corn Chips or **Pita Chips**
Beans, cooked, seasoned, chopped
   (pinto, black, red, or kidney)
Brown Rice, cooked
Lettuce, torn (leaf, romaine, bib)
Tomatoes, ripe, cut in chunks
Broccoli / cauliflower, small florets
Cucumbers, sliced lengthwise, cut in pieces
Peppers, diced (red, green, orange)
Onions, sliced or chopped (green, red)
Avocado, cut in cubes
Olives, sliced or chopped (black,
   green)
Pimento Cheese, shredded
Topping: Tofu Vegenaise,
   Salsa, or Tofu Sour Cream

Crush chips on plate, spoon on beans, rice. Then add layers of remaining ingredients. Top with your favorite dressing (see recipes).

Summer Salad Mold

1½ Tbs. agar flakes
1½ cups hot water
½ tsp. grated lemon rind
¼ cup fresh lemon juice

Mixed Greens with Tomato & Toasted Sesame

4 cups salad greens, bite size pieces
1 vine-ripe tomato, cut in wedges
¼ cup French dressing (see recipe)
2 Tbs. Toasted Sesame Seed (see recipe)

Place salad greens into individual bowls. Drizzle with French Dressing. Top with tomato slices. Sprinkle on Sesame Seeds.
Serves 2

Greens with Red Pepper, Pea Pods & Fresh Dill

(pictured below)

6 cups baby greens (arugula, red leaf, frisée, beet greens, oak leaf)
1 red or orange pepper, cut in strips
½ cup edible pod peas
¼ cup fresh baby dill, snipped

Lightly toss washed salad greens, sweet pepper and peas together. Cover and refrigerate. Just before serving, toss with your favorite salad dressing. Serves 3-4

Baby Spinach Avocado Salad

(pictured on left)

1-10 oz. pkg. fresh baby spinach
2 large ripe avocados, cubed
1 cucumber, thinly sliced
1 small red onion, thinly sliced

Toss all ingredients together. Serve with **French Dressing**, **Avocado Dressing,** or your favorite.

Rotini & Basil Pesto Salad

Pesto sauce is a specialty of Italy, where some of the most fragrant basil is grown.

8 oz. of uncooked rotini spiral pasta
Fresh Basil Pesto, see recipe p. 480
¼ cup diced sweet bell pepper

Cook 3 cups pasta as directed on package. Drain, rinse with cold water, drain again. Swirl in pesto, toss pasta to coat; garnish with orange or red bell pepper. Refrigerate to chill. Yield: 4 servings

to combine. Add broccoli, squash, peppers, olives and mushrooms; toss lightly, chill. Yield: 6-8 servings

Arugula Salad

The distinctive taste and fragrance of arugula (one of my favorites), adds a unique dimension to any salad. Grows well in any vegetable garden. Try it - you'll love it!

Arugula (rocket) baby leaves
Cucumber slices
Romaine lettuce
Sweet onion, pepper rings
Italian dressing
Toasted walnuts

Select young leaves that are dark green and about 4" in length. Wash thoroughly in cold water, drain, and pat dry. Cut off any thick stems. Combine equal parts of arugula and romaine. Add cucumber, onion, red pepper slices. Toss with **Italian dressing**. Garnish with **toasted walnuts** or **herb croutons**.

Pasta Salad with Veggies

There are several versions of pasta salad; this healthy one combines crunchy and smooth textures. Explore the possibilities and substitute tender asparagus tips or crunchy sugar snap peas for the broccoli.

8 oz. thin multigrain angel hair pasta
¾ cup Tomato Pesto, (see recipe)
2½ cups fresh raw broccoli florets
1 cup yellow summer squash, shredded
2 cups sweet red pepper strips
1½ cups black ripe olives,
broken pieces
1-6 oz. jar whole
mushrooms,
drained

Break pasta (multigrain or whole wheat angel hair) in half; cook according to package directions, being careful not to overcook. Drain; add pesto to warm pasta and carefully toss with 2 forks

Hot Spinach & Walnut Salad

Heart-healthy, rich in omega-3 and cancer-fighting antioxidants

16 oz. (1#) Spinach, fresh
½ cup walnut pieces, lightly toasted
1 recipe Italian Dressing*, to taste

Wash and dry fresh spinach leaves. Remove tough stems (save for juicing). Tear greens into bit-size pieces (about 10 cups). Heat salad dressing in pan; add walnut pieces. Pour over greens; toss until well coated, 10-15 minutes before serving. Good with whole grain **zwieback, breadsticks** or **crackers**.

*Walnut oil may substitute for the olive oil in recipe.

Four Bean Salad

A favorite make-ahead dish, perfect for pot-luck or picnic

1½ cups cooked dark red kidney beans*
1½ cups cooked garbanzo beans*
1½ cups yellow wax beans*,
  2" pieces, cooked
1½ cups fresh or frozen green beans,
  cut in 2"pieces, cooked
1 stalk celery, thinly sliced
4 green onions, chopped
¼ cup chopped fresh parsley
black olives, red onion, sliced, optional
2 cloves garlic, minced
1 Tbs. fructose or sweetener
1 tsp. onion powder; ¼ tsp. salt; cayenne
Herbed Lemon Oil Dressing, to taste

Mix beans, celery, onions, olives and parsley in a glass bowl. Make **Herbed Lemon Oil Dressing** (omit water in recipe). Combine dressing with garlic, fructose and seasonings. Pour over beans; toss together. Cover and refrigerate at least 3 hours to blend flavors, stirring occasionally and before serving. Serves 8.

Note: Canned beans* (drained) can substitute for home cooked beans.

Chickpea & Parsley Salad

Garbanzo beans (chickpeas) are an excellent source of protein, cholesterol-lowering fiber, and trace minerals.

3 cups cooked chickpeas
  or 2-15 oz. cans, drain liquid
⅔ cup diced celery
½ cup chopped tomatoes
⅓ cup fresh parsley, or spinach, minced
¼ cup chopped red onions
2 Tbs. dill weed, chopped or 2 tsp. dried
3 cloves fresh garlic, minced

Dressing:

3 Tbs. Lemon Juice
1 Tbs. olive oil
½ tsp. onion powder
⅛ tsp. cumin, to taste
¼ tsp. salt

Make dressing by stirring or shaking ingredients together. In a mixing bowl, coarsely chop garbanzos (or leave whole). Add celery, tomatoes, parsley, onions, dill and garlic. Mix all ingredients together. Pour on dressing, toss to combine; adjust seasonings to taste. Chill salad 1 hour before serving. Servings: 6

Tabbouleh & Chickpeas

*The classic Middle Eastern salad rich in
beta-carotene, protein, iron and B vitamins!*

1½ cups cooked bulgur wheat* or quinoa*
1½ cups cooked garbanzos or 1-15 oz. can
1¼ cups fresh minced flat leaf parsley
1 small cucumber, peeled, chopped (1¼ c.)
3 green onions, white part, thinly sliced
2 Tbs. fresh cut mint or 2 tsp. dried mint
1 tomato, diced or
  ¼ cup sun-dried tomatoes, finely cut
3 Tbs. fresh lemon juice + 2 Tbs. olive oil
½ tsp. sea salt, to taste
⅛ tsp. garlic powder
  or 1 garlic clove, minced
⅛ tsp. cumin and / or cayenne (opt.)

Cook bulgur*(see below). Set aside
while preparing the vegetables. Drain
the garbanzo beans, coarsely chop, if
desired. Mix cucumber, parsley, onions,
mint and sun-dried tomatoes. Combine
the vegetables with the garbanzo beans
and bulgur. **Dressing:** shake together
the lemon juice, oil, salt and seasonings. Pour dressing over bulgur mixture;
toss lightly to coat. Cover and chill. If
using fresh tomato, add just before
serving. Garnish with **sweet red pepper
rings**, if desired. Servings 4-6

*To prepare bulgur:** Place ½ cup bulgur in
saucepan, pour on ½ cup water, let set 10 min.
Add ½ cup boiling water. Cover, cook 5 minutes.
Turn off heat; leave covered.
*To cook quinoa:** ¼ cup quinoa + ¾ cup boiling
water. Cook low heat, covered, 20 min.

Quick Quinoa Salad

*Tiny, creamy white, and quick cooking. Quinoa
contains all the essential amino acids and is actually
higher in protein then any other grain. This salad is
light in texture with a delicate flavor.*

3 cups cooked quinoa*
1-15 oz. can garbanzo beans
2 fresh tomatoes, chopped
⅓ cup fresh chopped flat-leaf parsley
2-3 garlic cloves, minced
¼ cup lemon juice
2 Tbs. virgin olive oil
½ tsp. sea salt, to taste

Drain and chop garbanzo beans. Add
cooked quinoa, chopped tomatoes, parsley,
minced garlic, lemon juice and seasonings.
Garnish with **fresh parsley**. Servings: 4-6

*To Cook quinoa:** 1 cup quinoa, ¼ tsp. salt + 3 cups boiling water; cook covered, on low heat, 20 min. Cool.

Kidney Bean Salad

Excellent source of dietary fiber, iron, protein and calcium

1½ cups cooked (15 oz. can)
  dark-red kidney beans
1½ cups cooked (15 oz. can)
  light-red kidney beans
½ cup chopped red or sweet onion
½ cup sliced scallions
1½ tsp. sucanat or sweetening
3 Tbs. lemon juice, fresh squeezed
¼ cup watercress, fresh chopped
sea salt, to taste

In a bowl, mix all ingredients together;
refrigerate 3-4 hours to marinate flavors.
Serve on a bed of **mixed salad greens**.

Layered Summer Salad

Aunt Joan adds a designer's touch to this all-in-one, good-for-you, colorful, main dish salad.

Baby Spring Greens
(see- Salad Greens to Know and Enjoy- p.395)

Tomato wedges
Cucumber slices
Avocado slices
Red Bell Pepper strips
Black Ripe Olives
Parsley, chopped
Pumpkin Seeds

In a large shallow salad bowl, place a layer of Baby Spring Greens. Carefully layer remaining ingredients, alternating colors and shapes to create a salad with lots of eye appeal. Serve with your favorite dressing.

Crunchy Chinese Cabbage Salad

4 cups Chinese (Napa) cabbage, thinly sliced
½ cup diced sweet red or green pepper
2 Tbs. green onion or parsley, chopped
1½ Tbs. fresh lemon juice
1 Tbs. olive or peanut oil
  + ½ tsp. sesame oil
1 Tbs. Bragg Aminos® or light soy sauce
2 tsp. fructose or sweetening
½ cup toasted cashew halves, garnish

Using a long blade knife, slice cabbage

into very thin ⅛"slices starting at tip of whole head (this will form long curly shreds). Transfer to a bowl, add diced peppers and chopped onion. For dressing: Stir last 4 ingredients together, toss with cabbage in bowl. Garnish with toasted cashews; toss lightly. Serves 2-4.

Quinoa Greek Salad

1 cup cooked quinoa
  or whole wheat couscous
3 cups spinach, bit-size pieces (4 oz.)
½ cup cooked chickpeas (garbanzo beans)
½ cup diced cucumber
½ cup cherry or grape tomatoes, halved
¼ cup red onion, thin slices
¼ cup chopped kalamata or black olives
2-3 Tbs. Parsley Dressing (see recipe)

Rinse quinoa to remove bitter natural coating. Cook, set aside while preparing vegetables. Combine all ingredients in a salad bowl. Drizzle with dressing, to taste. Servings: 4

To cook quinoa: ¼ cup quinoa + ¾ cup boiling water. Cook low heat, covered, 20 min.
To cook couscous: ⅓ cup couscous + ⅔ cup boiling water. Cover, cook on low, 5-8 min.

Tossed Turnips
(Raw or Steamed)

Turnip slivers
Parsley frills
Carrot slivers

Combine equal parts of finely slivered raw turnips and carrots or lightly steam until crisp-tender.
Toss with fresh parsley, a little sea salt and olive oil if desired. Even children won't turn down turnips when prepared this way.

Fresh Wild Greens & Chickpeas

Many wild greens, often referred to as "weeds" are actually good to eat, and make interesting and tasty additions to the common variety of salad greens. Here's one wild combination!

Arugula leaves
Malva leaves
Sweet pea blossom heads
Miners lettuce
Dandelion greens
Comfrey leaves,
   optional
Baby spinach
   leaves, opt.
Chickpeas
Radish rings

Pick tender wildgreens in season, from fields and areas that are clean. Wash carefully. Mix greens together in salad bowl and toss with

fresh lemon juice and olive oil or your favorite salad dressing. Garnish with **chickpeas** and **sliced radishes**. Enjoy!

Oriental Sweet 'n Sour Pasta Salad

This simple, savory, make-ahead pasta salad is perfect for picnic or potluck.

1- 8 oz. pkg. buckwheat soba
   n oodles, angel hair pasta, or other
¼ cup each red and green bell
   peppers, diced
½ cup shredded zucchini
½ cup sliced black olives
¼ cup sundried tomatoes, chopped
¼ cup chopped green onion
2 cloves minced garlic, sautéed in olive oil

Dressing:

¼ cup each lemon juice, liquid aminos,
   toasted sesame seed + 2 Tbs. fructose

Prepare pasta noodles according to directions on package. Rinse with cold water, drain and set aside. Combine the peppers, zucchini, olives, tomatoes, onions, and garlic. Add dressing, then toss in a large bowl with pasta. Refrigerate to marinate flavors. Serve with a sprinkle of **"Parmesan Cheese"**, or toasted sesame seeds, if desired.

Tofu "Egg" or "Chicken" Salad

Good filling for sandwiches or pita bread

2 cups (1#) tofu, firm, *frozen / thawed, opt.
¼ cup finely chopped celery
2 Tbs. diced pimento
2 Tbs. finely chopped red onion
2 Tbs. minced parsley
1 Tbs. nutritional yeast flakes
½ tsp. each sea salt, onion powder,
   to taste
⅛ - ¼ tsp. each garlic powder, tumeric,
   celery seed
Soy Mayonnaise and lemon juice, to taste

In a bowl, smash tofu with fork, or
cut in very small cubes. Add next 5
ingredients and seasonings. Add Soy
Mayonnaise and lemon. Refrigerate to
blend flavors.

For a chewier texture: Freeze Tofu at least
24 hours, then thaw and squeeze out liquid
completely. Pull tofu apart in pieces or shreds.

Italian Artichoke Salad

*This hearty salad can serve as a main dish or
companion to pasta, beans, rice, or potatoes.*

1 small fresh head cauliflower, chopped
1 small fresh head broccoli, chopped
2 cups tender artichoke hearts,
   cut in quarters
1½ cups cherry or grape tomatoes, halved
1 cup black olives, sliced
   or broken salad-style
¼ cup chopped Italian flat-leaf parsley

tofu, diced, optional
red onion rings, optional

In a mixing bowl combine vegetables
together. Toss with **Italian dressing**.
Garnish with diced tofu (browned in
oven or skillet) or thinly sliced **onion
rings**, if desired. Servings: 8

Classic Green Salad

*Just green! Choose a combination of leaves-some crisp,
some sweet, some bitter, some peppery, some buttery, some
soft. Then choose the perfect dressing- that's important!*

4 cups mesclun salad mix
1 bunch arugula
1 romaine lettuce heart
1 Belgian endive
1 bunch watercress
Easy Italian Dressing or other,
   see recipes
3-4 Tbs. lemon juice, fresh squeezed
2-3 Tbs. extra virgin olive oil
¼- ½ tsp. sea salt
1-2 cloves garlic, fresh minced

Wash leaves if necessary, pat or spin dry
in salad spinner. Place in a clean towel
or plastic bag and chill 30-45 minutes to
crispen leaves. In the meantime, prepare
salad dressing in salad bowl; whisk with
fork. Add the leaves, and with clean
hands, gently toss (to avoid bruising
tender leaves) the salad with dressing
to lightly coat. Serve with crusty bread.
Servings: 6-8

Toss gently to coat. Cover and chill for 2 to 12 hours. Yield: 8 side-dish servings.

Easy Artichoke Salad

2-3 medium garden fresh tomatoes
14 oz. jar artichoke quarters
⅓ cup chopped fresh parsley
marinade (olive oil, lemon juice, sea salt, garlic)

In a medium bowl, cut tomatoes in ½" wedges. Add the artichokes (drained), chopped parsley, and marinade. **(1 Tbs. oil, 2 Tbs. lemon juice, 2 cloves garlic, minced or ¼ tsp. garlic powder,** and **sea salt** to taste). Toss together. Serve with crusty **Garlic Bread** or **Zwieback.**

Bow Tie Garden Pasta Salad

8 oz. bow tie pasta, uncooked
1 cup red and green peppers, chopped
½ cup celery, diced
⅓ cup black olives, sliced or chopped
¼ cup carrots, slivered, shredded or diced
¼ cup red onion, diced
2 Tbs. Italian parsley, minced
salad dressing or tomato pesto, to taste

Cook pasta according to package directions, drain. Rise with cold water; drain again. In a large bowl combine pasta, and remaining ingredients.

Garden Greens with Cucumber & Tomato

6 cups mesclun mix*
   (young tender greens)
1 garden cucumber, sliced with skin
3 vine ripened tomatoes,
   cut in thin wedges
Tofu-Lite or Creamy Cashew Mayonnaise,
   or your favorite-see recipes

Wash greens, pat dry and chill in refrigerator. Prepare salad dressing of your choice. Wash cucumber, score with fork, and slice thin. Slice tomatoes in ½" wedges. Place chilled greens in salad bowl, arrange slices of cucumber and tomato on top. Serve with dressing.

*Mesclun mix- see **Salad Greens To Know and Enjoy**

Fresh Spinach & Mushroom Salad with Sprouts

A simple salad for two - with lots of crunch, nutrition, and eye appeal

3 cups tender spinach leaves, packed
6 fresh button mushrooms, sliced
1 cup tender green sprouts
   (alfalfa, clover, radish)
¼ cup diced red bell pepper
Russian Salad Dressing, see recipe

Arrange a bed of fresh washed spinach leaves on 2 plates. Slice clean mushrooms over spinach; top with crisp sprouts, and diced red pepper. Serve with **Russian Dressing** or other favorite.

Red Leaf Lettuce with Spinach, Frisée & Avocado

1 part red leaf lettuce
1 part spinach
½ part frisée leaves
½ part avocado slices

Toss salad greens together. Top with avocado slices and serve with **Sesame Seed Salad Dressing** or other favorite.

Torn Mixed Greens Salad

tender green leaves variety (green and
    red leaf lettuce, radicchio, frisée,
    arugula, tat soi, etc.)
radish slices
cucumber slices
Thousand Island Dressing, see recipe
1-2 garlic cloves, opt.

Rub salad bowl with garlic cloves or
mince garlic and toss with torn greens.
Add radish and cucumber slices. Serve
with Thousand Island Dressing, or other
favorite.

Baby Greens Spring Salad Bowl

1 lb. baby spring mix (beet greens,
    chickweed, green ice, frisée,
    sorrel, lollo roso, royal oak leaf,
    ruby and red salad bowl)
½ cup whole baby carrots
½ cup mixed summer squash
    (yellow, zucchini)
handful of tender fennel tops
salad dressing (your favorite)

Carefully hand toss the tender green to
combine. Add the carrots, thin summer
squash slices, and fennel tops. Serve with
your favorite dressing. Tender and delicious!

Confused about Tomatoes?

In 1893, the U.S. Supreme Court ruled in the case of Nix v. Hedden that tomatoes fit the definition of vegetables. -Vegetarian Times

Vegetable Medley

A colorful combination of vegetables packed with lots of flavor, eye appeal, antioxidants, and anti- cancer fighting properties.

1 small head cauliflower, raw chopped
1 small head broccoli, raw chopped
2 cups sliced or whole baby
   carrots, steamed
2 cups cherry tomatoes, whole or halved
black ripe olives, sliced, optional
Herbed Lemon Oil or French Dressing

Lightly steam carrots until crisp tender. Chop the fresh broccoli and cauliflower into bite-size pieces. Toss and combine dressing to taste; refrigerate to chill and marinate to blend flavors. Layer the vegetables with tomatoes and olives in salad bowl.

Garden Salad with Lemon-Ginger Vinaigrette

3 cups fresh packed spinach leaves
2 cups torn red leaf lettuce
1 cup bibb lettuce, bite-size pieces
1 cup shredded Chinese napa cabbage
⅓ cup thinly sliced radishes
1 Haas avocado, sliced in wedges
Lemon-Ginger Vinaigrette, see recipe

Combine spinach and next 4 ingredients in large bowl. Add vinaigrette, toss well. Cover and chill. Transfer to salad bowl. Arrange avocado slices; serve, or toss in salad bowl and serve **Vinaigrette** on the side. Servings: 4

The age-old dictum "Eat your vegetables" is as important today as ever. Vegetables and fruits contain thousands of compounds or plant nutrients that can help protect and stimulate the body's natural immunity to disease. Most vegetables have little or no fat, cholesterol, or sodium, yet supply generous amounts of calcium, iron, folate, magnesium, other vitamins, minerals and fiber, that are essential for good health.

Salad Dressings & Dips

Index - CHAPTER 13

Salad Dressings & Dips

428

Ten Talents

Zesty Black Bean Dip,
page 432

Chapter cover photo: *Raw Veggie Finger Foods, Dilly Cucumber Dressing in Bread Bowl, page 433*

Salad Dressings & Dips

Dressings and Dips add a special finishing touch to salads and raw veggies. They can be as simple as a squeeze of lemon or lime juice with a dash of sea salt, a sprinkle of olive oil, a chunky Thousand Island Dressing, or an edible bread bowl filled with Dilly Dip. The homemade salad dressings, dips, and classic Vinaigrette (oil + vinegar combo) are all made with a combination of wholesome ingredients, with lemon juice instead of vinegar. In this chapter you will find a variety to dress your salad. So take your pick, the many choices are yours!

Lemon vs. Vinegar

Lemon is an excellent replacement for vinegar in salads and salad dressings. Lemon increases the secretion of gastric juices aiding digestion, and will not irritate or inflame the mucous lining of the stomach causing gastritis. Lime, another refreshing citrus is similar to the lemon in size and shape, but has a sweeter flavor and is less sour than lemon. (see more information on Lemons in chapter **Herbs and Seasonings**)

Salad Oils

You will notice, by reading this new edition of Ten Talents, the oil listed in some recipes including Salad Dressings, has been reduced, eliminated, or replaced with other ingredients such as avocado, seeds and nuts. Oils are fats found within the cells of seeds, such as sesame, sunflower and corn, or fruits such as olives, avocado and coconut. Although oils contain only a portion of the nutrients found in the whole seed, fruit, grain or nut, they do add flavor making foods more palatable. Listed is a brief description of some oils. Read more information on Oils in: Chapter 1 - Glossary of Natural Foods; Chapter 5 - Staff of Life - Breads; and Chapter 11 - Nuts, Seeds and Olives.

Olive Oil

A versatile oil made from pressed olives. Extra-virgin olive oil, made from the first pressing of olives, is considered the finest type. It is a rich golden-to-green color, with a full-bodied flavor and aroma. A good choice for drizzling on salads.

Sesame Oil

Is made from either natural untoasted sesame seeds, or toasted sesame seeds. The oil made from untoasted seeds is pale yellow and has a mild sesame flavor. The toasted sesame seeds yields an oil that is rich brown in color with a more concentrated flavor, used mostly in oriental cuisine. Refrigerate both to avoid rancidity.

Nut Oils

These are generally made from walnut, almond, coconut and hazelnut. The flavor and color of the oils may vary from a sweet delicate taste, light in color for almonds, to a more pronounced nut flavor, with rich golden color and aroma for walnuts.

Vegetable Oils

The most common varieties are made from corn, soybeans, peanuts, canola, safflower and sunflowers. These are light yellow and mild in flavor.

Avocado Salad Dressing

Avocados are used in making this favorite tasty salad dressing.

1 large or 2 medium ripe avocados
2-3 Tbs. lemon juice
2 Tbs. minced onion
½ tsp. sea salt, to taste
pinch of dill, crushed
2 Tbs. diced pimento or sweet pepper
2 Tbs. Tofu Mayo or Vegenaise®

Mash avocado with a fork. Add lemon juice, onion, salt, dill, mayonnaise, pimento or diced sweet red bell pepper. Stir to combine. Delicious on salad greens.

Herbed Lemon Oil Dressing

Good on salads, drizzle on vegetables and pasta, or use as a marinade when roasting vegetables.

½ cup lemon juice, fresh
¼ cup pure virgin olive oil
2 Tbs. pure water
3 Tbs. fresh parsley, minced
2 Tbs. fresh sweet basil, minced
1 Tbs. fresh rosemary, chopped
2-3 garlic cloves, minced
½ tsp. sea salt, to taste
⅛ tsp. paprika

Note: If using dried basil & rosemary, use ⅓ the amount.

Shake all ingredients together in a tightly covered container. Let stand ½ hour or more, to blend flavors. Shake well before using.

Chef's Chive Dressing

¼ cup chopped fresh chives
⅔ cup French Dressing, see recipe
¼ cup tofu soy cheese, opt.
lemon to taste, opt.

Mix well with a fork – breaking up the tofu cheese or blend in a food processor for 3 seconds. Good on cabbage salad.

Cucumber Salad Dressing

3 small cucumbers with peel
1-2 Tbs. fresh lemon juice
1 small green onion
½ cup mayonnaise, see recipes
1 Tbs. dill weed, fresh snipped

Process first 3 ingredients until finely chopped. Stir in mayonnaise, and dill weed. Good on salad greens, sliced tomato, potato salad or cabbage slaw.

Lemon-Honey Dressing

½ cup lemon juice, fresh
¼ cup honey, liquid warm
¼ tsp. lemon zest, opt.
¼ tsp. salt, to taste

Stir lemon juice and honey till well blended. Add lemon peel and salt to taste. This sweet-sour dressing is good served on beets, asparagus, parsnips, or lettuce wedges.

Lemon Juice

Tip: One medium fresh lemon will yield approx. 2-3 Tbs. of juice and 1 Tbs. grated peel. To get the most juice from a lemon or lime, it should be at room temperature. Before squeezing, roll lemon back and forth on the counter, with steady pressure, which helps the cells to release the juice.

French Dressing, Quick

½ cup fresh lemon juice
¼ cup pure olive or safflower oil*
2 Tbs. toasted sesame meal**
1-2 tsp. onion powder
2 Tbs. honey or fructose
1 tsp. paprika
1 tsp. sea salt
¼ tsp. garlic powder
dash of crushed fennel or anise seed, opt.

Whiz in blender for 2 seconds, or put in covered jar and shake vigorously until combined. Serve over tossed greens or any vegetable salad.

*Optional: To further reduce the fat- use **2 Tbs. oil + 2 Tbs. water.**
**Toasting sesame seeds before grinding improves flavor of dressing.

Creamy Italian Dressing

¼ cup Italian Dressing, see recipe
½ cup Tofu, soft or silken

Blend together in food processor or blender until smooth and creamy.

Italian Dressing

This simple, olive oil dressing is a Healthy favorite - used frequently in our home. We seldom measure the ingredients. The amounts depend largely on the variety of greens used, and individual preference. Here are my approximate measurements:

3-4 Tbs. lemon juice, fresh squeezed
2-3 Tbs. virgin olive oil
¼ - ½ tsp. sea salt, or 1-2 tsp. Bragg
    Liquid Aminos®
1-2 cloves garlic, fresh minced
sweet basil, dried or fresh minced, opt.

Drizzle ingredients directly on salad and toss lightly till all pieces are coated with dressing (don't be afraid to get your clean hands right in it). Or shake the ingredients together in a tightly covered jar. To avoid wilting, toss the salad just before serving.

Note: Salad dressing can be made ahead. Store covered in the refrigerator. Shake well. **Lighter Italian Dressing**: add 1 Tbs. water.

Zesty Black Bean Dip

(See photo on chapter index page)
Also called turtle beans; black beans are tasty, rich in iron, calcium, phosphorus, and B-vitamins. Black beans are popular in Mexican, South and Central America, and Caribbean cuisine.

2 cups cooked black beans, drained
¼ cup tomato purée + ½ tsp. paprika
2-3 slices dried tomatoes, cut in pieces
2 Tbs. lemon juice
1 Tbs. soy sauce or liquid aminos
½ cup onions, sautéed
3 cloves garlic; ⅛ tsp. cayenne, opt.
4 Tbs. red, yellow, or green minced pepper

Blend the beans, tomato purée and paprika,, dried tomato, lemon juice and soy sauce or liquid aminos, until smooth. Sauté onions, minced garlic, peppers, and cayenne in 1 Tbs.heated olive oil. Add the sautéed vegetables to blender and blend briefly. Use as a spread or dip for pita chips or crackers.

Dilly Cucumber Dressing or Dip

The texture of this lite oil-free dressing makes it suitable for a dip as well

6 oz. Tofu, silken firm
1 small cucumber, peeled
1 Tbs. fresh lemon juice
2 tsp. onion powder
½ tsp. dried dill weed or 1 Tbs. fresh dill
¼ tsp. sea salt, to taste

Blend all ingredients together until smooth. Pour into bowl or bread bowl. Sprinkle on more dill weed for garnish. Serve with fresh green salad, sliced tomatoes or pita chips.

Cashew Tahini Dressing or Dip

⅓ cup cashew halves or pieces
⅓ cup soy or cashew milk
1 Tbs. sesame tahini
1 clove garlic
1 tsp. onion powder
¼ tsp. sea salt, to taste
1-2 Tbs. fresh lemon juice

Blend cashews with some milk until smooth. Add next 4 ingredients and adjust liquid for desired consistency. Last, stir in lemon juice or blend briefly.

Serve your favorite Dips with Sesame Pita Chips. Simply cut healthy whole-grain pita bread in half, brush with olive oil or honey, then cut each half into 4 wedges. Press wedges in sesame seeds to coat. Place wedges on baking sheet. Bake at 300° until crisp and golden brown.

Avocado Edamame Dressing or Dip

⅓ cup edamame or green peas
¾ cup pure water
½ ripe avocado
1 Tbs. lemon + 1 Tbs. lime juice
1 clove garlic
1 tsp. onion powder
½ tsp. sea salt, to taste

Lightly steam green peas or edamame soybeans. Blend with water to combine. Add avocado and seasonings and blend again until very smooth. Adjust water for desired consistency.

Lemon-Ginger Vinaigrette

¼ cup lemon juice
¼ cup virgin olive or 2 Tbs. walnut oil
2 tsp. Bragg Aminos® or soy sauce
1 tsp. honey or fructose
1 clove garlic, minced
1 tsp. grated fresh ginger
pinch of sea salt or cayenne, opt.

In a screw-top jar combine lemon juice, oil, soy sauce, honey and seasonings. Cover and shake well. Serve on salad or store in refrigerator for up to 1 week.

Tofu Mayo

Fast and easy. Use as you would any mayonnaise.

1- 12 oz. pkg. silken firm tofu
2-3 Tbs. fresh lemon juice
1 Tbs. pure olive or grapeseed oil
1½ tsp. fructose or sweetener
½ tsp. sea salt

Blend until smooth. Store in refrigerator.

Garden of Green Dressing

¾ cup cashew nuts
   or dry roasted peanuts
3 small green onions + tops
½ tsp. veggie - salt
¾ cup pure water, approx.
½ small cucumber, with peel
3 Tbs. minced flat parsley
3 red radishes, diced

Blend first 5 ingredients until smooth. Stir in the parsley and the radishes. Use your imagination with different herbs. Add a squeeze of lemon if desired. Thinner dressing: add more water while blending, or less, for a thicker dressing.

Herb Dressing

⅔ cup fresh squeezed lemon juice
¼ cup cold-pressed virgin olive oil
¼ cup pure water
1 small stalk celery + leaves, minced
1 green onion + 1clove garlic, minced
2 sprigs Italian flat parsley, minced
1 tsp. vegetable salt
½ tsp. paprika*
1 tsp. fresh sweet basil**
¼ tsp. thyme or rosemary
⅛ tsp. celery seed, ground

Shake all ingredients together vigorously in a covered jar until combined. Allow to stand in refrigerator until flavors are blended. Drizzle on any vegetable salad.
*or use ½ tsp. sweet red pepper flakes
** or use ¼ tsp. dried sweet basil

Spinach Dip

10 oz. frozen chopped or fresh spinach
12 oz. silken tofu, firm
1 cup soy mayonnaise or Vegenaise®
⅓ cup minced fresh cilantro
1 Tbs. onion powder
¼ tsp. garlic powder
1 tsp. basil; ½ tsp. marjoram
1 tsp. lemon zest
2 green onions, chopped
½ tsp. sea salt, to taste
8 oz. water chestnuts, drained, chopped

Thaw frozen spinach and squeeze out liquid, or chop steamed spinach. Pat dry between paper towels. In a mixing bowl combine the spinach, tofu, mayonnaise and rest of ingredients. Cover and refrigerate to blend flavors.

Low-Fat Salad Dressing

1 cup plain soy yogurt
1 Tbs. chives, fresh or dried
1 tsp. fresh dill weed, snipped
1 tsp. onion powder
½ Tbs. lemon juice
salt and honey to taste

Stir all together to combine. Savory on sprouts, tomatoes, cucumbers, coleslaw.

Tofu-Lite Mayonnaise

12 oz. soft tofu
1 tsp. onion powder
¼ tsp. garlic powder
½ tsp. sea salt, to taste
2-3 Tbs. lemon juice, fresh squeezed

Blend all ingredients together until smooth. Refrigerate to chill; will thicken as it sets.

Silken Tofu

This creamy tofu is available in supermarkets as: Silken Soft, Silken Firm, Silken X-Firm. Pre-packaged in airtight sealed boxes; it can be stored on the shelf, needs no refrigeration. Best uses: **Salad dressings, Dips, Toppings, Desserts**

Tofu Vegenaise

8 oz. tofu, silken firm
⅓ cup pure water
⅓ cup Vegenaise®
2 Tbs. lemon juice, fresh
1 Tbs. onion powder
¼ tsp. garlic powder
¼ tsp. sea salt, to taste
¼ tsp. dill weed, opt.

Put water in blender. Add rest of ingredients. Blend to a smooth, creamy, consistency. Pour into a bowl or salad dressing container. Use as a salad dressing, topping for haystacks or salad.

Creamy Cashew Mayonnaise

⅔ cup pure water, hot
⅓ cup cashew pieces
1 tsp. onion powder
½ tsp. sea salt + ¼ tsp. paprika
½ tsp. lecithin granules,* opt.
1½ Tbs. lemon juice, fresh

Blend the cashews, with part of the hot water until creamy and smooth. (2-3 min.) Add remaining water and seasonings, blend again. Add lemon juice last, turning blender on then off.

*Lecithin adds a creamier texture- see notes in Glossary of Natural Foods.

Soy Mayonnaise - Eggless

1 cup Soy Starter* plain
1 clove garlic, small
1½ tsp. onion powder
½ tsp. sea salt, to taste
¼ tsp. paprika
¼ tsp. dill seed, opt.
3-4 Tbs. soy or olive oil
2 Tbs. lemon juice

In a blender or food processor combine all ingredients except oil and lemon juice. Cover and blend thoroughly. With blender running, slowly add the oil in a thin steady stream. When necessary, stop blender and scrape down sides. Add lemon juice last, turning blender on, then off. Chill mayonnaise to set.

* **Soy Starter** see chapter **Miscellaneous**

Guacamole

A favorite any time of the year. Serve with fresh cut vegetables, as a dip with chips, spread on crackers, sandwiches, or filling for pita bread.

2 large avocados, peeled, mashed
3-4 Tbs. lime or lemon juice
1 med-large tomato, chopped
3 Tbs. diced red or green onion
3 Tbs. minced cilantro or parsley
2 cloves garlic, minced
   or ¼ tsp. powder
2-3 tsp. onion powder, to taste
   ½ tsp. sea salt,
   cayenne, to taste

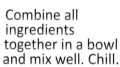

Combine all ingredients together in a bowl and mix well. Chill. Serve with chips, as a dip, salad dressing, topping, or filling for pita sandwiches.

Black Bean - Tomato Salsa

Black-eyed peas are a rich source of folate (folic acid)

1½ cups cooked black beans
   or black-eyed peas
3 cups Tomato Salsa (recipe next page)

Mash beans, mix together with Salsa. Chill and serve.

Fresh Chunky Tomato Salsa

Good served with chips, crackers, bean burritos, or crusty garlic bread.

5 ripe tomatoes, (4 cups chopped)
5-6 cloves garlic, minced
¾ cup chopped green, bell pepper
⅓ cup sliced green scallions
⅓ cup fresh chopped cilantro
¼ cup chopped red or sweet onion
3-4 Tbs. lime juice
2 tsp. onion powder
2 tsp. olive oil, to taste
½ tsp. sea salt, to taste
1 Tbs. fructose, opt.
¼ tsp. paprika or cayenne, opt.

In a bowl, chop solid ripe tomatoes (Beefsteak, Plum/Roma, Grape). Add rest of ingredients and mix together. Cover and chill 30-60 minutes to marinate flavors. Store in refrigerator up to 5 days. Yield: 5-6 cups

Tangy Tartar Sauce

1 cup tofu or soy
   mayonnaise
¼ cup sesame tahini
¼ cup chopped black olives
¼ cup chopped dill pickles*
   or 2-3 cloves garlic, minced
2 Tbs. diced pimentos
2 Tbs. fresh parsley, minced
2 Tbs. finely chopped onion
lemon juice, to desired taste

In a bowl stir together the mayonnaise and tahini. Add the olives, pickles, pimentos, parsley, onion and lemon juice. Mix well. Cover and chill 1-2 hours before serving.

*See recipe for homemade dill pickles

Tomato Dressing

½ cup tomato puree
¼ cup pure olive
or soy oil
¼ cup fresh lemon juice
1 clove garlic, minced
1 green onion, chopped
1 Tbs. honey or agave
1 tsp. sea salt,
to taste
1 tsp. Instant Clear Jel
or oat flour, opt.

Whiz in blender until smooth. Chill 1 hour.

Sure Mayonnaise

Bring to a boil while stirring until thick:

1 cup plain soy milk or cold water
1½ Tbs. arrowroot powder

Pour into blender and add:

½ cup pure water
¼ cup soy milk powder

With blender running, slowly add **cold-pressed oil**, in a thin steady stream, just enough to thicken. Add the seasonings, blend again. Last Stir in **lemon juice**.

1½ tsp. onion powder
½ tsp. sea salt, to taste
¼ tsp. celery seed
¼ tsp. garlic powder
⅛ tsp. paprika
Instant Clear Jel,* opt.
2-3 Tbs. fresh lemon Juice

Note: *For a thicker mayonnaise with little or no oil: Slowly add **2-3 tsp. Instant Clear Jel**, sprinkling in, while blender is running. Add the lemon juice last. Store in refrigerator. Makes: approx. 1 pint. This mayonnaise resembles store mayonnaise.

Parsley Dressing

3 Tbs. lemon juice
2 Tbs. virgin olive oil
⅛ tsp. sea salt
½ tsp. onion powder
1 clove garlic, minced
2 Tbs. chopped parsley

Stir together the lemon juice, olive oil, salt and onion powder until well blended. Add the minced garlic and chopped parsley. Good on salads, sprouts, or lettuce wedges.

Sesame Seed Salad Dressing

3 Tbs. sesame seeds, toasted*
1 small green onion
1 cucumber, peeled, chopped
2-3 Tbs. virgin olive or soy oil
juice of 2 lemons
salt and paprika to taste

Put all ingredients in a food processor or blender. Process until chunky or smooth. Good on avocado, tomatoes, sprouts, spinach or cabbage salad.

*Toasting see recipe chapter **Nuts & Seeds**

Thousand Island Dressing

1 cup Tofu Vegenaise or mayonnaise
¼ cup chopped red and green pepper
2 Tbs. chopped olives
2 Tbs. minced onion or chives
2 Tbs. chopped parsley
2 Tbs. diced cucumber
1-2 Tbs. spicy tomato sauce, optional
¼ tsp. crushed dill seed

In a mixing bowl, stir all ingredients together. If desired, thin with tomato juice to desired consistency. Makes a colorful and tasty salad dressing!

Pineapple Fruit Dressing

2 Tbs. almond or cashew butter
½ cup pineapple juice
   or crushed pineapple
¼ cup fresh lemon juice
½ tsp. orange or lemon zest
2 Tbs. honey
1 tsp. Instant Clear Jel®, opt.
pinch of sea salt

Blend all ingredients together in blender at high speed until combined.
Optional: Fold in ½ cup Soy Whipped Cream or **crushed pineapple**.
This dressing is good on any fruit salad, sliced bananas, or berries.

Avocado Lime Fruit Dressing

1 avocado, large
⅓ cup orange juice
2 Tbs. frozen pineapple juice concentrate
2 tsp. lime juice
½ tsp. lime or lemon zest
¼ tsp. sea salt
honey to taste, opt.

Put all ingredients in blender. Blend till smooth. Serve on fruit salad.

Tropical Palm Fruit Dressing

½ cup crushed pineapple
1 cup Cashew Soy Cream*
1 cup diced banana
¼ cup fresh grated coconut

Drain crushed pineapple. Fold pineapple into **Cashew Soy Cream** (*see recipe). Add diced bananas and coconut. Gently combine. Delicious on waffles and fruit salad.

Toasted Walnut Dressing
This simple dressing is low in sodium, and rich in omega-3 fatty acids

⅓ cup chopped walnuts, toasted
3 Tbs. lemon juice, fresh squeezed
3 Tbs. pure olive or walnut oil
2 Tbs. pure water
2 Tbs. Italian flat leaf parsley
1 large garlic clove, chopped
⅛ tsp. sea salt, to taste
dash of paprika or cayenne, opt.

Put all ingredients (except parsley) in blender or food processor. Blend 1-2 minute on high until smooth. Add chopped parsley, blend briefly. Serve dressing with mixed salad greens, or toss lightly in salad bowl. Drizzle on stuffed pita bread or veggie wraps.

Hummus

Chickpeas are the key ingredient in this Middle Eastern favorite. Serve as a dip, a spread, or sandwich filling. Our family enjoys this nutritious dish with crackers, pita chips, raw vegetables, or just about anything else we can find to dip into it - including our fingers!

1-15 oz. can garbanzo beans*
2-3 Tbs. sesame tahini**
2-3 Tbs. lemon juice
2 cloves fresh cut or roasted garlic
¼ cup chopped fresh parsley
1 tsp. olive oil, opt.

Place garbanzos, tahini, lemon juice and garlic in food processor or blender. While blending, add liquid from beans as needed to make desired consistency. Spoon into serving dish. Garnish with fresh parsley and olive oil, if desired. Serve as a dip, spread, or sandwich filling; or thin down with water for a dressing. Delicious over rice or pasta dishes.

* drain beans and reserve liquid
** ¼ cup toasted sesame can substitute

Soybean Hummus

In place of chickpeas, shelled edamame are used to prepare this hummus. Serve as a dip for chips, salad dressing, spread for flatbread or sandwich wraps.

1 ½ cups frozen shelled edamame
3 Tbs. fresh lemon juice
1-2 Tbs. pure olive oil
½ tsp. sea salt, to taste
2 cloves garlic, minced
2 Tbs. chopped flat-leaf parsley*

Thaw frozen ready-to-eat green soybeans or lightly steam 1-2 minutes. Combine soybeans with next 4 ingredients in a food processor until smooth. Add parsley, process until blended.

*Cilantro may substitute for parsley.

Russian Salad Dressing

1 cup tomatoes, whole canned
2-3 slices dried tomatoes, opt.
1 small green onion
**   or 1 tsp. onion powder**
1 Tbs. honey
½ tsp. paprika
¼ cup lemon juice
2-3 Tbs. virgin olive oil
1-2 clove garlic, chopped
½ tsp. salt; pinch of cayenne

Cut dried tomato in pieces. Put all ingredients in blender. Blend until smooth.

Note: Dried tomatoes can be reconstituted for puree, or juice (see Miscellaneous).

Avocado Dip

½ cup cashew nuts
1½ cups water
2 medium avocados
2 Tbs. lemon or lime juice
½ small onion or 2 green onions
½ tsp. sea salt, to taste
¼ tsp. garlic powder or 1-2 cloves garlic
fresh minced parsley and, or red pepper

Blend the cashews and water until smooth.
Add the avocado, lemon juice, onions, and
seasonings. Blend; stir in parsley and pepper.
The dip is good with chips, celery sticks, on salad,
sliced tomatoes and cucumber or alfalfa sprouts.

Tomato Yogurt Dressing

1 cup soy yogurt or mayonnaise
¼ cup tomato purée or paste
1 Tbs. minced onion or chives
1-2 tsp. fresh lemon juice
¼ - ½ tsp. garlic and onion powder
sea salt, to taste

Stir all together to blend flavors. Chill
and serve on cucumbers, tomatoes, etc.

Tomato Peanut Dressing

¼ cup peanut butter, lightly toasted
⅓ cup tomato juice
2 tsp. Bragg Liquid Aminos®
¼ cup Tofu Vegenaise or Soy yogurt
1 tsp. lime or lemon juice
1 clove garlic, minced

In a small saucepan mix tomato juice and
liquid aminos with peanut butter. Using
a whisk stir until combined. Add the tofu
vegenaise, lime juice and garlic. Good served
over pasta, baked tofu or fettuccini noodles.

Mineral-Rich Alfalfa Dip

½ cup fresh alfalfa sprouts, rinsed
1 Tbs. toasted sesame seed, opt.
½ cup lemon juice, fresh
2-3 Tbs. honey or agave
¼ cup virgin olive or soy oil
1 tsp. onion powder or ½ onion
1 tsp. celery seed
½ tsp. vegetable salt

Blend all ingredients together until
smooth. Serve as a dip for carrots or celery
sticks, cauliflower or broccoli florets,
cucumber spears, cherry tomatoes or
sweet pepper strips.

Creamy White Bean Dip

This nutritious dip is rich in protein, B- vitamins, and iron. Serve as a salad dressing or dip with pita bread wedges or raw vegetables.

2 cups cooked northern or navy beans
¼ cup chopped brazil nuts or almonds
2 Tbs. lemon juice
1 Tbs. onion powder
2 cloves garlic, chopped
1Tbs. plain soy yogurt or mayonnaise
1 slice soft bread, crumbled
1 Tbs. minced flat leaf Italian parsley
¼ tsp. basil, salt and cumin, to taste

In a blender or food processor combine the drained beans, nuts, and next 5 ingredients, adding some liquid from beans as needed to make a smooth consistency. Stir in the minced parsley and rest of seasonings to taste. Chill before serving. Garnish with fresh basil or parsley if desired.

Pimento Dip

½ cup pure water
¾ cup Brazil nuts or cashews
2 small green onions with tops
1-4 oz jar, 2 whole pimentos
¼ tsp. sea salt, to taste
lemon juice, to taste

Blend all ingredients together until smooth; (part of liquid from pimentos may replace the water). Add lemon juice. Store in refrigerator.

Raw Veggies below: *A bread bowl is filled with Dilly Cucumber Dressing, for dipping crunchy vegetables such as celery, summer squash or jicama sticks, baby carrots, cucumber or zucchini slices, tender green beans and broccoli florets. Nothing is wasted when serving this salad; even the carved bowl is eaten!*

Chapter 14
Sandwiches
& Spreads

Index - CHAPTER 14

Learn How to Cook

"Those who do not know how to cook (healthfully) should learn to combine whole-some, nourishing articles of food in such a way as to make appetizing dishes...without continually exercising ingenuity, no one can excel in healthful cookery; but those whose hearts are open to impressions and suggestions from the Great Teacher will learn many things, and will be able to teach others; for He will give them skill and understanding."
E.G. White, Medical Ministry, pp. 273-274

Chapter cover photo: **Super Sunburger Sandwich, page 467, also 311**

Sandwiches and Spreads

Sandwich Solutions

The choices for creating a satisfying sandwich include burger buns, stuffed pitas, rolled or wrapped sandwiches, filled tortillas, calzones, sandwich ingredients, layered, stacked or spread between two slices of bread, open - face sandwiches served with knife and fork, or cut in half or quarters. Sandwiches may be thin, hearty, or provide nourishment adequate for a full meal. Boost the nutritional value of the sandwich by using whole grain breads, buns and wraps. Be creative, vary the spreads and sandwich filling. Include leafy greens such as spinach, watercress or sprouts.

Super Stuffed Pitas

See recipe on page 463

Diets that include large amounts of fiber aid in the prevention of many degenerative diseases. Fiber is found only in plant foods: grains, fruits, nuts, seeds and vegetables.

Ways to Cut Bread

Pack A Picnic or Lunch

- Make it appetizing and attractive - vary the colors, shapes, and textures of food.

- Make it nutritionally balanced - a healthy salad, sandwich, soup, and raw nuts and seeds.

- Include some finger foods, such as carrot and celery sticks, radishes, cucumber, olives, zucchini, or bell pepper strips.

- Wilted lettuce in sandwiches? Use alfalfa sprouts. They will keep crisp in a sandwich. or wrap lettuce greens in waxed paper to retain freshness, then add to sandwich before serving.

Seven Sandwich Varieties

Burrito - shaping a softened flour tortilla up and over the filling, folding in the sides, and rolling up.

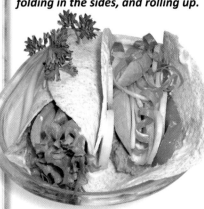

Burger Bun- a split roll having a filling in between

Two or more slices of bread with filling in between; may be cut in a variety of shapes

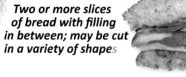

Wraps –usually include a variety of spreads, fillings and foods that are layered. Roll tightly in a jelly roll fashion. Cut in half, or in 1½" slices for an attractive presentation.

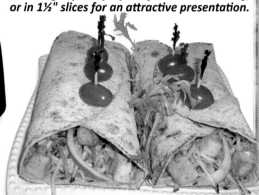

Open face - consisting of 1 slice of bread covered with food

Pita bread – a thin flat bread that can be separated easily into two layers to form a pocket, with food stuffed into pocket.

Calzones- a turnover of pizza dough stuffed with various fillings and baked.

Hass Avocado – *dark, pebbly skin, flesh rich and buttery, with a sweet nutty flavor. Smaller and creamier than many varieties.*

Florida Avocado – *smooth, lighter green skin, moist flesh, has less fat. (also called "alligator pear")*

Avocado Butter

Avocados, are a good source of natural unsaturated fat. Avocados contain Vitamins A, B, C, E, Calcium, Phosphorus, and Magnesium. Excellent replacement for butter– with no cholesterol!

448

Avocados, firm, ripe
Lime juice, dash of salt

Peel and mash avocado with a fork; add a little lime or lemon juice and salt; or for a sweeter version, slice avocado on toast; drizzle with honey. Delicious! Avocados are cheaper, pound-for-pound, than butter, and better for you!

Creamy Whipped "Butter"

The family will love this flavor-filled, ' just like butter' spread; contains zero cholesterol, compared with 30 milligrams of cholesterol in 1 Tbs. of real butter!

½ cup water, less 3 tbs.
3 Tbs. fresh carrot juice
2 Tbs. soy milk powder
½ tsp. lecithin granules
½ tsp. sea salt
1-2 drops butter flavor, opt.
¼ cup olive, soy or grapeseed oil

Blend water with carrot juice, soy milk powder, lecithin granules, salt and natural butter flavor until very smooth. With blender running on medium speed, slowly add the olive oil, in a thin steady stream (this should take about 3-4 min.)

Last, very slowly add while blending:
¼ cup cold pressed coconut oil
½ tsp. lemon juice, opt.
Pour into 8 oz. round container. Chill to set. Store in refrigerator or freeze. If separation occurs, stir. The amount of carrot juice used will determine the color.

Note: *It is better to use the natural cold-pressed coconut oil that melts at 75°-78°, (below body temperature). This spread will melt at room temperature, becoming a free-flowing oil, which is more desirable than the coconut oil with a higher melting point used in the confectionery industry. Coconut oil contains a variety of fatty-acids and although not hydrogenated, it is a more saturated fat; use sparingly, to replace butter. See description of Coconut Oil in Glossary of Natural Foods.*

Sandwich Filling Suggestions

1. Almond or Cashew Nut butter with dates on multi-grain, or raisin bread

2. Olive Spread, sliced cucumber or sweet red pepper, lettuce, spinach or sprouts

3. Apricot-Date Spread, Cashew, Pumpkin Seed or Brazil nut butter on toast

4. Grated carrots, almond or peanut butter and dressing on whole grain bread

5. + Monterey Jack cheese, sliced red onion, tomato, romaine lettuce, on rye bread

6. Mashed green lima beans, cucumber, dillweed, spinach leaves, mayonnaise

7. + Chopped garbanzo beans, avocado, tomato, sprouts, vegenaise, spelt bread

8. + Tofu Egg Salad, crisp lettuce, tomato, cucumber, whole grain bread or pita

9. Soya-Peanut Soufflé, chopped olives, celery, minced parsley, soy mayonnaise

10. Peanut Butter-Seed Spread, sliced avocado, dates, orange zest on raisin bread

11. Soya-Yeast Sandwich Spread, avocado, tomatoes, sprouts, on whole wheat bread

12. Sliced avocado, Cheddar Cheeze, red onion, watercress or spinach in pita pocket

13. + Baked eggplant slices, sliced tomato, onion, alfalfa sprouts, soy mayonnaise

14. + Browned Tofu slices, baby greens, sliced cucumber, tomato, vegenaise, in pita

15. Peanut Butter-Honey Spread and sliced bananas on sprouted whole grain toast

16. + Sprouted Wheat Burger on bun, tomato slices, onion, sprouts, soy mayonnaise

17. + Scrambled Tofu, spinach, tomato, olives, cucumber, vegenaise, on pita bread

18. Mashed avocado, lime juice, diced cucumber, pimento, spinach leaves, on rye bread

19. * + Super Sunburger, Health Ketchup, sliced tomato, avocado, onion, spinach or bib lettuce, multi-grain bun

20. * + Panelle- chickpea pancake, crusty bread or roll, romaine, lemon dressing

21. * + Caponatina - eggplant hearty sandwich –fill pita pocket (recipe- Side Dishes)

22. * + Artichokes w/onions, in whole wheat pita pocket, mayonnaise (see Vegetables)

23. * Leftover meatless loaf mashed with dressing, sliced tomato, onion, leaf lettuce

24. * + Soy-Not Meat, Tofu Mayo, sliced tomato, onion, spinach, multi-grain bread

*Make ahead fillings – see recipes in Index   +Pictured - see Index and Chapter

Simple Butter Substitute

This soft spread contains zero fat, is tasty and nutritious, very simple to make, yet looks and tastes like butter!

½ cup plain soymilk
¼ tsp. agar powder
2 tsp. lecithin granules
½ tsp. sea salt
½ - ¾ tsp. lemon juice, opt.
¼ tsp. butter flavoring, opt.

In a small saucepan heat soymilk and agar (¼ rounding tsp.) to a boil. Pour into blender. Add remaining ingredients and blend to combine. Pour into covered container. Refrigerate to set.

Note: For a more buttery, richer spread, add **1 Tbs. pure virgin olive oil.**

Maple Butter

⅓ cup homemade "butter"
3 Tbs. pure maple syrup

Combine homemade butter (see recipes) with maple syrup. Cover and chill until ready to use. Good on waffles, ornbread, pancakes, French toast etc..

Better Than Butter

This buttery spread made with cereal is cholesterol free- resembles soft margarine in appearance and texture, and has a pleasantly mild sweet flavor.

1 cup very hot water or soy milk
½ cup raw cashews
    or blanched almonds
1 tsp. sea salt
1½ tsp. light honey or sweetening
1 tsp. lecithin granules
⅛ tsp. turmeric
1½ tsp. lemon juice
2 tsp. Kojel®, plain, or agar flakes
1 cup hot cooked cous-cous*

In a blender, process the cashew nuts and the next 5 ingredients, using half the amount of liquid. Blend about 2 minutes until creamy.

Add the remaining hot liquid, **Kojel®** or **agar**, and cous-cous. Blend until smooth and creamy. Pour into container; refrigerate to cool and set. Use like butter or margarine on bread, potatoes, corn-on-the-cob, etc. Yield 1 lb. (pint)

 *Cous-cous: simmer ⅓ cup cous-cous + ¼ tsp. sea salt in 1 cup boiling water, 15 minutes, or until fluffy, and water is absorbed.

Note: *Hot cooked quinoa, cornmeal, or millet may substitute, if desired.

"My son, eat thou honey, because it is good: and the honeycomb, which is sweet to thy taste." **Proverbs 24:13 KJV**

Creamed Honey

Pure natural unclarified **honey** combined with **avocado** or your favorite **nut butter** makes a healthy spread on whole grain toast (see notes on **Honey** in *Glossary of Natural Foods*)

Peanut Butter-Honey Spread

½ cup crunchy peanut butter, lightly toasted
¼ cup honey, natural creamed
2 Tbs. ground sunflower seeds, opt.

Mix well all together in a food processor or with a fork. Spread on whole grain bread or toast. Top with chopped dates or bananas, if desired.

Date Butter

3 cups dates, pitted
1½ cups hot water
2-3 tsp. orange or lemon zest
1 Tbs. flaxseed, ground, opt.

Soak pitted, chopped dates in hot water until soft. Blend until smooth. Add orange or lemon zest and flax. This naturally sweet spread is good on waffles, pancakes, toast, etc.

Apricot and Date Spread

1 cup dried apricots, soaked
1 cup pitted dates, soft
1 slice dried pineapple, opt.
1 tsp. orange or lemon zest

Soak apricots until soft, whiz in blender with dates and pineapple, using just enough liquid from soaked apricots to blend into a thick, smooth or chunky spread.

Dried Fruit-Nut Spread

Make half of **Date Butter** recipe. Add 1 cup chopped figs, process until smooth. Remove from blender, add **1½ cups finely chopped walnuts, filberts, pecans** or **brazil nuts**. Add **orange juice** to moisten and make consistency for spreading. Delicious on **whole grain bread, raisin toast,** or **oat crackers**.

"If you find honey, eat just enough - too much of it, and you will vomit."
Proverbs:25:16 NIV

Wintergreen Honey

Take a stroll in the woods and gather **fresh Wintergreen berries**. Chop berries fine and add to raw honey. **(½ cup wintergreen berries to a pint of honey)**. Let stand in warm sunlight one or two days. Honey can be strained or used as is with the berries in it. For quick wintergreen honey, the berries can be blended with the honey in a blender or food processor until creamy. Wintergreen berries are not only delicious, but leave a refreshing taste when chewed. They are not to be confused with other red berries. Wintergreen berries are bright red, with one end shaped like a star, and slightly lighter in color.

Natural Peanut Butter & **Fruit Jam** makes a healthy filling for sandwiches. See **Miscellaneous** chapter for Strawberry and other Fruit Jams, also see **Index** for Fruit Spreads and Nut Butters.

Sesame Seed Sandwich Spread
(good source of calcium and phosphorus)

1 cup ground sesame seed
   or ¾ cup tahini
½ cup raw honey
½ tsp. orange or lemon zest
pinch of sea salt

Mix ground sesame seeds or tahini with honey. Add salt, lemon or orange zest. Refrigerate. Delicious alternative to peanut butter on toast, crackers or waffles.

Tofu Cheese for Spread

*(see recipes for making **Tofu - Soybean Curd** in chapter **Meatless Main Dishes**)*

Use firm soybean curd (tofu cheese)
Season by adding one of the following:

1. Fresh carrot juice, finely chopped onion, mayonnaise.
2. Beet juice, chopped nuts, and a little tofu vegenaise.
3. Chopped parsley, green pepper, celery and mayonnaise.
4. Tomato Pesto, minced onion, soy vegenaise.

Tofu with Herbs Spread

A light savory spread filled with the flavor of fresh herbs. A perfect spread on pita chips, crackers or toast.

**7 oz. (½ pkg.) soft tofu
2 Tbs. soy mayonnaise
2 Tbs. fresh parsley, finely minced
2 Tbs. fresh sweet basil, finely minced
1 small clove garlic, finely minced
sea salt and fresh dill weed, to taste**

Combine all ingredients with a mixer or food processor until smooth and creamy. Store covered in refrigerator.

Pineapple Tofu Cottage Cheese

**Tofu - Soybean Curd
Pineapple, crushed or chunks, in juice
Salad dressing, to taste**

Rinse tofu, drain. Mash and combine with some pineapple and juice to soften. Add salad dressing and sea salt to taste. Good served with avocado on bed of crisp sprouts.

Tofu "Cream Cheese"

**⅓ cup boiling water
1 Tbs. Kojel® plain gelatin or agar flakes
¼ cup almonds, blanched
½ tsp. scant sea salt, scant
½ pkg. (6 oz.) silken tofu, extra firm, rinsed
⅓ cup Silk creamer, vanilla
2 tsp. light honey, agave or fructose
1¼ tsp. lemon juice
   or ¼ tsp. lemon powder**

In a blender or food processor blend boiling water, gelatin, almonds and salt until very smooth. Add next 4 ingredients and blend thoroughly. Stir in crushed pineapple, if desired. Pour into container. Chill several hours to set before serving. Use as a spread on Bagels, French toast, Fruit Pizza, or layer with fruit and granola.

"Pineapple" Cream Cheese

Follow recipe for **Tofu Cream Cheese**
Stir in: **½ cup crushed pineapple, drained
Pour into container, chill to set.**

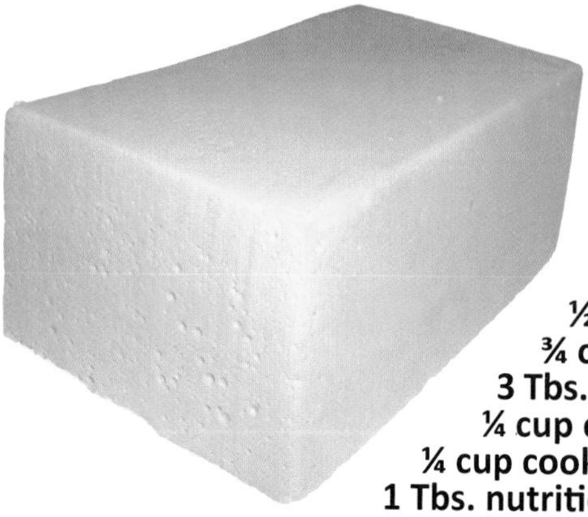

"American Cheeze"

This creamy version of non-dairy American Cheese can be grated, cubed or sliced. Use as a finishing touch on oven-baked pizza, in salads or sandwiches.

½ cup warm water +
¾ cup boiling water
3 Tbs. Kojel® or agar powder
¼ cup cashew nuts
¼ cup cooked carrots or squash
1 Tbs. nutritional yeast flakes
2 tsp. onion powder
¼ tsp. garlic powder
1½ tsp. sea salt, to taste
1 Tbs. sesame tahini
1 Tbs. olive oil or soy oil, opt.
3 Tbs. fresh lemon juice

Have all ingredients ready to assemble before starting to make cheeze. In blender soak 3 Tbs. **Kojel® or agar flakes** in ½ cup warm water for 2-3 minutes. Add ¾ cup boiling water, cashews, carrots, yeast, tahini, oil, and seasonings. Blend until smooth. Add lemon juice last. Blend briefly until smooth. Pour into mold. Chill to set.

Mock "Mozzarella"

1 cup warm water, divided
4 Tbs. Kojel® or agar flakes
½ cup soaked blanched almonds
or ⅓ cup almond butter
1 cup hot cooked couscous, barley,
or millet
2 tsp. onion powder
2 tsp. sea salt
¼ tsp. garlic powder
2 Tbs. lemon juice
1 tsp. crushed dill, optional

In a small pan, sprinkle **Kojel® or agar** in ¾ **cup warm water**. Stir and bring to a boil. Pour into blender. Add rest of ingredients and continue blending until thoroughly smooth. Heat remaining ¼ cup water to dissolve any remaining gel in pan, pour into blender. Quickly pour mixture into a plastic wrap lined pan or lightly oiled container. Cover and refrigerate several hours until chilled and firm.

454

Sandwiches & Spreads

Ten Talents

"Brick" Cheeze

(left) Make it mild and sweet or savory with a spicy tang. This savory version is for those who love garlic and chives, but it's still quite mild.

2 cups pure water, divided
6 Tbs. Kojel® or agar flakes
¼ cup sesame tahini
2 Tbs. nutritional yeast flakes
2 large garlic bulbs, roasted whole
2 Tbs. chives, minced fresh or dried
2 tsp. sea salt + 1 tsp. garlic salt
1½ Tbs. onion powder
dash of cayenne, opt.
3 Tbs. fresh lemon juice

In a small saucepan, soak **Kojel® or agar flakes** in 1 cup water for 1-2 minutes. Bring to a boil. Pour into blender. Add the cashews, tahini, yeast flakes, and garlic cloves (squeeze each clove to extract). Blend until smooth. In the meantime, heat remaining cup of water to dissolve any gel in pan, pour into blender; add rest of ingredients and blend briefly. Pour into a mold or loaf pan lined with plastic wrap. Cool thoroughly in refrigerator for several hours until firm. Lift plastic wrap to remove cheese. Slice, cut in cubes or grate as needed.

Herbed "Mozzarella"

Follow recipe for **Mock "Mozzarella"**. Add minced parsley, sweet red pepper, crushed dill, cumin, or caraway seed, to taste.

Cheese in general, is a most challenging article of food to trim from the menu when shifting to a totally vegetarian diet. Cheese, although a very concentrated food, does not contain all the nutrients found in milk or yogurt. In the commercial production and complex process of making cheese, a significant portion of protein, minerals and vitamins, is discarded with the whey. In addition, the drawbacks of cured cheese include:

● Fats (up to 60%) consist of predominately saturated fatty acids that increase cholesterol, tend to arteriosclerosis, cardiovascular disease, and obesity.
● High sodium content (common salt), in cured cheese tends to hypertension, and is harmful for the cardiovascular system.
● Microorganisms decompose into toxic substances which may acerbate allergies, eczema, and headaches. Risk of bacterial contamination; and antibiotics or hormones in dairy milk.
● Concentrated protein may lead to renal insufficiency and liver disorders, due to toxic substances produced as the proteins and fats decompose.
● Cheese is deficient in iron, and contains no vitamin C, or fiber.

This chapter includes recipes for non-dairy cheeses made with tofu, nuts, seeds, and other ingredients that are tasty and nutritious. They contain no cholesterol, lactose (the milk sugar that causes intolerance), harmful fats or other additives.

"Cheddar Cheeze"

This pimento slicing cheese has a rich, nutty flavor. Perfect for sandwiches, crackers or on pizza.

In a small pan, soak agar in water for 1-2 minutes. Bring to a boil, stirring until clear:

4 Tbs. agar flakes or Kojel®
1 cup pure water

While agar is soaking, blend the following until smooth:

½ cup pure water
¾ cup raw cashews
2 Tbs. sesame seed
1-4 oz. jar pimentos
¼ tsp. each garlic and dill seed
3 Tbs. yeast flakes
1 Tbs. onion powder
1¼ tsp. salt, to taste
dash of cayenne or paprika, opt.

Add agar mixture to blender. Boil **¼ cup more water** in pan to dissolve any

remaining agar, add to blender. Blend until creamy and smooth. Last add:

½ cup fresh lemon juice

Blend briefly. Pour immediately into a 3 cup prepared* container. Chill 4-6 hours to set.

Note: Have all ingredients (including lemon juice) measured and ready to use. For agar powder use 2 Tbs. *Prepare container before starting to blend. I use a small rectangular plastic container (size of a block of cheese) or small loaf pan, lined with plastic wrap for easy removal, or lightly brush/spray pan with oil or a non-stick spray.

Cashew-Olive Spread or Dip

1 cup cashews
½ cup salad olives with pimento
½ cup pure water, approx.

Drain liquid from olives. Blend all ingredients until smooth, adding water as needed, to make desired consistency. A tasty and simple veggie dip, spread for crackers, pita bread, or filled celery sticks. Yield: 1 pint

Almond-Olive Spread or Dip

Follow recipe for **Cashew-Olive Spread** using **blanched almonds** instead of cashews, and **green ripe olives** instead of pimento stuffed olives.

Monterey "Jack" Cheeze

A mild and mellow, non-dairy, semi-soft and sliceable cheese. Good in sandwiches, cube for salads or shred on pizza.

½ cup carrots, cooked in ¼ c. water
2 cups warm water, divided
3 Tbs. agar powder or 6 Tbs. flakes*
½ cup cashews pieces, washed
3 Tbs. food yeast flakes
1 Tbs. Bragg aminos® + 1 tsp. sea salt
1½ Tbs. onion powder
½ tsp. garlic powder
1 cup cooked couscous*
¼ cup tahini or 4 Tbs. sesame seed
¼ cup lemon juice

Slice and cook carrots until tender. Set aside. In a small saucepan, stir agar agar powder into 1 cup of warm water. Slowly bring to a boil, simmer for 1 minute. Blend ½ cup of hot water, cashews, food yeast, aminos, salt, onion, and garlic until creamy. Add the cooked carrots, hot couscous* and tahini and blend again until smooth. Add the hot agar mixture to blender, stopping blender to stir with a spatula. Heat the last ½ cup water in pan to dissolve any remaining agar. Pour into blender. Last add the lemon juice. Blend again to mix thoroughly. Quickly pour mixture into a loaf pan that is lined with plastic wrap. Refrigerate until firm. Yield: 2 lbs 6 oz.

*Kojel® kosher gel can be used in same proportions as agar flakes if desired.

*Couscous: Slowly stir ¼ cup into 1 cup boiling salted water. Cover, simmer 15 min.

"Farmer" Cheeze

Follow recipe for "Jack" Cheeze with the following changes:

Add ⅓ cup canned tomatoes in place of cooked carrots in water

1 cup soy milk, plain in place of 1 cup of water

1 cup cooked cornmeal in place of couscous

Variation:

Herbed "Farmer" Cheeze

Add dill weed, cilantro, parsley, pimento or paprika for a variety of flavors.

Olive Spread

1½ cups chopped ripe olives
½ cup finely chopped walnuts
¼ cup finely chopped almonds
¼ cup finely chopped celery
¼ cup toasted ground sesame
  or sunflower seeds

Mix all ingredients together with sufficient Soy Mayonnaise to make desired spreading consistency. Good sandwich filling, stuffing for pita bread or wraps.

Herb Butter

1 cup Creamy Whipped "Butter",
  see recipe
1 tsp. lemon juice
¼ tsp. onion or garlic salt

Cream butter, salt and lemon juice together. Add **3 Tbs. fresh minced herbs** or **1-2 tsp. dried herbs** for flavor desired.

sweet basil, chives, dill weed, oregano parsley, rosemary, savory, thyme

Use herb butters on sweet corn, as a spread for bread, or toss with pasta, rice, or vegetables.

Parsley Butter

1 cup soft butter
  substitute, see recipes
⅓ cup minced
  flat-leaf parsley
¼ tsp. sea salt
1 Tbs. soy or nut milk, opt.

Blend or whip ingredients to combine. Good on onion or garlic rolls.

Super Soy Sandwich Spread

2 cups soaked soybeans or soybean pulp
2 cups canned tomatoes or juice
1 cup toasted peanuts or ¾ cup peanut butter
½ Tbs. onion powder
2½ Tbs. arrowroot, soy or gluten flour
½ tsp. sea salt, ½ tsp. savory
¼ tsp. thyme, celery seed, to taste
2 Tbs. Bragg Liquid Aminos®
  or soy sauce

Blend all ingredients in a blender until smooth. Mix in soybean pulp with a spoon. Pour into oiled cans . Cover cans with plastic wrap or foil and secure with a rubber band. Set cans on a steamer rack or place in a kettle half filled with water. Simmer on medium-low 2½ hours. Cool, remove both ends from can, slide out. Slice loaf for sandwich filling or mash for spread with soy mayonnaise, chopped pimento, olives, parsley, diced celery.

Dilly Garlic Butter

1 cup homemade butter, see recipes
1 tsp. crushed dill seed
2-3 cloves fresh garlic, minced
1 Tbs. nut milk or cream, opt.

Put soft butter into blender or food processor; add remaining ingredients. Cover and blend smooth; add sea salt, to taste. Remove and put into refrigerator container. Chill.

Carrot Almond Paté

A tasty and nutritious fiber-rich filling for sandwiches and pita bread, or spread on zwieback, toast or crackers.

**2 cups finely grated carrots
1½ cups ground toasted almonds
1-2 green onions, finely chopped
¼ cup tofu, med-firm
2 Tbs. Bragg liquid aminos®
2-3 Tbs. soy mayonnaise**

Mix all ingredients in food processor to a smooth paste, adding water as needed. Line a small 6 x 3 x 2 loaf pan with plastic wrap, leaving a two inch overhang on sides. Carefully spread mixture in loaf pan, smoothing to corners. Press firmly. Cover with overhanging plastic wrap and chill for several hours. To unmold: lift paté out of pan using the plastic wrap. Invert onto serving plate lined with a bed of spinach. Remove plastic wrap; sprinkle with finely chopped parsley, if desired.

Roasted Red Pepper Hummus

Chickpeas, also known as ceci or garbanzo beans, are a rich source of protein, iron, B-vitamins, folate, and fiber. Serve Hummus as a spread, dip, sandwich filling, or with pita bread.

Follow recipe for **Hummus** in chapter *Salad Dressings and Dips, p.440*). Omit parsley and liquid from beans. Add 2 roasted red peppers, 1 tsp. ground cumin, 3-4 scallions (cut), and pinch of sea salt. Process ingredients to desired consistency in food processor.

Caponatina

This hearty eggplant relish is more like a filling for sandwiches or pita pockets. See **Caponatina** recipe, p.563 in chapter **Vegetables & Side Dishes.**

Garlicky Spread

Simply brush this savory spread on your favorite loaf and compliment the meal with this cholesterol-free version of garlic bread. Enjoy!

**6-7 cloves fresh garlic
2 Tbs. minced parsley
¼ cup pure water
¼ cup olive oil or other
2 tsp. onion powder or chives
¼ tsp. sea salt, opt.**

Blend together until smooth. Spread on toasted whole grain bread or brush on both sides of slice. Slip under broiler to briefly toast to a golden brown. Delicious! If a thicker spread is desired, add some **Silken Tofu (soy cheese)** before blending.

Calzones

Make dough for **Pizza Crust** - after first rising divide dough- let rest 30 minutes. Roll pizza dough into thin 7-inch circles or oblong shapes. Top half with seasoned vegetables (i.e. steamed cabbage, mushrooms, peppers, broccoli, tofu, beansprouts, or your favorite shredded non-dairy cheese). Carefully fold dough over vegetable filling; pinch, press with fork or flute edges together to seal stuffing securely. Place calzones on non-stick baking sheets. Bake at 375° for 25-30 minutes or until golden brown.

Peanut-Celery Spread

⅓ cup crunchy peanut butter
4 Tbs. finely diced celery
2 Tbs. finely chopped olives
2 Tbs. finely grated carrot
2 Tbs. minced parsley
1-2 Tbs. soy mayonnaise
onion powder, sea salt, to taste

In a mixing bowl, combine ingredients together with a spoon. Mix well, using mayonnaise as necessary to make desired spreading consistency. Good for sandwiches.

Nutritional food yeast may vary in color, flavor, and texture, containing 50% high quality protein (all the essential amino acids), a rich source of B-complex vitamins including Niacin, also Iron, Phosphorus, and trace minerals. Some types contain Vitamin B-12, an important factor in the total vegetarian diet.

Soya Starter
(base for Soya Yeast Spread)

1 cup soy flour
2 ¼ cups pure water
1 tsp. sea salt

Blend together the soy flour, water and salt. Double boil 1½ hours. Cool and blend to remove any lumps. Store in a jar in refrigerator. Use as a binder, base for spreads, etc. For mayonnaise: slowly blend in a little oil, seasonings, and lemon juice. A pinch of saffron or turmeric may be added for yellow color.

Soya Yeast Sandwich Spread
This favorite spread is rich in B-vitamins, tasty and nutritious – resembles the color of mustard

¾ cup soya starter, see recipe
1-2 Tbs. soy or olive oil
2 Tbs. lemon juice
6 Tbs. food yeast flakes
1½ tsp. onion powder
½ tsp. sea salt
¼ - ½ tsp. turmeric

Place soy starter in blender or food processor; slowly add the oil while blending. Remove from blender, stir in lemon juice, food yeast flakes, and seasonings.

Note: Lemon Juice in recipe may be replaced with ¼ cup diced dill cucumbers. A tasty and nutritious spread for zwieback, and filling for pita or sandwiches with: **Eggplant and Tomato, Alfalfa Sprouts and Olives, Sliced Tomato and Avocado, Soya Not-Meat**

Hi-B Yeast Spread

This quick-easy spread pairs well with pita bread, as a sandwich filling, on crackers, zwieback or toast.

½ cup soy mayonnaise
⅛ tsp. garlic salt or powder
1 Tbs. onion powder
nutritional yeast flakes

Combine mayonnaise, onion and garlic powder together. Add sufficient **nutritional yeast flakes**, stirring in 1-2 Tbs. at a time, to make a thick spread consistency. Good sandwich filling with cucumbers, sliced tomatoes, tofu, and spouts. Refrigerate.

Variation: Add chopped ripe olives, or minced parsley.

Not-Meat Layered Sandwich

Slice cold **Pea-Not-Meat***; layer the slices on **whole grain bread** with your **favorite dressing, non-dairy cheese, red ripe tomatoes** and **fresh spinach**. A hearty nutritious sandwich! *See recipes for not-meat.

Yummy Sandwich Spread

2 cups mashed Pea-Not-Meat*
½ cup diced celery
½ cup chopped cucumber
¼ cup minced parsley
¼ cup minced onion
mayonnaise or salad dressing*

Mix with just enough of your favorite mayonnaise to make spreading consistency. *See recipes for not-meat, mayonnaise, and salad dressing.

Baked Eggplant Sandwich

Select fully ripe eggplant without blemish. Wash, cut in ½" rounds or lengthwise slices. Brush lightly with oil, coat with breading meal if desired, or place slices on non-stick baking sheet single layer. Bake or broil in 400° oven until tender, turning once to brown on both sides. Make a hearty sandwich with baked eggplant, ripe **tomato, sweet onion slices, alfalfa sprouts, avocado** or **soy mayonnaise** on your favorite **whole grain bread** or **bun.** Celebrate a birthday, pack it for a picnic lunch; make it a special occasion with **Carob Pie (see Dessert chapter)** for dessert. Simple and delicious!

Tortilla Fresh Veggie Wraps

Try making whole grain flour and corn tortillas right at home (see recipes); or look for wholesome varieties available in natural foods stores. Then warm and fill with fresh garden veggies - enjoy!

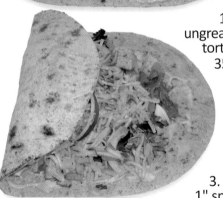

Whole grain flour or corn tortillas
Tofu, cubed or mashed and seasoned
Red and green bell peppers, diced
Fresh baby spinach leaves
Diced avocado or ripe sliced olives
Onions, sweet white, red, or fresh green
Celery, finely chopped or cilantro
Carrots, fresh long shreds or grated
Zucchini, fresh long shreds
Ripe tomato wedges or mushrooms
Sea salt, garlic and onion powder

1. Heat tortillas over med-high heat on ungreased skilllet 10-15 seconds to soften, or stack tortillas in a covered pan or wrap in foil; heat in 350° oven, 8-10 min. just to soften.

2. Meanwhile, in a bowl mash and season tofu with sea salt, garlic, onion powder, and a little mayonnaise to moisten. Add some finely minced sweet onion, celery, cilantro, and bell pepper or pimento.

3. Spread tofu mixture over tortillas, leaving a 1" space around edges. Top with avocado or olives, green onion, spinach leaves, grated carrot, sliced mushrooms, shredded zucchini and sliced tomato.

4. Fold ends of tortilla over filling. Anchor with toothpick or wrap to hold filling. Serve.

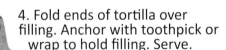

Note: Try other fillings: seasoned mashed beans, olive spread, chopped tomatoes, sliced mushrooms, cucumber, tender sprouts, watercress, variety lettuce leaves, etc.

Pitas - Garden Filled

3- 6" Pita Bread, whole wheat
3 ripe tomatoes, fresh chopped
1 ½ cups zucchini, chopped / shredded
1 ½ cups shredded carrots
1-2 cucumbers, thinly sliced
1 cup red bell pepper, sliced or diced
½ cup red or green onions + tops, sliced
1 large avocado, ripe, cubed
1 cup sliced mushrooms

1.Mix vegetables together and toss with enough **Lemon-Herb Marinade** to coat; let set 30 minutes in refrigerator.

2.Cut Pita Bread rounds in half crosswise, making 6 halves; open and spread with **Soy Mayonnaise, Soya Yeast Sandwich Spread, Tahini,** or **Hummus.**

3. Line pita bread with **garden lettuce** or **salad leaves**; fill each half with ½ -1 cup vegetable mixture.

Fresh sprouts may be added if desired.
Yield: 6 Pita, approx.

Super Stuffed Pitas

Follow recipe for **Garden Filled Pita**. Cut **2 Pita rounds** in half. Spread with **soy mayonnaise** and line with **leaf lettuce**. Add **⅓ cup seasoned scrambled tofu** to each pocket, then fill with **garden vegetable mixture**. Yield approx. 4 super stuffed pita halves.

Crispy Tofu Tomato Pitas

2- 8" Pita Bread, cut in half
1 lb. firm tofu, cut in 12-16 slices
2 vine-ripe tomatoes, sliced
1 garden cucumber, sliced
4 cups fresh baby greens
soy mayonnaise

Brown tofu slices in skillet with a little **Bragg Liquid Aminos** and a sprinkle of **Bill's Best Chik'nish Seasoning** or homemade **Chicken-style Seasoning**, turning slices over to brown on both sides. Spread soy mayonnaise in cut pita bread, line with tender salad greens. Place 3-4 crisp tofu slices in each pita half, with slices of tomato and cucumber. Serve with additional dressing if desired. Makes 4 stuffed Pita halves.

Bean Burritos with Avocado

A quick and easy meal for picnic or pot-luck. Take along ingredients to assemble or make ahead, ready to serve.

4 whole wheat tortillas
1½ cups cooked mashed beans
1 large or 2 small avocados
2 red ripe tomatoes
1 cucumber, thinly sliced
mayonnaise, see recipes
green leaf or romaine lettuce
parsley or green onion tops for garnish

Spread warmed, soft tortillas with mayonnaise. Divide seasoned or re-fried beans evenly down the center of each tortilla. Slice the tomatoes and cucumber; add to burrito. Top with avocado slices. Place lettuce leaf on top and roll up. Anchor with toothpicks; garnish with parsley or onion curls. Yield: 2 servings (2 burritos per serving).

Sandwich Relish

1 cup tofu vegenaise or other favorite
¼ cup chopped dill pickle, see recipe
¼ cup diced pimentos
¼ cup diced celery
¼ cup minced green onions
¼ cup minced parsley
2 Tbs. fresh dill weed, minced
2 Tbs. nutritional yeast flakes, opt.
Lemon and sea salt to taste, opt.

In a medium bowl, combine the chopped vegetables with tofu vegenaise or dressing. Store in covered refrigerator container. A tasty addition to veggie-burger sandwiches.

Garden Veggie Wraps

A variety of tortilla sizes, and flavors are available in some markets; ready-made selections include: whole wheat, fresh herb, spinach, tomato-basil. Wholesome wraps can be made with a choice of fillings.

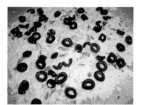

Large flavored tortillas
White/green onions + tops
Red/green bell peppers
Tofu, firm, seasoned
Celery, finely minced
Chopped cucumbers
Fresh spinach leaves
Black + green ripe olives
Tomato or spinach pesto
Carrots, zucchini, shredded
Shredded non-dairy cheese
Mashed beans, garlic, onion

1. Stack tortillas in covered pan or wrap in foil; heat in 350° oven, 8-10 min. to soften.
2. Meanwhile, in a bowl mash and season tofu with salt, garlic, onion powder, and a little mayonnaise to moisten. Add some chopped sweet onion, celery, and red bell pepper.
3. Spread tofu mixture over tortillas, leaving 1" space around edges. Top with sliced olives, green onions, spinach leaves, grated carrots, shredded zucchini or other toppings.
4. Roll up tortillas, gently pulling toward you, as you roll. Slice in 1½" pieces. Serve. For a main-dish serving, cut roll in half, serve on bed of lettuce leaves, and garnish.

Veggie Wrap Filling Suggestions

- Seasoned Tofu, sliced olives, shredded zucchini, carrots, spinach.
- Hummus, thinly sliced red onion, cucumber, tomatoes, sprouts.
- Basil pesto, steamed rice, diced tomato, cucumber, toasted sesame.
- Guacamole, steamed rice, sliced green onion, shredded carrots.
- Mashed beans, Tofu vegenaise, chopped olives, red pepper, spinach.
- Edamame pesto, sliced olives, mushrooms, carrot/ cabbage shreds.
- Tofu, salad dressing, mesclun greens, onion, shredded yellow squash

Note: Try other fillings such as mashed beans, chopped fresh broccoli, chopped tomatoes, shredded non-dairy cheeses, and variety lettuce leaves. Anything works!

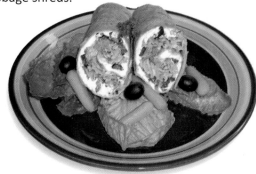

Tofu - Onion Sandwich

A quick fix sandwich that is healthy, satisfying, and super simple to make!

Whole grain bread, sliced
Tofu (bean curd) plain, seasoned or browned
Bermuda red onion, thinly sliced
Soy mayonnaise
Ripe tomato, sliced
Romaine lettuce leaves

Spread mayonnaise on toasted or plain whole grain bread. Cover with slices of tofu , and sweet onions, sliced paper thin. Top with slices of tomato and romaine lettuce leaves. Cover with another slice of whole grain bread, spread with mayonnaise, or cut and serve open face with a bowl of your favorite soup.

Super Spinach Sandwich

Whole grain bread / Avocado, sliced
Garden Veggie Pattie / Tomato, Sliced
Non-dairy cheese / Fresh Spinach leaves

Spread 2 slices of bread with **Tofu Vegenaise**. Place a **Garden Veggie Pattie** (pg 301), or your favorite, on top, next slices of non-dairy cheese, tomato, and avocado. Top with several layers of fresh spinach leaves. Cover with another slice of whole grain bread and cut in half. Enjoy this hearty wholesome sandwich by itself, or with a bowl of soup.

Tofu Parsley Scramble on Pita

(pictured left)

A hearty open-face sandwich can satisfy for a meal when served with a large mixed green salad.

1 lb. Firm Tofu, mashed
1 medium onion, chopped
1 Tbs. Bragg® liquid Aminos
2 tsp. Bill's Best Chik'nish® seasoning
1 tsp. paprika or sweet pepper flakes
3 Tbs. parsley, chopped

Brown onion in skillet with ½ tsp. olive oil, or soften with water. Add seasonings and tofu. Stir occasionally over medium heat, allowing some of the tofu to brown. Add the fresh parsley during the last 1-2 minutes of browning.

Super Sunburgers

My Favorite! (photos: baked, packed to freeze, or ready to eat)- see recipe **Meatless Main Dishes,** *pg. 311.*
The perfect burger to make, thick or thin, stack and freeze. Simply separate 1 or more, thaw as needed for sandwiches.

Hot Tomato Sandwiches

Hearty grain or dark bread
Vine-Ripe Tomatoes
Soy Mozzarella Cheese, or other
Vegenaise or Soy Spread
Seasoned Salt

Heat oven to 400°. Toast bread, opt.,
Spread with vegenaise or soy spread.
Cover with sliced tomatoes; sprinkle with
seasoned salt and top with soy cheese
shreds or slices. Bake or broil until cheese
is melted and bubbly. Enjoy hot!

Multi-Grain Sandwich Patties

(recipe in **Meatless Main Dishes***, pg 309)*
These multi-grain cereal patties can be
made ahead and frozen for instant use.
Simply thaw and sandwich between whole
grain bread with sliced avocado or your
favorite mayonnaise, fresh spinach, ripe
tomatoes and sweet onions. Yummy!

Tofu-Egg Sandwich Filling

You'll be surprised at the taste of this eggless filling – low-fat, cholesterol- free, perfect in sandwiches or pita bread.

2 cups (1#) tofu, firm
¼ cup finely chopped celery
2 Tbs. diced pimento
2 Tbs. finely chopped red onion
2 Tbs. minced parsley
1 Tbs. nutritional yeast flakes
½ tsp. each celery salt, onion powder
⅛ - ¼ tsp. each garlic powder, tumeric
soy mayonnaise and lemon juice, to taste

In a bowl, smash the tofu with a fork, add the celery, pimento, onion, parsley, yeast flakes and seasonings. Add soy mayonnaise, just to moisten. Refrigerate to blend flavors.

Roasted Garlic and Olive Paté

A savory spread to compliment pita bread or crackers

1-2 lg. garlic bulbs, oven roasted
1-7 oz can ripe olives, pitted
1 Tbs. sesame tahini
1-4 oz can mushrooms, drained, opt.
¼ cup fresh chopped parsley
1 Tbs. lemon juice, fresh

Process first 4 ingredients in a food processor until smooth, adding drained mushroom liquid as needed. Blend in parsley, lemon juice and salt, to taste. Spoon into a crock or mold. Cover and refrigerate several hours to blend flavors. Serve on crackers or pita chips with a relish tray of raw veggies for an appetizer.

Roasted Garlic

Whole garlic is relatively mild, but when minced or chopped, it releases juices and becomes stronger tasting. Roasted garlic has a sweet mellow flavor with all the goodness of garlic. I think you'll like roasted garlic. Try mashing it, for a healthy low-fat spread.

Select **garlic heads** that are firm, with tightly closed cloves showing no signs of green sprouts. Remove loose dry skin from garlic bulb. Cut off ¼" from top leaving garlic cloves intact. Place the head of garlic cut side up, in a garlic oven or muffin cup. Drizzle with olive oil, if desired. Cover; bake in 425° oven for 25 minutes, until garlic cloves feel soft. **For spread:** Squeeze individual cloves to extract the garlic paste. Mash with fork on crusty bread, crackers, or zwieback.

Pimento-Soy Chee Spread

Blend and cook 1 hour in double boiler:

1 cup pure water
1 cup soy flour
½ tsp. sea salt

Place in blender:

1 cup cooked mixture
1-4 oz. jar pimentos
2 Tbs. fresh lemon juice

Blend until smooth, adjust salt to taste, add a little **olive oil**, if desired. For a firmer spread add **2-3 Tbs. yeast flakes.** Refrigerate to set. Good sandwich filling.

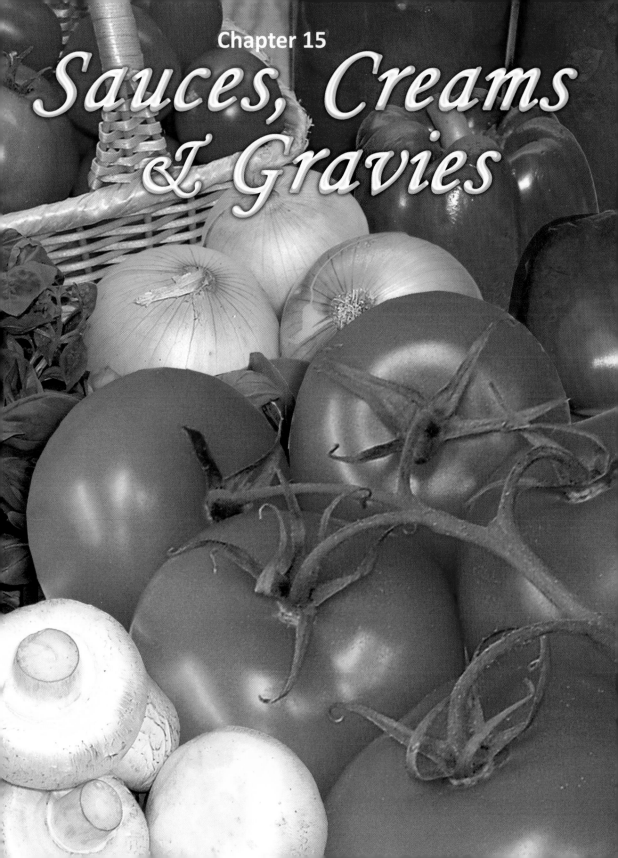

Sauces, Creams & Gravies

Index - CHAPTER 15

Today's Chuckle

**There are two reasons
why men leave home:**

**Wives who can cook and won't,
and wives who can't cook and do!**

Chapter Cover Photo: *Sauce Ingredients: Vine-Ripened Tomatoes, Mushrooms, Sweet Basil, Onions, and Bell Peppers*

Sauces, Creams, & Gravies

Sauces, Creams, **Toppings** and **Gravies** are like the "icing on a cake" that add a special finishing touch to plain food. The recipes in this chapter are fast, easy to prepare and made from wholesome ingredients that add nutrition and enhance the flavor of other ingredients in a dish.

Serve them on the side, like **Sweet and Sour Sauce** with roasted veggies or tofu kabobs; mix with food, as with **Tomato Sauce** layered in lasagna or as **White Sauce** for a creamy soup base; or spoon over the food as topping, like **Mushroom Gravy** over mashed potatoes.

The recipes include sweet and savory toppings to satisfy a variety of tastes.

"...eat what is good, and your soul will delight in the richest of fare." **Isaiah 55:2 NIV**

Gravies

Cashew Milk Gravy

(Creamy basic White Sauce)

2 cups pure water, divided
½ cup cashew nuts
1 Tbs. onion powder
1 tsp. soy or olive oil, opt.
2 Tbs. arrowroot powder
½ tsp. salt or 1 Tbs. Bragg Aminos®

Blend above ingredients together with half of the water until creamy and smooth. Pour into kettle. Whiz remaining water to clean blender, pour into kettle. Stir constantly over medium heat until thickened, adjusting water for thinner or thicker gravy as desired.

Garlic Gravy: Roast **1 head of garlic** (see recipe). Squeeze soft garlic out of cloves. Blend smooth with ingredients when making gravy.

Olive Gravy: Stir into gravy **¼ cup black olives, sliced or finely chopped,** and **1 Tbs. diced red pepper or pimento** for a dash of color.

Garbanzo Gravy: Add and blend **½ cup cooked garbanzo beans** or **¼ cup dry roasted ceci;** use only **1 Tbs. arrowroot** or **flour.**

Almond Milk Gravy

Use recipe given for **Cashew Milk Gravy** using **blanched almond**s instead of cashews; add **⅛ tsp. celery seed powder.** Just before serving, add **1 Tbs. toasted slivered almonds.**

Rich Brown Gravy

Choose any gravy, use browned whole wheat pastry flour to thicken. Add **2 tsp. pure olive oil, Bragg Aminos** instead of salt, and or **Cafix, Vegex,** or **Postum** to obtain desired color.

Mushroom Gravy

Follow recipe for **Cashew Milk Gravy** or **Rich Brown Gravy.** Add **8 oz. fresh sliced sautéed mushrooms**, or one **4 oz. can mushrooms with liquid**. Garnish gravy with **chopped parsley** if desired.

Creamy Country-style Gravy

2 cups water or veggie broth
⅓ cup cashew or Brazil nuts
2 Tbs. arrowroot powder
  or 3 Tbs. browned flour
2 Tbs. Bragg Liquid Aminos®
1 Tbs. onion powder
¼ tsp. celery seed or garlic powder

Blend the above ingredients together with 1 cup of the water, until very smooth. Pour into saucepan, add remaining liquid and stir over medium heat until thickened. Serve with potatoes, rice, patties, your favorite loaf or entrée. **Variation:** add **sliced sautéed mushrooms** or **browned tofu cubes.**

Chicken-style Gravy

Use **Creamy Country-style Gravy** recipe. Omit the Bragg Aminos. Add **½ tsp. sea salt** and **1½ tsp. of Chicken-style Seasoning.**

Parsley Gravy

1¾ cups pure water
  or broth
½ cup cashew nuts
2 celery sticks 4" long
¼ tsp. salt
¼ tsp. garlic powder
⅛ tsp. celery seed powder
1½ Tbs. arrowroot powder
  or 2 Tbs. browned flour
¼ cup fresh chopped parsley

Blend first 6 ingredients together until very smooth. Simmer in saucepan, stirring until thick. Add ¼ cup chopped fresh parsley.

Holiday Gravy

The finishing touch to "Thanksgiving Turkey Loaf" or your favorite meatless entrée.

2 cups diced celery, steamed
1 cup water or cooking liquid
⅓ cup cashew nuts
½ cup soy milk, plain
1½ tsp. onion powder + ½ tsp. sea salt
1 Tbs. arrowroot or tapioca flour
1 tsp. chicken-style seasoning
1 tsp. soy margarine, opt.

In a medium saucepan, steam or cook diced celery 2-3 min. until crisp-tender. Drain off liquid into a measuring cup. Blend cashews and seasonings, adding the water gradually, while blending smooth. (use leftover liquid from cooking celery as part of the water). Add soymilk, arrowroot. Blend again. Pour over the cooked celery in saucepan. Bring to a boil, stirring constantly until thick. Serve over your favorite entrée. Garnish with **chopped pimento, parsley, and toasted almonds.**

Pimento Gravy

Follow directions for **Cashew Milk Gravy**. Add:

½ cup diced pimento
½ tsp. paprika
¼ tsp. thyme

Stir until well blended. Serve over patties or brown rice.

Savory Sauces & Toppings

Golden Sauce

Blend leftovers into a tasty sauce!

¾ cup water
½ cup cooked potatoes
¼ cup cooked carrots
½ tsp. sea salt
1 Tbs. lemon juice
2 tsp. olive oil or nut butter
½ tsp. onion powder
1 small clove garlic, opt.S

Blend all the ingredients together until smooth. A good topping for vegetable patties, pilaf, roasts, steamed asparagus, cauliflower, etc.

Spicy Tomato Salsa

5 qts. vine-ripened tomatoes, chopped
3 cups fresh chopped peppers - Anaheim,
  banana, poblano, or green bell
3 large onions, (3 cups chopped)
1¼ cups (2- 6oz. cans) tomato paste
8 -10 cloves garlic, peeled, chopped
2 tsp. sea salt, to taste
¼ cup lemon or lime juice
½ tsp. cayenne pepper, to taste, opt.
1 cup snipped fresh cilantro

In a large stainless steel kettle, simmer chopped tomatoes, uncovered until thickened, about 1 hour, stirring frequently. Add rest of ingredients, stirring to combine; return to boil. Reduce heat, simmer uncovered another 15 minutes, to thicken and blend flavors. Fill hot clean pint canning jars with salsa, leaving ½" headspace. Wipe rims, adjust lids. Process in boiling water or steam canner for 15 min. Remove jars and cool. Yield: 9 pints

Cashew Pimento Cheese Sauce

Best sauce for macaroni and cheese, over rice, potatoes, cauliflower or broccoli. Use it when making lasagna, or as a topping on your favorite pizza! Delicious and nutritious!

1 cup raw cashews
1 cup pure water
3 Tbs. sesame seeds or 2 Tbs. tahini
4 Tbs. yeast flakes
⅓ cup fresh lemon juice
1¼ tsp. sea salt
1½ tsp. onion powder
⅛ tsp. celery seed
1Tbs. olive or soy oil, opt.
1 jar (4 oz.) pimentos or 1 cup tomatoes

Combine the cashews, water, and sesame seeds in a blender and process until very smooth. Add the yeast flakes, lemon juice, seasonings, oil, and last the pimentos and blend again until smooth. Can be stored in refrigerate 3-4 days or freeze for later use.

Tartar Sauce, Cheese

1 cup Soy Mayonnaise
  or Thousand Island Dressing
½ cup soy cheese, crumbled
1-2 tsp. lemon juice

Add the following if using **Soy Mayonnaise:**

2 Tbs. chopped pimento
2 Tbs. chopped dill pickle or cucumber
2 Tbs. minced chives or onions
2 Tbs. minced fresh parsley
1 Tbs. diced pimentos
1 Tbs. diced olives

Stir lightly – thinning with more mayonnaise and lemon juice as needed. Cover; refrigerate to chill. Good on baked tofu, burritos, veggie wraps or salad.

Note: For a sweet tartar sauce, add 1 Tbs. sweetening.

Tart Sauce for Asparagus, Broccoli, Cauliflower

Follow the recipe given for **Cashew Gravy/Creamy White Sauce**. Omit the soy sauce; just before serving add **1 Tbs. fresh lemon juice** (or more to taste), and **¼ tsp. celery seed powder**.

Savory Peanut Sauce

⅓ cup peanut butter, creamy natural
⅔ cup pure water
2 Tbs. lime juice
2 cloves garlic, minced
2 tsp. soy sauce or Bragg Aminos®
½ tsp. ground coriander
¼ tsp. ground cumin or paprika

Mix all ingredients together in a small saucepan with wire whisk. Warm over medium heat, stirring until smooth. Serve sauce over grilled tofu, vegetables or meatless patties. Refrigerate leftovers.

Avocado Fiesta Salsa

3 ripe avocados, peeled, chopped
3 vine-ripe tomatoes, chopped
1 cup chopped sweet peppers
1 medium red onion, diced
1 ¼ cups black beans, cooked, drained
1 cup frozen cooked kernel corn, drained
⅓ cup fresh chopped cilantro
3- 4 Tbs. fresh lime juice
2 cloves minced garlic
sea salt, cayenne, to taste

Combine all ingredients, adjust seasoning; chill 1-2 hours to marinate flavors. Serve as an accompaniment to meatless entrée, a topping, or side-dish salad.

Italian Tomato Sauce
(Savory- Sweet- Delicious!)

Garden fresh, or canned tomatoes with added herbs and vegetables provide a myriad of ways to use this basic sauce for pasta, pizza, casseroles, topping, stews, and a variety of other dishes.

2 qts. Red Tomatoes (Italian Plum are best)
1 lg. onion, chopped or sliced
1 small can tomato paste, optional
2 Tbs. dried sweet basil or
 ¼ cup fresh basil leaves, cut
1-2 Tbs. honey, to taste
1 Tbs. pure olive oil
1-2 cloves fresh garlic, minced
1-2 tsp. sea salt, to taste

Blend tomatoes to a chunky consistency or until smooth. Pour into a kettle; bring to a boil; add remainder of ingredients. Reduce heat, simmer uncovered 30-45 minutes, stirring occasionally, to desired consistency. The sauce should be quite thick if the tomatoes used are meaty or add tomato paste if needed. When using fresh tomatoes, blend, bring to a boil, then run through colander to remove skins and seeds if desired. Return to kettle, add remainder of ingredients and simmer to desired consistency.

Tomato Sauce Tips and Variations

- **Sweet Basil** is the secret ingredient in making a flavorful sauce; measure generously.

- If the tomatoes used are watery, blend tomatoes, let stand awhile, then pour off liquid that comes to the top (save for soup). Use thicker pulp that settles to the bottom for the best sauce or add tomato paste. The same applies to home-canned tomatoes.

- **Italian Tomato Sauce** can be made in quantity, canned and sealed in sterile jars, to be used on spaghetti, noodles, lasagna, ravioli, pizza, eggplant, stuffed peppers, artichokes, brown rice, and other dishes.

- When you have extra thick sauce, the cooking liquid from vegetables such as globe artichokes, and the sliced cooked stems, can be added, for a delicious sweet flavor.

- **Pizza Sauce:** Add dried or fresh oregano to sauce before spreading on pizza crust.

- **Tomato Sauce and Peas:** Add 2 cups fresh or frozen peas during last 7 min. of cooking.

Gremolata

A traditional finishing touch –good served with polenta, pasta, panelle, or mashed potatoes.

Parsley, fresh, minced
Sesame seeds, lightly toasted
Garlic cloves, minced
Lemon zest, sprinkle

Mix equal parts of ingredients; sprinkle on lemon zest and a little olive oil, if desired. Use as a topping for vegetables, beans, pasta, etc.

Sicilian Bruschetta

A fancy name given to a simple appetizer, The Italian name 'bruschetta' meaning to toast or grill thick slices of bread, which have been rubbed with garlic and olive oil, and often topped with tomatoes and herbs.

Topping tips: Tomato Salsa with peppers, chopped green and black olives, Roasted Garlic Spread, Sweet Basil Pesto.

Fresh Parsley and Sorrel* Sauce

*watercress or arugula, can substitute for sorrel

1 cup parsley, chopped
1 cup sorrel*, chopped
½ cup fresh chives, chopped
⅔ cup pure water
⅓ cup walnuts, chopped, toasted
2 garlic cloves, chopped
½ tsp. sea salt
½ tsp. dried celery leaves or ⅛ tsp. celery seed
¼ tsp. paprika or sweet pepper flakes
1 slice light bread

Combine all ingredients in a food processor, or blender, and process until smooth.

Note: The bread helps thicken the sauce, to a consistency similar to pesto. Sauce is good served on pasta, salads, etc.

Garden Vegetable Pasta Sauce

Follow recipe given for **Italian Tomato Sauce**. Add **chopped sautéed peppers, onions, zucchini, carrots,** and **mushrooms** to tomato sauce during last 10 minutes of cooking. Delicious on **buckwheat spaghetti, soy noodles,** or **steamed natural brown rice.**

Creamy Roasted Garlic Sauce

1 whole garlic bulb, roasted
½ cup cashew nuts
2 cups pure water, divided
1 Tbs. onion powder
1 Tbs. nutritional food yeast
½ cup silken firm tofu
1 tsp. olive oil, opt.
½ tsp. sea salt + 1 Tbs. Bragg Aminos®
1½ Tbs. arrowroot powder
garnish- fresh parsley, paprika or
**   toasted sesame**

Squeeze the roasted garlic cloves to release the garlic. In blender or food processor blend all sauce ingredients until very smooth (reserving ½ cup of water and the arrowroot until last). Pour into a saucepan, heat on stovetop to a low boil, stirring occasionally. Last add remaining ½ cup water blended with arrowroot powder; stir until sauce is bubbly and thick. Pour over cooked noodles. Garnish with fresh parsley, opt.

Note: For an extra cheesy Romano flavor sprinkle on toasted ground sesame seed.

Chickpea Parsley Dip or Sauce

An excellent topping or sauce for vegetables and rice; rich in protein, iron, vitamins B and A.

2 cups cooked chickpeas
1 Tbs. lemon juice
1 Tbs. sesame tahini
handful flat-leaf parsley

Blend first three ingredients until smooth, adding just enough liquid from beans for thick mixture. Add flat-leaf parsley and process again until almost blended.

Alfredo Cheese Sauce

A rich creamy Italian sauce to toss with fettuccine or other cooked noodles. This heart-healthy version is minus the cholesterol, butter, whipping cream, and cheese.

1 cup hot soy or tofu milk, unsweetened
⅔ cup blanched almonds or cashews
1 Tbs. sesame tahini
1 Tbs. nutritional yeast flakes
1½ tsp. onion powder
1 tsp. sea salt, to taste
1 cup (8 oz.) soft rinsed tofu, opt.
dash of garlic powder and cayenne
1 tsp. Instant Clear Jel®, opt.
1 Tbs. fresh lemon juice

Blend milk and almonds until smooth and creamy; add the rest of ingredients except lemon juice. While blending, sprinkle on Clear Jel, to make desiredconsistency (omit, if tofu is used). Last, add lemon juice; blend briefly.

Note: Pour sauce over cooked noodles and toss; sprinkle with fresh chopped Italian flat-leaf parsley and "Parmesan Cheese" if desired. (see recipe)

Health Ketchup

1 cup tomato purée, fresh or canned
1 Tbs. molasses or sucanat
1 Tbs. olive or soy oil
1 Tbs. fresh lemon juice
½ tsp. onion powder
½ tsp. sea salt
¼ tsp. garlic powder
¼ tsp. oregano leaves

Blend until smooth in blender. Good on roasted potatoes, eggplant, stuffed peppers, meatless loaf, **Walnut Burgers**, **Super Sunburgers**, etc. Refrigerate.

Marinades

Marinating is a simple process, in which foods are allowed to soak, in a savory seasoned liquid. By soaking foods in a zesty marinade, you will transform it from an otherwise bland food, such as tofu, into one that is flavorful. Marinating is especially tasty for broiled or oven roasted vegetables.

Marinated Vegetables

Pour **Sweet Sour Sauce** over vegetables or tofu cubes in a bowl or food-grade re-sealable plastic bag, set in a dish. Marinate 1-2 hours, tossing vegetables in bowl, or turning bag frequently. Store marinade in refrigerator; shake before using.

Lemon-Herb Marinade

3 Tbs. lemon juice
2 Tbs. olive or canola oil + ¼ tsp sesame oil
1 Tbs. Bragg Liquid Aminos®
1 tsp. lemon peel (zest)
1 garlic clove-large, minced
½ tsp. onion powder
¼ tsp. sea salt; 1 tsp.fructose
½ tsp. each fresh, minced,
    or ⅛ tsp. dry herbs: sweet basil,
    parsley, oregano, rosemary, paprika

Mix all ingredients together in a shallow glass dish, or re-sealable plastic food-storage bag. Add up to 1 pound tofu or vegetables. Cover dish, or seal bag and refrigerate. Allow foods to marinate, ½ hour or more, turning occasionally.

Sweet 'N Sour Sauce

This is a good sauce for sweet-sour tofu, and vegetable kabobs.

¼ cup pineapple juice, or concentrate
¼ cup lemon juice
1 Tbs. lemon peel, finely grated
3-4 Tbs. Bragg Liquid Aminos®
2-3 Tbs. honey or 3 Tbs. sucanat
2 cloves garlic, minced
1 tsp. light molasses, opt.
½ tsp. toasted sesame oil, opt.
½ tsp. grated fresh ginger, opt.

Briefly blend all ingredients together. Store in covered jar in the refrigerator.

Sweet Sour Sauce

2 Tbs. lemon juice
2 Tbs. Bragg Aminos® or soy sauce
1½ Tbs. fructose or honey
2 tsp. sesame seed oil or olive oil
1 tsp. fennel or coriander seed, crushed
1 Tbs. ketchup, see recipe, opt.

Shake or stir all ingredients together. Good on roasted vegetables, grilled tofu legumes or patties.

Barbecue Sauce

½ cup tomato or V-8 juice
½ cup tomato paste
½ cup finely chopped onion
4-5 cloves garlic, minced
¼ cup lemon juice
2 Tbs. soy sauce or liquid aminos
2 Tbs. dark molasses
2-3 Tbs. honey or other sweetener
1 Tbs. paprika + ¼ tsp. cayenne
½ tsp. sea salt, oregano, marjoram

Sauté onion and garlic in **½ Tbs. olive oil** until onion is tender. Stir in tomato juice, tomato paste, lemon juice, soy sauce, molasses, honey and seasonings. Bring to boiling, reduce heat and simmer uncovered for 20 minutes or until desired consistency, stirring occasionally. Brush on tofu or gluten steaks during baking, or serve with veggie burgers. Store leftovers in refrigerator 2-3 days.

Lime-Herb Sauce

2-3 Tbs. lime juice
2 Tbs. pure olive oil
½ cup fresh parsley, chopped
½ cup fresh cilantro leaves
½ cup fresh basil leaves
2-3 cloves garlic
¼ tsp. sea salt; ½ tsp. onion powder
dash of cayenne or paprika

Pack herbs in cup to measure. Combine all ingredients in a food processor until nearly smooth, stopping to scrape sides. Chill to marinate flavors. Good served with crusty polenta, pasta or pizza.

Pesto

Simple dishes become extraordinary as you swirl in pesto sauce. Try tossing it with penne pasta, add to spruce up pizza, top a baked potato, spread on crusty bread, or use as a filling for veggie wraps.

Edamame-Cilantro Pesto

This unique, simple sauce made with green soybeans instead of nuts is nourishing and tasty. Try it on spaghetti squash, pasta, or pizza with home-dried tomatoes

2 cups shelled edamame
　(green soybeans)
1 cup vegetable broth
½ cup fresh cilantro, chopped
½ cup fresh basil
　or Italian parsley, minced
2 garlic cloves, minced
2 tsp. olive oil
¼ tsp. salt; ⅛ tsp. paprika, to taste

Place the broth, cilantro, basil, garlic, edamame and remaining ingredients in a food processor. Pulse, until coarsely chopped or desired consistency.

Fresh Basil Pesto

Nutritious and delicious- made with
walnuts, pinenuts or part almonds

2 cups fresh basil leaves,
firmly packed
½ cup pine nuts, walnuts,
and/or toasted almonds
3 large cloves garlic,
minced
½ tsp. sea salt, to taste
1-2 Tbs. pure olive oil,
to desired
consistency
⅛ tsp. lemon
juice, opt.

Place nuts, garlic, basil, and
salt in a food processor or
blender. Cover and process
until finely chopped. Add olive oil and
lemon, if desired, and process until almost
smooth,
stopping
and scraping
sides as
necessary.
Color of pesto
will darken as
it stands. Use
immediately,
or store in a covered
container, in the refrigerator 3-4 days,
or freeze 1-3 months.

Spinach Pesto

Substitute **1½ cups fresh**
packed spinach for
part of basil; add
1 tsp. dried basil.

Sun-Dried Tomato Pesto

This rich pesto is full of flavor, and color- delicious on warm pasta, rice, vegetables, or as a sandwich spread or filling. A little goes a long way!

1 cup dried tomatoes*
½ cup pine nuts
3 cloves garlic, minced
1-2 Tbs. extra-virgin olive oil
¼ tsp. fresh lemon juice
pinch of sea salt, to taste

Process together in a food processor until smooth, stopping to scrape sides as needed. Good tossed with pasta, salad, on pizza, or as a spread for wraps. Store short term in refrigerator, or freeze 1-3 months.

*Home-dried or oil packed dried tomatoes. If home-dried, cut and re-hydrate in small amount of water.

Tomato Pesto Mayonnaise

Delicious mixed into potato or pasta salad, or use as sandwich spread or filling for wraps

⅓ cup light mayonnaise
2-3 Tbs. Tomato or Basil Pesto
⅛ tsp. sea salt
pinch of cayenne, opt.

Stir and combine ingredients together in a small bowl. Yield: ½ cup; erving size: 1 Tbs.

Tofu Sour Cream

*Replacement for sour cream
on baked potatoes, veggie haystacks, etc.*

½ cup cashews or blanched almonds
½ cup pure hot water
1½ tsp. onion powder
¾ tsp. sea salt, to taste
¼ tsp. garlic salt, opt.
10 oz. silken Tofu, extra-firm
3-4 Tbs. fresh lemon juice

Blend nuts, hot water, and seasonings until smooth. Add Tofu and lemon juice. Blend until creamy smooth. Pour into a bowl or jar; refrigerate to chill and set.

Note: Cooked, creamy brown rice may substitute for part of nuts

Pimento Sour Cream Topping

½ cup cashew mayonnaise
or Tofu Sour Cream
1-2oz. jar diced pimento or 1 oven roasted pimento
1 clove garlic, minced
1 Tbs. minced parsley, opt.

Stir all ingredients together or blend until smooth. Add **1 Tbs. minced parsley**. This simple tasty topping pairs well with stuffed pita, veggie wraps, or haystacks.

Soy Sour Cream

Try the variations of this simple sour cream to serve as a fruit or vegetable dip or topping

¾ cup Soybean milk #1
or ½ cup soy starter + ½ cup water
1-2 Tbs. soy oil, opt.
1 tsp. honey, to taste
¼ tsp. sea salt, scant
1 tsp. agar flakes or Kojel®, plain
2 Tbs. lemon juice

Pour the milk into blender, or use soy starter with ¼ cup of the water. Blend. Gradually add the oil, (opt. for a richer texture), the honey and salt. Boil remaining ¼ cup water; add the agar, stir to dissolve. Pour into blender, whiz to combine. Add the lemon juice, blend briefly (on and off). Chill to set.

Sour Cream Fruit Dip: add **¼ crushed pineapple** or **fruit preserves + ⅛ tsp. cinnamon substitute.** Serve with **apple, pear,** or **peach slices**, or use as a topping for fruit salad.

Sour Cream Veggie Dip: add **2 Tbs. snipped fresh dill** or **2 tsp. dried dill + 2 Tbs. finely chopped green onion + ¼ tsp. seasoned salt.** Serve with c**elery, carrot** and **zucchini sticks, broccoli, cauliflower florets, radishes, mushrooms,** and **red, green, orange pepper strips.**

Guacamole

A ripe avocado topping, rich in unsaturated fats, vitamin E, B6, and protein.

See recipe-**Salad Dressings & Dips, p.436**

Sweet Creams & Toppings

Cashew Soy Whipped Cream

¼ cup cashew nuts
½ cup soy milk
8 oz. silken tofu
2 Tbs. fructose or honey, to taste
½ tsp. pure vanilla (preferably clear)
pinch of sea salt
½ cup water, boiling
1 tsp. agar flakes or Kojel®
¼ tsp. lemon juice

Blend the cashews and soymilk until smooth. Blend in tofu, sweetening, vanilla   and salt. Dissolve agar in the boiling water; add and blend. Last add lemon, blend briefly. Pour into container. Chill. If desired, stir or whip before serving.

Note: Use pure vanilla powder or clear vanilla for a whiter cream.

Cream Variations

Orange Cream: Omit vanilla, add **1 Tbs. frozen orange concentrate** and **½ tsp. orange or lemon zest.**

Strawberry/ Raspberry Cream: Omit vanilla; stir in **¼ cup fresh berries** or **fresh fruit jam**; sweeten to taste.

Apricot Cream: Add **¼ cup apricot purée** or **chopped fresh apricots.**

Carob Cream: Omit agar and lemon; add **2 Tbs. carob powder**, and **honey.**

Coconut Cream: Replace the cashews, soy milk, and half the water with **1 cup coconut milk.** Omit the lemon juice.

Cashew Nut Cream

A simple delicious topping
to pour over hot cereal or fruit.

½ cup raw cashews
1 cup water or soy milk
1 Tbs. honey or 3 dates
⅛ - ¼ tsp. pure vanilla
⅛ tsp. orange or lemon zest
pinch of sea salt

Blend all together in blender till very smooth (about 2 minutes). May need a little more water when using dates. Delicious on brown rice, rye flakes, millet, buckwheat, and baked apples.

Note: For a thicker cream, reduce liquid to ½ cup and/or use **creamy coconut or soy milk**

Almond Cream

Follow recipe above using blanched almonds. Add the vanilla and replace orange zest with **pure almond flavoring**. Use **dates** (preferably) to sweeten.

Tofu Vanilla Crème

A simple and versatile topping - quick and easy to prepare.

½ cup soy milk
3 Tbs. cashew halves
½ tsp. white (clear) vanilla
2-3 Tbs. fructose or honey
⅛ tsp. sea salt
12 oz. silken tofu, x-firm

Blend cashews and milk till very smooth. Add vanilla, sweetening, salt, and tofu. Blend again. Chill and serve with fruit, or as topping.

Lemon Sauce

1 cup pure cold water
1½ Tbs. arrowroot powder
pinch of sea salt

Blend first three ingredients. Stir and simmer, over low heat, until thick and clear; remove from heat, add:

3 Tbs. lemon juice
3 Tbs. light honey
2 tsp. lemon zest

Good on brown rice pudding, brownies, cakes, fruit dishes, etc. If thicker sauce is desired, increase arrowroot to 2 Tbs.

Creamy Lemon Fruit Topping

Follow recipe for **Lemon Sauce** with the following changes: Use **1 cup pineapple juice**, instead of water; Add **1 (12 oz) package silken tofu, firm.** Process in blender until smooth and creamy. Use as a fruit dip, dessert topping or between layers of fruit in a tall parfait glass.

Peanut Coconut Cream

½ cup creamy coconut milk
2 Tbs. light peanut butter
⅛ tsp. pure vanilla
1 tsp. honey, to taste, opt.

Blend until creamy smooth . Add honey or dates to sweeten, if desired. Tasty on brown rice, rye flakes, quinoa, millet, and buckwheat.

Soy Whip Cream Topping

1½ cups soymilk, vanilla
1 tsp. agar powder or 2 tsp. flakes
2 Tbs. light honey
1 tsp. white or pure vanilla
¼ tsp. lecithin granules, opt.
¼ tsp. fresh lemon juice

Put soymilk and agar in a saucepan. Slowly bring to a simmer, stirring to dissolve agar. Pour into blender. Add honey, vanilla, lecithin and dash of salt, if desired. Blend to combine. Stir in lemon juice. Pour in container. Chill or lightly freeze to set. Re-whip.

Soy Whip Cream Variations

• Use **4 soft dates** instead of honey.

• In place of vanilla add **½ tsp. orange or lemon zest.**

• **Mint cream** - omit vanilla, add **1-2 drops of mint extract** and a **slice of avocado.**

Orange Sauce

A simple sauce with multiple uses. Add slices of peaches, bananas, or pineapple chunks. Serve over French toast, waffles, crepes or pancakes.

1 cup orange juice
1 Tbs. honey
1 Tbs. arrowroot
½ tsp. orange zest

In a small saucepan stir all ingredients together. Cook and stir over medium heat until thickened and bubbly.

Minted Honey

½ cup fresh mint, finely chopped
½ cup light uncooked honey

Mix together; put in a jar in warm sunlight. Honey will draw out delicious mint flavor. Ready to use in 1-2 days. Strain if desired. This stores well in pantry. Optional: Add a little lemon juice, to taste, to the portion being used. Mix well. Drizzle this simple topping on strawberries, avocado or fruit salad.

Carob Mint Sauce

Follow recipe for **Carob Peanut Butter Frosting (see Desserts).** Replace 3 Tbs. thick soy milk with **⅓ cup soy milk or cream + 1-2 drops mint extract.** Blend until smooth. For **Hot Carob Mint Sauce:** Pour into double boiler and heat on stovetop.

Caramel Sauce

¾ cup sucanat
¼ cup barley malt, rice syrup or molasses
¾ cup Silk Creamer®
1½ Tbs. all-purpose flour
2 Tbs. Earth Balance® soy spread
1 tsp. pure vanilla

Blend all ingredients together until smooth. Bring to a low simmer, stirring constantly until thickened. Pour into jar. Refrigerate. Use as topping for desserts.

Carob Fudge Syrup

Have a jar of syrup made ahead to add to hot or cold carob milk drinks, pies or frozen desserts.

⅔ cup soymilk or coconut milk
¼ cup carob powder
⅓ cup chopped dates or sucanat
1 Tbs. molasses or malt syrup
pinch of sea salt
1 tsp. pure vanilla

Combine first 4 ingredients in saucepan, heat and stir until bubbly. Add salt and vanilla. Blend until smooth, adjusting liquid to desired consistency. Use as needed or refrigerate up to 2 weeks.

Note: For ice cream sandwich coating, add 1 Tbs. cold pressed coconut oil while blending.

Carob Date Sauce

A rich topping for fruit bars, cakes, or fresh fruit platter.

½ cup creamy soy or nut milk
⅓ cup chopped pitted dates
¼ cup lightly toasted cashew
    or peanut butter
2 Tbs. carob powder
½ tsp. pure vanilla

Blend all ingredients until combined and very smooth, adjusting soy milk as needed for desired consistency. Store in refrigerator.

Blueberry Sauce or Topping

3 cups fresh or frozen blueberries
½ cup grape juice
  or frozen juice concentrate
⅓ cup water + 1 Tbs. arrowroot
½ tsp. lemon juice or ¼ tsp. zest

In a blender combine 1 cup blueberries with the grape juice or concentrate. Process briefly until almost smooth. Place water and thickening (arrowroot or flour) in a saucepan over medium heat. Gradually whisk in the blueberry mixture. Bring to a boil, stirring until thickened. Remove from heat, add remaining blueberries, lemon juice and sweetening if desired. Refrigerate.

Strawberry Topping

Replace blueberries with 4 cups strawberries. Use **white grape frozen juice concentrate.** Reduce water to ¼ cup.

Sesame Seed Sauce

½ cup plain or minted honey
½ cup toasted sesame seeds, ground
4-5 Tbs. lemon or pineapple juice
1 Tbs. shredded coconut, opt.
dash of sea salt

Warm honey. Add rest of ingredients. Stir and mix together. Good topping on fruit, salads, or vegetables. Refrigerate.

Fruit Juice Topping

¼ cup orange juice concentrate
¼ cup cashew butter or tahini
¼ cup pineapple juice
juice of 1 fresh lemon
1 tsp. Instant Clear Jel®, opt.
½ tsp. orange zest, honey to taste

Put all ingredients except Clear-Jel in a blender and blend until smooth. For thicker topping, sprinkle in Clear-Jel while blending. Chill and serve on **French toast** or **waffles.**

Our Kitchen Prayer

Please bless and use this kitchen, Lord
Let every meal I make
Build healthy bodies, loving hearts
In all who will partake.
I thank Thee for this house, our home,
So dear in every nook,
For here I've partnership with Thee
The food You make, I cook.

This door will see the fond farewells
As dear ones start the day.
And may each one who passes through
Return again, I pray.
And let each one who enters here
Find warmth and food and love
And go forth knowing that they have
Thy smile from heaven above.
Amen

Chapter 16
Soups & Stews

Index - CHAPTER 16

Soups & Stews

488

Ten Talents

Cooking – a Science

*"Cooking is no mean (an important) science, and it is one of the **most essential** in practical life...To make food appetizing and at the same time simple and nourishing, requires skill; but it can be done. Cooks should know how to prepare simple food in a simple and healthful manner, and so that it will be found more palatable, as well as more wholesome, because of its simplicity.*

Every woman who is at the head of a family and yet does not understand the art of healthful cookery should determine to learn that which is so essential to the well-being of her household. In many places cooking schools afford opportunity for instruction in this line. She who has not the help of such facilities should put herself under the instruction of some good cook, and persevere in her efforts for improvement until she is mistress of the culinary art." E. G. White, Diet & Foods, pp 257-258

Chapter Cover Photo: *Luscious Lentil Soup, p. 501; Garden Veggie Wrap, p. 465; Classic Green Salad, p. 422*

Savory Soups & Stews

Nothing is as satisfying on a cold day as a steaming bowl of soup and crusty bread. Soups can be main-course hearty, creamy, or mild and clear as broth, for a light beginning to a meal.

Stews on the other hand, tend to be chunky combinations of beans, rice or pasta and vegetables, or a flavored medley of vegetables alone. Many soups can be made-ahead from leftovers of a large recipe, simply frozen for later use.

Keep homemade vegetable broths on hand to make quick soups. Cook pasta or rice in simmering broth, add bite-size pieces of fresh or frozen vegetables, cooked beans, strips of seaweed, or cubes of tofu, and heat.

In this chapter you'll find a wide selection of soups and stews that will stick-to-your-ribs and satisfy just about every appetite and occasion.

Hearty Soups to Warm the Family

Clockwise from bottom left: Fresh Celery Soup, Sprouted Lentil Cream Soup, Soya Bread or Rolls, Fresh Green Pea Soup, Red Bean Soup, Cream of Tomato Soup, Yellow Corn Soup, Navy Bean Soup. Center: Alfalfa Sprouts.

Raw Soups

Peoples' tastes vary as much as their differences in disposition. This is known by the fact that Eskimos enjoy eating cooked bear feet; the Chinese enjoy overripe eggs and frog legs; the Russians love caviar; and Americans - eat everything! We can change our taste buds by educating them. The thought of raw soup may not make you feel hungry, but with skillful combining and seasoning, those who are careful to preserve health as well as the vital elements in wholesome natural food, will enjoy these savory soups.

Helpful Hints

1. If frozen foods are used, thaw in hot water before blending. When blending, be sure the water used is HOT.
2. Blend puréed soups until smooth. If your blender does not completely purée the vegetables, they may be put through a sieve or food strainer before warming.
3. When using raw nuts or seeds, blend them first, until smooth, before adding the rest of ingredients.
4. For seasoning, a variety of herbs may be used with sea salt (plain or vegetable), sea kelp or dulse, vegetable protein powder, unfermented soy sauce or liquid aminos.
5. Heat the soup thoroughly but do not boil. Stir soup while warming on stovetop or warm in a double boiler over hot water. Serve immediately in warm soup plates. (to warm plates - set in HOT water)
6. Cold soups are easy to make and great for summer; try **Gazpacho** or **Cucumber Soup**.
7. Be gracious and tactful when serving new foods; in rare occasions "Silence is Golden".

How To Thicken Soups

For raw soups, nuts do a fine job. When they are not used, try thickening soup like the European peasants often do, by soaking whole grain bread, toast, or zwieback in the broth and mashing it with a fork.

For soups that are cooked, Arrowroot Powder (*from the tuberous rootstocks of a tropical American plant* -see **Glossary of Foods**) browned flour, alphabet macaroni, and in some cases, agar flakes, may be used to thicken soup. The use of refined cornstarch, lacks nutrients and when used frequently, has a tendency to coat the intestines with a fine pasty substance, that may add to constipation and other problems. When thickening soups and stews with flour, or arrowroot, keep lumps from forming by mixing flour with a small amount of cold water or broth, before adding to the hot liquid you want to thicken.

Another way to thicken soup is to puree some of the cooked vegetables from the recipe with a little of the soup stock or liquid, then stir the thick puree back into the soup.

Fresh Green Pea Soup

Blend until smooth:

**2 cups pure hot
 water**
1 cup cashew nuts
1 Tbs. onion powder
1 tsp. sea salt
¼ tsp. celery seed
1 Tbs. olive oil
**dash of garlic, dill,
 thyme, opt.**

Pour into soup pan then blend & add:

1 lb. fresh or frozen peas
3 cups very hot water
 (adjust to desired consistency)

Heat thoroughly. Serve with **zwieback**, your favorite spread and **alfalfa sprouts**.

Cream of Tomato Soup

Blend until smooth:

1 cup cashew nuts
3 cups pure water
**2 Tbs. arrowroot
 (or thicken with
 bread when serving)**
1 Tbs. onion powder
½ tsp. sea salt, to taste
1 tsp. sweet basil
¼ tsp. oregano
1 Tbs. honey
1 Tbs. olive oil, opt.

Add:

**1 quart tomato puree
or solid pack tomatoes**

Blend again. Pour into soup kettle, bring to just under boil, but do not boil. Adjust seasoning, depending on tomatoes. Delicious served with crisp **alfalfa sprouts**.

Fresh Asparagus Soup

Blend together:

1 cup pure hot water
½ cup cashew nuts

Add and blend:

2 cups fresh raw asparagus
   or 1-16 oz. pkg. frozen asparagus
2 cups hot water or chicken-style broth
2 stalks of celery with tops
2 Tbs. minced parsley
1 Tbs. onion powder
1 tsp. sea salt, to taste
1 tsp. olive oil
pinch of thyme

Heat thoroughly but do not boil. Serve with toast cubes.

Yellow Corn Soup

Blend until smooth:

2 cups pure hot water
1 cup cashew nuts
   or blanched almonds
1½ Tbs. onion powder
1 tsp. sea salt, to taste
½ tsp. celery seed; ¼ tsp. garlic powder
⅛ tsp. cayenne or paprika, opt.

Add and blend:
3 cups tender corn, cut off cob
   or frozen corn
3 cups pure hot water,
   (adjust to desired consistency)
1 tsp. olive oil, opt.

Heat thoroughly. Garnish with **fresh chopped parsley**.

Seed Soup

1 cup seeds (from raw or baked
   squash or pumpkin)
1½ cups pure hot water or nut milk
1 Tbs. peanut butter
Chicken-style Seasoning
   or sea salt, to taste

Blend until very smooth and creamy. Strain. Add chopped **parsley, water-cress**, or **chives**. Dilute with more milk to desired consistency. Adjust seasonings. Blend briefly. Heat and serve with your favorite soup crackers or **zwieback**.

Variation: **½ cup tender fresh peas** or **fresh corn kernels** may be added.

Fresh Celery Soup

Blend until smooth; heat in kettle on stovetop:

1 cup hot water or plain soy milk
½ cup cashew nuts
1 small onion or 1Tbs. onion powder
1 tsp. sea salt + ½ tsp. celery seed
1½ cups fresh cut celery, lightly steamed
1 handful fresh celery tops

Blend, then add to above hot mixture:

½ cup pure water or more
½ Tbs. arrowroot powder, opt.
1 Tbs. olive oil, opt.

Stir until thickened and bubbly (just to boiling). Garnish with more **chopped celery leaves**. Serve with crackers or **bread sticks**.

Favorite Soups

1. Fresh Green Pea Soup, pg 491; 2. Veggie Broth, pg. 500; 3. Nine Bean & Barley Soup, pg. 510; 4. Best Barley Soup, pg. 497;
5. Potato Asparagus Leek Soup, pg. 511, 6. Lentil & Fennel Stew, pg. 503; 7. Escarole Garbanzo Noodle Soup, pg. 512;
8. Italian Minestone, pg. 505; 9. German Potato Soup, pg. 507; 10. Pumpkin Soup, pg. 508, 11. Borscht, pg. 509, 12. Cream of Broccoli Soup, pg. 499

ingredients, stir to combine, add sea salt to taste. Cover and chill before serving (1 hour or more). A great soup for a hot summer day! Serve with croutons, or avocado on toast. Yield: 6 servings.

* Bragg Liquid Aminos (1 Tbs.+ 1 cup water) may substitute for broth.

Cold Cucumber Soup

Cold soup? Pick some garden fresh cucumbers and try this on a hot summer day.

Follow recipe above for Fresh Celery Soup. Omit the arrowroot, celery seed, top leaves, and ½ of the celery. Add and blend in:

**2-3 cups cut garden cucumbers
    (skins may be left on)
1 clove fresh garlic, opt.
½ tsp. dill seed**

Serve soup cold or hot with your favorite zwieback or rolls. Garnish with **fresh dill weed** or **parsley**, if desired.

Gazpacho

A spicy cold summer soup, made from chopped raw vegetables, that is sure to refresh. Make-ahead in the morning, chill and serve during the heat of day.

**3 cups chopped tomatoes, fresh or canned
3 cups tomato or vegetable juice
    or part *broth
2-3 cloves garlic, chopped
2 Tbs. lemon or lime juice
1 Tbs. dried crushed basil
    or ¼ cup fresh chopped
¼ tsp. cumin and, or sprinkle of cayenne
1 ½ cups chopped cucumber
1 cup finely chopped green sweet pepper
½ cup finely chopped sweet onion
¼ cup finely chopped parsley,
    watercress or cilantro**

Place the chopped tomatoes in a large bowl. Blend the tomato juice, garlic, lemon or lime and seasonings until smooth. Pour into bowl, add remaining

Simple Tortilla Soup

In a hurry? Not sure what to make with those few garden veggies on hand? Use your own imagination and ingredients to create a speedy blender soup.

**Pure hot water or broth
Carrot, raw cut or shredded
Cabbage, sliced or shredded
Zucchini squash, sliced raw
Sweet bell pepper
Peas, fresh or frozen
Green onion with tops, cut
Tomatoes, ripe, chopped
Seasonings (fresh dill weed, watercress,
    fennel tops, sea salt, garlic,
    onion powder, cayenne, cumin)
Corn, canned, fresh or frozen
Black beans, canned or cooked
Tortilla chips**

Pour 1 cup hot water or broth in blender. Add the first 7 vegetables (your choice) and the seasonings. Blend until smooth. Add the corn, black beans and handful of Tortilla Chips. Blend to chunky consistency; add hot water or broth as needed. Serve soup warm. Enjoy!

Cooked Soups

Crock Pot Soups

When making hearty soups and stews, sort and rinse beans, soak with pure water for several hours until plump or *pre-cook* (depending on size and age of beans). Place beans in crock pot or slow-cooker. Cook on medium to low heat until almost tender. Add vegetables - your choice (carrots, celery, onions, tomatoes) and seasonings (garlic, onion, fennel, cumin, sea salt, etc). Cook until tender and flavors are blended.

* Dry beans cook more slowly in a crockery cooker than on the stovetop, therefore the beans should be *pre-cooked* for at least 15 minutes. Soaking is not sufficient for beans to cook to tender.

Pasta and rice will be at their best if you cook them first, then add them to the cooked soup or stew just before serving. Enjoy! On the next page you will find a few bean soup combinations to try:

9 Bean and Barley Soup - See Recipe on page 510

Calico Bean Soup Mix

**Pinto Beans, Small Red Beans,
Small White Navy Beans,
Pink Beans, Baby Lima Beans**

Light Soup Mix

**Green Split Peas, Yellow Split Peas,
Pearl Barley, Whole Green Peas,
Whole Yellow Peas, Red Lentils,
Lentils, Basmati Rice**

Chili Four Bean Mix

**Black Turtle Beans, Small Red Beans
Pinto Beans, Light Red Kidney Beans**

9 Bean & Barley Soup Mix

**Black-Eyed Peas, Small Red Beans,
White Navy Beans, Lentils, Black Beans,
Green Split Peas, Yellow Split Peas,
Pinto Beans, Kidney Beans and Barley**

Preparing Beans

Carefully sort beans to remove any stones, pebbles, grit or discolored beans. Spread out on clean tray and inspect before washing and tossing into soup pot. Cover beans with water, rise and drain in colander before using.

(See Bean Basics in chapter Meatless Main Dishes for soaking tips and additional information)

Sprouted Lentil Soup

1. Sprout ½ cup **lentils** to ½" long. (see **Sprouting** chapter)

2. Tenderize sprouts in skillet with a little **oil, lemon, soy sauce** or **Bragg's Aminos** and **onion powder**.

3. Make a thin **Cashew Cream Sauce** (gravy) and heat to thicken (bring up to boil).

4. Add tenderized sprouts to cashew sauce, stir to combine; serve in warm soup bowls.

Best Barley Soup

This simple colorful and attractive soup is a favorite at our cooking classes. A good stand-by for the family on those cold winter days or anytime. Make a double batch and enjoy!

¼ cup whole barley
1 cup sliced carrots
½ cup diced celery
¼ cup chopped onions
2-3 cloves fresh garlic, minced
2 cups tomatoes, canned or fresh
1 cup peas, frozen
    or fresh
sea salt, to taste
¼ cup minced fresh parsley

Cook barley one hour in 6 cups pure water. Add remaining ingredients and simmer until tender. Add peas last, and parsley just before serving. Drizzle with extra virgin **olive oil**, if desired. Good served with **Barley Burgers** and **Buns** and **Soya Yeast Sandwich Spread**.

Barley Broth

2 qts. pure water, boiling
½ cup whole barley
1½ cups chopped celery
½ cup cut green beans
½ cup chopped cabbage or onion
½ cup green peas + pods, opt.
1 cup tomato puree
1 tsp. vegex or sea salt
chopped parsley, optional

Simmer vegetables and barley in water until tender. Run through a sieve or strainer. Add tomato puree, seasoning or salt. Garnish with **chopped parsley** before serving.

Cream of Cauliflower Soup

Steam **1 head cauliflower** (about 2 pounds), separated into flowerets until tender. Reserve 1 cup of cooked cauliflower flowerets. Blend remaining cauliflower with first 7 ingredients as directed in **Cream of Celery Soup** (use half the amount of celery and carrots, or omit entirely). For the last seasoning, add **1 Tbs. lemon juice, and a sprinkle of celery seed**. Stir in the remaining 1 cup cooked cauliflower (tiny flowerets); adjust seasoning to taste. Garnish with **fresh chopped parsley** before serving.

Split Pea Soup

1 lb. (2¼ cups) split peas
2 Tbs. pearl barley
2 carrots, sliced or diced
2 stalks celery, diced
1 onion, chopped
1 tsp. sea salt, veggie
   or celery salt, to taste
2 cloves garlic, minced
pinch of red bell pepper flakes
   or cayenne, opt.
2-3 bay leaves

Cover the split peas with 3" pure water. Add the rest of ingredients. Simmer until tender and creamy, stir often. Last, add **½ Tbs. olive oil, opt.** Put through sieve for smooth soup or serve chunky with garlic toast or zwieback.

Eggplant Tomato Soup
(rich in potassium and iron, low in fat)

1 large eggplant, fully ripe
2 cups pure water
2 Tbs. barley, millet, or rice
1 qt. chopped tomatoes
1 Tbs. onion powder
2 cloves minced garlic or ¼ tsp. powder
½ tsp. sweet basil
2 bay leaves or ½ tsp. oregano
1 Tbs. molasses
sea salt, olive oil, to taste

Bake whole eggplant until tender when tested with a fork. Peel and cut in cubes. While eggplant is baking, simmer water and grain in a soup kettle on stovetop. Blend rest of ingredients, pour into soup simmer until grain is tender. Add cooked eggplant. Season with **sea salt** and drizzle with **olive oil**, if desired. Serve hot.

Note: To shorten cooking time, **½ cup cooked grain (millet, brown rice or barley)** may be added just before serving. In this case simmer blended ingredients only 10 minutes. Add cooked eggplant, grain, and sea salt oil to taste.

Almond Cream Bouillon

1 qt. almond milk, plain - see recipe
½ cup toasted wheat germ flakes
1 tsp. onion powder
½ tsp. vegetable salt, to taste

Blend till smooth. Add 1 cup diced avocado (firm, but fully ripe). Good served with a bowl of seasoned popcorn, toast or zwieback.

Mushroom Bouillon

1 cup chopped mushroom
¼ cup finely chopped onions
1 tsp. virgin olive oil
2 cups pure water
1 tsp. Vegex or liquid aminos

Sauté mushrooms and onion in oil. Add water and Vegex. Simmer 3-5 minutes.

Cream of Broccoli Soup

Steam until just tender:

**1 head fresh or frozen broccoli, chopped,
(about 4 cups)**

Reserve **1 cup of cooked broccoli.**
Blend remaining broccoli with first 7
ingredients as directed in **Celery Soup**

(use half the amount of celery and
carrots, or omit entirely). For the last
seasoning, add **¼ tsp. garlic powder**
and **½ tsp. grated lemon zest or a
sprinkle of cayenne, if desired**. Blend
well. Stir in reserved cooked broccoli;
adjust seasonings to taste. Good
served with toasted garlic bread and a
fresh green salad.

Cream of Celery Soup

**2 cups pure water with ½ cup cashews
    or 2 cups plain soy, almond or rice milk
2 cups Veggie Broth or Chicken-style broth
2 Tbs. arrowroot or 2 Tbs. browned flour
1 Tbs. onion powder
    or 3 shallots, peeled, sliced
1 tsp. vegetable salt, to taste
2 ½ cups chopped celery, steamed
½ cup diced carrots, cooked**

Blend the above ingredients together.
Stir over low heat to boiling, until
thickened. Then add:

**½ cup celery tops, chopped
½ tsp. ground fennel or dill seed**

Serve warm with seasoned croutons,
toast stars or zwieback.

*Note: A sprinkle of celery seed or powder may
be added. These tiny seeds from a wild variety
of celery called lovage, resemble that of garden
celery, but with a hint of bitterness. Use sparingly,
for these tiny seeds have a surprisingly big flavor.*

Cream of Mushroom Soup

**8 oz. fresh mushrooms (button,
    cremini, shiitake)
    or one 8 oz. can mushrooms,
    sliced or pieces, in water
1 recipe Cashew Milk Gravy**

Clean and slice fresh mushrooms; sauté
in **1 tsp. oil or water** (mushrooms
will give off liquid while cooking). A
**sprinkle of dried herbs such as sweet
basil** may be added; cook mushrooms
until tender. Set mushrooms aside (no
need to cook canned mushrooms).
Make 1 recipe of **Cashew Milk Gravy
(Creamy Basic White Sauce)** in blender.
Blend until very smooth; add half the
mushrooms and liquid and blend to
chunky consistency. Heat in saucepan
over medium heat, stirring constantly
until soup comes to a boil. Add rest of
mushrooms; adjusting liquid to desired
consistency. Yield: 4 servings

Golden Bouillon

1½ qts. (6 cups) pure water
1 cup diced carrots
1 cup diced potatoes
1 cup diced celery with tops
1 cup chopped onions
1 tsp. sea salt or kelp, to taste
1 cup squash puree
1 Tbs. almond or cashew nut butter
fresh parsley, optional

Simmer carrots, potatoes, celery, cabbage and onions in water until tender with sea salt. Strain. Pour broth into blender; add squash and rest of ingredients. Blend until smooth. Garnish with **fresh parsley**, if desired. Serve with **Bread Sticks** or **Sesame Crackers**.

Vegetable Broth #1

2 qts. (8 cups) pure water or more
2 cups sliced potatoes, with skins
1 onion, thinly sliced
2 cups thinly sliced carrots
2 cups thinly sliced parsnips
outer leaves of cabbage & lettuce, cut
½ cup fennel tops, opt.
1 tsp. pure olive oil, opt.

Wash the vegetables, discarding the damaged parts. Slice and put into a large saucepan. Add water. Bring to a boil; simmer 2 hours, then semi-blend or strain. Add **salt** or **vegex** to taste. Garnish

with **chopped fresh parsley,** if desired.

Variation: Return broth to kettle, add **1 Tbs. alphabets**, cook 5-8 minutes.

Soup Stock -Veggie Broth

You can dispense with the salty beef-flavored bouillon soup cubes, by making your own full-flavored, soup stock at home out of the snippets and trimmings from vegetables: **celery, onions, carrots, pea pods, the stems of parsley, spinach, kale and collard greens, outer leaves of artichokes, escarole, and other leafy vegetables, tips of green beans, potato peelings** and **squash, etc.** Homemade stocks create an ideal base of flavor for soups and stews as well as for a variety of other recipes. Wash the vegetable trimmings and store them in a plastic bag or jar, in the refrigerator. When you have collected 1-2 quarts, place them in a saucepan, cover with pure cold water, 2-3 cloves of minced garlic, and a little sea salt to release flavors. Cover and bring to a boil. Simmer on low heat for 25-30 minutes until vegetables are cooked. Strain while hot, into a glass jar. Seal and refrigerate. The resulting vitamin and mineral rich stock is ready-to-use and perfect for soups, sauces, cooking rice, and other grains for pilaf.

Vegetable Broth #2

4 cups pure water
1 cup diced carrots
1 cup diced celery with leaves
2 cups green pea pods
½ cup diced potatoes
½ cup turnips, cut fine
½ cup onion, cut fine
odd stalks of asparagus

Simmer vegetables in water until tender. Put vegetables through sieve to remove coarse fibers. Add a little **vegex** or **liquid aminos** and **chopped parsley.**

Note: Broth may be used as a base for other soups.

Luscious Lentil Soup

This hearty Italian-style soup was a standby when I was growing up. A rich source of B vitamins, iron, fiber, and other nutrients. It's colorful as well as delicious!

1 lb. bag lentils, dry
2 fresh carrots, cut in circles or diced
3 stalks celery, sliced or diced
1 medium onion, cut in rings or diced
3 cloves garlic, minced
1 cup stewed or chopped tomatoes in juice
1-2 tsp. virgin olive oil
sea salt, to taste

Sort and rinse lentils, cover with 4" water. Soak 1-2 hours. Start cooking lentils on med-low heat; add carrots, celery, onion, and fresh minced garlic. Simmer all together until tender (about 1½ hours), adding the tomatoes and a little salt during end of cooking. Last add olive oil and adjust salt to taste. Soup is thick; may be thinned if desired.

Note: For extra nutrition, variety and color, add tender leaves of fresh spinach during last 5 minutes of cooking, or make a small cavity in center of bowl of soup and fill with tenderized steamed spinach. Serve with garlic toast, wraps, rolls, or zwieback.

Rainbow Vegetable Soup

Green beans, fresh or frozen
Cabbage, shredded
Carrots, sliced or cubed
Celery, diced
Onions, small pearl
Red kidney beans, cooked
**   or frozen green limas**

In a large saucepan, barely tenderize vegetables in a small amount of boiling water and sea salt, reserving liquid. Blend a thin cream sauce with cashew nuts, water, arrowroot, onion powder, and salt; add to vegetables. Simmer a few minutes to blend flavors. Season lightly with fresh or dried herbs to taste; adjust liquid to desired soup consistency. Just before serving, garnish with **fresh chopped parsley** or **alfalfa sprouts**.

Broccoli with Beans and Spaghetti

(Hearty - Delicious Stew)

½ lb. northern dry beans
1 large onion,
    sliced or chopped
1 large tomato, chopped
4 cloves garlic, minced
1½ qts. pure water, boiling
2 lb. fresh or frozen
    broccoli, chopped
½ lb. buckwheat
    or soy spaghetti, 1" pcs
1 Tbs. Chicken-style
    Seasoning, to taste
½ tsp. sea salt
dash of cayenne, to taste

Sort, and rinse beans; place in a large saucepan, cover beans with 2" of water. Soak several hours until plump; bring to boiling; simmer uncovered 15-20 minutes. Remove from heat, cover, let stand 1 hour, then drain beans. In a 4 qt. saucepan combine beans, onion, tomato, garlic and 1½ qts. boiling water. Cover and simmer until beans are tender. Add the broccoli, spaghetti and seasoning; cook until tender and flavors blended. Adjust liquid as needed. Drizzle on **olive oil** if desired. Servings: 6

**"Avoid the use of
too much salt."**

E.G. White, **Diet and Foods**
pages 311, 340

Red Bean Soup

1 lb. dry kidney beans
2 stalks celery, chopped
1 Tbs. onion powder
pinch of garlic powder
2-3 bay leaves
sea salt, to taste

Rinse and soak beans for several hours. Add celery, onion, garlic and bay leaves; cover with 2" water. Cook on stovetop until tender, or pressure cook beans for 20 minutes. Season with salt, and lightly drizzle on **olive oil** to taste, if desired.

Garden Vegetable Soup

4 qts. pure water, approx.
3 potatoes, cubed
1 cup baby carrots or 3 carrots, sliced
3 stalks celery, diced or fennel with tops
2 parsnips, cut in slices
2 cups shredded cabbage
1 large onion, diced
3 cups peas, frozen
½ cup parsley, minced
sea salt or Chicken Style Seasoning, to taste

In a large saucepan or soup pot, sauté onion in 1 Tbs. olive oil until tender. Add rest of ingredients except peas and parsley. Bring to a boil; simmer until vegetables are tender (avoid overcooking). Add peas during last 5 minutes of cooking; add parsley just before serving.

Lentil and Fennel Stew

Plant some sweet fennel in your garden and use the lacey tops for soups and stews; adds a wonderful flavor. Fennel tops may be chopped and frozen or dried for later use.

Into a 4 quart kettle put:
1 lb. dried lentils
3 small green onions with tops
2 cups fresh fennel tops, chopped fine
2 cloves fresh minced garlic
1 carrot, thinly sliced, optional
1 tsp. sea salt, to taste

Sort lentils to remove any stones or debris then rinse. Cover with pure water 2-3" above lentils; let soak for 1 hour. Add rest of ingredients; simmer on low until tender (about 1 hour). When done, drizzle on a little **olive oil** to taste. Garnish with **fresh parsley** and **zwieback soup stars**, if desired.

Giant Lima Bean Soup

1 lb. lima beans, dry
3 qts. pure water
4 cups chopped celery with tops
½ cup chopped onion or 1 Tbs. powder
1 cup tomatoes, fresh or canned
1 Tbs. pure olive oil, opt.
1 ½ tsp. sea salt, to taste

Soak lima beans in soup kettle with water 4-5 hours. Add celery and onion. Bring to a boil and simmer until almost tender (or pressure cook for 20 minutes). Add the tomatoes and salt; simmer until tender. Add more water if desired and season with olive oil. Serve with garlic toast or hearty bread.

Note: If using a pressure cooker-soak beans with celery, onion and tomato. Cook together; last add olive oil and salt to taste.

Navy Bean Soup

1 lb. navy beans, rinsed
3 qts. pure water
4 stalks celery with tops, diced
1 large onion, chopped
2 cups tomatoes, fresh or canned
1½ tsp. sea salt, to taste

Let beans soak for 3-4 hours. Cook until tender in a stainless steel kettle or in a pressure cooker for 15 minutes. Add celery, onion, tomatoes, and salt during last part of cooking and more water as needed. When beans are tender, add 1 Tbs. olive oil if desired. If fennel tops are available, chop and add some while cooking. Delicious! Servings: 6-8

Variation: omit tomatoes; add **¼ cup barley** and **1 cup sliced carrots**.

Corn and Potato Chowder

1 ½ qts. pure water
3 cups cubed potatoes
⅓ cup diced carrot
2 tsp. onion powder
1 ½ tsp. sea salt; ¼ tsp. celery seed
½ tsp. savory herb
2 ½ cups creamed or liquified fresh corn
1 Tbs. nut butter, blended with corn

In soup pot bring all ingredients except corn to boiling, reduce heat, simmer to almost tender. Add blended corn

and nut butter, simmer 8-10 minutes. Garnish with f**resh minced parsley, chives** or **dill weed**. Serve with soup crackers or bread sticks. Servings: 4

Cream of Bean Soup

1. Blend until smooth and creamy any of the bean soups or vegetable soups containing lentils or other legumes.
2. Add a little plain unflavored **nut, rice** or **soy milk** to make desired consistency. Blend well. Heat and serve plain or with **alfalfa sprouts,** and **whole grain bread**.

Hearty Kidney Bean 'Chili'

3 cups celery, chopped
2 cups onions, diced
1 large green pepper, diced
3 cloves garlic, finely chopped
4 cups cooked kidney beans
3 cups cooked chopped tomatoes
1 cup browned tofu cubes, opt.
1 tsp. celery seed powder
½ tsp. cumin powder
½ tsp. dried oregano
½ tsp. sea salt, to taste
dash of cayenne and garlic powder, opt.

In a large kettle sauté the first 4 ingredients with **1 - 2 tsp. olive or soy oil**. When tender, add the beans, tomatoes, tofu and seasonings. Ladle into deep soup bowls. Drizzle with olive oil, if desired. Served with a fresh mixed greens salad, zwieback, or rolls would make a satisfying meal. Servings: 6-8

Vegetable Soup with Rice

3 qts. pure water
1 cup brown rice, uncooked
1 qt. tomatoes, chopped
2 cups winter squash, cubed
2 stalks celery with tops, diced
2 cups green beans, cut
1 Tbs. onion powder
1 clove garlic, minced
salt, savory, & chicken style seasoning to taste

In large kettle bring water to a boil, add rice, reduce heat and cook covered for 30 minutes. Add vegetables and seasonings; simmer for 20 minutes or until vegetables are tender. Drizzle on olive oil and sprinkle with fresh chopped parsley before serving.

Italian Minestrone

3½ qts. pure water, boiling
1 large onion, sliced
4 medium carrots, diced
2 cups chopped cabbage or fennel
2 large celery stalks, sliced or diced
1 pkg. frozen cut green beans (10 oz.)
1 pkg. frozen peas (10 oz.)
1 15-oz. can kidney beans or chick peas
1 can Italian tomatoes, cut (28 oz.)
1 bay leaf, 4 sprigs parsley or sweet basil
2 tsp. salt, beef style seasoning*, to taste
¼ lb. buckwheat or soy spaghetti,
   broken in 1" pieces

Bring water to a boil. Add all ingredients except spaghetti. Simmer for 30 minutes, then add spaghetti. Continue to simmer for 15 minutes, stirring occasionally, until spaghetti is tender. Drizzle with pure olive oil; sprinkle on *Parmesan "Cheese" before serving, if desired.
*see recipe in chapter Herbs and Seasonings.

Note: Frozen mixed vegetables such as Italian Blend can substitute for the vegetables in recipe.

Chick'n Noodle Soup

1 large stalk celery, diced
⅓ cup diced or sliced carrots
3 green onions with tops, thinly sliced
1 Tbs. onion powder or ½ c. chopped onion
2 cloves fresh minced garlic
    or ¼ tsp. powder
6 cups water or veggie broth
3-4 Tbs. Chicken-style Seasoning
1 cup thin spaghetti, 1"pieces
1-15oz.can chick peas
    or 2 cups home-cooked
¼ cup fresh parsley or chives, minced
sea salt, to taste

In a saucepan, lightly saute celery, carrots, onions and garlic in ½ Tbs. olive oil until soft. Add water, bring to a boil. Add seasonings, broken spaghetti, and cooked garbanzos. Reduce heat to medium. Cook until spaghetti is tender. Sliced browned mushrooms may be added, if desired. Garnish with **fresh or dried parsley** or **chives**. Servings: 4

Educate – Educate – Educate

"Let it ever be kept before the mind that the great object of hygienic reform is to secure the highest possible development of mind and soul and body. All the laws of nature – which are the laws of God- are designed for our good. Obedience to them will promote our happiness in this life, and will aid us in a preparation for the life to come."
E. G. White, Diet and Foods, p. 464

German Potato Soup

2½ qts. water or vegetable stock, divided
2 lbs. red potatoes (6 med.), sliced or diced
½ cup diced carrots
1 tsp. sea salt, to taste
1 large onion, chopped
1 cup diced celery
1 Tbs soy oil, opt.
2 Tbs. golden wheat flour
1½ tsp. paprika
1 tsp. dried dill or tarragon
¼ tsp. garlic powder
¼ cup fresh minced parsley

In a soup kettle, bring 2 qts. pure water, scrubbed or peeled thinly sliced or diced potatoes, carrots and salt to a boil over medium heat. Cover and cook 15-20 minutes until tender. Meanwhile in a heavy skillet, lightly saute onions and celery until crisp tender. Add flour, seasonings and remaining 2 cups water, stirring for 1-2 minutes until thick. Stir into the potatoes; simmer for 5-10 minutes. Last, add parsley. Servings: 6

Pumpkin Soup

A creamy American soup that is becoming popular world-wide. A rich source of vitamin A; also contains potassium, calcium, phosphorus, protein and fiber. When pumpkin is out of season, use butternut squash in its place.

1 pumpkin (approx. 2 lbs.)
1 cup sliced carrots
1 medium onion, sliced
2 cloves garlic, minced
1 tsp. fresh grated ginger, opt.
3 cups vegetable or chicken-style broth
1-2 bay leaves
sea salt and cayenne, to taste
1 cup creamy almond or soy milk, plain
1-2 Tbs. fresh cilantro or chives, snipped

1. Peel the pumpkin, remove seeds and cut in small pieces.

2. In a large covered pan, cook the carrots, onions, garlic and ginger, with 1-2 tsp. olive oil, soy butter, or water until soft, but not brown. Add the pumpkin and toss 1-2 minutes. Add the vegetable broth, bay leaves and seasonings; cover and simmer until pumpkin is tender.

3. Transfer to a blender or food processor (discard bay leaves); add the almond milk and blend until smooth; adjust seasonings. Garnish with chopped fresh flat leaf parsley, cilantro or chives. Yield: 4-6 servings

Minestrone Genovese
(Genoa Vegetable Soup)

2 cups dried white beans
2½ qts. pure water
4 mushrooms, sliced
2-3 Tbs. olive oil, divided
½ cup chopped onion
4 cups diced eggplant
4 cups shredded cabbage
2 cups sliced zucchini or squash
2 cups peeled diced or canned tomatoes
½ cup vermicelli noodles
2 tsp. sea salt, to taste
½ cup Italian parsley and, or sweet basil
½ tsp. dried Italian seasoning, crushed
2 cloves garlic, minced
⅓ cup pine nuts or slivered almonds

Wash the beans, cover with water, and bring to a boil; let stand 1 hour. Drain. In a large soup kettle, cover the beans with 2½ qts. pure water, bring to a boil; cook 1½ hours. Clean the mushrooms, slice. Heat 2 Tbs. oil in a skillet; sauté the onion and mushrooms. Add the eggplant, cabbage, and zucchini, cook until tender; add the tomatoes. Combine the vegetable mixture with the beans; bring to a boil, cook over low heat 30 minutes. Stir in the vermicelli, sea salt and dried herbs. Cook 10 minutes until vermicelli is tender. In a food processor, combine the parsley, basil, seasonings, garlic, nuts, and remaining 1 Tbs. olive oil until a paste is formed; or pound the ingredients to a paste. Stir this **pesto** into the soup slowly to prevent lumps from forming. Adjust seasonings.
Yield: 8-10 servings

Borscht

Also known as borsch, or borsht. A simple but hearty Russian soup made primarily of beets and cabbage. Served hot or cold, often with sour cream.

6 cups broth, veggie or beef-style
4 beets, cooked or 1-15 oz.can
2 medium potatoes, cubed
4 cups red and/or green shredded cabbage
1 large onion, sliced
4 cloves garlic, minced
1½ tsp. salt; dash cayenne, to taste
1 tsp. dill powder or 1 Tbs. dill seed
4 Tbs. lemon juice
tofu, 1-lb cubed, browned, opt.
fresh dill weed, chopped, opt.

Heat the broth, potatoes, onion, garlic, salt, to boiling. Cover and simmer until potatoes are tender. Shred cabbage and beets or cut beets into ¼"strips or cubes. Stir cabbage, beets, and dill into soup (add ground dill seed or tie whole seed in cheesecloth bag). Simmer 30 minutes until flavors are blended. Stir in lemon juice and tofu cubes if desired. Simmer uncovered 5 minutes; remove spice bag.

● Serve with a spoonful of soy sour cream if desired.
● Sprinkle with fresh chopped or dry dill weed.
● Good served hot or cold with **rye bread** or **crackers** and **avocado slices**.

"Right physical habits promote mental superiority. Intellectual power, physical strength, and longevity depend upon immutable laws.... In order to preserve health, temperance in all things is necessary."
E. G. White, Child Guidance, pg. 396

Broccoli Garbanzo Nori & Noodle Soup

A nutritious, simple soup containing seaweed, rich in vitamins, minerals and trace elements. Nori, a favorite seaweed, is very tasty, and can be added to soup, salad, or used as a wrap around vegetables and cooked rice as in sushi. (see Glossary of Natural Foods)

4 cups pure boiling water
4 cloves garlic, minced
1 Tbs. Chicken-style Seasoning, see recipe
3 cups broccoli florets
3 oz. healthy noodles or spaghetti 1" pieces
2 cups cooked garbanzo beans
2 Nori sheets (roasted seaweed)

In a large soup pan, bring water, garlic and seasoning to boiling. Add broccoli and noodles; cook until just tender. Add the garbanzo beans and nori strips (cut sheets in 4 pcs. lengthwise - stack, then cut in ⅛" thin strips). Yield: 6 servings

9 Bean and Barley Soup

This hearty bean soup with veggies is sure to stick-to your-ribs and satisfy hunger. Fennel herb tops, fresh, frozen, or dried, although optional, add a delicious wonderful flavor!

2 qts. pure water
2 cups 9 Bean Soup mix
(see bean combination)
¼ cup pearl barley
3 cups chopped celery, sautéed
1 cup onion, chopped
4 cloves garlic, minced
½ tsp. celery seed, ground
½ tsp. sea salt; pinch cayenne, opt.
handful chopped fennel herb tops, opt.
1-28 oz. can Italian plum tomatoes cut in pieces or chunks
1 Tbs. olive oil

Rinse beans in cold water; drain. In large kettle soak the beans 2-3 hours in 2 qts. water until plump. Simmer on low until almost tender (or place in crock pot overnight). Add the barley, celery, onion, garlic and seasonings and chopped fennel tops; simmer until tender. Last add the tomatoes and drizzle with olive oil. Serve warm. Good with crusty garlic bread, and a green salad. Yield: 8 servings

Potato Asparagus Leek Soup

This delicate spring soup tastes even better if made a day ahead. Good hot or cold!

1 lb. fresh asparagus, trimmed, cut in pieces
3 cups sliced leeks (3 large)
1 medium or 2 small red potatoes, cut
  in cubes
2 cups pure water or vegetable stock
1½ tsp. onion powder
1½ tsp. dried sweet basil
½ tsp. chicken-style seasoning

⅛ tsp. celery seed powder
¼ tsp. salt, to taste
1 cup diced celery
1 cup chopped onions
1 tsp. olive or soy oil, opt.
1-1½ cups cashew or soymilk, plain
¼ cup fresh chopped parsley

Trim about ½" from bottom of asparagus stalks, cut in pieces; set aside the tips. Place pieces of asparagus, sliced leeks (white and pale green parts only), potatoes, vegetable stock or water and seasonings in soup pot. Bring to a boil, then simmer covered on low heat 20 minutes or until vegetables are tender. In a skillet, sauté the celery and onions until crisp-tender. Blend the soup vegetables to a purée and return to soup pot. Add the parsley and cashew or soymilk sufficient to make desired consistency. Adjust salt and seasonings to taste; simmer on low 5-10 min. to combine flavors. Let soup stand for awhile, or refrigerate.Just before serving, steam the reserved asparagus tips to crisp-tender and bright green. Add to soup and serve. Yield: 4-6 servings

Escarole Garbanzo Noodle Soup

This thick-chunky vegetable and bean blend is bitter-sweet, delicious, and very easy to make. When pressed for time, I can finish this in less than 20 minutes. My family enjoys the wonderful flavor. Thanks mom for teaching me how to make it. It's one of my favorites!

1 ½ qts. pure boiling water
2 Tbs. Chicken-style Seasoning
5-6 large cloves garlic, finely chopped
6 oz. buckwheat or soy spaghetti,
   broken in 1" pieces
1-2 large heads (1½ lbs.) escarole,*
   fresh chopped
1-15oz. can cooked garbanzo beans
1 tsp. virgin olive oil, opt.

Wash and chop/slice escarole heads. In a large 4-qt. soup pan, bring water, seasoning, and garlic to boiling. Add spaghetti; stir and cook uncovered 3-4 minutes. Add chopped escarole, cover and continue to cook 10 minutes or until spaghetti and escarole are tender. Add can of cooked garbanzo beans; drizzle on olive oil, if desired. Yield: 8-10 servings.

Note: * *Escarole cooks down to less than ¼ in volume, so be generous (at least 8-10 cups chopped or sliced, tightly packed), the more the better. It may taste bitter in your mouth, but sweet in the stomach... and really good for you! Curly endive may substitute for escarole in recipe.*

Black - Eyed Peas and Vegetable Stew

1 large onion, chopped
3 cloves garlic, finely chopped
3 cups pure water or vegetable broth
3 cups vegetable
   or beef-style seasoning broth
2 tsp. onion powder
1 tsp. ground cumin
1 tsp. dried oregano
2½ cups dried black-eyed peas
   or navy beans
1 cup sliced carrots
2 cups Italian flat green beans,
   cut in 1"pieces
¼ lb. whole wheat or soy spaghetti,
   broken in 1"pieces
sea salt, to taste
2 cups chopped tomatoes with juice
Italian flat-leaf parsley, garnish

In a 4 quart soup kettle sauté the onion and garlic in 1 Tbs. olive oil until tender. Add the water, broth, seasonings and beans; heat to boiling. Boil 2 minutes; remove from heat, cover and let stand 1 hour. Add carrots, and green beans; cover and simmer about 2 hours until tender. Add the spaghetti and tomatoes, cook until tender; add salt to taste. Garnish with chopped parsley. Servings: 6-8

Sprouting

Index - CHAPTER 17

Sprouting

514

Ten Talents

My Kitchen Prayer

Bless my pretty kitchen Lord
And light it with Thy love.
Help me to plan and cook the meals
From Thy heavenly home above.
Bless our meals with Thy Presence
And warm them with Thy grace;
Watch over me as I do my work,
Washing pots and pans and plates.
The service I am trying to do
Is to make my family content,
So bless my eager efforts Lord
And make them Heaven Sent.

-Anonymous

Chapter Cover Photo: ***Sprouted Mung Beans***

Seed Sprouting

The Miracle of Sprouting Seeds

Sprouted seeds, the very beginning of new life, are one of the most nutrient rich, powerful, health building foods. No man is capable of explaining how one tiny seed can sprout and grow into a plant or large tree, except God made it so.

There is within a seed, life and power to reproduce in nature after its kind; and it's interesting to watch the amazing results of our meager efforts when combined with God's miraculous explosion of growth.

There are requirements on our part in helping the Creator fulfill His plan: 1. Secure good seed. 2. Provide warmth and moisture for the seed.

Sprouting is simple and fun, saving time when preparing a meal, as well as saving money on our food budget. Economical, and "chock-full" of nutrition; sprouts can easily become a staple food in the vegetarian's diet, providing fresh foods year round, right in your own kitchen. Start an indoor garden today; have some seeds sprouting in different stages and some sprouts ready to use. Sprouts will keep fresh for several days if covered and stored in the refrigerator. Try it – and Happy Sprouting!

Why Sprout Seeds?

God designed His creation to be very productive. Likewise, seeds when sprouted, have a greater biological value and give off more energy in the form of enzymes, vitamins, and minerals, which when digested, impart more vital energy to those eating them. Sprouts are the most alive and the freshest food we can put into our body.

As we age, our body's ability to produce enzymes declines. Sprouts are a concentrated source of vital enzymes that are lost when foods are not fresh, or over-cooked. Sprouts contain phytochemicals (plant compounds) that can protect us against disease. Sprouts are a powerhouse of nutrition and generally easier to digest than the bean or seed from which they came.

During sprouting, the starch is changed to simple sugar, and the proteins and fats are changed into simpler forms. This is the reason why many sprouts can be eaten raw. They are pre-digested and quickly assimilated; full of enzymes, anti-oxidants, vitamins and other nutrients.

Sprouts differ in texture and taste. Some are spicy, some are sweet, some are hardy, and some are delicate. The larger, sprouted beans - (soybeans, garbanzo, and fava beans) are best if steamed, just enough to tenderize (15-20 minutes); a much shorter time than the longer hours usually required to cook dry beans until tender and digestible. Sprouting is one of the fastest ways of improving the nutritional value of foods. Sprouting increases Vitamin C, B, Folic Acid, and other nutrients 4-10 times.

When seeds are sprouted their starch is reduced; the protein value of the seed

remains in the sprout. Chlorophyll (nature's great green deodorant) and pro-vitamin A develop in some sprouts (microgreens) as we uncover them to light in the latter stages of growing. England made a special study on the sprouting of grains because of her dependence on imported fresh fruits for vitamin C. English authors R.H.A and V. Plimmer, and Dr. Bailey of the University of Minnesota have the following information:

Vitamin C Value of Germinated Seeds
(100 grams)

Oats, whole   **11 mg.**
after germination of 96 hours   20 mg.
after germination of 120 hours   42 mg.

Peas, dry   0 mg.
after germination of 24 hours   8 mg.
after germination of 48 hours   69 mg.
after germination of 96 hours   86 mg.

Vitamin Increases in Sprouting Wheat

Vitamin	Ratio in wheat	Ratio in wheat sprouts
B1	7.0	9.0
B2	1.3	5.4
Niacin	62.0	103.0
Pantothenic Acid	7.6	12.6
Pyridoxine	2.6	4.6
Biotin	.17	.36
Folic Acid	28.0	106.0
Vitamin C	0.0	Higher

What Seeds Will Sprout?

Almost any whole natural seed with hull will sprout. Alfalfa seeds (king of sprouts) are among the best; others are lentils, mung beans, peas, garbanzo beans, soybeans and most grains – barley, corn, oats, rye, spelt, wheat (red, hard varieties not white wheat). Try high-protein buckwheat spouts, the sweet sunflower seed sprouts, aromatic fenugreek sprouts and the radish sprouts, they are all nutritious.

Radish seed sprouts are mildly pungent and have a delicious flavor, making them suitable for salads. Radish seeds may be mixed with alfalfa seeds and sprouted together, very rich in vitamin C.

Red Clover sprouts are much like alfalfa, except their taste is stronger. Obtain your seeds from local merchants, seed houses, or health food stores. Be sure that the seed is of good quality, free from insects, and has not been treated by harmful chemicals, or sterilizing heat. Heat-treated seeds sometimes sold in grocery stores do not sprout.

Broken seeds are worthless for sprouting, and for that reason, hulled seeds do not always sprout well, for many of the seeds may be broken or bruised. Pick out all broken or shriveled seeds, for they will not sprout.

Seed Sprouting Guide

Seeds	Amount in 2 Qt. Jar	Sprouting	Best Length
1. Lentils, dry	¾ cup	3 days	¾ -1"
2. Sunflower, whole	1 cup	2 days	⅛ - ¼"
3. Garbanzos, whole	1 cup	3 days	½ -1"
4. Mung Beans, whole	¾ cup	2-3 days	1 - 2"
5. Fava Beans, whole	1 cup	3 days	½ - ¾"
6. Alfalfa Seed	2 Tbs.	4-5 days	1 - 2"
7. Soy Beans	1 cup	3 days	½ - ¾"
8. Wheat, whole	1 cup	2 days	¼ - ½"
9. Large tray - Alfalfa	¼ cup	5 days	1½ - 2"
Buckwheat (not shown)	½ cup	2-3 days	1 - 2"
Fenugreek seed (not shown)	⅓ cup	4-5 days	1 - 2"

The variety of sprouts pictured below are arranged clockwise 1-9 beginning at lower left

Left to Right: Lentil Sprouts, Mung Bean Sprouts, Clover Sprouts, Alfalfa Sprouts

The hulls of beans, grains, and seeds, contain enzyme inhibitors, which are neutralized by soaking, and sprouting, aiding the body in the breakdown of these foods during the digestive process.

Methods of Growing Sprouts*

1. JAR –

This is the simplest of all; what you need is: a wide mouth jar and ring; wire screen or nylon stocking; and seed - whole, unsprayed, that's all! (Note: Seeds will not grow well if crowded; use only half the amount of seeds for a 1-qt. jar.)

A. Soak seeds in a jar with plenty of pure water overnight.

B. Drain water through screen, rinse seeds, drain well, divide in 2 jars if needed. (the water from draining sprouts can be used to water houseplants)

C. Turn jar on its side (or angle as shown) and put in a dark, warm place.

D. Rinse seeds through screen 1-2 times a day (2-3 in summer). Drain well. (Gently rotate jar to distribute seeds evenly around wall of jar).

E. Most sprouts are ready to use when they are ½ - 1" long. Sunflower seeds are sweetest when barely sprouted. Alfalfa sprouts are best at least 1" or longer. When alfalfa and clover sprouts are ½" long, place in sunlight to develop vivid green color (chlorophyl and vitamin A). Sprouts will keep fresh for several days (refrigerated) without wilting.

There are various sprouting systems and sprouting containers on the market. Check availability in your area, or contact the authors.

2. PAN or SPROUTER –
  A. Start seeds in jar (especially alfalfa – using method given for jar).
  B. After the second day, spread seeds thinly but evenly on the bottom of a pan.
  C. Sprinkle generously with water 2-3 times a day. Cover with wet cheesecloth.
  D. In about 5 days your alfalfa sprouts will look like a green carpet. They are so delicious! Method also works well for mung beans.

3. STRAINER –
  A. Line colander or wire strainer with cheese cloth.
  B. Put in soaked seeds and then cover with cloth. Put in dark warm place.
  C. Run cool water over them or sprinkle generously 2-3 times a day.

4. RAG DOLL –
  A. Spread soaked seeds on terry cloth; cover seeds with clean cloth.
  B. Roll up and keep well dampened and in a dark warm place.
  C. Using this method the sprouts should be used before they get too long. (Mildew may develop more quickly than in some of the other methods).

Note: When sprouts have developed to the desired stage, rinse well; drain completely and refrigerate in a covered jar. They will keep several days like any fresh vegetable.

5 Factors that Adversely Affect Successful Sprouting

1. Over or under-watering
2. Poor drainage
3. Overcrowded seeds in jar
4. Quality of seed (broken, treated)
5. Lack of warmth and sunlight

How to Serve Sprouted Seeds and Microgreens

Whenever possible use them without cooking. **Alfalfa, radish** and **clover** sprouts (microgreens) should not be cooked. Sprouts keep for days in the refrigerator. Add them to sandwiches, salads, veggie wraps, soups or blended vegetable drinks. **Sunflower seed sprouts** are delicious if eaten fresh, uncooked, when no longer than the seed. **Wheat sprouts** can be chopped and combined with dried fruit and nuts for healthy desserts, added to bread, or lightly steamed for hot cereal. **Sunflower, alfalfa** and **buckwheat sprouts** are delicious in salads, or use as a healthy garnish. (see serving suggestions)

Beverages: Add sprouts to beverages for a quick energy drink. Blend fresh, tender sprouts, with tomato juice, V-8 or other vegetable juices. Try adding some sprouted seeds to fresh, frozen or canned fruits / fruit juice, or non-dairy milk. Drinks made with sprouts are highly nourishing. Start with a small amount and blend until smooth.

Here are some simple healthy combinations:

Pineapple Juice **Sprouted Sunflower Seeds**	**Tomato Juice** **Alfalfa Sprouts**	**Carrot or Celery Juice** **Alfalfa Sprouts**
Strawberries or Pears **Sprouted Sunflower Seeds**	**Prune Juice** **Wheat Sprouts**	**Hot Carob (soy or cashew)** **Sprouted Sunflower Seeds**

Breads: Add sprouts to bread and rolls. Just grind or blend sprouts with water in recipe. See **Sprouted Wheat Bread, Ezekiel Bread, Sprouted Sunflower Seed Bread, etc.**

Desserts: Make healthy desserts by adding crunchy sprouts. Sprinkle chopped sunflower seed sprouts on ice creams and fruit desserts. See recipes: **Sprouted Wheat Surprises, Sprouted Wheat Candy, Sprouted Sunflower Clusters.**

Main Dishes: Savory Sprouts, Sprouted Lentil Casserole, Sprouted Wheat Burgers, Sprouted Garbanzo Sauté, Sprouted Mung Beans, Almond-Mushroom Chop Suey, Vegetarian Chow Mein, Green Bean Chow Mein, Vegetables in Casserole, Savory Stir-Fry with Fresh Bean Sprouts, Vegetable Chop Suey with Toasted Almonds (see recipes)

Salads: Tossed green salads and other vegetable combinations are tastier and more nutritious with the addition of fresh sprouts. **Mung bean sprouts** are crisp, and take the place of celery in salads. **Lentil sprouts** may be tenderized and added to vegetable salads. Add some alfalfa, clover, radish, sunflower or fenugreek sprouts for a crunchy fresh taste.

Alfalfa sprouts are delicious any way — plain, or in a variety of vegetable salads. Sprouted wheat and sunflower seeds are good in fruit salad. They add crunch and texture. Sprouts may be added to jelled or molded salads just before they begin to set. (see recipes)

Salad Dressings: Add tender sprouts while blending your favorite salad dressing or dip. (see recipes)

Sandwiches: Add variety and nutrition by using sprouts instead of lettuce.

Try alfalfa, clover, radish, or fenugreek sprouts; just reach into your refrigerated jar for fresh crisp sprouts. Add crunch to sandwiches, roll-ups, or pita bread; sprouts will remain crisp - not wilt like lettuce!

Soups: Blend sprouts with creamed soups, or add a handful just before serving. Avoid cooking tender sprouts such as alfalfa. Place a bowl of alfalfa sprouts on the table for a healthy addition to vegetable soup.

The larger sprouts, such as pea or lentil, may need to be tenderized before adding to soup. See **Sprouted Lentil Cream Soup** or add tenderized mung bean sprouts to **Cream of Celery Soup**, or other favorite soup. etc.

Alfalfa Sprout Gravy

1¾ cups pure water or broth
½ cup cashew nuts
2 celery sticks 4" long
¼ tsp. salt + ¼ tsp. garlic powder
⅛ tsp. celery seed powder
1½ Tbs. arrowroot powder
   or 2 Tbs. browned flour
¼ cup fresh chopped parsley

Blend first 6 ingredients until very smooth. Simmer in saucepan, stirring until thick. Remove from heat; add ½ **cup crisp Alfalfa or Clover Sprouts** just before serving.

Vegetables in Casserole

(pictured right)

2-3 cups mung bean, soy
   or lentil sprouts, tenderized
1 cup fresh or frozen peas, lightly steamed
½ cup sliced carrots, lightly steamed
1 cup diced celery, lightly steamed
2 cups sautéed onion
¼ cup bell pepper, sautéed

Combine vegetables with thick **Cashew White Sauce.** Top with:

½ cup toasted bread crumbs
¼ cup toasted sliced almonds

Bake at 350° until heated through. Serve with **steamed brown rice.**

Easy Lentil or Mung Bean Sprouts

(pictured- left)

Stir together in skillet:

2 Tbs. lemon juice
2 Tbs. soy sauce
1 Tbs. olive or soy oil
1 Tbs. onion powder

Add **8 cups Sprouted Lentils** or **Mung Beans;** cover and steam 3-4 min. until just crisp tender. Good served hot or cold as a main dish or side vegetable.

Sprouted Wheat Surprises

1 ¼ cups tender sprouted wheat
2 cups pitted dates
2 Tbs. honey or molasses
2 Tbs. nut butter (almond, peanut
   or cashew)
1 cup chopped nuts (filberts, cashews,
   walnuts)
2 Tbs. orange or lemon zest, unsprayed
¼ cup sesame seeds, lightly toasted
¼ tsp. sea salt

Put first 2 ingredients through food processor or grinder. Mix in the rest of ingredients. Form into balls placing a **filbert** or **pecan half** in the center. Roll each ball in **shredded coconut**. Ready to eat or freeze.

Healthy Advice

Stretch the food dollar – Every family can save dollars by getting into the habit of sprouting some seed every other day. Children will enjoy taking part in this and watching the seeds grow. Sprouts are so inexpensive. For example: Just 1 cup of dry lentils will yield 8-10 cups when sprouted; 1-2 Tbs. of alfalfa seed will overfill a 2 quart jar and yield enough sprouts to provide fresh salad for a family of 8. Seeds may be obtained in almost every part of the country – for very little cost. With just a little effort on your part, you'll be amazed at the healthy returns. We work by addition; the life-giver (our Creator God) works by multiplication!

Assist the digestive process – Legumes (beans + peas) are power-packed capsules of nutrition; an excellent source of protein for the healthy, plant-based vegetarian diet. However, some facts should not be ignored. Raw legumes contain toxic substances known as anti-nutritive factors because they interfere with the absorption of other nutrients.

Soaking in water and properly cooking legumes, or sprouting legumes destroys these undesirable substances. Many people who have difficulty digesting beans find that sprouting legumes and rinsing off the hulls, is beneficial in eliminating flatulence. In addition, the proper combining of beans (whether sprouted or not) with other foods, is of utmost importance for the proper digestion and assimilation of nutrients. (see chart - **Food Combining Made Easy**).

For better nutrition, try sprouting - without doubting!

A Talent of the Highest Value

"Good cooks are few. Many, many mothers need to take lessons in cooking that they may set before the family well-prepared, neatly served food... Unless the food is prepared in a wholesome, palatable manner, it cannot be converted into good blood..."
- E. G. White, Diet and Foods, p. 263-4

Chapter 18
Vegetables & Side Dishes

Index - CHAPTER 18

Chapter Cover Photo: *Sweet Roasted Vegetables, page 551*

Vegetables

Vegetables are a fundamental part of human nutrition, and with grains and fruits in proper combination supply the basic elements for a nutritious diet. Vegetables are generally low in fat, rich in fiber, vitamins, minerals, phytochemicals, and anti-oxidants.

Vegetables are blood builders, ideal for maintaining proper weight, and considered to be protective foods containing substances that boost the immune system and significantly reduce the risk of cancer and other diseases. A wide variety of vegetables should be included as part of the optimal or ideal diet. Ideally the best produce is organically grown.

Gardening is an excellent way to get exercise, reduce stress and grow your favorite vegetables. If that is not possible, an incredible array of fresh vegetables is now available in produce markets. At least five servings of fresh fruits and vegetables should be eaten each day.

In this chapter you will find helpful tips and suggestions about vegetables, and a variety of simple healthy recipes for preparing attractive dishes that are bursting with color and flavor.

The question is often asked:

What is a fruit? and What is a Vegetable?

All *Vegetables* come from Herbaceous Plants or Parts of Plants. For example, starting from the bottom up we eat different parts of plants:

Roots, Tubers and Bulbs of plant:
(carrots, beets, potatoes, onions, garlic, etc.)

Stems or Stalks of the plant:
(celery, asparagus, leeks, etc.)

Leaves of the plant:
(lettuce, spinach, turnip greens, kale, cabbage, etc.)

Fruits of herbaceous plants:
(tomatoes, eggplant, pepper, cucumber, squash, pumpkin, etc)

Flowers of the plant:
(artichoke, broccoli, cauliflower, etc.)

Seeds and/or pod of the plant:
(beans, peas, corn, lentils, flaxseed, etc.)

Vegetables (the parts of herbaceous plants we eat, known as garden vegetables, described above) are best combined with grains, nuts, and seeds, legumes, and some fruits such as avocado and olives. Keep the combinations simple. (see Food Combining Made Easy chart)

"For God, who gives seed to the farmer to plant, and … good crops to harvest and eat, will give you more and more seed to plant and will make it grow so that you can give more and more fruit from your harvest." 2 Corinthians 9:10 Living Bible

"To preserve the best health, we should avoid eating vegetables and fruit at the same meal. ....Have fruit at one meal and vegetables at the next." Diet & Foods p. 395

Give someone a meal, they eat for a day-
Teach them how to cook- they feast for a lifetime.
- Rosalie Hurd -

Kale, Mustard Greens, Collard and Turnip Greens, are rich in anti-oxidants, contain a host of vitamins, minerals (calcium, iron, etc.), protein, phytonutrients and fiber, to help protect against cancer, reduce high cholesterol levels, maintain strong bones, and a healthy cardiovascular system.

Parsley combined with **garlic** and **grated lemon peel** makes a tasty garnish for stir-fry, steamed rice, or roasted vegetables.

Lemon juice improves the flavor of green leafy vegetables and reduces the amount of salt needed to season greens. The Vitamin C in lemons prevents oxidation and enhances the absorption of iron in vegetables.

Cruciferous Vegetables - Members of the cabbage family that contain cancer-protective properties. This group of foods include: **Brussels sprouts, bok choy, broccoli, cabbage, cauliflower, collard and mustard greens, kale, kohlrabi, rutabaga and turnips.**

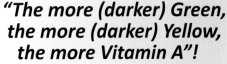

"The more (darker) Green, the more (darker) Yellow, the more Vitamin A"!

Chinese Snow Peas - are thin and crisp with tender sweet seeds. Both the pod and peas are eaten. When young and tender they are a tasty and colorful addition to salads and stir-fry vegetables. Eat raw or add during the last 1-2 minutes of cooking.

To prepare Snow Peas: Trim and remove any strings; blanch in boiling water 60 seconds, then plunge into ice water to stop the cooking; drain when cool. The brilliant green pods are a tasty, an colorful addition to pasta, salad, or stir fry. **Seasoning options:** fresh dill, chives, lemon zest, or mint.

Kabocha Squash (Sweet Mama) - The Orange flesh of this winter squash is fine textured, creamy and mild. Rich in beta-carotene and potassium; similar in taste but not as sweet as a sweet potato. Delicious baked, steamed, puréed or stuffed.

Garlic has long held a prized place in cooking and can be used to enhance flavor and reduce the amount of salt and spicy seasonings in cooking.

Escarole - Broad-leaf escarole (a variety of endive) is rich in folic acid, potassium, and fiber; also contains magnesium, calcium, iron, B-vitamins and trace elements including zinc. Aids digestion, stimulates the gall bladder. It's slightly bitter tasting in the mouth, but sweet in the stomach!

Sweet Basil - Superbly compliments all types of tomato dishes, zucchini, casseroles, pesto sauce, pasta, minestrone soup, steamed squash, carrots, cabbage, and beans.

Squash - Varieties differ in color, shape, and flavor. Squash is low in protein, and sodium, contains virtually no fat, however is rich in beta-carotene (provitamin A), minerals such as potassium, and soluble fiber. The properties of squash make it very digestible, suitable and beneficial for those with hypertension, kidney, stomach and eye disorders, and in the prevention of coronary heart disease and cancer. Squash can be baked, boiled, grated or puréed. The seeds and blossoms are edible.

Mushrooms - The similarities of edible to poisonous fungi are so close that only those who are capable of distinguishing the edible ones should attempt to gather them. Select mushrooms that are fresh or carefully pick your own, using a mushroom guide book. Look for caps that curl down and cover the fluted gills underneath. If the cap opens like a parasol, the mushroom is past its prime. Mushrooms are low in carbohydrates and fats; a source of protein especially-when dried; contain B vitamins and minerals. Common varieties include: Button, Cremini (Italian Brown), Portobella, Chanterelle, Morel, Shiitake, Porcini, Oyster, Enoki. The Oriental Shiitake, is valued for its medicinal properties and considered an elixir for long life.

"We need a genuine education in the art of cooking…, and how to put together ingredients to make healthful food combinations from the grains and the vegetables. Such an education will assist in creating a desire among the people to move out of the cities, to secure land in the country, where they can raise their own fruit and vegetables."
E. G. White, Medical Ministry pp. 267-8

• **Stir-Fry vs. Sauté:** *Stir-frying* and sautéing share similar techniques. Both methods cook food quickly in a small amount of oil, and because the food is cooked quickly, the flavors remain vibrant and the texture intact. Stir-frying cooks food in a dense bottom skillet or wok over intensely high heat, stirring constantly. *Sautéing* cooks small amounts of tender veggies over moderately-high heat in a wide pan (to avoid over-crowding) and food is stirred frequently (but not constantly), to promote even browning. Over- crowding pan should be avoided. Food releases steam while cooking; if the steam has no room to escape, it stays in the food, and ends up steaming rather than sautéing, and food will not brown. If the heat is too low, the food will release liquid and steam, rather than sauté.

• **Healthy Sauté:** Start with 1 Tbs. Broth, in hot skillet. Add onions, garlic, or other vegetables; stir frequently until tender. Using this sauté method, vegetables can be flavorful without oil.

• **To retain the bright color of vegetables when cooking them or in making soup, remember this simple rule:** Pour the boiling water over the vegetables, even when adding a small amount, add sea salt if desired. Cover and bring to boil, then turn heat down and simmer until tender. For vegetables such as broccoli, cauliflower or carrots, uncover when tender to keep vegetables from yellowing, or losing their brilliant color.

• Select **Eggplant** that are fully ripe, with glossy deep purple skin, and light in weight. Many super- markets err in selling eggplant by the pound. This may be a good time to buy (you'll need plenty to make Caponatina). Eggplant that are light in weight and dark in color have a delicate flavor, skins are edible. Those that are heavy or unripe (with green parts) are more likely to be bitter and seedy. Eggplant contains *solanine*, a toxic alkaloid that almost disappears when it is fully ripe and heated in cooking. For this reason, eggplant must always be eaten ripe and cooked. Best stored at room temperature. Eggplant, like tomatoes, are rich in phytochemicals (act as anti-oxidants) which perform numerous preventive and healing functions within the body.

Assorted Vegetables

Peas

Okra

Brussel Sprouts

Yellow Wax Beans

Rapini

Mustard Greens

Green Beans

Bok Choy

Red Chard

Kohlrabi

Peppers

Collards

Kale

Cucumber

Cauliflower

Artichokes

Asparagus

Tomatoes

Broccoli

Eggplant

Fennel

Cabbage

Sweet Corn

• Select **Globe Artichokes** that have a thick stem and a flat top. The smaller ones are usually tender; the larger ones can be tender, if the top is flat. When the artichoke has a skinny stem and pointed top, it usually has a large sharp beard (choke) and leaves are not as tender, creating more waste. Artichoke stems are tasty added to tomato sauce or soup. The composition of artichokes include significant amounts of fiber, folate, potassium, magnesium, phosphorus, iron, calcium, protein, vitamins, and many trace elements.

• **Jerusalem artichokes** (Sunchokes) have a smooth, crisp texture, similar to the radish. The larger tubers are best, and can be eaten raw, in salad, or cooked and prepared the same as potatoes by boiling and mashing into puree. Jerusalem artichokes contain inulin, a carbohydrate suitable for the diabetic diet. This herbaceous plant belongs to the same genus as the common sunflower; grows well in any garden.

• Select **Fennel** with a large round bulb and bright green tender tops. Avoid fennel with a flat bulb. These are woody and tough. Fennel enhances digestion. Just eat it raw. Save the tops for delicious soup. Tops can be chopped and frozen or dried for soups. (see recipes)

• Select **Broccoli** heads that are fresh, tightly formed, and deep green in color with firm stalks. Pale green or yellowing heads are past their prime. Broccoli, a member of the cruciferous family, is recognized as a cancer fighter. When properly cooked broccoli retains its vivid green color. Pour a little boiling water over spears. Cover; bring to a boil on high heat; reduce heat and steam until crisp-tender (5-7 min). Remove cover immedi ately to avoid it turning pale. Serve on a large platter, with a sprinkle of garlic powder, a drizzle of olive oil, and lemon wedges. Broccoli tastes good served hot or cold. Cauliflower florets are cooked the same way. Serve hot with cashew sauce or cold with lemon wedges.

• Cook the **fresh green tops** of garden radishes, beets, turnips, celery, outer leaves of lettuce, escarole, and other greens. These are a good source of nutrients and chlorophyll, and can be used in soup, broth, steamed or dried for veggie salt. If you have no garden, purchase fresh organic produce if possible.

• Clean **mushrooms** by "sweeping" them with a soft brush or damp paper towel (avoid soaking mushrooms as they will absorb water and get mushy). Avoid spongy-textured mushrooms. Store in their wrapped box or in a paper bag in crisper for up to 5 days. Mushrooms can be sautéed, stuffed, baked, sliced in salad, soup or gravy. The addition of a little sea salt, a little sweetening, and a little soy sauce or liquid aminos will magically enhance the flavor of stir-fried mushrooms. Firm small cremini or button mushrooms can be easily and evenly cut with an egg slicer.

• Avoid cooking **parsley**. To retain parsley's flavor and nutrients, chop the herb just before using and add it to cooked soups, potatoes, pasta, vegetables, hot dishes, salads, or for garnish. Freeze fresh parsley for instant use. Wash, dry, and chop the leaves. Freeze in zip-lock plastic bag or container; remove just the amount needed for each recipe.

• **Shallots** are sweeter and more mellow than regular onions, are very tasty sliced and eaten raw in sandwiches, minced and added to salad dressing, or sprinkled over soup, cooked vegetables, or gravy. When cooking, sauté or oven-roast to golden brown (being careful, like garlic, shallots can get bitter if overly browned). Delicious added to scrambled tofu, or add a dozen or more whole peeled shallots alongside your favorite meatless loaf, patties, or entrée when cooking.

• **Beets** add a sweet flavor and magnificent color to the meal. Wash beets thoroughly. Detach from greens. Cook separately. Boil, steam or bake beets whole. After cooking, hold beets under cold water. Skins will slip off easily. Slice or dice and season to taste.

• **Succulent Vegetables**
Finger-sized okra and other succulent garden vegetables are tasty, simply raw. When used as a garnish, these tender vegetables add a burst of color, interest, and nutrition to the finished dish.

Succulent Vegetables

Edamame

(green immature soybeans)

Young soybeans, shelled, or in the pod, are an excellent source of isoflavones, fiber, soy protein, iron and calcium. These versatile beans have a firm crisp texture, and may be eaten as a side-dish, or added to salad, soup, stir-fry, or combined with grains in casserole dishes.

**1 lb. fresh or frozen, soybeans in pod
seasoning: marjoram, chives, onion,
    rosemary
garnish: parsley, sweet red pepper, opt.**

Place one pound of green soybeans in a saucepan with 1" of boiling, lightly salted water. Bring to boil, reduce heat, cover and simmer 3-5 minutes until tender. Serve plain or remove pods; add seasonings.

Note: Enjoy beans in pod by pressing pod between thumb and forefinger to open and nudge the beans out. Pods may be discarded. Serves 4-6

Baked Butternut Squash

A very versatile vegetable, rich in beta-carotene (pro-vitamin A), potassium, vitamin C and fiber. Squash is excellent in diets that require low sodium and low fat, as in hypertension and coronary heart disease. Bake, boil, steam, mash and purée squash; or shred some varieties and- eat it raw!

**Butternut squash, or other
seasoning, herbs, to taste**

Select smooth-skinned squashes that are heavy for their size. Cut in half lengthwise, remove seeds. Place squash halves, cut side down, on oiled baking sheet. Bake in 350° oven 45 minutes or until tender, or place squash halves, cut sides up, in a baking dish. Pour water into dish ¼" deep; cover, bake at 375° 40 minutes or until tender when tested with fork. Season to taste **(sea salt, garlic, ginger, fennel, basil)** as desired.

Note: To steam or boil squash: Peel, cut into cubes. Cook in covered saucepan, with little water, 15-20 minutes or until tender.

Baked Winter Squash

Use **Hubbard, Kabocha, Gold Nugget, Buttercup, Acorn,** or other **winter squash**. Cut in serving size pieces; lightly brush with oil, sprinkle with sea salt. Bake at 350° 1 hour or steam until tender.

Sweet 'N Sour Veggie Noodles

A savory mix of vegetables and pasta that is delicious hot or cold.

8 oz. thin multi-grain spaghetti, cooked
1 small-medium zucchini, shredded
1 medium carrot, shredded
½ cup tender peas or pea pods
¼ cup chopped sweet or green onion
¼ cup finely chopped flat-leaf parsley
¼ cup toasted sesame seed
1 clove garlic, fresh minced
⅔ cup Sweet- Sour Sauce, see recipe

In a mixing bowl, toss all ingredients together. Serve warm or chill to marinate before serving.

Garden Vegetable Medley

A colorful side dish, with lots of nutrition. A tasty way to use extra zucchini.

1 cup diced green and orange pepper
1 med. onion, sliced
1-2 tsp. olive oil
2 lbs. zucchini, julienned
3 med. tomatoes, thin wedges
1 cup whole kernel corn
3 Tbs. minced fresh basil
½ tsp. salt, to taste

In a large skillet, sauté the onion and diced peppers in olive oil until crisp-tender. Add the zucchini, tomatoes, corn, sweet basil and salt. Stir and cook until vegetables are tender. Sprinkle with **toasted sesame seeds,** if desired.

Summer Squash Saute - recipe on right

Summer Squash Sauté

3-4 young summer squash, cubed
2 cloves garlic, minced
1 Tbs. Chicken-style Seasoning, to taste
1 Tbs. Bragg Aminos® or soy sauce
1 red pepper diced or red-pepper flakes
garnish: sweet basil

In a large non-stick skillet sauté the garlic and summer squash with 1-2 tsp. olive oil for 2-3 minutes until golden; cover and cook for 1 minute. Add the seasonings and diced pepper; stir fry 2-3 more minutes until squash is tender and browned, adding water if needed, to keep from sticking. A sprinkle of golden wheat flour can be added to enhance browning. Garnish with sweet basil, if desired. Delicious served with **green soybeans** or **lima beans** - a healthy combination and pretty contrast too!

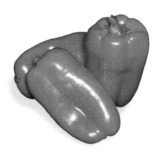

Roasted Sweet Peppers

Rich in protective antioxidant vitamins A and C

8 medium sweet red peppers
3-4 Tbs. lemon juice
1-2 Tbs. olive or canola oil
1 tsp. sea salt, to taste
2-3 cloves garlic, minced

1. Preheat the oven to 425-450° F. Wash red peppers, and drain them well.
2. Arrange whole peppers on a flat baking sheet; place 4 to 6 inches under broiler for about 10-15 minutes, or until the skins of the peppers becomes blistered and dark. Turn the peppers every 3-5 minutes, with tongs. (or cut pepper in half lengthwise, remove stem and seeds, and bake, cut side down in oven for 25-30 minutes)
3. Place hot peppers in a large covered pan. Let set 15 min. until cool enough to handle.
4. Carefully peel off charred skin with a sharp knife. Cut whole peppers in half or quarters. Remove the stems, ribs and seeds.
5. In large bowl, combine lemon juice, olive oil, salt, and garlic. Add the peppers, toss lightly to coat with lemon mixture. Layer into pint jars. Marinate in refrigerator several hours until ready to use, or freeze.

Suggestions or Ways to use Roasted Sweet Peppers: Serve as an appetizer with almond, cashew, or sesame butter on your favorite crackers or toast; add to pizza, tofu cheese, potato or macaroni salad, use as garnish, add to sandwiches or spreads, puree for cashew pimento sauce, or blend with a little mayonnaise for a quick dip.

Simply Broiled Eggplant

Select shiny dark fully ripe eggplant without blemish. (see Vegetable Tips)
Wash unpeeled eggplant. Cut off stem end. Slice in rounds or lengthwise ¼"- ½"
thick. Lightly brush both sides with olive oil. Sprinkle with sea salt and seasoning if desired. Layer slices in baking pans and place in oven, 3-4" under broiler. As the top slices brown and become tender, turn them over and brown the other side. Remove the slices that are tender and continue with the next layers till all eggplant is tender and browned.

Suggested uses:
Eggplant Roll-Ups, Eggplant Parmigiana, Eggplant sandwiches or serve with **Garden Veggie Tomato Sauce**. (see recipes).

Almond Eggplant Patties

2 medium ripe eggplant
2 cups whole wheat bread crumbs
1 cup almond meal
1 Tbs. soy sauce or Bragg's Aminos
¼ cup mixed fine cornmeal and flour
1 Tbs. onion powder
1 tsp. sea salt; ¼ tsp. garlic powder

Steam or bake whole eggplant. When cool remove skin and mash with fork. Add remaining ingredients and mix well. Form into patties; place on non-stick baking sheet. Bake at 350° 30-40 minutes, brown both sides. Yield: approx. 12 large patties

Squash & Pumpkin

Zucchini

Gold Nugget

Patty Pan

Chayote

Turban

Carnival

Yellow Crookneck

Buttercup

Spaghetti

Kabocha

Delicata

Acorn

Butternut

Winter Melon

Hubbard

Pumpkin

Zucchini & Tomatoes

6 small zucchini
1 bell pepper, diced, sautéed
2 tomatoes, peeled, thinly sliced
½ cup chopped green onion, sautéed
2 Tbs. fresh chopped parsley
½ tsp. sea salt or veggie salt
1-2 tsp. pure olive oil
2 Tbs. nutritional yeast flakes

Parboil whole zucchini 3-4 min. until crisp-tender. Cut in ¼" slices. Place in a shallow casserole alternating with green pepper, tomato, onion and seasoning - parsley and sea salt. Sprinkle with flaked yeast and olive oil. Bake at 350° for 10-15 minutes.

Pumpkin, Italian-style

1 pumpkin, medium size
garlic powder
sea salt, olive oil
3 lemons, freshly squeezed

Peel and slice pumpkin in wedges ½" thick. (opt: pre-steam 3-4 min. to partially cook). Heat non-stick or lightly oiled skillet. Lay slices of pumpkin side by side in skillet. Cover and cook until pumpkin is crisp-tender. Uncover and brown on both sides. Remove pumpkin from skillet and layer in casserole dish. Sprinkle each layer with a generous amount of garlic powder, sea salt, and fresh lemon juice. Repeat layers until all pumpkin is used. Pour lemon juice off and on to wet or baste slices of pumpkin. Chill to marinate flavors. Serve cold. Delicious!

Green Beans & Almonds

2 lbs. green beans
½ cup pure boiling water
½ tsp. sea salt
¼ cup toasted slivered almonds
1 tsp. onion powder
1 tsp. savory or dill weed
¼ cup chopped parsley
1 tsp. olive oil, opt.

Wash and cut beans in 1" pieces. Place beans and salt in saucepan, pour on boiling water. Cover, return to boiling, reduce heat and steam 5-7 min. until tender. Add the slivered almonds, seasonings, and parsley. Transfer to serving bowl, drizzle on olive oil and garnish with **pimento strips**, if desired.

Festive Green Bean Casserole

8 cups fresh cut or frozen green beans
1 medium onion, chopped
½ cup chopped sweet red pepper
½ recipe (1 cup) Cashew Milk Gravy
⅓ cup sliced almonds, toasted
1 tsp. grated lemon peel (zest)
1 8-oz. can sliced water chestnuts, drained
½ cup dry bread crumbs, seasoned
1 cup "American Cheeze" shreds
  (see recipe)

Cook green beans in 1 cup boiling water and ¼ tsp. sea salt until just tender. Drain, reserve liquid for making **Cashew Gravy**. In a large skillet, sauté the onion and pepper in olive oil; stir in 1 Tbs. flour, cashew gravy, almonds, lemon zest, water chestnuts and green beans. Transfer bean mixture to a casserole dish. Top with cheeze shreds and seasoned bread crumbs. Bake at 350° for 25 minutes or until heated through.

Baked Zucchini Steaks

Squash is low in fat, and when prepared with nutritional yeast is high in B-vitamins. Large tender zucchini rounds, breaded and baked look like steak. Baked slices make a delicious sandwich filling.

**zucchini squash, tender
nutritional yeast, seasoned
olive oil, sea salt**

Wash and slice whole zucchini in ½" rounds; slice small squash in half lengthwise. Brush or spray lightly with oil; press cut side down firmly into seasoned yeast flakes. Place on baking sheet. Sprinkle with salt and olive oil if desired. Bake at 375° or tenderize under broiler, until fork can be easily inserted. Turn and bake on both sides until crusty and golden brown.

Herbed Zucchini & Peas

**¾ lb. small zucchini, sliced
1 lb. frozen shelled peas
¼ tsp. sea salt
½ tsp. dried thyme leaves
olive oil, to taste, opt.**

In medium saucepan, cook zucchini in small amount of boiling water with sea salt and thyme 5 min. Add peas, steam just until tender. Drizzle with **olive oil**, if desired.

Skillet Rice & Sugar Snap Peas

Some of my favorite ingredients (sugar snap peas, tofu and red peppers) are included in this colorful dish that is quick-and-easy to prepare. At times I serve it as a satisfying entree with a side vegetable.

**3 cups blanched sugar snap peas
1 ½ cups firm tofu cubes, browned
2 tsp. soy sauce or liquid aminos
1 tsp. chicken style seasoning
1 tsp. onion powder
⅔ cup sweet red pepper rings
1 tsp. olive oil + ½ tsp. dark sesame oil
1 tsp. grated ginger, opt.
3 cups cooked cold leftover brown rice**

Blanch sugar snap peas by plunging into boiling water 60 seconds then toss into ice water; drain, set aside. In a non-stick skillet, brown tofu cubes in olive oil, sprinkle on soy sauce, chicken-style seasoning and onion powder. Add pepper rings, ginger, blanched peas and sesame oil; stir-fry 1-2 minutes. Add cooked rice, toss and stir 1 minute or until heated through. Adjust seasonings or add sea salt to taste. Yield: 4 servings

Fresh Sweet Corn with Herb Butter

What could be more flavorful than fresh picked garden veggies, especially tender sweet corn?

6 ears sweet corn, yellow, honey cream
herb butter, see recipe
sprinkle of sea salt

Husk and remove silk from fresh picked sweet corn. In a wide kettle, bring 1 qt. pure water to a boil.

Set corn on steamer rack or place corn directly into boiling water. Cook over medium heat 7-10 minutes or until tender. Remove from heat, serve with herb butter, sprinkle with sea salt or just eat plain. Delicious!

Note: For roasted sweet corn, leave husk on, cook over open campfire, or place corn on gas grill rack, cover and cook over medium heat.

Tender String Beans

Select fresh garden beans and eat raw in salad or lightly steam 4-5 minutes just to tenderize. Season with sea salt, garlic powder and a drizzle of olive oil and lemon juice. Garnish with bits of pimento or sweet red onion, if desired.

Stewed Okra Gumbo

Okra is rich in folate, other B vitamins, calcium, magnesium, iron and fiber.

Okra, sliced
Onion, chopped
Tomatoes, fresh or canned
Corn, fresh or frozen, opt.
Seasoning: sea salt, garlic, parsley
Corn meal, fine, opt.

In a saucepan, healthy sauté sliced okra and onion in a little water or olive oil. Add fresh chopped or canned tomatoes, frozen or fresh corn (opt.), and seasoning. For a thicker stew, sprinkle on corn meal, stir to combine. Cover, cook on low heat 20-30 min. until thickened.

Savory Herbed Polenta

Follow recipe **Polenta - Corn Meal** in **Grains** chapter. Add **1 cup mixed chopped green pepper, pimento, parsley** and season with **fresh** or **dried herbs** of your choice.

Minted Peas & Parsley

2 lbs. tender peas, fresh or frozen
2 Tbs. chopped fresh mint
2 Tbs. minced fresh parsley
1 tsp. pure olive oil, opt.

Steam peas until just tender. Add parsley, mint, olive oil and sea salt to taste.

Note: dried mint and parsley may be used instead of fresh.

Flower Vegetables

Serve steamed artichokes with a dipping sauce. The tender heart is the most favorite part. Enjoy!

Artichoke (globe) - a tall composite herb resembling a thistle, having an edible flower head, which is cooked as a vegetable. This elegant and remarkable flower vegetable is virtually fat-free. Contains many medicinal properties beneficial to the liver, kidneys, gallbladder disorders, and elevated cholesterol levels. Artichokes are a source of Potassium, Calcium, Phosphorus, Iron, Protein and Fiber. The majority of artichokes grown today are from Castroville, California, better known as the "artichoke capital of the world".

Steamed Artichokes

Getting to the heart of the artichoke is definitely worth the effort. This interesting thistle flower is delicious, as well as good-for-you.

Rinse **4 artichokes**. Trim stems, and remove loose discolored leaves. Cut off ½" from the top. Using kitchen shears, snip off sharp tips from remaining leaves. In a large kettle bring ½" of water to boiling. Set artichokes in pan or steamer rack stem side down; return to a boil. Reduce heat, simmer covered 20 minutes or until tender when tested with a toothpick, or a leaf pulls out easily. Drain artichokes. (Reserve remaining liquid; it's sweet and good to use in soup or tomato sauce).

Make **Lemon-Oil Dip**:

Stir together **4 Tbs. lemon juice, 2 Tbs. olive oil, ½ tsp. veggie or garlic salt.** Serve artichokes hot or cold, cut side up with dip or ***sauce**.

*Creamy Lemon Dill Sauce: Mix ¼ cup **soy mayonnaise** with **I Tbs. lemon juice, 1 tsp.fresh** or **¼ tsp. dried dill, 1 tsp.onion powder,** and **⅛ tsp. paprika.**

Note: To eat artichokes, pull off one leaf at a time and dip base in sauce. Draw base of leaf through your teeth, scraping off the tender flesh. Continue with each leaf until the fuzzy choke appears. Remove and discard the choke. Eat the remaining heart with a fork, dipping pieces of it in the sauce. A real delicacy! Stems are edible too.

Globe Artichokes with Onion

(Good as a sandwich filling or as topping for pizza)

Artichokes are a source of Potassium, Calcium, Phosphorus, Iron, Protein and Fiber.

4-6 globe artichoke, small tender onions, chopped
sea salt and olive oil
lemon juice, to taste

Clean artichokes - Cut off ½" from top and remove tough part of outer leaves. Quarter the artichokes, remove 'fuzzy choke'. Cut quarters and stems in small pieces. Sauté artichokes and onions in a non-stick skillet with a little water or olive oil and salt. Reduce heat, cover and steam together until tender, adding water as needed to prevent sticking. Add lemon juice to taste. Delicious hot or cold.

Note: Select artichokes that are flat, not pointed at the top. The flatter ones are more tender. Cold boiled artichokes can be used; cut in pieces, sauté with onions and seasoning.

Remove tough ends of outer leaves by cutting with scissors or with a twisting motion of the first two fingers.

Cut off ½" from top of leaves. Small artichokes are quite tender and may not need to be cut off very much. Select artichokes that are more flat at the top. Pointed artichokes have a sharp beard.

Notice the intricate arrangement of leaves and the different shades of green. Tender artichokes can be spread apart and stuffed – then cooked in tomato sauce until tender. (see Main Dishes)

Cut tender artichokes in quarters, remove choke, sauté with onion, or steam and use in dips.

Broccoli Italian-style

Rich in many nutrients including provitamin A, vitamin C, E, calcium, iron, potassium, and protein. Broccoli, a cruciferous vegetable is anti-carcinogenic.

1 head of broccoli
½ tsp. sea salt
½ tsp. garlic powder
1-2 tsp. pure virgin olive oil
lemon wedges, opt.

Select dark green bunches of broccoli, with no yellow flowers appearing. Wash broccoli, separate florets, peel tougher stalks at base (stalks may be eaten raw). Place in saucepan, add salt, and ¼-½ cup of boiling water. Cover, bring to boil, reduce heat and steam 5-6 min., just until tender when tested with fork. Uncover immediately (to retain bright green color). Arrange spears on platter, sprinkle with garlic powder, drizzle with olive oil. Serve warm or cold with wedges of lemon, if desired.

Cauliflower & Corn

4 cups chopped cauliflower
2 cups whole kernel corn
garnish: pimento or parsley

Steam cauliflower in a little pure water and sea salt until tender. Remove cauliflower, cook corn in same water until tender. Combine cauliflower and corn in serving bowl; sprinkle with olive oil and garnish with bits of chopped pimento or parsley, if desired.

Cauliflower & Peas

1 small head cauliflower
1 cup vegetable water
¼ cup cashew nuts
¾ Tbs. arrowroot powder
¼ tsp. sea salt
1 tsp. olive or soy oil, opt.
1 tsp. soy sauce
   or liquid aminos, opt.
1 cup steamed peas

In a medium saucepan, steam small cauliflower florets in pure water and sea salt, 5-8 min. until tender. Drain water and use in making the sauce. Blend the sauce ingredients until smooth. Bring to a boil, stirring until thick. Add tender peas. Pour sauce over cauliflower. Garnish with parsley or pimento if desired.

*Strengthen your immune system by eating vegetables rich in antioxidants such as **Broccoli, Carrots, Spinach, Kale,** and **Tomatoes.** Antioxidants help neutralize free radicals, and may assist in the prevention of cancer, arthritis and heart disease.*

Leafy Vegetables

Mixed Turnip, Mustard & Collard Greens

An excellent source of calcium, iron, vitamin A, C, E, fiber, and a host of nutrients that protect against cancer, heart disease, obesity and other diseases.

½ lb. turnip greens
½ lb. collard greens
½ lb. mustard greens
2-3 cloves garlic or ¼ tsp. powder
¼ tsp. sea salt, to taste
1 tsp. pure olive oil, opt.
2 Tbs. boiling water

Choose dark green, tender leaves, without blemish. Trim bruised leaves, cut off tough stems (save for juicing). Wash greens in cold water several times, drain. Cut or leave whole if leaves are small. In a deep skillet or pan, healthy sauté minced garlic in olive oil or water for half minute. Add the washed greens, salt, and 2 Tbs. water or just what clings to leaves, if waterless cookware is used. Cover, bring to boil, reduce heat, cook 8-10 minutes until tender (greens wilt down in volume). Transfer to serving dish, drizzle with **lemon juice** and **olive oil**, if desired. Servings: 4

Spinach Roman-style

3 lbs. fresh or frozen spinach
½ tsp. sea salt, to taste
1-2 tsp. extra virgin olive oil
2-3 cloves garlic, minced
3 Tbs. pine nuts or slivered almonds
¼ cup sliced green olives
¼ cup sliced black olives
¼ cup cooked sliced mushrooms

If fresh spinach is used, wash thoroughly and drain. Sprinkle with salt, cook 5 minutes, then drain and chop. If frozen spinach is used, steam 1 minute less than package directs, drain and chop (discard the water used in cooking to reduce oxalic acid in spinach). Heat the oil in a skillet, add garlic and nuts, sauté until golden. Add the olives and mushrooms, stir until coated. Mix in the spinach, heat and serve. Garnish with more pine nuts, and lemon wedges if desired. Serves 4-6.

Wilted Lettuce

My dear mother would never throw away the outer leaves of dark lettuce or escarole, but would wash, cut and lightly cook them in a little water, with a pinch of sea salt and one or two cloves of minced garlic, until tender. The warm wilted greens, served with a drizzle of olive oil in a soup bowl, were a stomach tonic when we children were feeling ill. Amazingly, the greens tasted pretty good; and we recovered. Mother uses this simple natural remedy herself; perhaps one more reason she is nearly 105 years old!

Cabbage Rolls

Core large head of **green cabbage**; place in boiling water until leaves drop off freely. Put leaves in very hot salted water 6-8 minutes, to soften for rolling. Place a large scoop of **Rice Stuffing** on each leaf. Roll up tightly. Tie with kitchen string to hold together, if needed. Place a little **sauerkraut** in baking dish with leftover cut cabbage. Place the cabbage rolls on top. Cover with more sauerkraut and sprinkle with **caraway seed**, if desired. Bake at 350° until tender. Serve with **Cashew** or **Almond Gravy.**

Wilted Spinach

Spinach tops the list as a very rich source of lutein, and zeaxanthin, two carotenoids that prevent vision loss. This protective food is best eaten raw in salads or sandwiches, or just lightly steamed or wilted. An excellent source of folate, vitamin A, C, and other vitamins and minerals.

1½ lbs. fresh spinach leaves
1 tsp. extra virgin olive oil
2 cloves minced garlic
¼ tsp. sea salt
1Tbs. lemon or lime juice

Heat oil and minced garlic in deep skillet, add salt. Gradually add washed spinach leaves, toss just until spinach is wilted. Drizzle with lemon or lime juice. Serve warm. Servings: 2-3

Collard Greens

(Rich source of Calcium, vitamin A and Iron)

Start with **1½ - 2 lbs. tender collard greens.** Wash greens thoroughly in cold water; drain and remove tough stems. Coarsely chop leaves to measure 6-8 cups, set aside.

Drizzle **1 tsp. olive oil** in a large saucepan, add **4 cloves sliced garlic or 4 shakes garlic powder.** Add **collard greens, a sprinkle of sea salt and ¼ cup boiling water.**

Cover with tight fitting lid. Bring to boil, reduce heat, simmer 10-12 minutes to desired tenderness. Serve with fresh lemon wedges. Delicious and good for you! Servings: 4

Potato Kale Casserole

Kale is an excellent source of vitamin A, calcium, iron and protective anti-oxidants.

Kale is a member of the cabbage family that does not form a head. Recognized by its sturdy, frilly leaves, usually dark green in color, tinged with blue and purple, with a mild cabbage taste.

1 lb. whole new potatoes
1 med. onion, chopped
2 garlic cloves, minced
1 lb. fresh chopped kale
sea salt, olive oil, to taste

Scrub and steam whole unpeeled potatoes until tender. Lightly sauté chopped onion and garlic in a little olive oil, add the washed, de-ribbed, chopped kale greens. Cover and steam until tender. Coarsely mash the potatoes, add the cooked greens and combine together. Season to taste with a little sea salt. Place in casserole, thread on olive oil, if desired. Bake in oven until warmed through, or serve as is. Delicious!

Beet Greens

The tender leaf tops of beets make a delicious pungent dish.

**Beet greens, washed
garlic cloves, minced
sea salt, to taste
olive oil, opt.**

Thoroughly wash and clean beet greens, removing any damaged or bruised leaves. riefly sauté garlic in a teaspoon of olive oil or water. Place greens on top and steam with just the water that clings to leaves, over medium heat 3-4 minutes

until tender. Transfer to a serving bowl, drizzle with olive oil if desired. Good served warm or cold.

Note: see Root Vegetables for preparation of beets.

Swiss Chard with Pine Nuts

A mild vegetable to steam or add to stir-fry. Raw chard may dominate a dish; use sparingly.

**Swiss chard, leaves and stalks
fresh garlic, chopped
sea salt, olive oil, to taste
pine nuts, walnuts or pecans**

Clean chard, rinsing in water several times. Separate the stalks from large leaves. (the two parts are sometimes cooked separately then tossed together and seasoned). Cut stalks in thick slices; cut leaves in strips. In a covered saucepan, cook stalks in a little water or olive oil and garlic until almost tender. Add cut leaves, lightly steam until just wilted. Season with a little sea salt; generously sprinkle with pine nuts. Serve.

Rainbow Chard

There is more than one variety of Swiss chard and both leaves and stalks are edible. Rainbow chard is colorful, good looking and good tasting! (Prepare in the same way as Swiss Chard above)

Sweet Sour Cabbage

One of my favorites. This dish actually tastes better cold!

4 Tbs. chopped onion
1 Tbs. water or olive oil
⅓ cup sucanat raw sugar or honey
⅓ cup fresh lemon juice
1 tsp. crushed caraway seed
1 tsp. sea salt, to taste
2 lb. red cabbage, shredded

In a large skillet, healthy sauté onion in 1 Tbs. water or olive oil. Add remaining ingredients, cover with lid. Steam 15 min. or until cabbage is wilted and tender. Cool or refrigerate to marinate flavors.

Super Asparagus Patties

Put through a coarse food grinder:

1 lb. chopped raw asparagus*
2 cups raw carrots, shredded
1 cup chopped almonds, raw or toasted
¼ cup chopped parsley

Pureé in blender:

1 cup plain soy or nut milk
2 cups raw oats, quick
1 medium onion, chopped
2 tsp. sea salt, to taste
2 tsp. paprika
½ tsp. thyme or marjoram

Mix all ingredients together. Drop by table-spoonful onto non-stick baking sheet. Bake at 400° for 20 minutes.
*1 lb. of asparagus or 1 bunch = approx. 3 cups.

Creamed Asparagus on Toast

One serving of Asparagus boasts the following daily requirements: Vitamin C and Calcium, 20%; Vitamin A, 8%; Dietary Fiber, 12%.

1 lb. asparagus spears
2 cups pure water
½ cup cashew nuts
1-2 Tbs. onion powder or flakes
1 tsp. veggie salt; ¼ tsp. celery seed
2 Tbs. arrowroot powder
1 tsp. soy or olive oil, opt.

Steam asparagus spears until tender in very little water and sea salt. Drain and reserve liquid to blend with remaining ingredients for **cream sauce or ***. Blend sauce, heat and stir until thickened. Pour over tender cut asparagus or asparagus spears on whole grain toast. Garnish with diced pimento, if desired. Serve as a main vegetable or side-dish with scrambled tofu and avocado.

* **Cashew Pimento Sauce** makes a nice topping for plain steamed asparagus spears (see recipe).

Steamed Brussels Sprouts

Fresh cooked Brussels sprouts have a delicate nutty flavor. The small cabbage-like heads, a member of the cruciferous family of cancer-fighting vegetable, very rich in phytochemicals, vitamins and minerals.

1 lb. Brussels sprouts
sea salt, onion powder, to taste
¼ cup pine nuts, lightly toasted

Select small to medium firm bright green heads that are compact. (the smaller ones are more tender). Rinse well, trim stem and remove any leaves that are yellow or withered. Place in a sauce-pan or on a steamer rack in pan. Add a small amount of boiling water and salt, if desired. Steam 6-8 minutes until crisp tender, avoid overcooking which may cause sprouts to be bitter. Season with onion powder and olive oil if desired; transfer to serving dish. Sprinkle on pine nuts.

"God is working in behalf of His people. He does not desire them to be without resources. He is bringing them back to the diet originally given to man. Their diet is to consist of the foods made from the materials He has provided. The materials principally used in these foods will be fruits and grains and nuts, but various roots will also be used."
E. G. White, **Diet & Foods**, pp 270 - 271

Root Vegetables

Sweet Roasted Vegetables

This versatile side dish is enhanced by the natural golden color and sweetness of these scrumptious vegetables. A favorite that compliments the most simple or elaborate meal.

1 lb. sweet potatoes, 3 cups, peeled, cubed
1 ½ cups parsnips, cut in ½" slices
1 ½ cups butternut squash, peeled, cubed
1 fennel bulb, sliced in thin wedges
1 cup baby carrots, whole or sliced
1 cup pearl onions or shallots, sliced
1 Tbs. soy butter or olive oil
½ tsp. sea salt; ¼ tsp. paprika
1 Tbs. maple syrup, agave or honey
1 tsp. lemon juice

Preheat oven to 450°. Combine first 8 ingredients in a large bowl; toss well. Spread vegetables in a prepared non-stick roasting pan or dish. Cover with foil. Bake at 450° for 50 minutes or until the vegetables are tender. Drizzle with maple syrup and lemon juice; toss and bake uncovered 5-10 minutes more, until golden and glazed. Servings: 4-6

551

Ten Talents

Potatoes (organic), are best cooked with skins. Bake, Steam, Boil, or Roast. If peeling is necessary, peel paper thin. Vitamins and valuable nutrients are just below the skin.

5 cloves garlic, minced
1 Tbs. pure olive oil
1 Tbs. Bragg® liquid aminos
2 tsp. onion powder
 or 1 small red onion, sliced
1 Tbs. rosemary, dried crushed
½ tsp. sea salt; ½ tsp. thyme
¼ tsp. cayenne
2 Tbs. lemon juice, 2 Tbs. honey

Pan Potatoes, Carrots & Onions

8 cups potatoes (3 #), cubes or strips
4 cups carrots, baby whole or strips
1 large onion, thinly sliced in wedges
5-6 cloves garlic, chopped
sea salt, olive oil, paprika, to taste
¼ cup parsley, fresh chopped

Simply combine first 4 ingredients in large mixing bowl. Add seasonings and mix together. Transfer to shallow baking pan; cover. Bake at 375° stirring often, or cook in a heavy skillet on stovetop with a little water, until potatoes are tender and golden brown. Add fresh chopped parsley. Serve hot, warm or cold. Delicious!

Herb-Roasted Root Vegetables

These sturdy textured vegetables are a rich source of vitamins, minerals and fiber. Their earthy flavors combine well with a variety of herbs and are a satisfying side to the main dish.

4 red potatoes, cut in ½" strips
2 cups parsnips, ½" round slices or strips
1 rutabaga, peeled, cut in 1" pieces
1 turnip, peeled, cut in ¾" cubes
1 red pepper, cut into strips
1 cup fennel stalks or bulb, sliced, opt.

Preheat oven to 450°. Combine all ingredients except lemon and honey in a large bowl; toss well. Spread vegetables single layer on a non-stick baking pan or heavy skillet. Cover, bake 40 minutes or until vegetables are almost tender. Uncover, toss veggies, bake 10 minutes to brown. Transfer vegetables to large bowl. Add honey and lemon juice; toss well. Servings: 4-6

Twice - Baked Potatoes

Select medium-large baking potatoes. Scrub, but do not peel. Pierce with a fork to allow steam to escape while potatoes are baking. Brush lightly with olive oil and bake in 350° oven until tender, about 1 hour. Cut potatoes in half; scoop out inside, leaving a thin shell, being careful not to tear the skin. Mash potato with a little plain soy or nut milk, until no lumps remain. Add chopped parsley, garlic salt or dill. Fill potato shells with potato mixture. Return to 375° oven, bake 10-15 minutes until heated through.

Variations: Mash potato, add chives or dill weed. Mash potato, add chopped sautéed onion. Mash potato with peas; sprinkle with paprika.

Root Vegetables

Sunchokes

Garlic

Radishes

Daikon

Carrots

Celery Root

Rutabaga

Turnip

Onions

Parsnips

Jicama

Sweet Potatoes

Beets

Shallots

Russet, Red & White Potatoes

Parsley Potato Patties

4 cups mashed potatoes, hot or cold
½ cup fresh chopped parsley
1 Tbs. onion powder
   or ⅓ cup minced onion
paprika and sea salt, to taste
1-2 Tbs. almond or cashew butter, opt.

Mix potatoes, parsley, seasonings and nut butter together (leftover mashed potatoes are fine). Form into flat patties, sprinkle with paprika. Bake or brown in skillet on both sides.

Variations: Add ½ cup mashed carrots, chopped sautéed onion, or dill weed.

Golden Roasted Potatoes

4 med. potatoes, cut in small chunks
2 small zucchini, slice in 2"long pieces
1 sweet red pepper, cut in bite-size pieces
1 medium onion, sliced or chopped
1-2 Tbs. pure olive oil
sea salt or chicken-style seasoning,
   to taste
pinch of saffron or paprika, opt.
2-3 Tbs. minced Italian flat-leaf parsley

In a bowl, combine unpeeled potatoes, zucchini, pepper, onion and seasoning. Transfer to non-stick pan; bake at 375° stirring often until potatoes are tender and golden brown. Sprinkle on parsley. Serve with **Italian Tossed Salad** and **crusty garlic bread.**

Roasted Garlic

Recipe:
see **Sandwiches and Spreads, pg. 468**

Garlic Mashed Potatoes

2 lbs.(6) medium red or white potatoes
6-8 cloves garlic, peeled
½ cup soy milk, plain
1 Tbs. soy butter or olive oil
¼ tsp. sea salt, to taste
½ tsp. dried dill weed, or chives, opt.

In a saucepan, place whole scrubbed potatoes (with skins). Add salt and water, just enough to half cover potatoes. Cover, heat to boiling; reduce heat. Simmer 30 minutes or until potatoes are tender; add garlic during last half of cooking. Remove potato skins, mash potatoes, add the soy milk and seasonings; serve with your favorite gravy (see recipes).

Oven - Browned Potatoes

Cook **potatoes** with skins, in lightly salted water until tender. Carefully remove thin skin. Place potatoes in non-stick baking pan; brush with **olive oil** and sprinkle on **sea salt**. Bake in hot 400° oven, turning 1 or 2 times until crusty and golden brown.

Christmas Potatoes

6 medium potatoes, unpeeled
2 medium carrots
1 large red beet, peeled
sea salt, to taste

Scrub potatoes, cut in quarters and steam with other vegetables until tender. Mash or whip until fluffy; add **2 Tbs. cashew butter**, a drizzle of **olive oil** and **sea salt** to taste, whip again. Sprinkle on **shredded coconut** if desired. These red potatoes are pretty served with a **colorful salad, yellow squash** and **green peas**.

Stuffed Sweet Potatoes

Sweet potatoes' rich orange color indicates their high level of immune-boosting beta-carotene (provitamin A).

Place clean **sweet potatoes** or **yams** on a steamer rack, so potatoes do not touch water below (½" water in bottom of kettle). Steam on stovetop, 30 minutes or until potatoes are tender. When cool enough to handle, slice ¼" off topside of potato. Scoop out half of the sweet potato, without tearing skin. Mash with a little **molasses** or **maple syrup** (1-2 tsp. for each potato) and **creamy cashew milk**. Add **1 Tbs. chopped parsley** and /or **toasted walnuts** for each potato. Stuff back into shells. Garnish with **fresh chopped parsley** or **walnuts** and serve.

Note: Steamed sweet potatoes retain their flavor, without becoming water logged. The entire sweet potato is edible, or if you prefer- just peel off the very thin skin.

Scalloped Potatoes

7 medium unpeeled potatoes (2 lbs.)
1 large onion, chopped or sliced
2 cloves garlic, minced
¼ cup gold 'n white flour
1 tsp. sea salt + ¼ tsp. celery seed
pinch cayenne or red pepper flakes, opt.
2 ½ cups soy milk or cashew milk gravy

In saucepan, cook onion and garlic in olive oil until tender. Stir in flour and seasonings; add milk or cashew gravy (omit flour if using gravy). Bring to boil, stir until thickened. Scrub potatoes, thinly slice. Place layers of potatoes and sauce alternately in prepared 2 qt. non-stick casserole. Bake covered at 375° 1 hour, uncover and bake 40 min. more or until potatoes are tender. Let stand 15 minutes before serving.

Jerusalem artichokes (Sunchokes)
Roots of a perennial plant in the sunflower family widely cultivated for its tubers and used as a vegetable. The ivory flesh has a crisp texture similar to water chestnuts. Just scrub and eat raw, slice or grate in salad. Globe and Jerusalem artichokes contain minerals including potassium, iron, and phosphorus. They are a good source of easily digested carbohydrates including inulin, and virtually contain no fat, protein or glucose. For this reason they are very suitable for the diabetic diet.

Mashed Carrots and Turnips

2 lbs. carrots, sliced
2 med. turnips, peeled, diced
1-2 tsp. Herb Butter or olive oil
¼ tsp. salt; dash of cayenne, opt.
parsley, fresh minced

Place carrots and turnips in a saucepan with a little water. Cover and steam until tender. Mash; add soy butter or olive oil, sprinkle with chives, if desired.

Glazed Carrots

Beta-carotene, a plant substance, which the body converts into vitamin A, is abundant in carrots, sweet potatoes, kale, and a variety of dark yellow and green vegetables. These foods, rich in anti-oxidants, strengthen the immune system, and protect against diseases of the eyes and skin disorders. In addition to vitamin A, carrots contain vitamin C, B, E, potassium, iron, other minerals, trace elements, protein and fiber! Good raw in salad, for juicing, stir-fry, combined with potatoes, parsnips and other vegetables.

1 lb. fresh carrots, cut
½ Tbs. honey, agave or sucanat
½ Tbs. maple butter, see recipe
⅛ tsp. sea salt
fresh dill weed, opt.

Select carrots that are fresh, slender and preferably with green tops. Scrub carrots, remove tops; leave baby carrots whole or cut carrots into julienne strips or "coins". In a medium saucepan, steam carrots or cook in very little water 5-8 minutes until crisp-tender. Drain, set aside, reserve liquid for soup or gravy. Combine rest of ingredients (except dill) in saucepan. Heat until bubbly; add carrots, cook 4-5 minutes until glazed. Transfer to serving dish; garnish with fresh chopped dill weed. Yield: 4 servings

Roasted Beets

Delicious served warm or cold, a colorful salad, rich in anti-oxidants.

3-5 beets, medium size
Lemon-Herb Marinade, recipe pg. 478

Cut top greens from beets leaving ½" of stem. Wash beets, being careful not to remove the tail (taproot). Place in baking dish with ½ cup water. Bake covered 45-60 minutes or until tender. Cool beets 5-10 minutes, then remove skins under running water. Cut beets into ½"slices then cut each slice in half to make half circles. Toss with **Lemon-Herb Marinade**. Serve plain or on a bed of tender mixed salad greens. Drizzle on marinade.

Simply Parsnips

(Pictured right)

The sweet, nutty, slightly piquant flavor of parsnips is sure to compliment that special dinner meal. Rich in dietary fiber and minerals, especially potassium.

**4-5 parsnips, medium size
soy butter and honey, to taste
¼ tsp. cardamom
     or fresh grated ginger, opt.**

Select young, firm, crisp parsnips without cracks. Scrape clean. Cut in half lengthwise, then in fourths, or 1/2" slices or strips. Cook in saucepan with little water, or steam. Bring to boil, then cook 5-7 minutes or until tender, being careful not to overcook. Season with a little soy butter, honey, or ginger to taste. Enjoy!

Beets with Lemon Sauce

Sweet and sour with lots of eye appeal. This colorful side dish is sure to compliment the meal and satisfy the taste for something sweet and sour.

Wash and steam 2-3 whole unpeeled beets until tender. Remove skins under cold water. Dice or thinly slice beets.

For **Lemon Sauce** stir:

**1 cup beet juice or water
2 Tbs. arrowroot powder
¼ tsp. sea salt**

Simmer until thick and clear. Turn off heat, add:

**2 Tbs. lemon juice + ½ tsp. lemon zest
2-3 Tbs. honey
beets, diced or sliced**

Serve warm or cold. Servings: 4-6

Sweet Potato Casserole

**4 cups cooked sweet potatoes
¼ cup almond, cashew or peanut butter
½ cup hot soy milk
2 Tbs. honey + 1 Tbs. molasses
¼ tsp. salt, to taste
¼ tsp. coriander, opt.
garnish: toasted walnuts, chopped parsley**

Steam or boil sweet potatoes in small amount of water until tender. Remove skins. Mash sweet potatoes in a pan until smooth, adding the soymilk and the rest of ingredients, a little at a time. Spoon into a (soy) buttered baking dish and bake; or mix nut butter and honey together and spread on the bottom of a non-stick or prepared baking pan. Top with the sweet potato mixture. Bake uncovered at 350° for 40 minutes. Garnish with chopped toasted walnuts and fresh parsley. Serves 4-6

Candied Yams

A festive dish, perfect for that special occasion and Thanksgiving dinner. Excellent source of vitamin A, and other nutrients including calcium, phosphorus and potassium.

6-7 yams or sweet potatoes, med. (3-4 lbs)
¼ cup honey or part maple syrup
**   + 1 Tbs.water**
¼ tsp. vanilla or orange zest, opt.
shredded coconut, medium fine, opt.
walnut or pecan halves

Slip off skins from cooked (baked, boiled, or steamed) sweet potatoes or yams. Slice into 1½" rounds. Roll in shredded coconut if desired. Place in a lightly (soy) buttered baking dish. Top with walnut or pecan halves. Thread on honey or maple syrup mix. Bake 30 minutes in 375° oven or until heated through, glazed and golden brown.

Note: Sweet potatoes may be candied in a skillet on stovetop. Remove skins from cooked sweet potatoes; cut in ½" slices. Heat syrup mixture in a non-skillet until bubbly. Add potatoes, gently stirring until glazed and hot.

Baked Sweet Potatoes

Bake whole sweet potatoes at 325°-350° for 45-60 minutes (depending on size) turning once in pan. When soft to the touch or a toothpick can be inserted easily, they are done. Cover with a towel, until serving time. Skins will peel off easily. Sweet potatoes are delicious eaten at room temperature, either hot or cold. Sweet potatoes can be baked the day before you plan to serve them. Enjoy the sweet taste by simply peeling them like you would a banana; no need to warm them again.

Note: It is not necessary to prick sweet potatoes before baking. Pricking them causes the naturally sweet syrup to spill out of the potato, losing flavor, plus a messy pan to clean up.

Baked Yams and Onions

Cook whole yams or sweet potatoes. When cool enough to handle, slip off skins. Dice and mix with a generous amount of sautéed sweet white or green onions and a pinch of sea salt. Spoon into a non-stick prepared baking dish. Bake at 375° 30 min. or until lightly browned. Garnish with fresh parsley or chives.

Combined Vegetables

Tofu Veggie Kabobs

An attractive, appetizing way to serve common vegetables

See Kabobs recipe in chapter **Meatless Main Dishes, pg 349**

Suggestions for Vegetable Cuisine - Conserving Minerals and Vitamins

Do's	Don'ts
Choose wide variety, prepare with care	Unattractive, dull, no variety or taste
Cook vegetables until they are crisp- tender...not mushy	Avoid overcooking vegetables
Cook waterless or pour small amount of boiling water over vegetables	Using large amounts of cold water- leaches out water-soluble vitamins
Use cooking liquid for soups, gravies, sauces, and bread	Draining and discarding cooking liquid into sink
Cook or steam vegetables properly to retain vivid color	Adding baking soda -destroys vitamin B^1,C and hinders digestion
Fresh, stir-fry, bake, steam, boil, roast	Fast-food, microwave, T. V. dinners
Serve vegetables as fresh as possible, and as soon as prepared or ready	Holding or storing vegetables too long, before preparing or serving
Store fresh leafy or garden vegetables in a cool place or refrigerate	Storing fresh garden produce in a warm place
Steam beet or turnip tops, green lettuce, broccoli, cauliflower leaves as veggies	Discarding the outer green leaves
Scrub potatoes – steam or bake whole. Eat skins.	Peeling potatoes - cutting away eyes.

Vegetables Crêpes

A combination of vegetables and browned tofu cubes make a nice filling for Crêpes

See **Savory Vegetable Crêpes** in chapter **Meatless Main Dishes**, page 358

Green Soy Bean Trio

A colorful combination of vegetables, rich in vitamins, minerals and fiber. Serve this tasty side dish to compliment any meal, at any season.

**2 ½ cups green soy beans
(frozen, fresh, canned)
2 cups carrots, diced or julienne sliced
1 ½ cups celery, diagonally sliced
basil or savory, fresh minced or dried
pure virgin olive oil, to taste
garlic, fresh minced or powder, to taste
sea salt, to taste**

Steam carrots and celery 5 min. in a little water. Add soy beans and cook until tender. Add seasonings and olive oil to taste. Garnish with fresh parsley.

Marinated Tofu

Tofu that has been frozen and thawed, has a unique spongy texture that is chewy and soaks up liquids easily. For this reason frozen tofu can easily substitute in some recipes for enhanced texture and works well for marinating. (see "Types of Tofu" in Main Dishes). Freeze Tofu in original container or plastic bag for 1-2 days up to 6 months. (I usually keep 2-3 containers of tofu in the freezer, to be thawed when needed). Thaw in refrigerator overnight, or in a bowl of hot water. Press or squeeze out excess liquid (tofu will be spongy). Cut tofu in cubes, strips, slices, or shred, as desired. Sprinkle, brush or place in a plastic zip-lock bag with **Sweet-and-Sour-Sauce,** or **Lemon Herb Marinade** (see recipes). Set aside for tofu to soak up liquid and marinate. Brown, broil, or bake in oven, or follow recipe directions.

Barbecued Tofu

Add a zesty sauce to bland tofu and transform it from a simple plain food to a savory dish. Freeze and thaw **Tofu** as indicated above, or use water-pack Tofu; rinse, blot dry, cut in strips or cubes, brush with **Barbecue Sauce** (see recipe in chapter **Sauces, Creams & Gravy-479**), then brown in oven or heavy skillet.

Lightly steam peeled onions until tender, add peas, steam 1 more minute. Blend and add cashew white sauce; heat to thicken. Serve over whole grain garlic toast or croutons.

Stuffed Baked Mushrooms

The flavor and meatiness of mushrooms make them a satisfying side-dish or tasty appetizer to compliment the meal.

**12 large Button or
Portobella mushrooms
1½ cups seasoned
bread crumbs
⅓ cup chopped walnuts
small can tomato puree
or 2 ripe tomatoes
3-4 Tbs. minced parsley
¼ tsp. garlic powder; sea salt, to taste**

Vegetable Casserole

**2 cups mung bean
or lentil sprouts
½ cup sliced onion,
sautéed
2 cups fresh or frozen
peas, steamed
1 cup sliced carrots, steamed
½ cup diced celery, steamed
¼ cup chopped red or green pepper
1 tsp. sea salt, savory, garlic, to taste
1 tsp. pure olive oil
¼ cup chopped parsley
2 cups Cashew Milk Gravy**

Stir-fry sprouts just until tender. Sauté onion, pepper and seasonings in olive oil, add steamed vegetables and parsley. Fold in Cashew Gravy, adjust seasonings. Place in casserole, cover with ½ cup seasoned bread crumbs and ¼ cup toasted slivered almonds. Bake in 350° oven until heated through.

Clean mushrooms with a soft brush or damp paper towel; remove stems. Combine stuffing of bread crumbs, walnuts or nut butter, mixed with tomato puree, parsley, garlic powder, and salt. Fill mushrooms; place in baking dish; thread on olive oil, if desired. Cover, bake in hot oven 425° until tender; uncover and brown lightly. Serve with rich **Parsley** or **Pimento Sauce**, if desired.

Creamed Onions and Peas

**1 lb. pearl onions
1 lb. fresh
or frozen peas
1 recipe Cashew
White Sauce**

Stuffed Peppers

The Anaheim chili pepper is generally mild in flavor and the size makes it ideal for stuffing.

Follow recipe for Stuffing Mushrooms; omit mushrooms, replace with **1 cup cooked brown rice**. Yield: 6 stuffed peppers.

Mixed Roasted Vegetables

Red, white, green, and orange- a splash of color and nutrients to compliment your main dish.

asparagus spears, tender
button mushrooms, whole or sliced
red, green, orange, yellow bell pepper
Lemon-Herb Marinade, see recipe

Heat oven to 375°. Cut asparagus spears into 4" pieces. Leave mushrooms whole or slice. Slice peppers into thin strips. In a bowl combine vegetables, drizzle on ½ of the marinade to coat.

Bake on non-stick roasting pan, uncovered, until vegetables are tender, tossing once or twice during baking. Drizzle on more marinade. Serve as a vegetable side-dish.

Note: In place of oven-roasting, vegetables may be quickly tenderized over medium-high heat, in a heavy pan, on stovetop, as in stir-fry.

Fresh Fava Beans & Sweet Pepper

Buttery, bright green, fava beans with a fresh springtime flavor; these quick-cooking Italian beans are great for soup or side dish.

1 lb. shelled fava beans, fresh or frozen
1 small onion, chopped
4 cloves garlic, chopped
1 tsp. pure virgin olive oil
1 bell pepper, cut in strips or diced
¼ tsp. sea salt

In a covered skillet sauté the onion and garlic in olive oil. Add the sweet pepper strips and salt, stir until crisp tender. Add the shelled fava beans and sufficient water (¼ cup for frozen; ½ cup for fresh). Cover, steam on low 5-8 minutes or until tender, stirring midway through cooking. (To retain shape and texture, avoid overcooking or over stirring) Garnish with more pepper strips and parsley, if desired. Servings: 6

Oriental-style Veggies with Toasted Sesame on Rice

2 small green onions, chopped
2 cloves garlic, finely chopped
1-2 tsp. cold-pressed sesame oil
1 small zucchini, sliced diagonally
1 small yellow summer squash, sliced
1 carrot, sliced diagonally
½ cup broccoli florets
¼ cup sliced mushrooms
   and/or water chestnuts
2 Tbs. sesame seed, lightly toasted

Heat a wok or heavy pan until very hot. Quickly stir-fry veggies in sesame oil until crisp- tender, adding a little water as needed. Serve over steamed Basmati, Jasmine, or Wild Rice. Sprinkle on soy sauce or liquid aminos. Top with toasted sesame seed. Servings 2-4

Baked Acorn & Limas

Bake halves of **Acorn squash** at 350° until tender. Fill center with tender **green lima beans** or scoop out squash meat and mash with **baby lima beans, a sprinkle of sea salt,** and **olive oil**; re-fill acorn squash shells, return to oven, bake 10 minutes.

Caponatina, Italian

Eggplant- a rich source of potassium and the key ingredient in making this Italian dish. A prolific garden vegetable and vegetarians delight, as its meaty, firm texture is an excellent replacement for meat in many dishes.

4 - 6 large eggplant, ¾"cubes
2 large heads celery, sliced
1 large onion, chopped
½ lb. ripe green olives, pitted
½ cup fresh basil leaves or 2 tsp. dried
1-2 qts. Italian plum tomatoes, solid pack
½ cup fresh lemon juice
¼ cup olive oil
3-4 cloves garlic or ½ tsp. powder
2 tsp. sea salt
1 small jar drained capers, opt.

1. Put cubed eggplant in colander. Sprinkle with a little sea salt, shake, let set 5 min.

2. Brown eggplant in 400° oven, under broiler (drizzle with a little olive oil). Toss and turn pieces occasionally to brown all sides, removing pieces as they are done.

3. Make sauce: Blend tomatoes. Put in kettle. Crush pitted olives with a jar. Add to tomatoes. Add the rest of ingredients, except the eggplant and lemon juice.

4. Simmer ingredients slowly – stirring often to prevent burning. When sauce is half done, add the lemon juice. Continue to simmer until celery is tender.

5. Add eggplant to the sauce mixture. It should be thick. Seal in quart jars. Enjoy this relish with bread, over polenta, or use for pita or sandwich filling. Yield: approx. 4-6 quarts

Tofu Parsley Scramble on Pita Bread

Transform ordinary bread into a healthy side dish with this protein- rich tofu topping.

Recipe in **Sandwiches and Spreads, pg** 466

Hash Browned Tofu

Good topping on pizza, pasta, or pita bread.

2 cups (1#) firm tofu
1 Tbs. Bragg Aminos®
1 tsp. chicken-style or Bill's Best® seasoning

Mash tofu with a potato masher or fork. Sprinkle on seasonings. Brown in pre-heated non-stick pan or lightly oiled skillet, until crusty and brown. Mix with vegetables, seasonings, and gravy for pot-pie filling.

Bok Choy & Spinach Stir-Fry Medley

This all-green stir fry is brimming with vitamin A; rich in iron, folate, and fiber. Bok Choy and star anise are favorite ingredients in Chinese cuisine. The star-shaped anise pod has a flavor similar to licorice, but more spicy.

1 head bok choy, about ¾ lb., sliced
8 oz. fresh baby spinach
½ cup snow peas, tender
1 small green bell pepper, sliced
1 large stalk celery, sliced diagonally

1 Tbs. olive or peanut oil
3 cloves garlic, minced
¼ tsp. ground star anise
½ tsp. sea salt, ½ tsp. onion powder
¼ cup chicken-style broth
½ tsp. sesame oil
garnish: cashews or sesame seed, opt.

In a large skillet or wok, stir-fry the garlic, star anise, salt and onion powder briefly in the olive or peanut oil. Add the celery, green pepper, snow peas, bok choy, and spinach. Stir fry for 2-3 minutes just until crisp-tender. Add the broth, cover and steam 1-2 minutes. Stir in the sesame oil; mix to combine flavors. Serve over steamed brown rice or as a vegetable side dish. Garnish with toasted cashews or sesame seed, if desired.

Roasted Sweet Peppers & Tofu

The sweet bell peppers, mushrooms, and crisp tofu cubes, add protein, color and texture to the meal

1 red bell pepper, cut into thin strips
1 green bell pepper, cut into thin strips
1 orange bell pepper, cut into thin strips
1 med. onion, cut in thin slices
1 lb. firm tofu, cut in 1" cubes, browned
½ lb. sliced fresh mushrooms, opt.
olive oil, lemon juice, sea salt to taste

Heat oven to 375°. Place vegetables in baking dish. Mix **1 Tbs. olive oil, 2 tsp. lemon juice and ¼ tsp. salt**. Drizzle evenly over vegetables. Bake uncovered 20-30 min. Toss, bake another 10-15 minutes or until vegetables are tender. Combine with browned tofu cubes. Serve over rice, pasta, or as a vegetable side dish.

Hummus

Chickpeas are popular in Middle Eastern cuisine. Serve Hummus with pita pockets, pasta, chips, or raw vegetables. This simple side dish is a rich source of protein, iron and calcium.

1-15 oz. can garbanzo beans*
2-3 Tbs. sesame tahini**
2-3 Tbs. lemon juice
2-3 cloves garlic, fresh cut or roasted
¼ cup fresh parsley, chopped
1 tsp. olive oil, opt.

Place garbanzos, tahini, lemon juice and garlic in food processor or blender. While blending, add reserved liquid as needed, for desired consistency. Spoon into a serving dish. Garnish with fresh parsley and olive oil, if desired. Serve as a dip, spread, or sandwich filling; or thin down with water for a dressing. Good served over rice or pasta noodles too!

*drain beans and reserve liquid
** May substitute ⅓ cup sesame seeds

Beta-Carotene, which the body transforms into vitamin A, needed for healthy eyes and skin, is abundant in dark green and yellow vegetables such as brocolli, carrots, kale, and fruits as dried apricots, and papaya.

Grilled Mushrooms

Mushrooms lovers are sure to enjoy the combined flavors of this baked version!

1 lb. Cremini or Shiitake mushrooms
1 Tbs. olive oil + ¼ tsp. sesame oil
2 Tbs. Bragg Liquid Aminos®
3 Tbs. parsley + ½ tsp. lemon zest
½ tsp. fructose or sweetening, opt.

In a bowl, combine the oil, liquid aminos, and sweetening. Add the cleaned, whole or sliced mushrooms; gently toss to coat. Place in a shallow baking pan.

Grill or broil in very hot oven, 450°, until mushrooms are crispy around the edges. Garnish with chopped parsley and lemon zest. Delicious served as an appetizer, with baked or mashed potato, tofu, vegetables, or rice.

Stuffed Grape or Cabbage Leaves

There are different methods and a variety of fillings for making this traditional Mediterranean dish. Here is one tasty, healthy version you will like!

**Grape leaves* tender, med-large size
4 cups cooked brown rice**
½ cup chick peas (garbanzos), chopped
⅓ cup red bell pepper, chopped
⅓ cup minced fresh parsley
¼ cup minced dill weed and, or 2 Tbs.cilantro
1 tomato chopped or 1 Tbs. tomato paste
1 onion + 2 garlic cloves, finely chopped***
½ tsp. salt; ½ tsp. garlic powder
¼ tsp. cumin; ⅛ tsp. cayenne
juice of 1 lemon, 3-4 Tbs., divided**

1. Soften leaves by dipping in boiling water for 30-60 seconds. Plunge in cold water. Drain, flatten and set aside, while preparing filling.

2. In a large skillet sauté the onion and garlic over medium heat in 2 Tbs.olive oil or water until tender. Remove from heat; add remaining ingredients, adjust seasoning to taste; add half the lemon juice. Stir thoroughly to combine.

3. Stuff grape leaves, shiny side down, vein side up, stem down. Place 1-2 Tbs. of filling (depending on size of leaf) in center. Fold bottom of leaf up over stuffing, and fold in sides. Roll up tightly from bottom to top of leaf. Continue stuffing leaves until filling is used up.

4. Place a layer of cabbage, dill sprigs or extra damaged grape leaves in the bottom of a large skillet, wide 4 quart saucepan, or baking dish. Arrange stuffed wrapped leaves, seam side down, side by side in layers;pack tightly together. Pour 1 cup water mixed with remaining lemon juice over the rolls. Arrange a few grape leaves on top, and place a heat-proof plate on top as a weight.

5. Cover. Bring to a boil, reduce heat and cook gently, for 35-45 minutes or place in oven at 350° for 45 minutes. Cool 1hour; remove plate; lift out rolls or place serving platter on top of pan and quickly invert so grape leaves come out in a nice mold. Refrigerate. Serve cold or at room temperature with **yogurt, tahini** or **hummus** for dipping, or enjoy eating plain. Yield: approx. 36 rolls.

Note: Rinse grape leaves in cold water (if pre-packed) to remove salt.

*Cabbage or Swiss chard leaves, may substitute for grape leaves.

**Use Long grain, Basmati, or brown Jasmine (1 cup rice + 2 ¾ cups water) Cook covered on low heat 50 minutes until tender and dry; let cool 10 min.

*** ½ tsp. garlic powder can substitute for 3 cloves of fresh garlic.

Meal Planning
& Menus

Index - CHAPTER 19

Meal Planning

568

Ten Talents

"Regularity in eating is of vital importance. There should be a specified time for each meal. At this time, let everyone eat what the system requires, and then take nothing more until the next meal. There are many who eat...at irregular intervals, and between meals...This is very injurious."   E. G. White, Life at its Best, pg. 74

Epitaphs of Many Men

"Scanty, ill-cooked food depraves the blood by weakening the blood-making organs. It deranges the system, and brings on disease, ... irritable nerves and bad tempers. The victims of poor cookery are numbered by thousands and tens of thousands. Over many graves might be written: 'Died because of poor cooking;' 'Died of an abused stomach.' "   E. G. White, Diet and Foods, p. 257

Chapter Cover Photo: *Rosalie Hurd, blending a delicious Strawberry Banana Smoothie, page 93*

Meal Planning & Menus

Dinner Meal: Spring Mix Salad, Turkey Loaf with Holiday Gravy, Candied Sweet Potatoes, Almond Wild Rice & Mushroom Pilaf, Broccoli Italian-style, Black Olives, Dinner Roll

What Shall We Eat? You have probably heard the slogan:
"Breakfast is Golden - Dinner is Silver - Supper is Lead!" or
"Eat Breakfast like a king - Dinner like a prince - Supper like a pauper."
Let's start with Breakfast. The meaning of Breakfast, or Break-fast, is exactly that - breaking the fast of the long night, by eating breakfast - the first meal of the day - in the morning.

A good breakfast can only be appreciated after a good night's rest. The need of most everyone, is to reverse the schedule of their lives, in order to accomplish this. It is not advisable to go to bed at midnight, with a full stomach of food to digest, tossing and turning, unable to sleep, and expect to enjoy a hearty breakfast at six or seven in the morning. The digestive system physiologically is not ready for food; which in turn sets a pattern for snacking the rest of the day. Try turning those habits around, by eating a good breakfast, and dinner, little or no supper, and experience how much better you will feel!

Healthy Food Guide

The **optimal diet** includes a wide variety of whole natural foods of plant origin. The **Healthy Food Guide** mainly emphasizes foods from the basic food groups (grains, fruits, vegetables, legumes and nuts), showing the category of food and comparative proportions needed for a healthy diet. A healthy diet, for most people, means eating more fresh fruits and vegetables and less refined sugars, starches, and saturated fats.

Protein Group
(legumes, nuts, milk products)

Fats & Oils

Sweets & Salt
(use sparingly)

Fruit Group

Vegetable Group

Grain Group

The US Department of Health and Human Services, and the National Academy of Sciences recommend eating a *minimum of 5-7 servings* of fruits and vegetables every day, 3-4 servings from the protein and milk group, and 6-10 servings of grains and grain products.

What is a Serving? One serving is: 1 medium apple, banana, or pear, 1/2 cup canned fruit or 1/4 cup dried fruit; 1 slice bread, 1/2 cup cooked cereal, rice or pasta, 1/2 cup cooked beans or tofu, a handful of walnuts or 1 cup of milk or yogurt; 1/2 cup cooked or chopped raw vegetables or 1 cup of raw leafy greens. Eating one large salad could contain several servings!

*Note: The illustration above serves as a guide to assist in meal planning. The relative amount of each category shown that should be consumed daily, is represented by the size of each section of the pie. In addition to a healthy diet see -Ten Principles for Abundant Health - chapter 21, **A Healthy Lifestyle.***

> ***"In Grains, Fruits, Vegetables, and Nuts are to be found all the food elements that we need."*** E. G. White, Diet and Foods, pg. 313

Breakfast (above): Fresh Fruit (peach, banana, figs), Crock pot Cereal (buckwheat-kasha with raisins), Soy milk, Whole-grain toast with almond butter and honey

"It is the custom and order of society to take a slight breakfast. But this is not the best way to treat the stomach. At breakfast time the stomach is in a better condition to take care of more food than at the second or third meal of the day. The habit of eating a sparing breakfast and a large dinner is wrong. Make your breakfast correspond more nearly to the heartiest meal of the day." E. G. White, **Diet & Foods**, p. 173

Advantages of Weekly Menu Planning

- saves time in meal preparation by thinking and planning meals ahead*
- save on budget by wise planning vs impulse buying; shop for foods on sale or in season
- many dishes can be prepared ahead, frozen or refrigerated for quick meals
- planning inspires including a greater variety of foods, reducing risk of meal monotony
- Compare menus with Healthy Food Guide to assure balance and adequate nutrition
- eliminates stress preparing for meals; allowing more time for family and friends
- be prepared on short notice to invite others or share hospitality

*Note: Jot down your menus on Menu Planner pg 582, using the category of foods and comparative proportions as shown on illustration - Healthy Food Guide.

Breakfast Suggestions

(Raw Foods Breakfast)
Orange Slices
Fresh Apple, Dates
Rosalie's Raw Granola
Almond or Nut Milk

Cranberry-Apple Fruit Relish
Avocado Halves
Rolled Rye and Wheat Cereal
Raisin-Nut Bread
Nut Cream

Papaya and Strawberries
Banana, fresh or dried
Millet with Dates
Almond Milk / Nuts / Bread

Unsulphured Apricots / Almonds
Applesauce / Avocado
Pecan Rolls, Zwieback
Hot Carob Soymilk

Peaches, fresh, frozen, canned
Blueberries, banana
*Oats, old-fashioned rolled (below)
Wheat Germ
Cashew Nut Cream

Prune Whip / Baked Apple
7-Grain Granola with Raisins
Almond Milk or Nut Cream
Whole-grain Toast
Nut butter/ Fruit Spread

* pictured

Sliced Avocado and Mango
*Oatmeal Waffles (right)
Fresh Blueberry Topping
Hot Carob Soymilk

(Raw Foods Breakfast)
Golden Apricot Nectar
*Swiss Muesli (below)
Cashew-Almond Milk
Fresh or Dried Figs

Fresh Peaches and Blueberries
Cornmeal, steamed / Cashew Cream
Sunflower Seeds
Breakfast Cupcake

Fresh Fruit Salad
*Millet with dates, (below)
or other steamed whole grains
4-Seed Cereal Topping
Soymilk, Almond Butter

Whole-grain toast / Zwieback
Strawberries and Soy Yogurt
Brown Rice / Dates / Flaxmeal
Oatmeal Squares / Seeds
Soy or Nut milk

*Sesame-Flax French Toast (below)
Apple / Pear Fruit Sauce
Fresh or Frozen Berry Topping
Pecans / Dates

Fresh Apple / Banana
Spelt, steamed
Sweet Raspberry Flax Muffins
Cashew cream / Brazil nuts

Pears, fresh / Thickened Cherries
Sprouted Whole Wheat Cereal
Seed Topping / Almond Cream
Zwieback / Date butter

* pictured

Fresh Pineapple and Papaya chunks
3-Grain Cereal combination
Flaxseed Meal, Raisins
Nut or Soy Milk

Fresh Grapes, Pear
*Mixed Grain Hot Cereal (below)
Almond Milk / Corn Bread
Raw Nuts or Sunflower Seeds

Fresh Grapefruit
*Berry / Fruit filled Crepes (above)
Almond butter, Agave or maple syrup
Soy yogurt, Sliced banana

Fresh Fruit Salad
*Baked Apples or Berry Crisp (below)
Corn Dodgers / Molasses
Walnuts, Nut Cream

Fresh Pineapple and Kiwi
Quinoa, steamed
Apple Oat Bran Muffins
Soy Milk / Almonds

Orange Juice – before breakfast
*Dried Fruit Compote (below) on
Whole-grain Toast Cubes / Nut Butter
Fresh Coconut, Avocado or Nuts

Grapes / Pineapple Slices
French Toast (multi-grain)
Banana mashed with avocado
Sesame Tahini / Honey, molasses

Grape Juice – before breakfast
Fresh Plums / Avocado Wedges
Steamed Oat Groats
Sesame Seed Spread / Oat Crackers
Almond Coconut Milk

* pictured

Dinner

Dinner has been commonly called "lunch" in our present day. Because it is the noon meal, our society has by-passed its importance in relation to our daily needs. Over half of families have members who carry lunches or eat hurriedly at fast-food restaurants, which encourages the rest of the family to neglect this meal. Something very light is snacked upon periodically during the afternoon, until a large meal is devoured at night. The dinner meal is best eaten 5-6 hours after breakfast, and should be substantial enough to assist the body in maintaining strength for the rest of the day. Plan the menus with variety, giving attention to color, shape, and texture of foods. Remember first and foremost - We eat with our eyes!

Thanksgiving Buffet:
Mixed Green Salad, Bread Dressing, Turkey Loaf, Holiday Gravy, Broccoli Italian-style, Almond Wild Rice Pilaf, Candied Yams, Dinner Rolls, Pimento-Soy Chee Spread, Ripe Black Olives, Pumpkin Pie, Soy Whip Cream

* pictured

Dinners without Dessert

Classic Green Salad
Tofu Veggie Scramble "Eggs"
Sprouted Wheat Toast
Baked Squash
Nut Butter and/or Olives

*Tofu Sunfaces
Millet-Barley Loaf
Beets with Lemon Sauce
Rye Bread / Olives

Sliced Avocado – Tomatoes
Green Pea Soup – Alfalfa Sprouts
Pumpkin Seed Patties
Whole Wheat Buns, Soy Spread
Ripe Olives

Classic Green Salad
*Mashed Potato with
*Mushroom Gravy (below)
*Collard Greens (below)
Zwieback / Garlic Spread

Summer Salad Bowl
Scrambled Tofu
Creamed Asparagus on Toast
Squash – baked

Vegetable Medley Salad
*Skillet Rice & Sugar Snap Peas (below)
Mixed Turnip, Mustard & Collards
Whole-grain toast, avocado

Fresh Escarole Salad
Baked Chee Spaghetti Casserole
Zucchini Steaks / Steamed Broccoli

Spring Mix Green Salad
Lentil Nut Loaf
Baked Acorn Squash
Stewed Okra

Fresh Wild Greens & Chickpeas
Sweet 'n Sour Veggie Noodles
Hummus / Pita bread
Glazed Carrots / Wilted Spinach

* pictured

Baby Spinach Avocado Salad
Wild Rice with Pecans
Mashed Carrots and Turnips
Zwieback with Hummus

Hot Spinach & Walnut Salad
Cream of Pea Soup / Bread Sticks
*Vegetable Kabob
Parsley Potato Patties

Sweet-and-Sour Coleslaw
Almond Rice Loaf / Cashew Gravy
Broccoli, Italian Style
Ripe Olives, Celery Sticks
Barley Bun, Soya Yeast Spread

Tossed Bouquet Salad
*Tofu Garden Quiche (above)
*Brussels Sprouts, (above)
*Baby Carrots (above)
Crusty Bread / Avocado Spread

*Italian Fennel Salad (below)
*Turkey Loaf / Holiday Gravy (below)
*Steamed Broccoli (below)
*Sweet Potato (below)
Zwieback / Spread, Olives

Cucumber – Avocado Salad
Sprouted Lentil Casserole
Collard Greens / Cauliflower with Peas

Italian Tossed Salad
*Tofu Spinach Lasagna (below)
*Asparagus with Pimento Cheese

Crunchy Chinese Cabbage Salad
Stuffed Peppers
Edamame
Steamed Simply Parsnips

Layered Summer Salad
Luscious Lentil Soup
Artichokes – Steamed
Zwieback / Olives

* pictured

Dinners with Dessert

"Olives may be so prepared as to be eaten with good results at every meal." CDF 349
Whole grain bread or zwieback may be added to dinner menus to complete the meal.

Stuffed Tomatoes / Alfalfa Sprouts
Sprouted Wheat Burgers w/ gravy
Roasted Sweet Vegetables
Pumpkin Pie with Soy Cream

Chickpea & Parsley Salad
*Oriental Stir Fry / Steamed Rice (below)
Peanut Butter Cookies

*Creamy Coleslaw (above)
*Bean Burritos with Avocado (above)
Red Pepper / Celery / Carrot sticks
Sesame Treats

*Haystacks - Veggie Salad (below)
Sweet Corn on the Cob
Carob Cream Pie

Summer Salad Bowl
Almond Rice Loaf w/Gravy
Tender String Beans
Carob Brownies with Ice Cream

Marinated Garden Vegetables
Yellow Corn Soup, Dinner Roll
Super Asparagus Patties
Oatmeal Cookies

* pictured

Raw Root Salad
Best Barley Soup
Baked Butternut Squash
Lima Beans
Easy Popcorn Cake

Tomato/Avocado/Alfalfa Salad
Garbanzo Croquettes
Herbed Zucchini & Peas
Anise Cashew Crumbles

Italian Tossed Salad
*3-Grain Oven Pilaf (above)
*Sweet Potatoes (above)
Vanilla Ice Cream

*Pitas - Garden Filled (below)
Ripe Olives / Celery Sticks
Carob Kisses

*Mini Veggie Pizzas (above)
or Calzones
Grilled Mushrooms
Lemon Sorbet

*One Dish Italian Meal (below)
Crusty bread / Garlicky Spread
No-Bake Cheese Cake

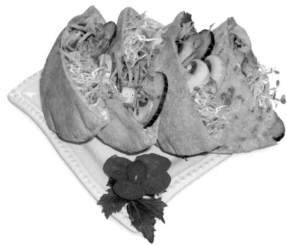

Quinoa Greek Salad
Summer Veggie Stir-Fry
Natural Toasted Brown Rice
Lemon Pie with Soy Cream

Spring Mix Salad
Boston Baked Beans
Hot Pasta Salad with Veggies
Simple Molasses Cookies

* pictured

Supper

The third meal of the day should be light and consist of foods that digest quickly and easily. Remember the body is tired after the day's work, and needs rest. The stomach is still part of the body, even at suppertime. Often this meal could be eliminated from the tables of most families, if a better plan were followed concerning the previous two meals of the day. The habit of eating late at night is injurious to the health of the body. If any meals are skipped during the day, it should be supper (best weight-loss plan). If your work habits require a third meal, it should be light and several hours before going to bed. When you retire to sleep, the work of the stomach should have been completed, so it may rest with you. The next morning you will feel hungry for breakfast.

"The practice of eating but two meals a day is generally found a benefit to health; yet under some circumstances, persons may require a third meal. This should, however, if taken at all, be very light and of food most easily digested." E. G. White, Counsels on Diet and Foods, p. 176

A Simple Supper Solution

Natural foods with minimal processing retain the most nutrition, color, and flavor. Since **fruit** is naturally colorful and sweet, naturally beautiful, naturally wholesome and delicious, naturally easy to prepare, and naturally light and easy to digest, it would naturally make sense to solve the supper dilemma, by simply serving **fruit**.

"Color Your Plate Like a Rainbow" with simply delicious **Fruit Kabobs** for a light supper (see recipe in chapter- *Fruits*)

"... Zwieback and fruit are the foods best suited for the evening meal." Diet and Foods, p.176

Supper Suggestions

(*pictured on left and below)

*Fruit Smoothies / nectars	Melon Chunks	Garden Veggie Drink
Popcorn / Apples	*Very-Berry Smoothie	Soup / Salad / Crackers
Fruit Filled Crepes	*Fruit Kabobs	Veggie Broth / Zwieback
*Peach / Granola Parfait	Fruit Pizza	Cream of Tomato Soup / Toast
Soy Yogurt Fruit Flavor	Summer Fruit Salad	Veggie Kabob / Corn Muffin
Baked Apple / Nut Cream	Blueberry Crisp	Pure Unsweetened Grape Juice
*Persimmon, Cherries	*Sleepytime or other herb tea	*Cantaloupe Cup / Blueberries
*Orange sections	*Red Grapes, Zwieback	*Ripe Banana / Barhi Dates
*Peach, Green Grapes	*Avocado, Crackers, Dates	*Grapefruit Half (or juice)

7-Day Menu Planner

	Breakfast	Dinner	Supper
SUN			
MON			
TUE			
WED			
THU			
FRI			
SAT			

Meal of the Day

BREAKFAST
(1st meal of day - hearty)

Fruits - Fruit Salad (1-3):
(fresh, frozen, canned, dried)
Grains: (Whole grain cereal,
granola, waffles, or other grain dish)
Nuts & Seeds (raw)
Toast or **zwieback**
Fruit Spreads, Nut butter
Soy, Nut Milk or other

DINNER
(2nd meal of day - main)

Fresh Green Salad
(leafy salad varieties, raw veggies)
Protein dish: (Legumes, Tofu, Peas/
Beans, Br. Rice, etc.)
Vegetables (2-3)
(dark leafy/green & yellow
vegetables, sweet potato, etc)
Whole grain bread
Spread, avocado, olives

SUPPER
(3rd meal - light choices)

Pure Water, Herb Tea
or
Fruit Smoothie, Fruit Parfait
or
Fresh Fruit, Popcorn
or
Melon Slices, Fruit Salad
or
Salad, Soup, Zwieback, Crackers

7 Meal Planning Pointers

• We eat with our eyes! If food doesn't look good- an opinion may be set in the mind that the food cannot taste good. Make each dish nourishing, tasty and attractive.

• Vary the colors, shapes, and texture of foods at a meal. This is easy- with such a variety in natural foods! Think of a beautiful rainbow of colors when planning the menus, then even simple basic foods, skillfully combined, can be a culinary delight.

• Planning meals in advance, a week at a time, saves dollars on the food budget, and eliminates impulsive buying. Shop when not hungry, and with a list of items needed.

• Purchase staple foods (beans and grains) in bulk if possible. These can be stored long-term. Purchase fresh vegetables and ripe fruits in season, in the quantity that can be consumed before spoiling, unless you plan to freeze, dry, or can them.

• Make-ahead foods (waffles in the freezer, a large kettle of soup, a crock pot full of whole grain cereal, an extra casserole, or dish of baked beans) can save you time in the kitchen on those busy days.

• Use leftovers wisely. Save cooking liquids for soup, hot cereal or starter for patties; mash leftover beans and season for a sandwich spread, or combine leftover vegetables for pot pie. Carefully using leftovers eliminates waste and a cluttered refrigerator.

• Two nourishing meals a day, in most cases, are preferable to three (those doing hard physical work may require a third light meal). The cooks who faithfully prepare 2 nourishing meals a day, would welcome a change at times, by suggesting that members needing a light meal, may serve themselves, by having extras on hand.

Beta-carotene is transformed by the body into vitamin A. This vitamin, needed for healthy eyes and skin, a healthy immune system, and protection against many diseases, is abundant in dark green and yellow vegetables (i.e. broccoli, kale, carrots), and fruits (such as dried apricots, cantaloupe, mango, and papaya).

Tofu Veggie Kabobs
(right)

Brighten up any meal with a colorful variety of vegetables. Serve as a light meal or appetizer. Tofu-Veggie Kabobs recipe in **Meatless Main Dishes** pg 349.

Tofu Mushroom Frittata

Add a green salad for a satisfying lunch or light supper

(**Tofu Mushroom Frittata** recipe in chapter **Meatless Main dishes** pg 337)

Calzone

(pictured below) See recipe in chapter **Sandwiches and Spreads** pg 460.

Patio Plate

(pictured below) Here's a rainbow of colors for a perfect lunch including stuffed pita bread and sweet corn-on–the cob. Enjoy!

Pita Bread-stuffed with scrambled tofu and garden green lettuce mix
Red tomato slices
Avocado slices on rice cake
Yellow Corn-on-the-Cob

Bean Burritos with Avocado

(pictured right)

Serve with soup or salad for a quick, satisfying meal; or take along ingredients for a picnic or pot-luck ready to assemble, or make ahead and wrap, ready to serve.

(see recipe in chapter **Sandwiches and Spreads** pg 464).

Veggie Crêpes

Filled crepes with **Stir-fry** and **Tofu cubes** makes this one-dish meal a winner! See **Savory Veggie Crêpes** recipe in chapter **Meatless Main Dishes,** page 358

Mrs. America – Winning Meal

This simple totally vegetarian meal, prepared and served by author Rosalie Hurd, won 1st Prize, competing with 50 other dinners which had meat and dairy on the menu.

**Summer Salad Bowl with Italian Dressing
Lentil Nut Loaf / Cloverleaf Rolls
Creamed Onion and Peas / Steamed Parsnips
Pumpkin Pie #1 with Vanilla Ice Cream**

"Let the table be made inviting and attractive, with the good things God has so bountifully bestowed. Let mealtime be a cheerful, happy time."
E. G. White, **Counsels on Diet and Foods**, page 231.

Miscellaneous

Canning, Freezing, Drying, Etc.

Index - CHAPTER 20

Proverbs 31:10-31

"Who can find a virtuous woman?
For her price is far above rubies."
She is loyal to her husband vv 10-12
She is faithful in her home vv 13-16
She is tireless in her responsibilities vv 17-19
She is generous toward the needy v 20
She is fearless about the circumstances vv 21-23
She is honest in business matters v 24
She is secured for the future v 25
She is wise in her utterances v 26
She is dependable in daily duties v 27
She is praised by her children v 28-29
She is beautiful in her conduct v 30
She is appreciated by her neighbors v 31

Miscellaneous

Canning, Freezing, & Drying

"Plant what you will
Till what you plant
Eat what you can
And Can what you can't."

Preserving Food at Home

Canning, freezing and **drying** foods that you have grown, picked, or purchased in season, is satisfying, simple and rewarding. Whether the result is from a desire to make healthy eating choices, or an alternative to the high prices of commercially prepared specialty foods, preserving foods at home can satisfy the need. A few easy steps in the process of preserving foods will assure success, as you "put up" your bountiful supply for another year.

Start with the Best – It only makes sense that great tasting preserved foods come from fresh, ripe, delicious produce. Select produce in season, at its peak, and preserve quickly to capture that fresh-picked taste.

Sterilizing Jars – *(This step is necessary if you are canning foods that will be processed in a water-bath or steam canner, such as fruit, jam, or dill pickles).* Select half-pint, pint, or quart canning jars. Check rims to be sure they are not cracked, damaged or chipped. Wash jars in hot soapy water. Rinse thoroughly. To sterilize, place jars upside-down in boiling water 10 minutes (keep jars and lids in pan of simmering hot water until needed).

Filling Jars – There are different methods of canning (raw cold pack for delicate fruits, hot pack for firm fruits). Pack raw food such as peaches, pears, blueberries, and cherries, firmly into jars. Add hot fruit juice (apple juice, or white grape juice) or water, if additional liquid is needed. Remove all air bubbles by sliding a narrow spatula or dull utensil several times down inside the jar, between the food and the sides of jar, to release trapped air. For hot pack method, food is first cooked in juice or water. Food that is pre-cooked, such as applesauce, requires less processing time, because it is already hot when it goes into the canner. The hot pack method is preferred for nearly all vegetables. Some general information and a few recipes are included in this chapter. The ***Ball Blue Book of Preserving Foods*** offers a complete guide of instructions.

Headspace – *(This is the amount of space between the top of the food and the rim of jar).* ½" headspace is needed for a vacuum to form and for the jars to seal correctly.

Equipment – Choose the best type of canner, depending on the food you are canning.

• **Boiling Water Canners -** Used for canning fruits and tomatoes. The old-fashioned

method of lowering rack of jars into simmering water. Water level should cover jar and 2-piece lid by 1-2 inches. Add boiling water if needed. Maintain water at rolling boil for the entire processing time. After processing, remove lid, let canner cool 5 minutes before removing jars. Let jars cool naturally 12-16 hours before checking for a seal.

• **Steam Canners –** The newest, easiest, cleanest, fastest method of processing foods. Used for canning all fruits, jams, pickles, and tomatoes. Jars are filled and placed on rack with only 3" of water below rack. Cover with dome lid. Water quickly boils; in just a few minutes, a stream of steam indicates jars are processing. After processing, lid

is carefully removed. Lift jars onto towel to cool at room temperature. Check for seal. Label. Store. This is a simple, preferred method, recommended and used by authors. See photo of steam canner. *(Contact the authors: 1-877- 442-4425 for information and availability)*

• **Pressure Canners –** Used for canning low-acid foods, vegetables, beans, soups. A heavy kettle and lid fitted with a safety valve, vent and pressure-gauge. Make sure all parts (weighted-gauge, steam vent, rubber gasket, and dial gauge) are clean and work properly. Read manufacture's instructions before using the pressure canner.

• **Steam Juicers – Stainless Steel:** *Pure undiluted fruit juice* is made from fresh grapes, apples, cherries, cranberries, etc. by steam extraction. Fruit is placed in the top holding pan; water is placed in bottom boiling pan. Juice will flow into middle pan, out through clear tube right into juice jar. Simply apply lid- finished! Cool, label and store. Delicious! See photo of steam juicer (Contact the authors for information or ordering)

Safety Check – After jars have cooled – check the seal by pressing on the center of each lid. If the center is pulled down and does not flex when pressed, the lid has a good vacuum seal. Remove the band, wipe jar and lid surface with a damp cloth to clean and remove any residue. Label jar with date to help identify inventory to be used first. Store jars in a cool, dark, dry place. It is important to inspect home-canned foods carefully before serving its contents. If the jar has a swollen lid, has leaked, or has any visible mold, discard it. Be sure there is a tight seal when opening the jar. The food should look good and smell good when the jar is opened. If you are unsure about the safety of certain home-canned foods, boil the foods for 10 minutes before tasting or using them.

Grape Juice – Homemade

*Enjoy pure undiluted juices-
made from your own fresh fruit.*

Concord Grapes – Blue-black, plump, round, and sweet-tart in flavor. They are most often used in making grape juice. Some varieties of white grapes are also used for making light sweet juice. Select juicy ripe grapes. Simply remove stems and discard damaged grapes. Wash, drain and place grapes in the holding pan of *Nutri-Steamer Juicer*. Cover and watch for the steam-extracted juice to flow in tube. Fill clean sterilized jars with the hot juice. Apply lid. It's finished! Cool jars and store.

Note: Other favorite easy-to-make homemade juices in Nutri-Steamer: Apple, Apricot, Blackberry, Cherry, Cranberry, Peach, and Pear.

"The pure juice of the grape, free from fermentation, is a wholesome drink."
E. G. White, Counsels on Diet & Foods, pg. 436

Grapes and pure **unfermented** grape juice contains anti-carcinogenic and detoxifying substances as well as protective nutritive properties that have been proven beneficial for cardiovascular health, **with no undesirable side effects**.

*Nutri-Steamer Juicer (Stainless Steel) -
available from authors- call: 1-877- 442- 4425

Apricot, Cherry or Peach Jam

6 cups fresh chopped fruit,
**   (peaches, apricots or cherries)**
1 cup white grape juice or water
3 Tbs. fresh squeezed lemon juice
1.75 oz. pkg. Ball Fruit Jell- No Sugar
**   Needed Pectin**
honey or other sweetening, to taste

1. Prepare fruit: Peel and crush ripe peaches with a potato masher; or pit and cut ripe apricots (do not peel).

2. In a saucepan combine prepared fruit, juice or water, and lemon juice. Slowly stir in Fruit Jell, until combined thoroughly with fruit.

3. Bring mixture to a boil, stirring constantly; add sweetening if desired. Boil on high heat 1 more minute while stirring. Remove from heat; skim off foam.

4. Ladle hot jam into clean hot jars. Adjust lids. Process 10 min. to seal jars or refrigerate.

Yield: approx. 6 half- pint jars.

Plain Grape Agar Jell or Jelly

Stir together:

2 cups pure sweet grape juice
1 Tbs. agar flakes
2-3 Tbs. honey or raw sugar, opt.

Let set 2 minutes. Simmer 2 minutes. Pour into bowl; chill in refrigerator to set. This is soft enough to spread on bread. For firmer jell, add 1 tsp. extra agar flakes. Seeded grapes (blue and red) may be added to jell before pouring into mold to set.

Note: If making Grape Jelly, juice can be sweeter: Replace 2 Tbs. grape juice, with 2-3 Tbs. honey or raw sugar. Pour into hot sterile jars. Process to seal.

Strawberry or Berry Jam
(freezer jam with agar-agar)

4 cups ripe mashed strawberries
**   or other sweet ripe berries**
1 cup water or juice (pour off fruit)
2 Tbs. agar flakes
1 cup honey or raw sugar, to taste
1 Tbs. lemon juice

Dissolve agar in water or berry juice. Bring to a boil and simmer until clear, stirring constantly. Add fruit mixed with sweetening and lemon. Heat to boil, simmer 1 minute. Pour into clean hot glass jars; adjust lid. Allow jars to cool thoroughly. Store in refrigerator up to 3 weeks or freeze up to 1 year. Yield: about 6 - 8 oz.jars.

Note: Increase or decrease agar flakes according to consistency desired

Freezing Fruits

Apples: Select crisp varieties. Peel and core. Slice and dip in pineapple or lemon juice. Drain. Pack dry in freezer bags. Ready to use for apple pie or crisp.

Apricots: Prepare as for peaches or wash, drain, cut in half / quarters/ slices/or puree. Freeze in plastic containers. Blend in fruit smoothies, or add to yogurt.

Avocados: Mash firm ripe fruit. Fill containers. Cover fruit with lemon or pineapple juice. Best used within a short time for guacamole, dressing or dip.

Bananas: Peel, freeze whole or cut in big slices. Freeze in plastic bags, ready to use for banana ice cream or delicious smoothies. Bananas can be mashed with lemon or pineapple juice. Fill containers to top. Best used within 6 months.

Blueberries: Pack whole, dry, unsweetened. If sprayed, wash and drain, Freeze in plastic bags. Add to fruit salad, waffles, muffins, smoothies, etc.

Raspberries: Clean and dry pack or rinse and drain. Freeze in containers Use in smoothies, salads, or thickened fruit topping. Sweeten when served.

Blackberries, boysenberries, currants, elderberries, huckleberries, loganberries, mulberries: Clean, dry pack or add honey syrup if desired.

Cranberries – Select firm ripe berries. Avoid soft, shriveled, or bruised fruit. Store in refrigerator up to 4 weeks, or pack and freeze in plastic bags up to 1 year. Use in cranberry apple relish, fruit drinks, muffins, etc. (see recipes)

Cherries, Bing or Red - Wash, drain and freeze whole, with or without tems or pitting. Fill plastic bags. Thaw quickly. Delicious! A bowl of thickened hot cherries is good eating too - just watch for the pits.

Dates: May be frozen whole to keep longer. Use as needed. Date bars freeze well.

Grapes: Simply wash and dry seedless grapes. Fill plastic freezer container or bag. Freeze. Best used within a short time. Enjoy frozen plain or in fruit salad.

Mangos: Cut in slices or chunks. Pack tightly in plastic containers. Use in fruit salads, desserts or smoothies. Sweeten with a little honey if desired.

Melons: Cantaloupe, honeydew, watermelon - Cut in chunks or melon balls. Dry pack or use a light syrup. Good in fruit salad, fruit sorbet and smoothies.

Papaya: Remove skin with vegetable peeler. Halve the papaya and remove seeds. Cut in cubes. Pack in freezer container or plastic bags. Thaw quickly. Serve with lime juice, mixed with other fruits or blended into smoothies.

Yellow/White Peaches:

Blanch peaches to remove skin, (ready to freeze or can).

To freeze: Slice peaches and freeze quickly in their own juice. Sweeten with honey if desired. Red haven variety freeze well. Many uses include: Fruit salad, pies, fruit cobbler, smoothies, ice cream, toppings, etc.

Pears: Peel, slice + dip firm pears in pineapple juice. Freeze quickly. Serve slices in hot fruit sauce over toast or whip frozen pears with avocado or banana.

Persimmons: Freeze whole ripe fruit on trays; or place single layer in plastic bags and freeze. When ready to use, hold under hot water; remove stem and skin, cut in pieces. Blend with juice for super smoothies, fruit parfaits or sorbet.

Pineapple: Peel, halve, remove core. Cut in cubes. Pack in freezer bags or container. Thaw quickly. Enjoy as is, in fruit salad, smoothies, ice cream or topping.

Strawberries: Best sliced or chopped. Freeze in own juice or add 1 Tbs. frozen orange juice or honey. Quick thaw; use plain, in smoothies, fruit salad or topping.

Note: Allow ½"- 1" headspace for expansion to avoid breaking the container or causing the lid to pop off.

Juices that Freeze Well

Apple Juice: In apple season - juice a variety of apples. Freeze in clean plastic containers, or freezer bags. Delicious when thawed.

Berry/Cherry: **Raspberry, Blackberry, Boysenberry, Cherry**, etc. Blend. Strain. Freeze in ice cube trays. Serve diluted with water; sweeten to taste.

Citrus Juices: **Lemons, Oranges, grapefruits, limes, tangerines**: Juice and freeze quickly in ice cube trays or freezer container. Transfer cubes to a plastic bag. Portion size cubes are convenient to use when making fruit smoothies, or float cubes in a punch bowl - a decorative touch.

Carrot Juice: Wash carrots well. Juice, extracting all liquid. Strain if necessary. Freeze and thaw quickly. Slight change in color. Flavor is good.

Grape Juice: Wash fresh grapes and process in press type juicer. Freeze juice in jars, containers, or ice cube trays. Transfer cubes to freezer bag. Cook remaining pulp with water. Press again to extract any juice.

Sauerkraut Juice: Remove liquid from crock after sauerkraut is ready to pack in jars. Freeze juice. Serve as an appetizer before a vegetable meal.

Tomato Juice: Blend ripe tomatoes in blender. Strain out seeds. Freeze juice in jars, containers, or plastic freezer bags. Very good flavor.

Watermelon Juice: When making melon balls, reserve juice from **watermelon, cantaloupe, honeydew,** etc. Freeze in containers or ice cube trays, for use in fruit smoothies, sorbet, or slush.

Quick Juice Tip:

Squeeze fresh lemon or lime juice. Freeze in ice cube trays; transfer to freezer bags. Ready-to-use in a variety of recipes: salad dressing, creams, dips, desserts or just drop 1-2 cubes in a glass of cold water for lemonade or limeade, in hot water for an instant morning drink or try these frozen juice cube combinations:

1. Lemon juice cube in hot or cold tomato juice
2. Orange or lemon juice cube in grape juice.
3. Pineapple juice cubes in coconut milk

How to Preserve Fresh Sweet Basil

1. Snip sweet basil leaves in season. Wash, pat dry with paper towels. Dehydrate.

OR:

2. Toss basil in bowl with a little olive oil until all leaves are coated. Pack in clean jar. Freeze. Use as needed for salad, soup, pesto, **Italian Tomato Sauce**, and other dishes.

OR:

3. Toss basil leaves with coarse sea salt. Layer leaves alternately with a sprinkle of sea salt; tightly pack in clean jar. Freeze or refrigerate up to four weeks. Use for soup or sauce.

Freezing Peppers

Select firm **bright red, orange, green or yellow peppers** in season. Wash, remove stems, seeds and membranes. To freeze: Dice or cut into strips. Fill freezer container or spread in single layer on baking sheet; freeze until firm, then pack into freezer bag or container. Use in stir-fry, soup, salad, for pizza topping, tomato sauce, dips, spreads, and dressings.

Freezing Parsley

Simply chop **parsley** and fill zip-lock freezer bag. Freeze and use as needed in soup, pasta, gravy, salad and dressing.

Refrigerator Dill Cucumbers

In the bottom of each pint jar put:

1 grape leaf
1-2 cloves of garlic
1 sprig of dill
1 rounding tsp. sea salt
1 Tbs. lemon juice
⅛ tsp. celery seed, opt.

Pack jar with slices or strips of firm cucumber. Fill jars with boiling distilled water leaving ½" headspace. Apply lid. Cool, store in refrigerator. May use in 3-4 days.

Kosher - Style Dill Pickles

Pickles made with lots of salt and vinegar are indigestible. This recipe less salt, and lemon juice in place of vinegar.

4 lbs. 4" pickling cucumbers (about 48)
1-1/2 quarts (6 cups) distilled water
1-1/2 cups lemon juice, fresh or bottled
4 Tbs. (¼ cup) canning or coarse sea salt
16-24 heads fresh dill or 8 Tbs. dill seed
8 grape leaves
8 cloves garlic, halved

  1. Rinse cucumbers. Remove stems.
  2. Combine water, lemon juice and salt in a stainless steel pan. Bring to boiling.
  3. Place 1 grape leaf, 2 -3 heads of dill or 1 Tbs. seed, and 1 clove of garlic at the bottom of 8 sterilized pint jars. Pack cucumbers into jars leaving a ½" headspace.
  4. Pour **Hot Brine (lemon juice, water, salt)** over cucumbers. Wipe jar rims and adjust 2-piece canning lids.
  5. Process in boiling water or steam canner for 10 minutes. (start timing after water comes to a boil). Remove jars and cool on racks. Let stand 1 week. Yield: 8 pints.

Homemade Sauerkraut

45 lbs. cabbage, shredded
1 lb. coarse sea salt

Remove wilted or damaged leaves from firm, mature heads of cabbage; wash and drain. Cut into halves; remove core. With food processor or sharp knife, cut cabbage into very thin shreds less than ⅛" thick. In a large bowl, layer cabbage and salt alternately. Mix thoroughly and let salted cabbage stand a few minutes to wilt. Pack firmly and evenly into a clean large pickling container or crock. Repeat shredding, salting and packing of cabbage. Fill to within 3- 4" from the top. Firmly press the cabbage with a wooden spoon, tamper, or hands, until juice comes to surface and covers cabbage. If juice does not cover cabbage, add brine (1½Tbs.coarse salt + 1 qt. water; bring brine to boil; cool) Place a clean plate over cabbage and weight under brine (a water filled jar works well). Cover crock with clean cloth and paper over it. Formation of gas bubbles indicates fermentation is taking place. Remove and discard scum formation each day. Set container in a cool place. Fermentation is usually complete in 3-5 weeks. Pack sauerkraut in clean jars, store in refrigerator or process for longer shelf life.

To Can: Heat sauerkraut in a large skillet, to low simmer (180°), but do not boil. Pack hot sauerkraut in clean hot jars, ladle hot liquid over kraut leaving ½" headspace. Remove air bubbles. Adjust 2-piece canning lid. Process in steam canner or boiling water 15 min. Yield: 12 quarts or 24 pints.

Dehydrating Fruits and Vegetables

Drying foods at home is simple and fun to do. Much of summer's harvest can be dehydrated, and nothing go to waste. Extra green vegetables and the outer lettuce leaves of salad greens can be dried, ground into powder and combined with sea salt to make a tasty 'green salt' (see chapter Herbs and Seasonings)

Dried foods are easy to use, weigh much less than fresh produce, and convenient to store- requiring very little space. For an example: a 40 pound box of bananas, when dried can be stored in 2 gallon jars. 10 pounds of apples will be reduced to 2-3 pounds when dried.

Preserving foods by drying removes 85-95% of the moisture found in food, inactivating the growth of bacteria and other microorganisms that cause spoilage. Generally vegetables are dried until they are crisp or brittle, whereas fruits are dried until soft or rubbery, being preserved by the natural sugars found in the fruit. Some foods require pretreatment by blanching (with steam or boiling water) or treating with an antioxidant, to set color, slow enzyme action or destroy bacteria.

Temperature plays an important role in the drying process. If the temperature is too high, foods may cook and harden on the outside, while trapping moisture inside.

Vegetables are usually dried at 125°F and fruits at 130-135°F, and take as little as 4 hours up to 14, depending on the size of the cut and thickness of the food, moisture content, pre-treatment, and efficiency of the dehydrator.

Choose a dehydrator that has an adjustable temperature control with a range from 85° to 160° for low temperature drying, a quiet fan that blows heated air evenly over the food, and drying trays that have adequate spaces for air circulation. Trays should be durable, made of food-grade material, and easy to clean. *Contact the authors for UL approved dehydrators with 12 year warranty. Ph: 877- 442-4425

Dried Apples

Select a sweet variety such as Golden Delicious, Honeycrisp, or Fuji that are firm and ripe. Wash, slice un-peeled apples in ¼" thick circles, or wedges. Dip in lemon water or pineapple juice if desired. Place on trays, dry at low temperature until pliable, being careful not to over-dry. Store in covered jar, refrigerator or freezer. Add to survival mix, and hot cereal, or rehydrate for pie, sauce, or fruit soup.

Dried Pineapple

Peel, core and slice pineapple into ⅜" rings. Dip into a light honey syrup if desired; place in dehydrator. Dry at 130° medium setting until pliable or crisp. Store in refrigerator container or for longer period of time, freeze to retain color.

Dried Fruits such as raisins, prunes, apples, pears, peaches, and apricots, contain protective health benefits, much like fresh fruit, and can be used as a staple article of diet.

Dried Raspberries or Blueberries

Simply place whole berries in a single layer on dehydrator trays. Dry on low setting until crisp. Store in glass jars in refrigerator. Dried raspberries or blueberries can be added to fruit salad, muffins, muesli, smoothies, or prepared as a topping for waffles.

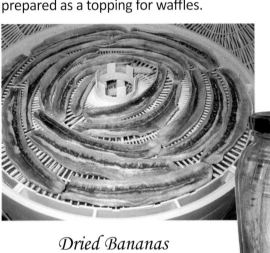

Dried Bananas

Choose lightly speckled yellow bananas, slightly underripe (dehydrator will continue to ripen fruit). Overripe fruit becomes very dark when dried. Peel and cut bananas lengthwise in half, dip in pineapple juice if desired, place on dehydrator trays. Dry at 130° until pliable. **For banana chips:** Cut large bananas into ¼" slices, pretreat by dipping into pineapple or lemon juice; dry until crisp. Use in trail mixes, in cookies or on cereal.

Dried Apricots

Select ripe apricots with a deep-orange color. Wash, cut in half, and remove pits. Place on dehydrator trays, cut side up. Dry at 130°F until pliable, with no moisture pockets, turning over once if needed, to dry evenly. Store in covered jar, refrigerator container or freezer.

Dried Persimmons

For drying, choose persimmons that are firm with deep-orange skin and not quite ready to eat. Slice unpeeled persimmons, in ⅜" circles. Dip in pineapple juice, if desired. The drying process will continue to ripen the persimmons while retaining their vivid color. Store in covered jar in the refrigerator or freezer.

Dried Kiwi or Strawberries

Peel and cut kiwi in ¼" slices; wash and cut strawberries lengthwise in ¼" slices. Pretreat by dipping in pineapple juice, if desired. Place on mesh screen on dehydrator trays. Dry at low temperature, until pliable, being careful not to over-dry. Peel fruit off screen. Store in a covered container in the refrigerator or freeze.

Fruit-Filled Thumbprint Cookies

Follow recipe for Thumbprint Cookies in chapter Desserts or your favorite cookie dough. Just before serving, fill centers with strawberry, cherry or apricot jam or preserves.

Home-Dried Figs

What could be more delectable than a sweet, fresh ripe fig? Figs vary in color from light yellow to green, purple, brown or black. Figs are very perishable and best eaten soon after picking, or preserved. Drying whole figs, fig syrup, fig fruit leather, or conserves; it's all worth the effort to relish the harvest all year. Dried figs, a concentrated source of energy also contain calcium, iron, magnesium, potassium, B vitamins and fiber.

10 lbs. fresh tree-ripe figs
½ cup honey or apple juice conc.
½ cup pure water
1-2 Tbs. lemon zest

Select tree-ripened figs. Cut stems to ¼". Wash figs, drain well and carefully place in a large kettle. Pour syrup (water, honey/juice) over figs. Cover and simmer for 30 minutes, occasionally swirling kettle back and forth to bathe figs with syrup. Remove from heat, uncover, allowing figs to cool several hours. Carefully transfer figs to another kettle (figs on top will now be on the bottom). Add lemon zest to remaining syrup and pour over figs. Simmer uncovered for 30-45 min., until figs are soft. Remove from heat, allow figs to cool thoroughly in the syrup. Drain figs in a colander (reserve the liquid). Place figs on drying trays to dehydrate (see note below). Enjoy dried figs plain, stuffed with walnuts, added to cereal, bread, desserts, or filling for cookies Yield: 3 lbs. fresh figs yields approx. 1 pound when dried.

Note: Dry figs to leathery consistency for long-term storage. Sticky for short-term. Refrigerate or freeze.

Variation: For a special treat, roll dried figs while still warm in shredded coconut. Store in freezer.

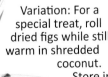

Fig Syrup

The liquid reserved from simmered Figs (see Home-Dried Figs) is sweet, thick and delicious. It can be canned or used to simmer more fresh figs for drying, added to fruit when making leather or conserves. Simply pour hot syrup into small clean jars and seal. Keep refrigerated or freeze. Delicious on waffles, crepes, pancakes, or as a topping for fruit salad or yogurt.

Fig Cakes

See recipe: Almond Fig Cakes in chapter Nuts & Seeds

Pineapple-Fig Conserves

2½ lbs. fresh or 2 cups dried figs
6 oz. apple juice concentrate
1-20 oz. can crushed pineapple
¼ cup honey, to taste
1-2 Tbs. lemon zest, to taste + ⅛ tsp. mace
1½ tsp. agar powder

In a saucepan combine coarsely chopped figs and frozen apple juice concentrate. Bring to a boil and simmer uncovered for 20 min. Remove from heat, cover, and let stand 30 min. Drain juice from pineapple and set aside. Add honey, lemon, mace and drained pineapple (approx.1¼ cups) to figs. Bring to a second boil and simmer uncovered for 20 min. Stir agar powder into ½ cup or more of the pineapple juice. Add to figs, stirring well to combine. Simmer to desired consistency; pour into hot sterile jars, apply lid and seal. **Note:** Amount of pineapple juice needed depends on the figs used (fresh or dried).

Fruit Leathers

Any fruit or combination of fruits can be blended to a puree, then dried in thin sheets resembling soft supple leather. The natural concentrated sugars of the fruit preserve the leather. Fruit leathers are nutritious, fast-energy foods, which can be enjoyed by the whole family. An excellent, convenient staple for hikers and backpackers, and when combined with crackers, nuts and seeds, provide the essential nutrients for a meal. Some favorite fruit leathers are: apricot, pineapple-peach, cranberry-orange, raspberry-apple, strawberry-banana. Lemon and orange zest, pineapple juice, or coriander, make tasty additions to fruit leather. If the puree is good, the leather will taste even better! Experiment with your own combinations! Fruit leathers keep indefinitely when stored in the refrigerator or freezer. Leathers can be used when making fruit soups, fruit sauces or re-hydrated for beverages. Roll and wrap different flavors to give as simple gifts!

Fruit Marmalade

1 lb. dried apricots
1 lb. dried pears
or peaches
1 lb. dried prunes
2½ cups crushed
pineapple

Soak all fruit overnight in hot
water *just to cover.* Remove
pits from prunes. Put fruit
through food grinder. Add
drained crushed pineapple and
honey to sweeten to taste. Store
in containers; refrigerate or freeze.
Process 10 minutes to seal in jars.

Fig Leather

Choose fully ripened, soft figs. Check
for any mold or decay. Cut figs in half
or pieces. Blend fruit with just enough
pineapple or white grape juice, and
a little lemon zest, to make a smooth
creamy puree. Pour puree on fruit
leather sheets or plastic wrap. Puree
should be about ¼" thick. Spread
evenly leaving ¼" around the edges.
Dehydrate the leather until it is no
longer tacky and can be easily peeled
off the fruit leather sheets or plastic
wrap. It should be dry, yet pliable.
Leathers dry in 8-10 hours, depending
on the thickness of the puree and
water content of the fruit. Roll flat
leather into a log
shape. Store
in airtight
container,
in the
refrigerator
or freezer.

Pineapple-Apricot Spread

*Here's a simple, nutritious spread you can make
using your own home-dried fruit. I think you'll like it!*

1 cup dried apricots, cut in pieces
3 dried pineapple slices, cut in pieces
2-3 tsp. orange or lemon zest, to taste
½ cup frozen white grape
or apple juice concentrate

Soak cut fruit and orange zest in warm
juice concentrate for 5-10 minutes until
softened. Whiz in blender or food
processor using part or all of the liquid,
until almost smooth or to desired consistency. Delicious on waffles, crepes, toast.

Drying Vegetables

Dried Onions, Mushrooms, & Peppers

Simply slice, chop, or dice vegetables as desired. Place on dehydrator trays. Dry at 125°F until vegetables are dry, crisp and brittle. Store in a glass jar in a cool, dry, dark place. **To Use:** Re-hydrate or simply add to soups, stews, grain pilaf, entrée dishes, etc., or for garnish.

Dried Tomatoes

Wash and slice firm, ripe, unpeeled solid tomatoes. Place on dehydrator trays, dry at 135°F until pliable or crisp. Store in a covered jar in the refrigerator. Use in soups, stews, cut in salads, sauce, or reconstitute in water and blend into tomato paste, puree, or juice. Rich in flavor, and nutrition, dried tomatoes are delicious eaten out-of-hand.

Dried Green or Wax Beans

Select any tender variety with small seeds. Wash, cut into 1" pieces; steam blanch 3-4 minutes, (may freeze 20 minutes to tenderize, opt.). Dry on dehydrator trays at 125°F until dry and brittle. Store in a covered jar in a cool, dark, dry place. Rehydrate and use in casseroles, soups, stews, or combine with other vegetables.

Drying Parsley, Chives or Dill Weed

Mince or Chop as desired. Place on mesh screen. Dehydrate at low temperature until very brittle- easiest culinary herbs to dry. To retain color, store in glass jars in cool, dark place.

Dried Carrots, Peas, Corn, Potatoes

Choose tender, peas and corn, mature carrots or potatoes. Wash vegetables, slice carrots and potatoes, shell peas, steam blanch vegetables, 5 minutes, Cool quickly. Cut corn off cob. Place vegetables on dehydrator trays. Dry at 125° until crisp and brittle. Use in soups, stews, casserole dishes, or combined in vegetable soup mixes. Grind sweet corn into cornmeal. Dried popcorn yields a deep yellow color cornmeal. Popcorn variety: Leave kernels on cob until dried. Dehyrate at 130° until shriveled.

Veggie Green Salt

Dehydrate dark leafy greens, lettuce and other vegetables to make this healthy, vitamin and mineral rich, seasoning salt.

1 part dehydrated green vegetables
1 part Celtic Sea Salt, fine
1 part onion powder

Use a nut and seed mill or food processor to pulverize dried vegetables (any variety of leafy greens, parsley, chives, watercress, cabbage, dill, fennel, peppers, etc). Mix with equal parts of sea salt and onion powder. Used to season pasta, rice, salad, potatoes, broth, soup, and popcorn!

Drying Herbs

Gather clean unblemished dry leaves or blossoms when tender and young. Place on dehydrator trays; set heat at lowest temperature and dry until all moisture is gone. Store in a clean dry jar or brown paper bag in a dark, cool place. Use in making herb teas. Herbs can be ground into powder with a nut and seed mill for filling capsules. (for more information on herbs- see chapter **Herbs & Seasonings**).

Croutons - Zwieback - Breadcrumbs

Try the dehydrator method for making zwieback and croutons, it's easy, no-risk-of-burning.

Twice-baked bread **(Zwieback)** is healthful and nourishing (see chapter **Breads)**

Croutons: Cut bread into slices, cubes, or other shapes; sprinkle on seasonings if desired. Dry in dehydrator or oven on low setting until thoroughly dry and crisp. Add to soup, salad or stuffing.

Breadcrumbs: grind croutons coarse or fine in a nut and seed mill.

Kitchen Notes

•**Healthy Sauté** – Start with 1 Tbs. Broth, in hot skillet. Add onions, garlic, or other ingredients; stir frequently until tender. Using this sauté method, vegetables can be flavorful without oil.

• **Quick sour milk** (buttermilk replacement) – For each cup: Add 1 Tbs. lemon juice to 1 cup (less 1 Tbs.) sweet soy milk. Stir; set aside 5 min. before using.

• **Beans** – 1 cup dry beans equal 2½ cups when soaked and cooked.

• **Canning with honey** – Cold pack: 1 Tbs. honey in bottom of quart jar; pack fruit with its own juice (i.e. peaches). Fruits needing syrup (berries, cherries, plums), add diluted fruit juice such as apple, or white grape, or make syrup using 1 qt. water + 2 Tbs. honey.

• **To measure Honey** – Dip spoon in oil or measure oil first. Use same cup to measure honey. Honey will easily slide off measuring utensil.

• **Bread Crumbs** – Bread to be used for crumbs should be dried thoroughly in a slow oven and stored in paper bags, or refrigerate crumbs in jars with tight fitting lids. Grape nuts cereal, finely fround, also works for bread crumbs.

• **Non-stick Pan Coat** – In a jar mix ¼ cup vegetable oil + ½ tsp. liquid lecithin. Stir well. Store in covered jar. Use as needed, instead of commercial cooking spray (it is less expensive). Brush lightly on bread pans, muffin cups, etc. for easy removal of foods.

• **No-stick Molasses** – Before measuring honey, molasses or maple syrup, apply pan coating to spoon or measure oil first. The sweetener will then slide off, rather than stick.

• **Leftover liquids** – When cooking rice or any grains, use other liquids for added flavor. Try vegetable broth, fruit juice combinations, or coconut milk.

• **Savory / Summer Savory** may help eliminate gas in beans. Watch food combinations!

•**Garbanzo Flour** mixed with a little water, will take the place of eggs in some recipes (cookies, patties, roasts). Experiment a little!

• **Canned beans** – may save cooking time, but adds extra salt to your dish. Eliminate the salty liquid by rinsing the beans in a colander under cold running water; drain well.

• **Hot oil** – To stop hot oil from splattering – sprinkle a little flour into pan.

• **Store onions, garlic, potatoes and other root vegetables** in a dry, cool, dark place in wire bins or racks that allow air to circulate around them.

• **Zest of lemons and oranges** (pesticide-free) can be frozen for later use. The peel contains flavonoids and natural aromatic terpenes having medicinal benefit. The zest (colored part of skin) is excellent and used to enhance the flavor of many dishes. Just grate rind, freeze in jar, use as needed.

- **Squeeze and freeze** fresh lemon juice in ice cube trays. Transfer frozen juice cubes to a plastic freezer bag. The portion - size cubes are handy and ready-to-use for salad, drinks, dressing, or a glass of refreshing lemonade!

- **Fresh Mint** – added to pea soup - has a refreshing flavor.

- **Nuts and Raisins** – Mix with dry ingredients to keep from sinking to bottom of bowl.

- **Rice, Brown** – Cook in boiling salted water, stir only once, to avoid rice sticking to pan

- **Leftover foods** – Best to refrigerate in glass jars. Will not pick up or give off odors.

- **Blanching Nuts** – Pour boiling water over nuts. Let set 1 minute, drain. Slip off skins.

- **Cabbage, Cauliflower, and Broccoli** – May leave odors in the air. Burn a piece of cotton string; carbon formed takes up the odor.

- **Bread making** – Grated raw potato, lecithin, and molasses, give bread a fine texture (prevents crumbling). Lecithin also acts as a preservative. Measure salt accurately- too much retards dough, not enough-dough runs away.

- **Date and Raw Sugar** – To keep soft - store in covered container with a piece of bread. If already hard, soften sugar in pan - very slow oven.

- **Garlic flavor for soups, etc** – Wrap peeled garlic cloves in small piece of cheesecloth or clean nylon stocking - remove before serving soup- saves time looking for it.

- **Cutting Dates** – Use wet or buttered scissors

- **Easy removal of cakes from pan** – Lightly coat with non-stick pan coating (¼ cup oil + ½ tsp. liquid lecithin). Substitute for cooking spray, or cut wax paper to fit bottom of pan.

- **To measure Margarine or Coconut Oil, etc**. – For ¼ cup of margarine, put ¾ cup water in measuring cup, add margarine until water reaches the 1 cup level. The same method can be used for ½ cup, ⅓ cup, or other amount.

- **Buttered toast** – cut leftovers in squares for soup, crumble and store in refrigerator for buttered crumbs- delicious base for stuffing green peppers, etc.

- **Cake (heavy)** – combine with day-old bread for a pudding. Make lemon sauce or carob pudding to go over it. Top with Soy Whipped Cream.

- **Icing** – save leftover icing that has dripped off the cake in the cutting – use as a start for the next batch of cookies.

- **Pan fried potatoes** – to make golden brown sprinkle lightly with flour before browning.

- **Firm small mushrooms** – can be easily and evenly cut straight with an egg slicer.

- **For plump raisins in cakes and breads** – Soak in warm water before adding to batter. If dry, sprinkle with flour; they will not stick together.

- **To avoid soggy pie crust** – Brush bottom and sides lightly with flax jell, sprinkle with flour, then add the filling.

- **Garlic Breath** – Chew fresh parsley, fennel tops, fennel or dill seed.

- **For golden brown pie crusts** – Brush top with milk before baking. Flaky crust: brush with cold water just before baking. To prevent over-browning-cover rim with 2" foil.

- **Bread making** – Use garbanzo, soy or lima bean flour for added protein and leavening.

- **Oat flour** – to cleanse and soothe tender skin. Relieves dry, itchy, scaly skin caused by hard water or soap. Make a smooth paste in hands, then put on face; leave on 2-3 min. Rinse. For Poison Ivy or Oak – Add to tepid bath water. Swish oats in water until gooey.

- **To color foods red** – Pink: Add raspberry or strawberry juice to fruit, beverages, or cream. Red: Add a few drops of beet juice or cooking water from beets. Yellow: Add a little tumeric; color intensifies with heat and mixing.

- **To easily clean a seed or nut grinder** – run with 2 tablespoons of uncooked rice, then wipe with a paper towel (the rice works as an abrasive, scrubbing the inside of grinder).

- **A quick fix for garlic and onion odor** on your hands – Rub with a lemon wedge or juice, then rinse with cold water.

- **To remove vegetable stains** – rub hands with a slice of lemon or raw potato.

- **Grapefruits and Oranges** – the heavier they are, the more juice they usually contain.

- **Vegetables and fruit**s – buy in season. Avoid buying perishables in large quantities.

- **Flour** – Mix with equal amount of cold water, raw sugar, or oil before adding to another mixture. These substances separate the flour particles.

- **Waste not, want not** – Use liquid left from cooking vegetables, as a tasty and nutritious base for gravy, sauce, vegetable soup, or broth. Contains vitamins and minerals.

Cinnamon Substitutes

Grind seeds together in a nut and seed mill. Use as cinnamon, in the same proportion. *(cinnamon stimulates the digestive process, however, its regular use can cause stomach inflammation (gastritis).*

#1

2 parts coriander seed
1 part anise seed

(Favorite for sweet rolls and apple pie. Grind together, or use coriander alone.)

#2

2 parts coriander, ground
1 part cardamom, ground

(Good in pumpkin pie)

#3

1 part coriander
1 part anise seed
1 part cardamom

(Use in fruit crisp, cobbler, breads, pies.)

Home-Made Baking Powder

Many of the recipes in cookbooks today, which call for baking powder, are largely made up of white sugar, white flour, hydrogenated fats, butter, etc.. These cakes and pastries are generally classed with "empty calorie" foods that are detrimental, rather than vital foods which promote health. These foods are unessential and require much time to prepare. As we experience the blessings of a simple diet, we will shun the rich cakes and pastries and be content to live on a more simple fare. The use of soda and baking powder is harmful. Soda causes inflammation of the stomach. Most baking powders contain harmful ingredients such as aluminum, lime, baking soda, and too much sodium. These affect the blood in an unhealthful way (Featherweight, Hain, Rumford and Ener-G, baking powders, contain no aluminum or lime). If you prefer to make your own baking powder, below is a recipe (for freshness, mix small batches). Ingredients available at health food stores or pharmacies.

2 parts arrowroot or cornstarch
1 part potassium bicarbonate
2 parts cream of tartar or tartaric acid

Sift 3 times. Store in airtight jar. Use in same proportion as other baking powders.

Note: For best results, add baking powder last to recipe and stir just enough to mix. Bake immediately.

Analysis and effect of the above ingredients are:

Potassium Bicarbonate: *An antacid salt and mild diuretic. (stimulates a greater flow of urine)*
Cream of Tartar: *(Potassium bitartrate) A diuretic, a cathartic (laxative), and refrigerant.*
Tartaric Acid: *A white powder from grapes and various plants. Rarely toxic (only in large doses)*

Note: **Ener-G® baking powder** consists of approximately 70% calcium carbonate and 30% citric acid, which produces calcium citrate (an absorbable form of calcium). The manufacturers recommend *double* the amount listed in recipes to achieve desired results.

Vanilla - Homemade

Vanilla- *A valuable flavoring made from the vanilla bean, commercially extracted by alcohol. Here's a recipe for those desiring to make a variation of this flavor at home.*

2 vanilla beans (8" long)
⅔ cup pure water
1 Tbs. raw sugar
½ tsp. liquid lecithin + 1 tsp. soy oil
1 Tbs. honey or agave syrup

Cut vanilla beans in small pieces. Blend in blender with warm water and raw sugar. Bring up to a boil in a covered pan, but do not boil. Put into a clean jar and cap tightly. Let stand overnight. Strain into the blender. Mix lecithin with oil and honey and slowly add this to the vanilla mixture while blending on slow speed. Pour into small 2 oz. bottles and cap tightly. Must be kept refrigerated.

Soya Starter (Base)

Dextrinizing the flour is optional but gives a nutlike flavor, making it more palatable. It may also improve its digestibility. Use dextrinized soy flour in recipes that call for it. **To Dextrinize:** Place Soy Flour ¼" thick in a dry baking pan. Lightly toast in 350° oven for 15 minutes, stirring occasionally to prevent burning flour. Store in cool, dry place.

2 cups pure water
1 cup soy flour
1 tsp. sea salt

1. Blend ingredients till smooth in blender.

2. Place in top part of double boiler and steam for 1½ hours - stirring occasionally.

3. Cool & blend to remove any lumps. Store in covered jar in refrigerator. Will thicken as it sets. Ready for quick use in making:

Tasty spreads (see Soya Yeast Sandwich Spread)
Soy beverages and creams
Mayonnaise and dressings
As replacer (1 egg) for binding: Use 2-3 Tbs. in vegetarian meatballs, patties, etc.

Egg Substitutes*

(Use one of these as a binder to replace 1 egg)

2-3 Tbs. Soy Starter (recipe pg. 611)
2 Tbs. garbanzo flour + 2 Tbs. water
   (thick paste)
¼ cup soaked soybeans or garbanzo
   beans + ¼ cup water-blend smooth
   (soaked beans can be frozen-ready to use)
2-3 Tbs. tapioca flour
2-3 Tbs. gluten flour
2-3 Tbs. potato flour or flakes
2-3 Tbs. oat flour (or blend quick oats)
2 Tbs. nut butter
   (almond, cashew, peanut, etc.)
Hot cooked oatmeal
   (½ cup oats in ½ cup water)

*Egg for leavening: ***Ener-g Egg Replacer***, a
blend of rising ingredients and stabilizers.
Glossary of Natural Foods - (see Ener-G®
Substitutes pg. 34)
Note: recipes for Scrambled Tofu "Eggs"
pgs. 353, 466, 468

Non-Stick Pan Coating

*Presto! - food will not stick when using this fool-
proof, inexpensive formula.*

¼ cup soy oil
½ tsp. liquid lecithin

In a jar, stir together the oil and lecithin.
Cover and use as needed. Use a small
pastry brush to lightly coat bread pans,
cookie sheets, muffin cups, griddles, fry
pans, waffle iron, etc.

How to Blanch Almonds

1. Boil 1 cup water or enough to cover nuts.
2. Pour boiling water over nuts in a bowl.
3. Let set 1-2 minutes. Drain.
4. Slip off skins by gently pushing with
thumb and index finger.

Flaxseed Jell

2 Tbs. flax seed
1 cup pure cold water

Soak flax in water ½ hour. Simmer 10
minutes. Strain. Set in refrigerator. Beat as
you would egg whites for meringue. It will
not hold its shape when heated, but can
be folded in jells and creams requiring no
cooking. Can also be used as a binder or
thickener in place of eggs in some recipes.

Preserved Persimmons

Persimmons, sliced
Raw honey or sucanat

Put a thin layer of honey in the bottom
of a jar. Then put a layer of sliced ripe
persimmons, then another layer of honey or
raw sugar. Repeat layer until jar is full. The
sugar will soon dissolve and form a syrup.
Press fruits down under syrup., or add more
honey to jars. Seal and store in refrigerator
until used. The syrup may be drained off and
the fruits served like dates, which they will
resemble in appearance and flavor.

Bring honey and water to a boil in saucepan. Add pitted cut fruit; simmer in the syrup until tender and glazed, stirring frequently. Remove fruit, drain, refrigerate. Use the candied fruit in fruit cakes, the same as candied fruit sold commercially. Try glazing whole apples and serve with **nut cream** and a sprinkle of **coriander**.

Glazed Fruit
(candied with honey)

1 cup honey
fruit, diced or cut
½ cup pure water

Fresh, canned, frozen or dried **cherries, pineapple chunks, orange** or **lemon peel, pears, apricots** and **apple chunks** are some of the fruits that can be glazed.

Helpful Substitutions – This for That

Baking Powder, and Soda
Use ½ Cream of Tartar, Rumford, EnerG, Featherweight low sodium, or homemade baking powder (see recipe)

Brown Sugar
Use sucanat (raw sugar), date sugar or honey (reduce liquid in recipe by ¼)

Butter or Margarine
Use oil (cold-pressed)+ liquid lecithin, coconut oil, non-hydrogenated soy spread or nut butter.

Buttermilk
Substitute sour milk. For each cup: Add 1 Tbs. lemon juice to 1 cup (less 1 Tbs.) sweet milk. Stir; set aside 5 min. before using.

Cinnamon
Use coriander, cardamom, anise (see cinnamon substitutes).

Chocolate, 1 square
Use 3 Tbs. carob powder + 2 Tbs. water + ½ tsp.oil, opt.

Cocoa
Use carob powder (medium roasted)

Coffee
Use caffeine-free beverages- Pero, Cafix, Bueno, Breakfast Cup

Cornstarch, (1 Tbs.)
Use 1 Tbs. arrowroot, tapioca or 2 Tbs.white or rice flour

Eggs, as binder
Use nut butters, soy starter, garbanzo, soy or oat flour

Eggs, for baking, 1 whole
Use 2 yolks and 1 tsp. water, or 4 Tbs. almond butter + 2 Tbs. lemon juice

Egg white, for meringue
Use Flax Jell, whipped

Flour, white
Use whole wheat pastry or barley flour

Flour, cake
1 cup, less 2 Tbs. all-purpose, unbleached flour

Flour, for thickening (1 Tbs.)
Use 1 Tbs. Tapioca, Arrowroot, or ½ Tbs. cornstarch

Gelatin, Jello, soft
Use 1 Tbs. agar flakes, Gefen® or KOJEL®, with 2 cups liquid

Gelatin, Jello, firm
Use 1 Tbs. granulated agar or 2 Tbs. agar flakes and 3 ½ cups liquid

Honey, processed (see Glossary of Natural Foods, pg. 35)
Use agave, brown rice syrup, maple syrup, or honey (natural in comb, spun or whipped)

Milk, sour (for baking)
Use 1 cup sweet milk (any kind) + 1 Tbs. lemon juice, or ¾ tsp. cream of tartar

Rice, white
Use natural brown rice, Basmati or Jasmine

Sugar
Use Sucanat, fruit juice concentrates, or (see chart below)

Tapioca
Use agar, arrowroot starch, brown rice or potato flour

Tea
Use Herb Teas (see chapter on Herbs and Beverages)

Vinegar
Use equal amounts of lemon juice

Substitutions for 1 cup Granulated Sugar

	Molasses	Maple Syrup	Honey (raw)	Agave Syrup
Other Sweeteners	1 cup	1¼ cups (reduce liquid by ½)	1 cup (reduce liquid by ¼)	½ cup (reduce liquid by ⅓)
Amount for Similar Sweetness	1½ cups = 1 cup sugar	1¼ cups = 1 cup sugar	¾ cup = 1 cup sugar	½ cup = 1 cup sugar
Miscellaneous Notes	Cakes heavier but stay moist longer	Good on cereals, puddings, sauces, desserts	Variety of flavors Good for bread, pies, canning fruit cakes, cookies, cereal, toppings	Use for cereal, fruit, beverages, baking, sweet sauces, topping Low glycemic Index (may be suited for diabetics)

Recipes using Milk & Eggs

Index - CHAPTER 20

Miscellaneous - Recipes using Milk & Eggs

Ten Talents

616

"*Let the people be taught how to prepare food without the use of milk or butter. Tell them that the time will soon come when there will be no safety in using eggs, milk, cream, or butter, because disease in animals is increasing in proportion to the increase of wickedness among men...God will give His people ability and tact to prepare wholesome food without these things.*"

"*Diet reform should be progressive. As disease in animals increases, the use of milk and eggs will become more and more unsafe. An effort should be made to supply their place with other things that are healthful and inexpensive. The people everywhere should be taught how to cook without milk and eggs so far as possible, and yet have their food wholesome and palatable.*"
E. G. White, Diet and Foods, pp. 460, 469

"*The brain is the organ and instrument of the mind and controls the whole body. In order for the other parts of the system to be healthy, the brain must be healthy. And in order for the brain to be healthy, the blood must be pure. If by correct habits of eating and drinking the blood is kept pure, the brain will be properly nourished.*" E. G. White, Counsels on Health, pg. 586

Chapter cover photo: *Farm Fresh Organic Eggs*

Animal Foods - Connection to Human Disease

Health improvement is a gradual process. A few recipes using milk and eggs are included in this chapter, for those who are in the transitional period. However, we encourage those who still cling to animal products to become acquainted with the facts concerning their use, and become weaned through this process.

Studies reported by the National Academy of Sciences' Food and Nutrition Board indicate that *total vegetarians* can have a nutritionally adequate diet if they carefully select a dietary which includes a proper balance of *essential amino acids (proteins)* and adequate supplies of *iron, calcium, riboflavin, Vitamins A, D, and B12.*

Replacement for flesh meats, eggs, or milk products should be made from the storehouse of natural foods given in God's original diet for man. Switching to a total vegetarian diet should include adequate amounts of a wide variety of *grains, fruits, vegetables, legumes, seeds,* and *nuts* in as natural, unrefined, state as practical, and in proper combinations.

There is conditional evidence linking the use of animal products (meat, eggs, milk, cream, butter, cheese, fish and fowl) with varied levels of cholesterol and saturated fat to the increased risk of numerous human diseases such as cancer, coronary heart disease, atherosclerosis, diabetes, arthritis, obesity, etc. Egg consumption is well known to be related to high blood cholesterol which increases heart attack risk.

Food producing animals are often concentrated in large flocks and herds, crowded stockyards, feedlots, and confining pens where they are force-fed for rapid growth and production. Such unnatural conditions often contribute to animal, and, in turn, human disease.

Milk is not for everyone. A pediatrician noted that a lactase deficiency can make milk-drinking hazardous. Mother's milk, he states is best for the infant. Beyond childhood, milk is not absolutely necessary. Many who suffer from various allergies have experienced better health by reducing or eliminating dairy products from their diet.

Some believe in order for them to obtain proper nutrition, milk, and eggs should be a part of their diet. For others, the restriction of these foods may not be practical or advisable. To such, we offer these suggestions:

1. Obtain the products from animals that are healthy, and from sources that allow the animals and chickens a natural as possible habitat.

2. Limit the use of eggs to 1-3 per week. Avoid the excessive drinking of milk, which may tend to replace other necessary and nourishing foods.

3. Keep dairy products and eggs under refrigeration, observing strict cleanliness in handling them during preparation, serving, and storage.

Scientific evidence today identifies the *vegetarian diet* as the *best possible* diet, and has proven the benefits and superiority of a vegetarian diet in the prevention and treatment of many diseases. Our main interest is to de-emphasize the use of animal products. With a reasonable understanding of the requirements of good nutrition, one may have a well-balanced dietary, and enjoy the adventures of eating a vegetarian diet and the advantages of a healthy lifestyle.

Fiber, soluble and insoluble, so necessary to good health, is found in whole grains, vegetables, fruits, nuts, seeds and beans. *There is no fiber in milk, eggs, cheese, or meat.*

Non-Dairy Cheeses

American
pg 454

Herbed Mozzarella
pg 455

Cream Cheese
pg 453

Brick, pg 455

Tofu, pg 350-1

Silken Tofu
pg 351

Cheddar
pg 456

American
pg 454

Pineapple Cream Cheese
pg 453

Farmers
pg 457

Monterey Jack, pg 457

Mozzarella, pg 454

Herbed
Mozzarella
pg 455

Dairy Substitutes

Butter

(see **Sandwiches & Spreads** pgs 448-452)

Avocado Butter
Better Than Butter
Creamy Whipped Butter
Dilly Garlic Butter
Herb Butter
Maple Butter
Simple Butter Substitute

Cheese

(see **Sandwiches & Spreads** pgs 453-457)

"American Cheeze"
"Brick" Cheeze
"Cheddar Cheeze"
"Farmer" Cheeze
Mock "Mozzarella"
"Monterey Jack" Cheeze
Pineapple Cream Cheese
Tofu "Cream Cheese"
Tofu - Soybean Curd #1
*(see **Main Dishes**)*
Soy Cheese Curd #2
*(see **Main Dishes**)*

Cheese, Other

(see **Sauces, Creams, & Gravy** pgs 474-477)

Alfredo Cheese Sauce
Cashew Pimento Cheese Sauce
Parmesan "Cheese" (pg. 298)
Ricotta Filling (**Main Dishes pg. 330**)

Creams

(see **Sweet Creams & Toppings** pgs 483-486)

Almond Cream
Cashew Nut Cream
Cashew Soy Whipped Cream

Soy Sour Cream
Soy Whipped Cream Topping
Tofu Sour Cream
Tofu Vanilla Crème

Ice Cream, Sherbet

(see **Desserts** pgs 191-199)

Egg Substitutes

(see **Meatless Main Dishes** pgs 299-368)

Scrambled Tofu "Eggs"
Soufflé, eggless varieties
Tofu-egg Sandwich Filling
*(see **Sandwiches & Spreads**)*
Tofu "Egg" or "Chicken" Salad
*(see **Salads - Vegetable**)*
Egg Substitutes - used as a
binder *(see **Miscellaneous**)*

Milk

(see **Beverages** pgs 102-107)

Almond Milk
Almond-Sesame Milk
Cashew Nut Milk
Coconut Milk
Malted Carob Milk
Rice Dream Milk
Sesame Milk
Soybean Milk
Tofu Milk
Milk Shake - varieties

Yogurt

(see **Beverages**
pgs 107-108)

Plain
Fruit Flavored
varieties

Vegetarians (Types of)

Semi-Vegetarian - A popular term used by those who include a lot of meatless meals in their diet, but still eat eggs, dairy products and occasionally fish, poultry and meat.

Lacto-Ovo Vegetarian - The diet includes fruits, grains, vegetables, nuts, seeds and dairy products (lacto), and eggs (ovo), but eliminates meat, poultry, fish and seafood.

Lacto- Vegetarian - Diet includes dairy milk and other milk-based products such as cream, butter, cheese, etc. Eggs, meat, poultry, fish or seafood are excluded.

Pure Vegetarian (Total) - Ideal diet consists of: Fruits, Grains, Vegetables, Legumes, Nuts and Seeds. The abundant variety of plant based foods may include beneficial herbs, oils, and natural sweeteners. (**TEN TALENTS** is based on this optimal diet)

Vegan Vegetarian - Strictest diet of all- includes no animal products *or by-products* (do not eat or wear anything that was ever part of an animal). Vegans may not use products such as honey, beeswax, wool, leather, fur, silk, most cosmetics or soaps. Diet includes vegetables, fruits, grains, nuts and seeds.

Note: *A few recipes are given here to facilitate the change to a total vegetarian diet.*

620

Meatless Dishes

Almond-Brown Rice Loaf

1 cup almonds, chopped
3 cups natural brown rice, cooked
2-3 small eggs, beaten
   (from free-range fed hens)
½ cup whole grain bread, soaked in
1 cup milk (soy or other, or tomato puree)
¼ cup onions, chopped, sautéed
½ cup celery, diced, sautéed
¼ cup parsley, fresh chopped
2 Tbs. peanut butter or soy flour
2 Tbs. soy sauce or Bragg's Aminos®
sea salt, to taste

Combine all ingredients in order given. Fill loaf pan. Bake 45 minutes at 375°. Serve with **Country Style Gravy** or your favorite.
Hint: Try omitting eggs, reduce liquid ½, add more nut butter or Soy Starter as binder.

Pecan-Nut Loaf

1 cup pecans, chopped
2 cups fresh bread, crumbled
2 cups celery, diced
¼ cup chopped onion
2 cups nut or soy milk
¼ cup chopped parsley
1 Tbs. soy oil, opt.
1 tsp. sea salt
1 tsp. Chicken-style Seasoning or other
pinch of savory or thyme
2 beaten eggs (from free-range fed hens)

Mix well all together. Bake in prepared loaf pans, at 350° for 1 hour or until set. Serve with **Country Style Gravy** or your favorite.

Natural Rice Carrot Loaf

½ lb. carrots
3 cups steamed brown rice
½ cup nut butter, peanut, almond
   or cashew
⅓ cup bread or cracker crumbs
2 eggs, beaten (from free-range fed hens)
1 Tbs. soy oil, opt.
1 tsp. sea salt

Finely grate carrots in mixing bowl. Add rest of ingredients. Combine together. Place in oiled loaf pan. Bake at 350° for 45 minutes or until set and golden brown (avoid getting too dry). Serve with your favorite gravy.

Oatmeal Seed Patties

2 cups rolled oats, quick
½ cup chopped walnuts
¼ cup ground pumpkin or sunflower seeds
1 medium onion, minced
½ cup thick milk or cream (nut, soy, etc)
¼ cup pure water
2 small eggs (from free-range fed hens)
sea salt and sage, to taste

Mix well. Form into patties. Brown on both sides in skillet, or bake in oven 45 minutes at 350°. Serve with your favorite gravy.

Breads

Sunflower Muffins

Into a bowl put:

2 Tbs. honey
2 Tbs. soy oil   or applesauce
½ cup fruit juice (apple, pear)
1 cup raisins
½ cup coconut
½ cup barley flour or rice flour
¼ cup toasted wheat germ

1 cup raw sunflower seed meal
2 egg yolks (from free-range fed hens)

Mix well. Fold in:

2 stiffly beaten egg whites

Pour into non-stick muffin cups and bake in 350° oven about 25 minutes.

Note: Sunflower seeds can be made into fine meal with a small nut grinder.

Swedish Limpa Rye Bread

Heat in saucepan until dissolved:

½ cup pure water
¼ cup molasses, raw or date sugar
1 Tbs. soy oil
1 ½ tsp. sea salt

Put in mixing bowl and add:

¾ cup buttermilk or soy sour milk*
2 cups rye / wheat flour, mixed
2 Tbs. grated orange rind

Then add:

1 Tbs. dry yeast dissolved in
¼ cup warm water + 1 tsp. honey

Mix well, then knead in sufficient flour (whole wheat, barley, golden white) to make a soft elastic dough. If desired, add ½ cup raisins. Let rise until almost double. Punch down and shape into round loaves. Let rise again to almost double. Bake 350° 50-60 minutes. Remove from pans; cool overnight. Dough with rye will be sticky. Add enough flour so it handles easily.

Note: For each cup of sour milk, place 1 Tbs. lemon juice in a glass measuring cup. Add enough milk to make 1 cup liquid; stir. Let mixture stand 5 minutes before using.

Raisin Bran Muffins

Stir together:

1 cup hot Soy Milk
1 cup Nabisco 100% Bran
⅓ cup raisins

Let set 5 minutes. Add:

1 egg, beaten (beat white separately)
3 Tbs. honey or raw sugar
3 Tbs. soy oil
½ tsp. sea salt

Sift and lightly stir in:

1 cup whole wheat flour
2 tsp. Rumford baking powder

Fold in egg white, beaten stiff. Fill prepared muffin cups ¾ full. Bake at 350° for 25-30 minutes.

Corn Bread

1½ cups corn meal
½ cup whole wheat pastry or barley flour
2 Tbs. wheat germ or whole wheat flour
1 tsp. sea salt
1 ½ tsp. Rumford baking powder
2 Tbs. soy oil + 1 tsp. lecithin
2 Tbs. honey
2 cups boiling water
2 eggs, divided (from free-range fed hens)

Combine corn meal, flours, salt and baking powder in a bowl. Mix oil, honey, and lecithin together and add to flour. Mix well. Separate eggs. Beat whites stiff. Beat yolks until lemon colored. Fold beaten yolks into the beaten whites, set aside. Slowly, pour boiling water over the cornmeal mixture while stirring. Gradually fold eggs in corn mixture, using as few strokes as possible. Pour into prepared baking pan. Bake in 375° oven for 30 minutes or until golden brown.

Double Corn Bread: Fold ½ cup whole kernel corn (frozen, thawed or cut off cob) into batter.

Zucchini Muffins or Bread

2 cups whole wheat pastry flour
¼ cup wheat germ, oat or barley flour
2 tsp. Rumford baking power
½ tsp. EnerG® baking soda
½ tsp. sea salt
1½ tsp. cinnamon substitute
¼ cup soy milk or other
¼ cup soy oil
½ cup honey
1 egg, beaten (from free-range fed hens)
1½ cups zucchini shredded, unpeeled
1 Tbs. pure vanilla
½ cup chopped walnuts or pecans

Pre-heat oven to 350°. Prepare muffin cups or loaf pan with non-stick coating. In a medium bowl, sift together all the dry ingredients. Make a well in center of flour mixture, set aside. In another bowl, combine milk, oil, honey, egg, zucchini and vanilla. Add to dry ingredients, stirring only until moistened. Add nuts. Spoon batter into prepared muffin cups, or loaf pan. Bake muffins 30-35min., loaf 50-60 min. or until toothpick inserted near center comes out clean. Cool in pan on wire rack for 10 min. Remove from pan, cool completely. Wrap and store in refrigerator. Yield: 8-12 muffins

Apple-Walnut Muffins

2 cups whole wheat pastry flour
1 tsp. cinnamon substitute
½ tsp. sea salt
1 Tbs. Rumford baking powder
1 egg, beaten (from free-range fed hens)
½ cup milk, soy or other
2 Tbs. soy oil
3 Tbs. honey or molasses
1 ½ cups grated raw apple
½ cup walnuts, chopped

Sift dry ingredients together. Combine egg, milk, oil, honey. Add to flour mixture stirring only until mixed. Fold in grated apples and nuts. Spoon into oiled muffin cups, ⅔ full. Bake in hot oven 400° for 20-30 min. Yield: approx. 12 muffin

Desserts

Perfect Cheese Cake

Crust:

2 cups graham cracker crumbs
   (recipe given)
½ cup oat flour, grape-nuts
   or granola crumbs
3-4 Tbs. honey or date sugar
⅓ cup soft coconut oil
   or cold-pressed soy spread
1 tsp. lemon or orange rind
⅛ tsp. sea salt

Mix ingredients with pastry cutter;
press into a square 8x8x2½" glass baking
dish. Chill while preparing the filling.

Note: Fine zwieback or granola crumbs may be
used instead of crackers.

Cheese Filling: Beat until fluffy:

3 lbs. soft cottage cheese

Add, while beating:

1¼ cups light honey
4 Tbs. arrowroot starch
¼ cup top milk or soy cream
½ tsp. pure vanilla
¼ tsp. sea salt
1 tsp. unsprayed orange rind
1 tsp. unsprayed lemon rind

Add to cheese mixture. Beat smooth:

3 eggs (from free-range fed hens)
or see egg substitutes - pg 612

Pour filling into graham cracker lined
pan. Bake 12 minutes at 500°. Reduce
oven to 200° (avoid opening oven door)
and bake 1¼ hours. Cool on racks away
from draft. Cakes will be set when
chilled. See variations for **Pineapple or
Strawberry Cheese Cake.**

Note: Soft or Silken Tofu can be used instead of
cottage cheese or cream cheese.

Pineapple Cheese Cake

Spread a ½" layer of crushed, drained
pineapple on chilled graham cracker
shell before pouring in the filling.

Strawberry Cheese Cake

When cake is chilled, cut into squares
and serve with a scoop of fresh or
frozen strawberries sweetened with
honey.

Banana Cake or Muffins

¾ cup honey
¼ cup oil or non-hydrogenated soy spread
2 eggs, divided (from free-range fed hens)
1 tsp. pure vanilla
½ cup soy milk or other
1 large mashed banana (¾ cup)
2 ¾ cups whole wheat pastry flour
½ tsp. sea salt
2 ½ tsp. Rumford
   or 1 Tbs. EnerG® baking powder

Cream oil and honey with an electric
mixer; add beaten egg yolks and vanilla.
Mix well. Combine milk and banana.
Add alternately with dry ingredients
to the oil and honey mixture. Beat egg
whites until stiff; fold into batter.
Pour into 2-layer cake pans (lined with
wax paper), or prepared muffin pans.
Bake at 350° for 50 minutes. Remove
from pans. When cool, cover with frosting
or cream. Serve with **Lemon Sauce**.

Coconut Macaroons

1½ cups coconut meal
¼ cup sesame seed meal
¼ cup sunflower seed meal
¼ cup barley or rice flour
½ cup light honey
¼ tsp. almond extract
2 egg whites, beaten stiff or substitute

In a mixing bowl stir first six ingredients
together. Fold in egg whites. Drop by
tablespoonfuls onto cookie sheet. Bake
at 350° 15 min. or until golden brown.
Remove from oven, cool completely.

Carob Nut Brownies

¼ cup soy oil or soy butter
⅓ cup honey
⅓ cup raw sugar or date sugar
1 egg or substitute
3 Tbs. milk, soy or nut
½ tsp. sea salt
1 ½ tsp. pure vanilla
1 tsp. ground coriander, optional
½ cup carob powder
1½ tsp. Rumford baking powder,
    or 1 Tbs. EnerG®
⅔ cup whole wheat pastry flour
1 cup chopped walnuts or pecans

Cream oil, honey, and raw or date sugar until smooth. Add egg, milk, salt, vanilla, coriander, and carob. Beat well. Sift baking powder and flour; stir flour and nuts into mixture. Spread batter in 9"x 9" pan lined with waxed paper or coated with non-stick spray. Bake 35-40 minutes at 350°. Cool in pan on wire rack; frost if desired. Cut into squares.

Oatmeal Coconut Cookies

Mix together and let stand 15 minutes:

2 cups quick oats
1 cup raw or date sugar
⅓ cup soy oil

Add and mix well:

1 egg, beaten or substitute
½ tsp. pure vanilla
½ tsp. sea salt

Stir in:

½ cup shredded coconut

Drop by spoonfuls on non-stick cookie sheet; bake 12-15 minutes at 350°. Remove from pan and cool. Yield: about 3 dozen cookies.

Apricot Sherbet

1 cup apricots, fresh or canned
1 cup pineapple juice, unsweetened
3 Tbs. light honey
1 Tbs. agar flakes
¼ cup pure cold water
½ cup evaporated milk or creamy soy milk

Blend fruit, juice and honey 2-3 minutes until smooth. Soften agar in cold water and dissolve by stirring over hot water. Add gelatin to fruit mixture. Chill until slightly congealed; beat in mixer until stiff. Whip milk and lightly fold into gelatin. Chill in glass cups or molds.

Note: 1 cup of **Soy Whipped Cream** may be used to replace the evaporated milk, if desired.

My Truest Friend

Why should I be discouraged?
    Jesus will not forget.
He knows my every trial,
    And He's never failed me yet.

Though shadows dark surround me,
    On Him I can depend;
For He will never leave me
    But will keep me to the end.

So I will ever trust Him,
    Though the way I cannot see;
For I know His hand is leading
    And His way is the best for me.
                    Eva J. Sharp

Chapter 21
Healthy Lifestyle

Trust in Divine Power

Exercise

Nutrition

Temperance

Air, Pure

Light, Sunshine

Energizing Water

Nightly Rest

Thankfulness

Service

Index - *Chapter 21*

Healthy Lifestyle

Ten Talents

**Today is God's gift to us...
That's why it is called the "present."**

Chapter cover photo: *Ten Healthy Lifestyle Habits*

Ten Principles for Abundant Health

T Trust in Divine Power

E Exercise

N Nutrition

T Temperance

A Air, Pure

L Light, Sunshine

E Energizing Water

N Nightly Rest

T Thankfulness

S Service

Quiz - Healthy Lifestyle Habits

How do you honestly rate yourself? Take this simple quiz. Add up your numbers and compare with the scores below. (use a scale from 1-10, with 10 being the highest).

1. I am attentively aware of my body, keeping it within a healthy weight-range, by proper habits of eating, sleeping, and exercising. _____

2. I drink at least 6-8 glasses of pure water every day: on arising, before, and between meals, not washing my food down with every bite, but chewing it well. _____

3. At least 5 days every week, I enjoy getting out in the sunshine, breathing fresh air, while walking 20-30 min.,or being actively engaged in some physical exercise. _____

4. I have a regular schedule for bedtime, and sleep at least 6-8 hours daily, resting naturally, without the aid of sleeping pills or medications. _____

5. Starting the day with the proper fuel for my body, by eating a nourishing breakfast, is important to me. _____

6. I eat no more than 3 wholesome meals each day, at regular times, with water between, thus avoiding late bedtime and between-meal snacks. _____

7. I treasure the gift of health, and choose to be temperate in all things, while abstaining from harmful habits such as: smoking, drinking or drugs. _____

8. My diet consists mainly of fresh fruits, grains, vegetables, legumes, and nuts, eating amounts suited to my gender, body frame, and daily activity, and to avoid overeating. _____

9. Knowing the stresses of life can be overwhelming, I take time for relaxation, mini - vacations, enjoying nature, sharing with family and building friendships. _____

10. I choose to be happy, peaceful and content; thus by living right, and believing and claiming the promises of God in His word, I can safely trust Him with my life. _____

My Score (Maximum score 100) _____

90-100 Congratulation! You are making wise choices.
70- 89 You are advancing in the right direction.
40- 69 There is room for improvement.
39 or less Are you ready for a change ?

What does the future hold for YOU?

"... In order to have perfect health, our hearts must be filled with hope and love and joy."
Ellen G. White, **Counsels on Health**, pg. 587

Nature's True Remedies - The Key to Health

"Pure air, sunlight, abstemiousness (temperance), rest, exercise, proper diet (nutrition), the use of water, trust in divine power – these are the TRUE REMEDIES. Every person should have a knowledge of nature's remedial agencies, and how to apply them...But in the end it will be found that nature, untrammeled, does her work wisely and well. Those who persevere in obedience to her laws will reap the reward in health of body and health of mind." - E. G. White, **Ministry of Healing**, p. 127

With all due respect for the inspired writings of Ellen G. White and the original quote above on Nature's True Remedies, the authors have included 2 more principles which reflect their belief in the importance of being "thankful" and giving in "service" for others. These 2 principles are essential in order to fully appreciate life and enjoy abundant health (see **Psalms 100** and **Isaiah 58:7-8**). The 10 Principles for Abundant Health have been arranged to form an acronym that coincides with the title of this book **TEN TALENTS** (see page 12, 627).

Psalm 144:15

1. Trust in Divine Power

This principle, I believe, heads the list for being the most important factor in our lives, and the very foundation or source of abundant health.

Throughout the world, everyone trusts in some sort of a power, often really quite undefined. In reality, the only safe power to trust in, is the one that connects us with our Creator. It is usually things that are done in or against the body that cause us not to recognize Who controls the power of our being.

Jesus said, "Without Me, you can do nothing." This means that it is only through our Creator that we can have divine power to help us in our pursuit of a healthy life-style that would include attainments of eternal value. All that is required from us is to first ask for divine help. After taking the first step, some sacrifices may need to be made, some indulgences given up, but the results are always beneficial to body and soul.

The only real security man can have today, is to trust in a higher being other than himself. This alone will assure him of a useful life here on this earth, enjoying the best physical, mental, and spiritual health and a hope for the future as promised to all who will inherit eternal life. Here are just two beautiful promise we can depend on: read John 10:10 and 14:1-3.

We all desire a deeper purpose and meaning in this life, but who can we safely trust? *"Trust in the Lord with all your heart, and lean not on your own understanding. In all your ways acknowledge Him, and He will direct your paths."* Proverbs 3:5-6 The Bible is God's love letter to us - in it we find hope, purpose in living, and help with the stresses of life. Radio co-host and counselor Dr. Laura Schlessinger comments by saying, "Humans find focus, purpose and meaning beyond creature comforts, needs and desires, through a relationship with God and adherencs to His commandments."

An inspired author wrote, *"The religion of the Bible is not detrimental to the health of the body or of the mind. The influence of the Spirit of God is the very best medicine that can be received by a sick man or woman."* E. G. White, **Medical Ministry,** pg. 12 (Since we have all been bitten by the disease of sin, that includes all of us).

Isaiah 40:30-31

2. Exercise

If you feel stressed, depressed, or unable to concentrate, walking may be the simple solution to your dilemma, and best of all- it's free!

It is amazing what a brisk walk in the open air will do. Studies show moderate exercise will improve digestion, alleviate stress, enhance concentration, improve mental health, slow down the aging process, and help maintain proper body weight.

In addition, many of the lifestyle diseases we face today can be reversed by proper daily exercise. Research suggests that a diet high in fiber helps you feel full while you exercise to lose weight. Exercise strengthens the heart, improves the circulation, lowers the blood pressure, and is an integral part, along with a proper diet, of a healthy weight management plan.

Everyone should do some physical labor every day. If you have nothing to do for yourself, then do it for a person in need, and charge it to exercise. Walking is the best way to get exercise, and recognized as an aid to health; but unfortunately many people hop into a car, even when going a short distance of three or four blocks.

"Walking, in all cases, ... is the best,...because in this exercise all the organs of the body are brought into use...There is no exercise that can take the place of walking. By it, the circulation of the blood is greatly improved." **Counsels on Health,** pg. 200

Other forms of exercise may include working in the garden, biking, swimming, lifting weights, or exercise on a stationary bike, or while sitting or standing in place.

Physical labor and exercise should be balanced in the life, to provide a better blood supply to the body. Perfect health depends upon perfect circulation, and good circulation depends upon the muscle tone of the body to a large degree. Circulation of the blood will be improved when more exercise is enjoyed on a regular daily basis. The path of fitness is measured in feet, that is, putting one foot ahead of the other!

Isaiah 33:16

3. Nutrition (Proper Diet)

Nutrition – what does it mean? It is the process of being nourished – the utilization of food substances for the proper nourishment of our body. The best diet for us today is still the same diet originally given to Adam and Eve at creation before sin, and after they sinned. What was this diet provided by the Master Designer of our wonderfully made and complex body? Let's take a look.

In the beginning of Bible books we read, "Then God said, 'I give you every seed-bearing plant on the face of the whole earth and every tree that has fruit with the seed in it. They will be yours for food.'" Genesis 1:29, and ... "you shall eat the herb of the field" Gen. 3:18. Our Creator, who carefully and wonderfully made us, also knew what foods would be best for us. Today, modern science supports a plant-based vegetarian diet, as being the optimal diet. This simple diet could prevent a heart attack, stroke, or cancer, and reverse diabetes, obesity, and hypertension.

To be able to look and feel alive and healthy, one must eat the kind of food that will give the body what it needs, rather than what you think it wants. Man is a fine network of automatic reactions that function best from raw material taken into the body, rather then the highly refined foods so commonly eaten today. The modern can opener and the fancy packaged dinners are fast taking the place of simple, wholesome, nourishing food.

When the blessings of health, that come from a simple and nourishing diet are appreciated, then all the unnecessary luxury can be dispensed with. Time in expensive and elaborate preparation of food is almost entirely wasted in the light of what our body really needs for proper nutrition. A diet rich in fiber, found in whole grains, fruits, nuts, vegetables, and legumes simply prepared, is still the most nutritious diet.

If the American people would live simply in their dietary habits, there would be little or no want of food in the world today. The state of health enjoyed would be on a higher and more productive plane.

Good health can only be sustained by good blood, which in turn comes from eating vital foods, rich in life-giving properties.

"Grains, fruits, nuts, and vegetables constitute the diet chosen for us by our Creator. These foods, prepared in as simple and natural a manner as possible, are the most healthful and nourishing. They impart a strength, a power of endurance, and a vigor of intellect, that are not afforded by a more complex and stimulating diet." E. G. White, **Counsels on Diet and Foods**, p. 81

I Cor. 10:31

4. Temperance (Abstemiousness)

Temperance is moderation in the use of that which is good, and the total abstinence from that which is harmful to our health. Temperance also includes the habitual moderation of the appetites and passions, including our thoughts, feelings and actions, and the exercise of our will power even in the restraint of some good things. "More is not always better." For example: Overeating, even of the best kind of food, is injurious to our health; also, too much exercise, work, sunshine, or rest, which are good and essential, can be harmful, in excess.

Anything or any habit that harms the body is counterproductive to good health. Research and various studies support why we should abstain from taking into our body addictive substances such as: alcohol, tobacco, drugs, tea, coffee, and popular sugar-laden caffeinated drinks.

"Tea, coffee, and tobacco are all stimulating and contain poisons. Tea and coffee do not nourish the system...Tea and coffee whip up the slagging energies for the time being, but when their immediate influence has gone, a feeling of depression is the result." E. G. White, **Temperance**, page 75-76.

"By the use of tea and coffee, an appetite is formed for tobacco, and this encourages the appetite for liquors." Harmful habits also include eating between the meals. Regularity in eating, should be established, to promote healthful digestion and assimilation of food. " **Ibid**, page 80

The history of Daniel in the Bible gives us a true picture of the positive results of practicing temperance in both lifestyle and eating habits. Read Daniel 1: 8-16

One of my favorite authors comments on this by saying:

"The erect form, the firm, elastic step, the fair countenance, the undimmed senses, the untainted breath,- all were so many certificates of good habits,- insignia of the nobility with which nature honors those who are obedient to her laws." E. G. White, **Diet and Foods**, p 28.

Eat and fill yourself; but don't overeat and kill yourself.

"LET YOUR MODERATION BE KNOWN UNTO ALL MEN." Phillipians 4:5

Genesis 1:6-8

5. Air (Pure)

Pure air is vital to all life and needed for all body functions. Without pure air life can be measured in minutes. The air we breath should come from a pure, non-polluted source. Results of breathing impure air bring on disease and death. Avoid smoking and the inhaling of chemicals and other toxic pollutants.

All nature works to produce pure air by taking in carbon dioxide and giving us back life giving oxygen. Fresh air should be breathed as freely indoors as outdoors. If necessary, open the windows and cover the extremities, so that pure air can ventilate every room of your your home and lungs at the same time. Pure air is necessary to accomplish good digestion and to rid the body of impurities. It takes pure fresh air, circulating throughout the body, to maintain good health.

"In order to have good blood, we must breath well. Full, deep inspirations of pure air, which fill the lungs with oxygen, purify the blood. They impart to it (the blood) a bright color and send it, a life-giving current, to every part of the body. A good respiration soothes the nerves; it stimulates the appetite and renders digestion more perfect; and it induces sound, refreshing sleep." E. G. White, **Ministry of Healing** p. 272

Ecclesiastes 11:7

6. Light (Sunshine)

Light was the first essential thing our Creator made, and it still divides the night from the day. Genesis 1: 3, 4. Sunlight was then added on the fourth day of creation week and is essential for healthy human beings as well as healthy plants. Our body needs at least 15- 30 minutes of exposure to sunlight each day to provide sufficient vitamin D, which is synthesized in the skin, when exposed to the sun. Other benefits of sunlight include:

1. Elevates the mood and gladdens the heart.
2. Kills germs, viruses, bacteria, and mold.
3. Stimulates melatonin output, and enhances restful sleep.
4. Strengthens the immune system.
5. Relieves pain and aids healing.
6. Imparts a healthy glow to the skin.
7. Improves home atmosphere.

The building of our homes should include plans that provide windows for letting in an abundance of sunlight. All rooms should be well supplied with pure air and the warmth of sunshine at various times of the day.

Avoid sunburn or over-exposure to direct sunlight, a leading cause of skin cancer. Sunlight is truly one of mother nature's gifts, we often take for granted. If possible, get out in the sunshine every day. What a dark, dismal world it would be, without it!

John 4:13-14

7. Energizing Water (The Use of Water)

Our bodies are composed of approximately 70% water, and is the vehicle which the cells of the body need to carry out all of life's processes. Energizing pure water quenches thirst, increases endurance, lubricates our joints, regulates body temperature and provides a medium through which pollutants are expelled from the body through our waste, breath, sweat and urine. Research indicates drinking lots of energizing pure water is an important factor in improving heart health and preventing coronary heart disease.

Of all the gallons of water used by humans today, we sometimes forget to take a drink. At least seven or preferably eight glasses of energizing, pure soft water, full of free, life-giving ions, should be taken into the body every day. The amount of water your body needs is recorded in this formula: ½ oz. water for each pound of body weight. (example: A person weighing 150 lbs. would require 75oz. of water each day) That's over 9- 8oz. glasses of water. That may sound like alot of water but some of it could include herb teas, juice, milk, and other liquid foods such as soup.

Many diseases that exist today, would be reduced, and more easily controlled in the body, if more pure soft water was used internally and externally. Water is a universal solvent. In addition to cleansing the body internally, the skillful use of water applied externally, would relieve pain and improve health. Water treatments such as: simple foot baths, hydrotherapy, fomentations, steam baths, etc., have an important place in assisting the body to recover from many ailments. The external application of water is one of the easiest and most satisfactory ways of regulating the circulation of the blood.

Drinking 7 to 8 glasses of pure water on arising and between the meals, as well as bathing frequently, assists nature in her efforts to rid the body of daily impurities.

"In health and in sickness, pure water is one of heaven's choicest blessings. It's proper use promotes health..." E. G. White, **Ministry of Healing** p. 237

Psalms 127:2

8. Nightly Rest

Everything in nature has a rest cycle. The span between sunset and sunrise provides ample time to include a regular schedule of 7-9 hours of rest each night. The fact that "Two hours of good sleep before midnight is worth more than four hours after midnight..." is still true.

We can enjoy the benefits of restful sleep by following a few simple suggestions:
1. Have a regular time for bedtime and for rising.
2. Get adequate exercise each day, preferably outdoors.
3. Reduce fatigue and stress.
4. Avoid eating a heavy meal at night.
5. Provide a dark, quiet, clean sleeping area with good circulation of pure fresh air.
6. Resolve differences in your life, thus having a clear conscience.
7. Give your anxieties and worries to God and be assured of peace of mind.

Getting rest for the body should be a well-planned program. During sleep hours, the immune system is revitalized, and the body is able to build up that which is broken down. It will be easy to go to bed early and get up early, once the habit is established, and you begin to enjoy the way you feel.

The old adage that "a change is as good as a rest" is often true. Following creation, our Creator gave us the Sabbath - a day of rest. This is to provide a special time to enjoy nature, and to communicate with our family and with God. Overwork, worry, lack of exercise, a fatigued mind, and overeating, are among the chief causes of lack of proper rest. Having a healthy mental attitude and a definite purpose for what you are doing in life, brings a kind of rest not otherwise acquired.

In addition to physical rest, the kind of rest most needful today is that from the cares of this life, rather than from work alone.

"When you lie down, you will not be afraid; when you lie down, your sleep will be sweet." Proverbs 3:24 NIV

Psalm 100:4

9. Thankfulness

"In everything give thanks (in all circumstances): for this is the will of God in Christ Jesus concerning you." 1Thessalonians 5: 18

Many people think of thankfulness as related to a special time or occasion as in celebrating Thanksgiving Day; however the spirit of gratitude should be in our hearts and expressed every day. The pilgrims who settled in the new world faced many hardships, and in the midst of a long cold winter, loss of loved ones, and meager supplies, still believed they were blessed and chose to give thanks in prayer and celebration to God for being alive.

Life itself is a precious gift, and no matter what the circumstances may be, there is always something for which to be thankful. The spirit of thankfulness could be read in the words of Helen Keller, who wrote *"The only thing worse than being blind is having sight, but no vision."* In the scriptures, king David wrote, *"It is a good thing to give thanks unto the Lord, and to sing praises unto His name..."* Psalms 92:1; and *"Praise the Lord, O my soul, and forget not all His benefits."* Ps. 103:2

A spirit of thankfulness is a sure remedy for overcoming selfishness, bitterness, depression, gloom and despondency. *"Nothing tends to promote health of body and prolong life than does a spirit of gratitude and praise."* Ministry of Healing, pg. 251

No matter how grim our outward circumstances, when we focus on who God is, and what He has done for us, we have reason to be overflowing with thankfulness. *"A cheerful heart is a good medicine, but a downcast spirit dries up the bones."* Proverbs 17:22 RSV (damages the bone marrow- or major portion of immune system)

If life could be reduced to one noble principle, a true spirit of THANKFULNESS would be able to generate more blessings from above than any other, and bring to us the joy of our salvation.

Isaiah 58:7-8, Matthew 25:40

10. Service

Someone once said *"We make a living by what we get, but a life by what we give."* How true that is! In our life here on planet earth, our greatest joy will be found in service.

Deeds of kindness whether great or small, and the unselfish performance of everyday duties for the benefit of others, will not go unnoticed. Be thankful for every opportunity to give and serve others, for in whatever position we may serve, or whatever our work may be, we are developing a character for eternity.

"Give and it shall be given unto you..." (Luke 6:38) is a divine law of reciprocity. This law of service is seen in all of nature. Consider the sun, moon, stars, rivers, lakes, animals, birds, trees, and flowers; they all provide something of benefit to another. Those who cease giving, block the channel from which all blessings flow.

The life of service Christ lived, and His love for us, sets an example for all who claim to be his followers. Jesus himself said, "It is more blessed to give than to receive" Acts 20:35. People who keep receiving, without giving for the welfare and benefit of others, soon become stagnant. In contrast, by living to benefit others, we conquer greed and selfishness; the law of service becomes the connecting link which binds us to God and to each other. It's **service,** not "serve us".

No man can be independent of his fellow men; for the well-being of each affects others. There is nothing but the selfish heart of man that lives to itself. All of our talents, if rightly employed, will be used in service for others; this will bring real joy.

Blessed are those who give without remembering; and blessed are those who receive without forgetting!

Take Time to Live

Take time to live,
The mad world rushes on;
    Yes, stop and think,
For life will soon be gone.

Take time to live,
For life is very sweet;
    So precious the hours,
With friends we meet.

Take time to live,
Fill every passing day;
    With all the good,
That you can give away.

Take time to live,
And never cease to pray;
    When life shall end,
You'll reach eternal day.

-Don Carlos Chamness

Time Is Running Out

The clock of life is wound but once,
And no man has the power
    To tell just when the hands will stop –
At late or early hour.

"Now" is the only time you own;
Live, Love, Toil with a will;
    Place no faith in "tomorrow" for
The clock may then be still.

-Author unknown

Reference and Recommended Reading

Bible texts - **Authorized King James Version** - Copyright ©1959, 1975, 1985, Collins Press - London and New York
New International Version - Copyright ©1978, International Bible Society
New Millennium Edition - Copyright ©1990, Thomas Nelson, Inc.
Counsels on Diet and Foods - E. G. White, © 1938, 1976
    Review & Herald Publishing Association, Hagerstown, MD.
Christ's Object Lessons – E. G. White, ©1900, Pacific Press Publishing Assoc., Nampa, ID
Ministry of Healing – E. G. White, ©1905, Pacific Press Publishing Assoc., Nampa, ID
Counsels on Health - E. G. White, ©1951, Pacific Press Publishing Assoc., Nampa, ID
Child Guidance – E. G. White, ©1982, Review & Herald Publishing Assoc., Wash., DC
Proof Positive – Neil Nedley, M.D. ©1998, 1999, Ardmore, OK
Encyclopedia of Foods and Their Healing Power - George D. Pamplona-Roger, M.D.
    ©2004, Editorial Safeliz, S.L., Madrid, Spain
Other excellent reading by E. G. White: **Steps to Christ, Desire of Ages, Great Controversy**

Sources of Natural Foods

*Bulk Foods, Grains, Dried Fruits, Nuts, Seeds, Beans, Flours, Cereals, Herbs & Seasonings,
Fresh Fruits and Vegetables, Misc.,Bakery and Specialty Items*

Azure Standard- 79709 Dufur Valley Road- Dufur, OR 97021 Ph: 541-467-2230
Bob's Red Mill- 13521 SE Pheasant Court- Milwaukie, OR 97222 Ph:503-654-3215
Country Life Natural Foods- P.O.B. 489- Pullman, MI 49450 Ph: 269-236-5011
GloryBee Foods-1120 N.Seneca Rd. P.O.B. 2744- Eugene, OR 97402 Ph: 541-689-0913
Natural Way Mills- 24509 390th St. N.E. Middle River, MN 56737 Ph: 218-222-3677
www.BulkFoods.com – 3040 Hill Ave- Toledo, OH 43607 (on line catalog of items)
www.Howellmd.com – Howell Mountain Distributors – P.O.B. 96 – Angwin, CA 94508
www.Littleladsonline.com –307 Main St.- Corinth, ME 04427 Ph: 207-285-3044
www.WholeFoodsMarket.com- 550 Bowie Street- Austin, TX 78703 (locate area store)

About the Authors

Rosalie Hurd, B.S., nutritionist and home economist, is actively engaged in promoting the principles of abundant health, the art of simple natural food preparation and nutrition counseling. She and her husband have conducted numerous seminars in the U.S. and various foreign countries, teaching natural methods, and demonstrating the preparation of whole foods in a simple attractive manner. Rosalie, a life-long vegetarian, is the mother of five, healthy, grown children, reared on vegetarian principles. In addition to caring for the needs of her busy household, she is primarily involved in the on-going ministry of Ten Talents, and serves as secretary and office assistant to her husband, Dr. Frank Hurd. She is a former Home Economics teacher, and food service director.

In a Mrs. America contest of culinary skills, Rosalie was chosen a winner selected from a group of 50 participants, being the only contestant who prepared a completely vegetarian dinner. For the Mrs. America winning meal - see *Meal Planning and Menus*, page 586.

Guests and friends served vegetarian meals in the home of Dr. and Mrs. Hurd have asked many questions from "How do you season those delicious Italian salads?" to "What do you eat to make your hair grow?" and a score of other questions on natural foods.

The ever-increasing interest in health, vegetarianism, lifestyle changes, and the simple preparation of whole foods, has inspired her to revise and expand TEN TALENTS which was first published over 44 years ago, in 1968. The foods pictured in this book were primarily prepared, arranged, and photographed by Rosalie Hurd.

Dr. Frank Hurd, D.C., M.D., has spent more than 49 years in the study and practice of lifestyle health and wellness. He has earned degrees in Chiropractic, Naturopathy, and Medicine, and still prefers preventive methods and natural remedies to promoting health. He is currently engaged in active practice, and lectures on healthful principles that support vibrant health through a vegetarian lifestyle, which he believes enhances man's relationship to our Creator.

Human Interest Story

Both Rosalie's parents, unknown to each other, immigrated from Italy - dad at age 16, then mother a year later in 1923. They came to America to work in our land of freedom and prosperity. Her mother was from a large family of 17 children, her grandmother one of 23 children, with 3 sets of twins, all born to the same mother and father.   Rosalie's mother will celebrate 105 years in 2011. Under the guardianship of family in the U.S. she met her husband and they were married and went on to have five children, Rosalie being next to the youngest of three girls and two boys.

Though life wasn't always easy in the U.S., there were many things they looked forward to. Rosalie enjoyed being with family, going to church, the park or zoo, skating, bike riding, helping mother at home, learning to cook, sew, design and make her own clothes. She has always been interested in caring for the family, creating healthy meals, etc. and enjoys many other activities including walking, sewing, learning computer skills, and memorizing bible promises, and is still learning precious lessons of dependence and getting to know Him more each day as her personal Savior and best friend.

She met her husband at Atlantic Union College during her college years. She, a city slicker from New York, and he a country boy who "knew what he wanted in life."   That is... it soon became apparent that Rosalie was the "one" that he could not live without, and after pursuing her at the tender age of 16, and winning her hand in marriage, he has faithfully loved and cherished her all these years since. They went on to have five children and have also been graced with 8 grandchildren. He has become a well-respected family physician, using natural alternative methods for restoring health and adding a better quality of life.

Family has always been important to them, and so it is no surprise that they have involved their family in some way in the ministry of Ten Talents . The daughters have helped with art work, office work, and were often found using their skills to critique the photography of the book, cooking or sampling the recipes. The boys have helped in the shipping deptartment, in building, carpentry, or doing mechanics to keep the vehicles in repair for their travel.

So what is the motivation behind this cookbook ? And why spend more years of hard work and countless hours completely re-doing Ten Talents and taking it to a new level, when most people would be satisfied to have retired?

Here is Rosalie's answer:

Rosalie - 10 years old

Frank & Rosalie- College Days

Sweet 16th Birthday

Wedding Day 8-16-56

Young Motherhood

"With so many other cookbooks out there and so much knowledge available through the world-wide web, magazines, cooking shows, etc. I really thought Ten Talents had lived out it's life span, and that when the last copies of Ten Talents in print were sold, we would retire—-but, God had a different plan."

"Repeated calls from the R&H requesting to reprint the Ten Talents book, for us.....was an indication that our ministry was not yet completed. God has given me a new desire, and that is to uplift Him through spreading a knowledge of the beautiful Bible diet that He has provided for man, and of the renewed health that is the result of following His perfect plan for our well being."

Rosalie is dedicated to sharing God's wonderful "Eden diet " that has brought renewed strength and health to so many people around the globe. They have received many beautiful letters from grateful people who are experiencing healthy lifestyle changes.

For examples: In the 1980's, a hippie couple living in a tent in Hawaii, enjoyed reading Ten Talents by candlelight, as their devotional every night. Eventually, they became vegetarians, finally married, and became "committed Christians."

A recent phone call from an owner and admirer of Ten Talents, inquiring about the due date for the upcoming book remarked: "It's the best cookbook I've ever seen - I'll wait forever for the new edition."

Bookstores and distributors far and near requesting the book say "There's something different about Ten Talents, it just keeps selling and selling, even after all these years"!

The ongoing demand for Ten Talents, has sparked a desire to revise the book into a pictorial edition. It has now evolved into an all natural foods healthy lifestyle manual, designed to inspire the reader to care for their body temple, and have a desire to someday soon, enjoy the bounties of Eden restored. With this thought in mind, and to this end, this book is dedicated. *-Les Derfler*

1968

1985 (1988 Spanish)

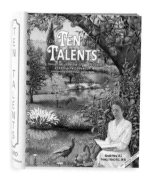

2008 (2009 Spanish)

Notes / Favorite Recipes

_____

_____

_____

_____

_____

_____

_____

_____

_____

_____

_____

_____

_____

50 Favorite Recipes

GENERAL INDEX

Ten Talents

N

O

ᵀ TEN TALENTS catalog

BOOKS

A taste of Eden

BETTER CHOICES

Raw Food & Favorites by authors of
Award-Winning Vegetarian Cookbook TEN TALENTS

FRESH & HEALTHY CUISINE

"I give you every seed-bearing plant on the face of the whole earth, and every tree that has fruit with seed in it. They will be yours for food."
Genesis 1:29 NIV

ROSALIE HURD, B.S. and FRANK J. HURD, D.C., M.D.

*Coming Soon!
Order now*

BETTER CHOICES

Eat well, live well, with this delightful collection of energy-packed foods simply prepared, along with favorite dishes and highlights from Ten Talents. Featuring naturally tasty and healthful recipes from God's original storehouse of plant-based foods including fruits, grains, vegetables, nuts, and seeds.

approx. 8 ⅛" x 10 ⅝" 160 pages **$24.95**

A Good Cook...TEN TALENTS

*Award-winning Classic Vegetarian Cookbook & Health Manual

A complete natural foods cookbook, emphasizing the Gen. 1:29 original diet for humans. TEN TALENTS is called "the perennial best-selling vegetarian cookbook" and "the all-time classic vegetarian's Bible." This 2009 ***Silver Medal Award Winner** is now in a new updated pictorial edition. TEN TALENTS is packed with information on natural foods, proper nutrition, diet, lifestyle, and more. Over 1,000 delicious, heart-healthy recipes. Endorsed by Dr. Neil Nedley, Dr. Hans Diehl, CHIP, the Vegetarian Society, and many others. A masterpiece and kitchen companion you will cherish! $34.95

· **Full Color · Pictorial Edition**
· **Lay-flat spiral binding**
· **7" x 9" · Illustrated · 675 pages**
· **Full chapter and General Index**
· **Over 1,300 color photographs**

Catalog & Ordering

667

Ten Talents

Una buena cocinera...DIEZ TALENTOS

Un completo libro de cocina con alimentos naturales y manual de salud que enfatiza la dieta original para el ser humano encontrada en Génesis 1:29.

Recetas vegetarianas que contienen frutas, cereales, hortalizas, nueces, semillas, hierbas y otros alimentos naturales. Más de 1.000 recetas deliciosas y saludables para el corazón. Bajas en grasas y sodio, sin azúcar y ricas en fibras.

Completo con información acerca de cómo usar y preparar alimentos naturales, como combinar alimentos, nutrición y dieta apropiada. Igual que la versión ilustrada y ganadora de premios en inglés. ¡Una obra maestra y un compañero en su cocina que usted apreciará! $34.95

·**7 X 9 pulgadas** ·**21 Capítulos** ·**675 Páginas**
·**Índice General y por Capítulo**
·**Más de 1.300 fotografías a todo color**
See website: www.dieztalentos.net

DVD'S & POSTERS

LIFESTYLE & NUTRITION DVD SEMINARS

Natural Foods - Vegetarian Cuisine

***Ten Talents 25th Anniversary series
as filmed on 3ABN- now on DVD***

1. Man's Original Diet
2. Food Combining / Wise Food Shopping
3. Kitchen Equipment & Gadgets
4. Beverages & Healing Herbs

5. Grains / Breakfasts / Healthy Ideas
6. Bread / The Staff of Life
7. Sprouting Legumes: How & Why

8. Meatless Main Dishes / Meal Planning
9. Salads, Fruit / Vegetable, Soups
10. Desserts / Something Special

$59.95 Set

5 Hours viewing (10 half-hour programs)

"These VIDEOS provide the 'ultimate' in Vegetarian Cuisine - for a healthy, natural lifestyle"

8 Natural Food Posters in Full Color

**Printed on quality matte finish poster paper
Set of 8 charts 9" x 12", $14.95; each $1.95**

Fresh Fruits, Grains, Nuts & Seeds, Legumes, Salad Greens, Assorted Vegetables, Squash & Pumpkins, Root Vegetables

HERBAL "SLIDE" CHARTS
Instant Reference

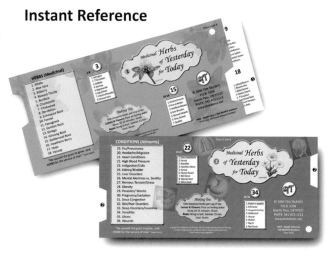

Chart #1 lists 36 healing herbs and names over 180 conditions for which each herb is beneficial.

Chart #2 lists 36 common conditions and over 90 herbs that can effectively be used as a remedy. Fast and easy to use, these slide charts give accurate, up-to-date practical information at a glance! Great gifts! Convenient size 4" x 9".

Set of two/ $6.95

Ten Talents FOOD COMBINING MADE EASY
Full COLOR Chart 18" x 24"

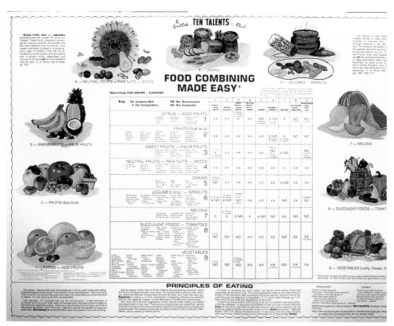

Learn at a glance how to properly combine natural foods. Enjoy better digestion and nutrition. Meal planning is fun and easy with this informative chart. Beautifully and clearly illustrated with original art drawings. Sample menus, simple principles. **Heavy textured paper**, $6.95; **Laminated Edition**, $9.95; **ENGLISH** or **SPANISH**

See items on website: **www.tentalents.net, www.dieztalentos.net**

SPECIALTY ITEMS

18" x 9" above
9" x 12" left
11" x 11" below

Catalog & Ordering

670

Ten Talents

Fine Art "GARDEN OF EDEN" Prints - frameable reproductions

Printed on Archival, acid-free Via Felt, distinctive textured paper
Reflections of Eden- 18" x 12" full cover $10.00; *Scenes of Eden-* 18" x 9" $8.00;
Eden- 11" x 11" $7.00; *Peaceful Eden-* 9"x 12" $6.00

Ten Principles for Abundant Health

T Trust in Divine Power
E Exercise
N Nutrition

T Temperance
A Air, Pure
L Light, Sunshine
E Energizing Water
N Nightly Rest
T Thankfulness
S Service

Ten Principles for Abundant Health

Quality matte finish poster paper
Chart - 8" x 11" $3.00; 2/ $5.00
Bookmarks - 2" x 8"; 10/ $2.00

5

Original Diet Plaques

9 Natural Food designs as shown on
Food Combining Chart, opposite page
$3.95 each; $10.50 set of 3

All-Occasion Stationery

5 variety sets: Nature Notes with Scripture & Leaves; Birds & Butterflies;
Original Diet Notes; Flowers; Promises and Leaves; $ 3.95 box; 16 notes/envelopes

New Era Electric Buffet Skillet – Pro-Health Ultra Oil Core skillet, large 11" or 13". Quality stainless steel evenly distributes heat to stir-fry vegetables, cook brown rice, etc.

L'Equip Blender – Features a German-designed stainless steel blade and shaft, heavy-duty 1.75 liter (7 cup) container; tachometer showing operating speed. 1 hp motor; 6 year warranty.

Champion Juicer – Heavy Duty all-in-one juicer. Make tasty nut butters, fruit sauces, frozen desserts, and flour with the optional Grain Mill attachment; 5 year warranty.

L'Equip Dehydrator – Compact, lightweight, computer controlled heat sensor. Fast, easy to use and clean. 12 square feet of drying space, add more trays. Full 12 year warranty.

Acme Juicer – Centrifugal action juicer. Separates nearly every drop of juice from the pulp of fresh fruits and vegetables quickly and efficiently; 10 year warranty.

Nut & Seed Mill – Multi-purpose compact, high-powered grinder for seeds, nuts, herbs, beans, etc. Stainless steel blades grind food coarse or fine. Easy to clean; 4 oz. capacity.

APPLIANCES, con't

Bosch Universal Plus Mixer – 6 ½ qt. bowl holds 15 lbs. dough. Includes dough hook, wire whips, cover. Blender container: 6 cups, 4-speed, pulse switch, 3 year warranty.

Vita-Mix Turbo Blend – Commercial quality ensures reliable performance. Durable components, stainless steel blade assembly, 64 oz. container. 2 hp motor, 5 year warranty

Kitchen Flour Mill – Capture the nutrition and save dollars by milling fresh flour and baking your own bread. Grind wheat, or any grain including hard popcorn, legumes and soybeans. Fast, easy to use and clean. 6 year warranty.

Nutri Steamer–Stainless Steel Steam Juicer efficiently extracts pure fresh juice from all softskin fruits and berries. Very easy to use, with multiple uses. Steam cook potatoes, fresh corn on the cob, green vegetables, or use as a colander, a soup pot, or roaster.

Steam Canner – Enjoy home canning with this revolutionary canner that saves time, energy and water. Very easy to use, clean and efficient. Holds 7- 1 quart or 10- pt. size jars.

Large Steamer

3 Qt. Dome

8 Qt. Dutch Oven with Cover

Large Skillet   Large Saute Skillet   Saucepan with Cover

2 Qt.

New Era Pro-Health Ultra Cookware – The ultimate 7-ply design is constructed of quality T304 surgical stainless steel. Energy efficient, even heat distribution cooks to perfection and eliminates hot spots. The finest waterless cookware (sets or pieces) with lifetime guarantee.

Sprouting Rings complete with screens – Two sizes of rings to fit wide or narrow mouth jars. Grow a fresh garden in your kitchen effortlessly and watch the miracle of seeds sprouting!

Deni Frozen Dessert and Ice Cream – Makes **1½ qts.** No salt or ice needed. Recipe booklet included.

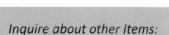

LeveLuk
KANGEN WATER

Enagic SD 501 – Enjoy the benefits of drinking energized, ionized, alkaline water to improve your health.

Raw Food Spiral Slicer – Cut carrots, parsnips, zucchini, cucumber, beets, and more into delicious ready-to-eat gourmet salad. Simply add a squeeze of lemon, pinch of salt, or your favorite salad dressing.

Inquire about other Items:

Saladmaker (with 5 cones)

Hand Grain Mill

Pressure Cooker

Water Distiller

Yogurt Maker

www.tentalents.net

Orders call: **1- 877-442-4425**

Catalog & Ordering

673

Ten Talents

TEN TALENTS

Dr. Frank J. & Rosalie Hurd
PO Box 5209,   Tel/ Fax: 541-472-1113
Grants Pass, OR 97527
www.TenTalents.net

Order from Publishers:
Mail to ➡
(or contact your dealer)

Order Form

NAME _____

ADDRESS _____

CITY _____ STATE _____ ZIP _____

PHONE (_____) _____ E-mail _____

☐ Send to another address other then above. (Name and address attached with my order)
☐ Please enclose a gift card at no extra cost. (Courtesy of TEN TALENTS)
☐ Please send me a Free color illustrated brochure on new items.   ☐ Quantity / Wholesale / Distributor discounts

Quantity		Total
	A Good Cook... **TEN TALENTS** • New Pictorial Edition • Updated • Expanded Award-Winning Natural Foods Cookbook / Vegetarian Health Manual - 675 pages........ @ 34.95	
	DIEZ TALENTOS (Spanish) • New Pictorial Edition • Updated • Expanded - 675 pages.. @ 34.95	
	*****BETTER CHOICES** - Favorite recipes and highlights from Ten Talents *****NEW** - 160 pgs @ 24.95	
	FOOD COMBINING CHART - Full Color - Illustrated - Simplifies Meal Planning Laminated Edition - 18" x 24" heavy 5 Mil Mylar - ENGLISH or SPANISH................ @ 9.95	
	Ten Talents **FOOD COMBINING MADE EASY** - 4 Color - Illustrated Wall Chart 18" x 24" Textured Heavy Paper - (same as above) ENGLISH or SPANISH.................. @ 6.95	
	HERBAL SLIDE CHARTS - Herbs of Yesterday for Today - Use of Medicinal Herbs Instant Reference, #1 Herbs, and #2 Conditions • New • Updated ....Set of 2 charts @ 6.95	
	DVD - NATURAL FOODS-VEGETARIAN CUISINE - Health Seminars Lifestyle & Nutrition -25th Anniversary Video Series 1-10 in DVD format ....Set @ 59.95	
	8 NATURAL FOODS POSTERS - Full Color - 9" x 12" New, Complete Variety........ Set of 8 @ 14.95 ☐ Fresh Fruits; ☐ Grains; ☐ Nuts & Seeds; ☐ Legumes; ☐ Salad Greens; ☐ Assorted Vegetables; ☐ Squash & Pumpkin; ☐ Root Vegetables ....each @ 1.95	
	TEN PRINCIPLES for ABUNDANT HEALTH - Charts/Bookmarks ☐ Chart 8" x 11" $3.00; ☐ 2 Charts $5.00; ☐ Bookmarks 2" x 8" (pack of 10) $2.00 .... choices	
	GARDEN of EDEN - Fine Art Prints - (Artist Cover Painting - Frameable Reproductions) ☐ Reflections of Eden - 18" x 12" $10.00; ☐ Scenes of Eden - 18" x 9" - $8.00; ☐ Eden- 11" x 11" $7.00; ☐ Peaceful Eden - 9" x 12" $6.00; ☐ 4 Art Prints $29.95....... choices	
	Original Diet Notes with Inspirational Quotes- Natural Foods in color- 16 notes/env ...... @ 3.95	
	Nature Notes - All Occasion Stationery-variety-16 notes/envelopes/gift box ....each @ 3.95 ☐ #1 Scripture and Leaves; ☐ #2 Birds and Butterflies; ☐ #3 Flowers; ☐ #4 Promises and Leaves	
	Original Diet Plaques - Natural Foods- Full Color- Wood/Brass hanger - 4-1/2" x 6" ...... @ 3.95 9 Designs- (✔ choices) -☐ 1, ☐ 2, ☐ 3, ☐ 4, ☐ 5, ☐ 6, ☐ 7, ☐ 8, ☐ 9, (set of 3 plaques) .. @ 10.50	
	Deluxe Vinyl Looseleaf Binder - Complete with 21 Index Dividers (1968-1999 editions) ... @ 9.95	

US Postage and Handling - $8.00 first item per address; $4.00 each add. item
International Postage - $20.00 first item per address; $10.00 each add. item

ENCLOSED IS A CHECK OR MONEY ORDER IN U.S. FUNDS   TOTAL $

Please Specify: ☐ CHECK   ☐ MONEY ORDER   ☐ CASH   ☐ VISA   ☐ MASTERCARD   ☐ AMER. EXP.   ☐ DISCOVER

In a Hurry?
Call: 541-472-1113

CREDIT CARD NUMBER ☐☐☐☐ – ☐☐☐☐ – ☐☐☐☐ – ☐☐☐☐   EXP. DATE ☐☐ ☐☐ MO.   YR.

SIGNATURE: _____ PHONE: _____

DISCOVER   MasterCard   VISA   AMERICAN EXPRESS   **PH/Fax Orders: 877-442-4425   Website/Orders: www.tentalents.net**